Buy, Keep or Sell?

Buy, Keep or Sell?

Judith Miller
and Mark Hill

DK

LONDON, NEW YORK,
MELBOURNE, MUNICH, DELHI

A joint production from **DK** and
THE PRICE GUIDE COMPANY

DORLING KINDERSLEY LIMITED
Senior Editor Paula Regan
Senior Art Editor Mandy Earey
Designer Dawn Terrey
US Editor Margaret Parrish
Managing Editor Julie Oughton
Managing Art Editor Heather McCarry
Publishing Director Jackie Douglas
DTP Designer Adam Walker
Digital Image Librarian Richard Dabb
Production Controller Rita Sinha

THE PRICE GUIDE COMPANY LTD
Editors Karen Morden, Emma Clegg, David Lloyd, Sara Sturgess
Photographers Graham Rae, Byron Slater, Steve Tanner,
Martin Spillane, Andy Johnson, John McKenzie

This work was created in conjunction with the
Reader's Digest Association Ltd.

First American edition, 2006
00 01 02 03 04 05 10 9 8 7 6 5 4 3 2 1

Published in the United States by
DK Publishing, Inc.
375 Hudson Street
New York, NY 10014

The Price Guide Company Ltd
info@thepriceguidecompany.com

Copyright © Judith Miller and
Dorling Kindersley Limited 2005

A CIP catalog record for this book is available
from the Library of Congress.

ISBN 0-7566-1338-8

Color reproduction by GRB, Italy
Printed and bound in China by SNP Leefung

Discover more at
www.dk.com

Editor-in-Chief
Judith Miller

Chief Consultant
Mark Hill

Specialist Consultants

CERAMICS
Jeffrey Snyder (Author), **Fiestaware**
Riley Humber (Cincinnati Art Galleries, Cincinnati, OH)
Maddy Gordon (Headhunters Newsletter, NY), **Lady head vases**
David Rago (David Rago Auctions, Lambertville, NJ)
Greg Belhorn (Belhorn Auctions, Columbus, OH)

HISTORICAL MEMORABILIA
Steve Allard (Allard Auctions, St Ignatius, MT), **Native American art**
Rowan S. Baker (usa-stamps.com), **Stamps**
Mike Pender (World's Fair Collectors' Society, Sarasota, FL), **New York World's Fairs**
Sharon & Joe Happle (Mill Antiques Center, Lafayette, NJ), **Holiday memorabilia**
Rick Coleman (Bloomsbury Auctions, London), **Coins and paper money**

HOUSEHOLD AND KITCHENALIA
Mercedes di Renzo (Jazzye Junque, Chicago, Illinois), **Cookie jars**
Amy Kraker (Port Antiques Center, Port Washington, NY), **Jadeite**
Andrew Truman (James D. Julia Auctioneers, Fairfield, ME), **Advertising and packaging**
Rick & Sharon Corley (Toy Road Antiques, Winchester, OH), **Advertising and packaging**
John Hainey (The Blue Pump, Toronto, ON), **Canadiana**

GLASS
Dudley Browne (James D. Julia Auctioneers, Fairfield, ME)
Mark Block (blockglass.com, Trumbull, CT)
Stephen Saunders (End of History, New York, NY)
Linda Richard (Cajun Collection, Temple, TX), **Factory glass**
Gordon Harrell (Collector), **Blenko**
John Walk (Walk Memory Lane, Mulberry Grove, IL), **Fenton**

BEAUTY AND FASHION
Stacey LoAlbo (Neet-O-Rama, Somerville, NJ)
Barbara Blau (South Street Antiques Center, Philadelphia, PA)
Roxanne Stuart (Dealer, PA), **Costume jewelry**
Alycen Mitchell (Fashion author)
Mark Laino (South Street Antiques Center, Philadelphia, PA), **Watches**
Julie Brooke (Price Guide Company UK Ltd.)
Esther Harris (Vintage Eyewear of New York), **Sunglasses**

TOYS, DOLLS, AND TEDDIES
Rich Bertoia (Bertoia Auctions, Vineland, NJ)
Noel Barrett (Noel Barrett Auctions, Carversville, PA)
Russ Burke (Milezone's Toys, Michigan City, IN), **Hot Wheels**
Robert Block (Auctionblocks, Huntington Station, CT), **Marbles**
Barbara Lauver (Harper General Store, Annville, PA), **Teddy bears**

ENTERTAINMENT AND SPORTS
Everett Cope & Paul Centofanti (Copes Sports Collectibles, Bozeman, NT)
Sports memorabilia
David Hunt (Hunt Auctions, Exton, PA), **Sports memorabilia**
John Kanuit (Vintage Sports Collector, CA)

THE WRITTEN WORD AND EPHEMERA
Erik DuRon (Bauman Rare Books, New York, NY), **First edition books**
Richard Mori (Mori Books, Amherst, NH), **Paperbacks**
John E. Petty (Heritage Comics, Dallas, TX), **Comics**
Vincent Zurzolo (Metropolis Collectibles, New York, NY), **Comics**
Diane Davison (Indispensible Pez, Baltimore, MD), **Pez**

TECHNOLOGY AND TRAVEL
David K. Bausch (Author), **Automobilia**
Victoria Campbell (Aurora Galleries, Bell Canyon, CA), **Space memorabilia**
Robert Pearlman (www.collectspace.com), **Space memorabilia**

MODERN DESIGN
Vanessa Strougo (Deco Etc, New York, NY), **Art Deco and Lamps**
Sasha Keen (Neet-O-Rama, Somerville, NJ), **1960s and 1970s**

Contributors
Sally Adams, Jessica Bishop, Julie Brooke, Andrew Casey,
Alexander Clement, Tarquin Cooper, Daniel Dunlavey, Catherine Early,
Sarah Foster, Philip Hunt, Nicholas King, Frankie Leibe, Alycen Mitchell,
Joan Porter, Nick Smurthwaite, John Wainwright, Sally Walton

Contents

Introduction 8
How to use this book 14

Half dolls, pp. 210–11

Ceramics

Automobilia, pp. 310–11

Glass

Snow globes, pp. 206–07

Amberina, pp. 126–27

Beauty and Fashion

Toys, Dolls, and Teddy Bears

Teddy bears, pp. 200–03

Entertainment and Sports

Rock and pop music, pp. 250–53

The Written Word and Ephemera

Technology and Travel

Modern Design

Radios and TVs, pp. 302–03

Nursery ware, pp. 50–51

Hats, pp. 152–53

Marbles, pp. 198–99

Hot Wheels, pp. 192–93

Depression glass
pp. 128–29

Introduction

I bought my first collectibles in the late 1960s, in a junk shop in Edinburgh, Scotland. Those inexpensive blue-and-white plates were just meant to liven up the walls of my rented student room. But I soon became intrigued as to who made them, when, where, and whether they were worth more than I'd paid. I was hooked, to the extent that since then much of my working life has been spent collecting, writing about, and broadcasting on antiques and collectibles.

The expanding market

The collectibles market has expanded enormously in recent years, fueled by the publication of annual price guides like mine, TV shows, collectibles shows, garage sales, and internet auction sites. The latter have created a global market for buyers and sellers.

Why collect and what's collectible?

People collect for many reasons: the pleasure of displaying beautiful or interesting objects in the home; nostalgia for items associated with

Sunglasses, pp. 158–59

childhood or youth, famous people, or events; and financial investment. All are perfectly valid. As the following pages reveal, the range of objects considered collectible is now immense. Traditional areas such as ceramics, glass, and textiles have been augmented with newer, equally sought-after categories as diverse as cell phones, jelly molds, sunglasses, and even shoes!

Desirability and value

The desirability and value of any collectible is determined by a combination of factors. Roseville pottery (see right) has become extremely popular in recent years thanks in part to the wide range that is available on the market, giving collectors a great deal of choice. Quality of design and manufacture are also important: many of Trifari's exquisitely made Jelly Belly pins of the 1930s have almost doubled in value (from around $450 to $900 or more) in the last three years, while their mass-produced, postwar pieces have only risen by around 15 percent.

Rarity is also highly desirable: a common piece of Blenko glass may fetch as little as $30 but a rare

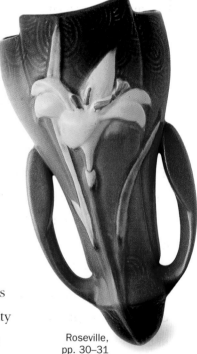

Roseville,
pp. 30–31

Character collectibles, pp. 232–33

Scottie dogs, pp. 94–95

Stoneware and redware, pp. 34–35

Coca-Cola, pp. 290–91

Snow globes, pp. 206–07

Fakes

Fakes and forgeries do appear on the market. You can avoid them by buying from reputable dealers or auction houses. Beyond that, the ability to spot fakes comes with experience. Beware of:

- Incorrect or no maker's marks.
- Wrong proportions or weight (too light or too heavy).
- Unrealistic simulations of natural patination and wear and tear.
- Poorer quality decoration or materials in comparison to an original.

volume means you won't get your money back in the foreseeable future. Remember—for values to rise, demand has to outweigh supply; for this reason, avoid "limited editions" of more than 1,000 pieces.

and exceptional example may fetch as much as $1,500. Provenance can be even more compelling: a baseball shirt worn by a star player *(see right)* can command a high price, especially if it has a certificate of authenticity to prove it. Aside from the rarest pieces with exceptional provenance, condition is also critical: "mint and boxed" toys and games can command 30–80 per cent more than damaged equivalents without original packaging. Desirability isn't conferred by age alone, and many new items become "instant collectibles." In 2000 the toy company Ty produced a limited-edition Thank You Beanie Baby as a Christmas gift for their retailers. In no time at all they were changing hands on auction sites for hundreds of dollars.

A note of caution, however, about limited editions. Some manufacturers advertise runs of 50,000 or more as "limited edition." While legitimate, the sheer

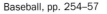

Baseball, pp. 254–57

Native American art, pp. 76–77

Paperweights, pp. 130–31

Blenko, pp. 136–37

Plastic dolls, pp. 214–15

Perfume bottles, pp. 120–21

Vintage advertising, pp. 286–87

Radios, pp. 302–03

What to pay

When I started out, deciding what to pay was often a matter of instinct. Today, there is far more specific information available. Publications such as the annual *DK Collectibles Price Guide* give current price trends, as do auction catalogs and internet auction sites such as eBay. You can also keep up with all the latest information by joining a collectors' club (*see Clubs and societies, pp. 338–39)*, and visiting fairs.

Where and how to buy

Always look first in your own home, especially the attic. Inherited, childhood, or previously overlooked pieces provide the starting point for many collectors. Scour "For Sale" advertisements in local papers and weekly magazines such as *American Classifieds* and *Thrifty Nickel*. Regularly stop by thrift shops and flea markets, and go to local yard and garage sales. In each case, make up your own mind as to authenticity

Buying at auction

Local auction houses are listed in the Yellow Pages, *while local newspapers often carry notices of forthcoming auctions. The major auction houses usually have their own websites. Alternatively try sites such as www.liveauctioneers.com or www.antiqueweek.com.*

- Buy a sale catalog through the mail or at the auction preview. Mark the lots you are interested in.

- Attend the preview and closely examine the lots, checking especially for condition. For more information, always ask a member of staff.

- Decide the maximum you are prepared to bid. Use the estimated low-to-high price bands in the catalog as a guide, or ask a member of staff, and factor in the auctioneer's "buyer's premium" (10–25 percent of the sale price plus any relevant federal or state sales taxes).

- Confirm acceptable methods and timing of payment—the latter is usually within one to three days.

- If required, register your name and contact details in order to bid; you will be given a numbered card or paddle to hold up if your bid is successful. This enables auction staff to note who won the bid.

- If you are unable to go to the sale,

leave a written bid (the highest price that you are prepared to pay) with a member of staff.

- Get to the sale in plenty of time for your first lot. Auctioneers can get through 80–120 lots an hour, sometimes more, so build in a margin of error.

- The auctioneer will start the bidding around the lower catalog estimate, but will keep lowering it until there is a bid. The bids will then be increased in regular increments, usually of around 10–20 percent of the bid amount ($10s, $20s, $100s, $1,000s, depending on the lot), until one bidder is left. The auctioneer ends the bidding by banging a gavel on his rostrum.

- Don't worry about coughs or twitches winning you an unwanted lot and a hefty bill. This is a myth. To join the bidding at any stage, catch the auctioneer's attention by holding up your card or paddle, or your catalog. After acknowledging your first bid, he will accept subsequent bids on the nod of a head—or your withdrawal on a sideways shake of the head.

- Don't get caught up in "auction fever." Stick to the price limit you set yourself at the preview.

- Having paid for your lots, you can remove them. Most auction houses request collection within three days, or storage may be charged.

Character collectibles, pp. 232–33

Salt and pepper shakers, pp. 108–09

Jewelry, pp. 176–77

PEZ, pp. 288–89

Cult TV, pp. 230–1

and value, and politely haggle over the asking price. Always ask for a written receipt, not only for your own records, but also to prove you bought in good faith in case, as very occasionally happens, the object turns out to have been stolen.

Of the various sources dedicated to collectibles, auction houses are the most intimidating to new collectors. Don't be put off! Buying at auction is fun, addictive, and allows you to compete with dealers and other collectors on equal terms. Stick to a few simple rules *(see left, Buying at auction)* and you'll be fine.

Professional dealers tend to concentrate on specific collectibles, such as those by certain manufacturers or designers. Some dealers trade from shops (names and addresses are listed in *Maloney's Antiques and Collectibles Resource Directory*; some are also listed at the end of this book). Others trade at local, national, or international collectors' shows (dates and locations are flagged on the internet, in local press, or in leaflets and booklets at many shows). Some trade from all these places and many also have websites and mail-order services. Establishing friendly relationships with reputable dealers will prove invaluable. They are a great source of information and expertise. If they don't

Tins, pp. 98–101

have a particular piece in stock, they can often find it for you through their contacts. After a while they may also offer you first refusal on new acquisitions, and sometimes the more you buy from them, the more generous their discounts.

The newest source of collectibles is the internet. Online auction sites, the most famous of which is eBay, have revolutionized the market. You can now bid for Murano glass in Denver or Staffordshire figures in Salt Lake City: location is no obstacle. Again, don't feel intimidated about stepping into this global shopping mall; most sellers are eager to help because they want to sell their

Cataloging and insurance

Since most household contents insurance policies exclude collectibles, you should take out an "All Risks" policy or a special independent policy that covers fire, theft, or accidental loss or damage, and values each piece by the cost of its replacement. To facilitate a claim, catalog each piece as follows:

- Photograph it, preferably from several different angles —also showing any damage or identifying features.

- Store photographic prints in a record book; if you use a digital camera, store image files on a disk.

- Keep all receipts, detailing the vendor, purchase date, price paid, and a full description of the piece. If bought at auction, also keep the sale catalog.

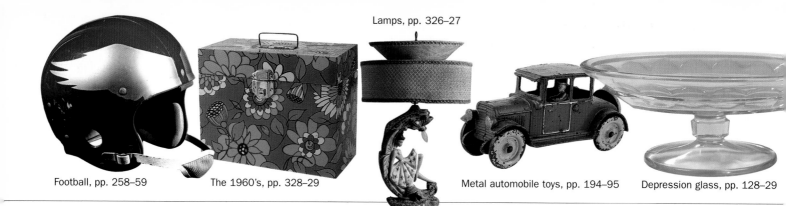

Football, pp. 258–59   The 1960's, pp. 328–29   Lamps, pp. 326–27   Metal automobile toys, pp. 194–95   Depression glass, pp. 128–29

Setting out your stall

When selling at a garage sale or collectibles fair, maximize the attractiveness of your wares and encourage buyers to return at a future sale, as follows:

- Cover your table with neutral, plain-colored fabric—patterns and vibrant colors won't show off your pieces to best effect.

- Ensure the table is well lit. Augment overhead lighting with desk lamps; an extension cable is invaluable.

- Don't overload the table so that pieces obscure one another.

- Label each piece with an asking price.

- Answer any questions as fully as possible, and in a friendly and enthusiastic manner.

- Be prepared to negotiate over price, but never accept less than your preset minimum (and only accept checks with a check guarantee card).

- Present fragile purchases in bubble wrap.

item. If you ask them questions such as whether they can supply further images of any damage or maker's marks, you should receive a reply. Each site provides user-friendly instructions on how to register, how to contact the seller for additional information, and how to bid. They also give instructions on when and how to pay (including more secure electronic systems such as Nochex, Bidpay, or Paypal).

Care and repair

Collectibles that are in good condition not only look better; they also command higher prices than their dirty, worn, or damaged equivalents. Equally, an incorrectly cleaned or badly repaired collectible is invariably worth much less than a slightly shabby or unrestored example. Always entrust any repairs to a professional restorer, and refer to one of the many books on caring for collectibles before starting to clean. These give specific do's and don'ts on cleaning the various materials from which collectibles are made.

Where and how to sell

Some of the sources for buying collectibles *(see pp. 10–11)* also apply to selling them. Consider a conventional auction house or an internet auction site if selling only one or two pieces. The former describes the object for you in a catalog and markets it to buyers as well as handling the sale for you (for a seller's commission of 10–25 percent plus applicable tax). The latter (usually for a small fee and commission rate) gives detailed instructions on

Vintage advertising,
pp. 286–87

Nursery ware, pp. 50–51

PEZ, pp. 288–89

Jadeite, pp. 104–05

Fiesta ware, pp. 22–23

Lady head vases,
pp. 56–57

Scandinavian glass, pp. 122–25

how to conduct, monitor, and close the sale but you must do all the work yourself, including photography. For both an auction house and an internet auction site, set a reserve price—the minimum you will accept. A good alternative can be selling direct to dealers: you may be offered as much as you would get at auction, but remember that they will price the object higher when they sell it, to cover their overheads.

For larger numbers of collectibles under $100—say, 20 or more—consider paying for a stall at a local sale (at around $20–60 for the day). For a similar number of more expensive pieces, apply for a stand at a local collectibles show or market. Forthcoming dates, locations, and organizers' details can be found in *Antique Week*. How well you do depends on the desirability of your pieces, and how realistically they are priced. But basic selling techniques *(see left Setting out your stall)*, also play an important part.

Enthusiasm and knowledge

Looking back over the last 30 years, I can conclude that enthusiasm and knowledge maximize pleasure and profit in the world of collectibles. The purpose of this book is to inspire that enthusiasm and convey that knowledge. If it does, I'm sure you will derive as much enjoyment from buying, keeping, or selling collectibles as I have.

Judith Miller

How to use this book

Buy, Keep or Sell?—The insider's guide to identifying trash, treasure, or tomorrow's antiques is divided into 10 chapters, covering topics from ceramics and glass to beauty and fashion. Within each chapter, pages focus on the work of a specific designer or manufacturer; on a subject area, such as Scandinavian glass; or on a general collecting field, such as the 1950s. Setting the topic in its historic and social context, each section also offers an insight into influences, styles, techniques, and current market values. Special feature boxes include *Top Tips*, *A closer look at...*, and *Collector's corners*. Central to the book's theme are the *Buy, Keep,* and *Sell* items which feature on every topic to help you make the right choices and investments.

Buy, Keep, or Sell identifies a specific type of collectible to buy, keep, or sell, and explains why.

The Essentials boxes show either the essential collectibles in a featured field, or key designs from a particular designer or manufacturer.

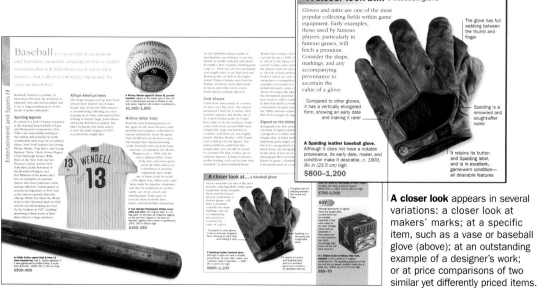

A closer look appears in several variations: a closer look at makers' marks; at a specific item, such as a vase or baseball glove (above); at an outstanding example of a designer's work; or at price comparisons of two similar yet differently priced items.

Top Tips gives expert advice on what to look for, care and storage, and how to recognize fakes.

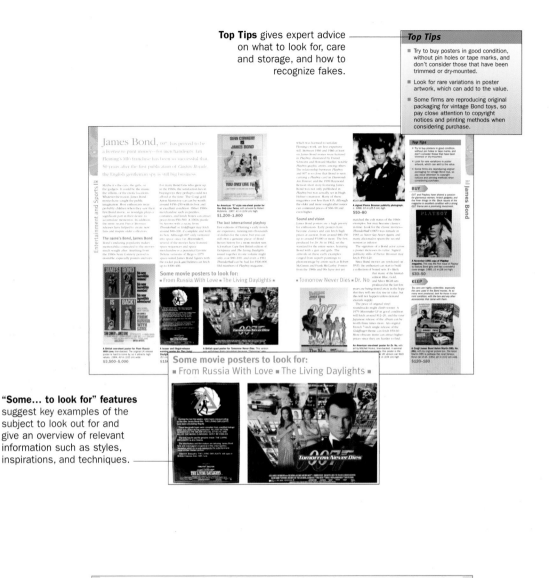

"Some… to look for" features suggest key examples of the subject to look out for and give an overview of relevant information such as styles, inspirations, and techniques.

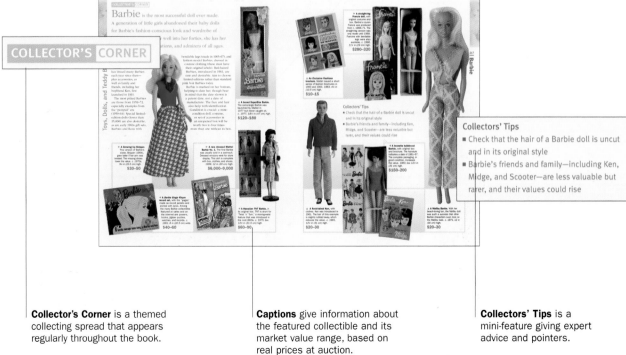

Collector's Corner is a themed collecting spread that appears regularly throughout the book.

Captions give information about the featured collectible and its market value range, based on real prices at auction.

Collectors' Tips is a mini-feature giving expert advice and pointers.

Ceramics

From the ornate, traditional styles of the 19th century to the colorful, excitingly modern forms of the mid-20th century, ceramic ware offers a huge diversity of styles packed into a relatively short time span.

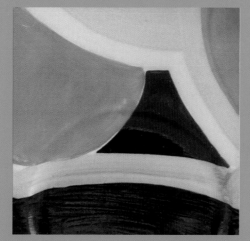

Jackie Kennedy
lady head vase,
p. 56

1

Satsuma
vase, p. 43

2

Clarice Cliff
pitcher, p. 20

3

The evolving styles of....

Ceramic ware styles are a faithful reflection of the rapidly changing world for which they were created. Industrialization in the 19th century gave rise to new markets for household goods, and an insatiable demand developed for new designs and modern styles.

7

Ceramics, whether functional or purely decorative, can be found in every American home. Many have become highly collectible and you may be surprised to learn their value today. Whether it's an old dinner service that you have inherited, or a 1950s lady head vase ①, it's well worth checking out.

Oriental ceramics ② have been exported to the West for centuries. Pieces salvaged from ancient shipwrecks are often sold at auction as salvage cargoes and there are still some bargains to find, if you're lucky.

Bold design

Ceramics really started to respond to Modernism in the 1920s and 30s, with an explosion of vivid colors and bold, geometric designs. Clarice Cliff ③, Royal Winton ④, Weller, and Fiesta ⑤ created sleek, streamlined pieces that encapsulated the Jazz Age and were the antithesis of traditional styles. Some makers continued to seek inspiration in the past: 1930s chintzware was based on the fabric designs imported from Asia in the 17th and 18th centuries. Lusterware ⑥, with

Ceramics really started
to respond to Modernism
in the 1920s and 30s,
with an explosion of
vivid colors and bold,
geometric designs.

8

Soldier Boy

Hummel figurine, p. 55

Roseville Futura
vase, p. 31

J.H. Cope & Co. wall
mask, p. 27

9

Royal Winton
vase, p. 25

④

⑤

Fiesta pitcher, p. 22

⑥

Maling bowl, p. 37

.ceramics

its dazzling, iridescent surfaces, is another example of how traditional elements have been reworked. Hummel figurines ⑦, produced from the 1930s onward, have great appeal and a strong collectors' following. Emphasizing form over decoration, the Art Deco Roseville Futura line ⑧ is stylish and highly desirable.

Floral and feminine

Pretty, feminine designs, such as those of ceramic wall masks ⑨ and lady head vases, are always a favorite with collectors. Roseville produced a huge bouquet of floral lines such as Sunflower, Wisteria, and Foxglove ⑩. Other popular ceramics include 1920s and 30s English cottage ware—pastoral nostalgia in reaction to the upheaval of

World War I—and nursery ware, which includes the whimsical characters designed by Mabel Lucie Atwell.

Made in America

While many admire the rustic charm of stoneware and redware, American art pottery from the Arts & Crafts era is immensely desirable. Makers such as Roseville, Fulper, Van Briggle, and Grueby embraced ideals of quality and craftsmanship. Rookwood ⑪ produced handmade wares and experimented with colorful matte glazes. Pieces can sell for large sums, but many of their Production line items are much more affordable.

⑪

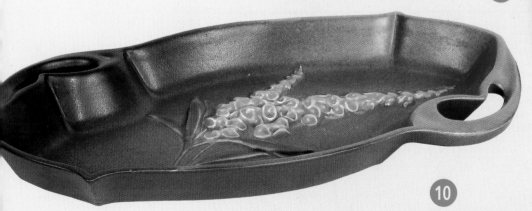

⑩

Roseville Foxglove tray, p. 30

Rookwood vase, p. 29

Clarice Cliff, the most famous and innovative English designer of Art Deco ceramics, was known as the Sunshine Girl, an expression that aptly conjures up the bold patterns and bright colors of her extraordinarily zestful output.

Bizarre salt and pepper shakers. The salt shaker is painted with stylized flowers, the pepper shaker with yachts under sail. *1930s, 3 in (8 cm) high.*

$150–200 for the pair

Clarice Cliff's designs were shockingly innovative for her era, with their cacophony of bright colors and jazzy geometric shapes. Cliff has grown in popularity over recent decades, and most people are familiar with her extrovert style. While a plate can fetch up to $1,500 and a pitcher $9,000 or more, small objects such as cruet sets or anything in the Crocus pattern are usually less expensive and make a good starting point for a collection.

A Bizarre tale

Born in 1899 in Tunstall, Stoke-on-Trent, England, Cliff began work aged 13 as an apprentice freehand pottery painter in a local factory. She then moved to the A. J. Wilkinson Royal Staffordshire Pottery, where she learned techniques of modeling and designing pottery. Colley Shorter, the managing director at the factory, recognized Cliff's talents. He became her protector, sponsor, lover, and, eventually, her husband. By 1927 Shorter had set up a small studio for Cliff at his own Newport Pottery in Burslem. In 1928 the Bizarre line, which had a distinctive, warm "honey" glaze, was launched as inexpensive domestic pottery. Cliff's fast-growing team of female painters became known as the Bizarre Girls. By 1930, Cliff was appointed art director of the Newport Pottery, the first woman to achieve such status in the potteries. Over the next decade Bizarre ware continued to be a great success.

World War II brought with it the decline of hand-painted pottery, with limited materials and a shortage of workers. After Shorter's death in 1963, both factories were sold to W. R. Midwinter Ltd.

Patterns and shapes

During her long career, Cliff designed more than 2,000 patterns. Although Bizarre is probably her best-known line, others such as Fantasque are also popular, as are her 1930s landscape designs rendered in the Art Deco style and using the same palette of bold, bright colors. Among Cliff's most sought-after patterns are May Avenue, Appliqué, Inspiration, Sunray, Mountain, and Solitude. Crocus, a best-seller of the time (available 1928–63), is still commonly

A closer look at... a Clarice Cliff Lotus pitcher with Sliced Circle pattern

This pitcher was made at the height of Bizarre-ware production using the Sliced Circle pattern on a Lotus-shape pitcher. It is fully marked with Bizarre stamping and signature on the base.

Geometric patterns are the most popular of Clarice Cliff styles

The enameled paint was applied thickly inside strong black outlines, leaving behind visible brushstrokes, although by 1930 these were slightly less prominent

The simple shape of Lotus pitchers shows off the pattern clearly—you get a lot of pattern for your money

This example is in perfect condition, with no scratches, chips, or rubbing of the paintwork

A Sliced Circle pattern Lotus pitcher. *c. 1929–30, 11½ in (29 cm) high.*
$7,000–10,000

Maker's marks

Rubber-stamped or printed (lithographed) marks were used from 1928 onward. The stamp sometimes printed unevenly.

HAND PAINTED Fantasque by Clarice Cliff WILKINSON LTD ENGLAND

This mark was used around 1929–30. It is a typical printed Fantasque mark.

found in different color schemes. Honolulu, Oranges and Lemons, and Windbells—all part of the Bizarre line—are also desirable, as are Secrets and Nasturtium. Collectible shapes include Bon Jour, Stamford, Biarritz, and Lotus, and, in particular, the 1930s Conical line of cone-shaped bowls, vases, and tea ware with triangular handles or feet.

The perfect marriage

The value of a Cliff piece is determined by the combination of shape, pattern, and condition. A circular bowl in the May Avenue pattern is common, so it will be worth less than the same pattern on a rarer conical sugar sifter. The earlier Bizarre pieces are most in demand and consequently fetch the highest prices. Changing trends play a big part: a stunning Bizarre vase will be less valuable if it is decorated in a pattern that is unfashionable today, such as Whisper.

Check spouts, handles, rims, and bases for signs of chipping. Look for a printed mark and signature on the base (except with smaller examples such as salt and pepper shakers).

Purely decorative Clarice Cliff reproductions are available, but these are not a serious collecting area and prices are unlikely to rise yet.

A Honolulu pattern side plate.
c. 1933, 7 in (18 cm) diam.
$200–300

A shape 362 vase, with colorful geometric and triangular design, and blue borders. *c. 1930, 7¾ in (19.5 cm) high.*
$700–1,000

Did You Know?

After 30 years on top of a closet, a never-before-seen c. 1932 Clarice Cliff charger in the desirable May Avenue pattern set a new world auction record. After much frantic bidding, it sold for $60,000 at Christie's South Kensington, London. Chargers are rare anyway, but the unusual color, large size of 18 in (46 cm) diameter, and immaculate condition made collectors the world over long to add it to their collections. The inspiration for the May Avenue design came from an oil painting by the Italian artist Modigliani, and the name of the design was taken from a street near Cliff's Tunstall birthplace.

Top Tips

- Opt for rarer color variations such as blue or purple. These can often fetch a higher price than the more common orange-colored pieces.
- Look for wares that are thickly painted with visible brushstrokes and have designs outlined in black. These typify early Cliff and are much sought after.
- Expand your collection with non-geometric patterns and shapes that show hallmarks of Cliff's typical designs.
- Beware of fakes. Telltale signs include wishy-washy colors, an uneven honey glaze, and artificial crackling in the glaze around the mark.
- On a pitcher handle, look for a blow hole, indicating that it has been hollow cast—a sure sign of a fake, as the handles on Cliff's originals were always solid.
- Check that all the pieces in a set are present and match. Examine lids carefully to make sure that they are original. Patterns should line up exactly, with the design sometimes flowing from the body onto the lid.

KEEP

The Crocus pattern is one of Cliff's most popular designs and was a best-seller in its day. Look for shapes that epitomize Art Deco, such as this cone-shaped sugar sifter. Pieces with appealing designs on typical Art Deco shapes are increasingly sought after and should rise in value.

A Crocus pattern conical sugar sifter. The brown band was meant to represent the Earth and the yellow band the Sun. *1930s, 5¾ in (14.5 cm) high.*
$500–700

SELL

Pieces in muted colors, such as this preserve pot, are not as popular with collectors, who want the colorful, stylized, geometric look. Sell this and invest in a piece more typical of Cliff.

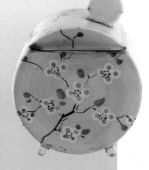

A May Blossom pattern Bon Jour preserve pot and cover. The piece is damaged, which reduces its value. *c. 1936, 4 in (10 cm) high.*
$60–90

Fiesta ware has been enjoyed by four generations of Americans, who love its modern, cheerful look. Designed to brighten kitchens during the Depression, these everyday wares are now very collectible, with pieces costing from $5 to $1,000.

A red sauce boat. *8½ in (20.5 cm) long.*
$50–80

Introduced in 1936 as tableware that was at once cost-effective and stylish, Fiesta ware was the brainchild of Homer Laughlin China, which, like all companies facing the Depression, had to rationalize manufacturing to survive. By limiting glazes to single colors and creating simple and streamlined pieces, the company actually came up with a line that was very much of its age—modern, striking, and highly desirable.

Created by British-born designer Frederick Hurton Rhead, the wares originally featured six bold, bright colors—red, yellow, cobalt blue, light green, ivory, and, just a year later, turquoise. The beauty of the concept, however, was that pieces could be mixed and matched. Tumblers accompanying a pitcher could be a rainbow of colors or all one shade. The colors chosen for the new line were very much the fashion in California art potteries—and

sometimes referred to as "old Mexico colors"—but until Laughlin took them up, they didn't sell well on the East Coast. The pieces had an architectural look as well, with many designs having sculpted concentric rings that gave the sense of having been handmade.

Of course, these dazzling dinnerwares were mass-produced and never meant to be expensive, selling at five-and-dime stores as well as Sears, Roebuck and Co., and Woolworth's. A 24-place setting cost about $11 in the 1930s, and it was the affordability of the wares that made them successful.

Today, a single 6-inch (15.25-cm) plate in a common color, such as light green, costs as little as $5–15 and a dinner plate $30–40. But, of course, plates, platters, and bowls are always made in greater quantities than, say, sauce boats, coffee pots, or casserole dishes, so basic pieces are inevitably cheaper.

In glazed semiporcelain, Fiesta wares are harder than earthenware and very

durable, but that doesn't mean they don't damage. Used for everyday purposes over many years, wares may often be chipped, cracked, or crazed—or even have glaze pops—and collectors prefer pieces that are in excellent condition. Since plates are so abundant, it's not necessary to buy pieces in poor condition. Minor factory faults are acceptable, since many wares are affected by these.

Splash of color

In the early 1950s, extra colors were added to the line, including rose, forest green, gray, and chartreuse, and, in 1959, medium green, which was produced for such a short time that it is considered a rarity. A medium-green casserole in mint condition can fetch up to $700–1,000, whereas a rose-colored

Some shapes to look for:
■ Vase ■ Candlesticks ■ Pitcher ■

A turquoise vase. Vases are sought-after shapes, particularly in certain colors such as ivory, and in the largest sizes. *8 in (20.5 cm) high.*
$500–700

A pair of chartreuse tripod candleholders, with stepped Art Deco styling. The modern yellow chartreuse was the third of Bloomingdale's three limited-edition colors. *c. 1996–98, 4 in (10 cm) high.*
$50–80

A cobalt blue pitcher. Spot older pitchers by a small dimple inside where the handle joins the body—modern pieces have large dimples. *1939–69, 7 in (18 cm) high.*
$200–250

one is $100 plus. Also rare are red pieces, which included uranium in their mix—a chemical that was requisitioned for military use during World War II and unavailable to potteries until the late 1950s. Expect to pay $30–50 for a red oval platter and less for a light green one. Ivory and yellow are also common.

Mix and match

Made in almost anything you could possibly want for the table, Fiesta ware was so popular that it was produced right up until 1973, although most collectors focus on the period up to 1969. There are condiment dishes, sauce boats, salt and pepper shakers, bowls, plates in many sizes, casseroles, coffee pots, and teapots. In addition to practical domestic items, decorative wares such as candlesticks and vases in different sizes—8, 10, and 12

inch (20, 25, and 30 cm)—and even a bud vase were made. Vases are popular with collectors and a 12-inch (30-cm) vase in a good color could fetch $1,000 or more. Also rare is the stick-handled demitasse coffee pot, which could be worth up to $800 in a desirable color. A cobalt blue example might run over $400 and a light green one up to $350.

Significantly, there is now a secondary market for new Fiesta pieces, which were reissued by Homer Laughlin China in 1986 in new, contemporary colors. These wares are also collectible, especially since some colors were introduced for a limited time before being discontinued; pearl gray, for example, finished production in December 2002. Some shades naturally become more sought after than others, but there is always a premium on the original, pre-1969 wares. Look for wares in the coveted lilac, made from 1993–95, and expect to pay $30–40 for a bowl and around $150 for a pitcher. Interestingly, this time around Fiesta production wasn't aimed at the lower end of the market, with New York stores like Bloomingdale's and B. Altman signing up to sell their customers the 50th anniversary reissue. That's a good sign that pieces will appreciate in value, since their popularity is still growing.

A pair of cobalt blue salt and pepper shakers. *Each 2½ in (6.5 cm) high.*
$30–50

■ Mixing bowls ■ Bowl ■

A yellow, No. 2-size nested mixing bowl. Mixing bowls come in seven sizes and are popular. *c. 1950s, 6½ in (17 cm) diam.*
$80–120

A red breakfast bowl. Although orange in color, collectors refer to this very popular color as red. *c. 1950s, 8¼ in (21 cm) wide.*
$50–80

Top Tips

- Fiesta wares (1936–73) were clearly marked: "Fiesta HLC USA"; "HLC Fiesta, made in USA"; "HLC Co., USA"; or, after 1986, "leadfree."

- New wares have distinctive colors such as cinnabar, rose, plum, and tangerine. On some hollow wares original molds were reused, so old marks may appear.

- Casserole dishes, carafes, and vases are almost always worth more than common shapes, such as dinner plates.

- Lids are on many collectors' wish lists, as so many were broken or damaged.

- Complete sets are very desirable, and ardent collectors want original sets, although many sets are made up.

KEEP ▶

With its unique and instantly identifiable shape and clean and modern lines, Frederick Rhead's pitcher design is one of the most desirable and recognizable Fiesta pieces. The concentric circle motif is also renowned and easy to spot. Pitchers in the different colors often form the core of many collections, ensuring strong and possibly even growing values.

A lilac pitcher, produced in a limited edition for Bloomingdale's. Lilac is no longer produced and, despite being modern, is a collectible and visually attractive color that may appreciate in value if demand increases. *1990s, 7 in (18 cm) high.*
$100–150

SELL ▶

Plates and platters in common colors are less valuable and unlikely to increase in value, as they are plentiful. Sell to another collector, but make sure the color isn't rare and pricier.

A light green platter. Light green is a common color but is often mistaken for the rarer medium green. *Plate 12 in (31.5 cm) wide.*
$30–40

1930s ceramics, like most other areas of the visual arts at the time, were hugely influenced by Art Deco. The vogue for Roseville Futura and Clarice Cliff has stimulated a growing interest in less expensive pieces by other manufacturers.

An early Crown Devon pitcher, handpainted with a geometric design. *1930s, 3½ in (8.5 cm) high.*

$100–150

The Depression of the early 1930s hit hard, with high unemployment and falling incomes. Yet there were many bright sparks of light amid the gloom. Architecture, cinema, and fashion flourished. The slogan of the New York World's Fair of 1939 encouraged citizens to look forward to "The World Of Tomorrow," and developments in technology, including new plastics and better refrigeration, contributed to the modernization of the home.

Art Deco on the map
To suit these modern homes, 1930s ceramics were bright and bold, often using the colorful geometric patterns pioneered by designers such as Clarice Cliff. The vogue for hand-painted decoration gave designers a broad palette with which to express new ideas. The influential 1925 Paris Exhibition, often seen as the starting point of Art Deco, featured pieces that imprinted the style on the popular consciousness. In the US, Art Deco was adopted by companies such as Cowan, Roseville, Lenox, and McCoy.

Smaller British makers, such as A. E. Gray & Co. Ltd., Myott, Crown Devon, and Wade Heath, also responded quickly to these changing tastes, and developed subjects and patterns that included ladies in crinolines, stylized floral motifs, leaping deer, sunray and geometric designs, budgerigars and parrots, and the ever-popular cottage scene.

Drawing a blank
Many smaller firms could not afford to invest in the production of new shapes, so used their new jazzy patterns on forms that had been created 30 years earlier. However, Art Deco decoration on 19th century shapes does not find as much favor with collectors today. A number of manufacturers, such as Gray's, often bought in blank wares on which to apply their own patterns, producing pieces in a style similar to Clarice Cliff's but painted with softer colors.

Geometry and relief
Susie Cooper, a very influential and prolific ceramics designer, flourished

A Wade Heath vase. Although better known for its nursery-ware patterns, this notable pottery introduced several Art Deco lines. *1930s, 7¼ in (18.5 cm) high.*

$400–600

Some makers and designers to look for:
▪ Wade Heath ▪ Cowan ▪ Weller ▪

A Cowan Persian blue Chinese Bird vase. Cowan made a variety of Art Deco lines, with limited-edition studio examples fetching the highest values. Lakeware pieces are less expensive. *1930s, 11¼ in (29 cm) high.*

$1,000–1,500

A Weller Tutone triangular vase, in red with green accents, faintly marked with a Weller Pottery half kiln stamp. Weller is known for its innovative glazes, such as Burnt Wood and Graystone. *Late 1920s, 11¾ in (30 cm) high.*

$150–250

in the 1930s. Cooper introduced bright geometric patterns, such as Moon and Mountains and Cubist, on a large range of beautifully practical household wares. These daring designs became her trademark and are still favorites among collectors. Pieces featuring her banding (juxtaposed thin and thick bands in muted or bright colors), the Patricia Rose and Endon patterns, and her later, more restrained plant form designs are also highly sought after.

Charlotte Rhead was a skilled tubeline decorator who created designs with a raised outline in liquid clay. She worked on many pottery lines, including Crown Ducal, and her pieces are also worth looking out for.

Fact or Fiction?

Colorful and typically Art Deco, Myott ware perhaps ought to be more highly valued. But collectors can't find any information on the factory, its production, or its designers, since all the company records and pattern books were destroyed in a factory fire in 1949. However, a keen-eyed member of the Myott Collectors' Club has reported seeing a pattern book in Leeds, England, recently. If it does exist, it would not only shed much-needed light on designers and production: it could also help values to rise.

The 1930s were a time for fun and frivolity—people wanted exciting colors and patterns to chase away their deeper forebodings.

A Susie Cooper for Gray's cup and saucer. Cooper was one of the most influential British Art Deco ceramics designers, and her brightly colored, geometric designs from the the late 1920s to the early 1930s are much sought after the world over. As well as patterns, Cooper also designed revolutionary shapes. *c. 1929, saucer 5½ in (14 cm) diam.*

$300–400

Top Tips

- Resist wares with plain decoration or chintzy patterns—they are less popular. Look instead for examples with angular, unusual shapes.
- Check hand-painted pieces for flaking, as any such damage will reduce value.
- Always look in thrift shops and yard sales: many people still ignore pieces unless they are by "big" names, such as Clarice Cliff or Roseville.

BUY

One notable yet lesser-known maker active in the Art Deco period was Myott & Son. It produced a diverse range of unusual shapes decorated with bold and abstract patterns reflecting the influence of ancient cultures, such as the Aztecs. Its most desirable pieces are still affordable and, as interest and knowledge grow, may rise in value (see Fact or Fiction?, left).

A Myott Star vase, hand painted. *1930s, 8¾ in (22 cm) high.*

$200–250

■ Royal Winton ■ Russel Wright ■

A Royal Winton vase. This hand-painted vase is quite different from the popular chintz designs that established Royal Winton's reputation and is testimony to the firm's ability to adapt to changing tastes. *1930s, 9 in (23 cm) high.*

$400–600

A Steubenville Coral water pitcher by Russel Wright. From the American Modern line, this is typical of Wright's streamlined, futuristic designs and muted colors, which were both revolutionary and successful in their day. *Late 1930s, 11¼ in (29 cm) high.*

$70–100

KEEP

Shelley used bone china, rather than earthenware, for its line of Vogue wares designed by Eric Slater, which borrowed their clean and streamlined shapes from the architecture of the period. This design is likely to become a period classic, so hold on to a complete set if you have one.

A Shelley Sun Ray Vogue-shape coffee set, 11742. The solid triangular handle is as overtly Art Deco as the Sun Ray pattern. *c. 1935, coffeepot 7 in (18 cm) high.*

$1,500–2,000

Ceramic wall masks

were inspired by the wooden tribal African face masks eagerly collected during the 1930s. Many lovers of kitsch and Art Deco find this unusual form of portraiture irresistible. It makes a striking feature on a staircase wall.

Unlike the tribal masks that inspired them, ceramic wall masks of the 1930s to 50s were given the bold colors and sharp contours of the period. Most masks were female, which allowed for a full exploration of flamboyant fashions in hair, makeup, and dress. The most important makers were the central Europeans Goldscheider, Goebel, and Royal Dux, based in Austria, Bavaria, and Bohemia, respectively. In the UK, the outstanding makers were Beswick, which had made its name in tableware and also produced popular animal figurines, and J. H. Cope of Staffordshire, which has a reputation for domestic ceramics. The masks often featured screen goddesses of the day, such as Marlene Dietrich, Dorothy Lamour, and Greta Garbo. Anonymous young women were also shown, modeling fashionable styles such as cropped, boyish hair. Masks were produced in various poses, as well as in groups, and faces often had idealized features such as arched eyebrows and almond eyes.

The 1950s examples displayed much more highly made-up faces, consistent with the postwar return to glamour in women's fashions. Dietrich, for example, was shown with high-arched, plucked eyebrows, almond eyes, yellow hair, and, on some of the Beswick models, a rakish French beret.

▲ **A plaster reproduction face wall mask of Betty Grable,** a favorite pin-up actress during World War II. This is a faithful reproduction of a 1950s example. *1990s, 10 in (25.5 cm) high.*

$60–90

► **A Beswick wall mask** with a high-fashion Art Deco look and a high-gloss glaze typical of a pre–World War II example. *1930s, 12 in (30.5 cm) high.*

$400–600

◄ **A rare Goldscheider wall mask** with finely modeled features and elaborate hair. This manufacturer is known for good modeling and painting, as well as fine materials. *c. 1925–28, 8½ in (21.5 cm) high.*

$1,000–1,500

▲ **A miniature Goldscheider wall mask** with short, black hair elaborately coiffed. The butterfly is a delicate feature and should be inspected for damage or repair. *c. 1925–28, 4½ in (11.5 cm) high.*

$500–700

▲ **A J. H. Cope & Co. wall mask** featuring a blonde with typically 1930s hair and makeup, wearing a hat with feather trim. *c. 1934, 12 in (30.5 cm) wide.*

$300–400

◀ **A Leonardi wall mask.** These were made in London, England, from the 1930s until the 1950s by a firm called Leonardene. *1940s, 20 in (51 cm) high.*

$280–320

◀ **A Goldscheider wall mask** with half-closed eyes and black, ringleted, "gypsy" hair. *c. 1925–28, 10 in (25.5 cm) high.*

$1,000–1,500

▶ **A faithfully painted plaster reproduction of a 1940s face wall mask.** *1980s, 10 in (25.5 cm) high.*

$60–90

▶ **A J. H. Cope & Co. wall mask** featuring a stylish lady in left profile with a hat and lustrous black hair. *c. 1934, 6½ in (16.5 cm) high.*

$120–180

◀ **A Goebel wall mask** with superb modeling and hand painting, further distinguished by the richness of the hair and the coquettish expression. *c. 1928–34, 8 in (20 cm) high.*

$280–320

Collectors' Tips

Look for these desirable features:

- Good-quality painting and modeling
- Period details including accessories, hair styles, and makeup
- Signs of aging that suggest a piece is genuine

◀ **A J. H. Cope & Co. wall mask** with high-gloss glazing, featuring a fashionable, typically 1930s woman. Cope is a popular manufacturer and this is one of its rarer right-profile masks. *c. 1934, 7 in (18 cm) high.*

$150–200

◀ **A miniature Goldscheider wall mask.** Black face masks are less common than white examples. *c. 1925–28, 4½ in (11.5 cm) high.*

$500–700

Rookwood, prized for its painterly look, is one of the biggest names in American art pottery. Early handmade wares are the most sought after, although there are plenty of more affordable Production pieces—for $100–400—to collect.

A porcelain scalloped bowl, painted with a bluebird on bamboo branches; marked on the base with a flame mark, "XLVI 6313," and an artist's mark. *1946, 8½ in (21.5 cm) diam.*
$400–600

Of all the art potteries started in the late 19th century, Rookwood is the most famous, influential, and collectible. At first, this distinctly American pottery made wares that were quite amateurish—gaudy in color and ungainly in shape—yet, only a few years into production its pieces had already acquired a wondrous synergy of decoration and form. The quality of the wares was so outstanding that the pottery won several prizes at expositions in Paris, St. Petersburg, and Buffalo, New York.

Established in 1880 in Cincinnati, Ohio, by a socialite named Maria Longworth, the Rookwood pottery was unique from the outset in that its owner was a woman. The main reason for its success, however, was the innovative atmosphere she created there, with artists—over 150 of them—encouraged to study abroad and experiment with

A carved, Matte cylindrical vase decorated by Rose Fescheimer, with stylized poppy pods in indigo and green; marked with a flame mark and "V 952E RF." *1905, 7 in (18 cm) high.*
$250–350

new ideas. The most dramatic development occurred in 1884 when decorator Laura Fry discovered the use of the atomizer, which made it possible to apply glazes evenly and with subtle gradations of color, giving Rookwood's glazes their special quality. Also key to the sophisticated look was the recruitment, from Japan in 1887, of Kataro Shirayamadani. He encouraged other Rookwood artists to cover the whole vessel with decoration, not just the front, as was the Western way.

Standard fare

The masterly use of glazes most distinguished the early pieces, which had a rich painterly look. One of the most recognizable styles is a chocolate-brown background fading to ocher and green, hand painted with slip to give a sense of texture, then glossed over. This look—called Rookwood Standard—was endlessly copied but never equaled.

Flower motifs are common, historical personalities and Native Americans less so, forcing prices for these into the thousands.

As with all art pottery, the wares were created to make handcrafted work accessible to all. Ironically, most of the early hand-painted wares are now the province of salerooms and museums, with a Flying Cranes vase from c. 1900 decorated by Shirayamadani selling for a world record $305,000 in 2004. Even if signed by a designer, however, early pieces can be had for much less ($600–3,000); a 9-inch (23-cm) Standard-glaze vase with blueberries and leaves, dating to c. 1901 and signed by Lenore Asbury, recently made just over $700.

Matte work

Luckily for Rookwood enthusiasts, the factory existed long enough to embrace cheaper production methods, and wares of all qualities and prices are available, with the earliest mass-produced pieces dating from c. 1905. The "Production" vases from the 1930s and 40s can be under $100. These are usually smaller (5–8 inches [12.5–20.25 cm]) and in matte glazes, although most run $100–200.

A Production creamer and sugar bowl, embossed with a four-square design under a shaded blue glaze; marked on the base with a flame mark and the date. *1912, 3 in (7.5 cm) high.*
$280–380

Vases are usually worth the most, although a collector would prize a vivid-blue gloss ashtray from c. 1931 ($30–50), a mottled bud vase from c. 1919 ($70–100), or a pair of Matte crystalline-glaze candleholders ($150–200). Look for paperweights, figurines, and bookends, which are going up in value.

Early Production pieces, of better quality than later ones, attract a premium. Matte finishes, too, are increasingly attractive to collectors. These were introduced in 1901, along with more naturalistic decoration, in response to changing tastes and the arrival in the United States of the Arts and Crafts movement. Another variation is the Vellum glaze, which, although matte, was translucent enough to allow for underglaze painting—often a landscape. Vellum wares by named designers can be expensive, costing $800–3,000. Also prized are Sea Green and Iris glazes, which are usually in pale hues.

End of the line

As the Depression took hold, glazes with hand-painted scenes became too labor intensive to make. Rookwood had to compete with other potteries, and more mass-produced pieces were made, many in the sensuous shapes of the originals. Using commercial techniques, however, didn't save the pottery from bankruptcy in 1941 and closure in the Sixties. Even so, any survey of Rookwood's wares will show that it stuck to its handcrafted ideals longer than most, and the look and quality the pieces still make them desirable. Today, the pottery has been revitalized, but collectors prefer pre-1967 Production pieces and early wares. Above all, they look for good condition.

A Vellum vase, painted by Sally Coyne, with stylized poppies on a gray background and fine crazing all over. *1908, 8¼ in (20.5 cm) high.*

$700–1,000

29

Rookwood

Top Tips

- Early Rookwood items bear an intertwined R and P. From 1886 an R-P appears, with a flame for each year. After 1900, the last two digits of the year (e.g., V for 1905) were in Roman numerals. Pieces from 1980 (made under license) have Arabic numerals.

- Works are in porcelain, earthenware, and clays. Marks show color or type of clay: P is for soft porcelain; Z for matte; V for vellum; X for factory "second."

- Artists' monograms (e.g., ETH for E. T. Hurley), attract a huge premium. Production pieces are unsigned.

BUY

Rookwood Production vases can be found in many Rookwood collections. With their classic colors and modern, simple forms, the pieces also fit well in modern interiors. Those decorated with stylized, molded designs are typical of Rookwood and tend to be more popular and valuable than plain examples.

A Rookwood Production narrow vase embossed with a band of modern, stylized seahorses under an appealing blue glaze; marked and dated. *1923, 6¾ in (17 cm) high.*

$250–350

KEEP

The Arts & Crafts movement in ceramics is widely popular, leading to consistently strong prices in general. The delicate Matte glaze is desirable, and only a few artists painted in this style since it was very hard to achieve. Flowers are typical motifs. Look for bright, strong colors, as these examples are likely to increase in value.

An aqua Dogwood Matte-glazed vase; marked "#906C" and Rookwood. Signed "A.R. Valentien" for Albert Valentien, who painted the first Rookwood Matte-glaze vase. *1900–10, 6½ in (16.5 cm) high.*

$700–900

A closer look at... a Standard-glaze vase

Although Standard-glaze pieces were more popular during the 1960s and 70s, certain pieces can still fetch high prices. Look at the design, since rare portraits, especially of Native Americans or statesmen, are extremely sought after. Unusual shapes such as the "pillow" shape and larger sizes also fetch a premium, as do those with added silver decoration, by the Gorham Silversmith Company.

At 10 inches (25.4 cm) high, this piece is comparatively larger than many others, making it more desirable

The "Old Master" style of painting in a brown palette is typical, and is further strengthened by showing the portrait of Van Dyck, an historic Old Master painter

A Standard-glaze vase painted by Grace Young, marked and dated on the base. *1902, 10 in (25.5 cm) high.*

$1,500–2,000

Standard-glaze pieces are usually decorated with floral designs; portraits are rarer and increase value

Roseville pottery—a virtual flower garden of pretty pieces—is distinguished by an endless variety of shapes and patterns. For a reasonable outlay, a collector can amass an impressive display from lilies and roses to poppies and pine cones.

A pink Foxglove tray, shape no. 424-14, marked "USA." *15 in (37.5 cm) long.*
$150–200

Of all the major art potteries, Roseville was the most mechanized. Far from diminishing the quality of the pieces, technology was used to stress the importance of the sculptural shape over expensive hand-painted decoration (that competitor Rookwood specialized in). Endlessly inventive, Roseville created a staggering range of lines—so varied were the styles, shapes, glazes, and patterns that there is something for everyone. And, as the most productive and long-lived of the art potteries, Roseville deserves a place in the display cabinet of any serious collector.

A rose is a rose

Begun by George F. Young in 1892, the factory was based in Roseville, Ohio (hence, the name), but later moved to Zanesville. As floral motifs were the basis of its designs, the name is quite inspired. Although it produced some handmade pottery, the factory was a commercial enterprise. It did have prestige lines such as Rozane and, from 1914, the marbleized Pauleo, but most vases cost just $5.

Today, expect to pay $60–90 into the thousands for a Rozane vase and up to $3,000 for an exceptional Pauleo piece, although many other lines also command good prices. Made from 1930, Sunflower is a moldmade ware that is appreciated for its bold floral motif; a vase can be worth $300–900 and a tall jardinière up to $3,500. A Pine Cone vase (1935–50) could

fetch $200–500. With its distinctive frieze of dancing cherubs, Donatello was successful in its day, but no longer has the cachet of the most-loved floral designs. Early Florentine doesn't fetch high prices, and the later designs decline in value. Mayfair, Wincraft, Foxglove, and Freesia are less popular than Ferrella, Wisteria, and Baneda.

Flower power

Hundreds of floral lines in several colorways were produced and, inevitably, there are favorites. Blue Pine Cone is more sought after than brown or green, and in Baneda green is preferred to pink. Vases are more popular than bowls. Enthusiasts try to collect all the shapes in a line, which is achievable with Sunflower but almost impossible with Pine Cone or Futura. Small floral vases range from $20–30 to

Some Roseville lines to look for:
- Blackberry ▪ Falline ▪ Pine Cone

A Blackberry vase, shape no. 571-6. This popular line is unmarked, except for a paper label or red crayon shape number, if they survive. *Introduced 1934, 6¼ in (15.5 cm) high.*
$400–500

A brown Falline amphora-shaped vase design; base marked "91." Look for the more sought-after blue colorway. *Introduced 1933, 7¼ in (18 cm) high.*
$350–450

A blue Pine Cone bowl, marked "Roseville 276-9" on the base. One of the best-selling designs, blue is one of the most desirable colors. *Introduced 1935, 11½ in (28.75 cm) long.*
$250–350

$100–150; wall pockets and bookends are also affordable. Look for crisp molded details, avoiding "flat" examples. Also consider glaze, which should be well applied, with no dripping. Strong colors and gentle color graduation are also prized.

One of the most collectible—and atypical—lines is the Art Deco Futura, with its bold colors, geometric designs, and streamlined shapes.

Shape was very important at Roseville, and the switch in 1919 from freehand decoration to moldmade pieces added to an already distinctive look of ruffled rims, exaggerated shapes, attenuated necks, and innovative handles.

Shape shift

Artists were not generally identified, although signatures can be found by decorators such as Katy Duvall, Hester Pillsbury, and the Timberlake sisters, Mae and

A Rozane vase, in standard glaze, decorated and signed by Walter Myers, otherwise unmarked; with a few light abrasions and firing mark from a kiln stilt. 14¾ in (5.5 cm) high.

$300–400

Sarah. Another important name is Frederick Hurten Rhead (later known for Fiesta ware). He emphasized the 3-D form over painted decoration, introducing the famous Della Robbia. This handmade line was never made in quantity, so pieces can go for up to $20,000.

Glazes also had their role to play: matte glazes were the most common, but marbleized or mottled finishes (seen on Dahlrose), and even luster or gloss were also used. Mongol is a striking *sang de beouf* (oxblood) and other early glossy glazes included the rich ochers and browns of Rozane and the pale blues of Azurean. These were similar to Rookwood, although are not considered as exceptional.

Top Tips

- Choose pieces with crisp detail.
- Go for a handsome glaze, strong colors, and clearly defined decoration.
- Damage reduces value; (minor) damage is acceptable only on the rarest pieces.
- Works after the 1940s will nearly always be inexpensive and less desirable.
- Early, hand-painted wares are often marked. Those from 1915–30 tend not to be, or have paper or foil labels. Later pieces may bear a shape number and "Roseville" or "Roseville USA."

BUY ▶

The current vogue for the Art Deco style has led to increased demand for the Futura line, with its angular shapes and designs. Its popularity among both Art Deco and Roseville collectors should ensure consistent prices and even steady increases. Look for unusual or outlandish shapes such as the "tank" and large pieces, as these are of greater value.

A Futura blue triangle vase, which exemplifies the Art Deco style in form and design. It would have fetched more had it not been restored. c. 1929, 9¼ in (23 cm) high.

$300–400

SELL ▶

Collectors look for examples with good levels of molding detail and strong, rather than insipid, colors. Values are also lowered if a line is not in demand and is readily available in the marketplace. Values are unlikely to go up, so sell to a collector who wishes to build up a more inexpensive collection of Roseville.

A gray Gardenia cornucopia vase. Produced in three colorways and introduced in 1950, the Gardenia line is not an early line. However, this is a desirable shape. 6 in (15 cm) high.

$80–120

Jonquil ▪ Zephyr Lily ▪

A Jonquil vase, shape no. 542-5½, but unmarked. Jonquil was only produced in this colorway, but remains popular. *Introduced 1931, 5½ in (13.75 cm) high.*

$250–350

A brown Zephyr Lily wall pocket, marked "USA 1297-8." Zephyr Lily was produced in three colorways and wall pockets are a very desirable shape. *Introduced 1946, 8¼ in (20.5 cm) high.*

$200–300

American Arts and Crafts

pottery is particularly vibrant. The early utilitarian style gave way to sophisticated pieces that capture the confidence of a nation growing up. Prices can be astronomical, but there's still room for the new collector.

A Fulper gourd-shaped, two-handled vase, covered in mottled blue and amber glaze, with some glaze bubbles. The piece bears a horizontal mark. *1909–15, 7½ in (19 cm) high.*

$350–450

Whether highly decorated, hand-carved, or molded with simple glazes, art pottery was a national phenomenon in the United States in the late 19th and early 20th centuries, when the country began to flex its industrial muscles and stretch its creative talents. Inspired by European styles seen at the 1876 Centennial Exhibition in Philadelphia, the look was a distinctly American take on the British Arts and Crafts movement. Anyone fortunate enough to own Arts and Crafts pottery should have it valued, as prices frequently run into the thousands of dollars. For those starting a collection, don't be daunted, as many beautiful pieces can be found for $100–500.

An art is born

The Ohio River Valley and East Coast are the birthplaces of American art pottery. The Ohio potters—the most famous being Rookwood and Roseville —initially favored painting their wares,

although other potteries saw their vessels as organic wholes and didn't distinguish between decoration and form. One such factory was The American Terra Cotta and Ceramic Co., makers of sewer pipes and bricks that formed a successful art line in 1901 called Teco. Pieces in good condition can fetch four figures, although those with slight damage can go for $500–800. Grueby of Boston—another brickmaker —also developed an art-pottery line that was so successful that its pieces are synonymous with American Arts and Crafts. Hand-thrown vessels are pricey, although, at $300–500 each, tiles by Grueby could be a good investment.

Glazed over

Glazes became a consuming passion for two eminent Arts and Crafts exponents —William H. Fulper Jr. and Artus Van Briggle. Fulper, who began making

wares in 1909, experimented with hundreds of glazes, from lusters and high-gloss glazes to mattes and crystallines. Today, collectors pay a premium for his highly original works: from $100–200 for a twisted-stem candlestick to $1,000 or more for a jardinière. Van Briggle spent years researching a rich-matte glaze. His Lorelei vase (c. 1901), which shows a long-haired woman almost flowing from the vessel, is a signature piece of American art pottery. As with all pottery, size, condition, and design matter, although date is important too, with early works fetching

Some makers to look for:
▪ Teco ▪ Marblehead ▪ Van Briggle ▪

A Teco pitcher with whiplash handle in matte green glaze, stamped "Teco." Plain, thickly potted walls and a silvery green glaze are typical. *1903–10, 4 in (10 cm) high.*

$500–800

A Marblehead squat vessel incised with Glasgow roses. Marblehead often uses stylized flowers, animals, or insects. The crack reduces value. *c. 1908, 5 in (12.5 cm) wide.*

$250–350

A Van Briggle bulbous vase, embossed with leaves under a Persian Rose glaze; typical of Van Briggle's style. Glazes tend to be in deep, rich hues. *1917, 7½ in (19 cm) high.*

$300–500

the most. Small, plain vases from 1905–15 can be had for $200–700. Pieces from 1920 on, made using old molds, are not generally of the same quality as earlier works, but, at $200–600, offer an affordable entry into the market.

Madness of George Ohr

Founded in Zanesville, Ohio, in 1871, Weller aimed to produce art pottery at affordable prices. Many lines resemble those of Rookwood and Roseville. The Louwelsa line from 1894, for example, imitated Rookwood's Standard glaze with its hand-decorated slip design. Prices are lower than for Rookwood, with an 11-inch (28-cm) floral-pattern vase costing around $400 and a pitcher going for about $250–300. The iridescent Sicardo line by Jacques Sicard can fetch $2,000–3,000, as can finer Hudson pieces. After the Depression, Weller made inexpensive molded wares such as the Woodcraft, Marvo, and Tutone lines, which can be $50–$500. Form and decoration merged harmoniously at the Newcomb College pottery in New Orleans (1895–1945). Wares feature bayou landscapes, lizards, waterbirds, and native crops such as

tobacco. Collectors love these pieces, and a 5-inch (12.7-cm) vase signed by the artist Joseph Meyer could fetch $2,000–2,500. Also sought after are wares by the eccentric potter George Ohr (the "Mad Potter of Biloxi"). His works, typically with thin sides strangled into asymmetrical form, can sell for $300 to $18,000, although a teapot went for $65,000 at auction.

Think small

Those looking to get into the field might want to steer clear of the big names. Hundreds of art potteries flourished: some, such as Hampshire, Niloak, and Marblehead, are well-known, others, like Clewell, Norse, and Shawsheen, are not. Since companies often stamped a monogram on the base of pots, identifying pieces isn't all that difficult.

A Hampshire early ovoid vase with leaves and buds under a fine green and blue feathered glaze; stamp marked. c. 1910, 6¾ in (17 cm) high.

$800–1,200

▪ Newcomb ▪ Fulper ▪

A Newcomb College fine bulbous vase, by Sadie Irvine, with white roses. Curving forms, inspired by Oriental shapes, dominate Newcomb's work. Hard-carved patterns focus on fruits, plants, flowers, and animals. *1917, 5¾ in (14 cm) wide.*

$1,000–1,500

A Fulper buttressed vase, with squat base covered in Moss-to-Rose flambé glaze. Fulper is known for its glazes. Different glazes and colors were combined for highly original effect. *1909–15, 8½ in (21.5 cm) high.*

$300–400

BUY ▸

Date is key to values for Van Briggle's work. As early examples become rare, pieces produced after his death in 1904 but before 1912 are more sought after and prices are rising. Learn to date pieces and invest now to take advantage of future increases.

A Van Briggle cabinet vase, embossed with leaves under a blue and green matte glaze. Although small, it is undamaged and in good colors. *1908–11. 3 in (7.5 cm) wide.*

$280–320

KEEP ▸

Tiles are a popular, growing collecting area and are a visual way to collect Arts and Crafts ceramics. Plus, they are often ignored, used simply as wall decorations or plant stands. Look for examples by notable factories or in typical Arts and Crafts styles.

A Grueby floor tile with a cornucopia-bearing putto design, in a wooden frame. The design in red clay and the thick yellow glaze are typical of both Grueby and the Arts and Crafts movement. *1900–05, 6 in (15 cm) square.*

$350–400

Stoneware and redware

were popular forms of utilitarian pottery that not only tell a story of America's development, but are also now loved for their rustic charm. Adding folk-art appeal to a home, there's a variety to suit all budgets.

An American stoneware crock, decorated with a blue daisy and marked "FB Norton & Sons, Worcester Mass." and "3." *c. 1890, 10 in (25 cm) high.*
$150–200

The settlers of North America needed durable wares to preserve farm produce, store liquids, and cook, and earthenware and stoneware vessels were just the answer. These wares required a type of clay abundant in New England, and European potters added their own styles and techniques, which eventually merged into a distinctly American look.

The simple life

Stoneware, fired at high temperatures, was preferred for utilitarian pieces, as it vitrified and did not require glazing. For this reason, many collectable stonewares are practical items such as bottles, pitchers, churns, and bowls.

Less common are chamberpots, spittoons, tablewares, and baking wares, in part because stoneware does not heat well. Plain pieces are loved for their simplicity, but detailed items are even more prized. Simple splash decoration and bands of brown slip or cobalt blue were often employed—expect to pay $10 for a 7-inch (17.75-cm) crock with a two-tone slip and $100 for a beehive 5-gallon pitcher. Pieces with finer work, such as figurative forms or hand-painted designs, fetch $300–500. Known makers such as Frederick Carpenter's Charleston Pottery (1793–97), marked "Boston"; the Meyer Pottery, c. 1900–40, of Texas; and J & E Norton of Bennington, Vermont, c. 1850–59, command a premium.

Home sweet home

Redware is the name used for American earthenwares. Also rooted in the European tradition of ceramics, redware differs from stoneware in that it is porous and needs glazing, although

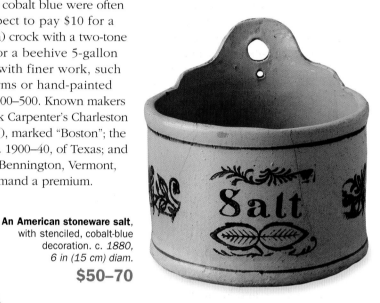

An American stoneware salt, with stenciled, cobalt-blue decoration. *c. 1880, 6 in (15 cm) diam.*
$50–70

Some shapes to look for:
■ Chargers ■ Animals ■ Bowls ■

A Breininger pottery charger with sgrafitto decoration, signed and dated on the back. Chargers display their patterns very well. Breininger is known for his folksy pastoral designs, moralistic inscriptions, and techniques that closely follow Pennsylvania Dutch redware traditions. *1992, 10¼ in (26 cm) diam.*
$150–200

A James Seagreaves pottery bird, in blue and yellow. Redware figures from the 19th century are desirable and scarce. His later works are becoming popular, with birds a hallmark. *c. 1950–70, 8 in (20 cm) long.*
$200–300

A Stahl pottery bowl, with a sgraffito design of tulips; signed "Made by I.S. Stahl Aug 5th 1941." Stahl pottery operated 1850–1956. *1941, 8½ in (21.5 cm) diam.*
$100–150

pieces can be fired in a very rudimentary kiln. It is the iron in the clay that produces the red color.

Tablewares are common in redware, with plates particularly popular and collectable. Highly decorated pieces, often in the style of the Pennsylvania Dutch potters, are the most prized and difficult to find. These wares are incised with complex designs, having first been coated in a contrasting slip, so that the red clay beneath was revealed as the design was scratched in—a technique known as sgrafitto. Other sought-after styles include slip-trailing, which was often done in a contrasting yellow (as well as green, black, or brown), creating squiggly lines, folk sayings, or flower motifs. Peoples' names, and especially bird motifs, are rare, and undamaged examples can fetch up to $8,000. More common and plainer 19th century redwares sell for $100–800. A modest Breininger black slip-trailed 7-inch (17.75-cm) plate can be found for $30–50, while a Foltz 10-inch (25.5-cm) bowl, incised with a bird motif, might cost $100-200. Beautiful pieces from the 20th century are also worth considering. Generally found for under $300, they are becoming increasingly hot and have great folk-art eye-appeal. Later producers to watch for include Stahl, Pennsbury, and Seagreaves.

■ Plates ■ Pitchers ■

An American pie plate, with black and yellow slip decoration. Plates are very collectible. If a piece is large and the pattern bright and complex, the value is greater. Damage reduces value considerably. *c. 1850–70, 8¼ in (21 cm) diam.*

$100–150

Plain Janes

Early pieces in basic, often undecorated, forms are usually still quite affordable. These include pitchers, pie plates, bean pots, bottles, and milk basins, finished with a clear lead glaze to render them waterproof. Canadian pieces are also usually less expensive than their American counterparts, although just as collectible. A plain mid-19th century redware jar or pitcher from Waterloo County can be found for as little as $50–80. Distinguishing two pieces made a hundred years apart can be difficult, since the basic style didn't change all that much, so the presence of a maker's mark adds huge value to a vintage piece. Die-impressed marks have been found for some notable makers including John Bell of Waynesboro, Pennsylvania, and the New York manufacturers Alvin Wilcox of West Bloomfield and Lorenzo Johnson of Newstead.

An American stoneware rolling pin, with a blue, transfer-printed wildflower design. *c. 1890, 17 in (43 cm) long.*

$300–500

A pitcher, with manganese splash decoration and incised bands. Pitchers with regular, colorful, and complex patterns, or those that are finely incised, such as an American eagle, are prized. *c. 1850–90, 10 in (25.5 cm) high.*

$350–550

KEEP

Stoneware decorated with finely painted and detailed cobalt designs is becoming scarcer and more sought after, especially if marked by a known maker. It is advisable to hold on to large, decorative jugs and crocks, particularly those decorated in strong colors, as prices look likely to go up in the future.

A four-gallon stoneware jug by the New York Stoneware Co., with an elaborate blue-scrolling flower decoration. *c. 1850–80, 14½ in (37 cm) high.*

$300–500

SELL

Small, plain, and functional, pieces such as these have a market, however, it is best to invest in pieces that show as many of the style hallmarks as possible. Sell and invest in more typical, and still affordable, pieces such as up-and-coming 20th-century wares.

An American redware mug with a brown glaze. Although small and unassuming, this mug's naïve charm would appeal to some collectors. *c. 1850–90, 3 in (8 cm) high.*

$80–120

Lusterware has a shimmering iridescence of color, mysterious and fascinating to the eye. This unusual quality, together with the great range of forms and patterns available, underlies its appeal.

Lusterware is produced by applying a thin metallic paint onto a pottery glaze. The technique can be traced back to Persia in 800 CE, and is also associated with Granada in Spain in the 14th century and northern Italy in the 16th. Most luster pieces on the market today were made from the 19th century onward, with many reasonably priced examples dating from the 1930s to the 1950s. Four different metals are used in lusterware: silver, gold, copper, and platinum. Only platinum produces a silver tint: silver yields a straw color; gold creates shades of red from yellowish to ruby; and copper yields a deep copper color.

Exotic appeal

The popularity of lusterware in the 19th century can be traced back to the British firm Wedgwood, which was refining ancient luster techniques in the 1770s for the market of the day. In the early 19th century, Wedgwood used mostly copper lusters, reserving the more costly platinum for a "silver-resist" effect, and gold for exotic pieces. The appeal of lusterware for the Victorians was its exoticism, combined with its heavy decoration and color. The early Victorians also covered whole items in silver-resist luster to give the impression that a piece was made of silver. The luster in such pieces can wear thin and become patchy. In this condition, they are not greatly valued.

The century turns

In the late 19th and early 20th centuries, developments in oxidization technology improved the purity of luster liquids. Other manufacturers in Britain—including the Staffordshire, Swansea, Sunderland, and Leeds potteries—adopted the technique, applying it to earthenware and porcelain. They gave their wares a uniquely British style, which met with a good response from their customers.

The "splatter" technique, in which only a little luster was applied, was

An A. E. Gray & Co. Ltd. silver-resist luster cigarette box and cover, made in England. *1930s, 4 in (10 cm) long.*

$30–50

A Wedgwood Fairyland bowl (shown inside and outside), decorated with the sought-after Lahore pattern by Daisy Makeig-Jones. The brilliant colors and Oriental-style pattern contrast with traditional Wedgwood designs. *1920s, 7¾ in (20 cm) diam.*

$800–1,200

Some makers to look for:
■ Wedgwood ■ Carlton Ware ■

▶ **A Carlton Ware bowl** with (scratched) mottled glaze and gilt highlights. Carlton's lusterwares typically have dark back-grounds, in blue, red, or black. *c. 1930s, 8¾ in (22.5 cm) diam.*

$200–300

used by the Sunderland potteries. Their lines of pink lusterwares, transfer-printed with pictures and mottoes or rhymes, are highly collectible.

Shimmering fairy tales

Wedgwood continued to produce lusters from around 1917, making a line of Ordinary Luster pieces decorated with dragons, fish, and butterflies. These were developed by Daisy Makeig-Jones, one of the firm's most respected designers. Ordinary Luster was followed by her Fairyland range of more intricate and sparkling effects. These were inspired by a mixture of fairy tales, exotic landscapes, and mythology—evoked in patterns such as Ghostly Wood, Candlemas, Bubbles, and Lahore. Their brilliant colors and designs gave the company a commercial edge. Expensive when launched, the Fairyland pieces are more sought after than the Ordinary Luster line and fetch high prices.

In Wedgwood's wake

The success of the Fairyland lusters influenced other manufacturers including Crown Devon, Royal Winton, and Carlton Ware, although these never achieved the quality of

Wedgwood, or the prices that Fairyland pieces command in today's market. Carlton Ware produced an outstanding line of Art Deco pieces in colorful lusters, such as Jazz, Rouge Royale, and Barges, and these can fetch good prices, depending on their size, pattern, and shape.

The smaller manufacturer A. E. Gray & Co. Ltd. produced lusterwares from the 1920s to 50s. Some of the earliest, most desirable patterns were designed by Susie Cooper and Gordon Forsyth, and feature dragons and leaping deer. These patterns appeared on plaques and ginger jars, which were probably used in showrooms and on trade stands, but many were also sold commercially. At the cheaper end of the market, in the 1950s, Gray's revived the "Sunderland Splatter" technique for a popular range of giftwares, often incorporating black-and-white prints of shells and ships.

A Maling luster bowl decorated in pattern 4075, with the Maling castle mark. *1930s, 10 in (25.5 cm) diam.*

$200–250

37

Top Tips

- Check the standard of potting and painting on pieces of copper lusterware. Fine examples of landscape and still-life painting can be found, but quality varies.
- Beware of thin, patchy areas where overzealous cleaning has removed layers of luster. Clean your own collection with care, using only distilled water.
- Look for silver-resist luster on a canary yellow or blue ground; this is less common than the more usual white ground.

KEEP

The condition of Sunderland lusterware greatly affects its value, since so much of it was produced. Look for marine or political themes that tell a story of the time.

A Sunderland pitcher with ocher luster ovals, printed and painted with the ship *The Unfortunate London* on one side and a verse on the other (both sides are shown). Slightly damaged. *c. 1850s, 5¾ in (14.5 cm) high.*

$100–150

■ Royal Winton ■ Ruskin Pottery ■

A Royal Winton luster floral centerpiece decorated with a yellow rose motif. Royal Winton is better known for lusterwares in brighter colors than this. *1930s, 12½ in (32 cm) wide.*

$120–180

▶ **A Ruskin Pottery vase,** glazed in a mottled mauve luster, with an impressed date. Ruskin Pottery was renowned for its high-fired glazes in vibrant colors. *1925, 10 in (25.5 cm) high.*

$600–900

KEEP

Carlton Ware went into lusterwares after the commercial success of Wedgwood's Fairyland range. Carlton Ware's luster pieces are immensely popular. Look carefully at the condition of this type of ware, as the enamel can easily be rubbed or chipped.

A Carlton Ware Rouge Royale ginger jar and cover decorated with chinoiserie scenes. The shape complements the oriental pattern. *1930s, 9 in (23 cm) high.*

$300–400

Floral ceramics of the 1930s

and 50s encompass a range of styles, from intricate, colorful, and complex patterns evocative of the past, to strikingly modern abstract designs that raced headlong into an exciting future.

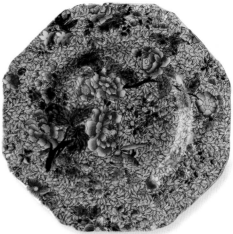

Among the most popular examples of floral ceramics are tea, coffee, and other tablewares printed with an all-over pattern. Known as "chintz" (from the Hindu word *chhintna*, meaning "to sprinkle with"), these intricate patterns were inspired by floral fabrics imported to the West on East India Company ships in the late 17th century. In the 1820s hand painting was superseded by an underglaze transfer-printing process. Improved multicolor transfer techniques were developed in the late 19th century.

A festival of flowers

Production of chintzware began in the early 19th century, with dressing-table washing sets (including wash bowl, pitcher, and candlesticks) and tableware. Most pieces were unmarked and produced in factories based in Staffordshire, England: those that

A Spode New Fayence chintz dessert plate, with sheet transfer background and large hand-painted flowers. *c. 1820, 8½ in (21.5 cm) wide.*
$100–150

are marked are often by Spode. Some of the chintzware produced during this period is characterized by ornate forms, muted colors, and spaces between the flowers. The background is often a transfer, and some flowers may be hand painted—in which case the petals will have slightly uneven brushstrokes, rather than the uniform color found on a transfer.

◄ **A Royal Winton Marguerite chintz cup and saucer.** *1930s, cup 3 in (7.5 cm) high.*
$50–80

▼ **A Royal Winton Summertime chintz sandwich tray.** *c. 1950, 12¼ in (31 cm) wide.*
$80–120

Production of chintzware peaked during the 1930s and 50s. Compared to 19th-century pieces, examples from this period have compact designs, with little space between the flowers, and bright colors. Patterns were given cheerful names evocative of the flowers themselves, such as Primula and Sweet Pea. Simple shapes were adopted to match the taste for clean-lined Art Deco.

Notable names

Most items are marked with a maker's name, one of the most notable being Royal Winton, owned by the Grimwade brothers, whose chintzware is extremely popular. Royal Winton developed a new lithographic transfer-printing process using flexible paper to transfer the pattern so that complex shapes could be covered without the paper tearing. Royal Winton ceramics always bear the shape name stamped into the base with the pattern name printed nearby. Other notable makers of chintzware include Wade, Crown Ducal, and Shelley.

The popularity of chintzware has grown dramatically over the past decade, especially in North America. As so many pieces were made in the 1930s and 50s, it is still widely available, with smaller, more common pieces in standard patterns such as Royal Winton's "Summertime" often priced at around $50. Look out for plates, trays, pitchers, and teapots, which, although intended for daily use, offer great display potential.

Radical change

The hand-thrown, hand-painted pottery produced by Carter, Stabler & Adams Ltd., now known as Poole Pottery, started a new movement against conventional style. Along with Clarice Cliff and Susie Cooper, the company

A Royal Winton, Hazel chintz, three-bar toast rack. *1934, 4½ in (11.5 cm) long.*
$200–250

A closer look at... a Poole Pottery vase

The designs produced by Carter, Stabler & Adams Ltd. in the 1930s are the most sought after of the Poole Pottery products. Prices have risen considerably over the past few years, making examples that show typical decoration and form valuable.

The Art Deco shape and decoration appeal to collectors

The zigzag pattern is highly desirable

A Carter, Stabler & Adams Ltd. earthenware vase decorated in an Art Deco pattern designed by Truda Carter. *c. 1934–37, 9¾ in (24.75 cm) high.*
$2,000–3,000

The blue, green, brown, and yellow colors are typical of Poole Pottery in this period

Maker's marks

All pieces are clearly marked on the base, bearing an impressed stamp with the factory name, a painted symbol identifying the painter of the piece, and a number-and-letter combination signifying the pattern name and period of production.

A typical impressed mark found on the base of a Carter, Stabler & Adams Ltd. piece from the 1930s.

offered a new interpretation of floral decoration, with bold, colorful, and often abstract designs in place of more traditional motifs. It swiftly earned a reputation for its bright, exuberant patterns, created chiefly by the designer Truda Carter. Most pieces are in soft yellows, bright blues, and greens on a glazed white body. The flowers are stylized and often combined with geometric motifs typical of Art Deco. Designs featuring birds and animals are much prized.

Rising prices

An increasing demand for 1930s pieces by Carter, Stabler & Adams Ltd. has led to rapidly escalating prices—the highest prices are paid for items with

A Carter, Stabler & Adams Ltd. pitcher, with a pattern by Truda Carter and painted by Ruth Pavely. Impressed "Poole England" and marked "321_ED." *1930s, 4¾ in (12 cm) high.*
$100–150

Top Tips: chintzware

- Examine chintz patterns closely, as many of them differ only minutely from others.
- Choose chintzware on which the pattern covers as much of the surface as possible, even the inside of handles—such pieces tend to be preferred by collectors, which makes them more valuable.
- Avoid chipped or cracked pieces, as these are worth substantially less. Since so much chintzware was produced, it is essential to find pieces that are in good condition.
- Examine pieces for gaps in the pattern (between transfers)—these can devalue a piece, although some collectors like them.

visual impact, such as large bowls, and heavily stylized decoration. Smaller or later pieces, which often lack the tight detail and energy of earlier designs, are less expensive, but may rise in value as demand for top-quality early examples outstrips supply.

Floral relief

William Moorcroft, a ceramicist working from around 1901 to his death in 1945, had a huge influence on floral Art Nouveau ceramics. He headed the art pottery department at Staffordshire's MacIntyre & Co., before founding his own factory in 1913. Moorcroft used a tube-lining technique to pick out his patterns—slip, or thin, liquid clay was squeezed through a narrow glass tube onto the surface of the ware. The Moorcroft company, still one of the leading manufacturers working with tube-lining, produced a variety of popular floral designs for long periods, such as Orchid, Magnolia, and Anemone. The rich

colors, subtle shapes, and stylized floral motifs underlie their popularity. Prices have risen considerably over the past decade, and remain high, as demand still exceeds supply. The best pieces (c. 1905–15), showcasing Moorcroft's exotic designs, are worth hundreds or even thousands of dollars, depending on size, period, and condition. His Florian ware is often influenced by Moorish designs or the work of the pioneer designer William Morris. Examples can fetch around $1,500 or more. More recently, Moorcroft has offered work by designers such as Rachel Bishop and

An earthenware A. E. Gray & Co. Ltd. pitcher, with hand-painted floral pattern. *1930s, 5¾ in (14.5 cm) high.*
$150–200

A hand-painted Radford dish. *1930s, 8½ in (21.5 cm) diam.*
$40–60

Sally Tuffin. Some of its limited-edition pieces sell for more than their original prices.

Flowery forms

If Moorcroft is one of the major makers, then Carlton Ware was one of the most prolific. Its less-expensive floral range of ceramics was aimed at the middle market, and many pieces can now be found for less than $100.

Carlton Ware is easily recognized— pieces are shaped like flowers, fruit, or vegetables, or else decorated with raised floral designs. In cheery yellows, greens, and pinks, Carlton Ware was mass-produced until the late 1950s. Cracks and chips are common, as this was pottery for everyday use, so search for undamaged pieces.

A satisfying collection of common patterns can easily be acquired, but anyone looking to invest should concentrate on what is scarce.

▼ **The traditional style of floral decoration** remained perennially popular. Here, youngsters enjoy a cup of tea from a floral tea set as they watch dancing at the Casino Dance Room in Birmingham, England, 1939.

Essential Moorcroft

FLORIAN WARE
Moorcroft's early Florian ware designs, such as this vase decorated with poppies, are sought after. Good examples fetch high prices. c. 1903, 4in (10cm) high.

$1,500–2,000

NATIVE FLOWERS
The Anemone pattern typifies Moorcroft's use of native flowers. Small items, such as this vase, are ideal for budget buyers. 1970s, 2¼ in (6 cm) high.

$200–250

ART NOUVEAU
The curling lines and stylized flowers of these Florian ware vases show the influential Art Nouveau style associated with Moorcroft's early work. c. 1902, 9½ in (24cm) high.

$2,000–3,000

RECENT PIECES
This Carousel ginger jar, by Rachel Bishop, shows the enduring popularity of Moorcroft's traditional style. c. 1990s, 16cm (6¼in) high.

$280–320

Cherries was produced in smaller numbers than Apple Blossom, making it more sought after. Colors are also important. A pink Buttercup trefoil dish *(see below)* is less common and worth more than one in yellow.

Not just the giants
Floral ceramics are not solely the province of the giants of chintzware—there is a whole range of smaller factories worth considering, such as A. E. Gray & Co. Ltd. (or Gray's Pottery), for whom Susie Cooper worked in the late 1920s. It is possible to find representative and attractive pieces for less than $150, although you should expect to pay up to $300 or more for designs by Susie Cooper. The boldly rendered, hand-painted floral pottery made by E. Radford of Staffordshire generally costs less than $150.

Ceramics by the Scottish firm Wemyss are slightly more expensive but may be a good investment, since they achieve consistently high prices and, depending on the condition and rarity, may appreciate in value in the future.

Top Tips

- Look for work by contemporary Moorcroft designers such as Sally Tuffin and Rachel Bishop, as they are becoming increasingly collectible.
- Search for sought-after boxed sets of 1930s floral Carlton Ware. Some collectors even buy the empty boxes to fill later.
- Check the base of Wemyss pieces for the signature of Karel Nekola, the chief painter until 1915, as this adds value—especially as few Wemyss pieces are signed by a painter.

BUY

Decorative and functional chintzware pieces that can still be used today should hold their value, if not rise, if in good condition.

A Royal Winton Cranstone-pattern, two-tier cake stand. Bright colors and a known maker add to desirability. 1930s, 8¾ in (22 cm) high.

$100–150

KEEP

The Wemyss pig is characteristic of the manufacturer, and animal shapes are desirable generally. Wemyss has a strong following of collectors, including Britain's Prince Charles, so prices are unlikely to fall.

A Wemyss pig decorated with roses. This is a rare piece in perfect condition. c. 1890, 6¼ in (16 cm) long.

$700–1,000

SELL

Standard Carlton Ware lines are commonly found and unlikely to rise much in value in the foreseeable future, so the best option is to sell and invest in rarer pieces instead.

A yellow Carlton Ware Apple Blossom bowl. Although this is jaunty and attractive, such pieces are easy to obtain and consistently fetch comparatively low prices. c. 1930s, 9¼ in (23.5 cm) wide.

$60–90

A Carlton Ware Buttercup trefoil dish. *1930s, 10½ in (26.5 cm) wide.*

$280–320

Oriental ceramics

bring an air of exotic sumptuousness to the home. Many pieces were made for export, with designs created to appeal to Western tastes of the time.

A **Kangxi period** *famille verte* **plate,** with birds flying over lotus flowers and a decorative band of flowers and butterflies around the rim. *1662–1722, 13¾ in (35 cm) diam.*

$700–1,000

Porcelain was first produced in China during the T'ang period (618–906 CE). The best-known pieces used the "underglaze blue" technique (blue painting under a clear glaze), which became popular during the early Ming dynasty (14th century). The export trade began in earnest in the 16th century and peaked during the 18th and 19th centuries. Much of this later ware can be found for $40 to $150.

A colorful history

The palette of colors used by Chinese ceramic artists during the 18th century is divided into *famille verte* (mainly green) and *famille rose* (largely pink). The *famille rose* palette took over from about 1718. The colors were mixed with opaque white to allow shading, adding depth and variety. Prices can reach thousands of dollars, but more common, smaller, inferior pieces with simpler designs can be found for less than $150.

Pretty in pink

In the 19th century, the *famille rose* palette was used for wares known as Rose Medallion, Rose Mandarin, and Rose Canton. These vibrant and detailed pieces often depicted birds, flowers, butterflies, and domestic interiors. Avoid the 20th-century pieces of inferior quality, which have less detail and brasher colors—these often bear square "seal" marks, or the words "Made in China" on the base.

Reclaimed from the sea

Hundreds of years after trade vessels from East Asia were shipwrecked, some of their cargoes have been recovered in superb condition. The Dutch ship *Geldermalsen*, wrecked in 1752, was salvaged in 1985. Its freight, the Nanking Cargo, included a huge quantity of porcelain. Prices start at around $75. Look for items from the cargoes of *Gotheborg*, *Diana*, and *Tek Sing*. Prices for these pieces are currently fairly low, but there is a finite supply, so values may increase.

An Imari bowl decorated inside and out with stylized trees and panels of dragons. *c. 1850s–90s, 5¾ in (14.5 cm) diam.*

$80–120

Essential shipwreck cargoes

HOI AN HOARD
Heavy pottery decorated in an underglaze blue is typical of this Vietnamese cargo, which yielded the earliest salvaged ceramics. c. 1450–1500, 9½ in (24 cm) diam.
$200–300

HATCHER Most of the items, such as this vase, were blue and white, and helped experts to understand Chinese ceramics from this era. c. 1643, 4¾ in (12 cm) high.
$200–300

VUNG TAO As well as formal Kangxi period blue-and-white ware, plainer, more humble "provincial" ware, such as this bowl, was also found. c. 1690–1700, 6 in (15 cm) diam.
$50–80

NANKING Utilitarian pieces dominated this cargo. Encrustations caused by saltwater have created abstract effects popular among collectors. c. 1750, 5 in (13 cm) diam.
$200–300

DIANA Most of this cargo was made to compete with cheaper European ceramics, so is of lesser quality: for example, these painted porcelain toys. c. 1817, 2 in (5.5 cm) high.
$120–180 each

TEK SING Bowls and dishes with blue designs were found on the *Tek Sing*. The freehand-painted design on this Spiral Lotus dish adds value. c. 1822, 7¼ in (18.5 cm) diam.
$280–320

Japanese style in demand

Early Japanese porcelain ranges from the sparsely decorated Kakiemon to the ornate Imari style. These wares were exported by Dutch traders from the mid-17th to the mid-18th centuries, as well as in the late 19th century, when there was fresh demand.

The quality can vary, so look for detail and fine brushwork, and choose examples on which the gilding is intact and follows the blue-and-red design beneath. Pieces from the 20th century have looser, less detailed decoration, and the iron red is less subtle. Large, well-painted 19th-century Imari wall plaques can fetch $120–300, but finely decorated 18th-century Imari costs thousands of dollars.

Japanese Satsuma pottery is known for its distinctive creamy colors and rich palette of iron red, burnt umber, and gold. Medium-quality 19th-century pieces can cost less than $150. Those signed on the base are more valuable.

Noritake goes West

Among the ceramics made for export were those from the Noritake factory, which was the main supplier of Japanese

ware for the US market by 1910. To appeal to Western tastes, it adopted Art Nouveau and Art Deco styles, and used decorative, raised gilding, and Western-style painted motifs. A good collection of Noritake wares from the first half of the 20th century need not be costly. Tea and coffee sets start at $50–80; better, more elaborate examples can fetch $150 or more.

Top Tips

- Examine each object with a magnifying glass and, when buying later Chinese and Japanese export wares, avoid even the tiniest chip or faintest crack.
- Tap each piece, or flick it gently with your fingernail and listen to its "ring." A dull sound indicates a crack.
- Be wary of dating Chinese ceramics by emperors' reign marks—earlier reign marks were used on some later pieces as a mark of respect for the past.
- Avoid wares marked "Made in China," "Made In Japan," or "Foreign." They're often of a late date and a low quality.

KEEP

After a period of strong popularity, prices for Satsuma ware have fallen because the heavy, ornate style is now seen as old-fashioned. But high-quality pieces could be worth keeping as an investment, especially if they have fine and intricate detailing—any signs of wear to the gilding or painting will reduce value considerably.

A Satsuma vase, probably from the late Meiji period, with pierced demi "mon" handles. Warriors, as seen here, or ladies in landscapes, are typical themes. c. 1900, 15¼ in (39 cm) high.
$500–700

BUY

Vases and other wares made by Noritake are likely to rise in value if they are representative of the factory's work, are influenced by Western Art Deco styles, and are of fine quality.

A Noritake cup and saucer with hand-painted gilt decoration and a lakeside scene. *1920s, saucer 5 in (12.5 cm) diam.*
$120–180

A Noritake vase with hand-painted pink roses and neoclassical motifs. It is Western in style and typical of Noritake production. *1930s, 7¼ in (18.5 cm) high.*
$100–150

Traditional ceramic ware

of the 19th and early 20th centuries includes some richly painted porcelain and pottery. Their sumptuous decoration makes them objects to covet, yet prices can be surprisingly low.

Decoratively gilded, and with floral, pastoral, and animal motifs, traditional ceramics were often "kept for best." Renowned British firms such as Royal Doulton, Royal Worcester, Royal Crown Derby, and Wedgwood began making items in the neoclassical style in the 19th century. If you have bought any such pieces—or are lucky enough to have inherited some—it may be well worth keeping them.

Setting the table

An amazing volume of tableware was made from the 1860s onward. In fact, these dinner and tea services fetch low prices compared with contemporary wares. A good dinner service from around 1890–1920, with six, eight, or 12 settings, may be worth $150–350;

a tea or coffee set, even less. Missing pieces or obvious wear and tear can lower the value considerably.

Dessert services, which were popular until the late 1930s, can be especially ornamental. Examine the painting carefully to ensure that it is not scratched or worn, and look for pieces with plenty of decoration rather than narrow border designs. Late 19th-century services featuring landscape paintings may fetch $80–400.

The better potteries employed established artists to paint finely detailed flowers, fruit, landscapes, and animals. Prices vary hugely, depending on the decorator, although the quality of painting might not. Many decorators specialized in one subject: at Royal

A Royal Worcester plate, painted by Harry Ayrton with fruit and berries, within a gilt rim that is gadrooned (edged in a cablelike design); with a black printed mark. *1951, 8½ in (22 cm) diam.*

$400–600

Did You Know?

Percy Curnock, the longest-serving artist at Royal Doulton, was famous for painting fine Italian landscapes on cabinet plates (made for display rather than use), but he never set foot in Italy. All his paintings on these now sought-after ceramics were inspired by picture postcards.

A closer look at... two Royal Doulton flambé vases

The flambé effect, introduced at Royal Doulton in 1902, was achieved by using a copper oxide historic formula. It was designed to mimic the Chinese *sang de boeuf* (oxblood) glaze. Flambé was used to decorate vases and won many prizes. Both these vases are valuable, but one is worth almost twice as much as the other.

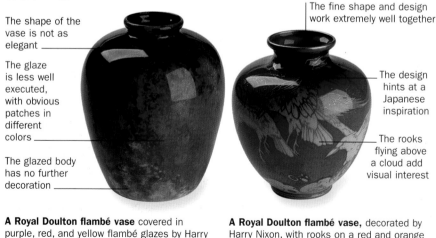

The shape of the vase is not as elegant

The glaze is less well executed, with obvious patches in different colors

The glazed body has no further decoration

The fine shape and design work extremely well together

The design hints at a Japanese inspiration

The rooks flying above a cloud add visual interest

A Royal Doulton flambé vase covered in purple, red, and yellow flambé glazes by Harry Nixon; with printed marks and painted monogram. *c. 1930s, 8¼ in (21 cm) high.*

$500–700

A Royal Doulton flambé vase, decorated by Harry Nixon, with rooks on a red and orange flambé ground, and printed marks including "HN" monogram. *c. 1930s, 7 in (18 cm) high.*

$800–1,200

A pair of Royal Doulton stoneware vases of waisted cylindrical form, with tube-lined decoration of cabbage roses on a graduated lilac ground, with impressed marks. *c. 1920s, 10¼ in (26 cm) high.*

$200–250

Worcester, John and Harry Stinton were known for Highland cattle, James Stinton for game birds, Harry Ayrton for fruit, and Harry Davies for landscapes. They often signed their work.

Popular patterns

Coalport is a favorite factory to collect. Prices can range from less than $150 for a 19th- or early 20th-century pitcher with a simple floral band to thousands of dollars for earlier and larger, more richly decorated pieces. Royal Crown Derby is known for its imitations of the saturated richness of Japanese Imari porcelain. The pattern numbers on Royal Crown Derby Imari are an indication of rarity: patterns still made, such as 1128 and 2451, are more common and less valuable.

Some Royal Worcester wares feature "blush ivory": printed or painted sprays of flowers or foliage outlined in gilt against an ivory-colored background. At present their popularity is on the wane, but this could change. Small

A Coalport, two-handled sugar bowl and cover, printed and painted with flowers in cartouches, on a blue ground. *c. 1920, 4½ in (11.5 cm) high.*

$200–300

pieces may fetch up to $80, while larger, more elaborate items range between $100 and hundreds of dollars.

Painting the lily

Minton & Co., a prominent Victorian Staffordshire porcelain factory, was known for its delicately painted and gilded wares. Look for examples encrusted with flowers, which imitate 18th-century Meissen originals—they can fetch $300–1,500, depending on size and quality. Its later Art Nouveau work is also desirable.

Royal Doulton wares are marked on the base with stamps and often incised initials to indicate the decorators. Look for designs by Florence and Hannah Barlow, Eliza Simmance, George Tinworth, and Harry Nixon. Baskets made by Belleek of Ireland, known for its creamy white china, are popular. Learn to spot valuable early items (1863–90) with the desirable black mark: the name "Belleek" printed in a rectangle surmounted by a dog, tower, and Irish harp.

A small Royal Crown Derby vase, painted with flowers in enamels and gilt on a blue ground, with red mark. *c. 1902, 4¼ in (10.7 cm) high.*

$200–300

BUY

Many museum exhibitions are based around particular aesthetic styles, and collecting within one of these areas is now popular with a younger generation. Striking pieces in the Secessionist style, an important strand of Art Nouveau, are an interesting part of Minton's work. Pieces typically cost around $250–750, so buy now while you still can.

A Minton Secessionist vase with tube-lined decoration in the form of stylized plant life and Minton's maker's marks on the base. *c. 1900, 12½ in (32 cm) high.*

$300–500

KEEP

Prices for Doulton Lambeth stoneware have dropped over the past five years, but this key maker could soon make a comeback. If your piece is signed by, and in the typical style of, a sought-after decorator, such as Hannah Barlow, it is likely to become even more desirable.

A Doulton Lambeth vase with a band of incised decoration of cattle, by Hannah Barlow. *1883, 12 in (30.5 cm) high.*

$1,000–1,500

Cups and saucers summon up

the elegance of British afternoon tea in more leisured times. Sometimes found with a matching plate for dainty sandwiches, they are less expensive to acquire and easier to display than whole tea sets.

Ceramics

Many manufacturers have produced cups and saucers as stand-alone items, which gives them extra cachet for collectors.

The production of British and European tea cups—made with handles from the 1720s onward—boomed after 1784 when the tax on tea was reduced, making tea drinking a more popular habit. Anna, the seventh Duchess of Bedford, is said to have invented British "afternoon tea" in the early 19th century by having tea with sandwiches at around four or five o'clock to stave off predinner pangs of hunger.

Fine cups and saucers produced by names such as Worcester, Meissen, and Minton command high prices, but there are many less expensive examples to be found, even from these makers. Check the bases for marks, which can help to identify the maker and date. When checking whether a cup and saucer are a genuine pair, bear in mind that popular patterns were often simplified over the years to reduce prices and thus appeal to a wider market.

Modern manufacturers often extend their lines by copying successful designs from the past.

▲ A Shelley Vogue trio set.
The set is pure Art Deco, with a solid triangular handle to the cup and simple decoration in a single, strong color. *1930s, cup 2½ in (6.5 cm) high.*
$200–250

▶ A Nautilus ware trio set. Made between 1894 and 1911 in Scotland, Nautilus ware has recently been rising in popularity and value. It is characterized by thin porcelain with crimped edges, floral decoration, and gilding. *c. 1900, cup 2½ in (6.5 cm) high.*
$200–250

▶ A Spode cup and saucer. Spode invented bone china in the late 18th century and is also famed for its excellent gilding and hand-painted flowers—a style of decoration perennially popular with collectors. *c. 1825–26, cup 2¾ in (7 cm) high.*
$100–150

◀ An Aynsley cup and saucer. Although many patterns produced in the 20th century were based on classical decoration of the past, they are often in stronger colors than the classical originals—like the deep pink on this cup and saucer. *c. 1900, cup 2½ in (6.5 cm) high.*
$60–90

◀ A royal-blue Coalport cup and saucer. Coalport is known for its bold, strong background colors, particularly the royal blue on this cup and saucer. Crimped edges and gilding are also typical features. *c. 1907, cup 2½ in (6.5 cm) high.*
$60–90

◄ A Hammersley trio set.
Produced as Europe teetered on the verge of war, traditional floral wares, particularly with gilding, were popular, as they evoked safer, more luxurious times. *c. 1939, cup 2½ in (6.5 cm) high.*

$350–400

◄ A Meyer & Sherratt (Melba China) plate, cup, and saucer.
The country style on such a geometric shape is unusual, as is the positioning of the design on the plate. *c. 1935–41, cup 3 in (8cm) high.*

$40–60

Collectors' Tips

■ Check gilding for signs of wear, cup rims for chips, and handles for evidence of repair

■ Where possible, buy cups with their original saucers, or the match may not be perfect

► A Mason's Regency cup and saucer. These "Patent Ironstone China" items were made of a hard earthenware produced by adding ironstone slag, making it strong and able to hold hot liquids well. *1930s, cup 2½ in (6.5 cm) high.*

$30–40

◄ An Orange Tree cup and saucer by A. G. Richardson Ltd., (pattern no. 439), produced from about 1925 onward. *c. 1928, 3 in (8 cm) high.*

$30–50

◄ An Alfred Meakin Cactus plate, cup, and saucer. 1950s ceramics often moved away from traditional flowers and gilt. The potted cacti here were a wry touch aimed at younger householders. *1950s, cup 2¾ in (7 cm) high.*

$20–30

► A Royal Crown Derby trio set, based on the porcelain made in Japan at Arita from the 17th century and known as "Imari." The underglaze decoration of iron red, blue, and gilt on a white ground is typical of the style. *c. 1885, cup 2½ in (6.5 cm) high.*

$80–120

▲ A Coalport cup and saucer.
The delicate floral design and heavy gilding are reminiscent of the popular French designs of the early 19th century. *c. 1940, cup 2¾ in (7 cm) high.*

$40–60

Cottage ware evokes the rustic idyll of rose-clad cottages and Tudor-style buildings of "Shakespeare country." This is an evocative and highly popular collecting area, suitable for anyone inspired by "Olde England."

Bone china and pottery cottage ware has long been a familiar sight in the homes of many who admire the quaint English country-cottage look. Perfumed pastille burners and nightlights disguised as cottages were produced by British manufacturers such as Spode, Coalport, and Worcester from the 1760s and throughout the 1800s, appealing to a population uprooted from their rural traditions by a mass exodus to the cities. Pastoral nostalgia survives to the present day, and the rustic styles of cottage ware continue to fascinate many collectors.

A comforting glow

In 1893 Goss introduced a line of seven nightlight cottages that were reproductions of period houses. The open back of each housed a candle-holder: when the candle was lit, smoke came out of the chimney and the extra thin porcelain windows glowed. These cottages were made until 1929, and were so successful that the line was extended to 35. Prices vary from less than $75 to around $300. Goss cottages dated after 1929, when the factory was sold, are worth much less than earlier models.

Country teas

Manufacturers also applied the cottage shape to tea and coffee sets, which usually consisted of a tea- or coffeepot, hot-water pitcher, milk pitcher, and sugar bowl. Extra items could be added to the set, such as cookie jars, cheese and butter dishes, jelly and preserve pots, cruets, and dessert plates. Individual pieces often fetch less than $150-200. Teapots, though, are a popular collecting field and are usually more valuable than other pieces. Pitchers also command higher prices.

An early Goss nightlight model of a Manx cottage, colored and with black-printed Goshawk mark and inscription "Model of Manx Cottage, Rd. No. 273243." *c. 1896, 4¾ in (12 cm) long.*
$150–200

Essential cottage ware

COFFEEPOTS
Teapots and coffeepots work well with the cottage shape and hold their value. This is a Price Bros. coffee pot. 1945-50, 10 in (25.5 cm) high.
$100–150

PITCHERS
Pitchers, such as this finely detailed Price Bros. Tudor-style creamer, are highly sought after. 1930s, 3 in (8 cm) high.
$200–300

CHEESE DISHES
A water mill makes a good cover for a cheese dish. This one, with desirable realistic detail, is by Royal Winton. 1930s, 7¼ in (18.5 cm) wide.
$400–600

PRESERVE POTS
A double preserve pot is worth more than twice the value of a single one. This one is by Kensington. c. 1930, 8 in (20.5 cm) wide.
$300–500

A dream of thatch

In 1933 Wade Heath launched its popular "thatched cottage" tableware, including items such as cookie jars and preserve pots. Since production lasted until 1971, pieces are easily found and prices start at $50. Beswick cottage ware, also produced from the 1930s, is not as collectible as Royal Winton (its decoration is often less fine), but Beswick teapots have a following—as do those by Burlington, J. H. Wood, and Price Bros.

An idyll lives on

Lilliput Lane, established in 1982, is renowned worldwide for its delicately painted, miniature resin cottages. As new models were launched, older ones were "retired" and have become collectible. Some of the early cottages were produced in small numbers, or the color was changed, or a chimney or window was added. The original versions can fetch a high price. For

Lilliput Lane's Sweet Pea Cottage, retired from production in March 1997. *c. 1994, 2 in (5 cm) wide.*

$20–30

example, Dove Cottage was produced in two versions between 1983 and 1988. Those produced in the first year have a nameplate and can be worth $400–600; the more common models produced until 1988, without a nameplate, often fetch less than $100. Some of Lilliput Lane's limited editions are highly valued: Cliburn School, produced in 1983 in an edition of 64, can sell for around $3,500. The most sought-after Lilliput Lane patterns include Drapers (first two versions); Crofters Cottage, also known as The Croft (first two versions); and any of the Roadside

America collection released in 1984, including Adobe Village, Grist Mill, and Covered Bridge.

David Winter is a name to watch, especially for special- or limited-edition cottages or the larger, rarer models. In 1981 Winter produced the best-selling Stratford House model, with rickety roof, wobbly walls, and giant chimneys—the trademarks of his style. Fairy Tale Castle (1982), The Bakehouse (1983), and The Bothy (1983) are enduring favorites. Also collectible are Sabrina's Cottage, Double Oast, Chichester Cross, The Coaching Inn, Little Mill (first mold—others followed), and Mill House (first mold). Many Winter cottages sell for $100–150; rarer pieces will fetch more.

Did You Know?

Most Lilliput Lane cottages are made to a scale of 1:76. The modelers have more than 200 different tools at their disposal (including dentistry tools) to create a wax model, which is then used to make a mold for the cottage. It can take more than two weeks for a modeler to make the basic wax model.

KEEP

Lilliput Lane cottages are collectors' favorites. Look out for variations from standard designs, short runs, or strictly limited editions. Mint-condition examples with deeds and box are preferable.

Lilliput Lane's Dove Cottage. This particular version was only made for one year in 1983; it is therefore quite rare. *1983, 5 in (13 cm) wide.*

$400–600

BUY

Teapots appeal to both teapot and cottage-ware collectors. They should at least hold their value and look promising for future appreciation. This example is valuable as the combination of colors is rare.

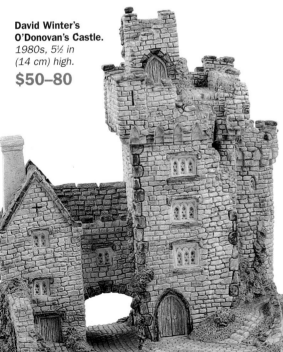

David Winter's O'Donovan's Castle. *1980s, 5½ in (14 cm) high.*

$50–80

David Winter's The Flower Shop, with its box. *1980s, 5½ in (14 cm) high.*

$40–60

A Price Bros. Ye Olde Inn teapot. The quality of the detailing, with leaded windows, makes this a desirable piece. *1930s, 8¼ in (21 cm) high.*

$400–600

Nursery ware from the 19th century onward is a favorite with collectors. Items scaled and designed for a child's use—from mugs to plates and divided dishes—reflect the changing fashions of their era. Many pieces are charming and unusual.

Illustrations of childhood stories and rhymes on ceramic nursery ware have a nostalgic appeal. The images adopted the style of children's book illustrations, which link them indelibly to their era. Victorian pieces often included designs based on nursery rhymes, especially those with a religious or moral message. Some of the earliest patterns, dating from the mid-19th century, were printed in single colors, such as black or sepia; others in multiple colors, such as black and green.

Painting and printing

By the early 20th century, the designs on nursery ware were often hand painted. In 1927 Susie Cooper designed her Quadrupeds line, printed in blue with hand-painted decoration showing animals among apple trees. A Quadrupeds plate might fetch around $250 and a mug around $150.

In the early 1930s Susie Cooper decorated children's mugs, cups, and porringers (small bowls) with images of lambs, rabbits, and other animals. Some of these hand-painted patterns were so popular that they were printed from 1935 to 1936. Many printed wares had hand-painted borders, to create a crafted look.

Between 1928 and 1939 W. R. Midwinter Ltd. produced a line of wares decorated with 12 nursery rhymes by William Heath Robinson. In the 1930s Eric Ravilious designed patterns for Wedgwood, including his notable Alphabet series of plates, mugs, pitchers, and bowls, on which each letter of the alphabet was represented by an illustration.

Chubby children

Shelley Potteries captured the market for nursery ware after 1926, when it introduced a line of patterns designed by Mabel Lucie Attwell, decorated with cartoons of small children. Today, an Attwell mug can cost up to $300. In 1995 fake Mabel Lucie Attwell plates began to appear. They are not hard to distinguish, since the transfers are applied on to the glaze.

Collecting themes

Although some collectors only seek early pieces, the popularity of nursery ware has less to do with age and value than with visual appeal, or a link to a certain manufacturer or subject. Many collectors focus on a particular line, such as the popular Bunnykins by Royal Doulton, a designer, or themed items such as egg cups or mugs, regardless of the maker, date, or style.

Side view

A closer look at... a Mabel Lucie Attwell nursery bowl

The work of Mabel Lucie Attwell is much prized. Particularly cherished are pieces from the 1930s adorned with painted figures, as well as her brightly colored novelty tea ware in the shape of children and elves. The value of either of these sets is not seriously affected by the large number produced.

The addition of a nursery rhyme was common, offering educational value as well as fun

A Mabel Lucie Attwell nursery bowl, designed for Shelley. *1930s, 6 in (15 cm) diam.*

$200–250

Attwell's children and elves are usually very rounded

Characters wear brightly colored clothing that appeals to children

Her elves are normally green. Yellow and brown elves are rarer and more sought after

IF THE FAIRIES CAME TO TEA, HOW VERY JOLLY THAT WOULD BE. THEY'D SAY "HULLO, I'D SAY "COME IN," AND THEN THE FUN WOULD ALL BEGIN.

Makers' marks

The leading companies were eager to promote their special lines (such as nursery ware) by giving them individual backstamps in a different style from the main company mark. The designer's or artist's name was often featured. Mabel Lucie Attwell's name was incorporated within the pattern, just like an artist's signature. This gave extra cachet to the item and was a strong selling point.

On the base of a Mabel Lucie Attwell nursery chamber pot the standard Shelley mark was used.

On the front of the same chamber pot the designer's name is featured next to a decorative motif.

Royal Doulton Bunnykins child's breakfast service, designed by Barbara Vernon Bailey. *c. 1934, plate 7 in (18 cm) diam.*

$50–80

Top Tips

- Be vigilant when buying a Susie Cooper nursery piece. Do not assume that it is hand painted: check for signs of hand painting such as brushstrokes and uneven paintwork.

- Be on your guard against fake Mabel Lucie Attwell plates. The colors are not as bold as on genuine examples and the transfers used are easy to scratch.

- Look for 19th-century nursery ware that sheds light on the social history of the time: this adds to its interest and value.

BUY

Nursery ware from the 19th century is popular with collectors, especially if it shows a childhood scene. Not surprisingly, ceramic nursery ware was often damaged. Surviving examples in good condition are often valuable.

A child's plate inscribed with the title "The Pet Lamb." Showing a girl playing with a lamb beneath a tree, the plate uses pastoral imagery typical of the period. *c. 1830–60, 5¼ in (13.5 cm) diam.*

$100–120

KEEP

The fresh style of Eric Ravilious, who worked for Wedgwood from 1936–40, is much sought after. Official reproductions have been produced and are marked as such. The Alphabet line included a pitcher, a plate, a porringer, a double egg cup, two sizes of mug, and a lamp base.

A Wedgwood Alphabet mug, designed by Eric Ravilious. It has a transfer print of the alphabet with images relating to the letters. *1938, 3¼ in (8 cm) high.*

$250–400

Royal Doulton figurines were

one of the company's most popular products, and are prized today. At one extreme are the "fair ladies," with their flounced petticoats and crinolines; at the other, the earthier charms of town criers and fictional characters from Dickens and Tolkien.

Despite having produced a few decorative figurines in the late 19th century, it was not until the 1920s that Royal Doulton began in earnest to release the pieces that have become so popular with collectors today. The series now numbers more than 2,000 different figurines.

Slender and small

Posed in expressive, carefree, or romantic postures, Doulton ladies can be found for less than $100 or as much as several thousand dollars, depending on the model, date, and color. Some enthusiasts choose to collect by color, others by modeler—certain modelers being well known for particular themes. In addition to the "fair ladies,"

Town Crier, designed by Peggy Davies, HN2119. *1953–76, 8 in (20.5 cm) high.*

$200–300

other popular topics include children and historical and literary personalities.

Miniature figurines, launched in 1932 and again in 1988, are also popular, especially for those with limited space. Two of the most sought-after series are the miniature Charles Dickens characters and "fair ladies." Some of these pieces have a rarity value and can command prices close to, or greater than, prices for the larger models.

Some designers to look for:
■ Charles Noke ■ Leslie Harradine ■ Peggy Davies ■

Charles Noke's miniature The Jester, originally one of his Vellum line but remodeled by Robert Tabbenor, HN3335. Noke was fascinated by entertainers. His original Vellum pieces, made in the 1890s before the HN series began, and named after their parchment color, can fetch more than $1,500. *1990, 4 in (10 cm) high.*

$150–200

Leslie Harradine's Paisley Shawl figurine, with red shawl and cream dress with painted flowers, HN1392. Designing at least one figurine per month from 1920, Harradine was one of Doulton's best modelers. Stylish "fair ladies" in crinoline dresses dominated his work. *1930–49, 8¼ in (21 cm) high.*

$200–300

Peggy Davies's Sweet Sixteen, from her Teenagers series, HN2231. Margaret ("Peggy") Davies created more than 250 figurines from 1946 to 1984. In addition to her teenagers, she is known for her 1950s figurines in period dress, historical personalities, and children. *1958–65, 7¼ in (18.5 cm) high.*

$120–180

The numbers game

Values tend to be high for early figurines, dating from the 1920s and 30s, and for those produced for limited periods of only a year or so. Every year, Royal Doulton announces a list of figurines to be withdrawn from production—a practice that was started just before World War II. When the first withdrawals were announced, many of the designs affected had been made in runs of fewer than 2,000, which makes them valuable today. A good example is Harry Fenton's The Newhaven Fishwife, produced from 1931–37.

Limited editions, specially produced in recent years for the Royal Doulton Collectors' Club, can fetch high prices, particularly if the figurines are attractive, small, or created by a noted designer.

A knowledge of color variations is essential when deciding whether to buy or sell a Royal Doulton figurine. A good example is Leslie Harradine's

The Newhaven Fishwife, designed by Harry Fenton, HN1480. *1931–37, 7¾ in (19.5 cm) high.*
$3,500–4,500

Paisley Shawl. If she is numbered HN1392, she will be wearing a red shawl and may fetch $200–300. If numbered HN1707, she will be wearing a much rarer purple shawl, and can be worth up to twice as much.

In Doulton's wake

Other makers produced similar decorative figurines. Wade issued a series of Art Deco dancing ladies in flowing gowns. The finish of these pieces was prone to flaking, so it is hard to find them in mint condition. Prices for Wade are generally low, which makes this a good place to look for stylish Art Deco figurines for less than $250. Arcadian produced a line of "fair ladies" along the same lines as Royal Doulton. Slightly less well modeled, but just as colorful, examples can be found for about $150 or less.

SELL

Although attractive and very popular with the original buyers, figurines produced for long periods are unlikely to rise much in value, since so many examples can be found. But look out for unusual variations in color on a particular figurine, as these are the exception to the rule.

Top o' the Hill, designed by Leslie Harradine, HN1834. This figurine was released in 1937 and has been in continuous production ever since. *c. 1990s, 7½ in (19 cm) high.*
$100–150

KEEP

Many people collect by series. Dickens miniatures are popular, and collectors are increasingly drawn to the Middle Earth series, inspired by Tolkien's Lord of The Rings, which are becoming scarcer and more valuable. TV programs have contributed to interest in the Dickens series, while Tolkien has gained fans thanks to the movie blockbusters. Many of these figurines were only produced for a short period. The price increases look set to continue, as demand outstrips the limited supply.

Barliman Butterbur, designed by David Lyttleton, from the Tolkien Middle Earth series, HN2923. The Tom Bombadil figurine is even more scarce and valuable. *1982–84, 5¼ in (13.3 cm) high.*
$400–600

▪ Nada Pedley ▪ Pauline Parsons ▪

Nada Pedley's Christine, HN3767. Pedley's figurines usually wear idealized and romantic Victorian and early 20th-century clothes. *1996–98, 7¾ in (20 cm) high.*
$100–150

Pauline Parsons' Susan, HN3050, boxed. Since Peggy Davies's retirement in 1984, Parsons has become the leading modeler of "fair lady" figurines at Royal Doulton. *1986–95, 8½ in (21.5 cm) high.*
$120–180

Hummel figurines

of endearing children are an enduring favorite. Over 500 models have been made, with variations in character, color, size, and form, therefore offering great scope and interest to collectors.

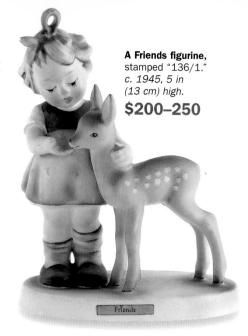

A Friends figurine, stamped "136/1." c. 1945, 5 in (13 cm) high.
$200–250

Perhaps the most widely collected ceramic figurines, Hummels were developed from sketches by a Franciscan nun, Berta Hummel (Sister Maria Innocenti), by the Goebel Company in Bavaria, Germany. Introduced in 1935, Hummel's figurines were an instant success. By the time she died in 1946, she had produced around 600 drawings—enough to keep the Goebel Company busy for decades.

It pays to be early

It is primarily the older pieces from the 1930s and 40s that are the most valuable, along with rare variations in color and form. Hummels from the 1950s and 60s can be bought for as little as $50–150, but earlier pieces can reach much higher prices. The first Hummel models included Puppy Love and Strolling Along, and early models from 1935–50 can be worth $500–700 or more. Rare, pale-colored doll faces or faience pieces can fetch up to $2,500 or more, and are very early in date.

Good variations

Figurines were produced in a range of sizes, and large pieces are worth more. Little Fiddler was one of the first line of 46 Hummels produced. A large 11-inch (28-cm) Little Fiddler figure (No. 2/II) from the 1970s can fetch over $800, while the standard 6-inch (15.25-cm) size from the same era is worth less than $200.

Look also for variations in color of certain parts of clothing. Village Boy is a popular model, which was first produced in 1936, withdrawn in the early 1960s, then reintroduced nearly 20 years later. A common 1979 green-jacketed figurine of Village Boy with a red kerchief can sell for $80–120. Earlier examples can fetch $250–800, while the rare, early version with a blue jacket and yellow kerchief can reach $800–1,200. Saint George,

Some Hummel figurines to look for:

■ Puppy Love ■ Merry Wanderer ■ Mother's Darling ■ Weary Wanderer ■

Puppy Love, stampled "1;" some damage. This is one of the first 46 models issued in 1935. This version, with the head facing right, is rare and valuable. *1950s, 4¾ in (12 cm) high.*
$200–250

Merry Wanderer, stamped "7," standard size. This model comes in three versions: the largest (9½ in [24 cm] high) can fetch more than $1,500. *1950s, 4 in (10 cm) high.*
$80–100

Mother's Darling. Stamped "175." Older versions, like this one, have light pink and yellow-green bags. Newer versions have blue and red bags. *1945–59, 6 in (15 cm) high.*
$100–150

Weary Wanderer. Stamped "204." This figurine has been made since 1949. A rare variation with blue eyes can fetch up to $300. *1940s, 6 in (15 cm) high.*
$120–180

designed by master sculptor Reinhold Unger in 1936 and different in style to most Hummel figurines, is normally worth around $250, but the rare red saddle version can fetch up to $2,000. Variations in the model also affect value. Early versions of Sensitive Hunter feature H-shaped suspenders used with the *lederhosen*, while the later ones have an "X" configuration. The "H" variation will increase the value by about 30 percent. Consult a reference work to understand what standard colors were produced in larger quantities and so learn to spot the unusual variations, which will often command higher values.

Revealing marks

Many designs are still in production today, so it is imperative to check the factory mark stamped on the underside of the base of a Hummel figurine in order to date it. The first mark used was a crown mark from 1934–50, with initials

"W. G." or the name "Goebel" in script underneath. Crown marks and marks with a large bee motif, used after 1959, denote early examples, which are among the most valuable. From the mid-1950s the bee became more stylized and smaller in size, and by 1960 had moved inside a V shape. In 1964, the entire motif was placed beside three lines of text reading "© by W. Goebel W. Germany," and from 1972, the motif sits on top of the word "Goebel" and the "G" becomes larger and almost circular in form. Examine the base for an impressed mark showing a number, as this helps to identify the modeler and the name of the piece, particularly if there is no transfer showing the name on the base.

The mold/shape number, e.g., 136, gives the name of the figurine, the modeler name, and the date of introduction. This information is listed in reference guides.

Fakes are few and far between, but some figures have faked marks painted on them in an attempt to make them look older.

Top Tips

- Always check the extremities of a Hummel figurine carefully for signs of damage and repair—the figurines are made of a brittle ceramic that chips, cracks, or breaks easily.
- Leave space between figurines when displaying to avoid damage.
- Intact models with easily damaged protruding areas, such as small birds, pigtails, and tree branches, may be harder to come by—and therefore more valuable.
- Fading and crazing decrease the value of a Hummel figurine: handle pieces carefully and display them out of direct sunlight.
- Bear in mind that the more recent or common the figurine, the more vital its condition in determining its value.

BUY

Look closely at color and smaller molded details on Hummel figurines, since even slight variations can cause values to rise.

A Soldier Boy figurine, stamped "332." The color of the badge on the cap changed from red to blue around 1970, with earlier red medal variants in limited supply—such as this one—fetching higher prices. *1964–72, 6 in (15 cm) high.*

$100–150

KEEP

Early Hummel figurines usually incorporate a bee motif, and the size and positioning of the bee counts.

A Chick Girl figurine, stamped "57." The incised crown and bee mark shows that this piece is early and also helps to date it more precisely. Its undamaged condition additionally makes it more likely to rise in value. *c. 1950, 3½ in (9.5 cm) high.*

$220–280

■ Skier ■

Skier, stamped "59," modeled and introduced in 1936. The ski poles were originally made from wood, but they can also be found in metal and plastic. *1950s, 5 in (13 cm) high.*

$280–320

Lady head vases were popular

from the 1940s to the 1960s, and these semiporcelain ladies epitomize the distinctive styles of their era. Prices are diverse enough to suit most budgets, making it easily possible to build up a satisfying collection.

Collectors adore the period elegance and allure of lady head vases. Often dressed in the feminine styles of the Fifties, the very best have extra details such as earrings and faux pearls, or sport extravagant hats or hair ornaments. Sometimes they hold one hand gracefully uplifted, perhaps covered in a white glove, but almost always they show only their shoulders, with just a glimpse of a delicate neckline. They can be had for as little as $20, but some rarities fetch up to $3,000. This is a fairly new collecting field, so bargains are out there, although values may rise swiftly.

Turning Japanese

Made in either a glossy-glazed or matte-finish semiporcelain, lady heads were vases sold by florists as gifts, holding bunches of flowers. Most were mass-produced by Japanese makers, then distributed to florists around the United States by American sales companies. One company in particular, Irving W. Rice Co., marketed lady head vases as a gift set—complete with flower sachet, net wrapping, and bow—from about 1955. These vases are usually marked "Irice Japan" on the bottom. A number of American manufacturers,

A Japanese Kissing Couple head vase; the base is marked 81708; the piece has a rare, brightly colored glaze. *1950s, 5¼ in (13cm) high.*

$180–220

A Japanese lady head vase with earrings, necklace, eyelashes, and molded bow. *c. 1950s, 6¼ in (5.5 cm) high.*

$120–180

including Betty Lou Nichols Ceramics of California, also produced vases that are popular with collectors, fetching from $150 to $600 for desirable examples such as the Floradorables series. The Ceramics Arts Studio of Madison, Wisconsin, is another popular name.

Model maidens

Some models came in several sizes, from around 4 to over 7 inches(17.75 cm), and many collectors try to amass the same design in all sizes, with a premium paid for the largest pieces. For instance, a blonde with her hair held in place by a tiara, marked "Lefton Japan," could be worth $60 in the 4¼-inch (11 cm) size, but as much as $250 for the 7-inch (17.75 cm) model. Look for 7-inch ladies

Essential lady head vases

PRAYING GIRL The praying hands are a rare feature. A Praying Boy was also made. This example is in mint condition. 1950s, 5¾ in (14.5 cm) high.
$100–150

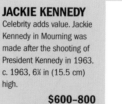

JACKIE KENNEDY Celebrity adds value. Jackie Kennedy in Mourning was made after the shooting of President Kennedy in 1963. c. 1963, 6¾ in (15.5 cm) high.
$600–800

ENGAGEMENT GIRL These were given, filled with flowers, to recently engaged couples. Loss of jewelry reduces value. 1950s, 5¾ in (14.5 cm) high.
$150–200

HEADACHE LADY If a wife was not "fulfilling her obligations," a husband could buy her this vase with flowers! 1950s, 5¾ in (14.5 cm) high.
$80–120

BETTY LOU NICHOLS These were handmade by a popular US maker. This is the Mary Lou; look for the larger Floradorables. c. 1950, 5½ in (14 cm) high.
$300–400

LITTLE SISTER Collectors like complete Big and Little Sisters series. Her gold eyelashes show she is Japanese-made, by Irice. 1960s, 4 in (10 cm) high
$100–150

in 1960s styles; these are popular and growing in value. Enthusiasts prefer vases that are pleasingly formed and nicely painted, with detailed moldings (often on hair that is elaborately styled and embellished). Painted-on gold jewelry or moldings imitating pearls, rhinestones, or precious gems can add value, as do hats, bows, and extra touches such as a delicately poised hand. Eye appeal and elegance count for a lot: a good Fifties-look example can run from $100 to $300.

Celebrity extras

Design choices abound, including religious themes such as Madonnas and nuns with sweet, placid expressions; southern belles with big hats; little girls with umbrellas; or babies in bonnets and bows. Celebrities tend to fetch the highest prices—most notably Marilyn Monroe, who can command around $3,000. Other popular designs include Lucille Ball ($500–900) and Disney characters such as Mary Poppins, Cinderella, Snow White, and Alice in Wonderland (at around $500 each). Jacqueline Kennedy in mourning clothes, with a hand stretched upward as if to wipe away a tear, is highly desirable and can fetch over $1,200, if the vase is in mint condition and she is accompanied by John-John and Caroline.

Vases in the shapes of exotic island girls or Asian beauties are scarce and desirable. A rare 6-inch (15.25-cm) island girl carrying a bowl on her head, marked "Shawnee, USA," and a small 4-inch (10-cm) Irving Rice Asian girl in elaborate

A Japanese Rubens Originals The Teenager, with realistic eyelashes and label to base. *1950s, 4¼ in (10.5 cm) high*
$150–200

headgear could be $50–60, while a 5-inch (12.7-cm) black woman in a turban and gold earrings can fetch $60–70.

Bargain buys

Men and boys are not as popular, but they make an interesting addition to a collection, since fewer were produced. Look for a 5¾-inch (14.5-cm) boy graduate with cap and gown, marked "Napco," from around 1959, or a 5-inch (12.75-cm) praying boy, marked "Inarco Japan," who is worth more with the praying girl. He can be found for $50–80, while she runs $100– 150. Also fun to collect are Christmas items: a fur-hatted lady in a red coat, marked "Napcoware," could be worth $50. First-time collectors can amass a fine collection of baby heads for as little as $25–50 each, and a display of clown heads for $20–40. At present, religious heads are not popular, but fashions may change, so at $5–15 each, now's the time to buy.

Top Tips

- An inscription or mark stating the country of origin, distributor, and, perhaps, the date and style number, can often be found on the bottom.
- Makers' marks or names, particularly from Japan, do not always add value; collectors look for form, size, and style.
- Examples without an inscription may have a paper label.
- Reproductions exist, so look for makers' marks, and consider colors, materials, weight, and form; when in doubt, compare to an original.
- Always examine protruding parts such as hair curls, hat brims, or flowers in hats for signs of damage or repair, since this reduces value.

BUY ▶

In contrast to the mass-produced Japanese vases, handmade and hand-painted US examples evocative of their period can offer value for money. They are all effectively unique, since each one was hand-painted. Most are also signed and dated, although check that the marks are there, as reproductions are not uncommon.

A Holt Howard Christmas lady head vase. The maker and signature, 1950s styling, and festive theme make this piece appealing. The value would be greater if the earring were intact. *1959, 4 in (10 cm) high.*
$70–100

KEEP ▶

Collectors look for detailed moldings and well-painted faces. Other added extras such as hands, jewelry, and hats increase desirability and add to value. Examples that have as many of these attributes as possible are the most likely to hold their value, probably even increasing in value as demand grows.

A Japanese Inarco lady head vase. The pleasing expression, pretty jewelry, and rare, easily damaged, curl in her hair make this example worth keeping. *1950s, 6 in (15 cm) high.*
$150–200

Historical Memorabilia

Historical memorabilia offers a tangible reminder of key events of the past. It encompasses mugs, pins, and decorative household items made to commemorate special events such as World's Fairs and political victories, as well as vacation souvenirs and the many stamps and coins that were once part of daily life throughout the last century.

New York World's Fair plate, p. 74 (1)

Coronation teapot, p. 63 (2)

Moments of history........

Historical memorabilia shows how important events have been commemorated through the decades. From coronation mugs to vacation souvenirs, coins, and special issue currency, these pieces were treasured when they were created and are highly collectible today.

Many of us have a mug we were given to celebrate a national event. Or perhaps we treasure childhood memories of a grandparent showing us a precious keepsake from an earlier event in his or her life. These mementoes are now extremely popular and highly collectible. Many of them have an interesting story attached, which can add to their appeal and value.

Souvenirs

Ever since the first international exhibition in London in 1851, World's Fairs have been commemorated with specially made ceramics (1). Likewise, the world has joined the British public in celebrating royal coronations with teapots (2), plates, and ornaments.

Stanhopes (3) were popular vacation souvenirs from the 19th century to the 1930s. These novelty items have a secret feature—a tiny window through which you can see images such as a town, monument, or person.

Many schoolchildren enjoy collecting postage stamps (4) and first-day covers.

George Washington candy container, p. 67 (5)

Ronald Reagan caricature coffeepot, p. 67 (6)

Storyteller Jemez doll, p. 77 (7)

Many personal mementoes have an interesting story attached to them that can enhance their intrinsic value.

Silver lantern Stanhope, p. 68

Space Shuttle Challenger STS-7 stamp, p. 73

..brought to life

If you still have a parent's or grandparent's collection, it's worth taking a closer look to see if any of the stamps they collected in the past have increased significantly in value over the years.

Americana

Enthusiasts are always eager to add to their collections of presidential memorabilia, from George Washington ⑤ to George W. Bush. Some of the most exciting objects date from election campaigns. You don't even have to be a fan to be a collector—there are plenty of whimsical and even downright disrespectful ⑥ items on the market!

Native American art can be prohibitively expensive, particularly for older artifacts. However, more recent pieces ⑦ can be just as evocative and much more affordable.

Minted treasures

Old coins and paper currency are sought after for their historical and aesthetic appeal more than for their face value. Rare coins can be valuable, however, and the scarcer paper currency increases in value as time goes by. There are plenty of other types of representations of wealth that attract just as much attention from collectors. Stock and share certificates, for example, can provide a fascinating record of industrial might, colonial adventure, and corporate intrigue. Silver certificates ⑧ and trade dollars ⑨ issued to facilitate commerce with the East are admired by many for their fine design as well as what they can communicate to us about a bygone era.

American silver certificate, p. 73

Trade dollar, p. 73

Elizabeth II of the United Kingdom

has had every stage of her life commemorated on a rich variety of ceramics. Such pieces represent the endurance of splendid pomp and ceremony through an era of tremendous change.

Thanks to the internet, commemorative wares featuring British royals are now easier to obtain. Pieces can be found in the United States and Canada through specialized dealers, or you might even have inherited some. Ceramics have also been produced to celebrate royal visits to North America. A 1959 Paragon bone china tazza, commemorating Elizabeth II's

A Wedgwood mug, designed by Richard Guyatt, issued to celebrate the Coronation. *c. 1953, 4 in (10 cm) high.*
$150–200

visit to Canada to open the St. Lawrence Seaway, can be worth up to $25.

Princess days

Wares produced to mark Elizabeth II's birth in 1926 are scarce, aside from a tea service produced by Paragon. Collectors are put off by its unusual decoration of magpies and the lack of personal imagery. A cup and saucer can fetch $90–120, a teapot more. Paragon later made a more popular set with a transfer portrait and the message "The Empire's Little Princess." Commemoratives of the princess's 1947 wedding to Lieutenant Philip Mountbatten are also rare, as postwar rationing meant few were made.

A Chiswick Ceramics earthenware mug, made to commemorate the Silver Jubilee. *c. 1977, 3½ in (9 cm) high.*
$40–60

Crowning glories

In contrast, a vast number of pieces were produced for the Coronation in June 1953. Mugs are unlikely to rise in value as they are common and often of basic quality. A Denby coronation mug, for example, is worth about $3.

Look for reputable makers, well-made bodies, fine detailing, and strictly limited editions. To commemorate the Coronation, Minton produced white orbs with gilt details in a limited

A closer look at... a Kaiser porcelain vase

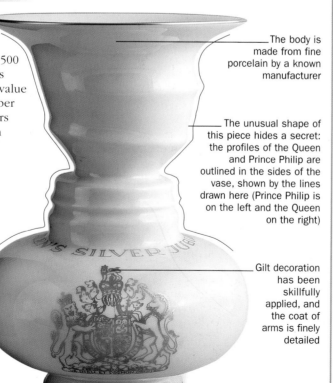

Commemorative pieces that were made in editions of 500 or fewer, such as this vase, tend to rise in value as soon as the number of potential collectors becomes larger than the total number of items produced.

The body is made from fine porcelain by a known manufacturer

The unusual shape of this piece hides a secret: the profiles of the Queen and Prince Philip are outlined in the sides of the vase, shown by the lines drawn here (Prince Philip is on the left and the Queen on the right)

A Kaiser porcelain bone-china silhouette vase, issued to mark the Queen's Silver Jubilee. It cost around $110 when it was first made. *1977, 8¼ in (21 cm) high.*
$150–200

Gilt decoration has been skillfully applied, and the coat of arms is finely detailed

A Crown Staffordshire bone-china mug, produced to celebrate the Silver Jubilee. *c. 1977, 4¾ in (12 cm) high.*
$30–40

edition of 600 that can fetch around $500–700. Colored examples in burgundy, cobalt blue, and green, which were limited to just 60 pieces in each color, can fetch a much higher price of up to $3,000 each. Wares were also produced by Aynsley, whose Deluxe coronation plates in different colors, all with gilt details and a photographic portrait, can fetch $300–500. Gold teapots in the shape of the coronation coach, made in 1953 by both Thomas Hughes and Garden House Pottery *(see right),* can be found for around $250–300 each, but the rarer white version with gold details and a musical movement can fetch more than $300.

Did You Know?

Elizabeth II's 1992 "Annus Horribilis" speech was commemorated by a Chown mug showing the lion and unicorn of her coat of arms being bombarded by arrows. It also has five slightly bizarre verses, which include:

"God save our Queen this
Christmastime From
the fanatic's knife and
bomb And from the more
self-serving crime Of perjured
Tess and Peeping Tom."

A Caverswall bone-china plate, issued to mark the Golden Jubilee, from a limited edition of 1,000. *2002, 10¾ in (27.5 cm) diam.*

$200–250

Silver and gold celebrations

The Silver Jubilee in 1977 was widely celebrated by manufacturers of commemorative ware. The high number of surviving pieces—the event took place less than 30 years ago—has kept prices down, so this could be a good time to start an inexpensive collection. Look for higher-quality pieces by Aynsley, Coalport, Royal Doulton, Worcester, and Wedgwood.

As part of her Golden Jubilee celebrations in 2002, the Queen visited 70 towns and cities throughout the UK, and many of these places issued commemorative pieces. A hand-painted, blue-rimmed, half-pint tankard by The Rye Pottery of Sussex can fetch $60. These Golden Jubilee commemorative pieces may become the treasures of the future.

Top Tips

- Avoid pieces with blemishes such as poor-quality transfers, rubbed gilding, chips, or cracks—unless they are particularly rare.
- Look out for reputable designers, unfussy designs, and unusual or attractive shapes. Generally, loving cups and cups are more valuable than mugs.
- To give your collection a focus, select a single manufacturer, a theme, or an event, such as a royal visit or jubilee.
- Aim to choose pieces with photographic images—they are often more popular than those with just coats of arms or ciphers.

An all-over gold-luster earthenware coach-shaped teapot, made by Garden House Pottery to commemorate the Coronation. *1953, 5 in (13 cm) high.*

$200–300

KEEP

Pieces that display fine quality, a restrained style, and skilled use of gilt decoration will at least hold their value—and may appreciate as collectors seek out the limited number available. If there are other items in the same line, you can start to build a good collection.

A Minton bone-china loving cup, produced to celebrate the Coronation. The design is by John Wadsworth. *c. 1953, 4 in (10 cm) high.*

$200–300

SELL

A plethora of low-quality mugs has been produced for the Queen's two jubilees. If the mug has a shoddy transfer, thick body, and gaudy colors, or if mass-produced by an unknown or poor-quality maker, its value is unlikely to rise even over the long term.

An English mug, issued to commemorate the Silver Jubilee. *1977, 3¼ in (8.5 cm) high.*

$7–15

Later royal commemorative ware

has often been produced in response to public interest in the sensational aspects of the British royal family's lives. Manufacturers have drawn on satire as well as affection to produce an inventive selection of collectibles.

A Chown mug, made to commemorate the divorce of the Prince and Princess of Wales, from a limited edition of 150. *1996, 4 in (10.5 cm) high.*

$100–150

Whether a grotesque *Spitting Image* mug, or a more respectful plate celebrating the wedding of Prince Charles and Lady Diana Spencer, much comparatively recent royal memorabilia has collectible appeal. Some pieces have undoubtedly appreciated in value.

Little was produced for Diana before her wedding, but hold on to any scarce items showcasing her birthdays. For example, a Caverswall mug with her portrait to celebrate her 21st birthday can be worth $100–150.

The most significant royal occasion involving Prince Charles before his marriage was his investiture as Prince of Wales in 1969. A Royal Crown Derby china bell, sold in a limited edition of 500 to mark this event, can fetch up to $600 in today's market.

Many inexpensive commemoratives were made for Charles and Diana's "fairy tale" wedding in 1981. Prices vary, as does quality—a plain Denby mug would be worth about $30.

Toward the other end of the price spectrum, manufacturers include Paragon, Spode, Royal Crown Derby, Coalport, and Royal Doulton. A Spode bone-china mug with a double portrait of the pair surrounded by floral and foliate wreaths can fetch up to $75.

Chronicling less happy times

After the couple separated in 1992, anything featuring an image of the princess alone doubled in price. These prices should at least remain constant and may increase. When the marriage ended in 1996, about six designs were produced to mark the divorce.

Although the quality of some of these pieces is only fair, the fact that so few were made has kept demand—and value—consistent. A mug made by Chown, showing Charles and Diana facing away from each other, is a typical example (*see above, right*). Any wares made after Diana's death

in 1997 should be examined with care, as the quality of portraiture and ceramics generally can be poor.

Colorful caricatures

A number of irreverent items were produced, and perhaps the best examples are those by Luck & Flaw. They were responsible for the 1980s satirical British TV series *Spitting Image*, which featured latex puppets of royals, politicians, and personalities. Egg cups based on the puppets, including Charles with huge, drooping

A Royal Doulton loving cup, made for the Queen Mother's 80th birthday. Despite the reputable manufacturer, unknown production numbers have kept values low. *1980, 3¾ in (9.5 cm) high.*

$30–50

Queen Mother commemoratives to look for:
■ 8oth birthday ■ 9oth ■ 99th ■

A Royal Crown Derby loving cup, made for the Queen Mother's 90th birthday. The high value is due to the intricate decoration and the limited-edition run of 500 by a well-known maker. *1990, 3 in (7.5 cm) high.*

$300–400

A Bradmere House mug, produced for the Queen Mother's 99th birthday. Only 99 mugs were made, but the maker is not well-known and the decoration is of poor quality. *1999, 3½ in (9 cm) high.*

$50–80

A J. & J. May mug, made to commemorate the birth of Prince William. *c. 1982, 3½ in (9cm) high.*

$100–150

ears, can be worth $100 today. Another well-known item is the 1981 Carlton Ware "Prince Charles ear mug." Mint, this can be worth around $70–100.

The young generation

Pieces associated with Princes William and Harry are currently in great demand. The company J. & J. May made a mug *(right)*, and a limited edition of 50 loving cups, for William's birth in 1982. The loving cup can fetch up to $800–1,200 because of its limited run and superior quality. More affordable items commemorating the young royals do exist—a Cardigan Pottery mug can be bought for $30–50.

The best of the rest

Interest in the Queen Mother remained strong as she passed the milestones of old age and many celebratory items were produced. Fewer pieces were made for other royal family members, so rarity value means that prices can be surprisingly high. A Coalport mug marking the bestowing of the title "Princess Royal" upon Princess Anne can be worth about $75.

Top Tips

- Avoid poor printing and smudgy images; production and finish are crucial.
- Watch out for hairline cracks, crazing, scratches, and missing bits of transfer.
- When buying royal commemorative wares for investment, note that many collectors prefer pieces with photographic portraits.
- Look for makers with an established name. Always check for the mark of the factory on the base of the piece.
- With modern wares, look for limited editions made in low numbers, preferably fewer than 100—these are more likely to rise in value.
- Focus on items that capture the style of their era, such as the *Spitting Image* pieces that epitomize the 1980s.

65

Later royal commemorative ware

BUY

Diana's children are eclipsing her in popularity. Fewer pieces were made to commemorate Prince Harry's birth than that of his older brother William, making them scarcer—a low production run often raises the value. Buy now while still affordable.

An Aynsley small loving cup made to commemorate the birth of Prince Harry. It shows a scene of Balmoral Castle. *1984, 2¼ in (6 cm) high.*

$80–120

KEEP

Any humorous commemorative wares, particularly those by Spitting Image such as this double-sided mug, which echoes Charles's large ears in Diana's "Queen of Hearts" frame, will probably rise in value. They are popular with many collectors.

A Kevin Francis Charles and Diana mug, made in a limited edition of 350 to commemorate the couple's divorce. Both sides are shown. *1990s, 6 in (15 cm) high.*

$120–180

▪ 100th ▪ 101st ▪ In memoriam ▪

A Caverswall lionhead cup, made for the Queen Mother's much-celebrated 100th birthday, in a limited edition of 500. *2000, 4¼ in (11 cm) high.*

$60–90

A Chown mug, made for the Queen Mother's 101st birthday. The limited edition of 70 and appealing portrait make this highly collectible. *2001, 3¾ in (9.5cm) high.*

$80–120

A Caverswall lionhead cup, made in memory of the Queen Mother, in a limited edition of 2,002 (matching the year in which she died). Values may rise as it becomes scarce. *2002, 4¼ in (11 cm) high.*

$50–80

Political memorabilia is

eyecatching and colorful, and offers insight into an era.
With campaign buttons costing as little as $2, it can
be a fun and affordable hobby, while important pieces
worth serious money can make it more than a pastime.

The razzamatazz of elections isn't new, although using mementoes to advertise a candidate wasn't considered proper until the 19th century. The change came when, after Andrew Jackson's defeat by John Adams in 1824, he came back in the next campaign by offering trinkets such as snuff boxes, clothing buttons, and ceramic plates. Ribbons were first used in 1828 in the Jackson era and, by 1840, William Henry Harrison made good use of parades and rallies as well. Of course, political memorabilia from those days fetches top dollar but recent pins, flags, T-shirts, mugs, and other merchandise can be had for relatively little. A Carter-Mondale '76 button can fetch $2–5, while a button with the black-and-white photographed heads of Reagan-Bush from 1984 can be

$15-25. The Kennedy name commands a premium, with a plastic badge fetching over $100. However, most pins cost $30–200. Don't forget the affordable mementoes of July 4th celebrations, which are often adorned in a Stars-and-Stripes theme and usually cost $30–150.

Looking for rarities

People may sell mixed lots of memorabilia associated with a particular campaign, so it's worth examining these for a rarity. Also consider objects that don't seem intrinsically valuable and that would normally have been discarded, as they have scarcity value. A bottle of sparkling water, used in the re-election campaign of George Bush-Dan Quayle in 1992, is not something many would have saved and, yet, the

A Sherwin & Cotton ceramic tile commemorating the centenary of Lincoln's birth. Printed image of an 1864 photograph of Lincoln on the front and impressed inscription on the back. *1909, 9 in (23 cm) high.*
$220–280

unused water, with its label intact and good graphics, can be worth $10 today.

Timely slogans

Earlier souvenirs are very sought after. Campaign buttons from 1896–1916 are particularly fine. These were usually metal disks with a color-paper design covered in celluloid; a rarity such as a Taft-Sherman elephant-ears pin could be $6,000–8,000. Pre-1896 campaign buttons tended to be real buttons with slogans; an early one (c. 1789) celebrating George Washington's inauguration might run $800. Medalets or tokens, with holes for ribbons, were introduced 1824–32 and are treasured for the slogans that recall concerns of the day, such as "Free Soil, Free Speech," "The Union Forever," or—alluding to Abraham Lincoln's man-of-the-people image—"The Rail Splitter of the West." Lapel pins also advertised issues; gold and silver bug pins (c. 1896) were worn to indicate preference in the Currency Standard debate, with Democrats favoring silver and Republicans gold. Some of the best ribbons, however, are from the late 19th century, and show likenesses of the candidates on silk. Most silk ribbons cost $80–300, depending on condition and graphics.

A closer look at... a campaign button

Campaign buttons are numerous and form a popular collecting area, marking important points in the political and economic history of the United States. While buttons can be had for as little as $10–20, early, rare, or desirable examples can be worth up to $1,000 or more. To begin assessing a value, examine the materials used, as well as considering the date a button was made and the event or reason for which it was made.

John Llewelyn Lewis was the president of the United Mine Workers. He had supported Roosevelt in the 1932 election and is shown next to him on the button

This button was made for a single day's event in one state, meaning fewer were made than for longer-running or national events

A Lewis & Roosevelt Labor day Celebration campaign button for an event at Sutterville PA on September 8th 1934. The first true campaign buttons were made for Abraham Lincoln's campaign in 1860. 1934 3.25in (8cm) high
$800-1,200 LDE

Surviving examples are extremely scarce, even more so in this condition, with bright colors and the original gilt printing on the ribbon

Wartime wins

Ceramic commemorative ware is part of many collections, much of it from World War II and bearing patriotic, "Allied" themes. Values depend on style and quality of decoration, as well as maker, date, materials, and rarity. Hence, poorly made transfer-printed pieces will be less than finely decorated ones from notable factories. Look for limited editions, the lower the edition number the better.

Make 'em laugh

Politicians will always be the subject of satires, sketches, and parodies, so any material with humor attracts a premium. Original material by cartoonists is mostly the realm of the top salerooms, but plenty of witty, inexpensive trinkets are out there. Peter Fluck and Roger Law of the UK had huge success with their *Spitting Image* puppets on TV. Ronald Reagan and Margaret Thatcher puppets from the show inspired a coffeepot and teapot that are now highly collectible.

A "Win With Kennedy" plastic campaign button. *c. 1961, 2½ in (6.5 cm) wide.*
$100–150

Collectors may enjoy the postcards (c. 1900–12) that regularly lampooned the other political party, with images of donkeys or elephants. A postcard campaigning for lower taxes or lower costs for saloon licenses could be worth $10–20. At the higher end, there is lots to collect, although much of it is traded by specialist dealers. Photographs always command good prices, particularly if signed. A black-and-white photo of the five presidents—George Bush, Jimmy Carter, Ronald Reagan, Gerald Ford, and Richard Nixon—and signed by all of them could be worth $3,700 or more. Objects owned by politicians will rise in value the more famous the personality. Objects owned by John F. Kennedy top the bill here, with his personal set of golf clubs fetching over $700,000 and one of his iconic rocking chairs going for over $450,000 at auction in 1996.

Cover story

Magazine covers and war propaganda posters frequently had political content. While illustrator Norman Rockwell's original artwork, *Rosie the Riveter*—which was used on the cover of the *Saturday Evening Post* in 1943—sold for $4 million, vintage and modern magazine covers can be had for reasonable prices. A *Saturday Evening Post* cover from October 1963 showing Richard Nixon could be bought for about $6–10. Since ephemera is by its nature fragile, amassing these now could be a worthwhile investment.

Top Tips

- With modern-day campaigns so reliant on TV and the internet, the colored cloth and trinkets traditionally associated with elections are on the wane. Snap up what you can; it may have rarity value later!

- When trading personal items of politicians, provenance is essential.

- Choose photographs with iconic images—showing important events or strong emotions—and eye appeal.

- Signed letters can make a great collection. Always consider content: Does the letter relate to a key career moment or an interesting personal fact? If so, it may well rise in value.

A George Washington cardboard and painted-plaster figural candy container made for Independence Day celebrations. *c. 1950, 9¼ in (23.5 cm) high.*
$150–200

BUY

Look for political propaganda and campaign material produced in the run-up to elections. These give invaluable insights into the issues of the time and how the candidates addressed them. If the candidate is shown and well-known or loved, so much the better. Many such items, especially made from paper, did not survive in quantity, making some scarce.

***Facts About the Candidate,* by Byron Andrews,** a miniature campaign book giving facts about Roosevelt's life and political career. Although many would have been distributed by the *New York Tribune,* its tiny size, inexpensive materials, and ephemeral nature mean few will have survived. *1904, 2¼ in (5.5 cm) high.*
$40–60

KEEP

Humor and satire have been historic and widely appreciated aspects of political commemorative items for centuries. Buy well made and designed items that combine a famous political figure with humor associated with that person, since these are likely to rise in value as well as be fun to own and display.

A Carltonware *Spitting Image* coffeepot of Ronald Reagan, designed by Fluck and Law. The great popularity of this coffeepot led to many similar copies, which can often be had for under $100. *1981, 10½ in (27 cm) high.*
$300–500

Stanhopes, first produced in the second half of the 19th century, are small, novelty mementos that contain a miniature peephole revealing a "mystery" photograph. They are an excellent theme for the budget collector.

A silver lantern charm, with a Stanhope showing four views of Exeter, England. *c. 1900,* ¾ *in (2 cm) high.*

$60–90

If you look carefully at the end of a bone needlecase or the top of a dip pen from the 1860s onward, you may find inset a tiny glass bead. This is the actual Stanhope—a lens just millimeters wide to which one or more minute photographs, that look like black pinheads, are attached. When held up to the light and close to the eye, the lens magnifies the microphotograph to reveal the picture as if projected on a tiny screen.

The pioneers

The name Stanhope comes from Charles Stanhope, the British politician and scientist (1753–1816), who invented a uniquely powerful hand magnifying lens, achieving enlargements previously possible only with microscopes.

About 50 years after Stanhope's death, his invention was adapted for use in souvenirs. An Englishman, John Benjamin Dancer, invented microphotography in 1839, but it was a Frenchman, René Dagron, who combined the Stanhope lens with the Dancer microphotograph in 1860 to make a tiny viewer with an image attached to the lens. He then began setting his device into everyday objects and souvenirs of locations or historic events.

Booming business

The public's response was so positive that Dagron opened a factory in Gex, on the Swiss border, just two years later. Soon he was employing more than 100 people, producing photographic miniatures known as *bijoux photomicroscopiques*, or "microphotographic trinkets," fitted into a huge range of inexpensive souvenirs containing views of personalities, resorts, and exhibitions.

The canny Frenchman realized that others might copy his idea once the patent expired, so he marketed Stanhope kits to encourage anyone else who wanted to produce Stanhopes to buy the equipment and supplies from Dagron. As a result, a great variety of Stanhopes was made by various companies during the late 19th century. Business declined from the 1920s to the 60s,

although Stanhopes were still manufactured—for example, to commemorate special events such as the Coronation of Elizabeth II in 1953. Production eventually ceased in 1972.

Exciting finds

Stanhopes were produced in the thousands, but they are relatively uncommon today because they were frequently discarded once the novelty had worn off, or left forgotten at the bottom of a drawer. Although the more commonplace Stanhopes often appear at sales and auctions, you do need to be alert to spot one elsewhere. If you are lucky enough to discover a Stanhope at a yard sale or similar, the likelihood is that the vendor is unaware of the trinket's

A pair of French bone binoculars, with Stanhopes showing views of the Isle of Wight, England. *c. 1920, 1 in (2.5 cm) long.*

$20–30

Did You Know?

Stanhopes such as rings, tie pins, watch fobs, and small pencils often contain racy nudes and other erotic images. Intended for gentlemen, they are a specialty and a valuable category with a crossover appeal to collectors of erotica.

A French, carved-bone measuring tape and pin cushion, with a Stanhope of a religious scene. *c. 1870, 2¼ in (6 cm) high.*

$120–180

A closer look at...

a two-lens erotic Stanhope

The view is always important to a Stanhope's collectibility but you should never neglect the object it is set into. This example has a decorative casing as well as several other desirable elements: it features erotic subject matter (a rare and valuable characteristic); and it has an unusual mechanism that gives the appearance of movement—a lady jumping into bed.

A French, pot-metal *cinématographe bijou* (cinematic jewel), in the form of a book with two views. *c. 1890, 1 in (2.5 cm) high.*
$300–400

The case is well made, with intricate detailing contributing to the value

Two Stanhope lenses are mounted in the moving metal bar, making it rare—pressing on the bar incorporated into the case alternates the views on offer: in this instance, a lady undressing and the same lady in bed

The "moving" image is viewed through this peephole

A cranberry glass perfume bottle with a Stanhope fitted into the hinge revealing six views of the town of South Shields, England. *c. 1900, 2¼ in (5.5 cm) high.*
$200–250

A silver, articulated fish charm, with a Stanhope showing extracts from the Torah. *c. 1900, 1¼ in (3.5 cm) long.*
$70–100

special secret. Most Stanhopes are valued at much less than $150, with only a few rarities exceeding this.

Lucky dip

Stanhope novelties are predominantly made from bone, pot metals, and silver, although plastic was usual after the 1920s. The most commonly found examples are sewing accessories, dip pens, jewelry, smoking accessories, and charms (including tiny binoculars for watch fobs). A pair of miniature bone binoculars with a view of a well-known personality might fetch $90 or more, but those with standard views of scenery may be worth as little as $15. Cigarette holders fall into the $50–150 bracket, depending on the material used (metal and wooden ones are worth slightly more than plastic). Larger items such

as canes are rarer and more valuable. Perfume bottles with Stanhopes can fetch up to $400, thimbles up to $600—these higher prices can be attributed in part to additional interest from collectors of perfume bottles and sewing tools.

The most frequently found images are of tourist attractions, historic cities, and spa towns. Portraits are rarer and are thus more sought after. Events such as the 1862 London International Exhibition are also unusual and have a wide appeal.

BUY

Views of personalities, such as royalty, are rarer and more valuable than scenic views. When the subject is a person, the Stanhope is likely to have been made to commemorate a historic event in their life, which helps to date the item, adding to its collectibility.

A brass monocular charm, with a Stanhope showing a portrait of Princess Alexandra. The charm commemorates her marriage to the Prince of Wales. *c. 1863, ½ in (1.5 cm) long.*
$70–100

Top Tips

- Before buying, check that the viewer is still set into the novelty. If it has fallen out, the Stanhope will be worth a fraction of a complete example.
- Examine the image carefully—it should be clearly visible, sharp, and unscratched. If it is blurred, bubbled, or crazed, the value of the Stanhope will be much less.
- Ensure that the novelty is in good condition before you buy. Don't wash a Stanhope after buying, since this can remove the gum attaching the image to the lens.

SELL

Dip pens, along with binoculars, are among the most widely found Stanhopes. They are a good starting point for a collection, but as dip pens are common, they are unlikely to rise in value, even if they are intricately carved.

A French bone penholder, with a view of Crystal Palace, England. The Stanhope is set into the shaft. *c. 1890, 6½ in (16.5 cm) long.*
$40–60

Philately is a long-established and popular hobby, and postage stamps are fun to collect. With their striking designs, American stamps are very desirable, celebrating key historical milestones and the icons of a nation.

The first American stamp was issued in 1847 and today that beloved 5¢ red brown stamp is worth up to $1,200, if in fine condition. In the world of stamps, however, age does not necessarily equate with value, and the later 10¢ stamp that followed could be worth about $2,500 in the same condition or more ($20,000), if in mint condition, as fewer were made. The rarest 1¢ stamp, a 1867 "Z" Grill, one of only two known, was recently sold at auction for $935,000. Some old stamps, however, can be found for just 25¢, while a rare modern stamp might fetch thousands.

In the eye of the beholder

Luckily for enthusiasts, stamps are not just collected for value but also for beauty. Since millions were printed, good examples can cost no more than $1, throwing the market open to all. The US Postal Service covers patriotic themes well and many handsome variations of the Stars and Stripes and bald eagles have been made over the years. Since American stamps never depict a living person, current politicians or movie stars won't be featured on stamps. Elvis Presley died in 1977, but didn't appear on a stamp until 1993.

Batter up

For sports enthusiasts, a series of 10 baseball stadiums (c. 2001) is worth about $10, and a set of four showing early football heroes (c. 2003) can sell for $5. Baseball heroes such as Babe Ruth, Lou Gehrig, and Jackie Robinson usually go for around $4–6. Look also for the Legends of Hollywood and Black Heritage series, issued once a year.

Pick a theme

American stamps are not overly commercial: don't expect to find a

A 5¢ red-brown stamp. The image on this stamp is well-centered and bears a lightly canceled postmark. This was the first American stamp ever issued. *1847, 1 in (2.5 cm) high.*

$800–1,200

US-issued *Star Wars* stamp, for example, although these have been issued by some countries in Africa. Disney is about as commercial as American stamps go. A set of four of Mickey Mouse, Donald Duck, Goofy, and Pinocchio, (c. 2004) stamps usually fetches around $3–7. Thematic collections, however, are fun to build as well as popular. Subjects range from aircraft, animals, explorers, and inventors to fish, flags, people, space, and sports.

A happy accident

Often the anomalies of a production run result in a rare—and therefore valuable—stamp. Sometimes stamps

Some American stamps to look for...

■ 3¢ Rose ■ 1¢ Kansas Overprint ■ Farley Series Unperforated ■

A rare block of 12 American 3¢ Rose stamps. In addition to being a hard-to-find block of stamps, this example retains its margin with the printed plate number, a rare and desirable feature. Single stamps may fetch up to $60. *1861–62, 5½ in (14 cm) wide.*

$800–1,200

A 1¢ Kansas overprint stamp. Stamps were overprinted with, and valid only in, Nebraska or Kansas to stop crimals from raiding post offices and taking stamps to sell in Chicago. *1929, 1 in (2.5 cm) wide.*

$5–8

are issued "imperforate," because the machine missed a sheet or a part of a sheet. A color shift or a missing color is another mishap that will make a stamp rare. A mistake in design can cause joy among collectors. In 1994, as part of the Legends of the West series, a stamp was issued ostensibly showing Bill Pickett, the legendary rodeo cowboy and first black cowboy movie star; in fact, it depicted his brother. Sheets of 20 corrected stamps sell for about $20, but the error sheet can be worth $400. For a short time, as collectors scrambled to get hold of these, they traded for a staggering $14,000.

Picture perfect

Most collectors are looking for quality, so a stamp should be in mint condition. Centering is very important among American stamp enthusiasts and very much affects price. Perfectly centered means that the image is placed evenly within the white perforated border, with an equal space on each of the four sides. An American 50¢ stamp, c. 1894, in typically average centered condition is worth around $1,000–1,500. A perfectly centered one that recently came on the market, however, sold for 22 times its catalog price, at $19,250. Modern commemorative stamps are fun to

amass, but since so many of them are issued to mark a special occasion they are highly unlikely to be a good investment, unless they contain some kind of irregularity. Event covers—envelopes mailed on the day of a special event—or first day covers—items postmarked the day a stamp is issued—are extremely popular. Some stamp enthusiasts collect nothing else.

A British Penny Black stamp, in very good condition. It has a light postmark cancelation, check letters "C" and "E" and clear, even top and bottom margins. *1840, 1 in (2.5 cm) high.*

$180–240

BUY

Learn the look of stamps and spot unusual anomalies. Errors can add value; these stamps are worth buying and should rise in value. Consider color, printing, and positioning.

A Family Planning 8¢ stamp. The printing shift raises the value from about 40¢ to up to $10. *1972, 1½ in (4 cm) high.*

$8–10

KEEP

Look for high value stamps since fewer were made. They are always worth keeping due to increased demand over time against a limited supply. Prices should rise, especially for those in lightly canceled or unused condition.

A $9.95 Airmail Definitive stamp, showing an American bald eagle. This high value stamp is made more desirable by the image of a bald eagle. Birds are a popular collecting theme. *1991, 2½ in (5 cm) wide.*

$25–35

■ $3 Definitive Space Shuttles ■ 3¢ Victory ■

A Farley unperforated 4¢ stamp. Postmaster James A. Farley printed quantities of perforated stamps for general use in the 1930s and a smaller number of unperforated ones for private use. He was later forced to print more unperforated stamps for general use. *1934, 1½ in (4 cm) wide.*

$1–2

A $3 Definitive stamp, showing the Space Shuttle Challenger STS-7 in orbit. Look for themed stamps, as these are popular with collectors. Like birds, space is a popular theme and this shows one of the most recognizable US space program icons. *1995, 1½ in (4 cm) wide.*

$7–10

A 3¢ Victory issue stamp. This stamp was produced to commemorate the victory of World War I in March 1919. This example is clean, unhinged, and perfectly centered, centering being of great importance to stamp collectors. *1919, 1 in (2.5 cm) wide.*

$8–12

Coins and paper money,

as well as stocks and bonds, are more sought after for their historical and aesthetic interest than for any intrinsic value—and there is always the chance that a rare coin might turn up in your home.

An American two dollar silver certificate, with red seal and in crisp and uncirculated condition. *1917.*
$300–400

The study of coins and medals is known as numismatics. This collecting area has broadened in recent years, and now includes paper money (notaphily) and stock and bond certificates (scripophily).

A penny saved, a penny earned

Some coin enthusiasts specialize in "type collecting," whereby one coin of each series and design issued for a particular period and place—such as American Antebellum coinage—is collected. Others concentrate on coins of the ancient world, commemoratives, minting errors, or other categories. The novice can begin by using coins in circulation to understand coins and learn the skills necessary to grade them.

A certificate for a 7 percent Confederate States of America Loan for $500.
1863, 13¾ in (35 cm) wide.
$50–70

When buying commemorative issues take the edition number into account. Those released in large numbers will appreciate less than strictly limited issues. Beware of facsimile collectors' coins, which are common. Although not necessarily made to deceive, they are hard to tell from the genuine article.

Condition is vital: coins that are uncirculated or in mint state are usually worth more, although collectors are fond of "toning." This is the natural blue-green discoloration that builds up, particularly on silver coins. A good, even tone will increase the value of a coin, so never clean or polish them—this can reduce value by half. Rarity is key: a half-cent Liberty cap from 1794–97 with a right-facing head can fetch up to $1,500, whereas the rarer left-facing version minted in 1793 only can fetch up to $5,000, depending on condition.

Paper chase

Paper currency is usually intricate, incorporating swirls and flourishes around finely detailed and colored vignettes, as well as additional security devices. Closer investigation will reveal many subtleties, such as the current US $100 bill, on which Franklin's lapels are microprinted with the words "United States of America." Possible collecting themes are historical period, special serial numbers such as palindromic or low numbers, currency with printing errors, or that created for special purposes, such as military currency.

Notes currently in use can be obtained for their face value; less common countries for as little as $30, whereas

▼ **In the York House club, London,** members watch fluctuations in the New York stock market during the Wall Street crash. Changes were chalked up by telephone operators in direct contact with New York. *October 31, 1929.*

A closer look at... a Romanian commemorative issue

Commemorative issues are often produced in large quantities, so to retain their value they must be kept in mint condition. If the paper currency or coin is issued with a presentation case or folder it should be kept safely stored inside. This colorful design by Nicolae Saftoiu depicts the path of the 1999 solar eclipse through Romania, which this note was printed to commemorate.

The unique serial number makes the note easier to trace in the event of fraud

Text is printed on both vertical and horizontal axes and in varying sizes, making it more difficult to counterfeit

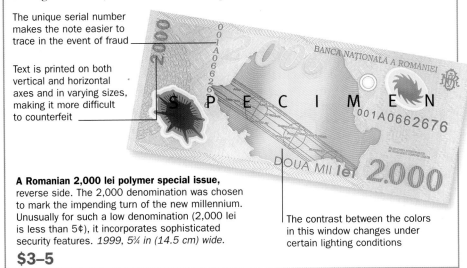

A Romanian 2,000 lei polymer special issue,
reverse side. The 2,000 denomination was chosen to mark the impending turn of the new millennium. Unusually for such a low denomination (2,000 lei is less than 5¢), it incorporates sophisticated security features. *1999, 5¾ in (14.5 cm) wide.*

The contrast between the colors in this window changes under certain lighting conditions

$3–5

rarer notes can fetch thousands of dollars. Bargains can be had by sifting through boxes of cheap currency kept by many dealers. Opt for the cleanest, crispest pieces available, preferably in unused or uncirculated condition.

Stock up on stocks

Stock, share, and bond certificates can be attractive, often featuring vignettes depicting the function of the issuing body—such as a ship for a shipping line. Generally, the more decorative the share, the more desirable it is. Most enthusiasts prefer certificates from the early 18th to the mid-20th century, the period when the great industrial and colonial powers flourished. Headline-making scandals can result in a rise in interest. Nominally worthless certificates for single shares of Enron stock have sold for more than $80 following the disclosure of irregularities involving the company in 2003.

Unlike paper currency, certificates in excellent condition are relatively easy to find, since they will probably have been kept in a bank vault for years. The denomination of

the certificate is also important. Higher denominations will be harder to find, since fewer were printed and so tend to be more valuable than lower ones. Applied items such as tax stamps and signatures can also add value. Crossover appeal can raise value too: for example, stock issued by the Great Western Railway Company is also attractive to railroad enthusiasts.

A Thai 60 baht issued to commemorate the King's 60th birthday, depicting the King of Thailand in state dress, enthroned, on the reverse. *1987, 6¼in (16cm) wide.*

$8–12

BUY

As coins and paper currency were made to be used, examples in close to mint, uncirculated condition are hard to find. These make excellent examples to buy since surviving numbers will usually be limited and they will always be more desirable to collectors than worn examples.

Prices should rise, particularly if the item has other interesting features that would appeal to collectors.

An American Trade Dollar; this example is in extremely fine condition with prooflike fields and only a few marks. This coin was also minted in 1874, the year the trade dollar was introduced for overseas use to encourage trade with other countries, particularly China. *1874.*

$200–300

SELL

Facsimile coins can be found in abundance and may lower the value of rare coins. The motives behind their creation are often entirely innocent—simply to make a reproduction of an attractive but expensive coin—but it can still be difficult to tell the genuine article from the counterfeit. A facsimile is unlikely to rise in value.

A silver facsimile Chinese coin with a military bust of Yuan Shih-Kai. Original coins with this design can cost about $200, but there are many facsimiles on the market. *1914, 1½ in (4 cm) diam.*

$2–3

New York World's Fairs, held

in 1939 and 1964–65, generated countless souvenirs. Visitors saw computers and touch-tone phones for the first time, and products from around the world. Memorabilia appeals to those wanting to relive the fun of discovery.

Celebrating the 150th anniversary of George Washington's inauguration, the 1939 fair had a futuristic theme—"World of Tomorrow." This was particularly forward thinking, considering the US was just pulling itself out of the Great Depression. Television was introduced here, with RCA broadcasting the first program. Futuristic design, dominated by the clean lines of Art Deco, also featured large.

To the Moon

With its 600 acres, 140 pavilions, and scores of amusements, the New York World's Fair of 1964–65 was an unforgettable experience for a generation of Americans. It also sparks curiosity among those too young to have been there, factors contributing to a booming collector's market. The brainchild of lawyer Robert Koppel, the

fair brought high-tech discoveries to young Americans and created a sense of pride in the country's achievements. The theme, "Man in a Shrinking Globe and Expanding Universe," focused on industry and technology, particularly on the newly launched Space Race.

Sites and sounds

The site for both fairs was in Flushing Meadows Park, Queens, where

A 1964–65 New York World's Fair vinyl inflatable child doll, by Alvimar, with a small bell inside. *c. 1961, 8 in (20 cm) high.*
$18–22

landmark buildings were constructed. Learn to recognize these, as it will make identifying memorabilia easier. The 1939 fair was dominated by the 700-ft-high, needle-shaped Trylon and its spherical Perisphere. The most common graphic representation of these is found in a plastic salt and pepper shaker ($40–60). The 1964–65 fair was overseen by the Unisphere. Constructed by US Steel, it was a vast model of the globe in 250 tons of steel, artfully poised on a three-pronged pedestal and encircled by

A 1939 New York World's Fair souvenir serving plate, with applied handle and transfer design highlighted with hand painting; back marked "MADE IN JAPAN." *c. 1939, 6 in (15 cm) diam.*
$30–40

A 1964–65 New York World's Fair license-plate style, printed-metal decal, with embossed Unisphere motif. *c. 1964, 4 in (10 cm) wide.*
$8–12

Essential World's Fair memorabilia

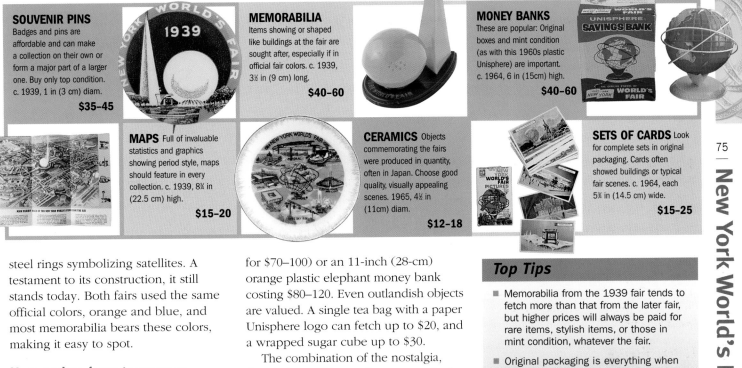

SOUVENIR PINS Badges and pins are affordable and can make a collection on their own or form a major part of a larger one. Buy only top condition. c. 1939, 1 in (3 cm) diam.
$35–45

MEMORABILIA Items showing or shaped like buildings at the fair are sought after, especially if in official fair colors. c. 1939, 3½ in (9 cm) long.
$40–60

MONEY BANKS These are popular: Original boxes and mint condition (as with this 1960s plastic Unisphere) are important. c. 1964, 6 in (15cm) high.
$40–60

MAPS Full of invaluable statistics and graphics showing period style, maps should feature in every collection. c. 1939, 8¾ in (22.5 cm) high.
$15–20

CERAMICS Objects commemorating the fairs were produced in quantity, often in Japan. Choose good quality, visually appealing scenes. 1965, 4½ in (11cm) diam.
$12–18

SETS OF CARDS Look for complete sets in original packaging. Cards often showed buildings or typical fair scenes. c. 1964, each 5¾ in (14.5 cm) wide.
$15–25

steel rings symbolizing satellites. A testament to its construction, it still stands today. Both fairs used the same official colors, orange and blue, and most memorabilia bears these colors, making it easy to spot.

Here today, here tomorrow

Souvenirs for the home, usually in glass or ceramic, are part of most collections and are commonplace and varied. A commemorative ceramic tankard for the 1939 fair, with a molded decoration of the Trylon and Perisphere can fetch up to $100, while a 1964–65 glass tankard with a transfer of the Unisphere goes for around $15. Other household objects include spoons, ashtrays, bookends, and trays. Most can be found for under $100, often for under $50.

Some of the most valuable objects are those associated with the day-to-day operations of the fair, many of which were damaged or discarded. These include common items such as admission tickets, signs and posters, and even bricks from the demolished Amphitheater, to rarer pieces such as uniforms and employee ID cards. A Greyhound employee's jacket from the 1964–65 fair could be worth over $250 and a staff ID pass bearing the Unisphere logo $25–$30 or more. Paper souvenirs, such as maps or postcard sets, which were produced in their thousands, are readily available and fetch around $20–30, making an excellent start to a collection.

Unusual objects are highly collectible, such as an 11-inch (28-cm) wastepaper basket showing the Unisphere (going for $70–100) or an 11-inch (28-cm) orange plastic elephant money bank costing $80–120. Even outlandish objects are valued. A single tea bag with a paper Unisphere logo can fetch up to $20, and a wrapped sugar cube up to $30.

The combination of the nostalgia, the plethora of items, the comparatively reasonable prices, and the importance of the fairs to American history make this a particularly thriving collecting area. With a popular society and websites devoted to collecting, it's easy for enthusiasts to learn more about the memorabilia and to build collections.

Top Tips

- Memorabilia from the 1939 fair tends to fetch more than that from the later fair, but higher prices will always be paid for rare items, stylish items, or those in mint condition, whatever the fair.

- Original packaging is everything when it comes to fair memorabilia. A clear plastic rain bonnet would be worth little without its case, but up to $15 with it.

- Look for souvenirs such as ceramics from the 1939 fair, since they are often particularly striking and collectable, many with streamlined 1930s shapes and Art Deco motifs.

BUY

Buttons, badges, and pins were produced as souvenirs of the fair itself and for special reasons, such as for visitors from different states, companies, or societies. More unusual examples such as the latter type are scarcer and thus likely to hold their value or even rise in value.

A 1939 New York World's Fair "Hi Neighbor, I'm from Connecticut" button. Few of these would have been made and, since it retains its original ribbon and is in excellent condition, it makes a great buy—that also shows the unifying friendliness of the fair. *c. 1939, 4¼ in (11 cm) high.*

$100–150

SELL

Many souvenirs were made to be bought and used and are functional rather than decorative. Decorative memorabilia often has a wider appeal due to its visual qualities and tends to hold value better in the long term. Sell to a keen collector and invest the money in something more decorative.

A 1964-65 New York World's Fair coaster and napkin set. Since it is in mint condition being still unopened and sealed in cellophane, this scarce survivor of ephemera would make a welcome addition to a hard-core enthusiasts' collection. *c. 1964, box 8½ in (21.5 cm) wide.*

$30–50

Native American art is

distinctive and prized for its beautiful workmanship. Prices can be high, although many works are still affordable and well worth snapping up before values escalate.

Arts and crafts were functional and ritual activities of indigenous peoples of North America long before they became an economic necessity. The growth of tourism has helped encourage creativity among artisans, and many items now collected date from the 20th century.

Paid by the pound

The peoples of the southwest are the biggest suppliers of handmade works. Navajo women are known for their colorful, patterned weaving—from rugs and saddle blankets with geometric designs to pictorial pieces made for the tourist market. A quality "pound" blanket—so called because they were sold by weight to traders—from 1885–1912 can cost $500 or more. Navajo men learned blacksmithing from the Spaniards and their jewelry is distinguished by its wrought silverwork and turquoise. Baskets vary greatly in shape and color. You can expect to pay $100–300 for a ceremonial example made of coiled yucca with a black-and-red star design, while a similar utilitarian piece (c. 1900) that is no longer made could be $300 plus.

A Navajo polychrome wedding basket, with three red coils, and a black, radiating, stepped inner and outer design and braided rim. *c. 1950, 13 in (33 cm) diam.*

$180–220

Hopi dolls

The Hopi of Arizona are famous for Kachina dolls. Made for religious ceremonies, Kachinas—over 200 characters in all—are reminders of the spirits. These are also made by Pueblo and Zuni Indians, who share the Hopi's beliefs. Others now make their own versions, which, strictly speaking, are just dolls, as they have no spiritual importance. Hopi Kachinas by famous artisans can cost $1,000, with rare figures fetching $10,000. The earliest examples—if they can be found—can be unexceptional visually, and some

Native American art to look for...
■ Dolls ■ Beadwork ■ Baskets ■ Pottery

Badger Kachina doll by Stacy Talahytewa. These dolls represent the spirits of nature that were venerated by the Hopi to ensure a good year. Look for hand carving, complex details, and use of natural coloring and materials. *c. 1975, 16 in (40.5 cm) high.*

$70–100

Platue-style Peyote bird design beadwork bag, probably by the Kiowa. Look for figural or animal scenes, which are scarcer than geometric patterns. Older bags are more valuable, but can be hard to identify. *c. 1960s, 12¼ in (31 cm) high.*

$250–350

Tlingit basket from Alaska, which can be identified by its geometric patterns. Baskets like this have been made for hundreds of years by many tribes. Look for bright colors and characteristic patterns, which may have symbolic meanings. *c. 1920s, 5 in (12.5 cm) high.*

$350–450

enthusiasts prefer designs from the Forties, when carving became more intricate. An Ogre Woman by Keith Torres might fetch $900 plus, while a simple corn maiden would be around $18, and a clown $120. The best place to buy these is from the Hopi. Their jewelry too is sought after: silver overlay pieces run from $40 to $1,000 or more. Pottery is a great buy, with striking examples going for $65–125 and up.

All that glitters

The Zuni of Arizona and New Mexico are the premiere jewelry makers of the southwest. Known for eye-catching settings of stone-to-stone inlay or channel inlay (with strips of silver), makers also set stones on silver backings or use many small, irregular stones (chip inlay). Turquoise, coral, jet, and pink shell are used to great effect. Carved "fetishes"—tiny animals imbued with powers—are also hung on necklaces. Jewelry can be expensive, but the carved creatures can cost

under $50. Zuni pottery is very desirable. As the culture is so dependent on rainfall, many vessels are decorated with symbols of rain such as tadpoles, frogs, and stylized water droplets. Another distinctive Zuni image is "The Deer in His House," which shows a heartline from the animal's mouth to his heart.

Primitive pots

To the east of the Zuni are 19 pueblos clustered along the Rio Grande River. These are abundant sources of primitive pottery, and styles are as varied as the artisans (the Cochiti pueblo, for instance, has 200 potters); prices reflect that diversity, ranging from $10 into the thousands. The Santo Domingans are known for small, rolled-stone beads or "heishi," made into multistranded necklaces and these, too, are prized.

A Navajo blue ground weaving, with red and white geometric design. *c. 1970s, 28 in (71 cm).*
$70–100

North and south

In Alaska and the far north of Canada, the Inuit are famous for soapstone carvings; small ones by unknown artists can cost around $50 up, while a 9-inch (23-cm) sculpture by a known artist could start at $400. The Plains Indians such as the Kiowa make exceptional beadwork; look for bags from $250 and belts from $100.

BUY ▶

Items that typify the traditions of Native American art in form, decoration, and function are likely to hold their value, if not appreciate. Storytelling dolls reflect the way children are taught verbally though song and are visually reminiscent of Native American pottery. A revival of their creation in the early 1960s has led to growing interest from collectors that looks set to grow.

A Jemez polychrome Storyteller doll, by Persingula Gachupin. The potter and style are well-regarded by collectors, making this early and charming example a find. *c. 1965, 6in (15cm)*
$180–220

KEEP ▶

Vintage Hopi pottery is already an established field, commanding high prices. Many collectors are now turning their attentions to newer potters who produce in the traditional manner. Those with skill, a feel for the medium, and an historic connection may prove winners in the future.

A Hopi pottery olla, by Clinton Polacca Nampeyo, with typically stylized polychrome bird and feather designs. The Nampeyo family is closely connected with Hopi pottery, with renowned potters dating back to the mid-19th century. *c. 1980 8¼ in (21 cm) high.*
$300–500

■ Jewelry ■

Hopi pottery vase from Arizona. Hopi pottery was one of the earliest Native American potteries and is the most widely collected. Geometric patterns, including those with eagles or the Sun, are typical. *1910–30, 7 in (18 cm) high.*
$280–320

Turquoise Navajo necklace. Crude workmanship often indicates a 19th-century origin, although authentic pieces are rare and valuable. Recent works, such as this necklace, are easier to find. *c. 1970s–80s, 25 in (63.5 cm) circ.*
$280–320

Household
and Kitchenalia

Vintage household and kitchen objects have immense appeal and charm. From the varied patterns and rich colors of wooden rural dairy items, to the urban sophistication of 1930s cocktail shakers, they are not only often decorative, but also offer a nostalgic reminder of daily life in days gone by.

Cookie jar, p. 96

Brass candlesticks, p. 82

Salt and pepper shakers, p. 104

SALT PEPPER

The lasting appeal of....

Many people appreciate the beauty and faded charm of vintage household and kitchen objects. There can be great pleasure in decorating the home with unusual pieces from the past, such as kitchen scales or an old sewing machine, and many can still be used.

Treen cup, p. 84

One of the advantages of collecting old kitchen equipment and household articles is that you don't have to be an expert to appreciate them. Many pieces are both decorative and highly nostalgic, such as mid-20th century cookie jars ① in the shape of animals or well-loved characters.

Familiar sights

Brass items like candlesticks ② are now purely decorative, adding warmth and a traditional feel to an interior.

Jadeite, a Depression-era opaque press-molded glass in shades of light green, is popular with collectors. Plates and cups can be picked up inexpensively, but rare containers and shakers ③ are more sought after. Kitchen implements such as bread boards, jelly and chocolate molds ④, pie birds, and toasters are all highly collectible. Old sewing machines ⑤ and sewing compendia ⑥ remind us of a time when needlecraft was an essential

Cough Checkers REGISTERED
CHECK HUSKINESS, TICKLING COUGH AND SORE THROAT.

Blue-and-white platter, p. 89

Cough drops tin, p. 99

Easter Bunny chocolate mold, p. 102

Singer sewing machine, p. 107

Sewing compendium, p. 107

.things for the home

skill for women. If you have inherited an old sewing box, it may well be worth something.

Carved wooden treen items such as butter stamps and cups ⑦ conjure up images of rural life in days gone by, and collectors especially prize original paint and the build-up of a rich patina on the wood. Colonial-style blue-and-white china wares ⑧ with intricate transfer patterns are also valued.

It's a wrap

Vintage packaging and tins ⑨ have become a hot collecting area over the last 30 years or so. Late 19th and early 20th century pieces tend to be valuable, but it is still possible to find bargains from the 1950s and 60s. Packaging reflects the styles and changing tastes of each period, from sinuous Art

Nouveau styles to the functional austerity of the 1940s and the colorful artwork of the 1950s and 60s. It also shows us how advertising has changed over the decades.

Drinking paraphernalia makes a varied as well as useful collection, ranging from vintage corkscrews ⑩ with their often ingenious designs, to sleek, silvery 1930s cocktail shakers ⑪ that encapsulate the languid glamour of Art Deco.

Many vintage household objects may be unearthed in your own home. Even everyday objects might be worth something and there are still plenty of fascinating bargains to be found in junk shops, thrift stores, and garage and estate sales.

You don't have to be an expert to appreciate kitchen equipment and paraphernalia. Many pieces are both decorative and nostalgic.

Button corkscrew, p. 110

Cocktail shaker, p. 113

Old brass and copper add

charm, warmth, and style to a home, and look good together. Stately brass candlesticks offer a hint of baronial splendor, while quaint copper pots and pans conjure up old-style rustic kitchens.

Aside from the pricey art metalware of Stickley and Van Erp, much old copper and brass is affordable yet attractive. Collectors often buy metalwork because of its affinity with oak furniture and to enjoy the reflected light of decorative pieces in period settings.

Shiny stories

The advent of electricity made many household items that our forbears used obsolete—which is partly why they are collectible. Copper or brass warming pans, filled with hot water or embers, were used to warm bedsheets. These sell for around $100–500, with larger, finely decorated pieces worth the most.

Candles were once a necessity. Many antique candlesticks have scratches where solidified wax was cleaned off. Beware of sticks in pristine condition and in bright yellow brass, as these are likely to be reproductions. An 18th-century brass candlestick could fetch up to $500, whereas a similar 19th-century one might be $100 or less.

Two brass saucepans with iron handles.
1860s–90s, top pan 6 in (15 cm) diam.; bottom pan 5½ in (14 cm) diam.
$50–80; $90–100

Kitchen heavyweights

Although cooking pots and saucepans were commonly made of cast iron, wealthy households owned sets made of copper. Vintage copper pots might cost from $80 for a small one, up to $500 for a large lidded pan by a noted manufacturer, such as Benham & Froud (1855–1906). A set of six copper pans, with a double boiler for making sauces, could be worth over $1,500.

Copper and brass kettles were rare before the 18th century. Prices now vary but can be high: an early 19th-century copper kettle could reach $500–800. Iron stands, for holding flat irons as they heated on stoves, were plain at first, but by the 1850s were decorated with complex patterns in brass or copper. The most sought after were made by craftsmen, sometimes incorporating a horseshoe in the platform.

Around the hearth

Brass and copper fireplace accessories included bellows, coal buckets, andirons, and fenders. A Federal brass and iron fender may be $400–600, while a pair of fine andirons from the same period can fetch from $700 to $6,000 or more. Bellows were made of brass and wood. Standard examples often fetch $60–90, while large, ornate, or mechanical versions can sell for over $150.

Lightweight reproductions

Pieces from the 18th and 19th centuries are the most collectible. Many 20th century items are also popular, although they are generally not as valuable. Because people like to keep brass and copper polished, it is difficult to use patina to date pieces. Modern pieces are often lighter than older wares because metal is now rolled

A pair of Victorian brass candlesticks.
c. 1850s, 11 in (28 cm) high.
$60–80

more thinly than it was in the past. Feel the surface of a piece: Is it smooth where expected, given its usage? Look for damage and wear: Is it believable, or might it have been contrived to fake age? The name on brassware may not be the maker's—many items were engraved to show ownership. Inscriptions are often unscrupulously added to genuinely old objects to make them appear more valuable. Modern lettering can be thin and scratchy compared with authentic lettering.

The thrill of the Chase

In the 1930s, the Chase Brass and Copper Company successfully mass-produced good quality, affordable metalware. Employing designers such as Walter Von Nessen and Russel Wright, the company took inspiration from older 18th and 19th century designs and

Collectors' Tales

"I once found a big box of brass items at an estate sale. Something poking out of the corner caught my eye. Although most of the pieces were uninteresting, a closer inspection revealed a pair of early 19th-century candlesticks. I sold them for $300— many times more than I paid for the whole lot."

Allan Coombes, Virginia

A closer look at... a Chase pitcher

The Chase Brass & Copper Company (founded 1876) produced homewares during the 1930s. Copper and chrome are the most common finishes, and styles are typically Art Deco. Chase homewares are hotly collected, particularly pieces with representative industrial styling by notable designers.

The striking design with its simple lines and clean surfaces lacking in ornamentation are highly Modernist, strongly representing the Art Deco period

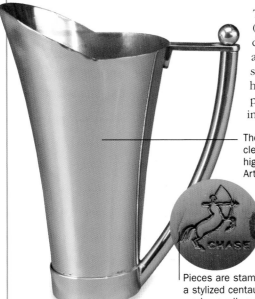

Pieces are stamped with a stylized centaur archer mark, usually on the base

A Chase copper-and-brass water pitcher. It was designed by Walter von Nessen, who is well-known for his lighting designs and is considered a pioneering industrial designer. *c. 1930, 10¼ in (26 cm) high.*

$200–300

added an Art Deco twist. The homewares included dishes, beer pitchers, cocktail shakers, lamps, coffee sets, and flower holders. Many attractive items can be found for $100–300, but some rare and desirable pieces can be worth up to $1,500 or more. Chaseware was distributed through major department stores and through Chase shops within stores in New York City; Portland, Oregon; Cleveland, Ohio; and Missoula, Montana. Chase pieces are still most easily found in and around these cities. Other Art Deco metalware makers of note include Revere, Manning Bowman, and Frankart.

A copper crumb tray and matching brush, *c. 1900, brush 13½ in (34 cm) long.*
$120–180

Top Tips

- Use a magnet when examining old copper and brass to make sure it is not merely plated. A magnet will not be attracted to solid copper or brass.
- Beware of overdistressed copper purporting to be old. New copper is often thinner than old, and so dents more easily.
- Ensure that any set of scales and weights is complete before buying.
- Keep copper pots and molds for decoration only: there is a risk of poisoning if the protective linings are no longer in perfect condition.
- Avoid common copper or brass items that are split. Repairs can be hard to hide and will reduce the item's value.

BUY

One of the joys of collecting vintage metal kitchenalia is that items such as brushes, candlesticks, and trivets can still be used. The range of designs available allows you to build a satisfying collection, adding a period feel to your kitchen. When buying a trivet, look for examples with attractive detail in the legs and the platform.

A brass trivet. The fine motif of a ship and the claw feet add value. *c. 1880s, 10 in (25.5 cm) wide.*

$20–30

KEEP

Kettles are among the most popular decorative brass and copper items. Many were so heavily used in their day that it is rare to find one in good condition. These should retain their value and may even rise, especially if they appeal to other markets or have extra decorative features.

A copper kettle. In addition to being in excellent condition, it was made by the notable maker Booth & Son, of Toronto, and so would appeal as much to collectors of Canadiana as to those looking for a decorative antique for a kitchen. *Late 1880s, 12 in (30.5 cm) wide.*

$220–280

Vintage wooden objects,

particularly those made for the dairy, hark back to our rural past. The homespun beauty of these satisfyingly tactile pieces and the social history they represent make this an immensely appealing field.

Most of us are attracted by the warmth and natural qualities of wood, and the way it changes so subtly with age. Wooden household objects conjure up images of busy farmhouse kitchens and a simpler way of life.

Of the tree

Miscellaneous small utilitarian items made from turned or carved wood are often referred to as treen, which means "of the tree," and are regularly

Did You Know?

Used hundreds of years ago, the word treen had become obsolete by the early 20th century. Enthusiastic collectors of wooden objects, such as Edward Pinto, helped bring treen back into usage.

included in the category of folk art. Most items available date to the 19th or early 20th centuries—18th century items are rare. Treen ware starts from around $40–60 for small items such as spoons, egg cups, or salt cellars, and larger or rarer items can fetch $2,000–5,000 or more, depending on age, condition, and decorative features.

Many objects are made of pine, which was commonly found and easily carved. Walnut, boxwood, and maple were also frequently used, and mahogany suited durable boxes. The look and feel of a vintage wooden item is very important. The patina that builds up on old wood through years of use has a subtlety and richness of color that is highly desirable and impossible to fake. Original paintwork and intricate, good-quality carving, also add value to a piece.

A treen cup, with a pedestal base and a handle, which would also be used to attach the cup to a belt when traveling. *1770s–1830s, 5 in (13 cm) high.*
$350–450

Dairy days

In the 19th century, butter was often decorated using a carved stamp or roller that was impressed into the butter pat. These stamps, sometimes featuring double-sided patterns, start from around $100, although rare examples in good condition, such as prized Pennsylvania items, can

Some dairy collectibles to look for:
■ Bowls ■ Molds ■ Stamps ■

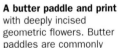

A butter paddle and print with deeply incised geometric flowers. Butter paddles are commonly found, but when combined with a print they are rarer. *11½ in (29 cm) high.*
$400–600

A sycamore dairy bowl. Most wooden bowls acquire an attractive patina and work well as decorative pieces. *c. 1910s, 13¾ in (35 cm) diam.*
$250–300

be worth $700–2,500 or more. Butter and sugar molds are also highly sought after, and vary greatly in price. Those with plain and simple patterns can be found for under $100, but if the pattern is intricate and attractive, and the carving is of high quality, pieces can fetch $2,000 or more.

Treen to please

Wooden spoons are full of character and make a good start to a treen collection. Found in many different shapes and sizes, and occasionally painted, they often feature attractive and useful carved handle ends, in the shape of hooks or hearts, for example. Spoons can be found for as little as $30–80, with most spoons fetching around $80–200, though some finely carved examples sell for $500 or more.

Wooden bowls are also popular, with prices starting from around $200. Burlwood bowls are especially desirable—they have an attractive texture and are very strong, since they don't crack along the grain. Good burlwood bowls can command prices of $1,000–8,000 or more.

Other wooden objects to look for include boxes, hand mirrors, cutting boards, cups, stools, and trays. Wall carvings and painted wooden business

signs have a big following, too. Weathered surfaces often add to the charm of these items, and they frequently fetch well over $1,000.

Wood advice

The provenance of a piece is worth noting. The area from which an item originates affects its value; for instance items from Pennsylvania and New England are more sought after and, hence, more valuable. When buying, keep in mind that items of Canadian origin offer excellent value for money, as they look similar to, but are currently less expensive than, many of their US counterparts.

Top Tips

- Look for decorative carvings and details. If original, they can increase the value, as can names and dates.
- Do not drill holes in wooden items so that they can be hung up, since this will reduce their value.
- Fake and reproduction wooden items do exist, but are fairly easy to spot; it is impossible to fake the wear of genuine age and long-term use.

BUY

Wooden objects wear extremely well if looked after, showing a rich and varied patina when gently polished. They make superb decorative items, and many are still useable. Good examples are sure to retain their popularity and values.

A Canadian treen salt cellar. The warm colors, the gently curving shape, and well-turned decoration make this a collectible and functional piece. *c. 1870s, 4 in (10 cm) high.*

$50–80

SELL

Items that are roughly carved and show little attention to form, those with limited decorative value, with an obscure function, or that are late in date are less collectible and unlikely to increase in value. Sell to a person who appreciates their naïve charm.

A fruitwood olive spoon with a perforated central bowl scoop and a drilled shaft in the handle for draining the liquid from olives. This piece has little decoration or style. *c. 1880s–1930s, 16 in (40 cm) long.*

$15–25

■ Milking Pails ■

An eagle butter stamp. Animal and wheat-sheaf designs are scarcer and more valuable than geometric patterns, as are double stamps. *c. 1880s, 4 in (10 cm) diam.*

$350–450

An oak milking pail, with a metal pint measure. *1880s–1920s, 14 in (35.5 cm) high.*

$150–250

Jelly molds, in all their wide variety of

materials and shapes, bring back memories of birthday
parties and feasts, and their appeal is both nostalgic
and aesthetic. Not all molds were just for gelatin
desserts—some were used for savory dishes as well.

The earliest jelly molds were made in the
18th century of thin white stoneware. Most
jelly molds found today though date from
the early 19th century to the 1950s.

In the late 18th century the British
Staffordshire potteries made deep and
increasingly inventive molds. Shapes
and motifs included fruit, animals,
wheat sheaves, and classical motifs.

Minton, Copeland, and Davenport were
all major manufacturers. They produced
cream-and-white wares from
the mid-19th to the early
20th century. Minton pieces
are often recognizable
by their glaze, which
has a bluish tinge.
Marked molds are
more desirable.

In the 1840s, decorated
earthenware and heavy, brown,
salt-glazed stoneware were
increasingly used. Prices are around
$45–90, but highly decorative molds
by major makers can exceed $150.

Copper was another material used,
since it was light, durable, and easy to
mold. From the 1920s onward, cheaper
materials were used and quality declined.
Designs also became less intricate, but
pieces can still be attractive and are
usually priced at around $30
or under. A notable 20th-
century maker is Shelley,
whose molds are
sought after today,
especially if they
are well shaped.

▲ **A salt-glazed rabbit
earthenware mold.** The use
of molded animal or vegetable
forms dates from an earlier time
when the the design of the mold
would have reflected the savory
ingredients of the jelly. *c. 1870s,
6½ in (16.5 cm) wide.*

$40–60

▶ **A Wedgwood
ceramic mold**
with bunch of
grapes motif. The
design may reflect
the ingredients of
the jelly, or the
conviviality of dinner
with wine. *c. 1880s,
6¼ in (15.5 cm) wide.*

$60–90

▶ **A Shelley
Star mold,**
shown upside down.
The known maker and
comparatively complex
shape increase the value.
1912–25, 5¾ in (15 cm) diam.

$60–90

◀ **A Shelley Acanthus mold.**
The acanthus leaf is a classical
motif that dates back to
antiquity. The attractive
design by a well-known
manufacturer makes this
pottery mold highly
desirable. *1912–25,
5¾ in (14.5 cm) wide.*

$60–90

◀ **An aluminum mold.** Many
molds of the 1920s and 30s
reflect the simple forms and
clean lines of the Art Deco
style. *1920s–30s, 6¾ in
(17.5 cm) wide.*

$7–10

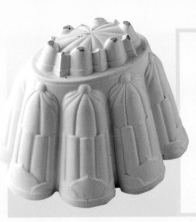

◄ A Shelley Ritz mold.
The Ritz Hotel in London was opened in 1906 to widespread acclaim. This is an early piece from a notable maker. *c. 1912, 7¼ in (18 cm) wide.*

$80–120

◄ A copper cylindrical Charlotte mold retailed by T. Aldridge of Brompton Road, London. Charlotte was a 19th-century jellylike dessert using bread or cake filled with chopped fruits such as apple. *1860s, 3¼ in (8 cm) high.*

$100–150

Collectors' Tips

- Look for makers' marks, since notable makers add value
- Feel the weight of copper molds before buying. Thin, light molds are probably reproductions. Avoid split and resoldered pieces
- Look for registered design marks to help date earthenware molds, but bear in mind that marks relate to the date of design, not manufacture

▲ A Green's, Newstyle Jellies, earthenware chicken-shaped mold. Jelly molds in the shape of animals are highly collectible, as are flower shapes. *c. 1920s, 6¼ in (16 cm) wide.*

$60–90

▼ A copper mold. Copper molds with complex designs such as this are more valuable than plainer examples. *1870s, 6¼ in (16 cm) wide.*

$200–250

► A Malin mold with swan motif. The well-known factory and pentagonal shape, combined with the swan motif, make this a desirable object. *1920s, 6¾ in (17 cm) wide.*

$80–120

▲ A Shelley Carlton mold. The deep indentation at the top created a well into which cream was poured. *1912–25, 6 in (15 cm) wide.*

$60–90

Blue-and-white ware had

its heyday in the 19th century, but its familiar, intricate designs still feature in many home ceramic collections. Whether for use or simply for display, it is available in a huge range of shapes, patterns, sizes, and prices.

A William Smith "Lion Antique" pattern jug. *c. 1835, 5 in (12.5 cm) high.*

$150–250

A collection of blue-and-white china is the perfect addition to a Colonial-style dining room. A late 19th- or early 20th-century plate with a common pattern such as Willow can fetch $50–80, but a large piece or one with a rare pattern or shape may be worth $1,500 or more. Early Anglo-American blue-and-white ware can command even higher prices.

From paint to print

In the 13th century, the Chinese began hand painting designs onto porcelain, with landscapes, flowers, and decorative motifs. Chinese blue-and-white ware became fashionable in Europe and the United States in the 18th and 19th centuries, although the labor-intensive production technique made it costly.

In the mid-18th century, the Worcester factory in England discovered a way of transfer-printing a design onto a piece before glazing, making it possible to produce inexpensive ceramics. Before long many factories, including some of the Staffordshire potteries, began printing blue-and-white designs onto mass-produced earthenware.

Patriotic plates

After the American Revolution, English Staffordshire potters were eager to increase business in the United States. Transfer-printed ironstone ceramics were made to appeal to the new sense of patriotism, and were popular from around 1820 to 1860. They featured heroes such as Washington, Jefferson,

Some patterns to look for:
■ Asiatic Pheasants ■

■ Death of the Bear

◀ **A Copeland & Garratt Death of the Bear pattern plate.** This pattern is the most commonly found from Spode's Indian Sporting line. *1833–47, 9¾ in (25 cm) diam.*

$300–400

▼ **An Asiatic Pheasants pattern sauce boat,** by an unknown maker. This delicate pattern was produced on a large variety of objects during the 19th century, making it an ideal theme on which to base a collection. *c. 1860, 4¼ in (11 cm) high.*

$150–250

▶ **A Copeland Italian pattern cusped dish.** This popular pattern was introduced by Spode c. 1816, and has been in continuous production ever since. The border is a copy of a Japanese Imari design. *c. 1900, 8 in (20 cm) diam.*

$150–250

and Franklin, as well as buildings, landscapes, railroads, and steamboats.

One of the first Staffordshire makers to print American subjects on his wares was Enoch Wood (from 1783). His work, characterized by a dark blue color and shell or grapevine borders, is in demand and his designs include over 40 American views. Other names of note are Andrew Stevenson, James and Ralph Clews, John and William Ridgway, Joseph Stubbs, and Ralph Stevenson. Colonial Staffordshire plates can be picked up for under $100, but large platters or pitchers in excellent condition by known makers can sell for $1,500–3,000.

Go with the Flow

Flow Blue describes blue transfer-printed earthenwares from Staffordshire, England, made primarily for export to the United States from the 1830s until the 1920s. American makers began producing it from the 1870s. Flow Blue is named for the underglaze blue transfer pattern that has "flowed" out of its sharp design, creating a blurred effect. Chinese patterns and landscapes were popular from the 1830s–60s; floral patterns from the 1860s–80s, and Japanese and Art Nouveau patterns from the1880s–1900s.

A Staffordshire eagle and urn cup and saucer by James & Ralph Clews, with a pagoda within a floral and urn border. The urn is decorated with a variation of the Great Seal of the United States and there is an impressed factory mark beneath saucer. *c. 1830, saucer 6¾ in (17 cm) diam.*

$350–450

▪ Italian ▪ Beauties of America ▪ Ponte Rotto ▪

▶ **A Ponte Rotto pattern tureen stand,** attributed to Rogers. Landscapes were popular subjects. *1815–42, 8¼ in (21 cm) wide.*

$150–250

A Beauties of America medium-blue William Staffordshire platter by John William Ridgway, showing the Almshouse, New York. The images of buildings for this collectible series of just over 20 designs were taken from an illustrated book of the same name. Plates cost less than platters. *c. 1820, 16¾ in (42.5 cm) long.*

$1,200–1,800

A Willow pattern ladle. This prolific Chinese-inspired pattern was introduced by Thomas Minton for the Caughley factory in the late 18th century. *c. 1830, 7 in (18 cm) long.*

$100–150

KEEP ▶

Collectors look for an even spread of flowing deep cobalt blue, with clean white areas in between. Keep pieces with typical patterns that display well, especially for when country-cottage styles return to fashion.

A Samuel Alcock Carlton pattern soup bowl, marked "SA & Co." With a deep blue, clean white, and printing on the outside too, this makes a superb piece to keep. *c. 1900, 10½ in (26.5 cm) wide.*

$150–250

KEEP ▶

Plates that depict notable personalities, politicians, or landmark buildings will have crossover appeal to collectors of political memorabilia or those interested in American history, so values may rise.

A Staffordshire commemorative plate, with Theodore Roosevelt. It is in excellent condition with a crisp transfer. *c. 1901–09, 9¾ in (25 cm) wide.*

$100–150

Quilts
have recently been raised to the realm of art, with dedicated museum exhibitions. Early and elaborate works attract big prices. However, as they were commonplace in many homes, adding warmth and decoration, they can be found at reasonable prices.

A pieced Compass quilt, with 25 blocks of brown and blue compasses on a white-quilted field and with a small blue binding, with a Kentucky family provenance and some staining. *c. 1860s–80s, 97 in (246 cm) long.*

$500–800

Made from scraps of clothes or furnishings and, when times were hard, even from old feed or sugar sacks, quilts were initially just a practical way to create warm, colorful, yet inexpensive bedcoverings for colonial settlers. While the quilts themselves were functional and visually pleasing, the making of a quilt also had a social purpose and a cultural importance. Groups of women quilters gathered to assemble them, and different needlewomen created a portion or a block of each bedcover. Moreover, a quilt was often imbued with great emotional significance, i.e., it was given to commemorate an important occasion, from a national event to a wedding, or as a token

of friendship, and could even serve as a visual record of a family's history. All these qualities are attractive to collectors, and many types of quilt are available across a wide price range—from as little as $50–70 right up to $5,000–15,000 or more.

Stitch in time

As a result of the growing appreciation for quilts as artworks, not all collectible quilts are antiques, and a new vogue for collecting modern "art quilts" by contemporary makers has sprung up. However, early pieces (c. 1770–c. 1850) are usually the most sought after, with many fetching considerable sums. A Baltimore album quilt of the finest quality, c. 1840, sold for $176,000 in

the late 1980s, a record that set a precedent for pieces of this quality.

Most early quilts were made in cotton, challis, or wool. The keys to pricing are how exceptional and detailed the workmanship is, how pleasing the design appears, and, of course, the condition of the quilt.

Birth of a notion

Quilts come in many styles, from whole-cloth, embroidered, stenciled, and appliquéd examples to representational,

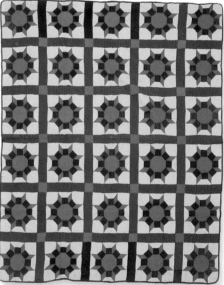

A pieced quilt, in a pattern similar to Castle Wall; with 30 blocks, brown sashing, and red at the intersections; some browning. *c. 1920s, 85 in (216 cm) long.*

$300–500

A Pennsylvania pieced quilt, with red and yellow flowers within a Sawtooth Diamond pattern. *1910s–30s, 97 in (246 cm) long.*

$1,000–1,500

friendship, or album quilts that have been pieced together. Thousands of recognized patterns exist, many with their own eccentric-sounding names, from the easy-to-assemble straight-edged piecework of Log Cabin, Bear Paw, or Tumbling Blocks to the complex designs using curved fabric scraps such as Double Wedding Ring, Star of Bethlehem, or Drunkard's Path. Generally, most quilts are pieced together using squares, triangles, hexagons, or diamonds, and tend to be geometric in design. Others may be appliquéd, which involves stitching and layering more figurative shapes such as birds, bows, flowers, and figures.

Canny collectors also prefer known designs that are easy to recognize, although, of course, the variations on popular patterns are endless, and what could be called "Bear Paw" in Ohio might be known as "Duck's Foot in the Mud" on Long Island and "Hand of Friendship" in Philadelphia.

Crazy for you

Simple, pieced designs from the late 19th and early 20th centuries—such as Log Cabin, Irish Chain, or Star—can be found for as little as $70–200. Lighter summer quilts are also accessible, with many examples from the 1920s costing $70–100. More complex designs such as the Crazy quilt—at its peak of popularity from 1876 to 1910—can fetch from $300 to thousands of dollars. The latter are prized for their random, often complex and brightly colored designs made from many materials cut into geometric shapes. The best are personalized with names and dates, or even embroidered with images of homes and pets, features that all add value. Some of the best album quilts—made of separate design blocks within a single quilt—are from Baltimore, while Kentucky also boasts a wealth of designs, including the highly original Graveyard pattern. Bedcovers by Amish quilters, particularly from before 1940, are prized for their distinctive look, which includes simple geometric designs, strong, rich colors, and intricate stitching. When valuing quilts it is important to choose textiles in good condition, so a near-mint condition, hand-stitched Star of Bethlehem quilt from the Forties at $200–300 is a better investment than an older, but shabby, 19th-century quilt of the same price.

A pieced quilt, with a Bear Paw or Lily variant pattern on a white field; some losses, browning, and staining. *c. 1890, 81 in (206 cm) long.*

$400–600

Quilts by African-American makers are popular with collectors of folk art, black Americana, and quilts. Identification can be hard, since styles were widely copied. Buy appealing examples in good condition; popularity is growing.

A patchwork quilt in Square-and-Star pattern; hand- and machine-stitched. Dated and bearing the name of its African American maker, Ivy Stanford of Brooklyn, New York, this is a great buy. *1873, 80 in (203 cm) long.*

$300–500

Crazy quilts dominated quilting fashions between 1876 and c. 1910 and represent a key part of quilting history. Those in fine condition and showing a variety of different, good-quality printed fabrics and methods of decorative stitching and embroidery should retain their appeal, and look set to be good investments.

A silk-and-velvet embroidered Crazy quilt made in the United States. The silk is still in good condition and the date and variety of the stitched and embroidered motifs make it a highly interesting example. *1885, 64 in (160 cm) long.*

$1,200–1,800

A closer look at... an Amish quilt

The Amish came to quilting comparatively late, around 1870, with communities quickly adopting the art. Designs and colors remained conservative, even when quilting elsewhere became more varied and vivid in design. Created primarily in the cold winter months, they today provide great inspiration to collectors and modern quilt designers.

An Amish quilt, with brown on green Sawtooth Diamond design and feathered scroll quilting. The strong bold colors and almost modern design fit well into today's interiors so widens interest from collectors to interior decorators. *1920s–60s, 83 in (211 cm) high.*

$700–1,000

Backs are typically plain, or bear a simple, unobtrusive design, such as dots

Large-scale, simple abstract or geometric designs are also typical of Amish quilts—the sawtooth edging adds interest

Plain areas of strong, deep colors are a characteristic of Amish quilt design

Vintage packaging chronicles

the long, colorful history of advertising. Appealing packages made for our favorite brands, particularly for products that have endured over the years, evoke not only a great nostalgia, but are also hot collectibles.

A wooden, **Two Orphans cigar box**, with printed color labels; patent dated 1875. *Late 1870s, 5½ in (13.5 cm) high.*
$50–80

One of the most popular areas for the advertising enthusiast is original packaging, which was so often ripped open and thrown away. This could be the box, bottle, crate, or wrapper in which an object was sold, or the label or top that was attached to it. Packaging is visually exciting and brightly colored, since it was meant to be an inducement to buy. Its appeal also lies in how the imagery, language, and typography chronicle social history—from the arrival of industrialization to the empowerment of women in the workplace.

A piece of the past
Anything ephemeral, with designs or themes typical of a period, is usually sought after. A design explosion began in the mid-19th century, with the advent of color printing. Indeed, the style of artwork, and even the wording, can help date an item. Consider the clean lines and crisp elegance of Art Deco (1920s–30s) against the detailed, ornate styles of the late 19th century.

Advertising aficionados often collect items by object—tins, bottles, or wrappers. They may also concentrate on a specific brand such as Kellogg's or Planter's Peanuts; a type of vendor including drug store, country store, or soda fountain; an industry—tobacco, beer, or gasoline; or even packaging associated with a specific character or celebrity. Some of the most valuable packaging relates to long-established, classic brands such as Heinz and Coca-Cola, although considerable enjoyment is also taken in now-defunct products—particularly medicinal ones—that have intriguing, outdated contents such as Dr. Kilmer's Swamp Root Kidney, Liver, and Bladder Cure, bottles of which can cost $20–50, depending on condition.

That's entertainment
Endorsements by known entertainers are much sought after and developed

---

A closer look at... a popcorn box

Away from larger, more well-known names, niche market rarities can command high values. Key factors include the origin and any nostalgic associations. Also consider other factors such as the artwork and condition, since these will also have a bearing on value.

The condition of the box is excellent, with no tears, stains, or crushed areas

A rare popcorn box from Idora Park. This box would appeal to adults who enjoyed the amusement park as children, as well as to collectors of vintage packaging. *1960s, 6¾ in (17 cm) high.*
$40–60

The graphics are typical of the 1960s; see, for example, the mother's hair and dress. Idora Park enjoyed its hey-day during this decade

The motif of the girl with her balloon was used across the Park, on everything from trash cans to posters

Although thousands of boxes were made and sold, the vast majority would have been thrown away, making survivors like this very rare

A Happy Dog Food Cubes cardboard and paper carton, from Happy Mills of Memphis, Tennessee. *1940s, 5¼ in (13 cm) high.*
$15–20

early, with Bing Crosby supporting Valley Farm vanilla ice cream and the child star Jackie Coogan appearing on a jar of peanut butter. Early comic-strip characters such as the Yellow Kid were also used to promote products and appealed as much to adults as they did to children. A 5-inch (12.7-cm) Buster Brown cigar canister from the Twenties recently fetched $3,000 at auction. Even more recently, companies like Post, Kraft, and Nestle used The Flintstones to sell products; the packaging is already collectible, even though some of it is from the 1980s and 90s. A Fruity Pebbles cereal box can now fetch $10–40, while a cheese slices container can sell for $5–15, depending on condition. In the mid-1990s Kraft appeared Bugs Bunny and friends on its macaroni-and-cheese box; he also featured on Betty Crocker Fruit Snacks. These items of packaging can now cost $15–20. Collectible characters used by advertisers were not just established ones, but also those specifically created for the brand: Mr. Peanut for Planter's Peanuts; Speedy for Alka-Seltzer; and Colonel Sanders for Kentucky Fried Chicken. Collectors will amass almost anything that strikes their fancies, and there are enthusiasts for relatively inexpensive treasures such as the bottle caps on soft drinks, juice, or beer, or even beer labels. If breweriana (which

A box of Mother Goose drinking straws by Maryland Paper Products, Baltimore. c. 1930s, 8¾ in (22 cm) high.
$50–80

generally fetches higher prices than wine-related objects) is of interest, there is a cache of items to collect, since it's an old industry with thousands of brands. After Prohibition, cans were introduced in 1935 and these are popular.

Chewing gum packs are also worth looking for, particularly key names such as Wrigley's or Fan Tan. A 1920s Wrigley's Spearmint pack, complete with sticks of gum, may fetch $2–3, while a rarer Fan Tan pack from the same period can make up to $50, depending on condition. In general, prices rarely rise above a few hundred dollars, tins aside, making this a very accessible area.

Up in smoke

Early tobacco packaging is popular today, perhaps in part because smoking is taking a final dive in popularity. The tobacco industry spawned a wealth of containers, in all kinds of sizes, colors, and styles—from flat-pocket tins to store bins. Vintage matchbooks are popular and can be found for $2 each, more for popular brands like the Playboy clubs or great artwork. Cigar bands with high-quality lithography and cigar boxes with ornately printed images on their inner lids are also collectible. Some cigar boxes can still be bought for modest sums, often under $100, although a rarity—such as special theme boxes showing Native Americans or sports-related subjects—may fetch big money, from the mid-hundreds upward.

A Wrigley's Spearmint gum pack, with five foil-and-paper-wrapped sticks of gum. *1920s. 3¼ in (8 cm) long.*
$2–3

Top Tips

- Avoid beer cans with rust or dings. Tabs should be intact. Cans with cone-shaped tops—e.g., from Schlitz—are worth more.
- Look for artwork with cross-market appeal; this increases demand.
- Condition is key, particularly with paper products, since they are so vulnerable. Buy the best you can afford.
- Look for giveaways (e.g., gifts in Cracker Jacks) or premiums, such as cutouts from cereal boxes, that came in series.
- Older packaging is rare and pricey. New packaging may be tomorrow's hot item.

BUY

Cereal boxes are a hot collecting area set to grow and appeal mainly for nostalgic reasons. Although millions were made, the majority would have been discarded. Reproductions, sometimes made for collectors, exist, so check materials, dates, and condition. When in doubt, compare to an original.

Kellogg's Sugar Smacks, with Dig 'Em the frog. Each cereal had a character such as Fruit Brute and Captain Crunch. *1970s, 9¼ in (23.5 cm) high.*
$20–30

SELL

Designs were often aimed at children in the hope that they would encourage their parents to buy; as such, they were tied in to timely trends. Over time, new themes arrive. Sell now and invest in up-to-date trends that may be less expensive and that will perhaps go up in value as new nostalgics start collecting.

A Nabisco cookie box. In the 1950s, cowboys were popular with children, who are now adults with disposable incomes. This design is rare and Nabisco is a popular name, with products that have been enjoyed by many. *1950s, 5 in (13 cm) wide.*
$70–100

Scottie dogs, always cherished by dog

lovers, endeared themselves to a wider public throughout the 1920s to 50s. Consequently, the Scottie motif charmed its way on to a vast array of household objects and some delightful advertising memorabilia.

The Scottie dog motif is still found today on sweaters, jewelry, novelties, and Christmas items, but the heyday of these collectibles was from the 1920s to 50s, thanks in part to successful advertising campaigns for Texaco and Black & White Scotch whisky that featured the fashionable Scottish terriers. The appeal of this feisty little animal was enhanced by the fact that many well-known personalities of the time, including Shirley Temple, Humphrey Bogart, and Zsa Zsa Gabor, owned Scotties. The most famous of them all was President Roosevelt's black Scottie, Fala, who went everywhere with him.

A huge number of items embellished with Scotties were produced, from desk accessories to hatpins, ceramic teapots, cufflinks, posters, compacts, and tape measures. Prices can range from around $7–15 for a small item such as a dog-shaped button to around $150–300 or more for a glass lamp, offering great scope for a collection.

Lamps are often the most prized and valuable articles, particularly complete examples from the 1930s and 40s. Other popular items include bookends, doorstops, and coin banks. Look, too, for Scottie dog artwork by British artist Marguerite Kirmse (1885–1954). An avid collector of Scottie memorabilia, she created pieces that are now highly valued.

▲ **A novelty lightbulb in an Art Deco-styled base.** Lightbulbs using special gases to create a "neon" effect are not common today, but were popular in the 1930s, often as advertising pieces. In this rare example, the Scottie glows bright orange. *1930s, 7 in (18 cm) high.*

$120–180

▶ **A German novelty tape measure** with a fabric Scottie dog on the spool. Sewing accessories are extremely collectible. *c. 1950, 2 in (5 cm) long.*

$30–40

▶ **A carved wooden ashtray** with a glass liner. Smoking accessories in the 1930s ranged from stylish and elegant to playful and amusing. *1930s, 6¼ in (16 cm) long.*

$80–120

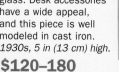

◀ **A painted cast-iron magnifier** with an adjustable magnifying glass. Desk accessories have a wide appeal, and this piece is well modeled in cast iron. *1930s, 5 in (13 cm) high.*

$120–180

◀ **A set of three framed Marguerite Kirmse Scottie dog etchings.** Kirmse was a noted British dog artist who bred and drew Scotties. Her work is popular and worth acquiring. *1920s, 14½ in (37 cm) wide.*

$150–200

◀ **A glass wall-hanging plaque.** A transfer on the back of the glass shows a fashionable lady in a 1950s A-line skirt and stylish bolero taking her Scottie for a walk. It captures the spirit of fun that brightened the post–World War II years. *1950s, 5 in (12 cm) high.*

$40–60

◀ **A ceramic teapot in the shape of a Scottie.** Teapots have a following in their own right, and this one will appeal to collectors of Scotties as well. *1950s, 6¾ in (17 cm) high.*

$40–60

Collectors' Tips

■ Since there is such a wide range of Scottie memorabilia, it's best to stick to one theme

■ Choose colorful items that represent the style of the period and show the dog clearly

SCOTTY
MILD LITTLE CIGARS
CANADA

◀ **A Canadian Barry Cigar Factory Scotty Mild Little Cigars tin.** Advertising products such as this have a perennial appeal. *1930s, 3¼ in (8 cm) high.*

$40–60

◀ **Four yellow Catalin buttons.** Early plastics such as Catalin are much sought after today, especially if, as here, they also appeal to specialized collectors. *1930s, 1¾ in (4.5 cm) long.*

$20–30 for four

▼ **A painted and carved wood-effect wall-mounted belt rack.** The American company Swank made a number of gentlemen's accessories that featured Scottie dogs. It is rare to find them on products designed for men. *1950s, 11 in (28 cm) wide.*

$40–60

Cookie jars come in every size and shape, from vegetables and fruits to people and popular cartoon characters. These cheery homewares are not just affordable collectibles, but also pieces of social history.

A clown cookie jar, by Maurice of California, marked "JA10." *1950s, 13 in (33 cm) high.*
$250–350

Cookie jars are a thriving area of collecting, with clubs and websites, and even a museum devoted to them. Although prices have dropped in recent years, this has more to do with plentiful supply, and a glut of reproductions, than with a wane in demand.

Most homes have a cookie jar and they are little relics of history. The Great Depression prompted American pottery makers to produce cookie jars for the first time. Before that, anyone with a sweet tooth would have bought at a bakery, but with the need to economize came more home baking and a demand for vessels to keep cookies fresh.

Interestingly, collectors are not so enamored of the earliest jars—either in plain stoneware or glass—although some do see their retro chic. However, early jars can be charming and, better still, inexpensive—as little as $10–50.

Quite a character

What most collectors want are ceramics from the 1940s onward that depict people, cartoon characters, or animals, but also fruits, vegetables, or themes. These are usually earthenware and decorated with glaze, hand-painting, airbrushing, or transfer-printing.

Novice collectors should look for figural jars dating from 1939–45 by American Bisque, APCO, and McCoy (usually $30–40). For character figurals, concentrate on American Bisque, which made very detailed jars; for vibrant vegetables, look for McCoy. Other names are Abingdon, Doranne, Red Wing, California Originals, and Roseville.

Some of the most highly prized, at $800–1,000, include McCoy's first figural cookie jar, a Mammy with Cauliflowers (c. 1939), and its undated leprechaun.

A Cow Jumped over the Moon cookie jar by Doranne of California, marked "J2USA." *1950s, 13½ in (34.5 cm) high.*
$350–450

A McCoy Native American, hand-painted tee-pee-shaped cookie jar; the base reads "McCoy USA." *1950s, 11¼ in (29 cm) high.*
$450–550

A closer look at... a cookie jar

Always pay close attention to the form and decoration of cookie jars, even on more common or familiar shapes. If you can spot a real rarity it could prove to be very valuable.

A rare Shawnee Smiley Pig cookie jar. This jar would have been from the top of the line of Shawnee's Smiley Pigs. *1950s, 11.5 in (29 cm) high.*

$1,000–1,500

Light green is a rare color for the neckerchief

He has gilt highlights and trim, which is an unusual feature

Smiley Pig was one of Shawnee's most popular jars; it was made in many colors from 1942

The strawberry details on his body are rare; flowers are much more common

Top Tips

- Reproductions are everywhere. Handle as many good jars as possible and know makers and markings. Fakes are often smaller than originals, as they are reproduced from a secondary mold, copied from an original piece.

- McCoy marked most jars; American Bisque and other makers did not. Brush sometimes used a brush and palette logo. Doranne markings include "CJ" or "J" and a two- or three-digit number.

- Check condition. Crazing is acceptable on rare pieces but not on common ones. Whatever the piece's rarity, it still reduces value, as do chips, cracks (by up to 40 percent), a missing lid, or even small factory flaws.

Other favorites are: American Bisque's Olive Oyl, ($800–1,000); a purple Brush cow ($300–400); and a Shawnee Smiley Pig, ($200–350), which is $400–600 in gold and $1,000 with hair. A real rarity—at $3,000–3,500—is the Regal China Alice in Wonderland.

Examples from the 1970s can also be valuable: a California Originals Superman can command $400–450. Some collectors look for new examples—with good ones available from Treasure Craft—as a way of amassing a good display on a budget.

The real McCoy

The market has of late been flooded with reproductions. Where they are marked, such as those by J. D. James of Buckeye Lake, Ohio, it is not a problem. Fakes, however, should be avoided; they are of inferior quality and deflate the market. A rare Mammy with Cauliflowers was once worth $2,000, but now goes for half that because it has been widely copied. Damaged pieces are also undesirable, although, since children handled them, some damage on rare examples and painted decorations is inevitable and acceptable.

Cookie jars appeal to other collectors as well, and will always be avidly traded. Quality pieces with detailed molding, bright colors, and interesting shapes or subjects are always a good buy.

BUY

Since cookie jars were aimed at children, bright colors, cheerful characters, and nursery rhyme themes are common. They feature in many collections and are perennially popular. Jars by notable potteries in the forms of figures are also desirable.

A Humpty Dumpty cookie jar by Brush Pottery, which introduced the cookie jar in the 1920s. This smiling egg figure is delightful and should rise in value. *1950s, 12 in (30.5 cm) high.*

$300–500

SELL

Cookie jars that cross collecting fields will often yield higher prices, since the demand from collectors is greater. This will cause prices to rise and remain high. If the character is popular with many different generations, the audience will be wider still, especially if the jar is very appealing.

Pinnochio cookie jar marked "Walt Disney Production." Pinnochio's sweet face appeals to Disney collectors. Sell to fund your collection. *1950s, 10 in (24 cm) high.*

$600–800

A Japanese, Napco Cinderella cookie jar, marked "1957 K2292." *c. 1960, 10 in (25.5 cm) high.*

$300–500

A Poppytrail calf head cookie jar by Metlox of California. *1950s, 11 in (28 cm) high.*

$400–500

Tins

of all shapes and sizes were used to store cookies, candy, tea, and tobacco in an age before plastic and card containers. Decorative as well as functional, their novel designs have immense nostalgic appeal.

In the 19th century, tins were used to store an increasing range of products, including precious commodities such as tea or snuff, because the near-airtight seal of the lid preserved the freshness of the contents. Early tins were usually plain and had paper labels, but these were easily damaged. From the 1870s, more advanced printing processes were developed, such as transfer printing and offset lithography. Toward the end of the 19th century, the decorative tin soon became a familiar form of packaging. Many of these early tins have highly complex and detailed printed designs, which makes them particularly desirable today. Because so few of them have survived the ravages of time, they are often valuable.

Ship shape

In the late 19th and early 20th centuries, tins were made in increasingly exotic shapes, and these are very collectible today, often worth $300–1,500 or more. Look for tins in the shape of cars, boats, or people. Lunch-pail tins, storage bins, and flat pocket varieties with hinged lids are popular. Moving parts, such as wheels, are especially desirable. Collectors look

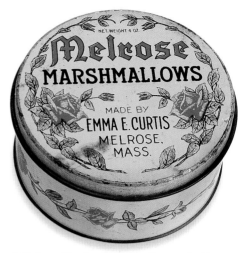

A Melrose Marshmallows tin, the smallest in a range of sizes, the largest having a glass top. *1920s, 4¼ in (11 cm) wide.*

$70–100

for early colored paper labels and embossed scenes, and it's important that a tin still has its original top. A 6-inch (15.25-cm) Towles Log Cabin Syrup tin with its original tin screw top can be worth as much as $80. Along with tobacco, toffee, and other confectionery tins, cookie and cracker tins are among the most creative, both in their shapes and their artwork. Prices can vary from under $50 to more than $1,500. Britain's Huntley & Palmers manufactured many remarkable shapes of biscuit tin, including soldiers, sentry boxes, and books, which are now sought after. A Huntley and Palmers shell-shaped biscuit tin from around 1912 may be worth more than $600. Other collectable British names include Crawford's, Jacob's, Carr's, and Peek Frean. French tins are also sought after; a French 1930s cookie tin of the *Normandie* liner can fetch $800–1,000.

Sign of the times

The designs adorning tins of different times document the development of graphic advertising. Bright colors and intricate designs are desirable, as are those representative of their era, such as Art Nouveau or the Fifties. Notable brand names, or images that appeal to another collectibles market, such as Scottie dogs, will add value. A particular illustrator can send the price of a tin soaring: a 1920s Maxfield Parrish Old King Cole tobacco tin can be worth

A toffee tin featuring a child in space, a theme typical of the period. *1960s, 4½ in (11 cm) diam.*

$15–25

A printed Mennen borated powder sample tin. *1930s, 2 in (5 cm) high.*

$35–45

A Checkers cough drops pocket-sized tin. *1930s, 2¾ in (7 cm) high.*

$70–90

$1,000–2,000, and a 1905 cookie barrel with Art Nouveau artwork by Alphonse Mucha can fetch $1,800–2,200. Nevertheless, there are all kinds of wonderful tins from coffee and cleansers to lozenges and toffee, costing no more than $20 to $150 on average. Spice tins can be found in great variety from $20–150. Their small size and colorful graphics make them ideal collectables.

Early tins are sought after, and the style of the artwork and typography can help determine age. Other ways of dating a tin include printed company names and addresses, the thickness of the steel sheet, and copyright information.

Some liked it hot

Many tins had intricate, charming designs, sometimes with images of people in far-off lands. A good example is a Mazawattee tea tin of about 1910 showing a bespectacled granny and her granddaughter sipping tea against an exotic background, which can be worth $25–30 today. Many cookie and toffee tins were designed to be used as tea caddies once the original contents had been eaten.

Tiny tins

Pocket-sized tin collecting has boomed in recent years and is now a huge collecting area. Pocket-sized and sample tins can be more affordable than their larger counterparts, and most can be found for less than $150 each. They are also small and easy to store, so can make a good start to a tin collection. Sample tins, given away as promotions by retailers, are usually simply smaller versions of the larger tin, using the same colors and graphics.

Pocket tins were produced in large numbers, but many are rare, since tins were often thrown away after use. Tins in mint condition can also be hard to find, as many have been damaged from being carried in pockets or bags. Small tobacco tins that were shaped to fit in a pocket are popular, fetching $50–500 or more. Also in demand are tins that once contained unusual products such as condoms or pesticides, and are usually worth around $40–150.

A closer look at... a peanut butter tin

Tins in novelty shapes are sought after, especially if they resemble toys or objects around the house and date from the golden years of the early 20th century. Some makers attract premium prices, but generally shape, decoration, and condition are the key indicators of value.

Bucket-shaped tins were often given to children as sand pails or toys, so became worn and rusty

Shaped tins are desirable as they were intended to be reused, so fewer survive

Nursery rhymes are popular themes both among children of the period and collectors of today

A Red Seal brand peanut butter bucket tin, by the Newton Tea & Spices Co., with nursery rhymes including "Old King Cole" and "Jack-Be-Nimble." The original lid and handle add value. *1900–10, 3¼ in (8 cm) high.*

$700–1,000

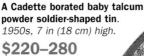

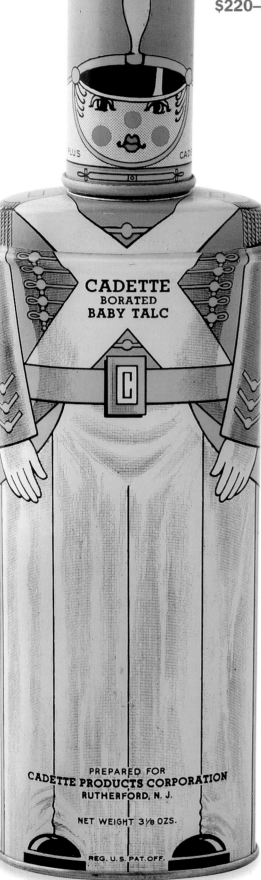

A Cadette borated baby talcum powder soldier-shaped tin. *1950s, 7 in (18 cm) high.*

$220–280

CADETTE
BORATED
BABY TALC

PREPARED FOR
CADETTE PRODUCTS CORPORATION
RUTHERFORD, N.J.

NET WEIGHT 3⅛ OZS.

REG. U.S. PAT. OFF.

▲ **A Huntley & Palmers Kate Greenaway biscuit tin,** with modified artwork by a mischievous employee. *1980, 8 in (20.5 cm) wide.*

$40–60

Did You Know?

In 1980 Huntley & Palmers sold a round tin with attractive artwork by Kate Greenaway on the lid, showing a tea party in a summer garden. A mischievous employee added his own unusual modifications. Once discovered, the tin was hastily withdrawn and reissued without the inappropriate addition. Today, a tin with the original, modified design can be worth around $50.

A Banner baking powder tin, by Geo. Hubbard & Co. of Pittsburgh, Pennsylvania. *1920s, 4½ in (11.5 cm) high.*

$80–120

A Buckingham smoking tobacco lithographed tin, by John J. Bagley & Co. *c. 1910, 5 in (12.5 cm) high.*

$60–90

Lighting up

By the 1880s smoking was a popular habit and there were hundreds of tobacco manufacturers. Countless tobacco tin designs were made. With prices starting from as little as $10–30 for a 1930s Player's Navy Cut tin with a printed paper label, tobacco tins are a good choice for a specialized collection. Some famous brands to look for are Lucky Strike, Uncle Sam, Tin Stag, Gold Dust, and Master Mason. Tins featuring such names can fetch $70–250 or more, depending on the intricacy and attractiveness of the artwork. The Roly Poly tobacco tins, made in six different characters for several brands in the 1890s, are much sought after, often fetching $600-$1,000. Some collectors enjoy finding the same design of tin in different sizes and styles: Tiger Brand cut-plug tobacco had store containers and small consumer pocket tins.

Needlepoint

The tiny needles used in early windup gramophones were sold in little tins, and today these containers are not very expensive, with values remaining well under $100. They form an ideal collection theme for people with limited space, as each tin is only about 1½ inches (4 cm) wide. The artwork is usually more important than the manufacturer, and its style can help to date a tin. A tin from the 1920s featuring Nipper, the dog representing HMV, may fetch less than $15, while a tin from the same decade decorated with, for example, a striking Art Deco image, can be worth up to $100.

Modern times

The heyday of decorative tins began to draw to a close in the 1950s, once cheaper packaging, such as plastic and plasticized sachets, was

A Salon-Tanz gramophone needles tin.
1925, 2 in (5 cm) high.
$60–90

introduced, but tins made before the 1960s are still collectible.

Look for tins with attractive artwork, particularly those in period styles, such as 1930s Art Deco or the Modern style of the 1950s. These are sought after not only by tin collectors but also by enthusiasts of graphic design and those with a special interest in collecting pieces from these eras. This tends to inflate the value.

Look, too, for tins with crossover appeal, such as British items commemorating royal occasions. A tin commemorating the Coronation of Queen Elizabeth II in 1953 can fetch $30–40, while a 1936 A. W. & R. Jacob biscuit tin in the shape of a royal coach, celebrating the Coronation of Edward VIII, can be worth $150–200.

Because so many more examples of recent tins exist, it is best to choose ones that are as close to mint condition as possible. Tins from the 1960s onward are not particularly popular at the moment, but there may be an increase in demand for them in the future. Tins that carry popular brand names, are unusual in shape, are decorated in attractive colors, or are for special occasions, are also worth collecting.

KEEP

Pocket tobacco tins are rapidly growing into a hot collecting area. Check to see if you have one, as prices are rising. Trade is particularly strong on the internet. Items with military or patriotic designs are the most popular, as are detailed, colorful examples.

A pocket tin for Brigg's Pipe Mixture by P. Lorillard Co. The excellent condition, pleasant and evocative artwork, and whimsical motto make this collectible. *1920s, 4¼ in (11 cm) high.*
$60–90

BUY

Biscuit tins are one of the most popular collecting areas. They have tins with a wide base of international collectors, meaning demand and prices are unlikely to fall. It is also a varied area, allowing plenty of scope. Look for examples in excellent condition by known names with interesting, attractive artwork.

A Sunshine Biscuits tin for Martini butter crackers, by the Loose-Wiles Biscuit Co. The style of the visually appealing artwork and inclusion of the Busy Baker helps to date this tin and makes it very collectible. *1920s, 6¾ in (17 cm) high.*
$80–120

Vintage kitchen equipment

can add a quirky touch to an otherwise modern kitchen. Many items have become objects of curiosity, because their original function has been superseded by new methods.

The kitchens of the 19th and early 20th centuries were packed with gadgets for every task, and there is a multitude of these vintage tools still to be found, many of them in working order. Look for vintage equipment at collectors' shows, junk stores, house clearances, and auctions.

Old molds

Old chocolate molds have become very collectible. A huge range of designs is available including holiday themes such as Santa Claus and the Easter Bunny as well as figures, animals, and cartoon characters. They reached the peak of their popularity from the early 1900s to the 1930s and began to tail off during the 1950s. Notable makers include Germans Anton Reiche (whose molds were imported

into the United States by T. C. Weygandt of New York), H. Walter, and Eppelsheimer of New York. Stamped marks can help to identify makers and date molds. Prices can be as low as $60–90 for a seated Easter Bunny mold, or around $150 for a standing Santa mold, but can rise to $600 or more for larger, or more unusual molds with good detailing.

The way the cookie crumbles

The first American-manufactured cookie cutters were made after the end of the Civil War. Some of these, and later examples, were marked by companies like Dover, Mason, Kreamer, Fries, and Hillson. In general, a cutter bearing a name is more valuable than a similar example bearing no inscription. Early tin cutters, often with a tin plate in the back, and sometimes a handle, are the most desirable. Many have one or two circular holes cut into the back for an easier grip, or to push stuck dough out of the cutter. Star and round, fluted shapes are common, and some cutters feature tiny, decorative holes in the backplate. A 19th-century iron or tin flatback cutter

A tin songbird cookie cutter.
c. 1880, 5 in (12.5 cm) long.
$40–60

will typically sell for $10–70, although collectors are willing to pay hundreds of dollars for rarer designs. Aluminum became the favored material for cutters in the 1920s, and plastic cutters were introduced in great number following WWII. Later cutters are sought after by collectors, but most fetch less than $20.

The search for perfect toast

Vintage toasters are growing in popularity with collectors. The electric toaster was developed in the US in the early 20th century. It became popular in wealthy households because toast made by servants in the kitchen was usually cold by the time it reached the table. The disadvantage was that early toasters only browned one side of the bread at a time, and needed to be watched constantly in case the bread burned.

A brass-and-cast-iron crimping machine, with heating bars, for crimping fabric. *1870s, 12½ in (31.5 cm) high.*
$500–700

A seated Easter Bunny form metal chocolate mold, in used but undamaged condition. *1900s–20s, 10 in (25.5 cm) high.*
$60–90

A closer look at... a goffering iron

The complexity of Victorian clothing and cooking led to the development of many implements that have long since fallen out of use. It is worth familiarizing yourself with some of them because they can make good investments.

Hot cylinders warmed in a fire or on a stove were inserted here

It is rare to have two cones. Single examples are more common and less valuable

A rare double-goffering iron, with a high-relief floral pattern on the base. A goffering iron was used to press ridges or pleats into a garment. In this example, fabric collars and cuffs were wrapped around the cones to set them into shape. The large size of this iron makes it unusual. *1850s–80s, 14 in (35 cm) high.*

$500–600

The cast-iron base is decorative, which is extremely unusual

103

Top Tips

- Research why and how an item was used originally to make sure you buy the right piece of equipment.
- Choose early examples, as well as transitional prototypes of a particular item, as these are the most desirable.
- Look for pieces bearing a maker's name, as they are often worth more than unmarked or homemade items.
- Check that the bowl of a coffee grinder is in good condition, as it is the weakest part and prone to cracking and splitting.

BUY

Early toasters are comparatively inexpensive, because the market is small and there is little specialized literature available. Toasters can often be restored to working order, even those with unusual features. Their simple design is attractive, and as interest in the area expands, they may prove to be a good investment.

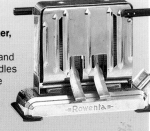

A Rowenta E 5210 folding toaster, with chrome-plated body and Bakelite handles and feet. The flap on the side opens downward, causing the toast inside to flip over, so both sides can be toasted by the central heating element. *1940s, 10 in (25 cm) high.*

$30–50

Manufacturers raced to introduce new features—turnover toasters, automatic toasters, and toasters that kept the toast warm inside the machine. Values vary from as little as $30 up to $250 or more. A rare blue-and-white transfer-printed porcelain toaster from the 1920s can fetch up to $1,200.

Crimpers, cutters, and scalers

There is a plethora of small tools for specific purposes, such as crimping the edges of pies, mincing meat, opening cans and bottles, and cutting vegetables. The more common tools, such as tin openers, can cost from as little as $10 up to around $80, depending on age, material, and decorative value. More unusual items, such as raisin seeders and fish scalers, generally raise higher prices, but they rarely fetch up to $250.

Baked in a pie

Also known as a pie funnel or pie vent, a pie bird is generally ceramic, glazed inside and out, and used in baking to prevent overspills. Most are around 4 inches (10.25 cm) high, with arches at the base to allow steam to enter, and a steam exit hole at the top. Novelty pie-bird figures from the late 1930s to the 1960s, shaped as bakers or colorful birds, can now be worth $20–150. One of the first novelty pie birds, the Nutbrown Elephant, is sought after and normally fetches $50–80, with the rare gray version commanding $220–280.

Before the development of steam irons, ceramic sprinklers were used to apply water to clothes before ironing. Original sprinklers shaped as soda bottles, animals, and figures can now be found for as little as $20 up to $300 or more.

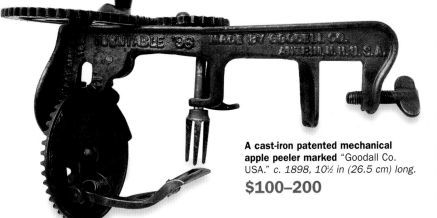

A cast-iron patented mechanical apple peeler marked "Goodall Co. USA." *c. 1898, 10½ in (26.5 cm) long.*

$100–200

KEEP

Kitchen collectibles from the 1950s and 60s are still generally affordable, yet rapidly increasing in popularity—you or a relative may even have one. Search cupboards for items that bring back nostalgic memories, or else that are still useable today. Colorful or whimsical items are also a hit with collectors, as they make great displays. Examples by known names in mint condition or in rare colors are highly desirable. Prices should increase as demand grows.

A ceramic pie bird by Californian Potteries, in unusual colors. If in the more common pink and green stripes, the value falls to around $50–60. *c. 1950–60s, 4¼ in (11 cm) high.*

$70–100

Jadeite kitchenwares, in their distinctive shade of pale green, epitomize the Depression-era glass of the period and are enormously popular. Plates and cups cost very little, but hard-to-find storage containers and shakers are worth a mint.

A pair of Jeanette Jadeite ribbed 8-oz salt and pepper shakers with aluminum screw-fit tops and original transfer lettering. *1950s–60s, 5 in (12.5 cm) high.*

$120–180 for the pair

Color fashions come and go, but in the Thirties—not just in the US—green was the key color for domestic wares. Perhaps its freshness appealed to consumers recovering from economic troubles and war, but whether it was spring green, forest green, or blue-green, green was the color that manufacturers most used for their products. Today, the pretty pale hues of Jadeite—an opaque, press-molded glass in pale greens—are, long after their original popularity, gaining favor with collectors. Jadeite can easily be found at flea markets, collectors' fairs and auctions, with all but the rarest examples costing under $100.

Green, green glass

Most of the kitchenware available in Jadeite—from storage containers to reamers and rolling pins—was produced in the 1930s and 40s by the Pennsylvania companies Jeannette Glass Company and McKee, and it is highly sought after. More common

is the dinnerware, made from 1945, by the Anchor Hocking Glass Company of Lancaster, Ohio, the biggest producer of Depression glass. Its Fire-King line includes dinner services in Jane Ray, Alice, Charm, Swirl, Shell, Sheaves of Wheat, and Restaurant Ware, as well as the breakfast service 1700 line. McKee also brought out a dinner service, called Laurel, which is paler than Fire-King.

For new collectors, Jane Ray, made from 1946–65 in great quantity, is easiest to amass and affordable. The most popular pattern, Restaurant Ware, sold in different thicknesses, which affect price: thin mugs are often $15–20; extra-heavy mugs $30–40; and a 9-inch (23-cm) dinner plate $25–30. A rarity such as the 10-inch (25.5-cm) Shell dinner plate may cost $30–40, as it is the only pattern to have it, very likely because it was produced later (until

1976), when portions were larger. Sheaves of Wheat is also rare, as it was made for just two years (1957–59). The spherical Ball pitchers are the priciest, often fetching $3000–1,500, but storage jars, canisters, and shakers, particularly sets, are also desirable. Whereas Jeannette produced these in dark and light green—with the darker more prized—McKee made just one color, but the shapes were more distinctive and modern than its rival's.

A small canister can cost $100, and a set of four up to $500. Building a

An Anchor Hocking Fire-King Restaurant Ware serving plate, with five compartments for different types of food in a meal. *1950s–60s, 10 in (24.5 cm) diam.*

$40–50

A closer look at... a Jadeite skillet

Certain shapes are rarer than others and prices can rise considerably for scarce items. In addition to considering the general shape, look at smaller details, since variations can push the price even higher.

This skillet has two spouts, making it rarer and, thus, more valuable than examples with one spout

Skillets are comparatively hard to find

Chips, especially to the rim or spout, are very common, since these items were used regularly; this is in undamaged condition

An Anchor Hocking Fire-King Jadeite double-spout skillet. The color and overall condition are excellent. A single-spout skillet in similar condition may fetch around $100. *1950s–60s, 6¼ in (15.5 cm) diam.*

$150–200

An Anchor Hocking Glass Co. Fire-King Jadeite Jane Ray-pattern cup and saucer. *1950s–60s, saucer 5¾ in (14.5 cm) diam.*

$8–12

Top Tips

- Not all Jadeite is marked. Jeannette didn't emboss wares; McKee pieces may have an "MCK" backstamp; Anchor Hocking used a "Fire-King" backstamp. Some items have labels.

- There are reproductions, but these are not the same style as the originals or, if copying Fire-King, lack a backstamp.

- The blue Delphite, Delfite, and Chaline by Jeanette and McKee were the same price as Jadeite when sold as new, but today are pricier. Anchor Hocking's Turquoise Blue and Azurite is cheaper.

BUY

Some common items were produced in a number of variations and it pays to learn to spot them, since many were produced in smaller numbers and are rarer or more desirable, making values more likely to rise.

An Anchor Hocking Glass Co. Fire-King extra-heavy Restaurant Ware mug. The C-shaped handle and very thick body show that this is a rarer mug than the more common, standard-bodied example with a squared-shaped handle, which is worth half as much. *1948–67, 3½ in (9 cm) high.*

$30–50

SELL

Examine pattern and form, since many pieces, such as plates, were produced in very large numbers. Providing it is not a rare size, such pieces are unlikely to rise considerably in value as so many survive today.

An Anchor Hocking Glass Co. Fire-King Jane Ray pattern dessert plate. This was the first pattern made for the home and is the most widespread. However, it would make a basic and useable addition to a new collection. *1950s–60s, 7¾ in (19.5 cm) diam.*

$8–12

---

custom set is perfectly acceptable, but aim to match form, decoration, and color as closely as possible. There are many variations to choose from—plain; with transfer-printed labels; with metal, crystal, or black-glass lids, or even lids with floral molding—all of which affect price. For example, McKee canisters with cursive lettering are more expensive than those with plain. Shakers and sifters are popular too, with a sugar or flour sifter fetching up to $60–80.

Bowled over

Refrigerator or leftovers boxes are fun to collect and may also be used, although, unfortunately, many lids didn't survive or are chipped. As a serious collector, don't buy worn pieces—a damaged leftover box is around $20, whereas in pristine condition it could cost $40–90. All Jadeite factories made these boxes.

Reamers for lemons, oranges, and grapefruits are loved by collectors. A lemon reamer goes for as little as $30–50, while a large McKee grapefruit reamer is $120–180. Eggcups are a good addition to any collection, as are rolling pins, spice jars, measuring cups, flower pots, and vases.

Mixing bowls by Anchor Hocking are a good buy, and nests of them look quite attractive. They are most common in the Swirl pattern—expect to pay $50–100—although the 5-inch (12.7-cm) bowl, even in this pattern, is rare and can fetch up to $300. A variation on the standard bowl is the lipped Swedish Modern bowl, which is a teardrop shape, but there are other styles—beaded edge, Colonial, vertical ribbed, and, in the Splashproof line, deep-sided bowls. Jeannette and McKee also made mixing bowls. For a monochrome range of glass, the choice and variety is great!

Four of a set of five Anchor Hocking Glass Co. Fire-King Swirl pattern nesting bowls. The smallest bowl, missing from this set, is the rarest size, at 5 inches in diam, and can be worth up to $300. *c. 1960s, largest bowl 8 in (20 cm) diam.*

$100–150

Vintage sewing tools

can be highly decorative and ornate. From thimbles to needle cases, they also serve as a reminder of the value once placed on household skills, which we are now in danger of losing.

Sewing tools have been produced for hundreds of years, and until around 30 years ago almost every woman would have owned a sewing box or basket.

Tools were made from wood, ivory, bone, metal, and mother-of-pearl. "Vegetable ivory," a dense yellow or beige material made from the tropical tagua nut, was typically used for carved needle cases and tape measure covers. Pieces dating from the late 18th and 19th centuries are sought after.

Values vary, depending on age, type of object, material, and decoration, but tend to lie between $30 and $800.

Thimble talk

Most of today's vintage thimbles date from the 19th century onward and were machine-made in metal or ceramic. A plain, mass-produced brass thimble may cost around $25–30, but a thimble in gold or silver can fetch up to $800. A number stamped into a thimble indicates its size.

Makers to look for include Charles Iles, Charles Horner, and Simons Bros. & Co. Iles was prolific and inventive, producing thimbles with liners and decorative features that can often be found now for $30–150. In the late 19th century, Horner developed the revolutionary Dorcas thimble, which had a strong steel core overlaid with silver and lasted longer than softer thimbles of pure silver. Dorcas thimbles may sell for $25–80. Simons Bros. & Co. thimbles are recognizable by the mark of an "S" on a shield.

Commemorative thimbles are popular. A British, non-precious-metal example made for Queen Victoria's

A mother-of-pearl, book-form needle case engraved with a floral motif, with a pink silk bow and pink fabric "pages" to hold the needles. It was assembled by its original owner. *c. 1850s, 2½ in (6.5 cm) high.*

$150–250

Diamond Jubilee (1897) may fetch around $60, while a silver thimble celebrating the Coronation of George V and Queen Mary in 1911 may be worth around $250–300. Ceramic thimbles are also common. Some examples by Royal Worcester featuring birds hand painted by William Powell can fetch $300–600.

Earlier thimbles do exist, but are rare. They can date back to the 16th century and are often made of leather, bronze, or iron, with domed or onion-

Some thimbles to look for:
■ Iles ■ Fenton ■ Horner ■ Dorcas ■ Simons ■

▲ An Iles Patent Ventilated pot-metal thimble. The ivorine liner—a form of early plastic that looked like ivory—served to ventilate the finger. *c. 1909, ¾ in (2 cm) high.*

$120–180

▼ An English silver thimble by James Fenton, showing a bicycle and a bird in foliage, hallmarked Birmingham, England, 1896. This is a valuable example as the bicycle is a rare motif. *1896, ¾ in (2 cm) high.*

$500–800

▲ A silver thimble by Charles Horner, with a punched-dot design, an inset carnelian crown (for decoration), and a Chester hallmark. *1923, ¾ in (2 cm) high.*

$80–120

▼ A Dorcas steel-cored thimble by an unknown maker, with a grid pattern and a registered mark for 1887. Hard-wearing Dorcas thimbles were produced by makers other than their inventor, Charles Horner. *c. 1887, ¾ in (2 cm) high.*

$30–50

▲ A sterling silver Scenic thimble by Simons Bros., featuring a village scene and an unengraved cartouche. This, like almost all scenic thimbles, is US-made. *c. 1880s, ¾ in (2 cm) high.*

$40–60

shaped tops. They can be worth $300–1,500, depending on their shape, condition, and place and period of origin.

Needle match

When choosing needle cases, look for well carved or finely modeled examples, made from quality materials such as ivory or mother-of-pearl, or those in the shape of figures. Examples can fetch $150–250 or more. Souvenir cases featuring scenic carvings or transfers can sell for $80–150, while beadwork cases can be worth more than $150.

Metal cases, often known as "Averys" (after the British maker W. Avery & Son), date from the 1870s onward. They came in three types: "flats," holding packets of needles; "quadruples," holding four rows of needles; and "figurals," which take the form of insects or other novelty shapes and are the most valuable, at around $300–800.

A Spanish walnut sewing compendium, including scissors, needle case, stiletto, bodkin, and booklet, all contained in a walnut shell. *c. 1850, 1¾ in (4.5 cm) high.*

$300–500

Needle boxes made from cardboard can cost up to $90 and feature a variety of printed and embossed decoration. Many cases were homemade, and, depending on the quality, can be worth $50–250. Pincushions were often made at home, too, but were also produced as commemorative items.

Other sewing essentials include scissors, tape measures, spools of thread, and thread winders. Values depend on materials and decoration, but rarely exceed $150–500. Tape measures are a popular collecting theme: novelty-shaped celluloid ones from the 20th century often fetch around $100–250, while commemorative tape measures tend to be worth $80–150 or less.

Box of delights

Compendia (compartmentalized boxes) are worth looking out for, as are cased *nécessaires*, which are similar to compendia, but small, often portable, and containing only a few objects. A case with two or three items may sell for $100–150, but a larger collection of finely made tools can be worth $500–800.

Mechanicals

Sewing machines are a specialized collecting area. Look for examples that were produced for short periods of a few years around the 1850s, since these are among the most valuable. Portable machines such as the 19th-century Moldacott fetch around $150–250 if they have all their accessories.

A cardboard needle box with a George Baxter print of Queen Victoria's eldest daughter, Vicky, the Princess Royal and Princess F. W. of Prussia. *c. 1880s, 2¼ in (6 cm) high.*

$30–50

Top Tips

- Beware of new thimbles advertised as limited editions or collectibles. They are seldom worth collecting.
- Use a magnet to test the authenticity of a Dorcas thimble—its steel core will be attracted to the magnet. A pure silver thimble won't attract, but is often more valuable.
- Examine bone or ivory through a magnifying glass. You should see blood vessels running through bone, while ivory has light striations of color.
- Make sure the contents of compendia and *nécessaires* are complete and original—replacements are hard to find.

KEEP

Needle cases were produced in abundance in various materials, including metal, bone, ivory, and wood. Finely decorated items, or those with mechanical functions, are likely to hold their value, or even appreciate, as demand is growing.

A W. Avery & Son needle case, The Quadruple Golden Casket, in gilt, with a leaf and butterfly design, for needle sizes 6, 7, 8, and 9. This is a typically intricate example of an Avery case. It has a sliding nodule at the bottom of the box that moves the rows of needles up and down for easy selection. *c. 1870, 2¾ in (7 cm) high.*

$200–300

SELL

Despite their often decorative finishes and colored transfers, sewing machines by makers such as Singer and Jones do not fetch high prices because so many were made. Sell now and consider investing in a rarer machine.

A Singer sewing machine. This example is in excellent condition and retains its decorative transfers; both these factors should lift the price if you choose to sell. *c. 1900, 14 in (35 cm) long.*

$50–80

Salt and pepper shakers

come in a wide range of shapes and materials, as well as prices. They can determine the mood of a table setting, from elegant to whimsical, and are also fun to display—a quality that adds to their appeal.

The salt shaker was a Victorian device invented after free-flowing granular salt was developed in the mid-19th century. The first glass salt shakers were made in the 1850s, with pepper shakers coming soon afterward. Rather like salt mills, early salt shakers had an agitator mechanism that broke down the lumps, a feature that reappeared in the 1960s and 70s.

From the 1930s onward, new methods of producing cheaper tableware led to the creation of colorful and imaginative shakers. Many were made inexpensively in Japan and East Asia; they are easy to find, often marked "Japan" or "Foreign." You can buy them for around $20–80.

Most collectors follow a theme, such as figures, cartoon characters, or advertising; others choose a maker— Royal Winton, Carlton Ware, Beswick, "Made In Japan" pieces—or a look, such as the 1950s. Shakers that overlap with other areas of interests, such as Disney characters, carry high prices, as their appeal is wider.

▲ **A pair of plastic, Homepride Flour, Fred salt and pepper shakers,** by Spillers. Homepride's bowler-hatted flour-grader, Fred, was a much-loved household name in the UK. The figures are now very popular in Japan. *1970s, 4¼ in (11 cm) high.*

$12–18

◄ **A Beswick Laurel and Hardy novelty cruet,** on a shaped stand impressed "375" and marked "Beswick England." Character-shaped salt and pepper shakers are a popular collecting theme. *1930s, 3¾ in (9 cm) wide.*

$60–90

► **A Carlton Ware fruity salt and pepper set.** Carltonware's inventive shapes and designs include novelty pieces such as these pear-and-lemon salt and pepper shakers in a banana dish. *1950s, 6¾ in (17 cm) wide.*

$40–60

▲ **A pair of coated-metal salt and pepper shakers,** with incised decoration showing the underlying metal. The 1960s fascination with space travel is reflected in the material and design of this pair. *1960s, 3½ in (9 cm) high.*

$15–25

◀ **A pair of silver-mounted ivory pepper mills;** made in Birmingham, England by Hukin & Heath. Luxury materials such as ivory and silver can fetch high prices. The waisted shape of these pieces is traditional. *1935, 3¼ in (8.5 cm) high.*

$150–200

◀ **An orange Catalin early plastic salt and pepper shaker set.** The new plastics of the 1930s brought previously unseen blasts of color and style to the dining table. *1930s, 2½ in (6 cm) high.*

$40–60

Collectors' Tips

- Look for animal or bird shapes; their wide appeal should increase value
- Choose complete sets—finding a match to replace a missing piece could take years

▶ **Guinness pottery salt and pepper shakers,** each in the form of a pint of Guinness. Advertising sets—particularly the perennially popular Guinness set—are highly desirable. *1930s–50s, 2 in (5 cm) high.*

$80–120

◀ **A Sydney Harbor Water Globe salt and pepper dispenser.** This souvenir of Sydney, with its sliding lid, is still in its original box. *Late 1950s, 2¾ in (7cm) high.*

$30–40

◀ **A Bonzo salt and pepper set,** marked "Foreign," probably Japanese. Cartoon character shakers are extremely popular. *1930s, 3 in (7.5 cm) high.*

$60–90

▼ **Japanese chrome-plated salt and pepper set, with plastic finials.** The use of chrome and simple shapes such as spheres are typical of the era, as is the use of the Scottie dog. *c. 1930s, 4½ in (11.5 cm) high.*

$500–700

▶ **A set of Venus salt and pepper shakers.** The use of black and white and of a nude, classically inspired female figure is typical of 1950s designs. *1950, 4 in (10 cm) high.*

$80–120

Corkscrews, bottle openers, and pourers can be plain, inventive, or quirky, and their intriguing mechanisms and decorative appearance appeal to many collectors. Corkscrews, in particular, are available in a huge range of materials and styles.

Worldwide, there are 1,000 patents for different types of bottle opener. But the most common form of bottle opener remains the corkscrew. There are two basic types—the straight pull, which relies on the strength of the user, and the often more sought after and valuable versions in which a mechanism of some kind takes the strain. The allure of corkscrews rests in part on the many different devices they use to extract a cork mechanically—including levers, cranked handles, and complex accordion-style contraptions. In addition, handles can be made from a variety of materials, such as silver, brass, steel, carved bone, and wood. Corkscrews come in many decorative forms, and some carry advertising. There are also artful novelty types, disguised as anything from keys to animals, to conceal their true identity.

New recruits are constantly joining the ranks of corkscrew collectors, so rarities are becoming increasingly difficult to find, but beginners should find many examples priced at $15–60. Numerous novelty or advertising examples sell for less than $15.

A Henshall-type button corkscrew, with a walnut handle and a brush. *c. 1840, 5¼ in (13.5 cm) long.*
$60–90

A Lund two-part lever corkscrew. *c. 1880, 7¾ in (20 cm) wide.*
$120–180

Keeping it simple

The first English corkscrew patent, issued to Samuel Henshall in 1795, lasted for 14 years and was for a T-shaped straight pull. Henshall's innovation was to add a cap, or button, to the screw. This limited the screw's penetration, but also gripped the cork on contact and turned it, breaking its adhesion to the neck of the bottle. Early versions are rare and can be worth thousands of dollars. When the patent ran out, other manufacturers produced variations on the type until around 1910. Simple all-metal examples can be found for less than $30, while those with ivory or bone handles often fetch $80–180, and those with a maker's name or fine detailing cost about $250. Present-day straight pulls are also collectible if they are decorative and made in fine materials.

A helping hand

A great many patents were issued in the 19th century for all manner of corkscrew with levers, arms, and twisting mechanisms. Some enjoyed limited success and are rare today. For example, Robert Jones's design of 1840, which has a brass "worm," or screw, and three prongs to pierce and grip the cork, can fetch as much as $6,000 if intact and in excellent condition. Another type,

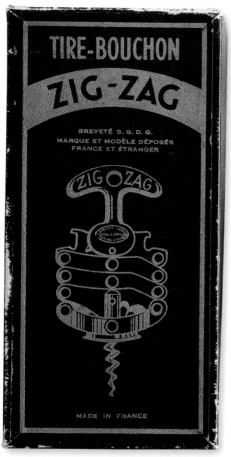

A French, chrome-plated Zig-Zag accordion corkscrew, with original box and instructions, *c. 1920, 6 in (15 cm) long.*
$80–120

A closer look at... a Thomason-type corkscrew

The inventiveness of corkscrew designs, such as Sir Edward Thomason's double-helix mechanism of 1802, has made 19th-century corkscrews very popular. The Thomason-type is one of the most desirable models.

The bone handle is original: a replacement handle of later date would lower the value

The plain decoration of the brass bottle barrel is relatively common—a more ornate style can add considerably to the value

The brush removes cork, lead, and dust from the bottle neck—the corkscrew's value is not seriously affected if the brush is missing

Thomason's double helix mechanism enables the user to insert the screw and withdraw the cork by turning the handle continuously

A bone-and-brass, Thomason-type continuous corkscrew by Wilmot & Roberts. *c. 1810, 6¾ in (17.5 cm) long.*

$200–300

often marked "Lund," combines a simple T-shaped screw and scissor-type handles with a ring to fit around the bottle neck and the screw. After twisting the screw into the cork, you grip the handle and squeeze, which forces the screw and cork up and out. When complete, these corkscrews may fetch around $150. The King's Screw has a top handle that is turned to insert the worm into the cork and a side handle that is turned to extract it. These often sell for $300–800.

Many new kinds of corkscrew, often of simpler design, were designed early in the 20th century. These can usually be bought for

$30–120 and could form a wide-ranging collection. Those marked with a maker's name, operated by an unusual mechanism, or finely crafted are all worth looking for.

Corkscrews in the shape of people or animals usually date from the 20th century. Since so many were made for the tourist trade, they tend to be inexpensive.

One for the butler

Not all openers for bottles with corks use a screw. There are many other types, and they are usually less expensive than corkscrews.

A good example is Converse's patent design, with two prongs that slide between cork and bottle. This "butler's cheat," valued from $50 to $120, enables the unscrupulous user to uncork a bottle, take a drink, then top it up with water and replace the cork.

After opening

Most bottle pourers date from the early 20th century on. Widely available and inexpensive, they often incorporate human figures or advertise products. Champagne taps were designed to retain the fizz in half-drunk bottles. They have a gimlet that can be screwed through the cork of an unopened bottle, allowing a glass or two to be poured before the tap is closed off. The heyday for these taps was from 1890 to 1920. Silver champagne taps are the most prized.

A Johnnie Walker whisky liquor pourer. *1950s, 5¾ in (14.5 cm) long.*

$12–15

Top Tips

- Before buying a corkscrew, carefully examine the sharp point; damage can reduce the value.
- Look for corkscrews with makers' marks and inscriptions—these always add value.
- Search for the big brass corkscrews used in bars; many collectors place a premium on these.

BUY

Colorful and amusing corkscrews that recall cancan dancers at the Moulin Rouge in Paris will appeal to collectors and to anyone who wants to pull a cork with panache. They can be found in a range of colors and should rise in value because of their wide appeal.

A German, celluloid, lady's-legs corkscrew, with striped, full-length stockings. *1880–90, 2½ in (6.5 cm) long.*

$200–250

KEEP

Bow corkscrews have swing-down accessories contained within a bow-shaped frame. The more accessories they have, the more valuable they are. These corkscrews offer excellent collecting potential, since they are available across a wide price range.

An English eight-tool folding bow corkscrew, with a hoof pick, leather hole-punch, gimlet, grooved helical worm corkscrew, spike, auger, screwdriver, and button hook. *c. 1820, closed 2¾ in (7 cm) long.*

$100–150

SELL

Amusing novelty corkscrews were made inexpensively and sold in great numbers during the 20th century. They are unlikely to appreciate in value, but if you have any, you might be able to sell them to collectors of animal memorabilia.

A pair of English novelty corkscrews, carved in pine as an alert cat and kneeling Scottie dog. *1930s, dog 5 in (12.5 cm) wide.*

$12–18 each

Decanters and cocktail shakers

conjure up two moods: the classic luxury of Victorian times and the contrasting dazzle of the Jazz Age. Either offers a way to live the past, not just look at it.

Serving wine in a decanter adds style to any formal meal; and cocktail shakers can create a party mood in, literally, a shake. Whether you want to add elegance or fun to your home, you are bound to find something special, whatever your budget.

The stamp of quality

Take time to familiarize yourself with the look and feel of a fine decanter. True Regency decanters are heavy for their size, and the quality and design of the cut-glass pattern are obvious when compared to later examples. Decanters from the 1800s to 1840s are most desirable and can be found in a variety of shapes and decoration, including classical-cut designs such as diamonds and "V"-shapes. Late-19th century pieces are often engraved with exuberant flowers, swirls, leaves, and birds. Prices start at $120–150, but the better the decoration and the quality of the glass, the higher the price. Beware of early 20th-century reproductions inspired by this style— molding, rather than cutting, is common; clear glass is brighter; and colored glass may have an ugly tinge.

Jugs and sets

Decanters with handles are known as claret jugs. Some tall, elegant

A claret jug and cover, with a rope-twist-shaped handle. The body is engraved with a design of grasses. c. 1880s, 13 in (33 cm) high.
$350–400

Victorian pieces are made entirely from glass, often with decorative engraving or faceting, and can fetch $120–300 or more. Bulbous early 20th-century pieces, made by firms such as Mappin & Webb, with silver mounts, can be worth around $250–800.

In the late 19th and early 20th centuries, decanters were sometimes sold as a lockable boxed set (or tantalus), for storing expensive liquors. Prices start at around $250 to $300. Novelty decanter sets, particularly those from the 1930s and 50s, can be found for around $150.

A carved oak tantalus and games box. c. 1910, 14½ in (37 cm) wide.
$600–900

Shaken, not stirred

During Prohibition in the 1920s and early 30s, the only way to render bathtub gin and bootleg whiskey drinkable was to sweeten them. So

A closer look at... two Regency decanters

Considering their age, Regency decanters are still not excessively expensive, and they add a dash of sophistication and historical interest to the liquor cabinet. It is important to look closely at the design, as well as the overall form.

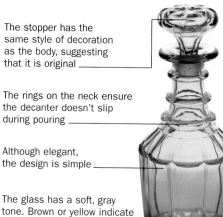

The stopper has the same style of decoration as the body, suggesting that it is original

The rings on the neck ensure the decanter doesn't slip during pouring

Although elegant, the design is simple

The glass has a soft, gray tone. Brown or yellow indicate impurities in the glass or a modern reproduction

Regency decanters typically have short necks

This decanter is far more decorative, with a number of patterns used in combination— fine-quality cutting always adds value

The body is pillar cut into rounded flutes. This expensive technique, introduced c. 1820, required thick glass to accommodate deep cuts

A flute-cut decanter with three neck rings, slice-cut shoulders, and flute-cut panels. c. 1835, 10¼ in (26 cm) high.
$120–180

A pillar-cut decanter with a step-cut neck. Its body is decorated with cut diamonds, pillars, and slices. The stopper is also pillar cut. c. 1825, 9¾ in (25 cm) high.
$280–320

cocktails were born. Bar accessories were later invented to accommodate the trend. The most essential accessory was the cocktail shaker. Here, novelty is important, and shape matters more than design. The best examples were produced during the 1920s and 30s and include imaginative forms such as skyscrapers. Such items can fetch $1,500–8,000 or more. If your budget allows (expect to pay $800–1,500 or more), look for rare "hidden" shakers allegedly used during Prohibition, such as the trophy shaker, where the trophy base turns into the shaker lid.

A mark of luxury

Shakers that are marked with names of luxury makers such as Asprey are valuable. Designs in chromed metal

and copper from the 1930s by the American manufacturer Chase are also popular. Some British makers include Mappin & Webb, Manning Bowman, Kensington, and Chrome Craft. A 1937 promotional Southern Comfort liquor-bottle-shaped shaker by Chrome Craft can fetch up to $300. American shakers tend to be plated in chrome, and British shakers in silver.

Plain and simple

Less expensive shakers from the 1940s and 50s were made in anodized aluminum and glass and they now cost about $50, while plain glass and silver-plated 1930s shakers start at around $45–80. Those with recipes printed on are desirable, provided that all the wording can be read.

◄ **A silver-plated cocktail shaker** with gilt details. The swiveling cover with windows allows individual cocktails to be chosen and the ingredients to be read in the windows. The photograph below shows a shaker in use. *c. 1935, 11 in (28 cm) high.*

$1,000–1,500

Top Tips

- Avoid decanters with a mismatched or loose stopper—the stopper should always fit snugly.
- Make sure that pairs of decanters are consistent in design and shape—pairs are more desirable and have a higher value, but only if they match.
- Buy in spring or summer for the best prices; decanters are more in demand around Christmas.
- Check that bases have light crisscrossing scratches consistent with wear through usage—a feature of genuine old decanters.
- Check the pourers on cocktail shakers. They should have closures that fit well, with either a button or screw top. Sadly, many have been lost over time.

KEEP

Novelty decanter-and-glass sets are growing in popularity. It is important for sets to remain intact. If they are still functional as well as being fun—few have survived in top condition—prices should rise.

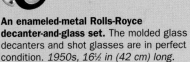

An enameled-metal Rolls-Royce decanter-and-glass set. The molded glass decanters and shot glasses are in perfect condition. *1950s, 16½ in (42 cm) long.*

$180–220

SELL

Cocktail shakers made from fine materials in novelty shapes from the 1920s and 30s have been fetching large sums recently, thanks to a small band of devoted collectors. Although prices may possibly rise a little further, they are unlikely to go much higher, making this a good time to cash in on your investment or family heirloom.

A silver-plated, stylized polar bear cocktail shaker, with a head that can be removed to reveal an internal strainer and to allow pouring. The amusing look and Art Deco feel of the design make this piece highly desirable. *c. 1930s, 10 in (25.5 cm) high.*

$3,500–4,500

Glass

Once the preserve of the wealthy, glass has long been prized. From the 19th century onward, mass-production made it affordable to all, and increased competition resulted in a multitude of different styles. More recently, talented artists developed new types of specialized glass that are now highly valued.

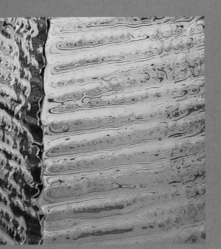
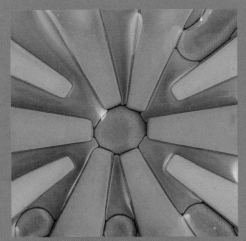
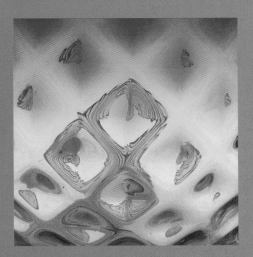

Higgins bird dish, p. 139

Perfume bottle, p. 121

Carnival glass dish, p. 119

2

3

4

The lustrous beauty of...

Industrialization and increased competition in the 19th century resulted in a riot of experimentation in glass. Since then, an extraordinary variety of new types and styles have evolved and are now considered highly collectible.

Whether you love the rich colors and distinctive forms of American factory glass such as Blenko or Viking **1**, the bold colors of a Higgins fused-glass piece **2**, or the sophistication of vintage perfume bottles **3**, this diverse collecting field offers something for everyone.

An explosion of color

The introduction of press-molding in the 19th century allowed glass to be mass-produced more cheaply, and the 20th century saw colorful and robust glass sold to a much wider market. Carnival glass **4** came in iridescent rainbow colors and was formed into bowls, vases, and dishes. It is now avidly collected. Fenton glass **5**, known for its Victorian-style frilled and Hobnail designs, is also prized, while many collectors can't resist the luxurious Aurene glass of early 20th-century Steuben **6**. Depression glass **7**, bought from dime stores or given away as promotions from the 1920s to the 1940s, provided some much-needed color and glamour in hard times and is now sought after.

1

Viking bottle p. 139

7

8

Depression glass Chintz candlesticks, p. 129

Steven Lundberg paperweight, p. 131

Fenton cranberry Hobnail vase, p. 134

⑤

Steuben Aurene bottle, p. 133

⑥

The introduction of press-molding allowed glass to be mass-produced more cheaply and sold to a much wider market.

..glassware

New inspiration

Art glass from more recent times can command high prices. Paperweight collecting is a perennially exciting area, and weights and spheres by respected contemporary glass artists such as Paul Stankard, John Deacons, Charles Kaziun, and Stephen Lundberg **⑧** may prove to be excellent future investments.

In the 1950s and 60s, Scandinavian glassmakers such as Orrefors **⑨**, Kosta, and Riihimäki experimented with colorful styles of glass, both plain and textured. This very modern glass is now firmly back in fashion.

The island of Murano near Venice has been a traditional center for glassmaking for more than a thousand years. The industry there received a creative boost in the 1950s and 60s, as designers such as Dino

Martens **⑩** at factories such as Venini and Barovier & Toso created innovative new styles. Pieces from these decades, many of them brought home by people who had been on vacation in the city, have now become highly sought after. As well as bowls and vases, there is also a market for postwar novelty animal and clown pieces.

Despite the appetite for modern glass, Amberina pieces **⑪** from the late 19th and early 20th century by US makers are holding value well. Patented in 1883, Amberina glass reddens when heated, and features a color spectrum from pale amber to rich ruby.

⑨

Orrefors Ariel vase, p.125

⑩

Dino Martens vase, p. 140

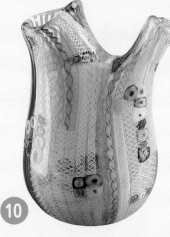

⑪

Amberina cruet, p. 126

Carnival glass has humble origins and was once seen as "Poor man's Tiffany." Its attractive patterns, cheerful colors, and generally low prices now make it eagerly collected worldwide.

With the light behind it, carnival glass can warm and beautify the home with its striking colors and flamboyant patterns. There is always scope for a lucky discovery or shrewd investment, even though these pieces were mass-produced during the 20th century.

Grand inspirations

At the beginning of the century, Tiffany art glass, with its bright, shimmering hues, was fashionable but expensive. To bring this look to the masses, from about 1905 American glass factories started to spray mass-produced, press-molded, colored glass with metallic salts. These iridescent pieces were a huge success, both in the US and in Europe.

The most popular colors at the time, and the most readily found today, are marigold (orange), amethyst (purple), green, and a rich cobalt blue. Rarer, and so more eagerly collected, are

Did You Know?

The name carnival glass was not used until the 1950s. It supposedly originated from glassware made in the US, Australia, Europe, and Argentina in the 1920s and 30s. These inexpensive items were often sold cheaply or given away at carnivals as prizes, hence the name.

pieces in amber, gray-blue, or with a marbled tortoiseshell effect. The rarest color is red, launched in the 1920s by Fenton Art Glass.

Patterns galore

Different patterns were associated with different makers; and although some apparently identical patterns were made by more than one maker, there are usually slight variations. Particularly collectible are patterns with unusual

A Dugan/Diamond Leaf Rays marigold "nappy," a form of shallow bowl. *1920s, 6¾ in (17 cm) long.*

$40–60

elements such as classical borders or Japanese-inspired decoration. Shapes are also important, as there are many variations. In general, small bowls and pitchers are common and less expensive. Large bowls or flat plates, which are harder to make, are more valuable, fetching up to $1,500 or more, depending on the color.

Prime colors

Collectors divide the glass found today into two categories. The "golden era" of 1911–25 provided the first and most collectible category, known as Prime carnival glass. Leading manufacturers were the Fenton and Northwood companies, both in West Virginia. Early Fenton carnival glass is unmarked but often has unusual patterns, such as

Some makers to look for:
- Northwood - Dugan/Diamond - Fenton -

A small Northwood Grape and Cable milk pitcher. A highly popular pattern by a prolific maker, this was made in more than 40 different shapes from 1910 until the 1920s. *c. 1920s, 3 in (7.5 cm) high.*

$60–90

A Dugan/Diamond Grape Delight amethyst bowl. After the Dugans left the factory they had bought from Northwood in 1913, it became the Diamond Glass Company. *c. 1913–30s, 7 in (18 cm) diam.*

$70–90

A Fenton Dragon and Lotus blue bowl. Along with Northwood, Fenton was one of the biggest producers of carnival glass, and this was one of its favorite and best-known patterns. *c. 1920s, 8½ in (21.5 cm) diam.*

$120–180

A Golden Harvest marigold decanter, possibly by the Diamond Glass Company. *1920s, 12 in (30.5 cm) high.*

$80–120

Cherries, and colors, such as red and Celeste blue; it also frequently had extra hand-finished details.

Grape and Cable

Northwood marked many (but not all) of its pieces on the base with an underlined "N," sometimes within a circle or, more rarely, a double circle. One of its best-known patterns was Grape and Cable *(see opposite, far left)*, found on a variety of forms from punch bowls to hatpin holders. As with most carnival glass, Northwood values depend on color and shape—a large green bowl in this pattern can be worth around $300–600 or more, while a marigold creamer will generally fetch under $50.

Other makers of Prime carnival glass include the Imperial Glass factory of Bellaire, Ohio, which made its name with its lines of Nucut and Nu-Art pressed glass, and the Millersburg

Glass Company, which was also based in Ohio.

From the early 1920s until about 1939, factories in France, Czechoslovakia, and even Argentina, made Secondary carnival glass. In England, the Sowerby's Ellison Glassworks in Gateshead also introduced a line. These European pieces tended not to be as crisp as the early American glass, since they were produced with inferior molds. The work of the Crown Crystal Company in Sydney, Australia, which produced patterns based on native flora and fauna in the 1920s, is often more appealing.

Look-alikes

By the 1960s, carnival glass had arrived as a popular collecting area. Some makers in the US, such as Fenton, created new lines using original molds. Unlike its earlier products, its new carnival glass is marked, with a script "Fenton" inside an oval cartouche. Imperial's more recent wares are also marked. Other new items have been made from fresh molds, or from old molds not originally used for carnival glass.

BUY

Pieces with a strong color, high-quality iridescence, and an identifiable pattern by a well-known maker, such as Northwood, are a good prospect for investment, since they are sure to at least hold their value and will probably appreciate.

A Northwood Good Luck amethyst bowl. The deep amethyst color and good-quality iridescence make this bowl a winner. *c. 1920s, 8½ in (21.5 cm) diam.*

$200–300

SELL

With so much carnival glass produced, it is important to invest in the best-quality examples. Pieces that lack a strong color (especially if also a common color), with a poor level of iridescence, and a faint or common pattern are not likely to gain value. Sell and invest in a more desirable piece.

A marigold dish with ruffled edge. The pattern on the dish lacks definition and the iridescence is poor. Marigold is also the most common color. *c. 1920s, 8 in (20.5 cm) diam.*

$15–25

■ Imperial ■ Brockwitz ■

An Imperial Luster Rose bowl. Imperial made carnival glass between c. 1909 and c. 1929 and exported many pieces from 1911 onward. *c. 1920s, 7¾ in (20 cm) diam.*

$60–90

A pair of Brockwitz Triands marigold vases. Brockwitz of Germany, opened in 1903, was the largest carnival glass producer in Europe by the late 1920s. *c. 1930, 7¾ in (20 cm) high.*

$50–80

Perfume bottles have a powerful allure. From the sparkling flasks of the 1900s to the doves of peace on the stopper of post–World War II L'Air du Temps, they capture the mood of the moment, with plenty of quirky flourishes to adorn the dressing table.

In the 19th and early 20th centuries, fragrances were generally light and refreshing. They were sold in plain packaging, then transferred to more attractive cut- or tinted-glass bottles for use at the dressing table. In the 1920s several leading Parisian perfumers, such as Coty, began to offer new perfumes in Art Deco bottles. The bottles were made by top glassmakers, such as Lalique, and were designed to complement the new, more sensual fragrances.

By the late 1920s many women aspired to own a bottle of French perfume. Paris couturiers, such as Poiret, launched the first "designer" perfumes to reach a mass market. Orientalism, then a fashionable style, inspired many perfumes and their bottles, such as Guerlain's Shalimar, which

was named after the gardens of Shalimar in India. The classic Chanel No. 5 bottle has hardly changed since 1921, so even early examples are inexpensive.

During the 1930s, streamlined Modernist designs captured the public's imagination and perfumes came in minimalist bottles, such as Patou's Joy. Surrealism also proved influential. Elsa Schiaparelli's perfume Shocking, introduced in 1937, was inspired by the movement and sold in a bottle shaped like a dressmaker's mannequin.

After World War II there was a taste for ladylike clothes and sweet fragrances, such as Miss Dior, which was launched in 1947. These perfumes came in bottles reminiscent of Victorian fashions.

▲ **A Victorian, cased, ruby-glass scent bottle,** with silver mounts. The deep red color and cut decoration are typical of Victorian styles. *c. 1880s, 3 in (7.5 cm) high.*
$280–320

▶ **An owl-shaped, Bakelite outer case for Evening in Paris perfume, by Bourjois.** By the 1920s manufacturers of inexpensive fragrances realized that stylish packaging and an upmarket name—preferably one with French associations— sold more perfume. *c. 1928, 4 in (10 cm) high.*
$120–180

▼ **A Venetian, *zanfirico*-glass scent bottle.** *Zanfirico* refers to the milky threads in the glass. *c. 1880s, 2½ in (6 cm) high.*
$200–300

▼ **A double-ended cut-glass bottle.** One end was for cologne, the other for smelling salts. *1900s, 4¾ in (12 cm) high.*
$200–300

▲ **A bottle for Caron's Les Pois de Senteur de Chez Moi.** The geometric shape is typical of Art Deco design. The original label enhances the value of this bottle. *c. 1927, 4½ in (11.5 cm) high.*
$150–200

▼ **A gentleman's Baccarat crystal scent flask,** one of a pair, with marks. Baccarat is one of the finest and most desirable French glassmakers. *1900s, 3¾ in (9.5 cm) high.*
$120–180 for pair

▲ **A Baccarat design for Miss Dior.** The urn shape harks back to mid-Victorian design and echoes Dior's clothes. *c. 1947, 5½ in (14 cm) high.*
$200–300

▲ **A Lalique L'Air du Temps bottle for Nina Ricci,** with box. This bottle by Marc Lalique—the son of René Lalique—is highly prized by collectors. *1960s–70s, 4 in (10 cm) high.*
$200–300

▼ **Max Factor's bottle for Chontrelle,** with original velour cat inside its plastic dome. The perfumer used this novelty styling for several inexpensive fragrances in the 1950s. *c. 1950s, 6 in (15 cm) high.*
$50–80

121

Perfume bottles

Collectors' Tips

- In pre-World War II bottles, look for novelty designs, or an established designer, or a bottle that reflects its period
- Keep current bottles that are celebrity-endorsed or innovatively designed—these may become collectibles
- Favor bottles that are full of the original perfume and still in their box

◄ **A Baccarat bottle for Guerlain's Shalimar,** which was launched at the International Exhibition of Decorative Arts in 1925. *1950s, 6 in (15 cm) high.*
$150–200

◄ **Guerlain's Parure bottle.** Limited production runs by leading perfumers always appeal to collectors, and this romantic bottle has been discontinued. *1975, 6¾ in (17 cm) high.*
$100–150

Scandinavian glass includes

some of the 20th century's most exciting work in this medium. With classic yet innovative designs, jewel-like colors, and tactile textures, it has become a magnet for lovers of clean, modern design.

A bark-pattern Finlandia vase by Timo Sarpaneva for Iittala. *c. 1964, 6¾ in (17 cm) high.*

$150–200

The twin forces of industrialization and urbanization had a huge impact on the West in the early 20th century, but in the Scandinavian countries tradition never lost its force. So, in the 1930s, Scandinavian glassmakers began a drive to bring handcrafted quality to factory-produced designs that were affordable to ordinary people. The result was the quiet, restrained elegance that has become synonymous with Scandinavian glass. The success of this initiative quickly led to a boom in design, production, and exports.

Thanks to its particular chemical formulae, Scandinavian glass has an extraordinary clarity of tone, and can be engraved, carved, and blown into molds. There are four categories: organic forms, geometric forms, textured glass, and engraved glass.

Budding designs

Curving, naturalistic shapes were considered cutting edge in the 1940s and 50s, and this style was adopted by Scandinavian glass designers. Sven Palmqvist's Selina line and Nils Landberg's Tulpenglas (Tulip glass) line for Orrefors, Sweden, are now classics, as are Timo Sarpaneva's asymmetrical vases for Finland's Iittala.

Per Lütken created fluid vases, bowls, and ashtrays, often with "pulled" rims—sections of the rim are pulled out, creating softly angular protrusions—for the Danish Holmegaard glassworks. His glass was typically cool, subtle, and transparent, in gray, smoked, or brown-tinged colors. These pieces can often be found for less than $150, as can his tableware. Other notable designers working in this organic style were the Swedish husband-and-wife team of Edvard and Gerda Strömberg at their factory Strömbergshyttan. Their pieces have a subtle blue, gray, or brown tint.

Some designers to look for:
■ Tamara Aladin ■ Nanny Still ■

◄ **Tamara Aladin's undulating, or flanged, vases for Riihimäen Lasi Oy, Finland.** Aladin is perhaps best known for the geometric style popular during the 1960s. *1960s, 11 in (28 cm) high.*

$80–100 each

Vases designed by Nanny Still for Riihimäen Lasi Oy, Finland. From the 1950s, Still's style became increasingly geometric, with strong, bright colors. *1970s, 11 in (28 cm) high.*

$100–120 each

Optical effects

Scandinavian designers were interested in optical effects, especially those created by internal bubbles. Cased within layers of clear glass, the linear or swirling patterns they formed appear like rows of little pearls. Gunnel Nyman at Nuutajärvi-Notsjö in Finland was one of the leading exponents, and her work is often copied. It is sought after today, and large vases can fetch more than $300. Other optical features include broad internal ribs or waves and thin swirling threads, a style most commonly associated with Vicke Lindstrand.

Solid geometry

Geometrical designs, with angular lines and projections and clean, unadorned surfaces, were commonly produced—in vibrant reds, blues, greens, and yellows. This style became hugely popular in the 1960s. Now easy to find, such pieces make a good subject for a new collection.

One of the key factories producing geometrical glass was Riihimäen Lasi Oy of Finland, whose pieces were nicknamed Lasi from the Finnish word for glass. Most of its glass is unsigned, but there may be a mark

A closer look at... an Erik Höglund Sun Catcher

Although designers were inspired by, and even copied, each other's designs, there are a few with unique styles, such as Sweden's Erik Höglund. Thickly rendered glass, deep colors, and primitive motifs are all trademarks of his work. Höglund designed for several Swedish firms including Kosta and Strömbergshyttan.

The glass is usually thick on pieces designed by Höglund

A Boda Sun Catcher designed by Erik Höglund, signed "H866/F," which was made to hang in a window with sunlight passing through it. *c. 1960s, 11¾ in (30 cm) high.*

$120–180

Höglund's designs typically incorporated impressed or molded primitive animal or human figures

His palette is strong, typically using orange, blue, or red

etched into the base incorporating a stylized lynx above the factory name. Prices are still low, usually ranging from about $25 to $150, depending on size, color, and form.

At Holmegaard, in addition to his naturalistic forms, Per Lütken created clean, sharp pieces in the Palette and Carnaby lines in bright colors such as pillar-box red. These can be bought for around $150, often less. Another successful and accessible Holmegaard line is the Gul vases designed by Otto Brauer. Price depends on size and color; cased-glass pieces often fetch twice as much as clear glass. A large green bottle may go for $150–180, a smaller one $50–60.

■ Vicke Lindstrand ■ Per Lütken ■ Helena Tynell ■

A Vicke Lindstrand vase for Kosta, Sweden. Lindstrand produced many styles, including glass with internal threads, as in this example. *c. 1960, 6¼ in (16 cm) high.*

$350–400

◄ **A Per Lütken vase for Holmegaard, Denmark.** Lütken is renowned for organic forms. His work is often signed. *1960, 5¼ in (13.5 cm) high.*

$60–90

► **A Helena Tynell vase for Riihimäen Lasi Oy, Finland.** Tynell is known for her vases with undulating rims or strong optical effects. *c. 1970s, 8½ in (21.5 cm) high.*

$100–150

Finlandia

The rugged landscape and harsh climate of Finland inspired the talented designers Tapio Wirkkala and Timo Sarpaneva. They translated natural shapes and textures—particularly from ice and bark—into custom sculptural studio pieces, as well as making inexpensive mold-blown production-line domestic glass. They worked for the three major Finnish glassworks—Iittala, Riihimäen Lasi Oy (sometimes referred to as Riihimaki or Lasi), and Nuutajärvi—from the 1940s until the 1960s. Look out for Sarpaneva's landmark Finlandia line with its barklike texture and clear, cool colors, and Wirkkala's evocatively named Stump vase. Colors are clear or in earthy green or smoked tones.

Wirkkala designed a wide range of textured tableware for Iittala from the late 1960s through to the mid-1980s. Look for his Ultima Thule carafe, with its textured surface and knobbly feet, introduced in 1970, and glasses produced from 1968; also, Sarpaneva's Iittala lines, which include Festivo candlesticks.

Textured pieces became popular in the 1960s and 70s, and the fashion spread overseas. Other designers such as Nanny Still, known by then for her geometric styles, began to follow the trend. Her textured pieces can still often be found for less than $200.

Even during World War II, Scandinavia had both the continuing resources and the political and imaginative freedom to create stunning designs.

A vase designed by Vicke Lindstrand for Orrefors, with an engraved decoration of a naked male swimmer. *1930s, 8¾ in (22 cm) high.*

$300–400

Cutting edge

Resilient new glass formulae stimulated Scandinavian manufacturers to produce engraved glass from the 1920s onward. The Swedish factory Orrefors excelled at producing clear-glass pieces with engraved designs using a spinning cutting wheel. Important designers include Simon Gate and Edward Hald, whose stylish engravings—often featuring figures or decorated bands known as friezes—were influenced by designs from Ancient Rome and Greece. Today, these can fetch thousands of dollars. You should also look out for engraved pieces with sparsely decorated, more modern designs by these two designers.

Vicke Lindstrand joined Orrefors in the 1930s. His line, including Art Deco-style figures and engraved nude divers, is as popular today as it was in the 1930s. Items usually sell for upward of $300, depending on the design and condition.

An aqua-blue vase from the Fossil line designed by Helena Tynell for Riihimäen Lasi Oy. *1960s, 6¼ in (16 cm) high.*

$100–150

A closer look at... an Ariel pattern cased-glass vase

From the 1930s, Scandinavian glass factories were centers of innovation. One of their major triumphs was at Orrefors, where a new technique known as Ariel was developed. Ariel patterns lent themselves to more dramatic effects than traditional engraving techniques.

An Ariel vase designed by Edvin Öhrström for Orrefors, with green glass decorated with bubbles. The base is engraved with the designer's initials, maker's marks, and pattern numbers. *c. 1960, 4¼ in (11 cm) high.*

$2,000–2,500

The pattern, composed of trails, or rows, of squares within the glass, was sandblasted onto a colored body known as a blank

The heavy, clear casing on the outside interacts with the colored glass inside to create interesting optical effects

Delicate lines

Engraved glass was not unique to Orrefors. Tapio Wirkkala, whose designs are most often inspired by nature, began his career at Iittala with a range including the mushroom shaped Kantarelle vase of the mid-1940s and the similar Foal's Foot vase in 1946. The surfaces of both are engraved with delicate lines. His original limited editions are museum pieces, but later and smaller items from the 1950s onward, including curling leaf-shaped bowls, can still be found for a few hundred dollars and are expected to rise in value.

After leaving Orrefors in 1950, Vicke Lindstrand joined the Swedish factory Kosta. His vases with finely engraved figures reinvigorated the business; many smaller items from the 1950s or later can be found for less than $150.

Innovative etchings

Abstract designs in glass were also produced using new techniques. Most important are the Graal and Ariel methods, which were used to create engraved, sandblasted, or etched designs in colored cased (layered) glass. If you are on a budget, look for good-quality examples that are either unmarked or by lesser-known factories—prices for these pieces will be much lower.

Top Tips

- If the lettering on a signed piece is hard to read, try examining it using a magnifying glass and a piece of black paper or fabric placed inside the piece.
- Learn to spot the style of leading designers by visiting museums and reputable dealers to look at their work.
- Engraving cannot be restored, so check the design all the way around the piece. Unusual flattened areas on a curved piece indicate restoration through polishing.
- Look for original engraved designs that capture the spirit of the time—such as skyscrapers, circuses, or skiers.
- Tableware is a good starting point for a collection. Sets can be built up over time and are useful and decorative.

BUY

Vases with pulled rims epitomize the Scandinavian interest in budlike forms and appeal to today's minimalist tastes. Even large pieces are still fairly inexpensive. Avoid scratched, scuffed examples, or those with limescale stains inside. These vases should increase in value as the demand outstrips supply.

A vase with a pulled rim designed by Edvard Strömberg for Strömbergshyttan. *1930s–50s, 8¾ in (22 cm) high.*

$100–150

KEEP

Natural forms were favored by many Scandinavian designers, as demonstrated in this vase shaped like a curling leaf. When considering pieces such as this, look for handmade and signed examples by notable designers, as these are more likely to increase in value.

A leaf vase designed by Tapio Wirkkala for Iittala, engraved with fine lines. It is engraved "Tapio Wirkkala-Iittala" on the underside. *1953–59, 7 in (18 cm) long.*

$400–600

SELL

Mold-blown vases in basic geometric shapes are typical of Scandinavian styling and love of color, and interest in them has grown. But because of the large number produced, the recent rise in value is unlikely to continue. Sell if prices do not rise soon.

A green mold-blown vase designed by Tamara Aladin for Riihimäen Lasi Oy. *1960s, 7¾ in (20 cm) high.*

$30–50

Amberina, with its pleasing, rich colors, is highly prized by collectors of late 19th century art glass. With pieces starting as low as $50 for a tumbler and $100 for a punch cup, pitcher, or other small utilitarian piece, there's something for every pocket.

In pale amber to rich ruby, the American art glass known as Amberina was manufactured for a short time at the turn of the last century and is sought after enough to hold its price levels—even with today's appetite for contemporary glass.

Its weight in gold

Always intended to be expensive, Amberina includes real gold in its molten mix, which when reheated turns red, purpley red, or even brown.

The shaded effect is created by partially reheating this reactive glass. The reheated part turns red—how red depends on the amount of heat applied.

Amberina was patented in 1883 by the English glassmaker Joseph Locke, who worked for the New England Glass Company in East Cambridge, Massachusetts. The glass was produced there until 1888, when owner Edward Libbey moved operations to Toledo, Ohio. At the renamed Libbey Glass Company, Amberina continued to be made in 1900, and again in the 1920s, as well as at the rival Mount Washington Glass Works in New Bedford, Massachusetts.

Red hot and Reverse

Collectors do not distinguish between factories when it comes to price. Value

A Libbey ruffled vase, with polished pontil and acid etched Libbey mark and Amberina signature. *1920s, 6 in (15 cm) high.*

$450–550

is determined mainly by coloration and shading, with connoisseurs seeking pieces with a rich red that isn't overfired and a clean, gentle changeover of shading from red to amber. If a piece is heated too long, it goes brown around the rim, which, although deliberately sought out by some collectors, is said to be overfired by others. When the bottom of a piece is reheated to create red at the base, this is known as Reverse Amberina.

Some patterns and designs to look for:
▪ ITP ▪ Plated ▪ Reverse ▪

A cruet, with amber stopper and applied handle. The rounded molded detail is known as ITP, which stands for inverted thumbprint. Cruets are often damaged since they were regularly used, so examine carefully. *c. 1890s, 6¾ in (17 cm) high.*

$150–250

A plated Amberina spooner, with vertical stripes and a layer of opaque white-glass inside. Patented by Locke in 1886, this type is rare and desirable, so fetches very high prices. *c. 1890, 4¼ in (11 cm) high.*

$4,000–5,000

A small, Reverse Amberina pitcher. The bottom of the piece, rather than the top, was reheated to make the color fade from fuchsia to amber from the bottom up. *c. 1900s, 4¾ in (12 cm) high.*

$50–80

Ds and Qs

Amberina was mostly free-blown, but was also cut or pressed into molds, creating wonderful patterns such as Diamond Quilted, (or DQ), Venetian Diamond, and Diamond Point. Occasionally glass was combined with silver mounting, which is very desirable, or the vessel was "plated" inside with a white opaque layer—a technique known as plated Amberina. Made for only a year and very fragile, plated Amberina commands as much as several thousand dollars a piece. Additions such as enameling also put up the price of a piece, as do extra fluting around the rim, swirled ribbing on the body, reeding on the handle, or an inverted thumbprint pattern.

A small lily vase, with delicate coloring, pull-down rim, and applied amber foot. *c. 1890s, 6 in (15 cm) high.*

$180–220

Extraordinarily for art glass, Amberina came in utilitarian objects such as toothpick holders, mustard pots, and water pitchers. There are a wealth of shapes, but large pieces always invite a premium. As to price, mid-range items vary from $700–1,000.

Rarities are sought after, particularly in plated Amberina; connoisseurs will pay as much as $15,000–20,000 for a particularly beautiful, large piece. There is plenty for modest budgets, too: a late 19th-century pitcher with an inverted thumbprint pattern and applied handle goes for $200; a goblet for $300–400; and a signed Libbey bud vase for $400–600.

Ultimately, the glass didn't survive the Depression because it was labor intensive to make compared to other types of glass and used expensive ingredients, but that note of late 19th-century luxury and opulence makes it highly sought after today.

BUY

Color, more specifically the variation and range of colors, is one of the most important factors governing value. The fuchsia should be strong and rich, fading to the palest of amber, with a full range of tones in between. Examples showing these tones are likely to be the best investment for the future.

A whisky taster. The warm and rich tones on this example make it a good buy. If the shape were more refined and the piece larger, the value would be higher. *c. 1890s, 2¾ in (7 cm) high.*

$180–220

KEEP

Consider the shape—some, such as trumpet vases, show off Amberina's color qualities better than others. Pieces made of carefully selected, differently colored parts can be stunning. Certain shapes are also rare. These qualities will remain popular with collectors, leading to rising prices.

A water goblet. The goblet is a rare shape, and the color strength and variation between the assembled bowl, stem, and foot is excellent. *c. 1890s, 6¼ in (15.5 cm) high.*

$250–300

▪ Diamond Quilted ▪ Ribbed ▪

An egg-shaped bowl with tricorn rim and three applied feet. DQ stands for Diamond Quilted, the centers of the molded diamonds being thicker and showing a deeper color than the edges. *c. 1900, 5½ in (13.5 cm) high.*

$400–600

A bulbous water pitcher, with applied reeded handle. Ribbed Amberina was made only by the New England Glass Company and is a sought-after pattern among collectors. *c. 1890s, 7½ in (19 cm) high.*

$180–220

Depression glass was designed to cheer the homemaker in hard times. The glass was mass-produced in great quantities and inexpensive. Nostalgia is fueling demand for the brightly colored pieces and prices are rising; now is the time to buy.

The perfect symbol of its age, Depression glass evolved out of hardship and, although it was made very cheaply, many people look upon it fondly as something that sparkled when all seemed drab.

Often given away as promotions, these vivid kitchenwares were used to sell everything from flour to gasoline to tickets (movie theaters often had "dish day"). Even when sold, for example, by Sears and Roebuck, at just $1.99 for a luncheon set, they were inexpensive.

Produced from 1925 to the 1970s, this press-molded glass was made by a technique that gave it the look of expensive cut glass, at a fraction of the cost. A gather of glass was fed from a

tank of molten glass into a mold, and a plunger pressed it against the mold as it cooled. The technique was used to produce streamlined and geometric wares that reflected Art Deco designs or those inspired by Victorian styles.

Six major makers

Knowing the output of the six major Depression-glass factories—which introduced over 40 patterns from 1930 to 1934 alone—is crucial for any collector. Minute differences matter, so find out what wares were created by Jeannette, Federal, Hazel Atlas, Anchor Hocking, Indiana, and MacBeth-Evans, as well as Fostoria, Lancaster, Westmoreland, McKee, and US Glass.

A Windsor, Diamond-pattern pink butter dish and cover; by the Jeanette Glass Co. Molded marks include a "J," usually in another motif such as a square. *1935–46, 6 in (15.5 cm) wide.*

$50–80

Rare patterns include Jeannette's Iris & Herringbone and Lancaster's Jubilee, any shape of which is hard to source. Even common patterns can be rare in some shapes—for instance, a sherbet dish in Starlight and a butter dish in Horseshoe. Parts of pieces are also popular, with an Anchor Hocking Mayfair sugar lid in pink running $1,000–1,500.

Most enthusiasts collect by pattern, aiming for a complete set. Currently popular are Macbeth-Evans's American Sweetheart and Dogwood; Jeannette's

Some makers to look for:
■ Anchor Hocking Glass Co. ■ Hazel Atlas Glass Co. ■ Federal Glass Co. ■

A rare, Hocking Glass Company Standard Floral Edging lemonade set, with pitcher and six tumblers. *c. 1927, pitcher 8¼ in (21 cm) high.*

$150–200

A Moderntone-pattern cobalt plate, by the Hazel Atlas Glass Co. of Wheeling, West Virginia, one of the most prolific makers of machine-made glass. Cobalt blue is a desirable color. *c. 1934–42, 8¾ in (22.5 cm) diam.*

$20–30

A Swirl-pattern ultramarine tumbler; Jeanette Glass Co. The factory also made carnival glass. *1937–38, 5 in (13 cm) high.*

$80–120

Cherry Blossom, Federal's Sharon, and Anchor Hocking's Mayfair, Open Rose, and Princess. Miss America and Manhattan have their fans, too.

Condition counts

Pieces to suit all pockets can be found at flea markets, antiques and collectibles centers, and collectors' fairs. It's possible to buy a plate or sherbet cup for under $20, particularly those pieces given away in bulk or sold in quantity. More valuable pieces go for $40–$60, and larger vessels, such as a Hazel Glass Company ice pitcher, for $100–120.

Chic bar accessories—available after Prohibition—make fun collectibles, as do soda fountain wares—banana split boats, sherbets, and malt glasses. There will always be a strong market for decorative pieces such as footed cake plates, candy jars, and comport sets, and these make great investments.

Condition is very important: it doesn't pay to buy chipped and cracked glass, as there are so many good pieces around. Take note of colors, since some collectors buy just one shade. Black, deep cobalt blues, and reds are more desirable than green, the most common color. Note too that patterns may have been made in one color more than another; Bubble is common in crystal, but rare in amber.

The most distinctive colors of the era are spring green and pink, which is always popular and similar in hue across companies. Transparent colors include amber, yellow, ultramarine, uranium green, forest green, amethyst, ruby, and the very rare cobalt. Opaque glass comes in white, cream, black, and Jadeite. Crystal became important in 1935, when the trend back to clear, colorless glass began.

A Sandwich, Daisy-pattern red wine or water goblet, by the Indiana Glass Co. with molded dot and floral design. *1920s–70s, 5⅛ in (14 cm) high.*

$40–60

BUY

Consider the shape of a piece as, for many different reasons, some are more desirable than others. If a piece is also in a collected pattern and by a sought-after factory, prices are unlikely to fall, and may even rise.

A Tearoom-pattern banana-split dish by the Indiana Glass Co. This popular pattern is found in green, pink, clear, and amber and the form is desirable with collectors for nostalgic reasons, making it an excellent buy. *7½ in (19 cm) long.*

$80–120

■ Jeanette Glass Co. ■ Fostoria Glass Co. ■

KEEP

Most current collectors have the more common patterns, making them less desirable and valuable today. However, the number of collectors building new collections is starting to rise, and this looks set to increase. Hold on for the time being and monitor the market. When prices begin to boom again, sell them to these new buyers and reap the benefits.

A Sharon pattern iced-tea tumbler by the Federal Glass Co. of Columbus, Ohio. *1935–39, 5¾in (14.5cm) wide*

$40–60

A pair of Chintz-pattern candlesticks, by Fostoria Glass Co. Fostoria was the largest producer of handmade pressed and blown glass tableware in the US until its closure in 1986. It also produced the first all-glass dinner service. *1928–44, 5¼ in (12 cm).*

$50–80 for the pair

A Colonial Block green goblet, by the Hazel Atlas Glass Co. The molded facets imitated more expensive cut glass. *c. 1927–1935, 5¾ in (14.5 cm) high.*

$12–18

Paperweights are perennially popular, produced unabated from the mid-19th century to the present day. These unique examples of virtuoso glassmaking are available in countless colors and designs, and suit a range of budgets.

Paperweights have a thick, clear, domed glass casing, which magnifies the colorful design within. The most popular type contains multicolored glass canes cut in short sections to create an effect known as *millefiori* (Italian for "a thousand flowers"). A different style of manufacture is the sulphide weight, which encapsulates a small portrait made from a white porcelainlike material.

The French factories of St. Louis, Clichy, and Baccarat produced superb paperweights in the mid-19th century. Today, they can fetch anything from a couple of hundred dollars for the simpler designs to thousands for the larger, finest pieces with dense, complex patterns. Many European glassmakers settled in the US in the 1850s, and the best American examples can also be expensive.

The collector on a budget has plenty of scope within the 20th century. One outstanding designer was the Spanish-born Paul Ysart, who worked for the renowned Montcrieff glassworks in Scotland. These weights bearing the label "Monart" can be found for little more than $150—a good investment, since prices are rising. Nineteenth and early 20th-century Chinese paperweights are still relatively modestly priced. High-quality, clear pieces may be a good long-term investment.

Look for weights by John Deacons, Charles Kaziun, Stephen Lundberg, and Paul Stankard, whose complex lampwork designs are sought after. Examples of the related art form of the glass sphere by top designers can be expensive and highly decorative, and are becoming increasingly popular with collectors.

▲ **A Cat in the Hat sphere,** by Jesse Taj, signed and dated. Many American paperweight artists have turned to the hot new collecting area of spheres and orbs that is rapidly growing in popularity with collectors. Taj is a glass artist known for his complex pictorial murrines. *2003, 1½ in (4 cm) diam.*
$250–350

▶ **A miniature Clichy *millefiori* paperweight.** Clichy often used soft colors, concentric rings of *millefiori*, and sometimes a cane with a "C" on the end, or a cane cut like an open rose (the Clichy Rose). *c. 1860s, 1¾ in (4.5 cm) diam.*
$250–300

▶ **A Chinese black clipper ship paperweight.** Among early paperweights, Chinese examples are probably the best executed outside France, Britain, and the US. *c. 1880s, 2½ in (6.5 cm) diam.*
$300–500

◀ **A New Zealand Coral Reef paperweight** by Lindsay Art Glass, signed on the base. California-based David Lindsay gained experience at the famous Nourot glass studio, and is now known for his complex, multi-layered paperweights. *2002, 3 in (7.5 cm) diam.*
$250–350

◀ **A Bohemian sulphide portrait paperweight,** with a cameo of the German religious reformer Martin Luther. *c. 1880s, 3¾ in (9.5 cm) diam.*
$250–300

◀ **A large, gold-foil Moon-and-cherry-blossom paperweight,** by Stephen Lundberg, signed and numbered on the base. An experienced American glass artist, Lundberg uses hot-torch techniques with colored glass to "draw" his designs. His work is sought after by a growing, devoted band of collectors. *1995, 3½ in (9 cm) diam.*

$500–600

◀ **A Baccarat Dupont garlands paperweight.** Dupont weights are often more affordable, and use smaller canes, than other Baccarat weights. *c. 1850s, 2¾ in (7 cm) diam.*

$500–600

Collectors' Tips

- Choose weights with closely packed canes
- Check canes for makers' marks or dates
- Look for canes bearing animal silhouettes
- Avoid cracked weights—they cannot be repaired (although tiny chips can be fixed)

▶ **A cherry blossom and dragonfly paperweight,** by Daniel Salazar, signed on the base. Many of Salazar's delicate and complex works are influenced by his interest in botany, such as this example. *2003, 2½ in (6.5 cm) high.*

$400–600

◀ **A Clichy posy weight,** with two pink roses and a pink-and-white cane set among five green leaves. *c. 1860s, 2¼ in (6.5 cm) diam.*

$300–500

◀ **A Perthshire scattered *millefiori* paperweight.** The canes are on a ground known as tossed muslin. Note the tiny elephant and kangaroo profiles—a desirable feature. *c. 1970s, 2 in (5 cm) diam.*

$150–250

▶ **A Charles Kaziun rose on muslin paperweight.** Kaziun was one of the most influential 20th-century paperweight artists. *c. 1955, 2¼ in (5.5 cm) diam.*

$1,200–1,800

▲ **A Paul Ysart butterfly paperweight.** This designer produced some of Britain's finest paperweights in the 1960s and 70s, most featuring *millefiori*. Animal subjects, such as this butterfly, are rare. *1970s, 2¾ in (7 cm) diam.*

$550–600

Steuben was a major player in American art glass, making sumptuous wares to compete with Tiffany. Pieces were mass-produced, and of such variety that Steuben wasn't just for the wealthy. Things have changed, and special wares fetch heart-stopping prices.

At the turn of the last century, glass enthusiasts adored the iridescent and sinuous Art Nouveau forms created by Tiffany, turning away from fussy Victorian pieces. Companies such as Steuben, founded in 1903 in Corning, New York, capitalized on this trend but, instead of making expensive studio glass, Steuben created mainly decorative wares, much of it factory-made.

Iridescent Aurene

A notable exception to this was Aurene glass, created by the company's art director of 30 years, Frederick Carder. Famed for its high-quality iridescent gold and blue—either pale and silvery or dark and inky—this glass was produced from 1904 to 1934. Vases are very collectible; expect to pay from $300 for a pair of bud vases to $5,000 and up for an elaborately decorated vessel. Also available are candlesticks, bowls, dishes, table lamps, and scent bottles, the latter being popular since they also appeal to scent-bottle collectors. Most prized of all, and much more valuable than plain Aurene, are pieces decorated in the Tiffany style, with trailing leaves or pulled feather motifs. Steuben's colors, however, tend to be brighter than Tiffany's. Other early types are also desirable, with a piece of Tyrian glass from around 1916 worth up to $30,000.

Hot off the line

Aside from such unique works, the pieces produced by Steuben embraced a larger audience and, although the decorative glass had the look of studio glass, even hand-blown pieces included production-line techniques. There were some 20 distinct glass types, but the forms were conventional, even romantic, rather than avant-garde. In his time as art director, Carder—an advocate of colored glass—created 100 new colors and 6,000 shapes in many finishes. He was followed, post-1932, by other talented designers including Walter Dorwin Teague, Sidney Waugh, and John Monteith Gates, although their aesthetic was very different from his, in that they favored clear, lead crystal.

A Steuben amethyst center bowl, with folded-over rim; unsigned. *c. 1930, 11½ in (29 cm) high.*

$300–500

Simply beautiful

Although iridescent glass made Steuben's name, collectors are equally fond of its other types of glass. Calcite, made from 1915, is a plated (cased) glass used for decorative wares and lampshades, often with an Aurene finish on an opaque opalescent ground. Cluthra, a mottled and bubbled variety is also desirable, as is *Verre de soie*, a clear glass with silky silver iridescence that is often seen on stemware. Some of Steuben's early colored glass is less costly if you avoid Aurene: a 6-inch 1930s Cluthra jade-green vase runs $350–450, although larger pieces in stronger colors can fetch $1,000. A colored crystal in French blue, Pomona green, or Bristol yellow is from $50 to several hundred.

A Steuben gold Aurene baluster vase, with etched signature on base. *c. 1925, 8 in (20.5 cm) high.*

$800–1,200

A Steuben bulbous blue Aurene small vase, with an etched "2048" and a triangular paper label. *c. 1925, 2½ in (6.5 cm) high.*

$400–500

A closer look at... a Steuben Grotesque vase

Grotesque vases are often overlooked in favor of the more traditional shapes in familiar lines such as Aurene. Said to be one of Steuben's founder, Frederick Carder's, favorite lines and produced in many different colors, Grotesque vases present a varied and comparatively affordable choice for a collection that may appreciate in value as popularity grows.

A Steuben Grotesque vase, with a gold ruby rim delicately shading to crystal. Other types of glass used include Aurene, opaque, transparent, and translucent. *c. 1930–32, 5¼ in (13.5 cm) high.*

$300–400

Graduated color Grotesque pieces like this example are found in one of five different rim colors; Pomona green, gold ruby, amethyst, and the rarer dark blue and amber

Although line drawings of intended shapes do exist, each form is free-blown by hand, so no two pieces are identical

It has no cloudiness or scratches and is typically unsigned, meaning the subtle coloration and clarity can be fully appreciated

This small size, at just over 5 inches, is rare

A Steuben jade green shoulder vase with swirl ribbing, signed with a Steuben *fleur-de-lis* mark. *c. 1925–30, 6¼ in (15.5 cm) high.*

$300–400

After 1934, the firm concentrated on elegant tablewares and ornamental pieces in its innovative 10M-lead crystal, distinguished by its clarity and brilliance. While many US glass companies went under, Steuben flourished. Influenced by Swedish simplicity and Art Deco geometrics, the pieces were often volumetric and weighty; a particularly beautiful example is Sidney Waugh's Gazelle bowl, which is typical of the engraved decorative wares and, although very desirable, not quite as popular as the Aurene.

Those favoring Art Deco crystal can pick up a Trumpet martini glass for $60–70. Fifties tablewares are also very collectable, with a set of 12 air-twist dessert plates costing $500–600 and a set of six wine glasses around $1,500.

Although utilitarian wares are still important to Steuben (even today) the factory introduced, in the 1930s–40s, a line of heavy, cast-clear crystal animals, and, in 1955, the Studies in Crystal line. Although the sculptures do not yet have a secondary market, the animals are enthusiastically bought and sold. A 2-inch mountain ram fetches about $150; a 5-inch pair of ducks $550–650; a swimming dolphin $200 or less; and a rare whale $350–400 or more.

BUY

A good knowledge of shapes and colors makes it easier to spot variations in standard production. If a form is attractive and shows hallmarks of Steuben, it may increase in value.

A Steuben, Pomona green trumpet vase. This is a common color and pleasing shape. However, it is usually in Aurene, rather than transparent, glass, making it a good and fairly rare buy. *c. 1925, 6 in (15 cm) high.*

$300–40

KEEP

Items that are representative or typical of a factory or production are likely to remain desirable. Those that appeal to other collecting markets will often fetch higher prices due to increased demand. Check your relatives' dressing tables for perfume bottles, as values should go up.

A Steuben gold Aurene perfume bottle. This type of glass is one of Carder's best-loved designs, and with its original matching stopper it is likely to be even more desirable among perfume-bottle collectors. *c. 1925, 6 in (15 cm) high.*

$650–750

Top Tips

- Look for red Aurene. Hard to make and unstable, little of it survived.

- Color and quality of finish determine value for Aurene. Look for bright, strong base colors and a satinlike iridescence.

- Before 1932, the glass had a *fleur-de-lis* and a script Steuben banner. Later pieces bear a signature (acid-etched, engraved, or paper label) or a small "S."

- Think small! Smaller pieces are cheaper to collect and easier to display.

Fenton, one of the most enduring art glass companies in the US, produced a multitude of wares from 1907 to the present day. There is a style of Fenton glass for every taste, with all but the most difficult-to-find pieces being still very affordable.

A scarce cranberry Coin Dot barber bottle, not listed in factory catalogs. *1940–c. 1950, 10 in (25.5 cm) high.*
$300–400

Art glass rarely comes as varied as it does at Fenton, where fluting, dots, and bubbles were applied to vases that fan extravagantly and bowls blown into melon shapes—not to mention wavy vessels shaped like top hats. The workmanship on each piece—usually mold-blown, but often with extra finishing touches—is admirable. Fenton has a luxurious look that is quite unmistakable, which probably explains why it is so enthusiastically collected.

In the know

Designs are many and varied, but some mainstays to look for include Coin Dot, Crest, and Hobnail, as well as less abundantly produced patterns such as Cactus, Diamond Lace, Polka Dot, Spiral Optic, and Honeycomb. Other very distinctive lines are the satin opalescent pieces, pastel milk glass, iridescent wares, and various styles of overlay glass (a milk glass cased in colored transparent glass). Hand-decorated pieces also exist, mostly done by companies such as Abels Wasserberg & Company, which bought Fenton blanks and painted them. Expect to pay extra for more elaborately decorated pieces: a peach Crest vase decorated with flowers could cost $100–150. Fenton—still based

today in its original West Virginia factory—revived its hand painting in the 1970s, and reasonably priced newer pieces can also be found; for instance, a pink Blossom basket can cost around $50–70.

Color, color everywhere

Knowing the factory's output helps to understand prices. A particular shape may be easy enough to get hold of in one design, but almost impossible to source in another. If looking for a complete table service in Hobnail, for instance, blue and French opalescent are the only colors in which it can be

A rose Crest melon vase. Colored rims, called crests, came in many colors. Rose Crest was made for Weil Freeman Co. from 1944–47. *9 in (22.5 cm) high.*
$80–120

Some lines to look for:
■ Crest ■ Hobnail ■ Overlay ■

A cranberry Hobnail opalescent vase. A popular line, Hobnail was made from 1939 into the 1980s. It came in opalescent, overlay, opaque, and transparent glass in many colors. *1939–77, 4½ in (11 cm) high.*
$70–100

A blue overlay double-crimped vase. Overlay pieces were made by covering opaque white milk glass with colored transparent glass. Also in rose, light and dark greens, yellow, and amber, and rare golden glass. *1943–53, 6½ in (16.5 cm) high.*
$70–100

found. Most shapes were sold in several treatments; for example, Coin Dot was available from 1947 in cranberry, French opalescent, and blue opalescent, while honeysuckle, introduced in 1948, and lime green (1952) lasted only relatively short periods. Blue opalescent Hobnail comes in three shades of blue, depending on the year of production. A topaz Hobnail decanter, being a rare shape, could fetch $500–700, while a small bonbon dish costs $20–40. Apple blossom in the Crest line (milk glass fluted with light pink or red) is scarce, simply because it was produced for one year only, in 1960. Expect to pay

up to $250–300 for a 12-inch Crest fan vase in this shade. Anything that's scarce inevitably increases in value, with pieces going for $100–500 or more. Still, there are plenty of affordable and beautiful pieces to amass, particularly in milk glass, as so much of it was made. Smaller, more common pieces can be found for $20–50, and some can be picked up for under $10.

First, best

Age is also a key factor in governing desirability, and, since Coin Dot is periodically reissued, connoisseurs will pay more for older pieces made from 1947 to 1964 than for reissues. Identifying post-1970s pieces is made simpler because it was after this decade that the Fenton factory began to mark its wares; before, pieces were sold with labels, many of which didn't survive. If the original label is present—there are at least 12 types—this can help date an object. Larger pieces such as fan vases, bowls, and pitchers are highly sought after, and anything a bit unusual, or with its lid, stopper, or handle intact is worth scooping up. Also prized are the earliest works—Fenton was a pioneer of iridescent pressed Carnival glass as well as stretch glass.

Top Tips

- Ware numbers, beginning at 14, were introduced in July 1952. Older pieces had mold numbers. IDs are useful for discussing glass, but are not marked on wares, so don't help to identify them.

- Know labels—there are over 12 types. From 1939–47, scalloped-edge oval stickers with gold on yellow or blue read "Hand/Made in America by Fenton."

- From 1974 glass was embossed with an oval mark with "Fenton" in script. Works from the 1980s bear an 8; from the 1990s a 9; and the 2000s 0.

KEEP

As popular colors, such as cranberry, in desirable lines become more expensive, many collectors look to other colors, causing their values to rise. Keep track of the market to see which colors are becoming more sought after and scarcer, since these should be worth keeping.

A topaz opalescent Hobnail vase. Topaz is perhaps second only to cranberry in desirability and also appeals to Vaseline glass collectors. It is also scarcer, being made for a shorter period of time, between 1940–43 and 1959–62. All Hobnail shapes were produced in this color, giving wide scope for collectors. *1940–62, 4½ in (11.5 cm) high.*

$80–120

BUY

Although most Fenton was mass-produced, experimental lines and one-time trials in unusual colorways do exist, particularly from the 1940s and 50s. Familiarize yourself with standard colorways, since any appealing, unusual departure should be worth buying, keeping future price increases in mind.

A peach Crest vase. Although peach Crest is commonly seen, it is very unusual to find a gold crest rim on a pink body, making this a good rarity for any collection. *c. 1942, 6¾ in (17 cm) high.*

$70–100

A Fenton Colonial blue Hobnail double-crimped basket, mold number "3837." 1963–c. 1973, 7 in (18 cm) high.

$30–50

■ Coin Dot ■ Decorated ■

A blue opalescent Coin Dot double-crimped bowl. Coin Dot was introduced in 1947. Blue was stopped in 1956; colors such as cranberry were discontinued and revived at intervals. *1947–56, 10¾ in (27 cm) diam.*

$100–150

A milk-glass Hobnail pedestal cake plate. Hand-painted decoration was applied in the 1940s and again later, but more rarely. Original work increases values by around 40–50 percent. This plate is marked with Fenton's name, dating it to the later period from the 1970s onward. *12¾ in (32 cm) diam.*

$80–120

Blenko glass is much prized for its opulent color and the unprecedented scale of its sculptural pieces. Rarer decorative wares by certain designers can command four-figure sums, but there is still plenty to amass for under $300—although not for long!

A Turquoise bottle with stopper, design number 657M, by Joel Philip Myers. *1965–67, 14¼ in (36 cm) high.*

$250–450

Originally a manufacturer of stained glass, Blenko only began making domestic blown glass in 1929. The founder of this family firm, William J. Blenko, had experience creating beautifully colored stained-glass panels, but had never made decorative wares. The new venture was a success, with the striking colors and bold shapes of the blown-glass pieces appealing to consumers. By 1932, Macy's of New York City was carrying the Blenko line and soon after department stores across the US stocked the colorful glass. Saving the firm from the grips of the Depression, the new line was also the making of a remarkable art-glass factory that still thrives in Milton, West Virginia.

Blenko collecting has recently become popular and has seen dramatic rises in values. Glass enthusiasts love Blenko for the striking modernity of its designs and for its strength and choice of colors. Today, the most sought after works can change hands for between $1,000 and $2,000 or more. This collecting field has not yet fully matured, however, so grab bargains while you can.

Bold forms

Early wares were often influenced by Swedish designs and can be uneven, with visible tool marks. These "idiosyncratic" pieces are snapped up by collectors, selling for $30–150 each. For investment buys, it is essential to know that the glass factory really hit its stride when it employed its first in-house designer, Winslow Anderson, in 1946. His revolutionary designs, made between 1947–53, are very collectible: for instance, his 948 bent-neck decanter and sculptural horn vase can be worth $150–400 each. The bent-neck decanter was selected by the Museum of Modern Art in New York City for the Good Design award at the Chicago Mart in 1952, firming up its reputation. Anderson designed many decorative pieces with free-form styling that is reminiscent of Scandinavian glass.

Bigger is better

The extreme designs of Wayne Husted (house designer 1952–63), such as his yard-tall bottles and architectural floor pieces, are prized by collectors, as are wares by the more traditional Joel Philip Myers (designer 1963–70). Part of the studio art glass movement,

Myers literally turned the Blenko factory into his own workshop. A very rare 587-L large spool decanter by Husted in hard-to-find Jonquil may sell for $2,000 or more, while a 6732-S decanter by Myers in Honey could fetch $300–500. Striking pieces can be had for less, however: a 1970s reissue of Myers' 6714 dented pitcher might be $20–50—albeit in the less prized shade of Emerald. Popular colors to watch for include Mulberry, Lime, Aqua, Nile, Plum, Lilac, Charcoal, Gold, and Rose—the latter favored by Jacqueline Kennedy. A Rose 5929-L decanter sold recently for $1,600, but smaller, more common pieces in this shade can be $200–300. Although rare, Chestnut is not favored by collectors, who tend to dislike the color.

A very large Tangerine bottle, design 5815-L, by Wayne Husted. *1958–70, (30½ in) 77 cm high.*

$1,200–1,800

A Wheat faceted bottle with a cased stopper, design 6934; Joel Philip Myers. *1969–72, 19¼ in (49 cm) high.*

$250–350

A closer look at... a cornucopia bowl

Blenko produced a large number of shapes, many of them decanters or vases, in a variety of colors. However do not ignore other shapes, as many are important. An understanding of forms, colors, and their histories can lead to a wise buy.

This piece was designed by Blenko's first, and arguably most important, designer, Winslow Anderson, around 1950

The design won a design award—an example is in the Museum of Modern Art, New York City

Called Charcoal, this color was only produced between 1954–57 and 1961–62, and in 1971.

A cornucopia gray bowl, design 964-S. This key Blenko shape can be found in all of Blenko's colors and is avidly sought after by collectors. *1954–57, 17¼ in (44 cm) wide.*

$200–350

BUY

One of Blenko's best-loved features, and one related closely to its heritage, is color. Pieces in bright and strong colors, such as red, are particularly prized. Look for works that show this feature off to its best, as these are likely to remain the most popular.

A tall Tangerine glass vase, model 6223. The vibrant graduated color, incorporating a strong red, twinned with the interesting texture makes this an excellent buy. *c. 1960, 11½ in (29 cm) high.*

$100–150

KEEP

Larger pieces such as floor bottles are among the most popular of Blenko's production. Those with unusual shapes with tapering or bulging areas are highly sought after. Hold on to any examples from the 1950s, as they are relatively scarce and likely to rise in value in the future.

A tall Persian-blue bottle, designed by Wayne Husted. Produced until 1964, it was made in this color in 1959 only. The crackle glass effect makes it more popular still among some collectors. *1959, 28¾ in (73 cm) high.*

$500–800

Splash of color

Identifying Blenko can be tricky since, with rare exceptions, it is not marked. Blenko used labels, which reflected its pride in the handcrafted work. A silver foil label that read "Blenko Handcraft" was used from the 1930s until 1983. From the 1970s, labels adopted a stylized "B" in black, pierced by a blowing iron. Other factories such as Bischoff and Pilgrim made similar pieces at the time. An sandblast-etched mark reading "BLENKO" was used from 1958-61, and can help to date pieces marked in this way. Blenko has some typical characteristics worth noting, including rough pontil marks on the bases (as the glass is usually free-blown), rounded and slightly uneven fire-polished rims, and thick walls. When looking through factory record or reference books, note that letters after a model number indicate the size, with "S" for small, "M" for medium, and "L" for large. Considering the actual sizes of a piece shown can help give a feel for the different sizes available. The first two numbers in the design number indicate the year of

An olive green daisy vase, design number 6115-L, by Wayne Husted, *1961-67 (14½ in) 37 cm high.*

$280–320

design. So the Tangerine decanter on the facing page, numbered 5815-L, was designed in 1958. In addition to solid colors such as Ruby, Persian Blue, and Sea Green there are many variegated tints including Blue Top Mountain, Big Sky, and Tangerine, which shades to red—Blenko's version of Amberina. Many colors have been discontinued and then reissued. Those seeking the classic colors should look for Turquoise, Sky Blue, Amethyst, Chartreuse, Ruby, and Sea Green, all sold prior to 1950.

Clarity is all-important with glass, so steer clear of pieces that have been marked by mineral deposits from water. Blenko glass is prone to water marks because it is soft and porous. The most valuable pieces combine named designers, rarity, strong colors, and an interesting design. Rialto wares have both unusual opalescence and desirable colors, and in recent years the oversized pieces have become increasingly difficult to find.

Other glassware from the 20th-century art glass movement offers a wide range of decorative collectibles. A form of creative expression in postwar Scandinavia and Italy, art glass was embraced by the pioneering glassmakers of the US studio glass movement.

Commercial glassmakers in the US couldn't make enough colored glass in the mid-20th century to satisfy consumer demand. Gone were the cheap, utilitarian designs of the Depression, as hundreds of factories in the Ohio River Valley (Pennsylvania, West Virginia, and Ohio) took to free-blowing and mold-blowing vibrant glassware. Most of the leading firms—Blenko, Pilgrim, Rainbow, Bischoff, and Viking—

A Bischoff yellow stoppered bottle. *c. 1960, 13¾ in (35 cm) high.*
$280–320

were in West Virginia. Blenko was the most original, and the most imitated; the pinched #39 ivy vase, gurgle bottles, and bent-neck decanters were widely copied, and the imitations are often prized by collectors. Tiffin is also worth looking for, with abstract pieces often fetching from $50 to $500.

Glass by any other name

Most American glass of the Fifties was mass-produced, but it deserved its soubriquet "art glass," with designers coming up with interesting, elongated forms and factories preferring free or mold-blown glass to pressed pieces. Crackle, plain, and satin-finish glass were popular, and every factory went in for strong, modern colors. Wares were decorative but useful, ranging

A Pilgrim orange square stoppered bottle. *1960s, 9½ in (24 cm) high.*
$100–200

from decanters and pitchers to vases and goblets, and can usually be found for under $250–500. Designs were repeated by all the factories, so identification is difficult, particularly since many wares are not marked. Enthusiasts refer to production catalogs or reference books.

A ware less ordinary

The most desirable items are those outside a factory's normal repertoire—anything a bit unusual or in a large size is valued. Pilgrim is known for cameo glass, an outstanding shade of pink, and interesting Venetian-style pieces created by the Italian brothers Alessandro and Roberto Moretti. A 9½-inch (24-cm) stoppered bottle could cost around $100–150, while a pitcher could be $50–80. Rainbow's mainstay was a line of miniature vases and pitchers, which sell for $20–80 depending on style and color, although canny collectors might go for the distinctive vessels featuring

A closer look at... a Higgins dish

Michael and Frances Higgins were pioneers in reintroducing the art of fused glass in the 1950s. Their bright and colorful designs, representative of the mid-20th century, have become enormously collectible recently, particularly those that best represent their style.

It contains an internal gold colored signature showing that it was made between 1957 and 1966, when the pair were at Dearborn Glass in Illinois

It was made by sandwiching shaped, colored-glass pieces between colored- and plain-glass panels and fusing in a kiln

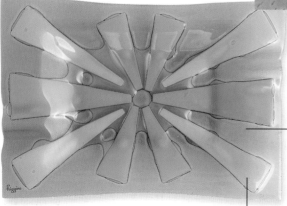

A Higgins green rectangular dish. The bold use of bright colors as seen here is a hallmark feature of desirable Higgins glass. *c. 1960, 10 in (25 cm) long.*
$150–250

The linear sunburst design is typical of the Higgins's designs

Three Viking amber mushrooms. *c. 1960, largest 5½ in (14 cm) diam.*
Small: $25–35 Large: $100–150

A Higgins dish with colored, bird-shaped applied decoration. *c.* 1970, 26 in (66 cm) high.

$300–500

Littleton and Dominic Labino began making glass pieces of almost any shape in small furnaces outside the usual factory environment. They forged the way for contemporary glassmakers such as Marvin Lipofsky, Lino Tagliapietra, and Dale Chihuly, and helped existing pioneers such as Michael and Frances Higgins—who began experimenting in 1948 with fused glass—to become appreciated as artists. They created sculptures and installations that evoke themes such as the environment, the material world, and emotion—often in an abstract manner.

Today, pieces by studio artists can fetch thousands of dollars, with bowls by Chihuly worth $5,000–50,000 and chandeliers $250,000–500,000. However, more affordable pieces exist. A pleasing collection of studio glass from the 1970s–90s could be built up by paying $100–200 or less for each piece by a currently unknown or underappreciated artist. Illustrative of the history of 20th century glass, early pieces can appear naively, but charmingly, made to today's eyes. Look for Dominic Labino, Sam Herman, Robert Eickholdt, Orient & Flume, and the Lundberg and Nourot studios. Examples can generally be found for around $1,000–3,000, but smaller pieces represent excellent value at around $200–500. Currently very fashionable are the Higgins's works, which sell for $40–800 or more. Studio and art glass from this period from Czechoslovakia has only recently become appreciated. Now may be a good time to invest.

BUY

Consider investing in the work of contemporary studio glass artists, since the market is extremely vibrant. By their nature, most pieces are unique, but make sure to buy typical designs from established or up-and coming artists to make the most of future gains in value.

A Josh Simpson New Mexico Blue Bowl with Red Lip. Simpson is a recognized glass-maker and this unique dish, inspired by the sunsets of New Mexico, is typical of his work. *2001, 9½ in (24 cm) diam.*

$250–350

KEEP

Shapes that typify the mid-century Modern look of the period, and that also have decorative appeal and are in bright colors, are likely to retain their value and possibly to increase in worth in the future. Because they also fit into today's modern interiors, they make an excellent buy.

A Viking purple stoppered bottle. Viking (originally the New Martinsville Glass Co.), is a prominent and collected name. The complex shape and large size also make this desirable. *c.* 1960, 26 in (66 cm) high.

$400–600

elongated or ball stoppers, and pitchers with three-ring handles. Bischoff made some idiosyncratic shapes, often with complicated ruffles and crystal stoppers or handles; a 1960s sky-blue epergne can be $100–150 and up. Many collectors will not buy Bischoff pieces without an identifying label. Viking (formerly New Martinsville) emphasized molding more than other companies, but upon changing its name in 1944 turned to vivid colors as its selling point. One distinctive Viking line, known as Epic, accentuated the liquid quality of hot glass; a 6-inch-deep bowl, #6962, in a satin finish might be $30–80, while an 11-inch split vase, #1171, can fetch $60–100 plus. Most pieces, however, sell for less than $100–150, many for under $100.

An artist is born

Out of this explosion of activity grew a movement that focused less on factories and more on individuals. In the early 1960s, Harvey

A Rainbow turquoise disk vase. *c.* 1960, 10¼ in (26 cm) high.

$200–300

Murano glass brought Italian

art glass back to the forefront of international design. Some of the best-crafted, most vibrant, and desirable examples were made during the postwar boom from the late 1940s to the 60s.

A Fratelli Toso *murrine* vase, with yellow and white *murrines* over an amber base and two yellow handles. *c. 1910, 4 in (10 cm) high.*
$400–600

If you are lucky enough to own some Murano glass from this golden period, it could be worth a small fortune—especially if it is by a top studio, such as Venini & C.

The small island of Murano in the Venetian lagoon has been home to glassmakers since the 14th century, and its glassworks have always borrowed freely from each other. Studying the best wares will help you to spot good-quality pieces by lesser-known designers and factories, which are available at more modest prices *(see overleaf)*.

Dramatic color combinations were used in stripes, patchworks, swirls, and free abstract designs. Talented designers used glass in original ways, sometimes applying traditional Venetian decorative techniques to new fluid forms.

Leading the revival

Paolo Venini, co-owner of the Venini & C glassworks, was also a designer, and his glassworks employed other fine designers such as Carlo Scarpa and Fulvio Bianconi. Scarpa developed the techniques that Venini was known for, such as *tessuto*, which uses crisscrossing, finely striped canes to create an effect resembling woven fabric. In 1934, he started using the *sommerso* (submerged) technique, casing (that is, covering) the main color with a thin layer of another color and then a layer of clear glass.

Bianconi used colored *tesserae* (tiles) to create the dramatic Pezzato (patchwork) vase and the bold stripes on the Spicchi (segments) vase. The *fazzoletto* (handkerchief) vase series—shaped to resemble a scrunched-up handkerchief—was designed by Bianconi and Venini and produced in various sizes and styles from the 1950s. Originals fetch around $300 or more but good copies are available for less.

A change of scale

The leading studios also produced less expensive, often witty, items. In the 1950s and 60s Venini made fish-shaped paperweights, giant eggs, and two-color egg-timers in different sizes. Prices start at $250 for smaller sizes.

Some designers to look for:
■ Paolo Venini   ■ Carlo Scarpa ■ Dino Martens ■

A Venini & C. flask designed by Paolo Venini, with red and green vertical stripes. Paolo Venini played a major creative role in adapting designs by others as well creating his own. *1952, 8½ in (21.5 cm) high.*
$500–700

A *tessuto* vase designed by Carlo Scarpa for Venini & C., with etched mark "Venini Italia 81" and labels. Scarpa's design dates from 1940. The 1980s reissues, like this one, fetch less than the originals. *1981, 12¾ in (32.5 cm) high.*
$700–1,000

A vase designed by Dino Martens for Arte Vetraria Muranese, with *zanfirico* and colored canes. Martens' designs in the 1950s are typified by his abstract use of bright, contrasting colors and by his asymmetrical shapes. He also created designs for the company Aureliano Toso. *c. 1952, 14 in (35.5 cm) high.*
$2,000–2,500

A closer look at... a *murrine* vase by Vittorio Ferro

The designer-led tradition in Murano continues today, with contemporary names becoming as sought after as their predecessors. One of the most prestigious designers of today is Vittorio Ferro. In addition to looking for notable designers, it is worthwhile learning about the decorative techniques they use. In a *murrine* piece, slices of glass canes are used to form a mosaic. A hot, clear-glass body is then rolled in the tiles, so that they stick to the glass surface.

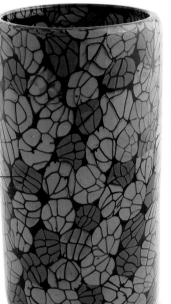

These tiles started off as long, multicolored glass canes, which the glassmaker cuts into mosaiclike pieces and "melts" onto the body of the vase in a furnace

The contrasting bright colors, which are typical of the 20th-century Muranese tradition, and the black lines in each section are hallmarks of Ferro's designs

A contemporary *murrine* vase, in blown glass, designed and made by Vittorio Ferro. Ferro comes from an established glassmaking family and his work is increasingly sought after around the world. The vase is signed and dated on the base by the artist. *2000, 10¼ in (26 cm) high.*

$1,200–1,800

Top Tips

- Check Venini pieces for an acid-etched identification stamp on the base—look closely because this mark can be difficult to find and read.

- If you find a Murano piece with a label (some Murano originally had a paper label with an outer layer of foil, often now missing), you can use the style of the label to help identify the period.

- Examine fine-quality Murano pieces to familiarize yourself with the size, weight, thickness, and close-up appearance of originals. This will help you to identify unmarked pieces.

- Because many top designs have been skillfully copied, only buy expensive investment pieces from reputable dealers or auction houses.

- If you cannot afford substantial pieces from the quality makers, consider smaller-scale items from anonymous factories. Small unmarked eggs can be picked up for less than $150. Egg timers can be found for $250–300.

▪ Flavio Poli ▪ Gio Ponti ▪ Fulvio Bianconi ▪

A *sommerso* vase designed by Flavio Poli for Seguso Vetri d'Arte in the shape of a teardrop. Poli, famous for his *sommerso* designs that use contrasting colored cased glass, often created curving, flowing forms. *c. 1955, 10¼ in (26 cm) high.*

$600–700

A Venini & C. bottle vase designed by Gio Ponti, marked "Venini Murano ITALIA." Work by Ponti is often characterized by broad bands or stripes in bright colors. *1946–50, 11½ in (29 cm) high.*

$400–600

A Venini & C. Pezzato vase designed by Fulvio Bianconi, made from joined panels of colored glass. His patchwork vases are among his most sought-after designs. *1950s, 8¾ in (22 cm) high.*

$3,000–4,000

Starting small

The color, vibrancy, and wit of postwar Murano glass was not the sole preserve of major factories and designers. A host of traditional, smaller workshops produced quantities of more affordable Murano pieces, and although these shared some of the same features as more luxurious pieces, they were often aimed at the tourist industry. They also borrowed and adapted new designs by the great names. These pieces epitomize the style and color of Murano glass, if not always the quality of the originals.

Modestly priced Murano glass can be found at collectors' shows, thrift shops, and flea markets. Striking colors and innovative designs are sometimes combined with traditional Venetian decorative techniques, such as stripes and *zanfirico* (colored glass made in thin threads and arranged into a spiral or net pattern), and cut facets and contrasting colors.

The *sommerso* menagerie

The *sommerso* technique used by the leading glass designers was also used by other Murano glassworks to make a wide variety of decorative glass items, including animals. While a signed piece by a well-known factory will be expensive, there are plenty of good unsigned or unattributed items

that cost much less than $150. Larger pieces are more likely to appreciate in value than smaller ones, as they are less common and their visual impact also makes them popular.

Sommerso ashtrays were produced in vast quantities in the 1950s and 60s at a time when smoking was still stylish. These are readily found in rounded shapes and with facet cutting, and often cost less than $100.

Sommerso vases come in a variety of shapes from geometric to abstract free-form, often incorporating generous curves. Free-form pieces with extending rims or peaks tend to cost more; they are also vulnerable to damage. The geometric vases have cut facets that reflect the light in eye-catching scintillations. They can be picked up for $40–150.

Colorful characters

Animals and character figurines have been a staple of novelty and souvenir items since the 1950s. They were produced in large numbers by skilled workers. Their appeal and price depend on the quality of workmanship and their condition. Look for fine detail, originality, and complexity of design. Clowns and musicians were favorite subjects. The figures were made in pairs, usually male and female, often depicted in elaborate historical costumes. A pair is more desirable and valuable than a single figure, and they can range from $25 to around $150 each.

A Murano *fazzoletto* vase, decorated with *zanfirico* canes. *1950s–70s, 4 in (10 cm) high.*

$60–90

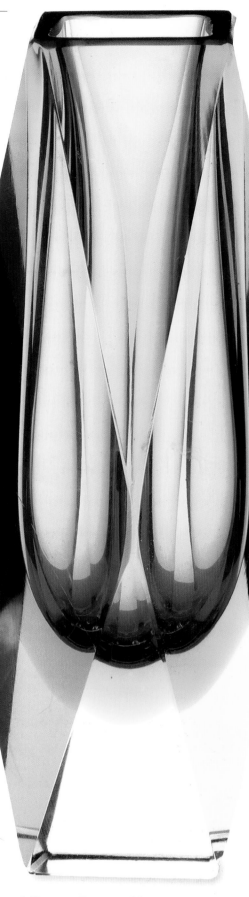

A Murano, yellow-geometric *sommerso* vase. *1960s, 6¼ in (16 cm) high.*

$50–80

A Venini & C. fazzoletto vase, decorated with internal twisted white threads. *1950s, 7½ in (19 cm) high.*

$300–400

Animals may be detailed and realistic, or more stylized. Dogs, cats, and birds are popular, as are fish. A 9¾-inch (25-cm) high Scottie dog from the 1950s may fetch around $100–200.

These wares were often assembled from small pieces of glass, so are vulnerable to breakage. Any damage or repair will reduce the value, so check before buying a piece by feeling along any potential fracture sites—sharp edges are a warning sign.

Novelty value

There are no hard and fast rules when it comes to collecting novelties. The more ingenious, charming, or humorous they are, the greater their appeal and the higher the price they are likely to fetch. Size and quality also affect price. Most pieces command less than $150. Typical Murano novelties include glass eggs (copied from the successful Venini line of the 1950s and 60s), egg-timers, and animals.

Many of these novelties are still made today. To be sure that you

buy a genuine vintage piece, check it carefully for signs of age, such as light and crisscrossing scratches on the base, accumulated from years of being placed and replaced on the surfaces on which they have stood.

Souvenirs and small novelties made in the last 20 years are unlikely to rise in value. It is best to buy or keep them because you like them, rather than as an investment.

A closer look at... two 1950s *sommerso* novelties

Many novelty-shaped *sommerso* pieces were produced in the 1950s and can make a colorful display. Smaller pieces are more common, as they were mass-produced as souvenirs—impulse buys that could easily fit into a tourist's well-packed suitcase. The larger pieces, more refined in design, were produced in smaller numbers and were also more vulnerable to damage, making them scarcer today.

The swan's neck is elegantly curved and long

The colors are not as clearly defined and the edges blur into each other

The definition between the colors is crisp, in contrast to those of the duck

This piece is less than half the size of the swan

The shape of the duck required less skill to form, so could be made more quickly

Three layers of glass are used in the casing: green, yellow, and orange

A Murano, triple-cased sommerso swan. *1950s, 14½ in (37 cm) high.*

$150–200

A Murano sommerso duck, with a green foil sticker. *1950s, 6¼ in (16 cm) high.*

$40–60

Top Tips

- Look for pieces with bright, contrasting color combinations, fluid shapes, and exuberant designs.
- Avoid *sommerso* glass with rough patches or scratches—the glass should be smooth.
- Run your finger along the top, bottom, and any sharper edges to check for tiny chips, often known as "fleabites."

BUY

Although many unsigned sommerso *pieces have been produced, large, impressive examples are worth buying, especially those with strong colors that show off the technique to its best advantage. Pulled, extending rims and fluid, curving forms are also popular. Pieces in excellent condition should rise in value.*

A Murano, triple-cased green, amber, and red sommerso vase. The shape of this vase resembles a stylized owl, with its typically large eyes. *1950s, 10½ in (27 cm) high.*

$80–120

KEEP

The fazzoletto vase is Venini's most popular design. Signed pieces are becoming harder to find and, with so many copies available, signatures are vital. It is worth keeping the larger pieces and those with differently sized frills. As demand outstrips the limited number of good signed pieces available, prices should rise.

A Venini cased fazzoletto vase, with red exterior and white interior, and acid etched mark. This piece is unusually colored, with a contemporary look. *1950s, 7¾ in (19.5 cm) high.*

$400–600

SELL

Murano glass is less likely to increase in value if it does not have the characteristic colors and forms. If a piece is made by a minor factory or is unsigned, its appeal lessens still further. But pieces that have retained their foil labels will be fairly easy to sell.

A light green Opaline vase by Fratelli Ferro of Murano, with foil labels. These vases were typical of the factory at this time. *1960s, 8¾ in (21 cm) high.*

$40–60

Beauty and Fashion

The whole spirit of a decade is captured in its fashions. From the frivolity of the 1920s to the austerity of the 1940s, the optimism of the 1960s to the brashness of the 1980s, clothes, jewelry, and fashion accessories are the perfect barometer of their time.

2

1950s nylon stockings, p. 150

3

Peter Max sweater p. 157

Art Nouveau pin, p. 176

4

Dedicated followers...

Fashions may change, but the trend for vintage clothing shows no signs of diminishing. Much of the attraction lies in wearing unique clothes that help you stand out from the crowd; another advantage is that they are often beautifully made.

1

Twenties flapper dresses ①, nylon stockings from the 1940s and 50s ②, 1960s miniskirts, and even punk slogan T-shirts from the 1970s are becoming increasingly sought after as more and more people want to own a piece of fashion history.

Look for pieces that are in good, and, where possible, original condition. Part of the appeal of flapper dresses lies in the beauty and cut of the fabric and the quality of decoration. Even vintage underwear has a market, so do not

overlook a pair of bloomers that has been passed down through the family.

All in a name

If you enjoy poking around in thrift stores and at rummage sales, bear in mind the names people look out for. For couture outfits, the crème de la crème—Chanel and Christian Dior from the 1930s onward, and Schiaparelli from the 1930s to the 60s—are the ones to spot. Iconic 1960s designs by Pucci, Pierre Cardin, Courrèges, Lilly Pulitzer, and Mary Quant are highly

Vintage silk dress, p. 149

1940s wedge-heeled mules, p. 162

6

7

1960s Gucci bag, p. 161

Look for pieces that typify an era and are in good and, where possible, original condition.

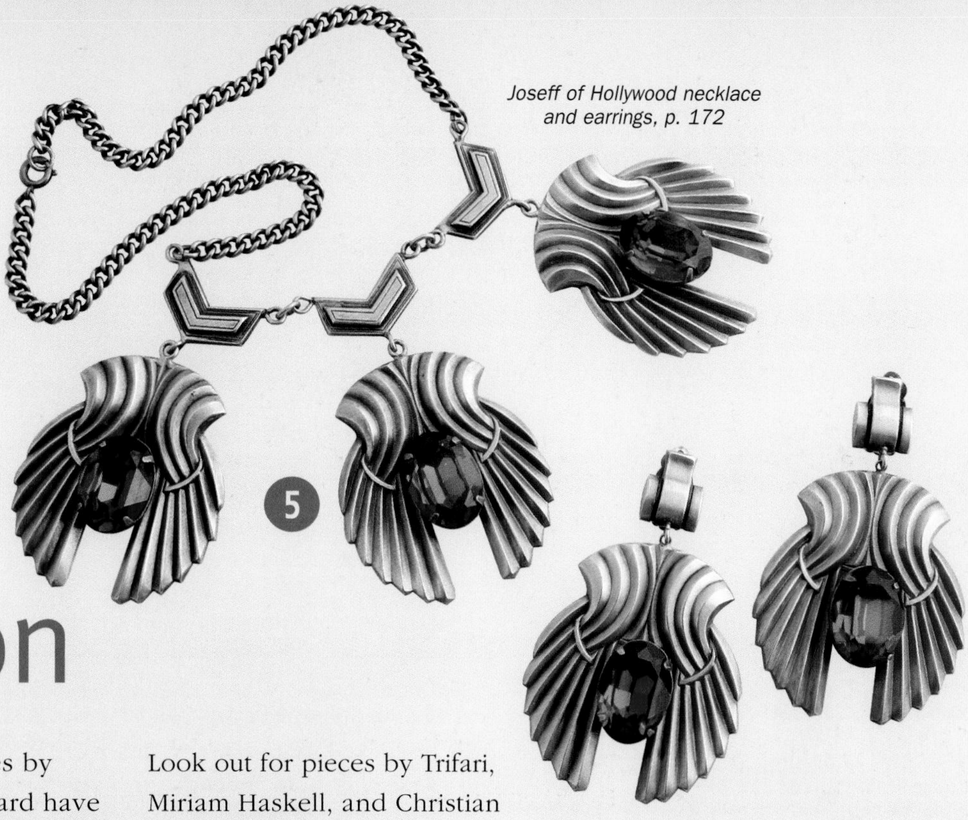

Joseff of Hollywood necklace and earrings, p. 172

⑤

...of fashion

desirable, while bold, colorful pieces by Peter Max ③ from the 1960s onward have become increasingly collectible. But labels are not everything. Flared jeans and platform shoes from the early 1970s are hotly contested when they come up for sale.

All that glitters...

Vintage jewelry ④, whether precious or costume, is another growing area. Gold and silver rings, earrings, necklaces, and pins set with precious or semiprecious stones have an intrinsic value that is enhanced by good design or a famous name. Although costume jewelry ⑤ is not made from precious stones, stylish pieces and those by named designers which typify a particular period are popular and can be very valuable.

Look out for pieces by Trifari, Miriam Haskell, and Christian Dior in particular.

Accessories such as shoes ⑥, purses ⑦, hats ⑧, and powder compacts ⑨ are also prized. Distinctive, well-made pieces that represent their period are always a good buy and are worth holding on to if you are lucky enough to inherit them. Labels are less important here; as many early 20th-century bags are not labeled at all and others are by makers who have long been forgotten.

Watches—ranging from gentlemen's hunter pocket watches ⑩ to early wristwatches—have always been collectible. Today, even 1970s analog and steel digital watches are sought after by enthusiasts.

Evans powder compact, p. 170

⑧

1950s Christian Dior hat, p. 152

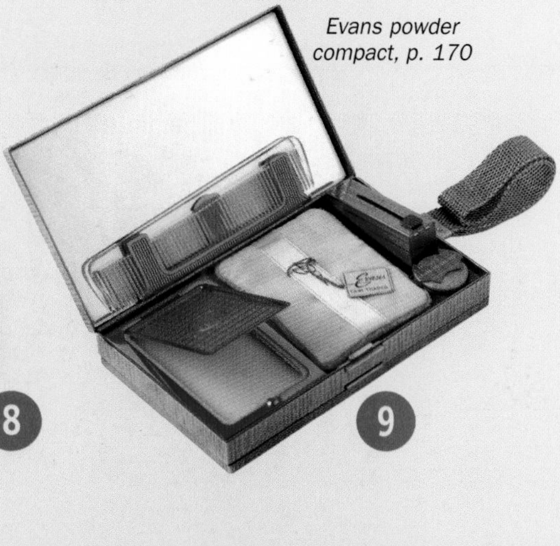

⑨

Waltham pocket watch, p. 178

⑩

WALTHAM

Vintage fashions

Vintage fashions from the early part of the 20th century reflect radical social changes, as well as being beautiful. Many pieces were worn only once or twice and it is still possible to find gorgeous garments at relatively low prices.

Black silk evening jacket, embroidered with ivory oriental motifs. *1930s, 24 in (61 cm) long.*

$120–180

Between 1910 and 1930 women went from wearing figure-hugging, full-length clothes made from reams of fabric to the slim shimmer of the beaded shifts beloved of the "flappers." Fashions changed so fast that dresses were often discarded after a season, so many are still in top condition. Prized pieces can be picked up in house clearance sales and from street markets. At the top end of the scale, auction houses and vintage clothing stores have established high prices for exquisite, well-preserved items.

In the early 20th century, women were tightly corseted into long dresses, or jackets and blouses with long skirts. Pastel colors were fashionable, but in an era when mortality rates

An *eau de nil* green chiffon dress, with train. *1910s, 50 in (127 cm) long.*

$60–90

were high, black predominated. Early 20th-century clothing is trimmed with buttons, bows, pleats, puffs, lace, and frills, all of which are easily damaged or lost. Expect to pay $300–500 for a black silk-velvet cape, and $300–800 for an embroidered white-cotton dress from the early 1900s.

One drawback with much early clothing is that it is usually small by today's standards, and unlikely to fit anyone taller than 5 ft 3 in (1.60 m) with a waist larger than 26 in (65 cm). This is irrelevant to some collectors,

A closer look at... a 1920s opera coat

Many sumptuous creations were designed for ladies to wear in the evenings, and some are still wearable today. In addition to shape, consider the material used and any decoration, since this can increase desirability and value.

The striking pink silk-velvet material is a hallmark of quality

The decoration is hand worked, with fine and intricate curling foliage and a geometrical pattern in metal beadwork, highlighted with pearls and diamanté

A pink silk-velvet opera coat. The value would be higher if it were by a notable designer and bore a label. *1920s, 40 in (101.5 cm) long.*

$600–900

The shape is both extravagant and typical of its period, with scalloped bugle-shaped sleeves and tails

A silk-velvet, rose-print dress, with decorative gathered panels. *1920s, 40 in (101.5 cm) long.*

$300–500

who feel that these clothes should be preserved, not worn.

Couture culture

Many women made their own clothes, or patronized a trusted dressmaker. Couture, which was worn only by the wealthy, was the finest custom fashion, and Paris was its capital.

Garments made from the mid-19th century onward by the top couturiers, such as Charles Frederick Worth, Paul Poiret, John Redfern, and Jeanne Paquin, originally had labels, so check any likely garments carefully.

Paul Poiret stripped away decoration and banished the corseted shape. He created straight, high-waisted, Oriental-inspired dresses and loose kimono coats, using jewel colors, bold prints, and rich fabrics. When the European dance company Ballets Russes took Paris by storm in 1909, its Arabian costumes gave the public a taste for exoticism. In response Poiret took his designs a step further, creating caftans, turbans, lampshade tunics, and harem pants. His garments are much loved but rare, with a powder blue chiffon and ivory silk tunic dress from about 1911 fetching upward of $2,500.

Gabrielle "Coco" Chanel gave fashion a sporty flavor, and her simple, chic creations suited the austerity of the World War I period. She designed sailor's-style boaters, berets, plain shirts, chemise dresses, overcoats, blazers, and two-tone shoes (based on men's spats). She also offered the earliest version of her famous cardigan suit, which came with an ankle-length skirt. Her early work (1910–20) is rarely seen outside museums: a major

auction house or dealer might sell a piece for $1,500–2,500 or more.

The Roaring Twenties

Postwar exuberance fueled the partying mania of the 1920s, when energetic new dances, such as the Charleston, raised hemlines to the knee. Flappers' dresses can be found for $300–1,200 or more, depending on the complexity of the design and decoration, and the quality of the fabric. In this decade, stylized floral and bold geometric prints were in demand for daytime dresses, which can often be found for less than $150.

Poiret's brand of exoticism and Chanel's casual elegance dominated clothing design in the 1920s. Shapes were simple and tubular. Well-endowed women bound their chests to flatten them.

Waistlines—if they existed at all—dropped to hip level. Sleeveless, beaded, shiftlike dresses were popular for evening wear. Bold young women started wearing wide-legged pajama-style pants on casual occasions. Examples can be found for $200–900, depending on the quality, but items by the top designers will cost more.

Sleek silhouettes

In the early 1930s women's clothes became more streamlined and elegant. Couturiers such as Madeleine Vionnet and Gilbert Adrian started using fabric "on the bias," particularly for evening gowns, since it enabled garments to be form-fitting yet comfortable. Hollywood stars promoted the look.

By the late 1930s couturiers such as Elsa Schiaparelli and Edward Molyneux began to look to Victorian styles for inspiration, and produced fitted suits and evening dresses with tight bodices and long, full skirts.

Good representative 1930s dresses can cost less than $100, but expect to pay around $1,500 or more for pieces by top designers.

Top Tips

- Store beaded dresses flat—hanging them will encourage tears. Wrap them carefully in acid-free tissue paper.
- Expect tiny holes or some staining on pre-1940s garments, but avoid any garment that has extensive damage.
- Avoid any silk items with splits in the fabric or missing sections of thread: once damage starts, it is irreversible.
- Treat clothing well: light, dust, dirt, and the stress of handling can lead to deterioration.
- Do not wash or dry clean clothes without consulting a textiles expert.

KEEP

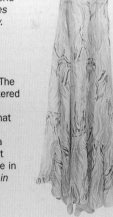

Dresses or other items of clothing that are typical of the period in both style and fabric are desirable. Prewar pieces were often altered during the austerity of World War II. This reduces value considerably.

A silk dress and matching bolero. The fabric of this unaltered day dress has an abstract pattern that was typical of the period, making it a desirable item that is likely to increase in value. *1930s, 47 in (119 cm) long.*

$400–600

SELL

Heavily beaded silk dresses were popular in the 1920s but they are difficult to keep in perfect condition—this is essential to retaining value. Prices have risen over the past decade for those garments still in top condition, so sell now while they are still looking good.

A beaded silk dress, decorated in an Art Deco pattern. This dress is attractively beaded in an intricate pattern, so it would be appreciated by a serious collector for as long as the beadwork survives. *1920s, 32 in (81 cm) long.*

$1,500–2,000

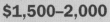

1940s and 50s fashions

for women encapsulate the contrasting styles of these two decades. From severe wartime suits to feminine, full-skirted dresses, there is a wealth of fabulous, wearable clothes for discerning buyers.

Many collectors focus on a particular decade or style of clothing, and garments from the 1940s and 50s are both stylish and easy to obtain. Austere wartime designs can be very different from the ladylike elegance of 1950s fashions, but pieces from both decades are highly sought after.

Rationed fashions

World War II had a tremendous impact on everyday life during the early to mid-1940s, and fashion was significantly affected. When Paris was occupied by the German army the fashion center of the world was cut off, and Hollywood fashions became more influential. Rationing forced American designers to be more creative. Natural fabrics were saved for the war effort, and domestic manufacturers geared up production of synthetic materials, such as rayon. US designers helped popularize the concept of coordinating separates, to give the illusion of more outfits than one actually had. Forties day dresses and separates, such as sweaters or clam diggers, fetch around $25–100 in good condition. Suits typically featured a short, narrow skirt and a short

jacket with padded shoulders. Sheath evening dresses replaced the fabric-rich gowns of the 1930s. Such low-key suits and evening wear range in price from $70–200 or more, depending on quality, material, and style.

Dressing down and up

In this era of utility and thrift, most people found it practical to dress down. With more women working for the war effort, the working-class look of Rosie the Riveter became popular, and headscarves were practical and inexpensive. Today, 1940s scarves are worth $15–150. Vintage Levis can fetch around $150–250.

Originally worn mainly on college campuses, classic sportswear designs became popular with all levels of society. Silk and nylon stockings were scarce, so ankle socks became popular.

Couturiers, such as Gilbert Adrian, Charles James, Pauline Trigère, Hattie Carnegie, and Claire McCardell, injected some longed-for glamour, and many increased their production of cheaper ready-mades in response to the war. Couture clothing from this period is highly sought after, and suits by lesser-known makers start from around $200. A desirable Gilbert Adrian cocktail dress can fetch $1,800–4,000 or more.

A pair of Missouri nylon seamed stockings, with the original packaging. *1950s, box 7 in (18 cm) high.*

$50–80

The "New Look"

After the austerity of wartime, Christian Dior's first collection in 1947 was an explosion of nostalgic opulence. Inspired by Worth, the 19th-century couturier, Dior produced crinolined evening dresses, fitted jackets, and long, full skirts, all in understated, elegant colors. He accessorized his outfits with wide-brimmed hats, gloves, and stiletto heels. With its structured lines, stiff fabrics, round, padded shoulders, and cinched waists, this style was so different from wartime wear that it was christened the "New Look." An original Dior suit can be worth $1,200–1,800 at auction and an evening dress up to $8,000. But clothes made by less well-known makers in imitation of Dior can often be found for under $150.

Collectors' Tales

"I was on the way home when I spotted a fantastic camel coat in a thrift shop window. I've been collecting vintage clothes for ages so I could tell it was late 1950s. It came from Saks Fifth Avenue, a store popular with 'ladies who lunch.' I bought it for $50, but it would probably have cost $500 from a specialist."

Rachel Bachmann, Philadelphia

An embroidered, black-velvet full-length dress. *1940s, 49 in (124.5 cm) long.*

$60–90

Fifties femininity

Early 1950s fashion took its inspiration from the "New Look" and was characterized by a feminine, hourglass silhouette, with full skirts over layered net petticoats, tiny, belted waists, and fitted tops. In reaction to Dior's retro corseted style, Coco Chanel came out of retirement in 1954 and relaunched her classic, straight-skirted suit to great acclaim. Chanel suits from the 1950s can now fetch $900–1,200 at auction.

Italian Emilio Pucci produced some of the first designer leisure wear and his ski slacks and cropped Capri pants are now synonymous with the 1950s. His simple sundresses and shirts were also widely copied.

Early street style

By the mid-1950s, teenage girls began to rebel against ladylike fashions. They wore circle skirts, ankle socks, and penny loafers. Artistic types dressed in a uniform of dark glasses, polo necks, skinny black pants, and ballet slippers. All this heralded the street styles that dominated fashion in the late 20th century.

Bargain hunt

As with all vintage fashion, general condition and the quality of the fabric affect prices, as do a piece's provenance and scarcity. It is also worth looking out for items made when a talented designer was working at a particular couture house, such as clothes designed by Yves Saint Laurent for Christian Dior in the late 1950s. Clothing by designers can be expensive, but if you avoid the big names, you can find some wonderful clothes at reasonable prices, often cheaper than their modern equivalents. The best places to look are flea markets, vintage clothing shops, thrift shops, and garage sales.

A red and green rose-print dress. *1950s, 39½ in (100 cm) long.*
$50–80

Top Tips

- Buy what you like and what suits you. Always try things on, as dress sizes have changed over the years.
- Check for damage and steer clear of clothing with major alterations, worn fabric, stains, or broken zippers or fastenings.
- Use a steamer to remove creases from clothing; do not iron, since this can leave a shine on some fabrics.

BUY

Worn by everyone from British royalty to Hollywood stars such as Grace Kelly, scarves are emblematic of the 1950s look. Hermès scarves were among the most popular, and today vintage examples are increasingly hard to find, especially in good condition, and their prices are steadily rising.

A Hermès Chiens et Valets pattern silk scarf, designed by C. H. Hello. The design of this scarf is typical of Hermès, reflecting its equestrian heritage: the company began as a saddlery. *1950s, 35 in (89 cm) wide.*
$120–180

KEEP

Fashions that are representative of their period are worth keeping. During the 1950s, teenage styling was a new force in fashion. Look for baby blue and shell pink clothes, which were among the decade's most popular colors.

A felt full skirt, with an appliqué poodle motif. Poodles are a classic feature of 1950s design. *1950s, 19 in (48.5 cm) long.*
$60–90

Hats appeal to our sense of drama—and there's nothing like a vintage hat for turning heads. No longer an essential accessory, hats are still desirable and are becoming an increasingly popular collectible.

At the beginning of the 20th century, the hat was integral to women's fashions. Going out bareheaded was unthinkable and classy ladies donned large hats decorated with finery ranging from ribbons to stuffed birds. Even in the 1920s, the emancipated flapper would not consider leaving home without her cloche hat.

In the early 1930s, wide-brimmed hats were in vogue, but by the end of the decade they had become much smaller and were accented with feathers and veils. During World War II, female factory workers wore scarves tied up in a turban style for safety reasons. Images of Rosie the Riveter helped this to become a fashion statement. Hats were more difficult to obtain during this period; some women contented themselves with eye-catching trims, while others felt justified in going bareheaded like their favorite screen actresses, such as Veronica Lake and Lana Turner.

Feminine styles returned during the 1950s, while—formal occasions aside—most 1960s women abandoned the hat in favor of exotic hairstyles or even wigs. But the hat was soon back. Designers of the 1970s emulated retro glamour—especially the famed New York milliner Adolfo.

▲ **A Christian Dior blue plush hat with netting over the feathers.** In the late 1950s, hats based on the cloche became chic. This hat was probably originally purchased to match a pea coat. *1950s–60s, 7½ in (19 cm) high.*

$60–90

▶ **A pale pink wool-felt hat decorated with a feather and a black dotted veil.** The hat's dramatic decoration is inspired by Victorian millinery. *1930s, 15¾ in (40 cm) wide.*

$200–250

▶ **A brown straw cloche hat decorated with a satin band and lined with silk.** Cloche hats were so popular during the 1920s that they came to symbolize the decade. *1920s, 5¼ in (13.5 cm) high.*

$180–220

◀ **A black woven-horsehair hat decorated with a velvet band and supported by a wire frame.** Older hats are often shaped using wiring or inner stuffing. Damaged or missing supports and linings lower the value. *1930s. 19¼ in (49 cm) wide.*

$70–100

◀ **A gray/blue wide-brimmed straw hat covered with organza.** Wide-brimmed hats such as this one accented the elegant 1950s silhouette perfectly. The organza decoration is a reworking of a popular Victorian design. *1950s, 13¾ in (35 cm) wide.*

$70–100

◄ A wide-brimmed straw hat decorated with a velvet band and roses. This would have been worn to complement a formal outfit. Beware of holes in straw hats; they cannot be repaired. *1950s, 15 in (38 cm) wide.*

$60–90

Collectors' Tips

- Look for 1920s cloche hats; these are now highly collectible
- Store hats in hatboxes, stuffing the crowns with acid-free tissue paper to retain their shape
- Use a handheld steamer to reshape straw and felt hats; if badly crushed, ask a professional

► An Adolfo blue straw hat decorated with simulated pearls, geometric shapes, and a simulated pearl hat pin. As one of New York's best-known milliners, Adolfo's hats appealed to conservative, wealthy socialites. *1970s, 12¼ in (31 cm) wide.*

$50–80

◄ A British Kaystyle rayon scarf decorated with a wartime pattern. Colorful wartime propaganda print scarves are now highly sought after. *1940s, 33 in (84 cm) wide*

$300–400

▲ An Elsa Schiaparelli multicolored turban decorated with beads and faceted blue "jewels." Shocking colors and outrageous designs were a Schiaparelli hallmark. Her best-known hats from the 1930s looked like lamb chops, ice cream cones, and shoes. *1950s, 8¼ in (21 cm) wide.*

$300–400

1960s fashions marked a

dramatic change in clothing styles for women. Today's designers are raiding the Sixties for inspiration, and authentic items by well-known names are in great demand.

Clothes from the 1960s represented either the dawn of the Age of Aquarius or a hippie trip to Marrakech. The first look was minimalist and futuristic. The second was flamboyant with ethnic overtones. Clothing in these styles and other key looks of the decade, including the A-line dress and the denim jacket, are collectible. Have a rummage through the closet of a willing "Sixties child" for items of value.

Futuristic designs

America's mission to send a man to the Moon propelled fashion into the Space Age. In the mid-1960s the Parisian couturier André Courrèges created a look for sci-fi heroines—pantsuits, tunic dresses, miniskirts, and white go-go boots. His designs were stark and angular, often in white accented with Day-Glo colors. He embraced new synthetic materials, such as wet-look vinyl. A Courrèges jacket in this material can fetch up to $500.

Pierre Cardin, another Parisian designer, made helmet hats, jumpsuits, and tunic dresses. He experimented with stiff, synthetic knits and used bold, contrasting colors, substituting black for Courrèges's white. Cardin introduced geometric cutouts and circular zippers. Paco Rabanne also designed Space Age wear, and has created clothes made from unusual materials such as riveted leather triangles, ostrich feathers, aluminum foil, and even socks and doorknobs.

Mary, Mary

British fashion designer Mary Quant opened her first boutique, Bazaar, on the King's Road, London, in 1955. She is credited with popularizing the miniskirt, and her inexpensive, cutting-edge fashions were bright, simple, and well coordinated. In the early 1960s she designed a line of coordinates, with sleeveless and pinafore dresses in unique color combinations.

A Levi's blue denim jacket. *1960s, 21¼ in (54 cm) long.*

$80–100

An André Courrèges "wet-look" turquoise jacket. *1960s, 21½ in (55 cm) long.*

$400–500

An American polyester dress printed with Art Nouveau-style ladies amid clouds. The "whiplash" Art Nouveau style was revamped during the 1960s with psychedelic colors. *1960s, 47¼ in (120 cm) high.*

$70–100

Emilio, Ossie, and Rudi

Emilio Pucci's widely copied clothing combines futuristic and hippie styles. This Italian designer was known for his psychedelic prints, inspired by stained glass and Aztec art. Pucci's tunics, kaftans, and harem pants regularly featured in classic 1960s *Vogue* photo shoots.

Ossie Clark, in his heyday (1965–74), rejuvenated the elegant bias-cut of the 1930s, and created floral gypsy dresses and peasant blouses with a sophisticated twist, and these items may now be worth up to $1,000.

Rudi Gernreich is credited with pioneering unisex clothes, see-through clothes, and inventing the topless bathing suit. A slightly less revealing 1960s knit bikini by this influential American designer can be worth $500–700 or more, and a lurex Gernreich dress can fetch $700–1,000.

Wearable fashion

It might be more economical to choose clothing inspired by the top designers. Shift dresses in bold colors inspired by Pulitzer or Quant can be found for $20–40, while low-rise bell-bottoms by popular makers such as Maverick are available for $30–100. Flea markets, thrift shops, and vintage boutiques are ideal places to search for 1960s clothing.

Top Tips

- Beware of rips and stains, particularly under the arms: these lower the value.

- Avoid repaired, altered, or customized items—these change the original nature and design of the piece, making it worth less.

- Get to know the key looks and labels of the period—those from less-expensive, lower-quality lines may not be so valuable now, but are likely to increase in price in the future.

- Be careful when handling clothing made of plasticized materials from the 1960s—these are fragile and may be brittle. Damage affects the value.

A closer look at... a Lilly Pulitzer dress

Always look for for dominant styles of the period, whether choosing to just collect or to wear vintage clothing. Famous names add value and designs worn by notable celebrities known for their great fashion sense will appeal to collectors and fans of the celebrity alike.

Pulitzer's hallmark shift dresses are typically sleeveless

They feature details such as lining and lace seam beadings around the neck

A yellow and green Lilly Pulitzer printed dress. When Pulitzer's old school friend Jackie Kennedy began wearing her designs, she shot to fame and her look became popular across the US. *1960s, 39½ in (100 cm) high.*

$70–100

The bright colors were originally conceived to conceal orange juice stains for her juice stand staff

Her name is always incorporated into the design of authentic examples—hidden in the green flower here

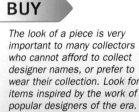

An Emilio Pucci silk jersey dress, made for Saks Fifth Avenue. *1960s, 44 in (112 cm) long.*

$800–1,000

BUY

The look of a piece is very important to many collectors who cannot afford to collect designer names, or prefer to wear their collection. Look for items inspired by the work of popular designers of the era.

A black and white minidress. The simple shape and the bold black and white printed stylized flower pattern were inspired by the designs of Mary Quant. *1960s, 35 in (89 cm) high.*

$40–60

KEEP

In the 1980s and 90s, Cardin leased his name for use on just about anything, including pans, and this promiscuity devalued his original designs. Nevertheless, he was an innovative fashion designer and couture pieces from his 1960s collections are a good investment.

A Pierre Cardin Space-Age green and black block dress. *1960s, 41¼ in (105 cm) long.*

$700–1,000

Post-1960s fashion is a new

collecting phenomenon among women. Clothing from the 1970s and 80s, once declared "the decades that taste forgot," is fashionable once again, and owners are eager to wear their amazing vintage dresses.

A Valentino print jacket from a two-piece suit. *1980s, 19 in (48 cm) long.*

$100–150 for two-piece suit

Although designer clothing from the 1970s and 80s can fetch top prices, some items are more affordable than others: a Sonia Rykiel knit dress can fetch about $200–300. Learn about the top designers to recognize elements of fashion styles that represent the era. The best designers were imitated by major manufacturers such as Banana Republic and Talbots: these copies are available at reasonable prices—look in vintage or secondhand clothing stores. Top-quality pieces are often found at dealers and auctions.

Romance and elegance

During the 1970s, the British fashion designer Ossie Clark introduced a romantic look—wraparound dresses tailored to drape around the body. Meanwhile, Ralph Lauren created beautiful clothing based on American Frontier fashions and the traditional styles of the prairies.

The Parisian Yves Saint Laurent was renowned for his chic pantsuits and *le smoking*—a tuxedo similar to those worn by glamorous 1930s stars such as Marlene Dietrich. Look for his flattering close cut and fit, using fine fabrics. The "sophisticated peasant" look of the 1970s Russian collection is popular, fetching from the low hundreds to many thousands of dollars for couture pieces or garments worn on the catwalk at major fashion shows.

American style

Wraparound dresses were as ubiquitous as bell-bottoms in the 1970s, and those by the American Diane Von Fürstenberg were best-sellers. Many can still be found for around $200. Roy Halston is another leading designer from this era. Look for his minimalist halter-neck dresses, kaftans, and flared jumpsuits, worth around $500–1,500. Clothing by New York designer Betsey Johnson is also desirable. Johnson is noted for her wide-ranging style, from floaty and

Some designers to look for:

■ Gianni Versace ■ Yves Saint Laurent ■ Diane Von Fürstenberg ■

A Gianni Versace matching top and pants. Versace's extrovert style is apparent in the bright pattern. He was also known for first-rate craftsmanship and using quality materials. *1980s, 49½ in (126 cm) long.*

$350–400

An Yves Saint Laurent Rive Gauche red woolen jacket, with black and white piping. The color and hallmark close-fitting style here with defined shoulders is typical of 1980s "power dressing." *1980s, 26½ in (67 cm) long.*

$100–150

A Diane Von Fürstenberg dress and matching jacket. Von Fürstenburg wore a green version of this print on the cover of *Newsweek* in 1976. Her trademark wraparound dress design sold more than 5 million in the 1970s. *1970s, jacket 28 in (71 cm) long.*

$120–180

A Hanae Mori blue diaphanous kaftan.
1970s, 53 in (135 cm) long.
$600–700

feminine to outrageously over-the-top. A Betsey Johnson dress is typically found for $150–300.

Disco fever

In the late 1970s, the craze for disco dancing was popularized by movies such as *Saturday Night Fever*. Disco fashion designs were often adapted from professional dancewear, and included hot pants and jumpsuits in stretchy materials such as Spandex and Lycra. Leopard skin prints were popular, as were light-reflective fabrics that shone under disco lighting. Disco items can usually be found for $30–150. The punk style appeared around the same time, and "cheesecloth" message T-shirts are

especially sought after, fetching from $15–50, or $500–800 for a Destroy or Anarchy T-shirt by British designer Vivienne Westwood.

Dressed to impress

In the 1980s, designer labels were attached to everything from jeans to ballgowns, reflecting the affluent mood of the decade. The Parisian designer Karl Lagerfeld joined Chanel in 1983, and his version of the classic Chanel suit, with a collarless jacket and short skirt, became a key look. These suits can be found for upward of $500. The Italian Giorgio Armani

is the other leading classicist. His suits were equated with success in business, and his early 1980s shoulder padding summed up the "power suit" look.

Gianni Versace, also Italian, had a reputation for exquisite craftsmanship and design, often using loud colors and unusual materials and styles to create extravagant, showy clothing.

Top Tips

- Choose garments that define the look of a designer or an era.
- Look for items that are well tailored.
- Check that designer labels are original—although rarely cut out of garments, as they add value, they are sometimes sewn into non-original clothing to increase the price.
- Avoid garments that are torn or stained—don't forget to check under the arms for perspiration marks.

BUY

The French designer Christian Lacroix is credited with introducing the lavishness that was a hallmark of 1980s fashion. He is well known for using fabrics printed with bright multicolored patterns. His distinctive pieces from the 1980s are increasing in popularity (and therefore value) as they sum up the era so well.

A Christian Lacroix *prêt-à-porter* jacket and shirt. The bright colors and bold pattern are typical of this designer. *1980s, 17¾ in (45 cm) long.*
$250–300

KEEP

Many collectors claim the 1980s look is returning in popularity, so values may increase. Search your closet for forgotten pieces by notable names and with bright colors that epitomize the decade.

A Peter Max unisex reversible jumper. Peter Max is a sought-after "pop culture" name. The exterior bears his printed "signature" and the interior is lined with yellow and red stripes. *1989, 23¾ in (60 cm) long.*
$40–60

▪ Jessica McClintock ▪

A Gunne Sax prairie-style cotton dress. Jessica McClintock's Gunne Sax label released Victorian-style "romantic" dresses that launched many imitators through the 1970s due to their immense popularity. *1970s, 49½ in (126 cm) long.*
$200–300

Sunglasses of vintage quality have never been more collectible. From early Ray-Bans to Aviators and 1950s novelty sunglasses, there is a huge variety of retro shades available and they may prove to be an invaluable investment.

Beauty and Fashion

Sunglasses first became popular in the late 1920s. Hollywood stars such as Joan Crawford and Cary Grant wore round sunglasses in the 1930s and the leading American brand Ray-Ban was founded in 1937. Aviator sunglasses, worn by military pilots, first became popular during World War II.

Wraparound sunglasses were popularized by jazz musicians in the 1950s. In the late 1950s, novelty shades with decorated plastic frames were all the rage and are now highly collectible. Classic styles by Foster Grant and Ray-Ban generally fetch from $10 to $300–500. In the early 1960s, the trend was for Space-Age sun goggles. Later in the decade, John Lennon sparked a trend for wire-framed "granny glasses."

Designer shades were the "must have" of the 1970s, especially those by Emmanuelle Khanh. *Playboy* was a big phenomenon in

the 1970s, and memorabilia connected to the name is collectible today, with sunglasses fetching around $50 to $200–300. The 1980s saw a return to shapes such as Aviator and Ray-Ban Wayfarers. Cazal produced large frames that are now popular with hip-hop lovers, and a vintage pair can be worth up to $750 today.

▲ French, plastic wraparound sunglasses. These glasses are made from a yellow snakeskin-effect plastic, and the "wings" wrap around the wearer's face—both are unusual features that add to the sunglasses' desirability. *1950s, 4¾ in (12 cm) wide.*
$200–300

► Women's novelty sunglasses. 1950s and early 1960s novelty shades, such as this pair with fabric petals around the frames, are now very collectible. *1950s, 5 in (12.5 cm) wide.*
$80–120

► Women's sunglasses with bronze, spotted-plastic frames. The movie star Lana Turner popularized this style and the "bow tie" shape was much seen in the 1940s and early 1950s. *1950s, 5¼ in (13.5 cm) wide.*
$20–30

◄ German, black- plastic-and-metal Playboy men's sunglasses. These fashionably shaped sunglasses, with a discreet bunny logo by the arms, would have been a big hit. *1970, 5½ in (14 cm) wide.*
$80–120

◄ Ray-Ban women's sunglasses with blue flecked frames. Vintage shades from Ray-Ban command a premium. *1950s, 5½ in (14 cm) wide.*
$100–150

◄ **Yves Saint Laurent, laminated-plastic Aviator sunglasses made in Italy,** with their original graduated colored lenses. This large squared-off look was fashionable in the 1970s, and the fact that these sunglasses were made by a designer of international renown makes them even more collectible. *1970s, 5½ in (14 cm) wide.*

$300–350

▲ **Italian sunglasses,** in tortoiseshell plastic. *Late 1950s, 5¾ in (14.5 cm) wide.*

$50–80

Collectors' Tips

- Watch out for scratched lenses or damaged frames, as these reduce value
- Look out for styles that are typical of a particular period
- Fakes of top names are common, so check a new pair against a pair you know is genuine

► **French, diamond-shaped, laminated-plastic sunglasses.** These sunglasses follow the avant-garde Op Art movement of the 1960s and are eye-catching and desirable. *1960s, 6 in (15.5 cm) wide.*

$200–300

◄ **French, 1960s plaid-plastic sunglasses.** Made from tartan fabric laminated between layers of clear plastic, glasses like these were all the rage in the 1960s. *1960s, 5 in (13 cm) wide.*

$120–180

◄ **A rare pair of André Courrèges sunglasses,** with white-plastic frames and slit lenses; marked "France." These are typical of the 1960s Space-Age look. *c. 1964, 6 in (15 cm) wide.*

$300–500

▼ **French, pearlized, bow-tie shaped, laminated-plastic spectacles.** Large sunglasses that covered the eyes, and often the eyebrows, were fashionable in the 1960s, as were bright colors. *1960s, 5 in (13 cm) wide.*

$150–200

Purses capture the glamorous fashions of the past century. A 1950s Hermès Kelly bag can be worth more than $1,500, but many desirable purses cost much less than $150.

A beadwork bag with a tortoiseshell-patterned plastic clasp and Art Nouveau shape and motif. *1900s, 6 in (15 cm) wide.*
$100–150

Purses have grown in size and complexity in proportion to women's independence. In the early 20th century, most women were largely financially dependent on men. Purses were correspondingly small and dainty, since they needed to hold very little. Some were so tiny that they could be clipped to belts or dangled from finger-rings.

The most popular styles from this period were the drawstring purse and the square, flat purse with a chain handle. Both types were often made of satin or leather, but most of the examples that survive are of fashionable beadwork, or metal mesh, which is like a delicate chain mail.

Floral-patterned beadwork bags generally cost $150–300, but rarer designs, such as those with an unusual beadwork picture, tend to be slightly more valuable.

Mesh was sometimes chemically tinted or decorated with enamel disks. Most mesh purses, made from base metal, fetch between $150 and $300; rarer gold and silver examples are usually worth substantially more.

By the 1920s a growing number of women were earning their own money, which gave them more independence. Meanwhile, smoking had become a fashionable pastime and the use of cosmetics was all the rage. This resulted in a trend for larger bags, to accommodate the necessities of women's busier lifestyles. Daytime purses were made of cloth and leather, while glamorous, brightly colored beadwork bags with Art Deco patterns were favored for the evening.

A beehive bag with a clear top inset with golden bees. *1950s, 5½ in (14 cm) high excluding handle.*
$400–600

Look, no handles

Clutches—purses without handles—were predominant throughout the 1930s. These were some of the first women's bags to be given interior divisions to organize their contents. Clutches came in many sizes and in simple, geometric shapes. Some examples can be bought for less than $150, but expect to pay more for fine-quality materials. Simple, modern designs were sometimes given an exotic twist with materials such as snakeskin. Finely made purses of this type may sell for more than $150, while standard pieces often start at around $75. Seek out models with brightly colored details such as clips in plastic (a new material at the time), as these can add value.

Wartime wonders

World War II limited bag production in Europe, so most surviving 1940s bags are American, since the US was less affected by rationing. British bags of the time were often made at home from items such as old clothes. Colorful felt appliqué purses, made

A closer look at... a Gucci purse

The Italian designer Gucci has produced quality leather goods since the early 20th century, but the price of success has been a flourishing trade in fakes. Genuine Gucci bags have a leather or suede lining, which bears a gold stamp reading "Made by Gucci in Italy." Below are some further tips for distinguishing the real thing from counterfeits.

A Gucci dark navy-blue leather clutch bag. The double "G" logo signifying the luxury Gucci brand is recognized—and copied—globally. *1960s–70s, 11 in (28 cm) wide.*

$120–180

Examine the stitchwork, which on genuine examples will be perfectly regular and tightly sewn. If the stitching is coming apart or the leather is cracking, the bag is probably a fake

Real Gucci is hand-finished and made from high-quality materials. The best leather is used—if the leather feels cheap, the bag may be a copy

Check the quality of the gold-plated trim—a fake Gucci bag will often have thin, worn gold plating even when the bag itself shows no signs of wear

from recycled fiber, were another wartime choice. These inventive bags tend to be less costly than those of the 1930s, since they are often inferior and less attractive.

From frivolity to women's lib

In the 1950s, austerity gave way to frivolity and unabashed elegance. Novelty purses were the latest craze, especially in the US—from wicker bags with felt fruit to rigid plastic box-shaped bags in bright colors. The latter were mostly made from an early transparent or translucent plastic called Lucite and are much sought after, with prices starting at around $200–300.

The Hermès Kelly bag (named after Grace Kelly) was hugely popular for dressy occasions, and is possibly the best-known and most luxurious bag in the world. Genuine examples can command prices of more than $1,500.

The 1960s "youthquake" favored futuristic designs and ethnic decoration. Enid Collins' wooden boxes and Emilio Pucci's psychedelic patterned purses are among the most desirable examples from this era and can fetch between $75–600, depending on the condition, design, and rarity.

In the 1970s, with the advent of the Women's Liberation Movement, tote and shoulder bags became popular as practical alternatives to the briefcase. As with bags from the 1960s, many

items are usually available for less than $75, although those by well-known names will usually be worth more.

Status symbols

In the 1980s and 90s, women rose to top positions in business for the first time and indulged in expensive outfits and luxury purses. These status items from élite makers are highly collectible in the current brand-conscious age. Names such as Gucci were popular in the 1980s, and the Prada rucksack was a highlight of the 1990s. Both often sell for more than $75–150. Look, too, for glitzy, witty, handmade evening bags from the 1990s. One top-of-the-line example is Judith Lieber's crystal-covered animal purses, known as minaudières, which often fetch around $800–1,500 or more.

Top Tips

- Don't buy mesh and beadwork purses with holes or missing sections—they are hard to repair.
- Avoid leather bags with dry, cracking, or rubbed surfaces—restoration is difficult and costly.
- Store purses flat to avoid damage, especially to the handles.
- Keep purses away from damp, heat, and direct sunlight, as exposure to these conditions can cause damage.

BUY

Many 1930s cloth purses, especially those made in costly metallic lamé, are still undervalued in comparison to beadwork examples. They make a shrewd buy for collectors on a limited budget.

A gold-lamé evening purse. The clip is made from paste, rather than precious stones. *1920s–30s, 6½ in (16 cm) wide.*

$30–50

KEEP

Collectors value 1940s felt bags, but it is difficult to find examples in good condition. If you have one that is, and you can keep it that way, the chances are that you will be rewarded with a good price when you eventually decide to sell.

A felt purse, with appliqué fruit. The fresh colors of the appliqué motif make this purse both eye-catching and collectible. *1940s, 13¼ in (34 cm) wide.*

$120–180

Vintage shoes appeal to women who want a unique accessory, as well as to collectors searching for display pieces. Whether for show or wear, there are plenty of styles to choose from.

Beauty and Fashion

Shoe styles have changed frequently since the 1900s, responding to the fashions of the day with startling rapidity. From delicate pairs dating back to the early 1900s to 1970s sneakers, there is something for everyone.

Fashionably French
In the early 1900s women's footwear was robust. Lace-up boots were the first choice for everyday wear and had sturdy, waisted "Louis" heels, a style that originated at Louis XIV's court in 17th-century France.

Shoes of the 1900s, which were reserved for formal occasions and evening wear, were also inspired by Louis XIV styles and modeled on 17th-century heeled slippers. They were often made of silk and decorated with embroidery, bows, and buckles. They came in pale colors, such as lilac and *eau-de-nil* green, and were worn with racy, patterned stockings. Prices start at around $150 and rarely exceed $500, unless the shoes are exquisitely decorated or made of fine materials; they can be found at auctions, dealers, and antiques and collectors' shows.

Straps and pumps
When hemlines rose in the 1920s, strappy shoes became fashionable. These came in dazzling colors, such as scarlet, emerald, and gold, and are highly collectible. Louis heels were still in vogue, and some shoes featured cutaway sides or peep-toes.

In the 1930s strappy designs were still popular, but streamlined pumps were the dominant style. Also known as court shoes, pumps were plain slip-on shoes with flat or raised heels, based on 18th-century footmen's slippers. They had rounded toes with slightly tapering heels

Platforms and wedges
In reaction to wartime rationing, designers came up with statuesque platform shoes, made from cork, wood, fabric-covered plastic, felt, and straw as alternatives to leather. Armed forces' pin-ups, such as Betty Grable, made platforms seem glamorous and hugely desirable. Examples can often be found in thrift shops, flea markets, and garage sales for around $75 or less. Finer items, or those in better

A pair of novelty wedge-heeled mules, made as souvenirs in the Philippines after World War II. *1940s, 12¼ in (31 cm) long.*
$120–180

condition, can also be found at vintage and secondhand stores and from clothing dealers.

The wedge heel, introduced by legendary Italian shoemaker Salvatore Ferragamo in 1936, was also popular. Examples by Ferragamo and his imitators can be found, generally at vintage clothing dealers, for around $75 and rarely exceeding $150–250.

The 1950s are associated with low-cut pumps with pointed toes and dainty stiletto heels. The heels on some stilettos were so sharp that women were banned from wearing them in certain buildings because of the damage they did to flooring. Roger Vivier, a Parisian shoemaker, made some of the finest examples. His gem-encrusted pumps

Essential shoes through the decades

1900s Glacé, kid-leather day shoes, from Lord & Taylor of New York, with eyelets and ribbons. The Louis heel is typical of this period. c. 1905, 8¾ in (22 cm) long.
$200–300

1920s Multicolored lamé shoes with Louis heel, ribbon laces, and rosettes. The colors and fancy lacings of these evening shoes sum up the times. 1920s, 8¾ in (22 cm) long.
$200–300

1940s A pair of gray, peep-toe, slingback platforms. Platforms of the 1940s were more streamlined than 1970s versions. 1940s, (9½ in 24 cm) long.
$20–30

1950s A pair of Pandora Footwear, purple dévoré-velvet evening shoes with stiletto heels. 1950s style is captured in these spiky-heeled shoes. 1950s, 9¾ in (25 cm) long.
$100–150

1960s A rare pair of Biba boots. A big fashion statement of the 1960s, boots were equated with youthful rebellion. 1960s, 23 in (58 cm) high.
$400–600

1970s A pair of wooden platform sandals decorated with plastic cherries. 1970s platforms scaled bizarre new heights. 1970s, 9½ in (24 cm) long.
$80–120

are highly sought after and often exceed $3,000. You can also find simpler styles from around $30–50 upward.

A decade for boots

The youthful styles of the 1960s were reflected in the Mary-Jane look (based on a child's button-up flats), often worn with miniskirts. Pumps with squared toes and heels were also typical of the time. Boots played a major role in 1960s style—from futuristic, white-plastic go-go boots to New Age hippie boots—and, with the current fashion for retro styling, they can be expensive. Boots by popular names such as Herbert Levine and Mary Quant may cost $150–500 or more, and those by their imitators can cost almost as much, since they capture the sought-after look of the decade. Despite this, good examples can be found for about $75–150.

Timeless soles

By the 1970s fashion had stepped back into platforms and wedge heels, and the new versions of these 1940s styles were more extreme than the originals. A pair of Terry de Havilland pale green, pink, purple, and orange snakeskin-effect

A pair of Anne Klein paisley pumps. *1980s, 10½ in (27 cm) long.*

$80–120

wedge sandals from the early 1970s may cost around $300–500 or more. These, and wooden-platform Candie's shoes, may be a good investment, as the profile of 1970s fashions is rising.

Discomania swept the US and Europe in the latter part of the 1970s, and dressy dance shoes became fashionable once more. The French designer Maud Frizon was acclaimed for the striking cone heels and colorful, decorative designs of her disco shoes, which can now be found in many secondhand clothing stores for around $80–120.

During the 1980s, styles such as the pump and strappy shoes with towering or Louis heels were dusted off and given a flashy makeover by Ferragamo and Chanel, among others. Examples of these can be found at around $75–150, or less. Manolo Blahnik, known for his dainty, open, strappy shoes with high heels, is still prominent, and his shoes from the 1980s can fetch £150–300 or more.

A pair of British sandals with marks reading "CC41." *1940s, 9 in (23 cm) long.*

$100–150

BUY

Sneakers are among the most desirable collectibles at the moment, and prices are rising rapidly. Look for retro sneakers like Puma Clyde, Adidas Superstar, and Nike Cortez.

A pair of Puma Clyde sneakers with their original box, named after the American basketball hero Walt "Clyde" Frazier. Vintage styles from the 1970s are being revived or adapted for today's sneaker-wearers. *1970s, 10¾ in (27 cm) long.*

$60–90

KEEP

Transparent-heeled shoes first made an appearance during the 1950s; most were made in the US to match plastic purses. Those in good condition usually increase in value over time.

A pair of La Rose of Jacksonville leather shoes with Lucite heels. Items made from Lucite are highly collectible. *1950s–70s, 8¾ in (22 cm) long.*

$100–150

Fans are worth getting into a flutter over—they have always been as much about the fashion and etiquette of the day as about keeping cool. These delicate and intriguing accessories still excite interest, and often display remarkable artistry and craftsmanship.

Gentlemen courted ladies with gifts of fans. Opera-goers hid behind them while watching each other. Lovers used them to flirt with. The language of the fan became so developed in the 18th century that you could converse without saying a word.

The fan's decorated fabric or paper is known as the leaf, while the framework upon which the leaf is mounted is made from sticks. Guards are the two outer sticks, and these may be decorated. Brisé fans are made entirely from sticks.

The painting and calligraphy on fans were prized by the Chinese centuries ago, but it was only in the second half of the 19th century that Western enthusiasts began to

collect them. Today, sought-after items include leaves painted by famous artists, such as Degas and Toulouse Lautrec, along with fans portraying special areas such as early ballooning and travel.

Unusual examples for any collection include celluloid fans from the 1920s that unfold to reveal lipstick, powder, and a mirror, and fans from the 1920s and 30s made from exotic materials such as feathers. Early 20th-century fans promoting products and places are also collectible.

▲ **An 18th-century paper fan,** with a scene of "Rebecca at the Well." The hand-painted scene from the Bible and the ivory sticks make this fan desirable, as does its age. *c. 1790, 11 in (28 cm) wide.*

$300–500

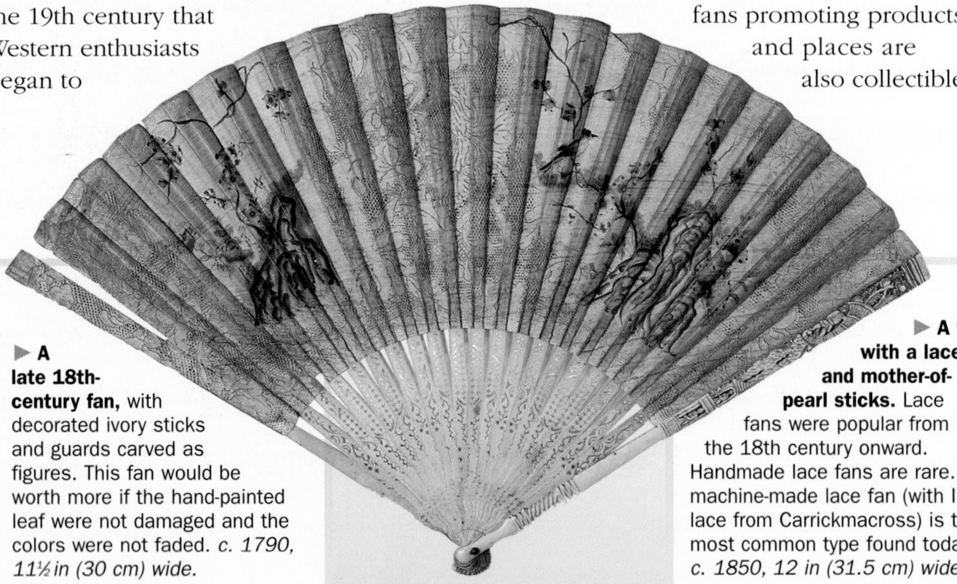

▶ **A late 18th-century fan,** with decorated ivory sticks and guards carved as figures. This fan would be worth more if the hand-painted leaf were not damaged and the colors were not faded. *c. 1790, 11½ in (30 cm) wide.*

$200–300

▶ **A fan with a lace leaf and mother-of-pearl sticks.** Lace fans were popular from the 18th century onward. Handmade lace fans are rare. This machine-made lace fan (with Irish lace from Carrickmacross) is the most common type found today. *c. 1850, 12 in (31.5 cm) wide.*

$350–450

◀ **A mid-19th century fan,** with a paper leaf printed with a picture of a fisherman flanked by two ladies next to a river. The fan has gilt detailing and pierced bone sticks applied with silvered decoration. One guard is damaged. *10½ in (26.5 cm) high.*

$120–180

◀ **A Victorian black fan,** with a leaf decorated with flowers, and ebony sticks. Somber fans were popular when Britain mourned the death of Prince Albert in 1861. *1860s, 12½ in (32.5 cm) wide.*

$100–150

◀ **A late-Regency, hand-colored fan** showing a typically French-style pastoral scene. The bright colors of the decorated leaf and the ivory sticks inlaid with silver make this fan a desirable item. *c. 1820–30, 10¾ in (27 cm) wide.*

$300–400

◀ **A Victorian printed fan,** with a scene showing a gathering of ladies. This fan is not as valuable as some: it has bone sticks (not ivory) and the design is printed, rather than hand painted. *1870s, 10 in (26 cm) wide.*

$120–180

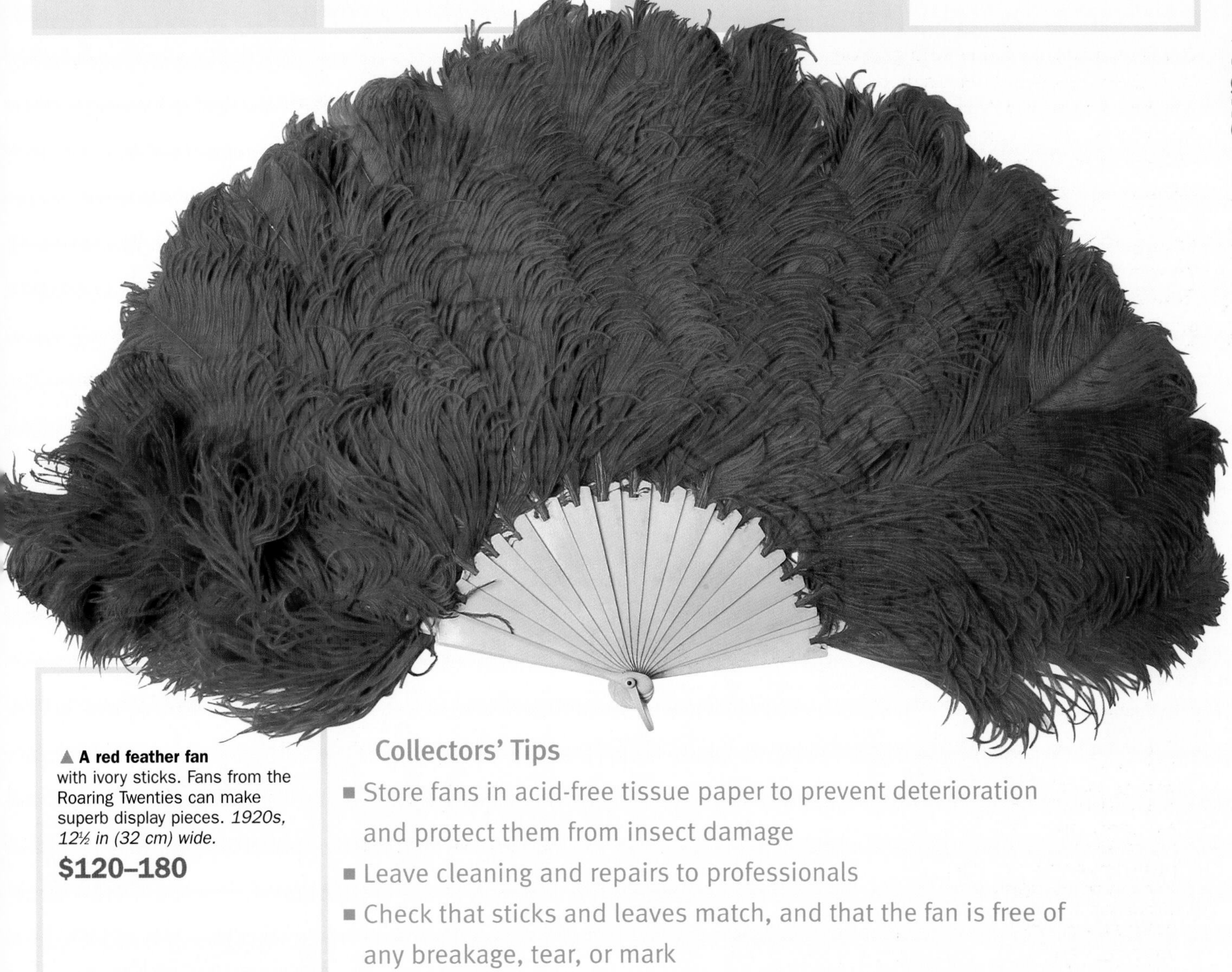

▲ **A red feather fan** with ivory sticks. Fans from the Roaring Twenties can make superb display pieces. *1920s, 12½ in (32 cm) wide.*

$120–180

Collectors' Tips

- Store fans in acid-free tissue paper to prevent deterioration and protect them from insect damage
- Leave cleaning and repairs to professionals
- Check that sticks and leaves match, and that the fan is free of any breakage, tear, or mark

◀ **A Cantonese lace-leaf fan.** The colors and scene, showing Asian people in typical dress, are characteristic of some East Asian fans, as are the ornately carved ivory sticks (detail shown in inset). *c. 1890, 11 in (28 cm) wide.*

$300–500

◀ **An Art Nouveau fabric fan,** with a painted pastoral scene of dancing figures. Mother-of-pearl sticks and gilt-highlighted period decoration add to its desirability. *c. 1910, 9 in (23 cm) wide.*

$450–550

Gentlemen's accessories

range from neckties and cufflinks to hip flasks and walking canes—the means by which men have displayed personality and flair for more than 100 years. Many of these are now highly collectible.

Cufflinks and neckties are still popular, but men looking for something special can also choose from studs (for shirts), tie clips, and even hip flasks. A pair of precious metal cufflinks or set of studs could cost $1,500 or more, but most items are much less costly.

Up your sleeve

Cufflinks are made in all designs and materials, including glass, mosaic, ivory, gold, enamel, and jewels. Collectors often focus on certain styles,

A pair of metal oval cufflinks decorated with ocean liners; they are probably a souvenir from the *Queen Mary*. 1930s, ¾ in (2 cm) wide.

$40–60

such as Art Deco, or jewelers such as Fabergé, Tiffany, Cartier, or Van Cleef & Arpels. Prices for such names can be high, often $500–1,200 or more, but there are many less expensive items at around $300–500 or less. Silver sets with simple enameling can cost less than $150. More modern items are generally less expensive than their original retail prices.

Look for "four vices" enameled cufflinks, with symbols representing the gentlemanly vices: playing cards, horse-racing motifs, cocktail glasses or champagne bottles, and elegant or scantily clad ladies. A gold Victorian or 1920s set can fetch up to $1,000–1,500 or more.

A set of sterling-silver Volkswagen Beetle cufflinks and tie pin. c. 1960s, button ¾ in (2 cm) wide.

$100–150

Early 20th-century cufflinks were sometimes gold-plated, with printed scenes under a clear-glass covering on one or both faces. These can fetch between $15 and $75. Similarly valued are plastic sets from the 1930s onward, often in novelty shapes.

All dressed up

Before the 1960s, men wore dress shirts with studs in place of buttons. There were two types: those for wear with tailcoats and white ties, and those for dinner jackets and black ties. White-tie sets are pale, usually made of mother-of-pearl or snowy enamel set in a platinum or white-gold mount. Black-tie sets are often set with onyx or ebony

---

A closer look at... two early 20th-century gentlemen's canes

A cane was an essential outdoor accessory for a typical middle- or upper-class Victorian gentleman. The materials used in canes and the quality of their decoration displayed the owner's wealth and social status. These factors also contribute to their value today.

The lid flips up to reveal matches and has a rough surface for striking them

The shaped horn handle has silver fittings

The gilt-lined hollow handle could be used for storing cigarettes

The inscription is worn, which reduces value

An American, gold-plated, tapered ebony cane with bright-cut scrollwork and a flaring knob; the top is engraved "W. L. Giffin From J. H. Herald & Family 1-18-24." Presentation canes to unknown people like this are common and are an excellent purchase for the budget buyer. *1924, 33½ in (85 cm) high.*

$150–200

The gold plating is worn; had it been solid gold, the cane would have been worth more

An unmarked, silver-mounted cigarette and matchsafe cane on a stepped bamboo shaft. Gadget canes are often more valuable than decorative canes, especially if the materials are fine, as on this example. *c. 1915, handle 4¼ in (10.5 cm) wide.*

$700–1,000

A painted silk necktie decorated with a dancing couple and a drummer, with the caption "Dance Pretty Lady," from a popular song. *1940s, 55 in (140 cm) long.*

$100–150

its own in the US in the late 1940s, with a craze for neckties with tropical scenes and risqué images. These are now sought after. Collectors also look for 1960s psychedelic designs from Emelio Pucci and Mr. Fish and Surrealist designs by Piero Fornasetti, as well as élite names such as Hermès. Values vary from $8–15 for 1970s and 80s ties, up to $250 or more for original hand-painted 1940s ties. Look for "peek-a-boo" ties, with a semiclad or naked lady on the underside of the tie.

Pinned down
Tie clips and pins were popular from the 1930s to the 60s, especially in the US. Most are plain with perhaps a single stone or paste to enliven them. They are usually gold- or silver-plated, but occasionally solid gold, silver, and platinum ones can be found. Solid examples can fetch several hundred dollars, or even $1,000 or more, while plated pieces will usually cost around $50–150, depending on the style and decoration.

All in a day's sport
The majority of vintage hip flasks found were produced between 1890 and 1930 and were designed to hold brandy or whiskey. Most are silver, silver-plate, or pewter. They come in a variety of shapes and sizes, including glass examples, encased in silver or leather. Values depend on the maker, the material used, the decoration, and the condition, but hip flasks can usually be found for around $80–500.

Top Tips
- Avoid enamel cufflinks that are chipped: they cannot be easily repaired, so the value falls.
- Look on the back of cufflinks for makers' marks and hallmarks.
- Make sure the stones in tie pins and clips are secure in their settings—missing stones are hard to replace.
- Fill hip flasks with water before purchasing to make sure there are no leaks.

enamel in a white- or yellow-gold mount. Cheaper variations, often pastes set in a silver or gold-plated mount, can also be found. Values vary from $150–300 for a paste set, to $1,500 or more for finer sets in precious materials.

Tied in knots
Bow ties have a limited following and prices are low, with fine silk or rayon examples costing less than $50–80. Look out for patterns from the 1930s with Scottie dogs, airplanes, or cars.

The long necktie was introduced between 1890 and 1900, but came into

BUY
Wearable or usable accessories are popular, especially if they are well made and in classic designs. Prices rarely fall and pieces in the best condition or by notable makers ought to rise in value over the years.

A silver- and leather-covered glass hip flask, with a maker's mark for "J. D. & Sons" and London hall-marks. This is a classic functional and decorative design for a hip flask; there is a small window to check the level of liquid. *1930s, 6 in (15 cm) high.*

$60–90

KEEP
Authentic hand-painted silk ties from the 1940s are now being reproduced and surviving originals are highly sought after by collectors. Prices for originals are climbing steadily.

A hand-painted silk tie decorated with a dancing girl among palm trees. The bright colors and well-posed naked lady make this an excellent example. *1940s, 55 in (140 cm) long.*

$150–200

SELL
Cufflinks by the best-known makers generally fetch the highest prices, but the style and design should be typical of the maker. Wearability aside, if you are looking for investment potential, sell these and buy more representative pieces.

A pair of Georg Jensen silver cufflinks decorated with horseshoes. The horseshoe, a symbol of luck, is not typical of this globally known company of Danish silversmiths. *1960s, ¾ in (2 cm) diam.*

$200–250

Smoking accessories

have become highly collectible, perhaps because of the decline in popularity of smoking itself. It is not difficult to find beautifully designed, imaginative, and unusual pieces at prices to suit all budgets.

Many desirable smoking accessories such as cigar, cigarette, and match cases, as well as lighters and cigarette dispensers, can be found at collectors' shows, antique stores, general auctions, and even flea markets. Finer or rarer pieces are available from specialized dealers or auctions.

An Italian clockwork cigarette dispenser with feet shaped like small devils' heads and an angel-shaped finial. *c. 1950s, 13½ in (34 cm) high.*

$300–500

From tin to tortoiseshell

Made for storing matches, vesta cases (named after a type of match and also known as matchsafes) have a rough or ribbed strip at the base for striking the match. They were made from a variety of materials including tin, brass, ivory, wood, and tortoiseshell. Silver and gold vesta cases—ranging from simple pieces with a scrolled engraving to a novelty shape such as a crown—are the most sought after. These can be found for as little as $30–60 for a plain silver or plated example, but generally cost around $50–250. Look for silver cases by Unger Brothers, Gorham, and Reed & Barton. Examples with ornate, repoussé designs are sought after, and tend to fetch $300–500 or more. High-quality cases were often decorated with colored enamels: these can sell for around $150 or more, depending on the complexity and quality of the enameling.

Cedar fresh

Rather than leaving cigars in the wooden boxes in which they were shipped, smokers stored them in elaborate boxes made of wood, silver, and hardstone. These were lined with cedar to prevent the cigars from drying out, and some—known as humidors—featured a water container to keep the cigars fresh. Values usually depend on type of material used, maker, decoration, and size.

A silver vesta case with an engraved foliate pattern and engraved initials; it has a hallmark for Birmingham, England. *1903, 2 in (5 cm) high.*

$60–90

A night on the town

Cigar cases were often molded in cigar shapes. Cases designed to hold three or four cigars were produced from the mid-19th century onward in materials such as leather, wood, papier-mâché, silver, and gold. From time to time, single cigar cases are found, sometimes with an extinguisher, so a half-smoked butt could be saved. As these cases are still usable today, prices can be high, even for leather examples. A mock-crocodile-skin holder can cost $120–300 or more, while silver and gold cases can cost upward of $200–400, depending on condition, maker, and decoration.

Cutting edge

In the late 19th century, novelty cigar cutters were made in such shapes as animals, people, and liquor bottles. Popular because they are still usable, silver table-mounted novelty cigar cutters can sell for $150–1,200 or more. There are also many pocket versions made from brass in shapes such as shoes and champagne bottles, which are available for around $50–300.

Slim cases

Cigarette cases were mainly of gold, silver, or were silver- or chrome-plated. The flat surface was perfect for decoration, including enameled or engraved designs. A simple, plated, early-20th-century case by makers such as Elgin or Evans can

A closer look at... a Dunhill lighter

Dunhill is one of the most collectible lighter manufacturers and has a heritage going back to the 1920s. Look out for unusual combinations of function and fine materials. The company marked many of the parts on complex examples with a matching serial number, so check that these are consistent.

The chimney protects the flame from wind, indicating that this is the Sports model

The casing is made from solid silver

The integral watch is a rare feature, introduced around 1927

The matching serial number is stamped on different parts

A Swiss-made, Dunhill Unique Sports, manual, gas pocket-watch lighter. If the filler cap that screws into the bottom had been a replacement, the value would have been reduced. *1927, 2¼ in (5.5 cm) high.*
$3,500–4,500

cost less than $50, whereas a finely lacquered piece from the same period made under a partnership between Dunhill and Namiki of Japan may be worth in excess of $800–1,200.

Need a light?

Portable lighters appeared in the early 20th century. Dunhill is the most collectible name: it first issued its Unique lighter (still produced today) in 1923. Look for lighters with extra functions, such as watches or powder compacts, especially if they are concealed. These can fetch high prices, often in excess of $1,500–2,000. Models with lacquer or coverings such as shagreen and leather cost around

$150–800 or more and are more sought after than plainer versions, which can be worth $100–250. Solid-silver or gold lighters can cost around $300–800. Later gas-filled versions, such as the brick-shaped Rollagas, are usually of less interest than 1920s–40s models, but precious-metal examples can fetch around $80–300. Zippo lighters appeal to specialized collectors due to the huge variety of decoration available. Early Zippos featuring applied chrome-plated brass *metallique* designs, produced from 1935 to 40, are particularly collectible, and can be worth over $2,000. Other names to look out for include Thorens and Ronson.

Did You Know?

In 1919 Frederick Charles Wise and Willey Greenwood developed a lighter that could be struck with one hand, using a horizontally placed flint and striking wheel. This prototype for the Dunhill Unique lighter was made from a discarded mustard can and can still be seen in London's Dunhill Museum. It marked a turning point for the Alfred Dunhill company.

Top Tips

- Check the interior of metal vestas and cigar and cigarette cases for signs of wear to the gilding; this reduces value.

- Learn to spot the difference between American, European, and English silver marks on vesta cases. US examples are stamped "STERLING," while English items are hallmarked, and European cases have numbers.

- Look for fine detailing and a deep striker on novelty, animal-shaped vesta cases; plainer pieces with shallow strikers are probably reproductions.

- Use vintage boxes for display or serving only—do not store cigars in them, as they are not usually airtight.

- Check lighters for major wear, dents, and splits, as well as missing or replaced parts, which lower the value.

BUY

Elegant pre-1960s silver cigarette boxes by respected companies are relatively inexpensive and make attractive dressing-table boxes. Prices are unlikely to fall.

A hallmarked silver cigarette box with a cedar- lined interior, made by Mappin & Webb of Birmingham, England. *1947, 10 in (25.5 cm) long.*
$150–200

KEEP

Prices for lighters by notable makers, in good condition, have risen over the past decade, and they should continue to do so as this area becomes more popular and attracts new collectors.

A Swiss-made, silver-plated, Dunhill Unique Standard pocket lighter. The plating on this example is in good condition and the casing has no scratches or dents, adding to its value. *1940s, 2½ in (6 cm) high.*
$120–180

Powder compacts first

appeared in the 1900s, but it was the growing popularity of the car in the 1920s and 30s that helped to take them out of the boudoir and into the realm of fashion accessories.

Increasing mobility after World War I created a demand for portable grooming kits. More women began to use cosmetics and it became socially acceptable to reapply makeup in public. The first powder compacts were made in the US and France, and by the 1930s they were being produced in vast numbers by many countries. Most compacts were made of silver plate, chrome plate, or gold plate, but other metals were also used, as well as tortoiseshell, mesh, and Bakelite.

Plain or heavily detailed, compacts came in all shapes, sizes, and prices. Some even had mechanisms that allowed them to play music. Elegance gradually gave way to souvenir-led designs and novelty items: both vintage soft toy and compact enthusiasts, for example, would relish finding a Schuco soft toy with a concealed powder container.

If these are a little extreme, however, you should aim to seek out stylish compacts with intriguing mechanisms and novelty value. Coty, Kigu, Evans, and Stratton are among the leading names. Slender compacts from the 1930s decorated in a typical Art Deco style are particularly popular.

By the 1960s, the advent of compressed powder and disposable containers meant that powder compacts had, for practical purposes at least, had their day. But their beauty and the nostalgia they evoke continue to appeal both to collectors and the fashion conscious.

▲ **An Evans silvertone-plated starburst-design Standard Carry All compact**, with chain-link handle and original cardboard tag. This compact was designed to hold other accessories and has space for cigarettes. *c. 1950, 5½ in (14 cm) long.*

$200–250

▼ **An Evans Tapset lady's compact**, with plated Scottie dog motifs on the lid. Scottie dog items are hugely collectible in their own right. *c. 1930s, 2¼ in (5.5 cm) wide.*

$50–80

▼ **A mother-of-pearl compact by Ansico.** Mother-of-pearl cases often have missing sections or splits in the covering—original and complete examples command a premium. *1950s, 2 in (5 cm) wide.*

$30–50

▲ **A musical compact and lipstick with musical mechanisms by Thorens.** The compact plays "The Night They Invented Champagne" and retains its original box (not shown). *1950s, 4 in (10 cm) wide.*

$150–250

▲ **A Schick Mfg. Co. mother-of-pearl covered compact**, with gold link chain. It is unusual to find compacts in mint condition and complete with all their accessories, such as the fabric pouch and lipstick holder. This one also has space for cigarettes in a compartment on the underside. *c. 1949, 6 in (15 cm) long.*

$150–250

A Georg Jensen silver compact. Jensen was a notable Danish silversmith, and anything by him is highly sought after. He often used animals and natural motifs. *c. 1925, 2 in (5 cm) wide.*

$800–1,200

Collectors' Tips

- Use an old toothbrush and cotton swab to clean powder traces from compacts
- Make sure the compact's hinge is sound and that it opens and shuts easily
- Do not wash any part of a compact, including powder sifter and puff

◀ **A Coty, brushed-gold compact and lipstick.** Manufacturers often ingeniously combined other features into compacts, such as the lipstick holder in the hinge. This can add value and interest. *1950s, 3¼ in (8.5 cm) wide.*

$50–80

▼ **An enameled compact and cigarette case** by Chelsea Cigarettes. In the 1920s, smoking was fashionable and combined cases were common. *1920s, largest 3¼ in (8.5 cm) wide.*

$150–250 for pair

▲ **A mirrored musical compact, with a carved glass oriental scene.** This compact still has its original box and fabric carrying case, which increases its value. *1950s, 3 in (7.5 cm) wide.*

$100–150

▲ **A Pilcher circular gold-plated compact.** Condition will usually determine the value—this compact, with its polished horse design on the lid, is in mint condition, which is unusual for such a practical item. *c. 1950s, 3¾ in (9.5 cm) diam.*

$70–100

▶ **A compact, lipstick, and leather case, by Dorset Fifth Avenue.** Light reflects off the finely engraved pattern on the surface of this compact, creating an interesting visual effect. *1950s, 6¾ in (17 cm) wide.*

$60–90

Costume jewelry was glamorized

by Hollywood in the 1930s and is still highly prized. Many women wear their glorious costume pieces as proudly as if they were crafted from genuine gold, diamonds, and precious jewels.

The fashion for "frankly fake" jewelry was popularized by Coco Chanel, who turned replicas of precious jewelry into accessories in their own right.

Paris leads the way

Chanel thought of jewelry as decorative rather than a display of wealth. She mixed the faux with the priceless and wore lots of bold jewelry. Wealthy trendsetters loved the look and by the early 1920s she was selling costume jewelry in her Paris couture house. Many of her signature designs—button earrings, outsized pearls, gilt chains, and *pâte de verre* (molded glass) crosses—date from this era. Pieces made during her lifetime are generally of fine quality, and sell for about $500–1,500 or more.

Fellow Parisian fashion designer Elsa Schiaparelli also produced costume jewelry in the 1930s.

Although her pieces had a big impact on fashions of the time, they were produced in limited numbers and can now fetch between $800 and $1,500. After the 1950s, her designs were produced under license by other makers who often featured abstract leaves, shells, and snails made from flamboyant stones and iridescent crystal. Pieces sell for about $150–800.

Chanel's and Schiaparelli's early works were exciting and innovative, but they looked like exaggerated versions of precious pieces. The impetus for change came from the US.

New York style

During the 1920s, New Yorker Miriam Haskell designed jewelry aimed at America's most stylish women. She used inexpensive materials, such as artificial seed pearls, in lavish quantities and daring new ways:

A pair of Chanel gilt button earrings, with Chanel's classic double-C motif. *1980s, 1 in (2.5 cm) diam.*

$60–90

necklaces, earrings, bracelets, and pins were layered with stones resembling glitzy bunches of grapes.

Jewelry by Haskell is extremely well made, being assembled by hand with hidden wires and attached to gold-plated filigree bases. Pieces from the 1920s to the 1940s are rarer than later items, but the complexity and detail in Haskell's jewelry are more important than the date. A small 1940s pin and earrings with large faux pearls surrounded by smaller pearls in the form of a fruit with leaves can be worth around $150, whereas a 1960s necklace from the Shooting Star line, with a built-up central motif and strings of faux pearls hand-wired to look like sheaves of wheat, can be worth $1,200–1,500.

Some designers to look for:
■ Joseff ■ Miriam Haskell ■ Hobé ■ Schiaparelli ■

A Joseff of Hollywood necklace and matching earrings. Bold, fanlike motifs are characteristic of Cocktail jewelry. The molded pattern and boldly set single-color stone typify Joseff's work. *1940s, earrings 3½ in (9 cm) long.*

$800–1,200

A Miriam Haskell diamanté and simulated seed-pearl pin, with matching earrings. A layered, three-dimensional effect is a classic element of Haskell's work. *1940s, earrings 1¼ in (3 cm) long.*

$400–600

Haskell started marking her pieces with "haskell" in an oval stamp in the late 1940s. Unmarked designs are attributed to her by the quality of workmanship and distinctive look. Values vary from around $120–180 for a simple pair of clip earrings to more than $3,000 for a complex necklace, earrings, and bracelet set.

The age of plastics

During the 1920s and 30s, Bakelite was used for costume jewelry. A wide variety of pins, bracelets, and chain necklaces with small fruit charms were produced in jazzy colors of jade, orange, yellow, red, and chocolate brown. Look for deeply cut pieces with geometric or whimsical designs,

or bright colors. Items can be found for $80–120 or less, and the majority sell for less than $800.

Bakelite jewelry is highly prized and modern copies abound. Vintage pieces rarely carried a maker's mark, but can often be identified by signs of wear, such as light, uneven, crisscrossing scratches on the surface. Most genuine articles are heavier than modern period-style pieces, and the clasps are usually attached with screws or pins rather than glue.

Hollywood greats

Movie moguls liked their stars to be seen wearing pieces that conveyed a larger-than-life glamour, both on and off the screen. Eugene Joseff, the leading supplier of costume jewelry to the movie industry, made pieces that photographed well. Using simple designs, he kept the stones to a minimum to show off the metal's shape and texture. Most Joseff pieces have a gold-matte finish, known as Russian gold, developed to minimize the glare from studio lights.

The majority of his designs are stamped "Joseff of Hollywood" or "Joseff." Pieces that once belonged to, or styles that were worn by, film stars are the most valuable. A Russian gold Sun-shaped pin set with clear

A laminated cast-phenolic bangle, in colored stripes. *1930s, 3 in (7.5 cm) wide.*

$250–350

rhinestones and worn by Pier Angeli can fetch around $500–600.

Joseff's fellow Hollywood designer, William Hobé, took 18th-century jewelry designs such as sprays, ribbon garlands, and floral baskets and reworked them in quality materials like silver and silver-gilt. Hobé is noted for his hand-setting and finely executed metalwork. His 1930s pieces can fetch $300–800, but those from the 1960s onward can cost as little as $50–80.

▪ Trifari ▪

A Hobé silver bow pin, set with multicolored crystals. Romantic bows covered with flowers are one of Hobé's hallmarks. *1940s, 4 in (10 cm) long.*

$200–300

A Schiaparelli red and iridescent crystal bracelet, with matching earrings. Unusual colors and leaf shapes are typical of 1950s Schiaparelli costume jewelry. *1950s, bracelet 7½ in (19 cm) long.*

$300–500

A Trifari pin in vermeil (gold-plated sterling silver), with rhinestones and blue enamel. Trifari often made fruit-shaped pins after World War II. *1940s. 1½ in (3.75 cm) long.*

$180–220

Cocktails for two

When the US entered World War II in late 1941, European supplies had already dried up and restrictions were placed on the use of materials such as base metals, which were needed for the war effort. Even so, costume jewelry thrived, with designers turning to new materials such as Lucite for stones, and using sterling silver instead of base metal.

The major makers of American costume jewelry in the 1940s were Coro and Trifari. Both started out making copies of Art Deco jewelry, then came into their own when they created Cocktail jewelry, worn by glamorous socialites to evening parties. This bold, sculptural style featured raised draped motifs and curving lines, along with bizarre combinations of vivid colored stones and the extravagant use of gold.

Coro's double clips (Duettes), which could be worn individually as two separate pins or combined as a single piece, were a huge hit. Values range from around $150 to $1,000. Other definitive Coro designs include a donkey cart pin, a blowfish pin, and a pin in the shape of a hand. Pieces from the 1950s onward can often be found for less than $80, while pieces from the 1930s and 40s often reach $300–500 or more.

Trifari is closely associated with "tutti-frutti" jewelry, set with carved pastes and *pâte-de-verre* pieces made from molded glass. Crowns, inspired by historical movies of the time, were specialties, made from the 1930s to the 50s. The Coronation Gems line was introduced in 1953 to mark the

Did You Know?

Metal-frame Christmas jewelry in seasonal greens and reds first appeared in the late 1940s. In 1950 the wives and mothers of American servicemen stationed in Korea sent their husbands and sons corsage-shaped pieces for Christmas or wore them as a reminder of their loved ones overseas. Even now, many designers introduce Christmas tree jewelry in their collections.

A closer look at... a Stanley Hagler necklace and earrings

Hagler's fantasy jewels have an international cult following. The New York City-based costume jeweler worked briefly for Miriam Haskell before setting up on his own in the late 1950s. Picking up on Haskell's layering and intricate design, Hagler took it one step further to create bigger, more opulent, highly colorful pieces.

Seed beads were combined with larger ornaments like glass leaves or crystals— a Hagler characteristic

The beaded areas are built up in the centers, so that they appear three-dimensional

The color is typically bright and eye-catching

A Stanley Hagler floral motif necklace and earrings, with faux-coral glass petals, beads, cabochons, and drops. Each individual piece is hand-wired to a filigree backing, a characteristic of Hagler's style. *1980s, necklace 22½ in (57 cm) long.*
$800–1,200

coronation of Britain's Elizabeth II. Trifari's "jelly-belly" animals designed by Alfred Philippe are by far the most sought after—these have Lucite centers modeled to form the animal's abdomen. Silver-gilt jelly-bellies from the 1940s and 50s command the top prices of more than $300–500.

To Europe and back

Christian Dior produced some of the most innovative costume jewelry of the 1950s, recreating 18th- and 19th-century designs with obviously nonprecious stones, such as iridescent crystals in place of diamonds. He made costume jewelry for two markets: exclusive couture pieces and the more easily found licensed pieces made for upscale stores. Mitchell Maer in Britain and Kramer in the US held the first licenses, and from 1955 onward the German firm Henkle & Grosse acquired all rights.

Dior designs are stamped with a date. Pre-1970s pieces are the most desirable, although post-1974 pieces are less expensive, at about $80–150, and offer an affordable way to start a collection. A pair of earrings simply set

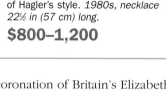

A Coro Duette bouquets of flowers pin, in enameled silver with red glass beads, green glass, and clear rhinestones (shown front and back). *1930s, 2¾ in (7 cm) long.*
$250–350

A Dior pendant pin, rhodium-plated with royal blue glass stones and iridescent rhinestones. *1958, 3 in (7.5 cm) long.*

$200–300

with colored stones may fetch around $60–120. Pieces that are intricate or date from the 1960s or before often sell for about $800–1,200.

When selecting a piece, check the quality of the stones, which are usually rhinestones. It is their clarity, cut, and sparkle that attract collectors.

Into the Space Age

The futuristic designs of early 1960s costume jewelry featured geometric forms in chic combinations such as black, white, and red. Enamel, plastics, and white metal were used, while designs included solid plastic bracelets and rings, rectangular and circular pendants on long chains, and necklaces and belts made from disks and squares. Geometric earrings were especially popular. The Parisian couturiers Pierre Cardin, André Courrèges, and Paco Rabanne are some of the most important names in Space Age costume jewelry. They produced limited-edition pieces as well as more readily available licensed designs. The more common mass-produced items can be found for around $80–150.

Larger than life

Kenneth Jay Lane's outrageous, outsized interpretations of valuable pieces were a big hit with the 1960s jet set, and they were often featured in the fashion magazine *Vogue*. Lane used flashy gilt and flamboyant enamels with abandon. He liked massive plastic cabochons in gaudy turquoise, pink, and coral. His larger-than-life panther pins and animal-head pieces now fetch $150 or more.

Look for pieces with bright colors and sparkling stones, as well as Oriental-inspired designs. A pair of earrings can usually be found for around $80–100, but many of Lane's

pieces, such as his necklaces, can exceed $150–300, with a few reaching $800.

Retro revival

The English company Butler & Wilson was at the forefront of the retro costume-jewelry revival of the late 1970s and 1980s, taking old favorites and updating them with a slightly brash 1980s twist. Its signature piece was a salamander pin. Many tip Butler & Wilson as a good name to collect, so it is worth keeping an eye out for its work, which can sometimes be picked up art flea markets. Expect pieces to command around $50–80 and upward.

BUY

Christmas tree jewelry is growing in popularity, with plenty of variety and scope for collectors. Pieces are available at a range of prices, and growing interest is likely to push up value.

An unsigned Austrian pin, with multicolored and clear rhinestones. This is an early piece in an unusual design, with clear, baguette-cut stones for the candles. *1950s, 3 in (7.5 cm) high.*

$60–90

KEEP

Classic pieces by Miriam Haskell are rising in value, since the look is in vogue and her work is usually of fine quality.

A Miriam Haskell three-strand necklace, with faux and baroque pearls and poured-glass beads. Haskell is known for her faux pearls, and combinations of faux pearls with colored beads are sought after. *1940s, 20 in (51 cm) circ.*

$250–300

BUY

Lobsters were a favorite with the Surrealists during the 1930s and the motif also features in much costume jewelry. Animal subjects are consistently popular, so they are likely to hold their value, or appreciate.

A pink-enamel lobster pin, with claws on springs. Look for lobster pins with spring "snapping" claws, like this one, as they command higher prices. *1930s, 3¼ in (8 cm) long.*

$80–120

KEEP

Butler & Wilson's pieces are still comparatively inexpensive, but values may rise as 1980s styles are being revived by fashion houses.

A Butler & Wilson dancing couple pin, with clear paste heads and black and clear rhinestones. The movement in the skirt and the classic glitzy black-and-white design make this piece typical of Butler & Wilson. *1980s, 4¾ in (12 cm) long.*

$60–90

Top Tips

- Look for makers' marks on clasps, earring backs, or pin backs, and inside catches or on closures.
- Avoid altered or damaged pieces.
- Ask a jeweler or specialized restorer to reset loose stones.
- Expect a bit of wear and tear on enamels, but avoid pieces with significant chipping or touch-ups.
- Keep hairspray, perfume, soap, and body lotion away from costume pieces.
- Do not soak costume jewelry in liquids, which can loosen crystals from their settings and discolor the finish.
- Clean paste jewelry with a lightly dampened cloth or cotton swab.
- Remove tarnish from silver-gilt pieces with a jeweler's polishing cloth; don't buff hard—gold plating can rub off.
- Store pieces individually in padded bags and boxes to avoid damage.

Jewelry ranges in style from the traditional to the avant-garde. Not only can pieces represent an excellent investment, but they can also be worn on special occasions without compromising their value.

An Art Nouveau enameled silver pin in the shape of a pansy. *c. 1890, 2½ in (6 cm) high.*

$100–150

The jewelry of the last 200 years embraces everything from sentimental remembrances of the late 19th century, through the groundbreaking fashion changes of the 1920s and 30s, to sleek modern-day designs.

Victorian keepsakes

Nothing epitomizes Victorian jewelry more than the cameo: a carved miniature relief sculpture, usually made from a hard stone, a gem, or a shell, with the subject in a color that contrasts with the background. Good-quality 19th-century examples can be worth $500–800 and upward. Early 20th-century pieces, often made as souvenirs, can be found for $80–150, although the carving can be crude.

Mourning pieces were often inscribed with the name of the deceased and contained a lock of his or her hair. Jewelers favored enamel, amethysts, and seed pearls (a symbol of tears). Carved jet chains, crosses, and pins were especially popular. Prices start at about $60–90 for small, rolled-gold mourning pins, but can rise

to $300–1,200 or more for earlier 18th-century items.

Finely crafted jewels

Originating in the 1890s and recognizable by their flowing lines, Art Nouveau pieces often depict sinuous plants and mysterious maidens. Art Nouveau jewelers were highly skilled with enamel, especially *plique à jour* (a technique similar to *cloisonné*, which created a stained-glass effect). Pieces of this type can be found from $800 upward. Objects by leading makers such as René Lalique, Tiffany, Unger Brothers, and Kerr & Co. start around $150–500, but can fetch between $3,000 and $100,000 or more.

Much Arts and Crafts jewelry from the 1890s to about 1910 was handmade, and fine hammer marks were often left on the finished piece deliberately, to endorse the authenticity of the craftsmanship. Silver was often used, set with cabochons of agates, moonstones, or mother-of-pearl. Small pins and pendants can be found for less than $300. Pieces by Kalo Shop, Carence Crafters, Frank Gardner Hale, Edward E. Oakes, or Robert Jarvie can be worth $200–800, rising to $7,000–$10,000 or more.

Dazzling days

The bold Art Deco style of the 1920s and 30s gave rise to dazzling jewelry. Platinum was popular, along with diamonds, clear rock crystal, and pearls. The look was sometimes accented with black onyx, red coral, and stones such as sapphires, rubies, and emeralds. Jewelers who embraced the Art Deco style included Oscar Heyman & Brothers, Jacob Mehrlust, Bonner

Manufacturing Company, Walter P. McTeigue Inc., Hirsch & Leff, J. Milhening Inc., W. R. Anderson & Co., Dorst & Co., and Letwin & Sons. Look also for pieces sold through prestigious retail outlets such as Marcus & Co., Saks Fifth Avenue, and Gattle. Numerous inexpensive pieces often of avant-garde design were produced by a number of companies such as The Elgin American Manufacturing Co. of Illinois, Victor A. Picard & Co., and Whiting & Davis. Prices start at around $20–30 (e.g., for a pair of Whiting & Davis silver earrings). In contrast, an Oscar Heyman pin could set you back $10,000 or more, while a J. E. Caldwell & Co. diamond and ruby bracelet could fetch $20,000 plus.

A Victorian-style gold, ruby, and seed-pearl charm in the shape of a lady's hand, with a later 18kt-gold chain. *c. 1910, pendant 1½ in (4 cm) long.*

$120–180

A mourning pin, with human hair in the form of a wheatsheaf, in a gold-plated mount. *1880s, 2¼ in (5.5 cm) high.*

$50–70

A closer look at... a Georg Jensen silver pin

Pins, also known as brooches, have long been popular. Art Deco pins are particularly sought after for their striking, modern design. In order to buy wisely, look at a number of features, including the material, form, details, and maker.

A Georg Jensen silver pin of a grazing deer, with the design number 298 and bearing the maker's mark. The popularity of the maker and the fact that this is typical of his work make this a sought-after piece. *1930s, 2¼ in (5.5 cm) wide.*

$700–1,000

The simple form, clean lines, and lack of intricate surface decoration are typical of Art Deco design and Jensen's style

The legs crossing the roots of the tree add perspective— a sign of good quality

Daring designers

Values for jewelry made during the 1950s and 60s depend on the maker, material, and design, and can range from around $250–500 up to many thousands of dollars for names such as Boucheron, Van Cleef & Arpels, and Asprey. Designers to look for include Tony Duquiette, a Hollywood interior decorator (a small piece may be found for $3,000–5,000), and Courts & Hackett, who began designing custom pieces for rock stars, and whose items can often be found for $300–500 or less.

Jewelry by the Danish company Georg Jensen continues to be popular, with its Modernist styles, usually in silver, incorporating naturalistic motifs and themes. Examples can be found for around $150 for a small, simply designed 1950s silver pin, to $3,000–6,000 for a more decorative pin from the 1930s.

Contemporary names

One notable contemporary jewelry designer is Dinny Hall. Characterized by a simple elegance, her pieces are handmade, usually from silver, resin, gold, and gold plating. Pieces from the late 1990s can be found for $80–300 and look likely to become classics. Other names to look for include Joseph Nolen, Kelly Pearce, Bill Schiffer, Vivienne Jones, and C. L. Sherman. Pieces can often be found for $100–300.

Did You Know?

Diamonds were rare until the discovery of abundant South African mines in the late 19th century. Some antique diamonds have as few as three facets and can be mistaken for glass or marcasite. Older diamonds tend to be less sparkly and have fewer facets than modern equivalents, and you may just pick up a bargain if you spot one that has been mistaken for an imitation stone.

A pair of Dinny Hall gold-plated silver earrings in the shape of elongated, stylized leaves. *c. 2001, 1½ in (3.5 cm) long.*

$100–150

Top Tips

- Look for original cases for antique pieces. These may be stamped with the jeweler's or retailer's name.
- Ask a specialist to test gold content.
- Check the back of a piece for repairs and alterations, which reduce value.
- Watch out for "improvements," such as replacement modern stones, which can look out of place in older settings.

BUY

Silver pins from the 1880s and 90s are representative of the era, yet comparatively inexpensive. No two hand-engraved pieces are identical. These pieces may increase in value as demand grows.

A silver double-horseshoe pin. The good-luck theme of the horseshoe is as popular today as it was 120 years ago. *1880s, 1½ in (4 cm) wide.*

$80–120

KEEP

Many Art Deco diamond and platinum designs were reproduced in paste and silver. Paste pieces with fine workmanship and good detail are highly collectible. They offer excellent value for money if you want the sparkly Art Deco look but can't afford diamonds, and they will remain in demand as period pieces.

A paste-and-silver bow pin. The simplified shapes, strong lines, and bold contrasts of color are characteristic of the period. *1920s, 2 in (5 cm) wide.*

$150–200

SELL

Many 19th century pieces can be worn in more than one way—a pin might convert into a hairpin or pendant, for example. If the design is unbalanced or has been altered, sell it and buy a better piece.

A gold almandine garnet-and-pearl pin. The design is uneven and the pendant fitting is missing. *1860s, 2 in (5 cm) wide.*

$700–1,000

Watches

Watches evolved from 19th-century pocket timepieces, through 1930s Art Deco wristwatches, to designer sports models. Although they all share the same basic function, they include remarkably varied examples of human ingenuity and craftsmanship.

A gold-plated Waltham gentleman's full-hunter pocket watch.
c.1910, 1½ in (4 cm) high.
$100–150

Large numbers of pocket watches were produced in the 19th and early 20th centuries. Most were open-faced, but there was also the hunter (with a flip-open cover protecting the entire face) and the half-hunter (a flip-open cover with a central aperture so that some of the watch face is visible).

Pocket pieces

A pocket watch's value is affected by its maker, and its functions, materials, and decoration. A plain silver- or gold-plated example from the 1890s to the 1920s, either unmarked or by a prolific maker such as Waltham or Elgin, can be found at collectors' shows, auctions, or antique stores for about $60–150. Those made of precious metals such as silver, gold, or platinum are worth more—gold watches can cost $300–800 or more. Decorative features such as enamel or jewels can add value, depending on the quality of workmanship. Look for marks inside the casing, but take care when opening the back, or ask an expert.

Something for the ladies

Ladies' pocket watches, introduced in the late 19th century, are smaller and more decorative and are often enameled or set with stones. Novelty case shapes, such as beetles or violins, or pendant watches hanging from a pin can sell for $250–800 or more.

Rectangular purse watches, which were carried in a bag, are popular. A plain leather-covered example can cost $120–180, while finer models are worth about $300–500.

Aside from timepieces by notable names such as Abraham-Louis Breguet or Patek Philippe—whose watches can reach a staggering $15,000 or more—the most valuable pocket watches are often those with added features. An extra dial showing the current phase of the Moon, a chronograph, a calendar, and features such as a repeating mechanism, add to the value. An unmarked gold watch with all these functions from around 1900 can sell for $1,500 or more.

Changing shapes

Wristwatches became popular in the 1920s, especially those with square-, rectangular-, or octagonal-shaped faces, often with Art Deco styling. In the 1940s, watches often matched a

Some 1970s watches to look for:
■ Spaceman ■ Pierre Cardin ■ Sicura■

A Spaceman Audacieuse automatic wristwatch by OMAX, with a date function, on a metal bracelet. This model was designed by André Le Marquand in 1972, originally for the Catena watch company. When these watches were released at the 1973 Basel Watch and Jewelry Show they caused a sensation—nobody thought that such avant-garde angular lines would sell. *c. 1974, face 2 in (5 cm) wide.*
$400–600

A Pierre Cardin wristwatch, with a movement by Jaeger-LeCoultre. This watch combines a stylish look with a fine-quality mechanism. The strap has been replaced. *1970s, face 2 in (5 cm) wide.*
$300–500

A Sicura windup wristwatch, with a gold-filled bezel and bronze dial, on a black-patent plastic strap. Sicura are known for their stylish period designs and quality mechanisms. *1970s, face 1½ in (4 cm) wide.*
$120–180

woman's jewelry, or were designed for military use. Futuristic styling arrived in the 1950s.

Watches made from the 1930s to the 60s by known makers range from $80 to $1,000 or more. A stainless-steel Rolex from the 1950s may sell for around $500–800. Gold watches by the Swiss company Longines can be worth $300–700.

Top watches

Many people collect by the maker: Rolex, Patek Philippe, Audemars Piguet, Vacheron & Constantin, and Jaeger-LeCoultre are the most notable and expensive. A gold Patek Philippe chronograph from 1939 can command up to $30,000. Look for watches by American companies such as Elgin and Hamilton, whose prices are commonly up to around $150–500.

Watches from the 1960s and 70s often have visually exciting cases. The top names and finest-quality examples can command high prices ($1,000–1,500 or more), but sports models often cost less and are a good way of owning a top brand-name watch—a 1970s Heuer Carrera can be found for around $300–600.

An Art Deco Movado lady's silver gilt and black enamel purse watch. There is damage to one corner. *1928, case 2 in (5 cm) wide.*

$300–400

Top Tips

- Keep all sales material and any details of restoration work; these add value.
- Check the condition of the case, since this is vital, and remember that a clean dial may indicate either a well looked-after watch or a replaced dial.
- Buy from reputable dealers—there are many fakes on the market.
- Look for the British government-issue arrow mark inscribed on the back or printed on the face of a watch; this denotes that it is a UK military watch.
- Look for popular makes that combine cutting-edge design, representative of the era, with a good-quality mechanism.

Collectors' Tales

"I knew a dentist who went to an antique market and bought a Rolex as a present for his wife. It was an 18kt-gold perpetual watch. He got a jeweler to check the strap and it was genuine, so he assumed the rest of the watch was too. He thought he'd gotten a good deal for $9,000, so he bought it. But when he showed it to a watchmaker he discovered that the strap was the only part of the watch that was genuine and it was only worth about $800–900."

Mike Pullman, New York City

BUY

Watches produced from the 1930s to the 50s by big names, with simple styles and little ornamentation, are growing in popularity. Examples in good condition with original cases and mechanisms will hold their value, if not rise.

A Rolex gentleman's watch. This example has a 9kt-gold case, which makes it highly desirable. Both the dial and the movement were made and signed by Rolex, which adds to the value. *1950s, 1¾ in (4 cm) high.*

$400–600

SELL

Accessories for pocket watches such as "Albert" chains and watch stands are of little practical use today. Sell to a collector with an interest in period accessories and invest in a watch from an area that is growing in value.

■ Sorna ■ Buler ■ Vulcain ■

A Sorna windup wristwatch, on its original steel bracelet. Watches by good makers with extra features, such as an alarm, are desirable. *1970s, face 1½ in (4 cm) wide.*

$300–400

A Buler windup wristwatch, on a black leather strap. The face is shaped like a TV, a design feature characteristic of the era. *c. 1970, face 1¾ in (4.5 cm) wide.*

$100–150

A Vulcain lady's wristwatch, on a gold-plated bracelet and with its original tag. The known maker, the 1970s shape, and the bracelet make it desirable. *1970s, face ¾ in (2 cm) wide.*

$80–120

A 9kt-gold pocket watch fob chain, with an older unengraved revolving citrine seal fob. The addition of the Victorian seal makes this piece attractive to specialists. *c. 1900, 8 in (20 cm) long.*

$150–200

Digital watches are stylish, often chunky, and typical of the 1970s. They were the first watches to adopt the advances in electronic microcircuitry—state-of-the-art 1970s technology that introduced light emitting diode (LED) displays.

When quartz-driven LED digital watches arrived at the beginning of the 1970s, American and Swiss manufacturers were the first to harness the new technology. In 1971 the Hamilton Watch Company in the US started producing the Pulsar, the world's first wristwatch with no moving parts. Limited-edition 18-karat gold Pulsars can now fetch anything up to $1,000–1,500. A year later, Longines released its first LED model and by the mid-1970s most Swiss makers had begun introducing digital ranges.

Other notable early digitals include Omega's 1601, 1602, and 1603 models and Citizen's Quartz Crystron LED; a mint-condition Omega 1601 can fetch upward of $800. But the ever-lowering cost of the technology meant that liquid crystal display (LCD) digitals from Asia soon flooded the market. By the end of the decade, most quality watchmakers in Switzerland had reverted to making traditional watches.

Compared to mainstream watch collecting, the digital market is not yet widely known or understood. Pieces can still be found for sale in a range of venues from flea markets and collectors' shows to vintage clothing and accessory shops. But increasing interest from both those subscribing to retro fashion trends and hard-core collectors is already pushing up prices.

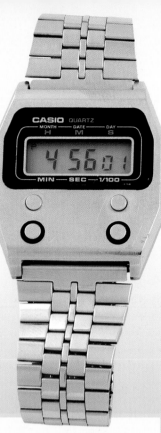

▲ **A rare, Casio 52 LCD wristwatch on a steel bracelet.** Casios with original metal bracelets are always worth keeping—this watch includes time, day/date, stopwatch, and chronograph functions. Casio produced many versions, and collectors are eager to collect all the variations. *c. 1981, face 1½ in (4 cm) wide.*

$60–90

▶ **A Casio 505 Data Bank LCD wristwatch on a steel bracelet.** Casio is a leading name in the digital watch collecting market—always look for the original papers and labels. *c. 1980, face 1¾ in (4.5 cm) wide.*

$80–120

TELE-MEMO 30
5 MULTI-FUNCTION ALARMS WITH 8-LETTER MESSAGES

5 yrs.

CASIO

CASIO Module No. 671/871

CASIO DATA BANK
WATER RESIST

▼ **A Fairchild LCD wristwatch with a hexagonal steel bezel, on a stainless-steel bracelet.** Watches by Fairchild, an upscale specialty company, are always sought after. *1970s, face 1½ in (4 cm) wide.*

$80–120

▶ **A Fairchild Timeband LCD wristwatch with gold-plated bezel on a gold-plated bracelet.** One of the earliest, and top line, LCD watches. Its value is likely to rise in time. *1978, face 1½ in (4 cm) wide.*

$40–60

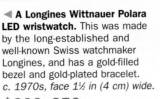

◀ **A Longines Wittnauer Polara LED wristwatch.** This was made by the long-established and well-known Swiss watchmaker Longines, and has a gold-filled bezel and gold-plated bracelet. *c. 1970s, face 1½ in (4 cm) wide.*

$200–250

◀ **A Junghans Mega 1 LCD wristwatch with a hexagonal steel bezel on an original black-leather strap.** This is the British version of the first radio-controlled watch and was fashioned by Frog Designs. It synchronizes itself daily between 3 a.m. and 6 a.m. to the atomic clock in Frankfurt, Germany. *1991, face 1¾ in (4.5 cm) wide.*

$280–320

▶ **A Fairchild LCD wristwatch with a steel bezel and black face on a steel bracelet.** This is one of the earliest LCD watches, and from a prestigious manufacturer. *c. 1970s, face 1½ in (4 cm) wide.*

$100–150

Collectors' Tips

■ Before buying a vintage digital watch, check that all the functions work and that there is no battery leakage

■ Replace or remove watch batteries as soon as they run out

◀ **A Pulsar Sport Timer LCD wristwatch on an original black-plastic strap.** This rare watch was novel at the time: it can time four people at once, thanks to the combined stopwatch settings. *c. 1970s face 1½ in (4 cm) wide*

$80–120

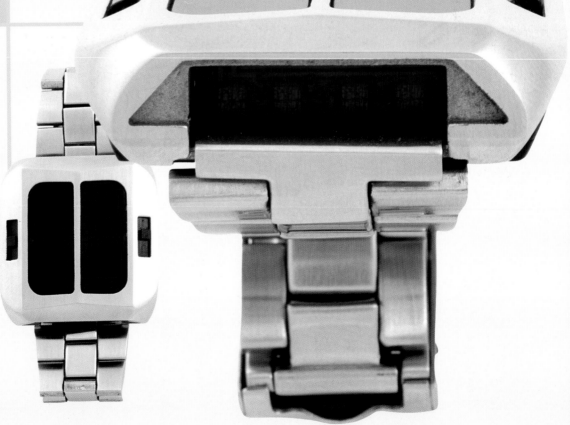

▶ **A Synchronar 2100 solar-powered driver's watch with a LED readout on a stainless-steel bracelet.** This unusual watch designed by Roger Riehl has two solar panels *(see right)* that power it for up to a year. The digital display *(see far right)* on the side can be read while driving a car. The watch is calendar-programmed until 2100, hence its name. *1973, face 1½ in (4 cm) wide.*

$1,200–1,800

Toys, Dolls, and Teddy Bears

Nothing evokes childhood more immediately and vividly than an old toy. Each generation harks back to the playthings it enjoyed—the old-fashioned cars, dolls, and teddy bears of the early 20th century, or perhaps the Barbies and Tiny Tears of the 1960s and 70s.

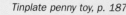

Tinplate penny toy, p. 187 ①

Dinky van, p. 189 ②

The nostalgic charm of...

Toys bring back fond memories of rainy afternoons in the past spent playing with a dolls' house, a favorite teddy bear, or a fleet of model cars. Each generation harks back to the playthings it especially enjoyed, and many of them are now sought-after collectibles.

Toy cars and trucks are not only fun to play with; they also show how real cars have changed over the years. From early tinplate toys ① to die-cast versions—the Dinkys ② of the 1930s onward, Corgis ③ of the 1960s onward, and Hot Wheels toys of the 1970s and 80s—they offer a parade of vintage cars for the living-room floor. Although early tinplate toys can be scarce and

valuable, later toys and those that are smaller are still affordable. But to reach the highest values, toys should be in good condition and retain their original box.

Some manufacturers have devised highly successful lines of dolls that prove irresistible to collectors. Many Annalee dolls ④, first sold in the early 1950s, had limited production runs and individual dolls were constantly replaced with new models, in much the same way that Beanie Babies are today.

Accessories with depictions of classic toy brands such as Hot Wheels ⑤ often have

Mattel Hot Wheels Mantis pin, p. 192 ⑤

Bisque doll, p. 209 ⑥

Madame Alexander doll, p. 215 ⑦

Just as toy cars show how technology has developed over time, dolls from the past century show how fashion has evolved.

Corgi gift set, p. 191

③

④

Annalee soft toy, p. 204

.toys and teddy bears

colorful graphics and can be an inexpensive way of reawakening the child within.

From bisque to Barbie

In the early 20th century, bisque dolls ⑥ were the preserve of the wealthy and were cherished. As a result, dolls by makers such as SFBJ, Jumeau, Heubach, and Kestner can fetch high prices when they are found today.

By the 1950s, these dolls had been replaced by affordable, mass-produced fabric and plastic dolls ⑦ dressed in more casual clothes. Makes such as Lenci, Barbie ⑧, Sasha, and Tiny Tears were on every young girl's wish list.

Many of these dolls were advertised on television, which became commonplace in homes in the 1950s. The spread of TV also brought a new range of characters to life. Companies such as Pelham Puppets had already been making toys under license from Disney, and it wasn't long before a host of new, popular TV characters were also made into toys.

Childhood friends

Teddy bears ⑨ are the kind of childhood friends that often accompany us into adulthood. From the Steiff bears of the 1900s to the Chad Valley and Dean's Rag Book Co. teddies of the 1930s onward, there is always a market for old bears, even those that have been so well loved that they look a little ragged. In fact, some toys ⑩ were even designed to look that way!

Raggedy Anne doll, p. 213

⑧
Barbie doll, p. 216

⑨
Blonde mohair bear, p. 200

⑩

Tinplate toys

are among the earliest mass-produced toys available. They evoke nostalgia for a childhood of imaginative games. The best combine fine detailing, period styling, and renowned makers.

Tinplate toys began to eclipse wooden toys in the early 19th century. Formed of sheets of tinplated steel, which were cut out, shaped, and then decorated, they were easier and cheaper to make. Although tinplate toys from the early 19th century onward are scarce today, and mostly expensive, later, smaller toys are accessible to many. Expect to pay $80–150 for a small, windup, animal-shaped toy of the 1930s–50s.

The toy pioneers

The late 19th and early 20th centuries are the Golden Age of the tinplate toy. Many of the most important producers were German—notable names include Märklin (founded 1856), Gebrüder Bing (1863–1933), Carette (1886–1917), and Ernst Planck (1866–c. 1935). Toys by Märklin and Bing are particularly sought after. The American makers Marx, Strauss, and George W. Brown, and C. I. J. in France, also made fine examples.

Before the 1890s, tinplate toys were hand painted, which allowed for a high level of detail. Boats were among the most popular toys at this time.

Often expensive in their day (with portholes that opened and convincing rigging), examples can now fetch $5,000–30,000 or more. Similarly detailed early toy cars, produced as the automobile gained popularity in the early 20th century, featured lamps, doors that opened, running boards, and wheels with rubber tires. Today these can fetch around $1,000–6,000 and often more.

From the 1900s, makers increasingly used the printing technique of color lithography to decorate their toys with a transfer. It was faster and more economical, but tinplate toys became lighter and less complex. Prices for such toys remain comparatively high today, fetching from a few hundred dollars to thousands of dollars, depending on the type and size of toy, and its complexity and condition.

Penny for them

If you are looking for an inexpensive way to start collecting tinplate toys from the Golden Age, try "penny toys." Often based on their larger counterparts, these small, simply made toys were sold by street vendors. They included trucks, cars, and horse-drawn carts, as well as novelties such as gramophones and babies in carriages. They measure around 4 inches (10 cm) long, are often brightly colored, and are usually decorated with a lithographic transfer. Production peaked around the beginning of the 20th century. Today, examples with detailed designs and embossed areas are the most valuable. A tiny German Meier sewing machine on a stand might fetch $60–80, while a detailed car or truck by a noted maker can be worth up to $800 or more.

The later years

Although quality had declined by the 1920s and 30s, there are still many excellent examples from this period and the from 1950s and 60s. Again, German manufacturers, such as Schuco, Karl Bub, and Distler, led the field. US

A Distler Goose on Platform penny toy with embossed lithographed decoration and an amusing bobbing-head action.
c. 1900, 3½ in (9 cm) long.
$250–300

A battery-powered Bristol Bulldog airplane, by Straco of Japan. The powered action includes a stop-and-go switch and a turning propeller. There is some minor rubbing to the finish. *1950s, 12 in (30.5 cm) long.*

$120–180

BUY

Penny toys in the form of cars, trucks, and buses are worth seeking out. Look for undamaged pieces with intricate decorative details applied by transfer lithography and finely cut details such as a driver, passengers, and opening doors.

A German Meier limousine penny toy, with embossed lithography, a fully modeled driver, and cutout passengers. The toy is in excellent condition, but needs cleaning by an expert to reach its full potential. *c. 1900, 4¼ in (11 cm) long.*

$200–250

makers such as Marx, J. Chein & Co., and Wolverine, also produced colorful, often less expensive models. Cars and motorcycles are often seen: examples by Schuco or Japan's Masudaya could fetch $150–300 or more. Many were driven by windup or (from the 1950s) battery-powered mechanisms. Small, basic, windup vehicles or animals have a whimsical charm. These can be less costly—though if in their original boxes the value can range from $50 to $250, depending on maker, size, date, and condition.

A closer look at... a clockwork tinplate motor coach

Tin cars are among the most collectible type of tinplate toy. Before the classic "limousine" styles of 1900 to the 1920s, cars were made that mimicked the earliest "horseless carriages." These can be highly desirable and valuable.

A painted French motor coach, with a clockwork mechanism, original glass, tufted upholstery, and opening doors. The paint wear on the roof and dashboard exterior does not affect the value much, since the age, size, and shape of the coach make it highly desirable. *c. 1890, 15½ in (39.5 cm) long.*

$5,000–7,000

The model has a clockwork motor drive (detail above), making it one of the earliest automotive toys seen.

The decoration is hand painted, indicating an early toy

The motor coach is finely detailed with lamps and opening doors

KEEP

Pieces like this clockwork motorcycle and rider are sure to retain their popularity. Their bright colors, realistic lithographed detailing, mechanical movement, and automotive subject matter make them immensely popular. If in excellent condition, they're likely to grow in value.

An Arnold Mac 700 clockwork motorcycle, with a movable rider in period clothing. In good working order, and only slightly worn, it has its key and original instruction sheet. *c. 1948, 9 in (23 cm) long.*

$280–320

Dinky toys have enthralled children since the 1930s. Many of us love to acquire and handle the models that once so tantalizingly tempted us in toyshop windows.

Dinky 1:25 SCALE MODELS | **Ford Capri Rally Special 2214**

Dinky toys were still produced until recently, but the pre-1980s models are the ones to look for. Those dating from pre-World War II are especially desirable. Dinkies can be worth $10 to $10,000 or more, so any old play toys or flea-market buys are worth close examination.

Transport your imagination

The forerunners to Dinky, known as Modelled Miniatures, were launched by Hornby in 1931 as accessories to its train sets. The first cars appeared in 1933 and were such a hit that by the following year they were given their own brand name—Dinky.

With the growth in the auto industry, toy cars caught the imagination of children everywhere. The line, made in 1:42 scale, expanded rapidly: by the late 1930s there were more than 200 varieties of car, as well as planes and boats. By 1939 wayside buildings, road signs, and animals were available.

The 1930s is often deemed Dinky's Golden Age, but production was halted

A Ford Capri 1:25 Rally Special, 2214, in red with a black hood and roof. Its original bubble pack is slightly damaged, but the car is in excellent condition. *1974–76, 6¾ in (17 cm) long.*

$100–150

during World War II. After the war some prewar models were reissued; these tend to have fatter wheels, black-finished base plates, and dull colors.

On the right lines

In 1947 the smaller Dinky Supertoys were launched—with a 1:48 scale. Clear plastic windows and spring suspension were introduced in the late 1950s, while the 1960s brought opening doors, hoods, and trunks, and working steering wheels.

A Supertoys Euclid Rear Dump Truck, 965, with its box. *1955–61, box 6 in (15 cm) long.*

$120–180

A closer look at... a Dinky Big Bedford Heinz van

Minor design variations (in particular, in colors and transfers) affect the value of Dinky toys, sometimes leading to great disparity in value between two similar pieces.

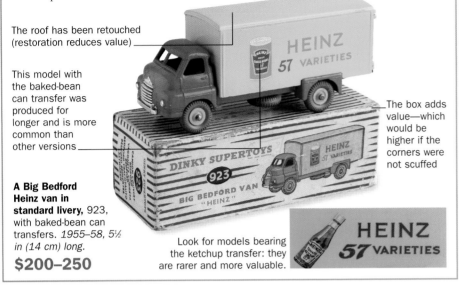

The roof has been retouched (restoration reduces value)

This model with the baked-bean can transfer was produced for longer and is more common than other versions

The box adds value—which would be higher if the corners were not scuffed

A Big Bedford Heinz van in standard livery, 923, with baked-bean can transfers. *1955–58, 5½ in (14 cm) long.*

$200–250

Look for models bearing the ketchup transfer: they are rarer and more valuable.

KEEP

Gift sets are sought after if the set is genuine (all the models are correct) and with its box. Since models were often lost by children playing with them, only a limited number of complete sets survive.

A Post Office Services Gift Set, 299, complete, with its box, all in excellent condition. Unusually for a British post-office set, a pillar-box model was not included. *c. 1957–59, box 11¾ in (30 cm) wide.*

$600–900

SELL

Even popular toys, such as those produced to accompany a TV series, will be of limited value if there is any wear, such as dents, chips, or scratches to the paintwork. The absence of a box will lower the price further. But these items may be attractively inexpensive to a buyer on a budget.

A Lady Penelope's FAB 1 Rolls-Royce, 100, from the *Thunderbirds* TV series, in well-used condition. *1967–75, 5¾ in (14.5 cm) long.*

$20–30

By 1963 competition from Corgi had resulted in financial trouble, and the company was bought by Tri-ang, which continued making Dinky toys until 1980. In 1988 Matchbox acquired the rights to the name and relaunched some of the Dinky line.

Survivors

Pre–World War II toys in good condition are rare and can be worth up to $800 or more. Series 25 trucks and series 28 delivery vans are particularly desirable. Individual Dinky toys were not sold boxed until the mid-1940s (before then they were sold unboxed, out of "trade boxes" containing six models). Gift sets comprising models and accessories were always sold in boxes. Original packaging, in good condition, can add 40 percent or more to the value.

Most of the standard toys from the 1950s to 70s tend to fetch $50–150, with values unlikely to rise. Boxed toys in excellent condition from the 1950s and early 60s make better investments, as do toys with rare variations. Uncommon transfers can add value—a Supertoy 514 Guy Van with a Slumberland mattress transfer (1950–52) can fetch around $250 in mint condition with a box, but the value could be tripled if the van had a Weetabix transfer (1952–54).

A perfect match

Matchbox-made Dinky toys are of high quality, although perhaps lacking the charm of earlier models. In 1991 Matchbox decided to restrict output and limit color reissues in order to enhance collectibility. Its limited editions often fetch $15–50 or less and are unlikely to gain much as so many have been kept pristine.

A P47 Thunderbolt, 734, with red plastic propeller, in excellent condition, complete with bombs. The blister pack is slightly discolored. *1975–78, box 6 in (15 cm) wide.*

$200–250

Corgi toys, launched by Mettoy in 1956

to rival Dinky's domination of the toy car market, have an extra touch of refinement that has won them a loyal fan base. Tiny working parts, combined with generally low prices, make for a winning formula.

To differentiate its models from Dinky, Corgi produced vehicles with clear plastic in the windows—a dramatic departure! Later innovations included Glidamatic spring suspension, hoods and trunks that actually opened, and "jeweled" headlights.

Details like these were thrilling to boys all over the world and by the end of the 1960s Corgi was exporting its toys to more than 120 countries.

In collecting terms, the 1960s currently has an edge over later decades. The key factor is a vehicle's rarity—some were only produced in six-month runs.

A standard Corgi in mint condition, still in its box, can fetch between $50 and $130. Boxes add as much as 40 percent to the value, but, as with other die-cast toys, even the condition of the box has to be taken into account. In general, prices have leveled off in recent years; no one should expect to make a quick profit in this field. But the good news is that many Corgis can be bought for under $30.

Rise and fall

In the 1960s Corgi prospered. A new range, called Corgi Classics, issued to celebrate Mettoy's 30th anniversary in 1964, won the Queen's Award to Industry. But after a warehouse fire in 1969, which destroyed stock and upset the distribution system, many retailers turned to Dinky. In 1983 the receivers were called in, but the company was re-formed as Corgi Toys Ltd. in early 1984.

In collecting circles, Corgi has traditionally been overshadowed by Dinky. During the 1980s and 90s even Matchbox eclipsed Corgi in popularity. But the balance is now shifting, partly because people who loved these toys

A BMC Mini Cooper S 1966 Monte Carlo winner, 339, in red with white roof and with a roof rack and spare wheels; mint, in its box with paperwork. *1967–71, 2¾ in (7 cm) long.*

$60–90

Some TV and film Corgi toys to look for:
■ Batman ■ Popeye ■ James Bond ■ The Avengers ■

A Batmobile with Batman and Robin, 267, the first issue, with its pictorial box. The Batmobile was made from 1966 until 1979 in many variations. Later Batmobiles produced for longer periods would fetch half this value or possibly less. *1966–67, box 6 in (15 cm) wide.*

$600–800

A James Bond Aston Martin DB5, 270, silver with tire slashers, ejector seat, front-mounted machine gun, and other accessories, all in good condition, with box. This variant of the box was fragile, so few have survived. *1968–76, box 6 in (15 cm) wide.*

$600–900

A Popeye Paddle-wagon, 802, with all its original parts and in working order, in a reproduction box. The Popeye, Olive Oyl, Swee' Pea, Bluto, and Wimpy figures move as the toy is pushed across the floor. The price reflects moderate wear and chipping. *1969–72, box 6 in (15 cm) wide.*

$100–150

as children of the 1960s have become adults with cash to spend.

TV times

Where Corgi had the edge over Dinky was with its TV- and film-related toys. This is another reason why Corgi's star is rising: many people are nostalgic for the films and TV shows these playthings represent. Reaching much higher prices than many ordinary cars, such toys are worth looking out for. One of the most successful models of all time, reaching sales of 5 million, was the 1966 Batmobile *(see opposite, far left)*. Other top earners included the 1969 Noddy car (now worth around $1,000 boxed and in mint condition), the *Chitty Chitty Bang Bang* car (around $250–400), *The Man from U.N.C.L.E.'s* Thrush-buster Oldsmobile (around $400–600), and Dick Dastardly's Mean Machine racing car from the *Wacky Races* cartoon series (around $120–180).

Special gifts

Keep your eyes open for Corgi's gift sets. A complete transporter set, with a truck and four cars, can be worth up to $500, whereas the same models sold

A Ford Consul Cortina Super Estate Car, 440, in dark metallic blue with "wood" side-panels, complete with golfer, caddie, clubs, and hand cart; mint, in its box. *1966–69, box 6 in (15 cm) long.*

$150–250

separately might only raise about $400. Also of interest are the variants that were released; most tend to be more valuable, often because they are rarer. The 1964 line of Corgi Classics was discontinued after 1969 but rereleased in 1985 with "Special edition" on the base plate. Originals are usually worth $25–40, while rereleases fetch less than $10. In the Chipperfield's Circus line, released in 1960, animals add an extra dimension, and many collectors relish the challenge of building up the complete set.

The Avengers, a gift set, 40, with Bentley, Lotus Elan, two figures (John Steed and Emma Peel), and three umbrellas; the box is damaged, which reduces the value. The set with a green painted Bentley is worth around 20 percent more than this. *1966–69, box 6 in (15 cm) wide.*

$280–320

Top Tips

- To fetch the highest price within its range, a model should come with its box and both should be in mint condition.
- Look out for rare variations, such as in the body color, hubcaps, and seats, as these increase value.
- Avoid unattractive cars, such as the Marlin Fastback. They are unlikely to rise in price.
- Keep abreast of new Corgi releases. Most of them are limited editions and they often sell out within a matter of weeks.

BUY

Corgi's Whizz Wheels line offered wheels that turned faster so vehicles traveled faster for longer. Examples can be bought for $15–150, but prices look set to rise.

A Rover 2000TC Whizz Wheels, 281, mint; with its window box (the back is shown). This model is uncommon, since it was only produced for about a year. *1971–72, 3¾ in (9.5 cm) long.*

$100–150

KEEP

Corgi's Chipperfield's Circus line is popular. Some models were heavy and damaged their packaging, so few boxes have survived. Demand for the line looks likely to outstrip supply, so prices may rise.

A Chipperfield's Circus Scammell with Menagerie Trailer, 1139, with three animal cages, with its window box. This model is harder to find than other examples, so its relative scarcity makes it more valuable. *1968–72, 9 in (23 cm) long.*

$280–320

Hot Wheels

have become the world's most popular die-cast toy car. Many cars cost just $1–5, but you may be holding on to a gem worth hundreds, so it's well worth finding out if your wheels really are hot.

A Mattel Hot Wheels Mantis pin. The last year buttons were sold with cars was 1971. *c. 1969, 1½ in (4cm) diam.*

$7–10

Toys, Dolls, and Teddy Bears |

Billed as the "fastest metal cars in the world," Mattel's Hot Wheels first entered the die-cast toy market in 1968, quickly becoming more popular than the Matchbox cars by Lesney and toys by other makers. At 1:64 the scale of a true vehicle and less than 3 inches long, Hot Wheels boasted a special torsion-bar suspension and low-friction wheel bearings. Often based on real models, they were very desirable.

Spoiler for choice

Collecting Hot Wheels can be a fun and inexpensive hobby, with thousands of models to choose from, most selling for $10–40. A 1978 Packin' Pacer can be scooped up for $8–15, and cars from The Heroes series of 1979—such as The Hulk or Captain America—for around $30 each.

The most collectable models cost $50 and up, and usually boast hard-to-find variations in paintwork or on the windows, interiors, or base. The variety of wheel—there are over 25—is another factor in determining the value. For example, the Peterbilt Dump Truck No. 100 normally costs $3–5,

but an example with white basic wheels can sell for over $30–40. Consult a reference guide to get acquainted with the many subtle variations and find out what's rare and desirable.

Easy rider

As with many collecting fields, early examples are prized. Many Hot Wheels enthusiasts nostalgically hark back to the Sixties and want the Volkswagen buses and bugs, as well as the Camaros that Mattel made in a number of spectraflame colors (discontinued in 1973 in favor of enamel paint). The Classic '32 Ford Vicky, No. 6250,

A Mattel Hot Wheels red Mercedes Benz C 111, No. 6196, with plastic baseplate. *1972, 3 in (7.5 cm) long.*

$80–120

produced in 1969, came in four colors, while the Custom Volkswagen, No. 6220, c. 1968, was made in seven color variations, although there were 21 vivid colors in all; later models were available in fewer colors. Early models can be identified by a red stripe on the tires that is known as redline. Redline tires were phased out in 1977, and vehicles with this feature are eagerly sought after by collectors. Pre-1972 models also came with a now-desirable collector's button in each blisterpack.

Rev your engines

Special features can drive up the price of Hot Wheels, whether it be detachable or moveable parts or a limited production run. The Sky Show Fleetside, No. 6436, c. 1970, not only had redlines on its truck, but also planes and a launch ramp at the rear, and can be worth

A Mattel Hot Wheels metallic blue Deora, No. 6210. *1968, 2¾ in (7cm) wide.*

$80–120

A closer look at... a Mattel Volkswagen Beach Bomb

Rare or unusual models are the most likely to hold their value or even increase in value. Consider the type of vehicle, the paint, and any accessories it may come with to ensure that you buy or sell wisely.

These were made in the US and Hong Kong. The Hong Kong version has rear-mounted surfboards and is extremely rare, worth thousands of dollars

The detachable surf boards were often lost—if they are missing the value is more than halved

A Mattel Hot Wheels green Volkswagen Beach Bomb, No. 6274. This model came in different colors, including blue and green. Pink is rare. c. 1969, 2½ in (6.5cm) long.

$120–180

A desirable early piece, this model was released in 1969, one year after Hot Wheels were launched

$600–1,000 if complete. The Army Staff Car, No. 9521, c. 1977, sporting an American flag, can sell for $1,000. Extremely hard to find, it was only sold as part of a set, as was The Road King Truck, No. 7615, c. 1974, which can be over $300–400. Cars made in 1973 are valuable, since few models were sold that year: a Show-Off, No. 6982, or Alive '55, No. 6968, worth $150 plus, are good finds. Look too for models from the Real Riders series (1983–86), which can fetch $30–130. With real rubber tires, gray or white hubcaps, and Goodyear markings, they were expensive to produce and are popular.

In on the action

Rare is the company that has not tied in with Hot Wheels for a promotion—Kellogg's, McDonalds, and Shell included—and collectors like these models, since the cars often have extra features. Some collectors prefer early US-made models (production ceased in 1971), although cars made in Hong Kong, Malaysia, France, Italy, Mexico, and Canada also have their enthusiasts. Even today, with Mattel long ago producing its one billionth car, the company continues to make limited editions, commemoratives, and replicas of older models, often with packaging reminiscent of early blister packs. To celebrate the US mission to Mars, an Action Pack with a Mars Rover, marked July 4, 1997, was produced. Limited editions could well become tomorrow's hot buy.

A Mattel Hot Wheels orange and silver Peterbilt Tank Truck, No. 1689. *1981 3¾ in (8cm) long.*

$10–15

KEEP

Some models were made only for short periods, meaning that there are fewer examples on the market. Keep these models because, as demand grows, they are most likely to increase in value.

A Mattel Hot Wheels Heavyweights Funny Money, No. 6005. This model with a silver finish was produced in Hong Kong in 1972 only, so will be harder to find than other models. *1972, 2½ in (6.5 cm) long.*

$150–200

SELL

Colors such as pink and purple were considered too feminine by boys at the time and as such weren't very popular. This makes them rare and highly desirable today, and prices can be surprisingly high. Sell to a collector and invest the money elsewhere.

A Mattel Hot Wheels neon-pink Classic '36 Ford Coupe, No. 6253. The redline wheels also make this more sought after by collectors. *1969, 2¾ in (7 cm) long.*

$220–280

Metal automobile toys

were produced in huge quantities from the 19th century, reaching top speed in the 1920s–40s. Children delighted in bright colors and details. Now these cars are hot collectibles, rather than children's playthings.

An orange Hubley Golden Arrow racer, with white rubber wheels. *c. 1935, 7¼ in (18 cm) long.*
$120–180

The coming of the automobile was greeted enthusiastically by the toy industry. As each new car came on the market, toymakers would replicate it in miniature, so well, in fact, that collectors love these vintage toys not just for nostalgic reasons but also for their social importance. Naturally, toy cars and trucks reflect the era in which they were manufactured, and that couldn't be more true of the Hubley Manufacturing Company's 1929 Packard Straight Eight sedan in cast iron. Based on one of the most luxurious cars ever made, it was an expensive toy that was withdrawn after the Wall Street Crash. With its hinged hood, replica engine, opening doors, and spare tire, the 11-inch sedan is usually lacking its original parts. A complete one recently sold for $24,000. Many of the metal cars and trucks are worth $500–5,000, however, and some can be picked up for less.

Cast-iron quality

By the 1880s toys in cast iron were being produced in large quantities, and remained on the scene until plastic took over in the 1950s. Values of cast-iron toys are affected by complexity, rarity, size, condition, and, sometimes, maker. The casting of older toys was of extremely high quality and pieces had great detail, sharp lines, were very durable, and usually featured strong, bright colors. Desirable details include stenciled phone numbers on yellow cab doors, nickel-plated grilles, electric headlights, spare tires, license plates, and hood ornaments, plus a host of working parts—particularly on construction vehicles—and sometimes passengers inside. One Kenton concrete mixer truck, for example, has a revolving nickel drum like that seen on the genuine article.

The real deal

Many companies made cast-iron cars and trucks, with the heyday of production being from the 1920s to 40s. Names to look for include Arcade, Dent, Kenton, Kilgore, Hubley, Vindex, and A. C. Williams. Arcade even made a virtue of its realistic modeling, marketing the toys under the slogan "They Look Real." Also made around the same time—and no less valuable—are toys in pressed steel. Names to collect include Kingsbury, Buddy L, Keystone, Metalcraft, Kelmite, and American National. It is the pre-World War II Buddy L toys, however, that are really

Some makers to look for...
■ Kilgore ■ Kenton ■ Hubley ■ Arcade ■ Kingsbury ■

A Kenton cast-iron sedan, in blue and black, with separate driver and in excellent condition. Founded in 1890, Kenton began toy production in 1894. Its toys were successful from 1920 to the 1930s, but the factory closed in 1952. Some shapes later appeared under the Utexiqual name c. 1953–82. *c. 1925, 6½ in (16.5 cm) long.*
$500–700

A Kilgore cast-iron Blue Streak roadster, with rubber tires and nickel hubcaps; in excellent condition. Known for its "Toys That Last," the Kilgore Mfg. Co., of Westerville, Ohio, made cast-iron toy cars from 1928, until production ended in 1944. *1930s, 5¾ in (14.5 cm) long.*
$500–700

A green painted Hubley car with yellow hubcaps. Founded in 1898 in Lancaster, Pennsylvania, Hubley is known for cast-iron cars, fire engines, horse-drawn wagons, and, from 1909, cap guns. Toys became smaller in the Depression to make them affordable. Plastic was used from 1942. *1930s, 8½ in (21.5 cm) long.*
$350–450

desirable.

Identifying genuine items is relatively easy, since many factory names—such as Arcade or Hubley—were stamped on the undercarriage. Dent and A. C. Williams didn't mark their toys, but the excellent quality of the casting is obvious and tells even a novice that this is a quality vintage piece. Good cast iron is smooth, not rough or grainy. Pressed-steel toys generally had factory decals on them, most of which have not survived.

The bigger the better

Larger examples tend to fetch more: construction vehicles and buses often reach prices in excess of $2,000. A rare 15-inch Arcade Mack Chemical Truck can fetch up to $6,000. More affordable, however, are examples with some wear and tear or the smaller, plain models that were 4-inches (10–cm) long (the average was 6–8 inches [15.25–20.25 cm]). A

Kingsbury dump truck with some replaced parts could go for $400. Models in one paint color are also more affordable, although as soon as there is extra detailing—such as a nickel-plated grill—the car would attract a premium, so expect to pay $200–500 or more for those pieces. A pleasing collection can be built by spending between $200 and $2,000 on each piece, with the higher prices reserved for special purchases such as rare models, large, more detailed examples, or mint-condition items.

Condition counts

Collectors may focus on a particular period or prefer one material over another, perhaps choosing cars with nickel-plated detailing or in similar colors. Some opt for a single type of vehicle—for example, farming or racing—while others concentrate on one manufacturer. The one aspect, however, that all enthusiasts agree on is condition. The value of a toy is severely reduced if it is worn or damaged. Some wear is accepted on the very rarest pieces, and many collectors prefer mottled original paint to any kind of repainting, but the more common the toy the better kept it should be.

Top Tips

- A heavier, less detailed piece—perhaps with artificial aging such as rust or bright paintwork—could be a reproduction. Look at molding and signs of age and compare to an original.

- Do not repaint, even if paintwork is chipped—collectors want original finishes. Repainting diminishes value.

- Completeness is important. Original moving parts, such as tires or decals, add value.

- Look for matching boxes. Few survived, so today they are hotly sought after.

- Consider size, color, and detail—features that delighted yesterday's children will likely excite today's collectors.

KEEP ▶

Variations in detail or color are important considerations. Buy a book and learn how to spot unusual colorways. Large sizes are more visually impressive and generally have more details than simpler, smaller models. Values should rise if the toy is kept carefully.

A Kingsbury painted, pressed-steel, windup Pickup Truck, #359, with original decals. The blue finish is rare, as is the larger size, making it an excellent keep. It also retain its original decals, further adding to desirability. *c. 1930, 14 in (35.5 cm) long.*

$1,000–1,500

SELL ▶

Shape and condition count toward value. Classic vintage cars, trucks, and fire engines are among the most popular. Less visually appealing shapes can fetch less, especially if condition is poor. These are unlikely to increase in value, so sell now and reinvest.

A Dent cast-iron road grader, with rider. This shape is not as appealing as other cars or trucks. The paintwork is also in poor condition and the frame has been repaired. However, since it is a rare shape, it should appeal to an avid Dent or cast-iron toy collector. *c. 1930, 5¼ in (13.5 cm) long.*

$80–120

An Arcade cast-iron No. 8 silver racer, in great condition. Founded in Freeport, Illinois, the Arcade Mfg. Co. existed from 1885–1946. Look for the Yellow Cab, from 1922, and the Mack truck series. The "They Look Real" slogan said it all. *c. 1933, 5½ in (14 cm) long.*

$200–300

A Kingsbury windup dump truck, in painted pressed-steel, with replaced tire and tailgate rubber. Based in Keene, New Hampshire, the Kingsbury Mfg. Co. produced toys from 1919–42, when the factory was turned over to wartime work. Its use of lightweight steel for bodies allowed for more authentic and sharper details. *c. 1930, 11 in (28 cm) long.*

$400–500

Model trains

by makers such as Lionel and American Flyer are as popular with enthusiasts as they were with yesterday's children. If you have assembled a collection over the years, whether on a working track or stored in the attic, it may prove an excellent investment.

An American Flyer S-gauge 21088 Franklin 4-4-0 electric locomotive and tender, from the Old Timer series. *c. 1960, 10 in (25 cm) long.*
$200–300

Model trains were first produced in the mid-19th century. Early trains of cast iron, wood, or tinplate were often made for the well-to-do, and could be very expensive. Since then, toy trains have been driven by steam, clockwork, or electricity, and made in a variety of sizes, or gauges. They can be picked up at toy shows, garage sales, and specialized auctions.

On your Märk-lin

One of the most respected names is the German company Märklin, which made its trains out of decorated tinplate. The earliest from the late 19thC are hand painted and usually the most valuable; later examples from the 1910 onward tend to be lithographed. In 1891, Märklin standardized track gauges and sold ready-made track sections, engines, and accessories. Early models were made in three gauges: I, II, and III; the very successful smaller gauge of 0 was introduced around 1910. Of the early models, scarce, large, and fine-quality trains fetch the highest prices, starting at around $500–2,000; larger steam-driven trains often command $5,000–30,000. An example of the earliest known set made by Märklin for the American market, a gauge II Eagle passenger set, recently sold for over $70,000!

Electric trains

Ives (1868-1928) in Bridgeport, Connecticut, produced a wide variety of well-known model trains, ranging from tinplate and cast-iron carpet trains to the first 0-gauge electric system in the US, launched in 1910. Ives passenger sets can be worth $300 to over $3,000. Exceptional early models can fetch over $10,000. In 1928 the company was taken over by the Lionel Corporation (1900–69) of New York. Lionel dominated the American market after World War I, producing trains in 0 gauge (1⅜ in/35 mm) from 1915.

Collectors' Tales

"I once saw a guy pay $900 for an empty box at Christie's. I thought he was crazy. But it turned out he had the Märklin prewar engine to go in it. The engine on its own would be worth about $2,700, but the box would push the price up by much more than what he paid for it!"

Lee Young, Philadelphia

The firm also introduced its own nonstandard size, cleverly named the American Standard Gauge (2⅛ in [57 mm]) in 1906. Today pre-1969 Lionel trains are some of the most sought after, renowned for their accuracy and fine build-quality. A Lionel electric 0-gauge metal die-cast steam locomotive from the 1930s can be worth $150–350, depending on the model and condition. An 1835E Standard-Gauge steam locomotive in excellent condition can fetch around $800–1,000, while rarer locomotive-and-tender sets can sell for $1,500–6,000 or more.

All change!

Lionel's main rival was American Flyer (1907–c. 1960) in Chicago, Illinois, which from 1918 produced a popular line of electric-powered 0-gauge trains.

A Märklin 0-gauge B-1 steam locomotive with tender, made for the American market; hand painted in black; with some wear and original paint. *c. 1905, 12½ in (31 cm) long.*
$4,000–6,000

A closer look at... a Lionel Train

It has a large six-wheel tender—they are usually smaller, with four wheels

Gray is less commonly found than black

A late 1930s Lionel Standard-Gauge gray locomotive and tender; the tender is stamped "392W." It is in very good condition, with only a few scratches, so was played with very carefully, making it desirable to a collector. *c. 1937, locomotive 15¾ in (39.5 cm) long.*

It dates from the late 1930s—prewar trains are harder to find since there are fewer of them than postwar trains, especially in good condition

$800–1,200

197

Model trains

KEEP

Big names and complex designs do not always equal value and desirability. A simple design of tin or iron construction can indicate an early date. Check the attic for hidden treasures. Also, keep an eye out at fairs and flea markets, since less eye-catching rarities can still be found and are well worth keeping.

A Secor clockwork train, in hand-painted cast iron. The very early date and unusual maker make this train a keeper. Secor later sold his Connecticut-based business to Ives, which is very well known for its trains. *c. 1882, 9¼ in (23 cm) long.*

$1,500–2,000

SELL

Trains from the late 20th century are usually of little interest to most collectors. As many were made in large quantities, they can still be found comparatively easily and are unlikely to increase in value in the near future. If you have one, sell to an enthusiast who wishes to use it or is nostalgic for the train set of his or her youth.

An American Flyer 0-gauge Chicago clockwork passenger set may fetch $800–1200, and a No.16 cast-iron clockwork passenger set with tender and two coaches, truck, and box around $400–600. Later examples fetch less, with an S-gauge Franklin locomotive and tender from c. 1960 costing $200–300. Other brands to look for include: Marx, known for its tinplate trains and toys; Lima; Carlisle & Finch; Voltamp; Rivarossi; early US maker George W. Brown; Britain's famed Hornby, Carette, and Bassett-Lowke; and Germany's Fleischmann and Bing.

Gauging value

Older, heavier trains that are more realistic in appearance tend to be more desirable, and the rarest trains can be worth thousands of dollars. Trollies and coaches are sought after, and often reach high prices: an Ives No.804 Suburban tinplate trolley can fetch up to $1,000, while a Märklin hand-painted tin Electric Tramway trolley can fetch over

$15,000. The manufacture of reproductions can affect value: the largest Lionel Standard-Gauge electric locomotive, the 381E from 1928 used to be very expensive, but value has dropped due to a reproduction by Williams. Larger size trains are normally the most collectible, followed by Standard Gauge and S gauge. With the exception of brass locomotives and some limited-run plastics, many more modern HO and N scale trains are normally worth less than half of their original retail value, no matter how old they are.

Looking good

Condition is key: an old Lionel train that is immaculate but won't run is worth more than the same train in scruffy condition in perfect working order. For Voltamp trains, heavy enamel paint was used that tended to flake, so prices rise significantly for trains in excellent condition. The original box, parts, and paperwork also add value. Some examples might merit restoring, though the majority do not—a restored train is often worth less than the same item in untouched condition. Major variations in body type, exterior color, and the size, color, and placement of graphics also affect value. Join a collectors' group, attend train meetings and shows, and consult price guides and online auction sites to get acquainted with current prices for specific models and variations.

A Lionel No. 3 General Electric locomotive and tender. Since this train is in excellent condition and retains its original box, it would be of interest to an avid Lionel collector. *c. 1975. 10 in (25 cm) long.*

$70–100

Marbles strike a chord, not only for their vivid, swirling colors, but also because they are so evocative of childhood. These multicolored glass toys produced from the mid-19th century onward are avidly sought after.

The most desirable marbles are handmade, mostly in Germany from around 1850 until c. 1914. Made from brightly colored glass rods that created swirling patterns of color, they can be identified by a slightly rough area called a pontil mark where the marble was removed from the rod. There are many different types of marble, all with descriptive names, such as swirls, onionskins, or corkscrews.

Collectors look for marbles with complex patterns. Symmetrical patterns increase a marble's value and large marbles command a premium. Sulphides are also highly sought after. These clear marbles contain a small white figure, human or animal, and can fetch from $120 to more than $3,000.

World War I cut off supplies of marbles to North America, and this stimulated the machine production of glass marbles in the US. Machine-made marbles can usually be distinguished from handmade ones because they do not have a pontil mark. They have become popular because of the increasing scarcity and expense of handmade marbles. Nostalgia also plays a role, since many of today's collectors played with machine-made marbles when they were young.

Look for marbles by the Akro Agate Company, M. F. Christensen & Son, and the Peltier Glass Company. Values vary enormously, ranging from $2–8 for an Akro Agate Co. Slag marble to more than $300 for a Christensen Guinea. It is also worth looking at the innovative work of today's marble makers; these marbles have become increasingly popular since the 1990s, with brisk trading via the Internet.

▲ An Akro Agate Company machine-made Swirl Oxblood marble. During the company's lifetime (1910–1951) Akro Agate was the US's largest marble producer. Oxblood refers to the deep rust color with black striations. *c. 1940s–51, ½ in (1.5 cm) diam.*

$15–25

▶ A German, handmade Orange Latticinio Core Swirl marble. The pontil mark, which shows where this marble was removed from the rod, can be clearly seen. Made from twisted strands of colored glass, a marble's most common core color is white; orange is comparatively scarce, and blue extremely rare. *1860s–1920s, ½ in (1.5 cm) diam.*

$30–50

▶ A handmade Indian marble, with a black base and swirls of navy and white and green and yellow. Indian marbles usually have dark glass bases with colored strands applied on top. The more colors there are, the more valuable the marble usually is. *1860s–1920s, ¾ in (2 cm) diam.*

$120–180

◀ A German, handmade Solid Core Swirl marble. This fairly complex example has a pink, white, and blue inner swirl overlaid with an outer swirl made up of thin white strands in white glass known as *zanfirico. 1860s–1920s, ¾ in (2 cm) diam.*

$30–50

◀ A German, handmade, End of Day onionskin marble. End of Day marbles use stretched flecks of colored glass rather than rods, which are used in Swirls. The flecks tend to be red, blue, or green; other colors are rarer. *1860s–1920s, ½ in (1.5 cm) diam.*

$120–180

◀ **A German, handmade Banded Lutz marble,** with yellow and white bordered Lutz swirls. Lutz marbles have copper flakes suspended in glass, creating the impression of gold. *1860s–1920s, ¾ in (2 cm) diam.*

$150–200

◀ **A German English-style Joseph's Coat marble** with blue, orange, and white strands and two pontil marks. Named after the biblical coat of many colors, handmade Joseph's Coat marbles have a layer of tightly packed colored strands beneath the surface. *1860–1920, ½ in (1.5 cm) diam.*

$80–100

Collectors' Tips

- Seek out solitaire boards, but ensure that the marbles are old, as sets are often replaced
- Avoid marbles such as Cat's Eyes that were mass-produced after the 1960s
- Look for original packaging. It adds value but is usually only found for machine-made marbles

▶ **A German china marble with blue painted circles** and a band of brown elongated teardrops. China marbles from around the 1860s tend to be glazed and have more complex designs, but as time passed and competition grew, the designs became simpler and glazing stopped. *1870s–80s, ¾ in (2 cm) diam.*

$30–50

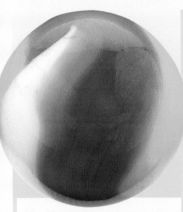

▶ **A contemporary glass marble by Edward Seese,** with a ribbon swirl and a green aventurine band; signed "FES 2003" *1¼ in (3 cm) diam.*

$30–50

▲ **A machine-made Corkscrew marble,** made by the American Akro Agate Company. Akro Agate made the most marbles during the 1930s and Corkscrew marbles were the most common, with over 1,000 color variations. *1930s, ½ in (1.5 cm) diam.*

$15–25

◀ **A German, handmade sulphide marble** with a white standing lion. Making sulfides took great skill. Named personalities, colored glass, and painted figures are the most valuable. *1870s–1920s, 1½ in (3.5 cm) diam.*

$150–200

Teddy bears have comforted the young since the early 20th century, but now they can offer financial solace, too. Vintage bears may fetch thousands of dollars, but post-1940s, miniature, and promotional bears can be found for much less.

The special appeal of teddy bears is that each one has its own characteristic charm. Enthusiasts may benefit from learning to recognize shapes and forms of different makers, but "hug" appeal should not be underestimated. Original pads, eyes, and stitching and intact fur are all desirable. Also vital are size, maker, and condition.

Bear essentials

Pre-World War I bears are rare and expensive. President Theodore "Teddy" Roosevelt was the inspiration behind the creation of the teddy bear, and teddy bear fever swept the US during the early years of the 20th century. The Ideal Novelty & Toy Company is reputed to have made the very first teddy bear in the US. Early Ideal bears feature a wide triangular head, short mohair, very long limbs, long muzzles, and large narrow feet. Other early

An American blonde mohair bear, with boot-button eyes and stitched black wool nose and mouth. *1906–08, 11½ in (29 cm) high.*
$800–1,200

US makers include Harman, Aetna, Bruin (BMC), and Columbia Teddy Bear Manufacturers. The latter was known for the Laughing Roosevelt Bear, which was designed c. 1907 to reproduce President Roosevelt's grin, and featured wooden or glass teeth. It can now be worth around $4,000. Novelty bears made around this time by various manufacturers, which could growl, whistle, or tumble, or had eyes that lit up, are sought after.

A Steiff mohair bear, with a stitched mouth and claws, a black felt nose, a button in the left ear, and a swivel head. Typical of this maker are the humped back, long, bent arms, and pointed snout. *c. 1909, 12¼ in (31 cm) high.*
$1,500–2,500

Some makers to look for:
■ Steiff ■ Bing ■ Chiltern ■

A Bing plush bear. Before 1920, these bears resembled Steiff's in shape and appearance, but later the smile grew wider. *c. 1920, 27¼ in (69 cm) high.*
$8,000–12,000

A Chiltern mohair bear. The two stitches at the top of the nose are typical of the bears that Chiltern made in the 1920s and 30s. *c. 1930, 20 in (51 cm) high.*
$600–900

A closer look at... a 1920s and a 1950s teddy bear

Becoming familiar with the different features of bears will make it easier to distinguish between early examples and those of the 1940s and beyond. Early bears are especially desirable and often fetch a premium. Convincing signs of wear and tear are a reliable sign of authenticity.

A golden mohair bear with a fully jointed body, felt paw pads, and wood-wool stuffing. Early bears were made from mohair and stuffed with materials such as kapok. *c. 1920s, 13 in (33 cm) high.*

$1,500–2,000

The snout is longer than on later bears _____

The arms are long and bend slightly at the wrist _____

The paws are slightly upturned _____

An Austrian light-brown mohair bear, with jointed limbs and head, a black stitched nose and mouth, and plush pads. Postwar bears were usually made from shinier, softer plush. *c. 1950, 24 in (61 cm) high.*

$200–300

_____ The rounder face and shorter snout suggest a post–World War II bear

_____ The arms and legs are shorter

_____ The round, plump body is typical

Even interwar bears can fetch high prices, especially those by German makers such as Steiff, Gebrüder Bing, and Schuco (trademark of Schreyer & Co.). Prices start at around $300–500 for a 1920s or 30s bear, rising to $15,000 or more.

British bears made by Chiltern Toys, Dean's Rag Book Co., and J. K. Farnell can fetch $300–900 or more. Chad Valley and Merrythought bears usually cost upward of $150, depending on age, size, and condition. Small, much-loved bears with balding fur and replaced pads, eyes, and noses usually sell for well under $200, unless by a notable maker.

Lifelong friends

Steiff bears are the most sought after. They are usually solid and well stitched (but stuffing and stitching can degrade over time), with thick mohair, long, slim bodies, elongated arms, large feet, a humped back, and a pointed nose. They have a Steiff

Top Tips

- Always sniff an old bear—it's impossible to fake the smell of years of love, attention, and accidents.
- Get to know the defining features of well-known makers.
- Avoid suspiciously clean "old" bears, or any bear with an old label on new paw pads—pre–World War II bears are often faked.
- Beware of fake logo buttons and incongruous modern logo buttons that look shiny and new.

▪ Schuco ▪ Merrythought ▪ Chad Valley ▪

A Schuco Yes/No bear made out of mohair with a straw filling. The tail controls his head movements. Damage has reduced the value. *1920s, 15 in (38 cm) high.*

$280–320

A Merrythought jointed bear, by one of the most popular and prolific makers of the post-World War II era. A Merrythought label is typically on the right foot. *1950s, 15 in (38 cm) high.*

$300–500

A Chad Valley mohair bear. This popular British manufacturer made bears that typically have flat ears and chunky limbs. *1930, 20 in (51 cm) high.*

$800–900

COLORED BEARS Unusual fur colors (such as red, or the white mohair on this Steiff bear) may prove more valuable, especially if by a good maker. c. 1920, 3½ in (9 cm) high.

$280–320

BERLIN BEARS First made in the 1950s, Berlin mascot bears wore a crown and a "BERLIN" sash. This Schuco bear's lost sash lowers its value. 1950s, 3 in (7.5 cm) high.

$150–250

NOVELTY BEARS Two-faced Janus bears by Schuco feature heads that turn around, revealing a second face, complete with protruding tongue. 1950s, 3½ in (9 cm) high.

$600–1,000

GADGET BEARS Schuco was master of the miniature jointed bear, which was often designed to hold items such as lipsticks or perfume bottles. c. 1950, 5½ in (14 cm) high.

$200–250

UNKNOWN BEARS Miniature bears in standard colors by unknown makers can be an effective and economical way to expand a collection. c. 1940s, 3¾ in (9.5 cm) high.

$60–90

PANDAS Panda bears became popular from the 1930s onward, when live pandas started appearing in zoos. This model was made by Schuco. 1950s, 3¾ in (8.5 cm) high.

$200–250

Toys, Dolls, and Teddy Bears

202

button in the ear or a hole where it once was. Unusual colors or variations add value, such as the rare "center seam" bear (1905–07), which can fetch up to $8,000: every seventh bear had a seam down the center of its head, to avoid fabric wastage.

Bing's plush-covered bears (c. 1920s) usually included a mechanical element (walking or kicking), and often wore stylish outfits. Many Schuco bears also had mechanical parts, such as the nodding Yes/No bear.

In addition to Ideal, American makers of note include Knickerbocker, Gund, and the Character Toy Company.

▼ **Children listen to the radio** at home with their child-sized teddy bear. *1920s.*

American bears typically have triangular heads, long firm bodies, and straight limbs placed low on the body. Bears from the 1930s to the 1950s, in good condition and by a desirable maker, can fetch up to $1,000 or more.

Tiny treasures

Miniature and novelty bears are popular collectibles. Schuco specialized in miniatures—sometimes designed to store makeup. Steiff also made miniature bears, as did several other makers. Prices start at about $50–80 for a good unmarked bear.

Man-made

From the 1950s onward, most bears were given washable fillings and synthetic fabric bodies. Many had rubber and plastic

A gold mohair American teddy bear, with black boot-button eyes, cardboard inserts in the feet, original felt pads, woven nose and claws. The triangular shape of his head and snout hint at the maker Ideal. *c. 1905–10 24½ in (62 cm) high.*

$2,500–3,500

noses and, by the late 1960s, locked-in plastic eyes. Makers such as Wendy Boston, which pioneered the safe eye and the washable bear in 1954, even abandoned jointed arms and legs. Most collectors prefer traditional jointed teddy bears, made in mohair, so post-1940s bears, except those by the main makers, usually fetch around $150 or less. Colored bears exported from East Asia after the 1950s are usually poor in quality and are not collectible at present.

Old Smokey

During the 1950s, bears with painted features on soft molded vinyl faces were popular, and such bears can be worth $50–200 today. Ideal produced vinyl-faced Smokey the Bear toys, in association with the Cooperative Forest Fire Prevention Company. R. Dakin & Co. and Knickerbocker also made Smokey bears in a range of styles, and any merchandise associated with the character is collectible.

Cheeky chaps

Post-World War II teddy bears by Steiff had a printed fabric label in the left ear (as well as the traditional button), and a cardboard swing tag around the neck. As with other makers, the form of these bears grew rounder during and after the 1940s and 50s. Examples can be found between $250 and $1,200. Chad Valley bears from the 1950s are also sought after, especially the rainbow-colored range, which normally fetches $200–300 or more. Look for Merrythought's 1950s Cheeky bears, with wide, stitched smiles, costing from about $150 to $1,500 depending on size and age.

A Merrythought Cheeky bear, with a fully jointed, dark-gold mohair body, brown felt pads, a black wool-stitched mouth on a velvet snout, and a printed label reading "Merrythought/ Ironbridge, Shropshire" on its right foot. *1970s, 15¼ in (39 cm) high.*
$400–500

Chiltern was taken over by Chad Valley in 1967, and bears were marked "Chiltern Chad Valley."

Barely collectible

Around the late 1970s bears started to be made as collectors' pieces, as distinct from toys. These "new" bears fall into two broad groups: artist's bears, created by designers, and limited editions and replicas, made by leading names. Both may be good investments, but the majority are yet to show any significant gain. Top of the line is Steiff, which launched a limited-edition series in 1980, and added replica bears in 1991 (offering the chance to own an example of rare early designs, such as the Somersault Bear of 1909). Limited-edition bears in low runs (fewer than 1,000) may yet provide good returns. An Ideal collectible bear made in 1978 to commemorate the company's 75th anniversary can fetch around $120. But beware, replicas can be confused with, or occasionally even misrepresented as, original early bears.

Top Tips

- Look for homemade bears from the World War II period, as they offer charm and are growing in popularity.
- Never immerse a bear in water, whatever its age. This can cause damage, and may affect the stuffing.
- Keep bears you have bought brand new for investment in the original, unopened packaging, together with receipts. Mint condition and paperwork are important.
- Look for bears with an interesting or heartwarming provenance. A photograph of the original owner and the bear together adds to the value.

BUY

An appealing or unusual face often adds to a bear's value. Many such faces are unique to the individual toy, so if you find a characterful bear in good condition, it is likely to be a sound investment.

A "glum" bear cub. Although by an unknown manufacturer, this bear's striking face makes it a desirable purchase and a worthwhile investment. *c. 1950, 11 in (28 cm) high.*
$550–600

KEEP

Early American-made bears are desirable among collectors and early examples are generally rare and valuable. Knowing the maker is not always important as the date, shape, condition, and "huggability" of the bear count for a lot.

An early American bear, by an unknown maker. His unusual face and arm placement hint at a US origin. His friendly face and superb condition makes him an excellent keep. *1906–08, 12½ in (32cm) high.*
$1,000–1,500

KEEP

Rare bears with an interesting story behind them can be valuable. These two bears were produced to celebrate the birth in 1949 of Brumas, the first polar bear cub to be bred at London Zoo.

Two Dean's Rag Book Co. mohair plush polar bears, Ivy & Brumas. It is very unusual to find this mother-and-cub set still intact. *c. 1949, cub 6½ in (16.5 cm) high.*
$400–600

Soft toys, with their simple, nostalgic charm and sometimes bizarre appearance, appeal to young and old alike. It is possible to find many unexpected treasures, by major makers, at affordable prices.

An early Annalee soft toy of an orange chipmunk, with poseable tale and painted eyes. *1950s, 7 in (18 cm) high.*
$150–250

Traditional soft toys date from the late 19th century. Their Golden Age was from the 1920s to the 50s, after which quality declined as inferior goods were imported from Asia.

Unwavering quality

Steiff, a German company established in 1877 and best known for its teddy bears, started out making other soft toys. The firm has produced some of the best-quality animal toys, including cats and dogs, wild animals, dinosaurs, lobsters, reptiles, and insects. Margarete Steiff's first toys were homemade presents for her family. A felt elephant made as a pin cushion for her sister-in-law in 1880 trumpeted the beginning of the Steiff empire and was featured on the button used on toys from 1904–05.

Penguins joined the Steiff line in the 1920s, with King Peng. Some toys, such as the insects, produced in the 1950s to 60s, are often undervalued by those who associate Steiff with bears, and can be found for $80 or less; others have fetched $600 or more. Well-known characters are sought after—a felt Steiff Mickey Mouse from the 1930s can fetch $3,000–5,000, depending on size and condition.

Monkeys and acrobats

Germany was also home to Schreyer & Co., known as Schuco, established in 1912. In addition to bears, it made a line of miniature monkeys. Some valuable examples were designed to conceal hidden features such as compacts or perfume bottles, and others had windup mechanisms that made them tumble or perform acrobatics. The limbs on toys made in the 1950s are sometimes shorter and the bodies and heads rounder than on earlier models, but this is not always the case. Look for Schuco monkeys in unusual colors such as blue—they are more valuable than those in traditional colors.

Some makers to look for:
■ Steiff ■ Schuco ■ Merrythought ■ Chad Valley ■

A Steiff elephant. Even after World War II, when many makers were using cheaper fabrics, Steiff continued to use quality materials, so it is safer to date these toys from the style, tag, or button in the ear. *c. 1918, 9¾ in (25 cm) high.*
$300–500

A Schuco Yes/No monkey, with felt clothes, painted metal eyes, and a tail lever that makes its head nod or shake. Many of Schuco's soft toys had such mechanisms, enabling them to move. *c. 1920, 7¾ in (20 cm) high.*
$200–250

A velveteen Merrythought Jerry mouse, with a label. This top British maker is noted for its wide and varied line of soft toys. *1930s–70s, 9 in (23 cm) high.*
$300–400

A Chad Valley golly, with printed label. The royal coat of arms of the UK's Queen Mother appears on labels from 1938 onward. *1960s, 24½ in (62 cm) high.*
$40–60

Did You Know?

When the traditional black golly became increasingly unacceptable in the 1960s, Dean's Rag Book Co. produced an alternative white-faced Mr. Smith golly to challenge the traditional Chad Valley version. The white-faced golly never enjoyed the same popularity. Far fewer were made and so they are now rare.

Pick your favorites

In addition to seeking out favorite makers, many people collect by animal type—cats, dogs, and monkeys being especially popular. Cartoon and comic characters are also sought after. Gund, an American toymaker established in 1898 and still active today, was one of several companies that made soft toys based on cartoon characters such as Mickey Mouse, Pluto, and Felix the Cat. A Gund Bambi from the mid-1950s in good condition can fetch around $50–80. A 1950s Winnie the Pooh by Agnes Brush, of Long Island, New York, can be worth up to $300–500.

Knickerbocker toys can be found from as little as $5, although its vintage Disney toys can fetch $100–1,000 or more.

Annalee animals

Stuffed, often hand-painted, animals by Annalee are popular, and include mice, ducks, pigs, and rabbits. Many are available for as little as $15–50, but some toys fetch much higher prices. Early examples from the 1950s are particularly sought after, as are those from small editions, or that are signed by Annalee herself. A Hot Pink Monkey made in 1970, signed and from a limited edition of 70, can be worth as much as $800–1,000.

Stuff it

Collectors look for excellent condition, with all parts, including ribbons or tags, complete. Larger toys, and rarer, early limited editions tend to fetch more. Toys with festive themes, such as Annalee's Christmas Frog, are also popular.

Look for toys made from early materials: mohair, felt, and kapok or wood-wool stuffings are generally pre-1950s, while silk plush and softer stuffings date from the 1950s onward.

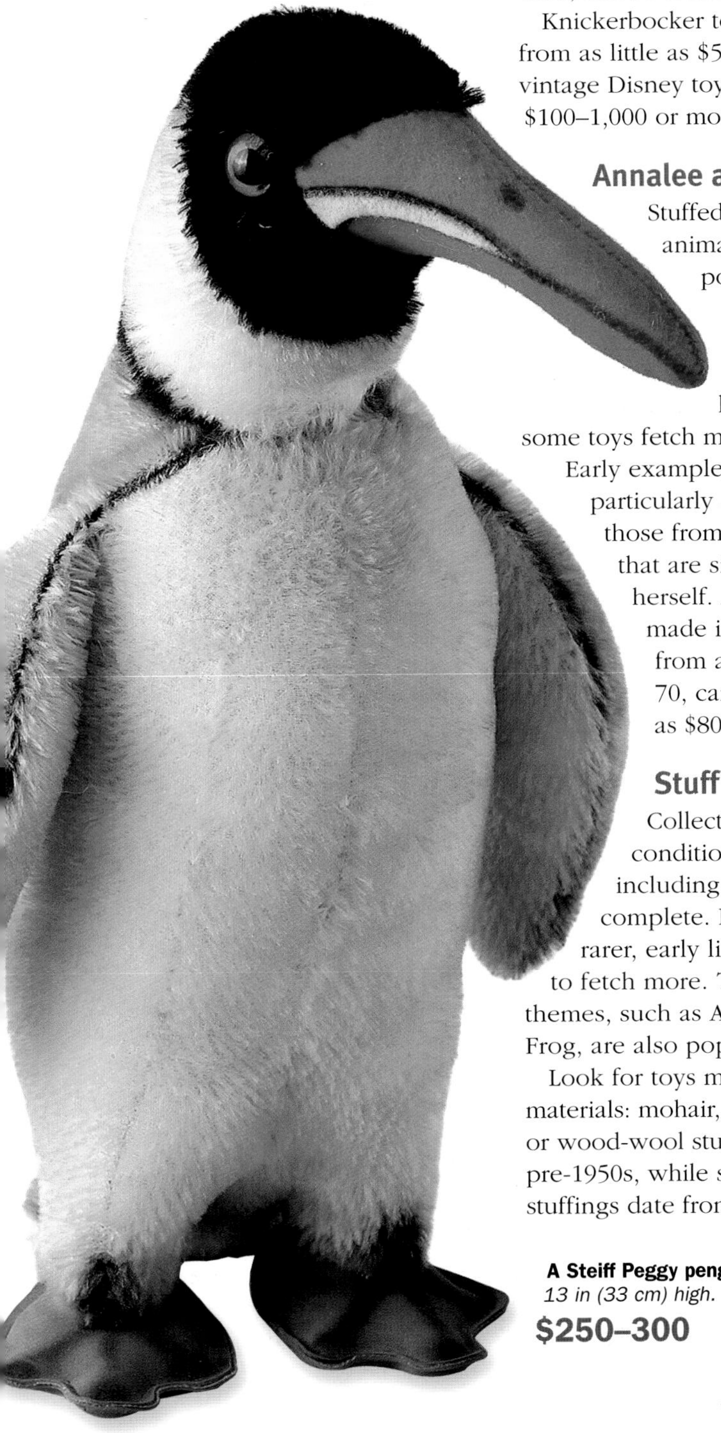

A Steiff Peggy penguin. *1950s, 13 in (33 cm) high.*

$250–300

Top Tips

- Choose a soft toy that is undamaged, clean, and retains its button or label if it had one. Condition is all-important.
- Invest in unmarked early toys if they are in good condition and come with an original box. If they also have a pleasing appearance, it is likely that they will retain their appeal and make sound investments.
- Don't undertake restoration work yourself, such as sewing up a split seam, as this can reduce value. Also, never immerse a toy in water. Find a teddy bear or doll hospital to restore or clean a soft toy.
- When storing a soft toy collection, use lavender bags rather than moth balls to deter moths, as the smell is more pleasant. Destroy insects by sealing toys in plastic bags and putting them in the freezer overnight.

BUY

When buying modern limited editions, look for low edition numbers, short-lived editions, or those that commemorate events such as anniversaries. Always keep the toy in mint condition with its tags, paperwork, and box, if applicable, as these will ensure the highest prices if you sell in the future.

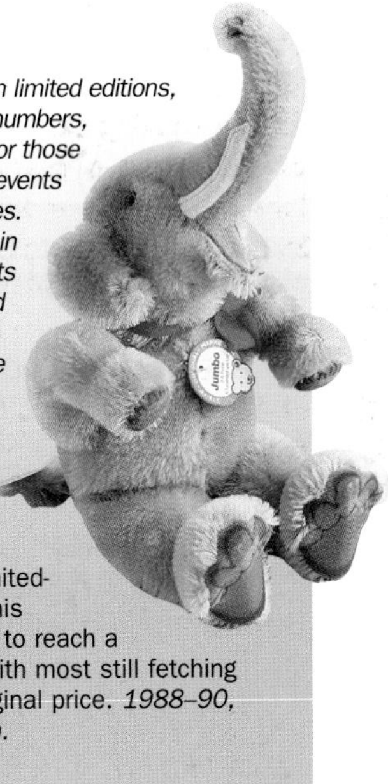

A mechanical Steiff elephant from an edition of 4,000. Modern limited-edition toys, like this elephant, have yet to reach a peak in interest, with most still fetching less than their original price. *1988–90, 13 in (33 cm) high.*

$200–300

KEEP

If characters from literature or the media remain popular in the long term among a wide audience, prices will rise as demand grows against a limited supply.

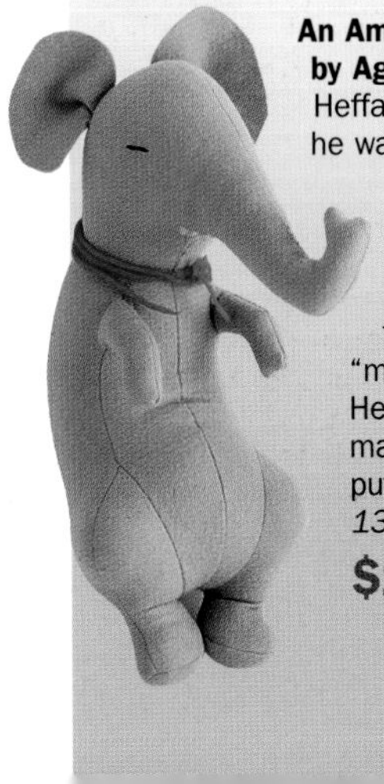

An American Heffalump by Agnes Brush. The Heffalump is rarer since he was less appealing at the time than popular characters like Winnie the Pooh and Piglet, meaning fewer were sold. The "mythical" status of the Heffalump in the books makes him desirable if put up for sale. *1950s, 13¾ in (35 cm) high.*

$1,000–1,500

Snow globes and domes capture

charming, miniature little worlds. From religious subjects to the frankly kitsch, they make delightful souvenirs and are even more popular now than they were when they originated in France in the 1870s.

The first souvenir snow globes were sold at the 1889 Paris Exposition and featured miniature Eiffel Towers. But, sadly, none appear to have survived.

The central subject is key to a snow globe's appeal, and today these tiny worlds feature everything from Hawaiian snow scenes to Harry Potter.

Early globes were made from hand-blown glass and filled with water. They had a wooden, ceramic, rubber, metal, or marble base and plaster-molded interior scenes. The "snow" was made of chipped bone,

porcelain, treated wax, rice, or sand. Today, it is comprised of fragments of white plastic or glitter in distilled water. The water evaporates over time, affecting values to some extent. Later models may be refillable, though.

Production accelerated in Europe during the early 20th century, followed by the US in the late 1920s, and Japan in the late 1930s. Since the late 1950s, globes have been made of plastic with injection-molded interior scenes. Taiwan, Hong Kong, and China have led production since the 1970s.

▲ **A rare, early 20th-century, European, glass snow globe.** Globes with religious themes were most popular at the turn of the 20th century. This one has wax angels on wire tremblers with gold leaf "snow flakes." *c. 1910, 5 in (12.5 cm) high.*

$100–150

▶ **A souvenir sailor-and-sea-captain snow globe.** Appealing characters are always popular. This piece has a seesaw fishing scene. *1970s, 5 in (12.5 cm) high.*

$50–80

▶ **A Walt Disney Productions Mickey and Donald snow globe.** Mickey Mouse and Donald Duck, two of Walt Disney's most popular characters, sit astride a moving seesaw. *Early 1970s, 3 in (7.5 cm) high.*

$30–50

◀ **A Walt Disney Productions Pinocchio snow globe,** one of a set that includes Raggedy Anne and Bugs Bunny. *Early 1960s, 5 in (12.5 cm) high.*

$80–120

◀ **A set of three McDonald's snow globes.** These globes were given away with Happy Meals in Germany only. *1980s, 2¼ in (5.5 cm) high.*

$25–35 each

◀ **A book-shaped snow globe with Santa.** Although not global in shape, this novel commemorative Christmas item has an unusual shape and a festive theme. *1970s–80s, 3½ in (9 cm) high.*
$30–40

◀ **A "Jerry" glass snow globe by Rosarium.** Cartoon characters, especially well-known ones, are highly collectible and have a wide appeal. *Late 1970s/early 80s, 4 in (10 cm) high.*
$15–25

Collectors' Tips

Look for these desirable features:

- Attractive designs featuring both a foreground and a background
- Globes with unusual shapes, moving parts, or scenes that fill the entire globe

▶ **An illuminated religious snow globe.** Religious subjects and souvenirs from pilgrimage sites, such as Lourdes, are still in demand. This globe shows the Last Supper and the Crucifixion. *c. 1970s, 3½ in (9 cm) high.*
$30–40

◀ **A snowman snow globe with seesaw action.** There are plenty of Christmas scenes around. The rocking action of this globe gives it extra charm, as does the cheerful snowman. *Late 1960s, 5 in (12.5 cm) high.*
$30–40

▼ **A limited-edition Millennium snow globe.** Commissioned by Hollywood actor Corbin Bernsen, 2,000 signed copies of these were made. *c. 1999, 3½ in (9 cm) high.*
$30–40

◀ **A Helsinki, Finland, souvenir snow globe.** Don't underestimate the interest in basic tourist-attraction globes—even if inferior in quality, these items are still collectible. *1990s, 2 in (5 cm) high.*
$7–10

WELCOME TO THE NEW MILLENNIUM

2000

SUN 3 1 DEC

Take the Next Step

HELSINKI FINLAND

Bisque dolls were first made in France and Germany, but soon captured the hearts of children everywhere. With their period costumes redolent of childhoods long past, they represent an important area of interest for doll enthusiasts and investors.

Bisque, the material used to make the heads of these dolls (and sometimes their hands and feet, too), is unglazed tinted porcelain. Bisque dolls were popular from about 1850, and were made by all the leading French and German dollmakers.

Bisque basics

There are three types of bisque doll: French fashion dolls (miniature adults), *bébé* (baby) dolls, and character dolls, which tend to be more expressive or dressed as a certain type of character. Fashion dolls are extremely expensive today. Early *bébés* are perhaps the most popular type of bisque doll, with prices to suit all pockets. Later *bébés*

can be expensive, but those by lesser-known firms are more affordable. Character dolls offer the widest range of prices and styles. An appealing face or expression will always add value.

Bonny *bébés*

French *bébés* reigned supreme from 1860 to the 90s. Leading makers include Jumeau, Bru Jeune et Cie., Gaultier, and Steiner; early examples from any of these now cost thousands of dollars. Early *bébés* often have no identifying marks, and authentication is a matter for experts.

In 1899 French dollmakers formed the Société Française de Fabrication de Bébés et Jouets (SFBJ) to produce

◄ **A late 19th-century character doll** in contemporary sailor dress. It has a cloth body, an open mouth, and a mark that looks like "Alma." *c. 1880s, 12¾ in (32 cm) high.*

$50–80

"economy" dolls to compete with German imports. SFBJ dolls tend to have cruder faces, with rosier cheeks and parted lips. The bisque heads (often made in Germany, ironically) are usually attached to jointed wooden and composition bodies. Most SFBJ dolls made after 1905 bear these initials on the back of the heads. Prices often start at about $300.

Some makers to look for:
■ **Armand Marseille** ■ **Simon & Halbig** ■ **Steiner** ■ **SFBJ** ■ **Jumeau** ■

◄ **An Armand Marseille Dream Baby doll.** Marseille often manufactured in high volumes to meet the demand for less expensive dolls. In series such as the Dream Baby line (from 1926) the company maintained high overall quality. *c. 1930s, 6¾ in (17.5 cm) high.*

$200–300

A Simon & Halbig girl doll, with original ► Edwardian clothes. Examples made before the early 20th century have open mouths and solid heads. Later dolls have closed mouths and socket-type heads. *c. 1920, 12½ in (32 cm) high.*

$400–600

◄ **A Steiner doll,** incised "SCS," series C. Steiner dolls always have the nose set close to the mouth and hands with stubby fingers. *c. 1870, 24½ in (62 cm) high.*

$7,000–9,000

An SFBJ toddler doll, 236. ► SFBJ's character dolls tend to be popular. *c. 1911, 20 in (51 cm) high.*

$800–1,200

Living dolls

Character dolls with more expressive faces appeared around 1900. This market was dominated by German makers, such as Kammer & Reinhardt, which issued its first dolls of this type in 1909. Rare examples of these early dolls can fetch tens of thousands of dollars. Look for dolls with mold numbers 117 or 117/A.

The character dolls made by Simon & Halbig carry the initials "SH" on the back of the head. Its black and Asian dolls are much sought after.

Hello dolly

Character dolls by the German maker Armand Marseille are less expensive. From 1890, it made bisque heads, usually marked "AM," both for its own company and others. Its Dream Baby (produced until the late 1940s) came in many sizes, as well as in four ethnic types. The 341 model, up to 24 inches (60 cm) high and with a composition body, is the most popular and can fetch around $150–800. Black versions are desirable, especially those with colored and fired (rather than painted) bisque heads. They can fetch around $300–900. Other makers include J. D. Kestner and Gebrüder Heubach. Kestner dolls are largely known by their mold numbers, with very few having names. One exception is the highly prized Hilda, which can fetch $1,000–1,500 or more. Prices for genuine Gebrüder Heubach dolls have suffered from the existence of good fakes made from molds taken from the originals.

A Jumeau bébé, in size 9. Jumeau dolls are prized for their delicately painted faces and charming expressions. *c. 1885, 24 in (61 cm) high.*

$3,500–4,500

Top Tips

- Check the back of the bisque head for a mold number and perhaps a maker's mark.
- Examine dolls for pale-colored bisque and detailed painting—bold colors and crude features are less valuable.
- Try to buy dolls with original bodies and original or appropriate clothing.
- Look for black and Asian dolls still in their original costumes, since they are much sought after.
- Avoid dolls with repainted facial features or details—the repainting will reduce value.
- Choose dolls with jointed limbs—they are easier to stand or sit for display.

KEEP ▶

Character dolls are popular, especially those with expressive and cheerful faces. Larger sizes by known makers are the most sought after and should go up in value.

A 1920s SFBJ French character doll, known as a Laughing Jumeau. (Jumeau was one of the firms in the SFBJ). Its mint condition and original body both add to the value. *1920s, 16¼ in (41 cm) high.*

$800–1,200

SELL ▶

Armand Marseille dolls from the 390 mold series (from around 1900) are among the most common antique dolls and are unlikely to rise in value over the foreseeable future. Finely painted dolls in larger sizes, with more realistic faces, will have more potential.

An Armand Marseille doll, 390, with original clothing. It is larger than the smallest size, which is 9 inches (23 cm), but the quality is below that of many dolls of the period. *c. 1910s, 23½ in (60 cm) high.*

$200–250

Half Dolls, dainty porcelain figurines,

were fashionable early in the 20th century and were produced in the thousands at the height of their popularity. By the end of the 1940s, however, production had virtually ceased.

Intended for ornamental use around the home, half dolls were usually made from porcelain or bisque: they had upper bodies, heads, and arms, but no legs. They were sometimes known as pincushion, dresser, or tea cozy dolls, as the voluminous skirts sewn onto them were used as decorative covers for everyday household objects, such as powder boxes, pincushions, and teapots. The most popular half dolls were modeled on pretty ladies, but male dolls were produced too, in addition to children and a variety of animals.

The most prolific manufacturers of half dolls were German factories, such as Dressel & Kister, Heubach, Goebel, and Kestner.

Values start from around $15–30 for basic dolls (made from a single mold so the arms lie against the body). Mid-price dolls have arms set farther away from the body, while the finest dolls have delicately sculpted, outstretched arms and can be worth up to around $500. Detailed painting and smooth bisque are also good indicators of quality. Large dolls are particularly sought after, as are those with their original skirts, which are often elaborate and made from a wide variety of fabrics.

▲ **A porcelain half doll of a lady wearing a pink dress.** Although it is neither particularly well painted or modeled, this doll's fan and tall wig enhance its appeal. *c. 1925, 3¾ in (9.5 cm) high.*

$30–40

▼ **A porcelain half doll** of a lady wearing a hat and dress. Unusually, this doll has legs and her original clothing. She is sitting in an attractive position with her arms bent, and her dress and hat have an attractive, lustered finish. *c. 1910, 3½ in (9 cm) high.*

$80–120

▼ **A ceramic half doll** of an elegant young woman mounted on an upholstered fabric skirt. Dolls dressed in their original clothes, usually homemade, are much sought after. *c. 1935, 5½ in (14 cm) high.*

$50–80

▲ **A porcelain half doll** of a lady holding a rose. The wide-brimmed hat makes this simply modeled doll more collectible. *c. 1925, 4 in (10 cm) high.*

$50–80

▲ **A porcelain half doll** of a naked lady with painted feathers in her hair. This finely painted doll has expressive arms, which makes it very desirable. *c. 1910, 4 in (10 cm) high.*

$100–150

◀ **A porcelain half doll of a blonde lady mounted on an upholstered, fabric-skirt base**. The addition of porcelain legs is unusual, making the doll more desirable. *c. 1935, 5¼ in (13 cm) high.*

$40–60

◀ **A pair of porcelain Dutch boy and girl half dolls**. National dress is a feature much sought after by collectors, as are pairs of dolls. *c. 1925, 1¾ in (4.5 cm) high.*

$30–50 each

▶ **A porcelain half doll of a young lady**. This doll's finely modeled face, thoughtful expression, and the rose she is holding in her outstretched hand, make it valuable. *c. 1910, 3 in (7.5 cm) high.*

$200–300

Collectors' Tips

- Look for dolls with period details and clothing, such as 1920s hairstyles or 1930s outfits
- Dolls' features were prone to damage, so check them carefully for signs of chips or regluing
- Examine dolls' back waists for manufacturers' identification marks

◀ **A porcelain half doll of a "flapper" in a yellow-painted 1920s cocktail dress**. This doll's hairstyle dates it to the 1920s, a period when half dolls were extremely popular. *c. 1925, 2¾ in (7 cm) high.*

$60–90

◀ **A porcelain half doll of a lady in Art Deco dress** with incised marks "10039." This elegant doll epitomizes Art Deco style and is appealing because of her carefree expression, stylized hair, and vivid coat with black-and-white lined collar and cuffs. *c. 1925, 3¼ in (8.5 cm) high.*

$300–400

▲ **A porcelain half doll of a young lady** with incised marks "15460." The wealth of detail, from bows on the doll's chest and sleeves to her floppy, wide-brimmed hat, make it desirable. *c. 1925, 4¾ in (12 cm) high.*

$40–60

Fabric dolls

are direct descendants of the homemade rag doll—that huggable confidante of children down the centuries. While some fabric dolls can have a high price tag, many colorful cloth character dolls—to take just one of the numerous types—can be found for less than $50.

Dolls made of plush, pressed cotton, or printed felt are classed as fabric dolls. These materials are fragile, so older examples are rare. Prices for dolls with maker's labels or marks by well-known companies, such as the Italian firm Lenci, rose in the 1990s, but inexpensive dolls still exist.

Early dolls

Early fabric dolls are much sought after by collectors. Folk art cloth dolls from the 1800s to the 1930s can be worth $200–1,500 or more, and rag dolls, for example, those made by Art Fabric Mills, normally fetch $100–300. Izanna Walker's primitive sculpture dolls,

made in Central Falls, Rhode Island, can be worth $8,000–30,000. Another early maker of note was Ella Smith, a skilled seamstress who developed a technique for making very strong dolls using heavy cotton and fleece, plaster of Paris, heavily applied paint, and clever stitching. These Alabama Indestructible Dolls can be worth $2,000–12,000 or more, and black dolls are particularly sought after.

From 1920 until 1934 the Volland company produced Raggedy Ann and Andy dolls, to tie in with the illustrated stories of John Gruelle, and these can command $500–2,000. Raggedy Ann and Andy dolls by other makers, such as Molly-'es, Georgene, and Knickerbocker, are also worth looking for, as they can fetch from around $70 up to $2,000 or more.

Wardrobe of felt

Felt dolls made by Lenci, established in 1908, were designed for display. Typically, they have elaborate costumes and expressive painted faces, often with sideways glancing eyes. The most desirable Lenci dolls, made in the period from 1920 to

A Käthe Kruse child doll, in excellent, clean condition with extra clothes and her original box—all of which add to her value. *c. 1930, 20 in (51 cm) high.*

$1,200–1,800

A Nora Wellings Mountie doll, with original hat and clothing. *c. 1930s, 10 in (25 cm) high.*

$25–40

1941, tend to fetch $300–800, but rare examples can be worth up to $8,000. Those made after 1941 are usually valued at less than $300. Reproductions of early designs, issued in the 1970s, may prove to be a good investment if kept in mint condition.

Lenci dolls have a black or purple stamp on the foot and often a label attached to the costume. Early dolls may have a Lenci pewter button sewn on to the costume.

Poses and paint

Annalee dolls are popular with collectors. Barbara Annalee Thorndike and her husband, Chip, created a unique internal wire frame so that their dolls could be poseable. Production of these "mobilitee" dolls began in the early 1950s, and the company steadily grew, selling dolls in over 40 states in the 1960s. Further expansion followed, and the dolls are still produced today. Annalee dolls start at around $15, but can fetch $500–1,000 or more. Look for early dolls from the 1950s, 60s, and 70s. Those from a small edition or one-of-a-kind examples, and dolls

A closer look at... an Annalee doll

Annalee dolls, made since the 1950s, have attracted a large number of dedicated collectors. As so many dolls have been made over the decades, it is important to look for unusual features that may push the value upward.

Dolls with closed eyes were not so popular with the public and as fewer than expected were sold, they were discontinued in 2000; they are now becoming collectible

Many Annalee doll faces are hand-painted with great character

At 18 inches (45.5 cm) high, this is a large example

It is a vintage example, dating from the 1970s, and it was part of a limited edition

An Annalee clown doll. Part of a limited edition of 2,343, this clown is still bright and its colors have not faded. *1970s, 18 in (45.5 cm) high*

$200–300

Top Tips

- Be wary of unmarked "Lenci" dolls—they may be Chad Valley copies.
- Do not wash a fabric doll in water.
- To store dolls, wrap them in acid-free tissue paper and pack them in a box.
- To eradicate insects, seal the doll in a bag and place it in a freezer overnight.
- Look for characters from fairy tales, nursery rhymes, and stars of stage and screen: these are especially collectible.
- When examining a Lenci doll, check that the pewter button from an early doll has not been attached to a later one. A telltale sign is new stitching.

BUY

Look for a Lenci doll that has a face full of character—a scowling child can be worth up to $900. A rare costume and the original label also add value.

A Lenci Mascotte doll holding a red rose, in good condition. *c. 1930s, 20 in (51 cm) high.*

$250–300

SELL

Many companies produced sailor dolls, including firms that made advertising props. They are too common to appreciate in value, so it is worth selling to a collector of advertising memorabilia.

An Invicta marine doll. This late example was produced as an advertising doll and is not by a noted maker. It has no maker's label or stamp. *1950s, 23 cm (9 in) high.*

$15–25

that are signed by Annalee herself, are also worth searching for, as they reach the highest prices.

Fireman, soldier, dreamer

The German company Steiff made felt dolls such as firemen and military figures. They have distinctive painted felt faces with a center seam, sewn-on ears, and felt hands. Recent limited editions of its earlier dolls from the 1920s to the 50s have the script Steiff button, used since 1986. Larger dolls can fetch $800–1,000.

Another famous German maker is Käthe Kruse, who introduced her cloth dolls in 1912. Look for early examples produced before 1929 with three hand-stitched seams on the head. Her *Du Mein* (You are Mine) and *Traumerchen* (Little Dreamer) dolls are desirable. Early dolls in good condition are very expensive. Dolls from 1948 onward have plastic heads and tend to fetch prices of $150–500.

A Raggedy Ann doll, by Georgene, wearing an unusual dress. Although she is in original condition, she shows signs of wear and could stand to be be cleaned professionally. *c. 1940s, 15 in (38 cm) high.*

$300–400

Plastic dolls have delighted generations of little girls since they first appeared in the 1940s. The huge numbers produced over recent decades allow plenty of scope for anyone interested in adopting these pretty characters.

Plastic was the toymakers' ideal material, allowing them to produce dolls that were light, hygienic, hard-wearing, and inexpensive. Post-World War II dolls in this novel medium were snapped up by an enthusiastic public. By the late 1950s, the hard plastic of the early years had been replaced by a softer vinyl. With so many of these dolls still in existence, condition is vital. Desirability is also increased by a rare or appealing design, or by a well-known maker.

American beauties

The American doll designer Mary Hoyer began making hard-plastic dolls in 1946. They were distinguished by curled hair and elaborate outfits, often homemade by their owners, using special knitting or sewing patterns.

In 1948 Beatrice Behrman—trading as Madame Alexander of the Alexander Doll Co., New York City (established 1923)—introduced one of the earliest lines of currently collectible plastic dolls. She featured characters from movies, books, and cartoons, as well as personalities. Her dolls are marked either on the back or elsewhere on the body, and some have name tags attached to their clothes. Among her most sought-after dolls are

the Little Women series based on Louisa M. Alcott's books. Examples in mint condition with their original clothing and hairstyles can fetch anything between $50 and $800.

Dolls made by the Vogue Doll Co. in the 1950s will now generally cost $300–800, again, if in good condition with their clothes and hair unchanged.

Sasha dolls were a triumph of the 1960s. These realistic-looking dolls—a boy (Gregor) or a girl (Sasha)—had dark or fair hair, brown or blue eyes, different skin colors, and everyday play clothes. They were designed to break down cultural stereotypes, and were made by different manufacturers in different countries. Authentic clothing and a swing tag on the wrist will add value, as will the doll's general condition, especially if the long hair on the female model is uncut.

Did You Know?

Kewpies began life as doodles in the love stories that Rose O'Neill illustrated for the American magazine, "The Ladies' Home Journal." Asked to develop them into a children's series, Rose redesigned them as dolls. They were so successful that they were even commemorated on a postage stamp.

▶ **A vintage, Mary Hoyer, hard-plastic doll,** with her original dress and tag, and marked on the back with the maker's mark. *1950s, 14 in (35 cm) high.*

$300–500

◀ **Two plastic Rosebud Kewpie dolls,** with molded hair. *1950s, 6 in (15 cm) high.*

$30–40

A closer look at... a Madame Alexander doll

Dolls produced by this renowned New York maker are known for their detailed costumes and accessories—the example here even has a hairnet and hair curlers.

The doll still has its presentation box, which is in excellent condition

The hair is set in its original style and retains its floral band and hairnet

The clothes and accessories are still intact, including the hatbox

The tag is still attached, which adds value.

A Madame Alexander Margot Ballerina doll, with her original clothing, accessories, and box. She is in mint condition, which is rare for a doll of this age. *c. 1953, 14 in (35.5 cm) high.*

$700–1,200

Top Tips

- Avoid any doll with hair that has been altered by its owner—cut, restyled, or damaged by washing or brushing.
- Choose dolls that are clean, with unstained plastic. But also make sure that overenthusiastic cleaning hasn't damaged the surface of the plastic.
- Look for original accessories and packaging—especially the box—as these will enhance the value.
- Search for dolls with makers' tags still attached, as this also adds value.
- Marks indicating Madame Alexander dolls include: "Mme. Alexander," "Alexander," or "Alex."
- Beware of unauthorized Japanese-made Kewpies without a proper label.

KEEP

Madame Alexander is now one of the most desirable names in the plastic-doll market, and those models with eye-catching, brightly colored clothing are especially popular. Prices are rising fast, as interest in plastic dolls grows, so an example such as this is sure to at least retain its value.

A Madame Alexander, Morocco, bent-knee doll. The original clothing is in excellent condition and the doll still has its tag, making this piece well worth keeping. *1950s, 8 in (20 cm) high.*

$300–400

BUY

Many dolls made since the 1960s do not currently fetch high prices, but good-quality examples of models that were particularly popular in their day have the potential to rise in value as yesterday's children become tomorrow's collectors.

A Tiny Tears doll by American Character Doll Co. The saran hair is in good condition and Tiny Tears dolls are becoming increasingly sought after. *c. 1963, 12 in (30 cm) high.*

$100–150

Effanbee good

Effanbee dolls have been popular since the New York City-based company began production in 1912. One of the first plastic dolls was its Dy-Dee baby with applied ears, which can fetch from $150 to around $600 for an original, boxed, early rubber version. The Legends series, featuring dolls of stars such as John Wayne, Mae West, and Liberace, can be worth $70–280. Dolls are usually marked "Effanbee" on the head or torso, and a heart-shaped bracelet or label adds value.

Baby love

Companies such as Ideal, Horsman, and American Character Doll Co. produced early vinyl dolls, including "drink-and-wet" and "squalling" baby dolls, which were well loved by many children. The condition of such vinyl dolls is therefore often poor—check them for damage to fingers and toes. Make sure that hair hasn't been spoiled by any washing and that it is still in its original style. Sleeping eyes should open and close, and eyelashes should be intact. Missing or replaced clothes will lower the value.

Kewpie cuties

Cartoons and illustrations gave rise to many character dolls. One of the most popular was Kewpie, with her starfish-shaped hands, small "wings" over the ears, tiny eyebrows, and appealing face. As a result of the variety of different types, sizes, and materials available, as well as the range of prices, Kewpie dolls make an excellent collection on their own. Licenses were issued to various companies that produced inexpensive plastic Kewpies from the late 1940s and 50s; some pirate versions were also made.

The eyes have it

Googly dolls, with their large "goo-goo" eyes, were first produced in bisque by various German makers. Later plastic versions were made by a number of lesser-known manufacturers. These plastic dolls can often be found for under $100. Googly dolls with mischievous expressions are more collectible.

Barbie is the most successful doll ever made.

A generation of little girls abandoned their baby dolls for Barbie's fashion-conscious look and wardrobe of "must-have" clothes. Now well into her forties, she has her own website and publications, and admirers of all ages.

Toys, Dolls, and Teddy Bears

Launched at the American Toy Fair in New York City in 1959, Barbie was the first teenage doll. Her maker, Mattel, has issued many Barbies each year since then—plus accessories, as well as family and friends, including her boyfriend Ken, first launched in 1961.

The most prized Barbies are those from 1959–72, especially examples from the "ponytail" era (1959–64). Special limited-edition dolls (fewer than 35,000) are also desirable, as are early 1960s gift sets, Barbies and Kens with bendable legs (made in 1965–67), and fashion model Barbies, dressed in couture clothing (these must have their original labels). Red-haired Barbies, introduced in 1961, are rare and desirable. Aim to choose limited editions rather than standard pink box Barbies today.

Barbie is marked on her bottom, helping to date her, though bear in mind that the date shown is a patent date, not a date of manufacture. The face and hair also help with identification. Condition is crucial: a mint-condition doll, costume, or set of accessories in an unopened box will be worth two to four times more than one without its box.

▲ **A boxed SuperSize Barbie.** The extra-large Barbie was launched by Mattel in 1977 but never caught on. *c. 1977, 18½ in (47 cm) high.*
$120–180

▶ **A Growing Up Skipper.** This version of Barbie's sister, Skipper (1964), grew taller if her arm was twisted. The missing shoes lower the value. *c. 1970s, 9¼ in (23.5 cm) high.*
$30–50

▶ **A rare dressed Mattel Barbie No. 1.** The first Barbie was usually sold in a swimsuit. Dressed versions were for store display. This doll is complete with box, clothes, and shoes. *1959, 12 in (30 cm) high.*
$6,000–9,000

◀ **A Barbie Sings 45rpm record set,** with the "pages" made as record jackets and printed with lyrics. Among the many Barbie collectibles featured at sales and on the internet are posters, books, jigsaw puzzles, watches, and records. *c. 1961, 8 in (20.5 cm) wide.*
$40–60

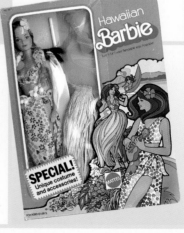

◀ **A Hawaiian TNT Barbie,** in its original box. TNT is short for "Twist 'n' Turn," a moving-waist feature that was introduced in the mid-1960s. *c. 1975, box 12½ in (31.5 cm) high.*
$60–90

▲ An *Exclusive Fashions* **brochure.** Mattel issued a short series of fashion brochures in 1963 and 1964. *1963, 4¼ in (10.5 cm) high.*

$10–15

▶ **A straight-leg Francie doll,** with original costume and box. Barbie's cousin Francie was produced from c. 1966–71. The straight-leg version was only made until 1968. Francies with bendable legs were also available. *c. 1966, 11¼ in (29 cm) high.*

$280–320

Collectors' Tips

- Check that the hair of a Barbie doll is uncut and in its original style
- Barbie's friends and family—including Ken, Midge, and Scooter—are less valuable but rarer, and their values could rise

▲ **A flock-haired Ken,** with clothes. Ken was introduced in 1961. The hair of this example is slightly rubbed away, which reduces the value. *c. 1961, 12¼ in (31 cm) high.*

$20–30

◀ **A brunette bubble-cut Barbie,** with original box and brochure. The hairstyle indicates a date of 1961–67. The complete packaging, in good condition, increases the value. *1963, box 12¼ in (31 cm) high.*

$150–200

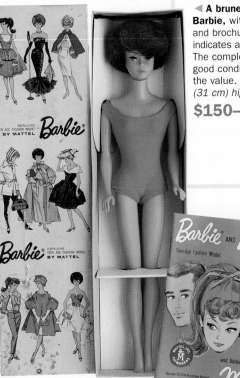

▲ **A Malibu Barbie.** With her beach-loving tan, the Malibu doll was such a success that other Barbie characters soon took on the Malibu look. *c. 1971, 12 in (30 cm) high.*

$20–30

Dollhouses reached the peak of their popularity from the late 19th century to the 1950s. Many mass-produced examples—and their furnishings—survive in good condition, and they are much sought after.

The first dollhouses, constructed by cabinetmakers in the 16th and 17th centuries, were models of the homes of the wealthy, created purely for display. The earliest surviving American dollhouse is dated 1744. It was a special commission for a wealthy Boston family, and now resides in the Van Cortlandt Museum in New York City. It was not until the 19th century that the dollhouse became a toy. Many examples made from the 1930s to the 1950s can be found today for about $200–600 or more.

Where the heart is

The age and rarity of early dollhouses make them valuable; a simple 17th-century European dolls' cabinet was sold in 1999 for more than $26,000. Size, quality, and original furniture and decoration contribute to the overall value, whatever the era. A modest late-19th-century house may be found for between $800 and $1,500, but many will cost around $1,500–9,000 or more. In the mid-19th century, very fine wooden dollhouses were carpenter-made in the style of

A wooden dollhouse bureau by Walterhausen, with a drop-down writing slope, in good condition. *1890s, 5½ in (14 cm) high.*

$280–320

grand New York brownstone townhouses. They were often extremely sumptuously furnished, and can command prices of $1,500–4,000. Many houses were repainted or repapered, and these are worth less.

A Shaker-style wooden Trustee's Office dollhouse, the interior complete with miniature Shaker furnishings, some signed "Don Crossen." *c. 1920s–40s, 36 in (90 cm) wide.*

$7,000–10,000

An American Bliss-type dollhouse, with a color lithographed paper decorated exterior and fully decorated interior, with minor damage. *c. 1895, 10¼ in (260 cm) high.*

$450–550

A closer look at... a dollhouse

Bliss is one of the best-known and sought-after US dollhouse manufacturers. Rufus Bliss of Pawtucket, Rhode Island, began making dollhouse furniture in 1832, and turned to making houses in 1889. His houses were modestly priced, and due to their success they were copied widely at the time, and later. Take a closer look at examples you come across to make sure you're buying the genuine article.

The design always includes typical characteristics of American houses of the period such as porches, balconies, gables, and balustrades

Certain characteristics of the printed design, such as turned wooden balusters, help to identify authentic originals

Bliss dollhouses are constructed from wood that is covered with richly colored printed paper with brickwork and other architectural features

A Bliss two-story dollhouse, opening to reveal children asleep in their beds on the second floor and children playing with dolls on the first floor. There is some bubbling to the paper, which is, generally still brightly colored. The house is missing its front steps and a piece of the railing paper has possibly been replaced, which reduces its value. *c.1900 16½ in (42 cm) high.*

$800–1,200

Look carefully in the printed designs for Bliss's name—it is often hidden, found on floors, doors, or under gables

Household names

Introduced in 1889, Bliss houses were made of lithographed paper glued to a wooden frame, and came in a range of styles (*see A Closer Look, above*). In 1894 the McLoughlin Brothers of New York launched a New Folding Dollhouse. This cardboard house could be assembled from flat board printed with wallpaper and floor coverings; flat cardboard furniture was also supplied. Bliss and McLoughlin houses are rare, and consequently valuable. Other manufacturers to look for include Gottschalk, Christian Hacker (both German), the English Lines Brothers, and US makers Schoenhut, Ideal, Plasco, Bluebox, and Marx. Items of original dollhouse furniture can fetch $50–400 or more, but later pieces can cost less than $20. Cast-iron furniture by J. & E. Stevens (c. 1870–1930) of Cromwell, Connecticut, is particularly desirable.

Prices for later houses from the first half of the 20th century range from $200–800 up to around $3,000, while an accessible area for new collectors is the wide range of mass-produced plastic houses from the mid-20th century onward. These include the shocking-pink and blue Barbie house by Mattel, and the Fisher Price house based on the TV series *Sesame Street*.

Top Tips

- Start with modern replica period furniture if you are on a tight budget.
- Always have any electrical components checked by a qualified electrician.
- Examine the style, decorative features, materials, size, and condition to date a house. Look at real houses of the era to identify period features.

BUY

Original period dollhouse furniture is always worth buying, as it is usually well proportioned and often detailed. Objects connected with the running of a house, such as domestic appliances included to help educate little girls, are particularly popular.

A lithographed tinplate sewing machine on a stand. The transfers are in comparatively good condition, particularly on the machine itself, and add to its value. *c. 1900, 2¾ in (7 cm) high.*

$100–150

KEEP

Small dolls made as accessories for dollhouses add realism and life to a house. Period examples were handled a lot, so those in good condition with their original accessories and clothing— usually indicating their role in the house—should at least hold their value.

A cloth dollhouse cook doll, with original clothing and holding a knife and fork. This example is clean; a dirty, worn, or damaged doll will be worth less. *1920s, 6½ in (16.5 cm) high.*

$50–60

Nursery playthings,

especially traditional toys such as rocking horses, wooden building blocks, and Noah's arks, have seenan upsurge of interest in recent years, but many inexpensive objects can still be found today.

Nursery toys first became popular in the late 18th century. In the following century vast numbers were produced, and pieces from this era are valued, both for their charm and craftsmanship—especially if they are undamaged. Toys from the 20th century can be a desirable, and less costly, option.

A stable market

Rocking horses are great favorites, and values have remained steady. The finely crafted bow rockers made

Did You Know?

For many children in the 19th century, play was forbidden on the Sabbath. Instead, a child read Bible stories with the family, or enjoyed a special Sunday toy with a religious theme, such as a Noah's ark.

in the 18th and 19th centuries are rare and can cost thousands of dollars. By the 1870s the bow-shaped stand had been largely replaced by a metal cradle on a wooden stand. F. H. Ayres, Bauer & Krause, and Lines Brothers mass-produced rocking horses into the 20th century. Prices for these normally range from $150 to about $1,200, but early examples with attractive, expressive features and fine painting can command more than $1,500–3,000. Look for horses in good condition with tail, saddle, and bridle intact.

Rocking horses from the 20th century offer value for money—a good example can cost about $200–300. Horses with a connection to popular culture, such as those made to tie-in with TV shows such as *Roy Rogers* or *Hopalong Cassidy*, can be worth around $500 or more. Rocking/ride-on horses made by mid-20th-century toymakers in materials other

A Victorian toy baby carriage. *c. 1880s, 33 in (84 cm) long.*
$200–300

than wood, such as metal or rubber, can often be found for under $200, although these are usually less than full size.

The animals went in two by two

Noah's arks were popular during the 19th century. Few craftsmen had seen the creatures they were carving, so animal figures can be oddly shaped. Prices depend on quality of decoration, condition, age, and size; the type and number of animals are also factors. A large, complete 19th-century ark will cost at least $900–1,500, and a rare, top-quality, near-complete model up to $15,000.

Moveable wooden animals featured in Schoenhut's much-loved Humpty

A closer look at... a rocking horse

Rocking horses make delightful and enchanting toys for children, and buying one can prove to be an excellent investment. Consider the condition, shape, and the maker to ensure that you make the best choice.

The horse is realistically modeled with flared nostrils and bared teeth, as well as pricked-up ears

The red cloth, as well as the bridle, saddle, and stirrups, are original

The real pony-skin coat is unusual—most were painted—but it must be in good condition, otherwise value is lowered

The original horsehair mane and tail are still full and intact

An Ayres piebald rocking horse, with clear glass eyes. There are minor bald patches to the coat. The wooden safety rocker bears a plaque reading "Manufactured by Ayres, London," which adds value. *c. 1900, 53 in (135 cm) high.*
$800–1,000

A German painted wooden Noah's ark, with eight wooden people and 90 pairs of animals. *c. 1870s, ark 7½ in (19 cm) high.*

$900–1,500

Dumpty Circus, along with clowns and acrobats. Made between 1903 and 1935, these figures are highly sought after, and fetch $200–1,500, with some rare pieces valued at around $3,000.

Piecing it together

Jigsaw puzzles originally showed a world map, but in the 19th century other themes such as animals and nursery rhymes were introduced. With chromolithography, which was widely used by the 1870s, puzzles became more colorful and varied. Hand-cut, hand-painted wooden puzzles sell for the most—from around $300–400 to $1,500 or more for special examples.

The introduction of cardboard in the late 19th century, and new die-cutting techniques, led to an increase in puzzle production. Puzzles by McLoughlin, Par, Milton Bradley, Ives, and Parker Brothers are sought after. If a puzzle has crossover appeal, such as a sporting, military, or Wild West theme, it can sell for $80–500 or more.

Learning to build

Children's ABC building blocks from the 19th century in original boxes can be worth up to $800 a set, but early 20th-century examples often cost as little as $15–50. Vintage nesting block sets can sell for $400–800 if colorful and in good condition. More recent sets of non-wooden blocks also have some value; large sets of American Plastic Bricks by Elgo from the 1960s have changed hands for $30–100 or more.

Playtimes and teatimes past

Children's tea sets have great appeal, and can cost anything from less than $30 to $800 or more. Sets featuring Disney or other popular characters can fetch $300–600 or more, depending on the date, with the 1930s being the most desirable.

Baby doll carriages and other wooden or metal toys, from cup and ball games to musical instruments, are popular—look for good quality and condition and original boxes.

BUY

Toys made in the 19th and early 20th centuries include spinning tops and tee-totums—a six-sided top with numbers. Items such as these are often ignored and sold in boxes of assorted pieces for a few dollars. Check carefully as pieces can sometimes be worth more than the price of the box, especially if they are in good condition, or in materials such as fruitwood or ivory.

A carved ivory spinning top. This example is desirable as it is made from ivory rather than bone. Most were made from wood or tin. *c. 1910, 1 in (2.5 cm) high.*

$30–40

KEEP

Since toys and games from the 19th century and before are consistently popular, cherish any that you find or inherit. Prices may well rise, especially if the game is complete and in good condition.

A child's miniature white glazed ceramic tea set, with floral decoration, in original box. *c. 1950s, box 8½ in (21.5 cm) wide.*

$20–30

An early Victorian English jigsaw or "dissected puzzle," of the British Isles, in a painted wooden box. As well as being complete, this puzzle has its original box, making it desirable. *c. 1820s, box 6¾ in (17.5 cm) wide.*

$150–250

Games

played by the whole family celebrate childhood and the best aspects of family life. Vintage card games, board games, and chess sets are in demand, especially those in good condition.

The mix of chance, skill, and rivalry that characterizes indoor games has fascinated people for centuries. Games that are visually interesting, such as decorative 19th- and early 20th-century examples, are generally the most desirable. Many vintage games can cost $50–200 or less and rarely reach more than $1,500.

Keep in check

Many chess sets were produced in the 19th century; earlier examples are hard to come by. Prices for collectible sets start at $50–80 for a plastic example from the 1950s. By contrast, a 19th-century ivory set can raise $1,200 up to $12,000 or more depending on age, quality, and condition.

Sets made of ivory, decorative glass, and exotic woods, such as rosewood, are prized, while more basic examples made of bone or common woods, such as boxwood, are generally less desirable but form the staple of many collections.

Sets by the English maker John Jaques & Sons (known as Staunton sets because they were endorsed by the chess celebrity Howard Staunton) are almost a collectible area in themselves. They were made from the Victorian period until the early 20th century and vary in value from around $250 to $900. Look for original boxes with green labels and stamped pieces to indicate an authentic Jaques chess set. Similar sets were produced by other makers; these are known as Staunton pattern and can be found for about $120–500.

A Tiddly Winks game by John Jacques & Sons, with its original box. c. 1890, box 4 in (10 cm) wide.
$40–60

A Famous Five card game, with its original box. The popularity of Enid Blyton's storybook characters and the superb artwork on each card make this set highly sought after. *1950s, box 3½ in (9 cm) high.*
$50–80

Some card games to look for:
■ Famous Five ■ Happy Families ■ Snap ■

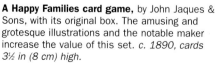

A Happy Families card game, by John Jaques & Sons, with its original box. The amusing and grotesque illustrations and the notable maker increase the value of this set. *c. 1890, cards 3½ in (8 cm) high.*
$50–60

A Snap card game, with its original box. Each of the 24 color-lithographed cards depicts a strongly characterized figure. Early sets with well-drawn figures in period clothing are collectible. *c. 1900, cards 3¼ in (8 cm) high.*
$40–60

A John Jaques & Sons carved boxwood and ebony Staunton chess set. The white king is stamped "Jaques London." *1880s, king 3¼ in (8 cm) high.*

$300–400

On the board

McLoughlin board games from the 1870s to the 1910s feature lithography of an impressive quality and are highly desirable. Games such as District Messenger Boy, Steeple Chase, and Magnetic Fish Pond can fetch $200–400, while the rare Bulls and Bears game can sell for over $10,000.

Board games from the 1940s–60s that feature characters from comic strips, movies, and television are very collectible and are normally valued at around $100–200. Games of cult TV shows can fetch higher prices: a Game

Gems *Gilligan's Island* game can be worth as much as $600. Invest in board games of this type from the 1970s onward—most can be found for under $50, but prices are set to rise as demand increases over time.

Holding the right cards

Limited-run, high-quality, and unusual card games from the 19th century are desirable. Packs of playing cards from the 1890s, such as Happy Families by John Jaques & Sons, or Matchmaking, or Marrying For Mone" by McLoughlin, can fetch $30–60 each.

Top Tips

- Look for vintage editions of games at antique centers, flea markets, and garage sales.
- Avoid exposing board games and playing cards to sunlight, heat, damp, and dust—they are easily damaged.
- Don't try to repair boxes or boards yourself—seek help from a professional paper conservator.
- Look for vintage board games in their original boxes with all their original pieces, dice, and instructions.
- Examine chess pieces closely to see whether any have been repaired or are replacements.

■ Playing Cards ■

A set of De La Rue playing cards. These cards do not have numbers, suggesting that they are pre-1900. The two-headed figures were first used in the late 19th century. *1870s, cards 3¾ in (9.5 cm) high.*

$25–40

BUY

Small hand-held games from the 1920s and 30s rarely survive in good condition, as parts were often broken and pieces lost. Commonly found for $10–80 or less, those in original condition make an excellent and amusing collection and may be a good investment for the future.

A Ringtail Cat Puzzle dexterity game. This paper-covered wood, card, and glass game was made by R. Journet & Co., a highly collectible name, which adds to its value. *1920s, 4¼ in (11 cm) high.*

$50–80

KEEP

Magic sets are as popular with children today as they were more than 50 years ago. The subject has become a collecting area in its own right and the market looks set to grow. Look for vintage sets with attractive artwork and ensure that all the pieces are present.

A Hokus-Pokus magic set complete with its box and lid depicting a young magician entertaining his friends. The attractive artwork on the box, as well as the age of the set, adds to the value. *1930s, box 15½ in (39.5 cm) wide.*

$120–180

007
Tomorrow Never

Entertainment and Sports

Entertainment and sports memorabilia is a diverse area that covers many modern passions. From rock groups and football teams to movies, TV shows, and even computer games, the interests that have filled our spare time are intriguing to look back on and experience all over again.

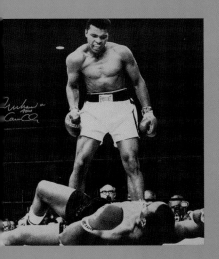

Dukes of
Hazzard *toy car,*
p. 231

1

Items connected to the
plethora of modern boy
bands will probably hold
no more than curiosity
value in future.

*Donald Duck coin
bank, p. 241*

2

Spotlight on the world..

Entertainment and sporting memorabilia such as film posters, signed
record albums, football programs, and old golf balls are the sort of
mementoes we all keep as reminders of special events in our lives.
But these items may have a value that is more than just sentimental.

Cult TV series and films have a loyal
fan base eager to own props and original
merchandise. *Star Trek, Mork & Mindy,* and
The Dukes of Hazzard ① have all had a
dedicated following over the years. As old
films and TV shows such as *Charlie's Angels*
are remade or rereleased, spin-off
items such as lunch boxes,
toys, and annuals
emerge from attics
and garages to be
appreciated again.
Walt Disney films

have been delighting children for over
80 years. Since the 1930s the company
has licensed toy and other manufacturers
to create products to complement its films.
These include soft toys, puppets, and money
banks ②. The biggest names of all when
it comes to movie merchandise must surely
be *James Bond* and *Star Wars* ③. Toys
and other spin-off items related
to the first films in these series
can be worth large sums,
particularly when complete
with original packaging.

5

*New York Mets
official yearbook,
p. 256*

NEW YORK METS

6

Wilson tennis balls, p. 262

7

*Football player
money bank, p. 258*

③ Star Wars *toy and box, p. 228*

④

..of entertainment

All in a name

Film props offer an exciting way for fans to own a piece of their favorite movie—be it dishes from the dining room on *Titanic*, a sword from *Gladiator*, or a letter addressed to Harry Potter.

Film posters ④ also attract a dedicated band of enthusiasts, who look for examples from blockbuster, cult, or classic films, or those that are typical of their era or have a striking design.

Sporting souvenirs

Souvenirs such as Superbowl tickets, signed bats, balls, or gear and official yearbooks ⑤ connected to popular teams and players are often valuable. There is also a thriving market for vintage sports equipment ⑥ and household items such as money banks ⑦ depicting any popular sport.

Era-defining icons

Whether or not you harbor a soft spot for Big Bird or Kermit the Frog ⑧, you will certainly have heard of them both. Stars of children's TV attract loyal fans long after they first appear on our screens. Likewise, if you were a fan of Elvis ⑨ and still have old memorabilia you are fortunate; most items associated with the King are worth at least a little money today to fans old and new. Children of the 1980s who held onto old video games could also find themselves in the money—the first pioneering consoles ⑩ are continually rising in value as advances in technology make earlier examples rare.

⑧ *Kermit the Frog soft toy, p. 233*

⑨ *Signed Elvis Presley card, p. 247*

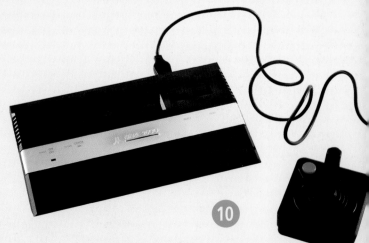

⑩ *Atari game console, p. 244*

Star Wars is one of the most merchandised movie franchises of all. An immense variety of products can be found with a *Star Wars* theme—from soaps and lunch boxes to toy figures, vehicles, and spacecraft. Any collector is spoiled for choice.

For collectors of *Star Wars* items, there are two names to look for: Kenner in the US and Palitoy in the UK (both now part of Hasbro). Their products are the most popularly collected and include action figures, board games, and puzzles. Many other companies secured *Star Wars* licenses too, and because of the strict control that the movies' creator, George Lucas, exercises over the rights to his trademarks, quality is high.

The figures add up

There are many tales of mothers disposing of supposedly priceless *Star Wars* toys. In reality, Kenner/Palitoy's original 1977 lineup of 12 figures are still available for $15–30 each,

although the less common characters and variations can raise $80–300, or more for truly exceptional items, such as an original vinyl-caped Jawa or Power of the Force Yak Face. The highest prices are reserved for figures still sealed in their packaging. Today, these figures can realize from $150 to $1,200. Again, rare variations can be worth more, depending on the figure. Look for packaging that shows the original 12 figures on the back of the pack, as this usually indicates an early example from the first series. Han Solo is one of the rarest figures from the original lineup and a sealed and unopened example in mint condition can be worth $500–800.

A *Star Wars* R2D2 figure and C-3PO action figure. *c. 1978, largest 3¾ in (9.5 cm) high.*

$15–25 each

Completing the scene

Star Wars figures were complemented by a line of vehicles and play sets based on scenes from the movies. Many contained small parts that were easily lost, and so intact surviving examples are valuable. There is even a thriving trade in the accessories, and the tiny guns that came with the figures can now sometimes fetch up to $15–30.

The Power of the Force line—the figures made by Kenner/Palitoy after the first trilogy of movies had come and gone—are also sought after. These did not sell in such high numbers as

Star Wars toys to look for:
■ AT-AT ■ Luke Skywalker ■ Jawa ■ Han Solo ■

▼ **A *Star Wars: The Empire Strikes Back* AT-AT (All Terrain Armoured Transport) by Palitoy, with its box.** An AT-AT must be in near-mint condition and complete with its box and all parts to reach this price. *c. 1980, 18 in (45.5 cm) high.*

$250–350

A *Star Wars* C-3PO bath-size bar of soap, unused and in its box. *c. 1978, 5½ in (14 cm) high.*

$3–5

previous lines and so are harder to find. A collector's coin was included in the packaging and these coins are among the most eagerly pursued newer *Star Wars* secondary collectibles.

The lunch box strikes back

For children in the early 1980s, a *Star Wars* lunch box was the height of fashion. Today, an *Empire Strikes Back* thermos and lunch box can sell for $120–180 if in excellent condition. Other household items that bore the *Star Wars* name include soap, toothbrushes, and bedclothes. Items made by better-known companies tend to be more valuable, and perishable items must be unused to retain any value. In general, the price for a *Star Wars* product that falls outside the more clearly defined categories of toy

figures and comic books depends largely on what a particular enthusiast is willing to pay to own it.

A galaxy of pictures

So many *Star Wars* posters were printed, and yet so few saved, that there is always a chance of coming across something new. Categories include posters for movie releases from various countries, advertising, and commemorative posters produced after each movie's release. Values vary widely, depending on age, condition, and, crucially, rarity. The original poster from the US release of *Return of the Jedi* bore the movie title "Revenge of the Jedi," until George Lucas decided that revenge was something a Jedi knight would not seek. Comparatively few survive, so prices are high: around $500–800. A different, more common, US one-sheet poster for the same movie can cost up to $150.

Original props from all the movies are hard to come by, as their availability and sale is strictly regulated by George Lucas's production company.

KEEP

Older Star Wars *merchandise, particularly anything from the early 1980s or before, has powerful nostalgia value for today's generation of thirty-somethings.*

An *Empire Strikes Back* thermos and lunch box made by Thermos. Condition is all-important —dents, scratches, and other damage reduce value. *1981, 8¾ in (22 cm) wide.*

$100–150

BUY

The Kenner brand has come to be a badge of quality among Star Wars *merchandise, and portable computer games are becoming more collectible and valuable. Early spin-off games that straddle these two collecting fields may well increase in value over the coming years.*

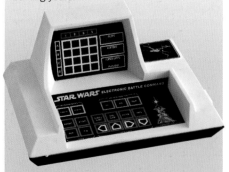

A Kenner *Star Wars* electronic Battle Command game. *c. 1979, 8¼ in (21 cm) wide.*

$100–150

A *Star Wars* Jawa action figure with a vinyl cape, by Kenner. If the cape were missing, or made of fabric, the figure would be worth less than $25. *c. 1978, 2½ in (6.5 cm) high.*

$280–320

◄ A *Star Wars* Luke Skywalker Early Bird action figure by Palitoy. This example, from the first batch of toys, is a rare variant with a long, extending light saber. *c. 1978, 3¾ in (9.5 cm) high.*

$250–350

▲ A *Star Wars: The Empire Strikes Back* Han Solo (Bespin Outfit) action figure by Palitoy, with packaging. Out of its packaging, the figure would be worth less than a tenth of this value. *c. 1981, card 9 in (22.5 cm) high.*

$200–250

Cult TV

From *Charlie's Angels* to *Buffy*, certain TV shows inspire a loyal and enduring following. Because of their nostalgia value and the cult status of their protagonists, the merchandising associated with them is a major source of interest.

Entertainment and Sports

It is probably our age that determines the period of TV history that really interests us. Anyone who grew up in the 1960s is likely to remember *Bewitched* or *Gilligan's Island* with affection, while children of the 1980s may have a soft spot for *Knight Rider* and *The A-Team*. The current trend for reruns, new movies based on TV classics, and even pastiches of TV shows, often creates a boom in prices for original memorabilia.

Cult collections

Enthusiasts tend to be fanatical about their collections, which may include storybooks, annuals, magazines, original toys, or posters based on characters or series. Owning a prop used in the filming of the original series is the dream for many, but prices are in a higher league than

those for general memorabilia and fetch from $300 to $1,200, or even thousands of dollars. Annuals, books, and other memorabilia, however, can often be found for under $100.

Cars and action figures are often a good place to start a collection. Many are still available, so look for examples in mint condition complete with their original boxes in similar condition. Values can range from $10 to $800, depending on condition and the popularity of the series. Corgi was known for its popular line of TV- and movie-related vehicles produced during the 1960s. Mego made a variety of figures, including characters from *Starsky and Hutch* and *Wonder Woman*. Hasbro's 1970s range of *Charlie's Angels* figures sold particularly well because they were the first major TV action heroines. Dolls

A button showing "The Fonz" from *Happy Days*. 1970s, 1 in (2.5 cm) diam.
$12–15

of the main cast members are likely to appreciate in value; they are currently available for around $30–90 each.

Memorabilia from *The Avengers* of the 1960s and *The New Avengers* of the 1970s attracts a lot of interest. Always look for pieces representative of the characters: Steed, for example, was known for his umbrella, which doubled as a sword stick; the toy version produced by Lone Star can be worth $500–600. Even the packaging card attached, with artwork of Steed brandishing the umbrella, can fetch around $100.

Some cult TV toy cars to look for:
- Knight Rider
- The Man from U.N.C.L.E.

A *Knight Rider* die-cast, **Knight Industries Two Thousand,** by ERTL. KITT, the talking sports car, was the real star of this 1980s show. *c. 1982, 5 in (12 cm) long.*
$60–80

A Corgi, No. 497, *The Man From U.N.C.L.E.* blue Thrush-buster, in excellent condition and boxed. Look for the rarer white version of this car. *c. 1966, 5 in (12 cm) long.*
$300–400

A **Charlie's Angels** lunch box and thermos, by Aladdin Industries. c. 1978, 8 in (20 cm) wide.

$150–250

Look ahead

More recent cult TV shows include *Buffy The Vampire Slayer*, *The X-Files*, *Xena: Warrior Princess*, and the new series of *Star Trek*. When buying merchandise, consider which shows are the most popular, because the children who watch them today will often become the nostalgia-driven collectors of tomorrow.

Bringing back memories

Other TV collectibles include tie-in books and comics, especially those with stories based on existing series. Books and comics from the 1970s and 80s in good condition range in value from $1–5 to $30–50. Cigarette cards and old copies of *TV Guide* featuring the main characters from TV series are also popular, but it can be hard to find a magazine in good condition. Copies of *TV Guide* from the 1960s to 80s usually sell for $10–20.

A growing trend since the early 1990s has been to collect lunch boxes decorated with images from popular children's shows. A 1979 *Buck Rogers* box could be worth more than $150, while complete boxes in mint condition from the 1950s, such as *The Lone Ranger*, may fetch up to $500–600.

Did You Know?

You can reenact favorite scenes from "The Prisoner" on the perfect stage: the bizarre and colorful village some of it was filmed in is not a set, but a real place—Portmeirion—built between 1925 and 1975 on the Welsh coast south of Snowdonia, in the UK.

Top Tips

- Look for memorabilia from the most popular or cult shows.
- Always look for products in original packaging, particularly toy cars.
- Beware of fake boxes and packaging. If a box looks new, it probably is.
- If you buy a jigsaw puzzle or game, make sure that all the pieces are there.
- Look for pieces that are representative of the characters or the series.

BUY

Buffy the Vampire Slayer has a cult following. If in mint condition with its box, a limited-edition piece that has gone out of production such as this figurine should rise in value.

A **Buffy the Vampire Slayer** limited-edition figurine, by Steve Varner, from an edition of 4,500. *2000, 9 in (23 cm) high.*

$90–100

KEEP

The planned Warner Bros. remake of the 1976 movie version of Logan's Run may attract renewed interest in items linked with the original movie and TV series, so hold on to those old annuals.

A **Logan's Run** annual, featuring cartoons and photographs, including many close-ups of the interiors of the vehicles used in the show. *1979, 10 in (25 cm) high.*

$5–6

▪ The Dukes of Hazzard ▪ The Prisoner ▪

A **Dukes of Hazzard** Hazzard County Sheriff car, by Ideal, in its original packaging. *1981, 5 in (12 cm) long.*

$20–30

A **Dinky Toys 106** *The Prisoner* Mini-Moke, boxed and in very good condition. *1967–70, 3 in (8.5 cm) long.*

$280–320

Character collectibles

include the thousands of products that were inspired by familiar characters of TV and film. Ideal for a child collector or anyone on a budget, they offer many treasures, from stickers to stationery.

Whether it's a Cookie Monster hand puppet, a Flintstone's lunch box, or a Snoopy dog bowl, the merchandise inspired by cartoons or comics is so varied it's almost bewildering. What makes a character appealing is hard to quantify, but it usually happens when a TV series becomes a classic or when a character is imbued with a special quality, such as Popeye's strength. Nostaligia is also a key factor.

Collectors look for quality, usually licensed, products, that are faithful to the original character. Some focus on a particular character, while others collect all characters from a show. Areas include figurines, toys, or kitchenalia. "Soakies," empty, character-shaped bottles of bubblebath, are a common collectible and generally cost $5–50. With toys, choose companies known for

A Canadian "I Read Hopalong Cassidy in the Toronto Star" pin. *1950s, 1 in (3 cm) wide.*
$120–180

quality such as Fisher Price Toys, Knickerbocker Toy Co., Remco, and The Ideal Toy Corporation. If the toy is clean and the original packaging is intact, all the better, as this is rare. Even advertising packaging is collectible, with companies like Kraft, Nestlé, and Post using characters to endorse everything from cheese to cereal. These can be scarce, as so many were thrown away. Prices tend to be low, however, usually under $30–50.

Howdy Doody favorites

One of the most popular characters is Howdy Doody, a boy puppet featured on the much-loved children's show that enjoyed a 13-year run from 1947. Vintage memorabilia in good condition is rare, but new material is still being made,

A Cookie Monster plush hand puppet, with a pull-string operating his mouth and googly eyes. If in better condition, he would fetch up to $30–40. *1980s, 10¼ in (26 cm) high.*
$15–25

including a figurine celebrating the 50th anniversary. An 18-inch vintage marionette of Howdy Doody from the 1940s, with some crazing, might be $40–80, while a vintage 4-inch figure of his friend Dilly Dally $10–20, and a rare 28-inch plush doll of Zip the Monkey $150–200. The show's sponsor, Wonder Bread, produced collectible stickers and an original 1950s one, showing Don Jose Bluster, would fetch $7–10.

Howdy Doody collectibles to look for:
■ Accessories ■ Clothing ■ Puppets ■

A plastic key-chain puzzle. He holds an NBC microphone so is post-1960, when NBC took over copyright. *1960s, 2½ in (6 cm).*
$35–45

A pair of ear muffs. Clothes were usually worn, becoming easily rubbed or damaged. On this example the fur and delicate celluloid are in mint condition, hence the high value. *1950s, 3¾ in (9.5 cm) high.*
$180–220

An articulated, printed-cardboard puppet. Puppets are desirable. This period example of Howdy Doody is valuable since, despite being in delicate cardboard, it is still bright and intact. *1950s, 13¾ in (33 cm) high.*
$70–100

Yaba Daba Do!

The first animated comedy on primetime TV, The Flintstones began in the Sixties and is part of most people's memories. It has spawned jewelry, mugs, salt and pepper shakers, cookie jars, toys, games, books, puzzles, and stickers—at least 3,000 products licensed by Hanna-Barbera. Available from $5–100, plastic figurines of the characters are an accessible collectible. Look for the 2-inch Kinder figurines—placed within chocolate eggs—as these are nicely crafted and easily found. Also inexpensive are mugs and glasses (from $10), and metal pins ($15–40). Lunch boxes will cost more ($100–150). Very coveted items include: cookie jars by top makers (an American Bisque Dino with Golf Clubs can make $550–650); early toys (a 1962 Fred Riding Dino mechanical toy by Louis Marx & Company can be $500–650); and hard-to-find toys (Frankonia Toy's battery-operated Fred Flinstone's Bedrock Band, c. 1962, can be $1,000).

Even older than the citizens of Bedrock are the cast of Looney Tunes including Porky Pig (1935), Bugs Bunny (1940), and Tweety Bird (1944). Making their debut in movies, these characters were an instant success, cheering a nation hard hit by the Depression. Of the 17 characters, Bugs Bunny is the

A Fred Flintstone soft vinyl-and-fabric doll, by Knickerbocker Toy Co., with plush and felt clothing, cardboard inserts in his feet to make him stand, and an original tag. *c. 1961, 17 in (43 cm) high.*

$70–100

favorite and the first Looney Tunes character with his own US postage stamp. Again, the selection of merchandise is diverse. Ceramics seem to be near the top of the price scale. A set of McCoy cookie jars from the Seventies with transfers of Bugs Bunny, Yosemite Sam, and Popeye can be worth $100 each, while a late 1940s M & H Novelty Corp. Bugs Bunny as a baseball player can fetch $150–200, if it's complete with carrot, bat, and ball.

Of course, here are many other characters to collect, from Charles Shulz's Peanuts characters (from 1950) to *The Muppets* and the Disney animation classics (usually pricey). New characters such as Garfield (1978) and *The Simpsons* (1987) are also on the scene. *The Simpsons* are a hot tip for the future; look for items relating to favorite character traits or sayings.

■ Cookie jars ■ Games ■

A rare Puritan cookie jar, which appeals to both cookie jar and Howdy Doody collectors. Lids were easily broken so mint-condition examples like this one are hard to find. *1960s, 7¾ in (19.5 cm) high.*

$500–700

An Electric Doodler game. Finding a game in good condition after play and a few decades' storage, and also with its box is hard, making this example desirable. *1960, 13½ in (33.5 cm) wide.*

$30–50

Top Tips

- If purchasing a battery-operated toy check for corrosion. Also make sure the battery cover is included.

- On items made up of many parts, check that all the pieces are there.

- Minor damage on rare items is acceptable, but be aware that cracks and chips should be reflected in the price. Hold items to the light and examine them closely.

- Don't ignore minor characters that were less popular as toys than main characters—devoted collectors often want rarities to complete sets.

KEEP

Characters that have endured in popularity, entertaining many generations, ensure that a wide audience of fans will be interested in them and that they will remain popular. Endearing or amusing character traits help to etch a character on many people's minds. Check the attic for licensed toys by known makers, as they are usually better made and truer to the look of the character.

A Jim Henson-licensed Kermit the Frog soft toy, by Fisher Price Toys. The unforgettable Kermit, with his funny voice, starred in the popular show. Keep toys that are complete and clean. *c. 1976, 19¾ in (50 cm) high.*

$22–28

BUY

Objects associated with popular characters are likely to appreciate in value. Look for original packaging. Classic characters still in the public eye through product endorsements, comics, or cartoons have the best chance of increasing in value.

Official Popeye wooden pipe. The rare packaging would appeal to Popeye collectors. He no longer endorses smoking, making this an item of its time. *1950s, 9 in (22.5 cm) wide.*

$60–90

Sci-fi TV memorabilia

has been in demand since science fiction shows first burst onto the small screen in the late Fifties. The appeal is just as strong today, as new viewers discover the magic.

When Yuri Gagarin became the first man in space in 1961, children everywhere dreamed of becoming astronauts, rocketing into the unknown. It's not surprising that science fiction shows on television soon became very popular.

Thunderbirds are go

Gerry Anderson was responsible for several 1960s science fiction puppet series, of which *Thunderbirds* is the best known and loved. A new generation of fans is created every time it is aired on TV. The recent movie has given *Thunderbirds* an even wider audience, and renewed interest may help prices of original memorabilia to rise.

From the earliest days, themed merchandise was popular and included everything from games and comics to action figures and toy versions of the vehicles. Original toys in good condition are sought after, and merchandise in perfect condition can command astonishing prices because of its rarity—few toys are left untouched in their original packaging. A 1966 *Thunderbirds* rifle in boxed and mint condition made by Crescent was sold a few years ago for $3,000. Given its rarity, even a used rifle without its illustrated box can fetch $500–900. Lady Penelope's FAB 1 car by Dinky from the same period can fetch around $150–300 or more, provided that it is in mint condition with its packaging.

Stickers, buttons, trading cards, and other small items are often available for $10–15 or less, and original 1960s annuals usually cost about $2–15.

Shrewd investors may prefer to gamble on more

A plastic Mork From Ork Eggship, with removable Mork figure, copyright Paramount Pictures Corp. c. 1979, egg 4½ in (11 cm) high.

$15–20

recent lines. A mid-1990s *Thunderbirds* model by Matchbox, kept in immaculate condition with its box, can now cost $30–50. When choosing current toys, look for lots of detail, gadgets, and moving parts; toys that are popular now are likely to be collectible in years to come, but only if kept boxed and in excellent condition.

Beam me up

Star Trek launched a galaxy of movies, spin-off shows, merchandise, and fanzines. First shown in 1966, the show has a huge following. The continued interest in all things "Trekkie" means it is still worth searching for bargains. A complete set of the five 1960s promotional cards distributed by TV stations can fetch up to $50–90, while a 1970s Mego action figure can be worth $80–250, depending on rarity and condition. Later figures, such as those issued alongside *The Next Generation* series, are generally less expensive. Try attending *Star Trek* conventions to learn what's popular.

A few Bucks

The successful television series *Buck Rogers in the 25th Century* and *Battlestar Galactica*, both by Glen A. Larson and featuring live actors, also have their fans and a band of devoted collectors. Despite the success of the television show, *Buck Rogers* toys by Mego did not take off, making them difficult to find today. Carded action figures can cost $20–30

A Star Trek Champions pewter figure of Captain Kirk, inspired by the 1979 film *Star Trek: The Motion Picture*; from a limited edition of 9,998. 1998, box 9¼ in (23.5 cm) high.

$60–90

A closer look at... *Star Trek* figures

Mego Corp is one of the most collectible names in action figures. They are not as widely collected as Kenner's *Star Wars* toys, but nevertheless attract a cult following since they are well made.

It is "carded," in its original packaging with its accessories. Loose figures are worth a fraction of this value

Mego designed this figure; it did not appear in any *Star Trek* episode

A rare Star Trek Aliens Neptunian carded action figure, by Mego Corp. This was the only figure that Mego designed; all other characters in the line were taken from the TV series or films. *c. 1976, card 9 in (23 cm) high*

$200–250

A Star Trek Klingon carded action figure, by Mego Corp. This popular character appeared in all five TV series, although its appearance changed from this original version over the years. *c. 1974, card 9 in (23 cm) high.*

$30–50

Look for Romulan and Andorian figures, which are rarer and more valuable

This is one of the most common figures found, along with the popular Kirk and Spock

---

each, but the market is small and prices are not likely to rise much in the near future.

Model kits are reasonable buys, but only if they are boxed and in mint condition. Airfix kits from the 1970s Anderson live-action series *Space 1999* and the 1990s *Battlestar Galactica* kits by Revell can often sell for $15–30, if unused.

A Dinky Lady Penelope's FAB 1 car, 100. The car is in excellent condition but the box is damaged. *1967–75, box 8 in (20 cm) long.*

$150–250

Lost and found

Irwin Allen shows of the 1960s such as *Lost In Space*, *Land of the Giants*, and *Voyage to the Bottom of the Sea*, have acquired cult followings, and original merchandise is sought after. A *Land of the Giants* annual from 1969 can fetch $15–30, while a complete set of bubblegum cards from 1968 can be worth $600–900. A 1960s Remco toy of the robot from *Lost In Space* can command $500–600. Interest in *Lost In Space* may increase amid rumors of a new TV series in the works. Newer items, such as a limited–edition 1998 lunch box, currently valued at $40–50, may therefore be worth investing in.

"X" marks the spot

Collectibles from more recent, popular series may also rise in value. Go for limited editions and rare items. Props used in TV series are always sought after: a sword used by the Berserker character in *Xena: Warrior Princess* can fetch $600–700. *The X-Files* has a large fan base, so merchandise such as complete card sets (currently valued around $15), or collector's issue comics ($15–25 in mint condition), may rise in value in the future.

Top Tips

- Always keep modern toys and memorabilia in their original packaging if bought for investment. Also aim for limited edition numbers with low edition sizes.
- Keep an eye out for Gerry Anderson characters from the 1990s line of "candy toys" by Konami, since these look set to rise in value.
- Hunt for sci-fi-related board games at garage sales—not everyone recognizes their value as collectibles.
- Look for Playmates—the most collected *Star Trek* figures. Expect to pay about $8–25 for characters in good condition.

KEEP

The price of original memorabilia can leap following rereleases and remakes of movies or series. Pieces linked to the original series may rise in value as a result.

A *Battlestar Galactica* story book, dating from the original series. The revamped recent series has renewed interest in the show. *1978, 10¼ in (26 cm) high.*

$4–5

SELL

Buck Rogers is not a favorite, and there are no revivals planned. Pieces may not increase in value, so sell now and invest in promising items, such as those from Star Trek.

A Buck Rogers Laserscope Fighter, made by Mego Corp. As this is in mint condition with its box, it will appeal to an avid collector. *c. 1979, box 12 in (30 cm) high.*

$50–60

James Bond,

007, has proved to be a license to print money—for merchandisers. Ian Fleming's MI6 franchise has been so successful that, 50 years after the first publication of *Casino Royale*, the English gentleman spy is still big business.

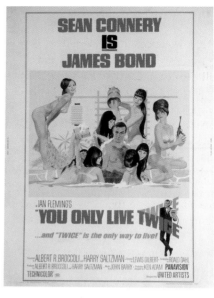

An American "C"-style one-sheet poster for *You Only Live Twice,* with artwork by Robert McGinnis. *1967, 41 in (104 cm) high.*

$1,200–1,800

Maybe it's the cars, the girls, or the gadgets. It could be the music, the villains, or the exotic locations. Whatever the reason, James Bond movies have caught the public imagination. Most enthusiasts were probably children when they saw their first Bond movie, so nostalgia plays a significant part in their desire to accumulate mementos. In addition, the more recent Pierce Brosnan releases have helped to create new fans and inspire older collectors.

The name's Bond, James Bond
Bond's enduring popularity makes memorabilia connected to the movies much sought after. Anything from the 1960s Sean Connery period is desirable, especially posters and toys.

For many Bond fans who grew up in the 1960s, the satisfaction lies in buying toys they perhaps could not afford at the time. The Corgi gold Aston Martin toy car can be worth around $150–250 with its box and in excellent condition. Other 1960s merchandise such as puzzles, costumes, and lunch boxes can attract prices from $50–500. A 1960s puzzle by Arrows with a scene from *Thunderball* or *Goldfinger* may fetch around $80–100, if complete and with its box. Although 007 only ventured into space once (in *Moonraker*), several of the movies have featured space sequences and space merchandise is a perennial favorite. Deluxe versions of Mego's 1979 space-suited James Bond figures with the rocket pack and helmet can fetch up to $300–400.

The last international playboy
First editions of Fleming's early novels are expensive, running into thousands of dollars for the rarest, but you can still own a genuine piece of Bond literary history for a more modest sum. A Jonathan Cape first British edition of *Octopussy* and *The Living Daylights* issued together in one volume might only cost $80–100, and even a 1961 *Thunderball* can be had for $500–800. Old numbers of *Playboy* magazine,

Some movie posters to look for:
▪ From Russia With Love ▪ The Living Daylights ▪

A British one-sheet poster for *From Russia With Love,* linen-backed. The original UK release poster is hard to come by, so it attracts high values. *1964, 40 in (102 cm) wide.*

$3,500–5,000

A teaser and illegal-release warning poster for *The Living Daylights.* *1987, 20 in (51 cm) wide.*

$150–180

A British quad poster for *Tomorrow Never Dies.* This version was withdrawn from circulation because "Tomorrow" was spelled incorrectly in the credits, making the poster hard to find. *1997, 40 in (102 cm) wide.*

$100–150

which was licensed to serialize Fleming's work, are less expensive still. Between 1960 and 1966 at least six James Bond stories were featured in *Playboy*, illustrated by Daniel Schwartz and Howard Mueller, notable *Playboy* graphic artists, among others. The relationship between *Playboy* and 007 is so close that Bond is seen carrying a *Playboy* card in *Diamonds Are Forever*, and the 1999 Raymond Benson short story featuring James Bond was not only published in *Playboy* but was actually set in Hugh Hefner's mansion. Many of these magazines cost less than $15, although the older and more sought-after issues can command prices of $60–90 and even higher.

Sound and vision

James Bond posters are a high priority for enthusiasts. Early posters have become classics and can fetch high prices at auction, from around $80–150 up to around $5,000 or more. The first, produced for *Dr. No* in 1962, set the standard for the entire series, featuring Bond with a gun and girls. The artwork on these early examples ranged from superb paintings to photomontage by artists such as Robert McGinnis and Frank McCarthy. Posters from the 1980s and 90s have not yet

A signed Pierce Brosnan publicity photograph. *c. 1996, 10 in (25.5 cm) high.*
$50–80

matched the cult status of the 1960s examples, but may become classics in time. Look for the classic movies— *Thunderball* (1965) was remade in 1983 as *Never Say Never Again*, and many aficionados spurn the second version as inferior.

The signature of a Bond actor across a poster increases its value. Signed publicity stills of Pierce Brosnan may fetch $50–120.

Since Bond movies are rereleased on DVD, the enthusiast can start to build a collection of boxed sets. It's likely that many of the limited-edition Blue, Gold, and Silver MGM sets produced in the last few years are being stored away in the hope that they will one day rise in value, but this will not happen unless demand exceeds supply.

The price of original vinyl soundtracks might climb sooner. A 1979 *Moonraker* LP in good condition will fetch around $12–20, and the rarer Japanese release of the album can be worth three times more. An original French 7-inch single release of the *Goldfinger* theme can fetch $50–60. More obscure items can attract higher prices since they are harder to find.

■ Tomorrow Never Dies ■ Dr. No

An American one-sheet poster for *Dr. No*, with art by Mitchell Hooks; linen-backed. A seminal piece of Bond iconography, this poster is the one that started it all. The UK version can fetch $8,000–9,000. *1962, 41 in (104 cm) high.*
$2,000–2,500

Top Tips

- Try to buy posters in good condition, without pin holes or tape marks, and don't consider those that have been trimmed or dry-mounted.
- Look for rare variations in poster artwork, which can add to the value.
- Some firms are reproducing original packaging for vintage Bond toys, so pay close attention to copyright notices and printing methods when considering purchase.

BUY ▶

007 and Playboy *have shared a passion for glamorous women, hi-tech gadgetry, and the finer things in life. Back issues of the magazine in excellent condition with a strong 007 theme are a promising investment.*

A November 1965 copy of *Playboy* magazine. This was the first issue of *Playboy* to feature Bond girls and has a wonderful cover image. *1965, 11 in (28 cm) high.*
$30–50

KEEP ▶

Toy cars are highly collectible, especially the cars used in the Bond movies. As so many were produced, look for those in near mint condition, with the box and any other accessories that came with them.

A Corgi James Bond Aston Martin DB5, No. 261, with its original picture box. The Aston Martin DB5 is perhaps the most famous Bond car of all. *1964, 40 in (102 cm) wide.*
$120–180

Movie memorabilia, from

classics of the studio era to today's blockbusters, yields a rich variety of collectibles; enthusiasts want a piece of their favorite motion picture. The range is huge, with objects and prices to suit everyone.

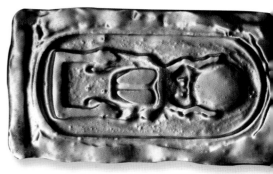

Once the sets are cleared, props and memorabilia can be sold at auction. The market is extremely volatile, and although simply owning a keepsake from a movie can be fun, it is even better if it is likely to go up in value.

The big screen

Some people focus on a particular star, while others collect by genre, such as horror movies. Objects linked to leading movie stars go for the highest prices and make the best investment. Props, autographs, posters, photographs, and costumes are the mainstays, with photographs and autographs often costing $80–150. Almost anything is collected, including movie scripts and crew T-

shirts—a T-shirt from *A.I. Artificial Intelligence* can cost around $15–30.

More common or numerous props that play a small role in the movie can be inexpensive. A life jacket from *Titanic* can be worth $60, and an ammunition clip from *Saving Private Ryan* can cost $15–30. Iconic items can carry a heavy price tag: Harrison Ford's whip from the *Indiana Jones* movies raised $18,000 at auction.

Poster appeal

Movie posters have evolved their own collectors' cult, with prices to match. An original *King Kong* poster was sold for a staggering $53,000, because of its rarity and stunning artwork. Values depend on the featured stars, the popularity of the

A gold-colored "gold ingot" from *The Mummy*, impressed with the design of a scarab beetle. *1999, 11 in (28 cm) wide.*

$80–120

movie, and the impact of the artwork. Look for foreign posters with striking designs; studios sometimes produce different layouts for each country, although this practice is dwindling.

US one-sheet posters (27 in/68.5 cm x 41 in/104 cm) and British quad posters (30 in/76 cm x 40 in/ 101.5 cm) are the most popular sizes. Only pristine original posters will fetch high prices, although it is difficult to find mint-condition pre-1970s examples. Creases, tears, pin holes, and tape damage all reduce value.

Some movie posters to look for:
▪ The Godfather ▪ The Shining ▪ Gladiator ▪

◄ **The Godfather,** British quad poster. This is a classic image from a seminal film that united some of the best talents working in the industry at the time. A poster for this film is very likely to hold its value. *1971, 40 in (101.5 cm) wide.*

$600–800

▼ **The Shining,** British quad poster. Posters showing key scenes or central characters are desirable. This image of the deranged Jack Torrance (played by Jack Nicholson) breaking through the bathroom door with his fire ax is evocative of the terror inspired by this film. *1980, 40 in (101.5 cm) wide.*

$300–400

Gladiator, promotional poster. The addition of important signatures, such as on this poster, signed by Russell Crowe, can add value, particularly if it is a less common pre-release promotional poster. *2000, 42 in (106 cm) high.*

$800–1,000

Costume collection

Prices for clothing vary. A suit worn by Al Pacino in *The Recruit* sold for about $800, but, interestingly, there was more demand for costumes worn by his up-and-coming co-star Colin Farrell. At the other end of the scale, a pair of beige pants worn by James Dean in the 1955 classic *East of Eden* sold at auction in the US for $15,000.

Quality goods

The quality of movie memorabilia varies greatly. Props that featured prominently in a scene or were in the foreground of a shot are likely to be more detailed and better made than background props, and so are more valuable. Weapons are especially sought after.

When buying props or costumes, look for studio tags or certificates. For example, large numbers of props from *Titanic*

were sold, but a studio certificate accompanied each item. Any item that does not come with a guarantee is probably not authentic.

Popularity shifts

When a blockbuster opens, there can be a clamor for collectibles and prices can rise, then fall when the publicity dies down. If the movie is released on video or DVD, interest—and prices—may soar again. There are exceptions, such as the James Bond movies, but price fluctuations are common.

Look for items linked to cult (or potential cult) movies. *Blade Runner* bombed at the box office, so few props were kept. Today it is a cult movie and anything associated with it is now sought after—and difficult to find.

A used, prop White Star Line, Moët & Chandon champagne bottle from *Titanic*. 1997, 12 in (30 cm) high.
$250–350

Top Tips

- Autographed photographs may not be genuine—many are signed by assistants, or stamped, or printed.
- Before buying, carefully track prices for memorabilia linked to Hollywood blockbusters, such as souvenirs given away before the film is released.
- Posters are often reproduced—these fetch lower prices than originals. Check sizes, printing method, and paper carefully.

BUY

Look for props from key moments in a movie, as these are likely to have enduring popularity and consistent values. Certain movies and characters never fall out of fashion, but inexpensive items can be found and may rise in price if they fulfill these criteria.

A prop copy of the *Daily Planet* from *Superman III* recalls the memorable scene from the picture in which Superman straightens out the Leaning Tower of Pisa. 1983, 23 in (58.5 cm) high.
$150–250

BUY

Observe what children—tomorrow's collectors—are watching, since nostalgia is an important motive for collecting. Buy pieces that are present in key scenes, or that give a strong flavor of the movie as a whole.

A wand box from *Harry Potter and the Philosopher's Stone.* This first Harry Potter movie is almost certain to become a classic. 2001, 14 in (36 cm) long.
$700–1,000

▪ A.I. ▪ The Lord of the Rings ▪

A.I. Artificial Intelligence, advance US one-sheet poster. The film was preceded by interactive hype on the internet and in other media. The credits on this poster contain hidden symbols that unlock information on a website. 2001, 41 in (104 cm) high.
$100–150

The Lord of the Rings: The Fellowship of the Ring, style A, teaser one-sheet poster. Teaser posters, issued before the film's release, are more desirable than a standard poster. The style B poster shows Frodo looking down at the ring. 2001, 41 in (104 cm) high.
$100–150

Animation—in particular, animation art—is a popular collecting area, with often high prices justified by good investment prospects. The emperor of the craft is Disney, whose artifacts and merchandising attract a passionate following.

When Mickey Mouse first appeared in the black-and-white cartoon short *Steamboat Willie* in 1928, who could have foretold that this endearing little rodent would one day become a collectible with extremely good investment potential?

The mighty mouse

Mickey Mouse's creator, Walt Disney, must have had some inkling of his invention's commercial potential, since the great Disney merchandising machine started to roll as early as 1930. If you want to start collecting Mickey memorabilia, it's worth familiarizing yourself with his changing looks over the years. Early, desirable Mickey Mouse figures have ratlike bodies, large hands, and a tail. Mickeys that have eyes shaped like pies with one slice removed usually indicate an early date. But this look can be faked, so also check for signs of aging, such as old scratches or wear. Genuine scratches acquire grime and dirt over time, while chips on old ceramics are less sharp around the edges than new ones.

Steiff made soft Mickey Mouse toys from 1931–36, and these are very desirable. In good condition, these toys can be worth around $5,000–8,000, with rarer versions—such as those dressed in blue pants—fetching $12,000–18,000.

A golden decade

Any piece of merchandise from the first 10 years of Disney output—

A Wade Heath miniature tea set for the nursery, comprising six pieces with transfer-printed Walt Disney designs. *c. 1940s, teapot 3 in (8 cm) high.*
$30–40

A baby's rattle, with painted celluloid figures of Snow White and the Seven Dwarfs suspended from the brass ring. *1940s, 3 in (8 cm) high.*
$40–60

much of it made in the US, Germany, and Japan—is collectible and can fetch high sums, provided it is all in one piece. Look for printed marks indicating Disney's copyright details, as these help to date pieces. Officially licensed items produced before 1938 should be marked with "Walt Disney Enterprises" or "Walter E. Disney." Look for

A yellow Catalin Disney Donald Duck pencil sharpener. *c. 1930s, 1½ in (3.5 cm) wide.*
$40–60

Mickey and Minnie windup toys, ceramic figures, dolls, and utility items such as egg cups and toothbrush holders from this period, since they are very scarce today. Figures of characters from early Disney movies are also highly sought after—for example, a good, vintage set of cloth *Snow White and the Seven Dwarfs* dolls can fetch more than $1,500, while a large, early wood and composition Pinocchio figure by Ideal can be worth $800–1,200. Disney tins from the 1930s and 40s are also desirable. Available in many shapes, sizes and designs, they can command anything from $30 to $600 or more.

Disney for the masses

Because of the increasing scarcity of pre–World War II Disneyana, collectors have turned to merchandise from the 1950s, 60s, and 70s. During this period plastic

Essential Mickey Mouse

EARLY DESIGNS
This Micky Mouse soft toy with an angular face is early and by Steiff, making it highly desirable, despite its missing tail. c. 1930s, 12 in (30.5 cm) high.
$5,000–8,000

CERAMIC FIGURES
The value of ceramic figures like these depends on their age and size. Early and large figures command the highest prices. c. 1970, largest 3 in (8 cm) high.
$40–60

TINS
Mickey Mouse tins can fetch a considerable sum. This example is early, has bright, attractive artwork, and is in good condition. 1930s, 6 in (15 cm) wide.
$300–400

DIE-CAST
Toys in die-cast include novelties such as this Mickey and Minnie barrel organ. The figures are separate from the organ. c. 1940s, box 4 in (10 cm) high.
$280–320

COIN BANKS
Early coin banks were often used as toys, rather than for saving. This rare French cast-aluminum model is by the Depeche Company. 1930s, 6 in (15 cm) high.
$200–300

BUTTONS
Many buttons were made and they are still common. This one is marked "Walt Disney 1937" and made by Kay Kamen Ltd. c. 1937, 1¼ in (13 cm) diam.
$20–40

overtook tin as the preferred material. Disney characters from movies such as *The Lady and the Tramp* (1955), *101 Dalmations* (1961), and *The Jungle Book* (1967) became major subjects for merchandising. Items such as lunch boxes, card games, and cereal bowls from this era can still be found for less than $100, with boxed plastic toys fetching $300–400 or more.

Inexpensive and commonly found items such as buttons, pens, erasers, and greeting cards may rise in value in the long term, particularly if from the 1930s–50s. But the best investment potential for modern pieces lies with larger or more unusual items and strictly limited editions, provided they are in mint condition with original packaging.

Computer creatures
Is it worth keeping merchandise and memorabilia from the computer-generated cartoons of today, such as *Toy Story*, *Dinosaur*, and *Monsters Inc.*? It certainly is—provided you keep the presentation box and the item is well preserved, be it a stuffed toy or a comic book. Such classic animations represent the nostalgia of tomorrow.

A painted Donald Duck coin bank, the paint showing serious wear. *1940s, 6½ in (16.5 cm) wide.*
$40–60

KEEP
Attractive boxed sets with all their original pieces are likely to appreciate, even if produced comparatively late.

A boxed set of Mazda Disneylights, manufactured by the British Thomson-Houston Co. This consists of 12 bell-shaped Christmas-tree lights, each printed with Disney characters, including Mickey Mouse, Dumbo, the Seven Dwarfs, and Bambi. The box adds value. *c. 1960s, box 10 in (25 cm) high.*
$60–90

BUY
Although produced in vast numbers, early paper and cardboard items are often damaged. When in good condition, they make excellent display pieces, showing artwork characteristic of their period.

A Hallmark Cards Disney Mickey Mouse 5th birthday card. Well preserved and with a charming subject, this is likely to appreciate in value: its current price is low for a vintage piece. *c. 1930s, 4¼ in (11 cm) high.*
$12–18

Did You Know?
Walt Disney originally wanted to call his mouse Mortimer but his wife felt that was rather pompous and preferred Mickey.

A limited-edition Disney On Ice serigraph of Mickey and Minnie Mouse skating, taken from a 1935 original production cel. *c. 1998, 13 in (33 cm) wide.*

$400–500

The animation craze

Interest in animation art has greatly increased during the last decade, with characters such as Homer Simpson becoming the cultural mascots of the digital age. Not only has original artwork from cartoons increased sharply in value, but limited-edition prints have also become eminently collectible.

The most popular animation art collectibles are "cels" (individual celluloid frames used in the animated movies), or the drawings they were based on. Originals can fetch thousands of dollars, but there is also a thriving market in limited-edition replicas.

In the 1970s, when values for original cels started to rise, Disney was prompted to launch its own art program. Today, Disney produces limited-edition cels taken from digitally produced images, then reduced in size and hand painted. These are not used in the movie, being produced strictly for the collectibles market, but they are becoming valuable in their own right.

Cartoon classics

Of interest to collectors are (in order of the production process) production sketches, storyboards, production cels, limited-edition, hand-painted production cels (as already described in relation to Disney) and the less expensive serigraph

A Pinocchio doll by Ideal, fully jointed and made from wood, with its original oilcloth collar and felt bow tie. *1940s, 7½ in (19 cm) high.*

$150–250

cels (machine produced using silk-screening), and giclée prints (mass-produced using a digital technique).

Disney, Warner Bros. (*Looney Tunes*), and Hanna-Barbera (*Tom and Jerry, The Flintstones*) fetch the highest prices because their cartoons are the most recognizable and loved, are internationally renowned, and, hence, have the largest followings. They can also offer desirable earlier items, but old and new animation artwork, prints, ceramics, and interpretive work from other studios such as Fox, Cartoon

"I hope that we never lose sight of one thing: that it was all started by a mouse." Walt Disney

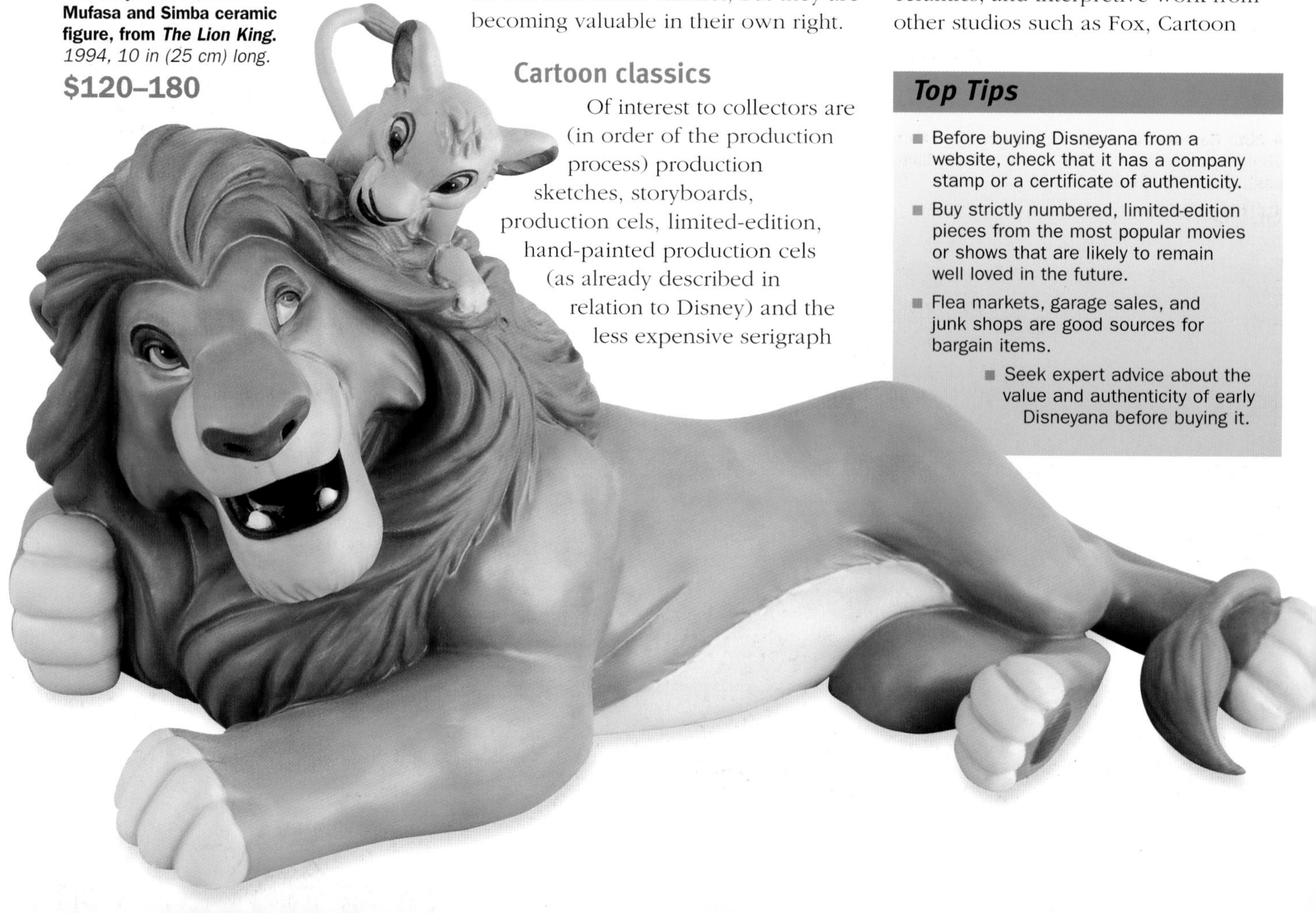

A Disney Pals Forever Mufasa and Simba ceramic figure, from *The Lion King. 1994, 10 in (25 cm) long.*

$120–180

Top Tips

- Before buying Disneyana from a website, check that it has a company stamp or a certificate of authenticity.

- Buy strictly numbered, limited-edition pieces from the most popular movies or shows that are likely to remain well loved in the future.

- Flea markets, garage sales, and junk shops are good sources for bargain items.

- Seek expert advice about the value and authenticity of early Disneyana before buying it.

Did You Know?

All production artwork at Walt Disney was drawn by hand until Beauty and the Beast in 1991. From that date, only certain elements, such as characters, have been hand drawn, and were used in conjunction with computers. 2004's "Home On The Range" was declared to be Disney's last hand-drawn movie, and the company is now concentrating on 3-D computer animation. These new processes have made production cels obsolete, increasing collectors' interest in them.

Network, Dreamworks, and Universal are of interest. Popular subjects include *Futurama, The Pink Panther,* and *Spongebob Squarepants.*

The Simpsons probably has the biggest mass-market appeal at the moment, and many pieces are released for sale to dealers, galleries, and websites by Fox, including original production cels, drawings, storyboards, and special-edition prints. Prices can start at around $300–500 for a production cel. Pieces probably won't appreciate in value quickly, but your collection may be the start of a generous bequest to your grandchildren.

A 20th Century Fox original production cel from The Simpsons, featuring the family in their Sunday best. *c. 2000, 16½ in (42 cm) wide.*

$600–900

Top Tips

- Look for cels that show the typical poses or expressions of famous characters: a good example is Homer Simpson's "Doh!"
- Invest in first-rate, limited-edition prints, since they can sometimes be worth as much as an original cel.
- Display original cels out of direct sunlight as they can fade, and consult a professional framer on the use of conservation glass and mounts.
- Concept artwork or sections of a storyboard are also collectible. Look for strong images, ideally showing faces.
- When storing cels keep them flat and covered with acid-free tissue paper. Other materials such as polythene and normal paper can damage them over time.

A Marvel Studios official Marvel Collector's Edition cel, given away in a magazine. *1990s, 10¾ in (27.5 cm) wide.*

$280–320

KEEP ▶

Choose cels of famous characters, such as Tom and Jerry, especially if depicting characteristic activities. If a cel is hand painted, reproduced from a rare production cel, or from a notable limited edition, its value will hold, and may well rise.

A limited-edition, Hanna-Barbera, hand-painted cel from Yankee Doodle Mouse, signed by animators Bill Hanna, Joe Barbera, and Iwao Takamoto. *c. 1996, 12 in (30.5 cm) wide.*

$1,200–1,800

SELL ▶

Look for animation art of characters with staying power. Although by Disney, Hercules has not become a classic as other movies have, so popularity and prices could fall further.

A limited-edition Walt Disney Studios sericel. Sell to a fan who would enjoy its size, subject, and title: "Portrait of a Hero." *1997, 19 in (48.5 cm) high.*

$350–450

Computer games have

fascinated adults and children since the 1960s. Even the simplest and earliest games still appeal to today's high-tech enthusiasts, and, as their popularity is likely to increase, so is their value.

Entertainment and Sports

The first significant computer game, the outsized Space Wars, was introduced in the early 1960s, but it was only in the 1980s that manufacturers started producing compact gaming systems for the home. By 1990, Nintendo and Sega had introduced their first consoles and the popular game Tetris was on sale.

The Nintendo Game & Watch series, and other simple games that use liquid crystal displays (LCDs) are popular among enthusiasts. The first of almost 60 Game & Watch consoles, Ball, was released in 1980. Widescreen versions included Snoopy Tennis, Fire Attack, and Popeye. These games can be worth $30 to $250, with rarer

examples fetching more than $300. From 1991, Nintendo concentrated on developing its Gameboy console.

Of the huge range of games consoles, the Sega Dreamcast is popular, despite being made until recently. Peripheral Dreamcast objects and attachments, generally issued in small numbers, have increased in value.

Neogeo's consoles have become popular with enthusiasts. Its Pocket Color, a rival to the Gameboy, can fetch from $30 upward, while the company's home system often fetches around $300–500.

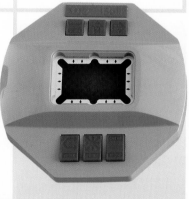

▲ **A Bambino, UFO Master-Blaster Station handheld game,** with a uniquely designed "space ship" plastic body and a large screen. *c. 1980, 5 in (13 cm) wide.*

$50–80

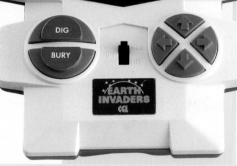

▶ **A CGL Earth Invaders handheld game,** based on the successful Space Invaders and similar games. *c. 1980, 7¾ in (20 cm) wide.*

$60–90

▶ **A Palitoy Alex Higgins Cue Ball tabletop snooker game.** Games that recreated sports were fashionable in the 1980s. *c. 1980, 6 in (15.5 cm) wide.*

$60–80

◀ **An Atari 2600 game console.** This is a smaller version of the "woodgrain"-cased model, which is more common and usually worth around 20 percent less than this version. *c. 1986, 15 in (26.5cm) wide.*

$80–120

◀ **A Grandstand Munchman tabletop game,** with two skill levels. The success of the arcade game Pac-Man led to companies releasing similar games such as this one, which even has a Pac-Man-shaped case in identical yellow. *c. 1981, 7¾ in (20 cm) wide.*

$50–60

◄ A Bambino Boxing tabletop game, with a six-button control that enabled the players to attack their opponents from various different positions. *c. 1979, 11¾ in (30 cm) wide.*

$40–60

◄ A Nintendo Snoopy SM-91 panorama-screen Game and Watch. As well as being one of the desirable "Game and Watch" series, the addition of popular characters such as Snoopy adds interest. Other versions of the game use Disney characters. *c. 1983, 4¼ in (11.5 cm) wide.*

$120–180

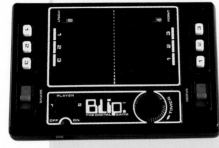

► A Tomy Blip handheld analog game. Early games often used simple graphics of a randomly moving dot that had to be kept from the sides of the screen. *c. 1977, 6¾ in (17.5 cm) wide.*

$30–50

Collectors' Tips

■ Games should be complete, have their battery covers, and be in full working order

■ Remove batteries when games are not in use

■ Try to protect serial numbers and stickers

◄ A Nintendo Micro Vs. Donkey Kong Hockey HK-303, two-player "Game and Watch" with two controls (not shown). *c. 1984, 6 in (15.5 cm) wide.*

$100–150

◄ An SNK Neogeo, Pocket-Color, 16-bit portable game console. First released in Japan, this console enjoyed limited success in the US and Europe. Features include an alarm clock and customized horoscope. *c. 1999, 5 in (13 cm) wide.*

$60–90

◄ A Tomy Skyfighters 3-D handheld game, with a neck strap. This game required the player to hold it up to his or her eyes like a pair of binoculars. *c. 1983, 8¼ in(21 cm) wide.*

$30–50

▲ A Nintendo Parachute PR-21 wide-screen from the highly collectible Game and Watch series. The player has to save parachutists falling from a helicopter by catching them in a rowboat. *c. 1981, 4¼ in (11 cm) wide.*

$60–90

Elvis Presley dominated the pop charts in the

1950s and his movie-star status in the following decade created a
multimillion dollar industry, generating a wealth of memorabilia—
from wristwatches to Christmas cards—for his fans and
enthusiasts to explore.

In addition to records, items including buttons, watches, and postage stamps have been adorned with Elvis Presley's image. There's even a Monopoly game based on him. If you know fans who followed the star during his lifetime, find out if they have any memorabilia —it might be worth something.

A Summer Festival at the Las Vegas Hilton souvenir concert menu, signed by Elvis Presley. *1970s, 15 in (38 cm) high.*

$400–600

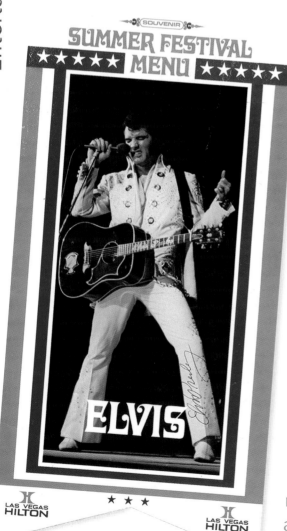

The King

Presley was brought up in a poor, working-class family in Tupelo, Mississippi, where he was influenced by the pop and country music of the time, as well as the gospel music in his local church. In 1953 he paid $3.98 to make his first record, "My Happiness." The following year he signed up with the Sun Records label in Memphis, Tennessee, and his singing career began in earnest, managed by the self-styled "Colonel" Tom Parker. Presley's bluesy vocal style, sexy image, and electrifying live shows opened up a new era in popular music and culture. In 1956, at the age of 21, Elvis had his first No.1 hit with "Heartbreak Hotel." In the same year he made his movie debut in *Love Me Tender.*

In 1958 Presley was drafted into the military. While this interrupted his career as a live performer, it heightened his appeal among his legions of fans. Items used by Elvis during his army service are extremely rare, but Tom Parker produced a run of ankle bracelets with replica Elvis Presley army dog tags, which can be found for less than $30.

When he left the army, Presley embarked on his

A Swiss-made, "Forever Elvis" commemorative wristwatch by the Precision Watch Company Inc. *c. 1980s, 2 in (5 cm) diam.*

$30–40

A Graceland security badge, marked "Caughley 5." James Caughley was a security guard at the Presley mansion. *c. 1961, 4 in (10 cm) high.*

$700–1,000

Hollywood years, making 27 movies between 1960 and 1969. Original Elvis movie posters and lobby cards are highly sought after and can fetch upward of $150.

The Vegas years

After an 11-year hiatus, Elvis returned to live performance with the 1968 "Comeback Special." This final period of his career was characterized by

Elvis remains the undeposed *King of Rock 'n' Roll.* It is estimated that he has sold more than one billion records, and his Memphis mansion Graceland attracts more than 600,000 visitors each year.

ELVIS PRESLEY

An Elvis Presley, Panel Delux, double-album boxed set (RP-9201-2), produced by RCA for the Japanese market. The albums are in near-mint condition. *c. 1970, 15¾ in (40 cm) high.*

$1,200–1,800

Top Tips

- Be cautious when buying souvenirs relating to Elvis's most famous performances, such as his 1968 "Comeback Special," as these items are commonly targeted by forgers.
- When buying concert memorabilia, note that Elvis performed only five concerts outside the US in the whole of his career—in Canada in 1957.
- Seek third-party authentication— particularly for high-price items.
- Do not buy any item originally sold in the 1999 Graceland auction unless it comes with a certificate of authenticity.

BUY

Key events in the Presley story, including his untimely death, are still being commemorated in various media. Attractive pieces by well-known makers, in limited-edition runs of 1,000 or fewer, are likely to rise in value, mainly thanks to Elvis's enduring popularity even among people born after his death.

An enamel box depicting Elvis, made by Halcyon Days, with Andy Warhol-style artwork. The box was issued in a limited edition of 500 to mark the 25th anniversary of Presley's death in 1977. *2002, 2 in (5.5 cm) long.*

$120–180

---

extensive touring and his downward spiral into obesity and ill health.

Elvis played throughout the US in the 1970s but was particularly popular in Las Vegas, where the glitzy atmosphere suited his style. Souvenirs from his Vegas shows, such as the menus printed for his two- and four-week residencies at the Hilton Theater, are highly collectible. Presley died at his home, Graceland, in Memphis, Tennessee in 1977 at the age of 42.

Sweet charity

Items that belonged to or were used by Presley himself are far more valuable than the merchandising. In 1999, at a charity auction of 2,000 items from the Graceland archives, a set of balls from Elvis's pool table fetched $7,500, his old football helmet sold for $10,000, and a credit card raised $11,000. Even a receipt for a TV set went for $650.

Here comes the Sun

Prices for Elvis memorabilia may level out as lifelong fans get older, so it is essential to invest carefully.

Personal items are valuable if the link can be proven beyond a doubt, and any merchandise from the 1950s will command impressive prices. Souvenirs produced since Elvis's death are less likely to fetch large sums of money.

The collectibles market is swamped with Elvis Presley's music. Most of his records are worth less than $80, with some fetching as little as $3–8.

Among the most valuable items are mint-condition Sun singles, which can sell for up to $4,000. Few of Elvis's LPs reach these dizzy heights: the rarest can sell for around $800–2,000.

KEEP

Seasons Greetings
Elvis and the Colonel
1966

Keep items with strong visual impact, such as any showing a young Presley in the first phase of his career in the 1950s. An authentic Presley signature will make the item even more desirable. The piece is likely to rise in value, especially if it was produced in limited numbers and can be displayed easily.

A Christmas card signed by Elvis. This is addressed to "Mary," and the picture shows a typically moody Elvis. *1966, 6¼ in (16 cm) high.*

$600–800

The Beatles

burst onto the scene in 1962 and changed pop music forever. Their superstar status, especially in the 1960s, led to a huge array of memorabilia, and this—along with their records, of course—can make an impressive collection.

A painted plaster figure of John Lennon, with a nodding head. *1960s, 8 in (20 cm) high.*
$60–80

The Beatles—John Lennon, Paul McCartney, George Harrison, and Ringo Starr—dominated the popular music scene from the early 1960s until they disbanded in 1970. Today, their domination of the rock and pop memorabilia market is similarly pronounced. John Lennon and Paul McCartney's pianos headlined the first rock memorabilia auction in 1981, and Beatles items continue to lead the way.

Marketing the Beatles

Countless products bearing their portraits were manufactured, from souvenir buttons and coins to dolls, serving trays, and even a *Yellow Submarine* pop-out decoration book. You may still have some item of memorabilia in your family. If so, it could well be worth many times more now than the price originally paid for it. A cloth button, made to tie in with the 1967 *Sgt. Pepper* album, could have been bought with pocket change at the time, but today can fetch $200–300.

Spin city

Collecting Beatles records can be a minefield. For example, the American edition of "She Loves You" (released on Swan in 1964) was pressed at several factories, resulting in a number of label variations. To increase the confusion, this single was frequently forged. An authentic, signed "She Loves You" recently fetched $2,500 in mint condition—the signatures making up most of the value.

Millions of Beatles records have been released over the years, so most are of relatively low value and rarely fetch more than $80, but some, at least, are highly sought after by serious collectors. For example, any records produced in small runs, such as promotional copies of singles used by DJs, have a high value, as do those withdrawn from sale, such as the notorious edition of the American compilation *Yesterday and Today*,

A Beatles toy guitar by Selcol; made of orange and cream plastic. *1960s, 24 in (60 cm) long.*
$150–200

with a cover showing the Beatles in butcher's coveralls, surrounded by dismembered dolls. It is said that the band requested this cover as a protest at the way in which their American record company, Capitol, was "butchering" their albums by recompiling them. Early copies were withdrawn and replaced with an innocuous version showing the band standing around a storage trunk, with Paul sitting inside it, but in some cases the new image was simply pasted over the offending cover.

Other collecting areas include programs, magazines, and posters. A program for the group's 1964 Australian tour can be worth $120–180,

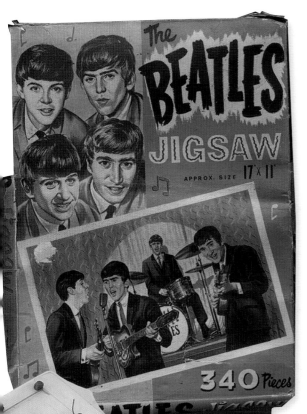

A **Beatles jigsaw puzzle** with a worn box. *1960s, 12 in (35 cm) high.*

$120–180

valuable, particularly if they are representative of their lifestyle at the height of Beatlemania. Examples include clothes, musical instruments, and documents such as contracts and plane tickets. The provenance must be cast iron, though.

Autograph alert

A band member's signature or handwriting will increase the value of any item it appears on. A note by Paul carrying lyrics from "Penny Lane" sold for $2,000, and a copy of the album *Please Please Me* signed by the entire band can be worth $1,500–2,500. A cartoon Christmas card of John and his first wife, Cynthia, drawn by Lennon, with an eight-page letter enclosed, fetched $12,000.

Band members were known to sign for each other in the early days, and many items were signed by staff, too. A photocard signed for all the Beatles by Paul has sold for $800. Beatles autographs are among the most commonly faked, so be sure that any signed item is from a reliable source.

and a complete set of the original 77 issues of *The Beatles Book Monthly* magazine, published from 1963 to 1969, can fetch $600–800. A movie poster for *A Hard Day's Night*, signed by Paul, George, and Ringo, has fetched more than $2,500.

Personal touches

Items of significance to, or owned by, members of the band are usually

Top Tips

- Join a Beatles fan club to keep informed about collectors' events and auction sales.
- Stay up-to-date with current album prices by checking auction sites on the internet.
- Familiarize yourself with the distinguishing features of the most collectible pressings, such as misspellings of song titles and minor variations in recording credits.
- Don't be fooled by 1970s reprints of *The Beatles Book Monthly*. Each reprint issue contains four extra pages—these can be removed. Other telltale signs are that the photos are less clear than the originals; and some copies vary slightly in size from the original 6 x 8¼ in (15.25 x 21 cm).

BUY

Beatles images appeared on the packaging of a vast variety of products. Relatively few disposable items survive, so they may well rise in value. Look for items that show the faces and signatures of the Beatles and that are representative of the styles of the time.

A Beatles talcum-powder tin. Tins such as this are prone to damage, which makes one that is in mint condition especially valuable. *1960s, 7 in (18 cm) high.*

$200–250

KEEP

If you were lucky enough to have seen the Beatles in concert, hunt out any memorabilia you might have kept. Original programs, or even ticket stubs, can be of value and, as they are in limited supply, prices are likely to continue rising.

A program for the "Another Beatles Christmas Show" season at the Hammersmith Odeon, London (December 24, 1964, to January 16, 1965), together with a ticket stub from the show on January 8. The printed artwork on the cover is by John Lennon. *1964–65, program 12 in (30 cm) high.*

$150–200

Essential Beatles

MERCHANDISE The Fab Four were so famous that their faces appeared on even mundane objects. This dish towel captures "Beatlemania." *1960s, 23¾ in (60 cm) wide.*

$60–90

SIGNATURES Genuine signatures are desirable, especially if, as with these framed with a photo, they don't overlap each other. *1960s, frame 16 in (40 cm) wide.*

$2,000–3,000

PERSONAL ITEMS Even pre-fame artifacts, such as John Lennon's employment card from his job at a waterworks, can be highly sought after. *1959, 10 in (25 cm) wide.*

$8,000–12,000

RECORDS Rare pressings and unusual foreign editions, such as this Italian version of the album *With the Beatles*, fetch high prices, but only if in excellent condition. *1965, 12½ in (32 cm) wide.*

$350–400

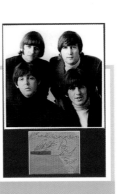

Rock and pop music

has commanded an often fanatical following since the birth of rock 'n' roll in the 1950s. More and more fans are turning to collecting memorabilia relating to the artists they most admire.

Collectors of rock and pop memorabilia usually specialize in particular artists, eras, or genres, and although reports of record-breaking sales suggest otherwise, this remains an accessible area of the collectibles market. With thousands of artists, and more than half a century of material to choose from, there is plenty to collect for those of every popular music persuasion. Even fans of artists who have died (which increases the value of memorabilia associated with them) are able to pick up items such as ticket stubs and concert programs at relatively low prices.

Rock 'n' roll is here to stay

In the late 1950s, artists such as Elvis Presley, Buddy Holly, and Bill Haley ushered in the rock 'n' roll era. Although memorabilia associated with Holly and Haley is not as highly priced

A limited-edition Jerry Lee Lewis poster, reading "Springhill Salutes The Founders of Rock 'N' Roll," with Lewis's signature. *c. 1990s, 22¾ in (58 cm) high.*

$70–100

as Elvis material, collectors still expect to pay up to around $150–500 for tour brochures and concert programs. A signature adds value: a signed Buddy Holly program can cost up to $800.

An Official Monkee Puzzle, by E. E. Fairchild. The Monkees are known for classic hits such as "I'm a Believer." *c. 1967, 13 in (33 cm) wide.*

$80–120

Like a rolling stone

Along with The Beatles and other bands, The Rolling Stones emerged in the 1960s as part of the "British Invasion." Early Stones memorabilia, such as guitars and items of clothing, is rare and sought after, but there are less expensive alternatives. Souvenir booklets and tour brochures from the mid-1960s are available for around $40–100, and a program with a ticket stub can often fetch $120–180. Unlike most bands of the era, The Rolling Stones are still recording and touring, so there is 40 years' worth of material to choose from. In general, items from the 1960s have the highest value (a 1960s guitar signed by the original members might fetch $5,000–8,000 or more, especially if it was used by the group), but memorabilia from later decades will also attract premium prices if rare.

Sixties treasures

Other artists from the 1960s whose memorabilia still attracts great interest include The Doors, The Grateful Dead, The Monkees, The Who, The Byrds, and Bob Dylan. Merchandise for these artists can fetch $150–1,000 or more. A Monkees signed record jacket can be found for around $200, while autographed Bob Dylan photos may be worth up to $600. Concert tickets and programs for leading bands and artists start at around $20, but some can fetch $200–400 or more.

Writing on the wall

Original late-1960s concert posters that employ psychedelic patterns and colors have become highly collectible, especially those by renowned designers such as Rick Griffin, Randy Tuten, Victor Moscoso, David Singer, Bonnie MacLean, or the pairing of Stanley Mouse and Alton Kelley. Griffin's work is found on

A closer look at... a psychedelic concert poster

Sixties psychedelic posters have become eminently collectible, especially classic designs by US artists such as Stanley Mouse, Victor Moscoso, Rick Griffin, and Randy Tuten. Values depend on the type of artwork, the artists, and significance of the concert or band advertised.

Bright, acidic colors were most often used

Janis Joplin was performing with Big Brother and the Holding Company at this point, making it desirable to her fans

A blue version of this poster is also known, as are handbills. Many psychedelic posters took older styles such as Art Nouveau: here the look is inspired by vintage music hall posters

An Earthquake poster designed by Stanley Mouse of Family Dog for a Bo Diddley, and Big Brother and the Holding Company concert on August 12 and 13, 1966, printed by the San Francisco Poster Co. and with design number FD21. *1966, 19¾ in (50 cm) high.*

$500–800

posters for seminal events such as the 1967 "Human Be-In" in San Francisco, as well as for many of the early San Francisco shows by bands such as Jefferson Airplane and the Grateful Dead. He was also a prolific record-jacket artist. As with other deceased artists, the value of his work increased after his death in 1991. Any damage such as rubbing or wear to the design

(especially on "mirrored" or reflective areas), tears, or fading, reduces value considerably. Rarer examples can fetch $2,000 and more, but others with the same look can be found from about $50–80, with the majority worth around $150–600.

Rock giants

Artists such as The Who, Led Zeppelin, and Deep Purple developed a heavier guitar sound in the late 1960s, and became rock superstars in the 1970s. Any musical instruments or clothes connected with these artists or other notable rock bands, such as KISS,

A Jimi Hendrix Experience *Axis: Bold As Love* songbook, published by A. Schroeder Music Publishing Co. Ltd. *1968, 12 in (30.5 cm) high.*

$30–50

Axis: Bold As Love was the second album by The Jimi Hendrix Experience. The song "Little Wing" has been covered by Stevie Ray Vaughan, Def Leppard, and Sting.

Aerosmith, Van Halen, Black Sabbath, and Metallica, command top prices. A guitar autographed by members of The Who can fetch $1,500–2,500 or more. A KISS gatefold album jacket signed by the four original members can fetch $120–180. Concert tickets tend to be less expensive, but significant gigs attract a premium. A ticket for a 1970 Led Zeppelin show in Dallas can be found for under $100, yet one from Madison Square Garden for the same year—when lead singer Robert Plant dedicated a song to Jimi Hendrix, who had just died—can be worth more than $150.

A set of four KISS dolls, by Mego Corp. The backs of the boxes were printed with cutout instruments for the band. A complete set of figures is more desirable than individual dolls, which are worth up to $200 each. *c. 1977, each 13¼ in (33.5 cm) high.*

$800–1,000

A David Bowie "Serious Moonlight" tour concert program. *1983, 12 in (30 cm) high.*

$20–30

Global superstars

From 1981, MTV was a key influence on the development of popular music. Through videos channeled into people's homes, pop artists such as Michael Jackson, Madonna, and Prince became global superstars with greater emphasis on image. New music styles such as rap and dance also emerged, so the period from the 1980s onward provides collectors with a rich variety of material.

Awards memorabilia has attracted much interest. A silk suit worn by Prince, for example, at the 1998

A closer look at... a Grateful Dead signed print

Signed photographs and autographs are hotly sought after by fans. Images dating from a band's early or best years, or hard to find signatures, are especially desirable and more likely to rise in value. Examine features such as band members and signatures carefully to spot valuable examples.

A black-and-white publicity print signed by members of the Grateful Dead. The photo was taken by Bob Seidemann in 1971. It was used on the double album *The Grateful Dead*. Today the group tours without Garcia and Pig Pen and is known as The Dead. *c. 1971, 10¾ in (27 cm) wide.*

$4,000–5,000

It is cut down, and half of Bill Kreutzman's signature has been cut off—if it were complete its value would have been higher

Instrumentalist and singer Ron McKernan's signature is very rare as he didn't like to sign. He was known as "Pig Pen," and died in 1973

Did You Know?

A sale of The Who memorabilia in 2003 included 180 guitars, the largest number ever sold at one auction. The highest price was paid for a 1958 Gibson Explorer, which fetched more than $150,000.

Grammys can be worth around $8,000, partly because a global television audience saw him wearing it. For the budget buyer, programs for the same event are available for just a few dollars.

Variations on vinyl

Along with the growth of the picture disc and colored vinyl, recordings made for individual markets offer plenty of scope for collectors. Rare promotional records, limited editions, and first pressings are also sought after. A colored vinyl edition of the rock band Nirvana's debut album, *Bleach*, can sell for up to $200. Hüsker Dü's rare "In A Free Land" EP, released on the New Alliance label, changes hands for around $50.

Cult followings

Some bands gain a mystical aura that generates a passion in their fans for everything and anything to do with them. The Grateful Dead is one example: "Dead" memorabilia has

A giant color Madonna poster for the Spanish leg of her 1990 "Blond Ambition" world tour. *1990, 54 in (137 cm) high.*

$60–90

always been highly prized, but the death of lead singer Jerry Garcia in 1995 pushed prices even higher. While items from the 1980s and 90s are within the price range of most collectors, memorabilia from the 1960s can be expensive: a ticket for a 1966 Grateful Dead concert in San Francisco can be worth up to around $500–800 and one of Garcia's Hawaiian print shirts can fetch more than $1,500.

Nirvana has enjoyed a huge cult following, and the suicide of lead singer Kurt Cobain in 1994 has done little to dampen fans' zeal. The rare German Geffen "Penny Royal Tea" CD single was withdrawn before sale because of Cobain's death, and can be worth up to $400 in mint condition. Pieces signed by Cobain generally fetch $200–300, though Nirvana tickets and original photos might sell for $20–30 or less.

An eye to the future

Memorabilia from recording artists who have been successful for a long time, for example David Bowie, Madonna, and Bruce Springsteen, will almost always be worth more than that from performers who have been "manufactured" by record companies. Signed photos of today's pop artists, such as Britney Spears, Usher, or Beyoncé, can be found from $20 up to around $400, depending on the star's status and how inclined they are to sign autographs. Whether prices of merchandise associated with current pop performers will rise is debatable, as so much material is produced, and the continued popularity of many cannot be guaranteed.

BUY

Pop stars come and go, but those who adapt to, or lead, changing tastes become iconic and are likely to remain popular. Memorabilia relating to notable periods or tracks should rise in value if demand continues.

A Madonna "Crazy For You" picture disc, W0008P, Sire Records. This is one of her best-known hits, originally released in 1985 and rereleased in 1991. *1991, 11 in (28 cm) high.*

$20–30

KEEP

Comics that are associated with popular bands attract attention from fans, especially if they are early editions, have appealing artwork, or are in excellent condition. These have the best chance of rising in value in the future.

Kiss: A Marvel Comics Super Special, No. 1, September 1977. This issue, with its great cover, was printed with ink containing the band's blood and is in near mint condition. *1977, 11 in (27.5 cm) high.*

$100–150

SELL

After initial success, some stars gain a cult following but rarely regain widespread popular acclaim. Sell to constantly loyal fans, as such memorabilia is unlikely to rise in value much in the long term.

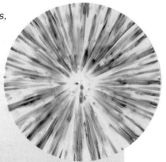

A Frank Zappa *Marvellous Stunner* multi-colored bootleg LP, released by Angry Taxman Records. It is from a limited edition of 50, with tracks recorded in 1976 and 1979. *1980s, 12 in (30.5 cm) wide.*

$70–100

Baseball is a sport full of excitement and legendary moments, inspiring its fans to gather souvenirs that will help them reach out to their heroes—and collectors often pay big money for such memorabilia!

A Mickey Mantle signed B. Brown AL portrait baseball, signed on the sweet spot in blue ink, with a hand-painted portrait of Mantle on the side panel, together with a letter of authenticity.
$1,000–1,500

Baseball, America's pastime, is more than 150 years old, its history is extremely rich and well recorded, and it has a long-standing place in the hearts of sports enthusiasts.

Sporting legends
If a player is a Hall of Famer—honored at the National Baseball Hall of Fame and Museum in Cooperstown, New York—any memorabilia relating to that athlete will normally be worth considerably more than for an ordinary player. New York Yankees Lou Gehrig, Mickey Mantle, Yogi Berra, and George Herman ("Babe") Ruth; Honus Wagner of the Pittsburgh Pirates; Willie Mays of the New York and San Francisco Giants and the New York Mets; Jackie Robinson of the Brooklyn Dodgers; and Ted Williams of the Boston Red Sox are examples of superstar players who have particular cachet among collectors. Certain games or seasons are legendary as well, such as the famous episode when the Chicago White Sox threw the World Series to the Cincinnati Reds in 1919 and the record-breaking year had by the Yankees in 1927. Anything pertaining to these teams at these times attracts a huge premium.

African-American heros
The Negro League—set up after black players were pushed out of major league play in the late 19th century—is an interesting collecting area that is going up in value, and memorabilia relating to Satchel Paige, Josh Gibson, and Jackie Robinson is prized. The latter, being the first black player to join the major leagues in 1947, is particularly sought after.

Million-dollar baby
Baseball cards featuring players of the sport are the most obvious—and probably most popular—collectible for anyone enthusiastic about the game. Over 10,000 sets are known to exist, and despite their unprepossessing looks, baseball cards can fetch huge amounts: an extremely rare Honus Wagner card, c. 1909, sold for over a million dollars. Some of the first cards were given out in the 19th century by a distributor of baseball equipment and a single one of these could be worth a five-figure sum. Other early cards were made by cigarette companies and also by producers of caramel candy, ice cream, cereal, and chewing gum. Some types of card are more desirable than others, with desirability depending

A Turk Wendell Philadelphia Phillies home white knit shirt, with original Sept. 11 US flag patch on the back and Majestic tagging on the tail front; signed on the back by Wendell, together with a letter of authenticity. *2001, 30½ in (80cm) high.*
$150–250

An Eddie Collins signed Stall & Dean 11 store baseball bat, with E. Collins signature. If it were game-used by Eddie Collins, it could fetch $15,000. *1930s, 31¾ in (81 cm) long.*
$500–800

on the distributor, player, quality of reproduction, and whether or not the picture is evenly centered and retains its bright colors. Goudey chewing-gum cards, (c. 1933–34), are very handsome and sought after, as are later Leaf and Bowman sets, as well as the larger-format Topps. Certain cards from the Thirties, however, most often those in black and white, fail to excite much interest among collectors.

Card sharps

Cards have been made in a variety of sizes over the years: the earliest measured 1 inch by 2 inches; then 2-inches square; and finally, the 2-by 3-inch format made by Topps that came to be the standard. Some early cards from around 1890 were untypically large and known as cabinets, and these are also highly prized. Mickey Mantle's 1952 Topps card could go for six figures, but mint-condition cards from this sought-after set can still be found for around $70 plus, if they are of ordinary players. A famous player's rookie trading card can become very desirable. A mint-condition Barry

Bonds Fleer rookie card from 1987 can sell for up to $350. One way to invest in the future is to amass current rookie cards and hope that the players will one day make it to the top of their profession. Also, look for errors on cards since any anomalies—a misspelled name, for example—can result in a card being withdrawn and a rarity created. Those not especially interested in the investment potential of cards may want to collect cards that are in less-than-perfect condition or concentrate on items made from the 1980s onward—expect to pay $10–40 for images of regular players.

Signed on the dotted line

Autographs are also treasured, and any kind of signed ephemera, from a program to a ticket stub, can be sought after. A ticket stub for an important game might cost $30–75, but if it's autographed it will fetch much more. An autograph is usually worth more if it is on an action photograph that's evocative of the player or game, a handwritten letter, a document such as a contract, or a

KEEP

Examine forms, details, and identifying features such as manufacturers' labels carefully, since rare or unusual details can add value. If such details prove to be rare or else attract a cross-market interest, as here, keep the item since values should be maintained and may even rise.

A rare Winchester "goggle-eye" catcher's mask. Goggle-eye masks are desirable and early. Winchester made sporting goods for only a short time during the 1920s. If this were not made by Winchester or didn't retain its label, the value would be around $400–500. *c. 1925, 10¼ in (26 cm) high.*

$700–1,000

BUY

Although game-worn or signed items are sought after, unused items can be valuable, especially if they were meant to be used. Vintage items such as baseballs in their boxes and in mint condition can fetch surprisingly high sums, as few will have survived.

A J. DeBeer & Son of Albany, New York, baseball in mint condition in original cardboard box. The appealing graphics on the box and the unopened condition make this a great buy. *1940s, box 3 in (7.5 cm) high.*

$50–70

A closer look at... a baseball glove

Gloves and mitts are one of the most popular collecting fields within game equipment. Early examples, those used by famous players, particularly in famous games, will fetch a premium. Consider the shape, markings, and any accompanying provenance to ascertain the value of a glove

The glove has full webbing between the thumb and finger

Compared to other gloves, it has a vertically elongated form, showing an early date and making it rarer

Spalding is a renowned and sought-after name

A Spalding leather baseball glove. Although it does not have a notable provenance, its early date, maker, and condition make it desirable. *c. 1900, 9¼ in (23.5 cm) high.*

$800–1,200

It retains its button and Spalding label, and is in excellent, game-worn condition—all desirable features

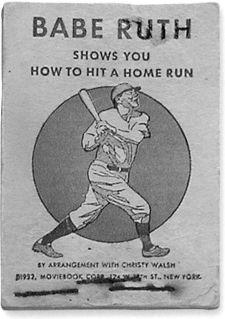

A Babe Ruth flipbook, interior with great images of Ruth in his pinstripes swinging for a home run. *1932, 6 in (15 cm) high.*

$100–150

magazine cover with striking graphics. Photographs are all the more desirable if they show an important game or moment and the player in mid-action. Most photos can be had for $5–50 if unsigned, but if signed might be worth $10–200, and much more if showing a superstar. A rare photo of the All-American Girls Pro Baseball League, signed by 75 players at a reunion would be worth $1,000 or more.

From the Babe

As the game became more commercial, marketeers hired players to attend baseball shows and sign anything that the public gave them and, as a result, a wide variety of autographed merchandise is available including balls, gloves, bats, jerseys, shoes, and hats. Anything signed before the 1920s—when Babe Ruth popularized the signing of baseballs—is usually very rare and expensive, since much less was autographed. Some players are very shy of signing, so anything with their names may attract a premium. As well, signatures of superstars who were very generous with their autographs—such as record-breaking hitter Babe Ruth—will always be valuable because of their legendary status.

How sweet it is

Balls are best signed on the "sweet spot"—the narrowest white area between the stitching—and ideally a superstar's signature should not be crowded out by other signatures. Balls should also be official American or National League baseballs, identified by the stamped signature of the league president, or, after 1999, the commissioner. Multiple-signature balls are not as desirable as single-signature balls—unless, of course, they are signed by a fabled team. A ball autographed by a current player would be $20 to $250, depending on his status, and as much as $300 or more for the greats of the game. Souvenir balls, sold at ballparks and stamped with signatures, are worth very little.

A Mickey Mantle's Backyard Baseball Stick game, by L. C. Toy Distribution, in mint condition, complete with original packaging. *c. 1960, 22½ in (57cm) high.*

$220–280

Well worn

Game-used equipment is worth more than unused signed objects. For example, Mickey Mantle's old glove went under the hammer for a staggering $239,000 and this sum is on a par with other Hall of Famers' signed belongings. Game-used bats, or those made to players' specifications, for current or recent players might fetch anything from $70 to $1,500, although an earlier

Essential baseball memorabilia

CARDS such as this T-206 Ty Cobb with a Piedmont back are valued on condition, popularity of the player, image, and rarity. 1909-11.

$350–450

YEARBOOKS like this 1971 New York Mets book provide team history and bios, and are good references. 1971, 11 in (28 cm) high.

$30–50

ADVERTISING and packaging with fun artwork or players endorsing products is popular. Condition is all-important. Yankee boy tin. c. 1910.

$150–200

PENNANTS vary in value depending on their team, age, look, and condition. This one is missing a tassel. 1950s.

$125–175

PHOTOS of top players in dynamic poses, such as this of Joe DiMaggio, are desirable. Signatures add value. c. 1949, 20 in (51 cm) high.

$180–220

PINS are affordable and varied. Look for popular players, vintage pins, and rare press pins. Chicago White Sox pin. 1959, 3 in (7.5 cm) diam.

$20–30

date or a genuine signature will put the price up even higher. A Joe DiMaggio-signed Rawlins Slugger bat may be worth $1,500–2,500. Bats can be linked to players using factory stock numbers, since manufacturers will always mark the bats ordered by major league players. The same is true of gloves, which are also custommade. Jerseys can be bought, too, since team clubhouses sell off old clothes to fans. To ascertain if a jersey is authentic, check that the label inside is the right manufacturer for that team—Rawlings made uniforms for the Pittsburgh Pirates, for example, but not for every team, so look for the label. Game-worn jerseys by known players from the 1940s to 60s are often worth $1,000–4,000 or more. Also worth considering are replica jerseys, which are less expensive than authentic ones, but still prized. Even a superstar might have signed one for a fan, so it could be an inexpensive way to obtain a great jersey for a few hundred dollars that might otherwise cost six figures.

Geared up

Of course, not all baseball collectibles need a signature to be valuable. Early equipment can be very collectible as well as unused, still-packaged objects in mint condition. Pre-WWII fielder's gloves, identifiable by laced fingers, are sought after, and early gloves (c. 1900) can be worth $800–1,200. A 1940s mint-condition baseball in its original box can fetch $60–70. Many other baseball souvenirs have been produced that are worth adding to a collection including yearbooks, scorecards, pennants, lapel pins, and coins. Buttons featuring sought-after players can cost $10–120. Since baseball stars are household names they often lend their images to advertising packaging on everything from Wheaties cereal boxes (around $15) to Christmas ornaments ($15–30). Early baseball advertising signs and displays can fetch big prices: a 1926 World Series tobacco advertising display can be worth up to $6,000. Postage stamps in mint condition featuring heroes such as Jackie Robinson, Babe Ruth, and Lou Gehrig can cost around $2 each. Toys and games shouldn't be overlooked, since many baseball board-game boxes can have eye-catching graphics that could increase values. Some fans collect so widely that they even hoard disused stadium seating—almost anything connected to this sport is valued!

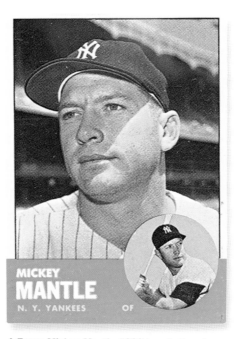

A Topps Mickey Mantle #200 baseball card. 1963, 3 in (7.5 cm) high.
$280–320

Top Tips

- Current players will sign equipment and ephemera at specially organized shows, but may charge more for a bat or baseball than a photograph. Another tactic is to approach a player at spring training, or mail a letter to his home team and hope for a handwritten reply.

- Run your finger over signatures and examine them closely, since printed or stamped facsimiles are common—with an authentic signature, you should be able to feel where the pen indented the piece and see variation in terms of the ink and pressure used when signing. Also consider the size.

- Big names command big prices. Track promising, up-and-coming players; one of them may be the next Babe Ruth.

BUY

Look for memorabilia that was produced in quantity, but that was most often thrown away later. Items such as scorecards, paper cups, and banners are typical, and ardent fans will love to add this extra ephemera to their collections. Vintage pieces in complete and mint condition will always be sought after

A woven straw hat, worn at opening games for the Mets. This one retains its badge and plastic New York figure, which is rare, making it a great buy. *c. 1960, 10½ in (27 cm) wide.*
$70–100

KEEP

Nodders have become very sought after, with examples produced in the Golden Age of the 1960s being the most desirable. Look at the shape of the base and examine the paintwork, head, body, and stem for damage. Black players or character heads add value. Those from the primary period in undamaged condition look set to rise in desirability and value.

A Boston Red Sox ceramic nodder, made in Japan. The white round base dates this to the early 1960s, and the mint condition also makes it an excellent keep. *1961–63, 4½ in (11.5 cm) high.*
$200–300

Football memorabilia could become just as highly sought after as baseball's and, as with that game, items used or signed by famous players can command big money. However, you can easily kick off a great collection for under $100.

A rare and early Philadelphia Eagles Kra-Lite helmet, by Riddell, undrilled for facemask, with original chin strap and letter of authenticity. *c. 1961–66, 12¾ in (32 cm) high.*
$600–700

Although its history is not as long and illustrious as baseball's, football has a huge following. The sport developed from a hybrid of Association Football and rugby. While professional baseball began relatively early (in 1871), football didn't come into its own until later. The American Professional Football Association was formed in 1920, becoming the National Football League (NFL) in 1922. Harold "Red" Grange's exciting play for the Chicago Bears after 1925 drew crowds and helped popularize the sport, as did later TV coverage, which conveyed the action and excitement of the game.

Used goods

Equipment worn or used by famous players in games—such as jerseys, helmets, or the ball itself—are worth top dollar. The uniform of Jim Brown, a fullback for the Cleveland Browns in the 1950s and 60s, sold for over $50,000. An item used in play can be worth considerably more than its unused equivalent, and a signature by a football hero drastically increases value. Anything associated with Hall of Fame players, or with those who have shined in some way, will always be more desirable. Red Grange, Beattie Feathers, and Johnny Unitas are big names of the past, while Brett Favre and Peyton Manning are recent stars.

Local boys

Signed mini-helmets typically cost $150–250, while jerseys can sell for $300–500. Footballs are always something a fan would treasure and usually cost from $150 to $800. A football signed by Joe Namath of the New York Jets, with a photo of him signing, might fetch $400

A rare Moyer football player ceramic money bank, marked "© Moyer" on the side of the base. *c. 1970, 7½ in (19 cm) high.*
$80–120

or more. Sports fans set great store by their local teams, so memorabilia connected to John Elway, for example, who played for the Denver Broncos until 1998, is usually worth more in Colorado than elsewhere. Also, once a famous player is deceased, the price of related memorabilia tends to increase.

Autographed photographs are also very popular with collectors, particularly action shots, and these can be $15–150. A photo of Brett Favre of the Green Bay Packers is likely to cost at the upper end of this, as he signs very little and plays for a team with wide appeal.

Historical records

Historical memorabilia showing the development of the sport is a prevalent collecting area. Objects from championship games, the Superbowl, and the Rosebowl, are highly prized. Team plaques of the winners or illustrated programs with striking

Essential football memorabilia

VINTAGE GEAR either unused or worn by a noted player, is desirable. These cleats have wooden spikes. c. 1910–20, 11½ in (29 cm) long.
$120–180

EPHEMERA with amusing or dramatic artwork—like this moving-football Valentine's card—add life to a collection. c. 1935, 9¾ in (24.5 cm) high.
$25–35

FIGURINES in bright colors and appealing shapes, such as this bisque figurine by notable German factory Heubach, are popular and often valuable. c. 1930, 6¾ in (17 cm) high.
$450–650

BALLS make superb display pieces. Real signatures add value; here the signature is printed. c. 1950, 12¾ in (31 cm) wide.
$100–150

CATALOGS with great cover artwork are desirable, particularly if they show period styles, as with this athletic equipment catalog. 1925, 7¾ in (19.5 cm) high.
$80–120

PROGRAMS offer insight into games, players, statistics, and seasons. This Super Bowl I program also has appealing artwork. 1967, 12¾ in (32 cm) high.
$250–350

graphics add to a collection. The 1938 Superbowl program (New York Giants vs. Green Bay Packers) celebrates two popular teams, and could cost a fan $1,500–2,000, whereas a championship game program from the Sixties might be $600–800. The program from the first Rosebowl in 1925 (Notre Dame vs. Stanford) could be up to $3,000. By contrast, the much more recent 2003 Rosebowl program (Oklahoma vs. Washington) could be snapped up for $15, and might be a good investment.

In the cards

While football cards don't reach the heady heights of the million-dollar Honus Wagner baseball card, a rare example can be $800–1,000. Others are more affordable, with common players of the Fifties found for $5–50. Cards have been made since the 1890s, but it was not until 1935 that National Chickle of Cambridge, Massachusetts, produced the first full set of football cards. The chewing gum and tobacco manufacturers that made baseball cards—Bowman, Leaf (both from 1948), and Topps (from 1950) —also provided fans with pictures of football stars. Condition is everything and pristine cards are the most desirable. Again, player popularity affects value. Rarities such as misprints also count for more.

Ad-ed value

Football players have lent their images to products from cereal boxes to bottle caps, and advertising and packaging are still affordable areas to collect. A six-pack of Coca-Cola, c. 1988, endorsed by the Oakland Athletics, could be worth $20–25. Other types of memorabilia include magazines, postcards, books, toys, board games, figurines, and glassware. Vintage plastic football-player nodders can sell for $50–200; avoid those with damage, however, unless they are extremely rare. Some pristine 1940s pennants are $200–300, although many felt examples are under $10.

KEEP

Don't ignore memorabilia produced for college games, as this area is growing. It can form a fascinating and valuable collection of its own, or add variety to a general collection by charting the full history of the game. Much of it is still affordable but prices, particularly for early or attractive examples, are rising so buy now.

A rare Harvard fold-out pennant postcard. The unusual, but highly relevant, pennant shape, appealing artwork, and early date make this an excellent addition to a collection. The notable college name is also a very desirable feature. *c. 1909, 5½ in (14 cm) high.*

$70–90

BUY

Players' uniforms and equipment are among the most desirable and appealing items, and often the most valuable. Follow the careers of promising young stars, especially if they begin to make great achievements. Pieces acquired early in their careers can be excellent investments. If they go on to become widely known and famous, especially in the long term, values for these items will take off.

A Barry Sanders Detroit Lions knit jersey, which shows some wear and lacks an NFL shoulder patch; with letter of authenticity. Playing for the Detroit Lions from 1989–98, Sanders was one of the game's most exciting running backs. In 2004 he was inducted into the Pro Football Hall of Fame. *1994–95, 5½ in (14 cm) high*

$1,500–2,000

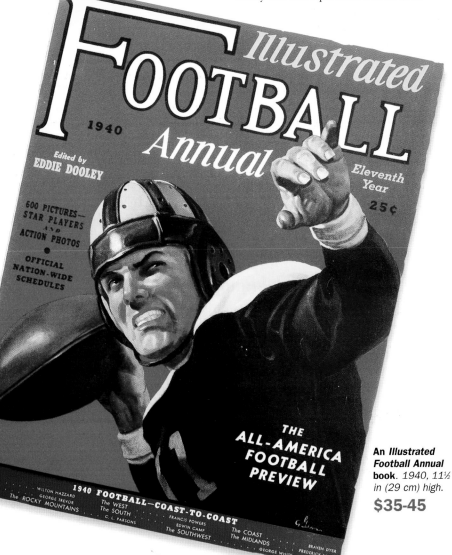

An *Illustrated Football Annual* book. *1940, 11½ in (29 cm) high.*

$35-45

Golf has a long history, and its enduring popularity has produced a wide variety of equipment and related items to collect. Although antique pieces are rare and expensive, there is plenty to suit even the most modest budget.

A German ceramic bottle in the shape of a golfer. *1920s, 5 in (13 cm) high.*
$200–250

Many of us have inherited a passion for golf from our parents or grandparents. Some may even have been lucky enough to have been passed on something more tangible, such as a well-worn set of clubs or a cherished memento of an early Open tournament.

A time-honored pursuit

By the early 20th century, golf had become tremendously popular. Enthusiasts eagerly pursue the wide range of equipment, such as clubs, balls, bags, and club-head covers, sold during the 19th century.

Absolutely anything with a golfing theme—including books, artworks, ceramics, and silverware—is of interest. Antique equipment catalogs make a fascinating addition to any collection, for example, with some dating from the late 19th century available for $250–400; later examples usually cost less.

Established ceramic factories such as Royal Doulton, Spode, and

A silver, golf-themed smoker's companion, with an attached lighter and covered ashtray in the shape of golfballs. *1923, 5 in (12.5 cm) high.*
$850–1,000

Clifton started producing wares decorated with golfing images in the 1890s. Early pieces in perfect condition can sell for $150–1,500 or more, whereas golfing ceramics from the 1950s onward can often be bought for around $20–150.

Competitive edge

Not a week goes by without a professional golf tournament being played somewhere, and each one produces more memorabilia: tickets, trophies, programs, and posters. Many of these items can be picked up relatively inexpensively—a Masters Championship program from the mid-1980s might set you back around $10–20.

Older pieces, or those linked with significant competitions and golfing landmarks, will attract higher prices—a program from the 1962 Open Championship might sell for $600–900, but one from the 1930s or earlier will generally be worth about $1,200–1,800 or more.

Clubbing together

Clubs, of which there are 14 distinct varieties, form a central feature of many collections. Market prices are linked to age,

rarity, quality, and condition. Iron-headed clubs that predate the introduction of the steel shaft in the 1920s are particularly prized, as are the early long-nosed woods that were in use until the mid-19th century. These can be worth from $3,000 up to $80,000. Later examples, such as 1930s steel-shafted clubs, can be found for less than $80, but they may rise in value as they become rarer.

Modern clubs can also be collectible. Rare early Ping putters from the 1960s can sell for more than $1,500, with some more recent examples from the 1980s already reaching around $150–300.

A featherie in your cap

The first golf balls, called featheries, were made by hand from stitched animal-skin casing stuffed with boiled feathers. Featheries with no identified maker can be picked up for around $1,200–1,800, but the mark of a recognized manufacturer such as Andrew Dickson or Henry Mills can often boost this to $15,000 or more.

Featheries were replaced in the mid-19th century by balls made

Collectors' Tales

"One of my better buys was a table croquet set for $70. When I got it home I discovered that instead of four croquet balls, there were two croquet and two golf balls. The golf balls turned out to be two beautiful, hand-hammered, Forgan-pattern gutta-percha balls in mint condition and worth around $1,500 each."

Bennie Weightman, Detroit

A closer look at... a Spalding jigger

This jigger (old-fashioned golf terminology for a club that gives high loft) is a good example of an early steel club. The famous name and distinctive features make this a valuable piece.

The hexagonal shaft was bored through the center and drilled with more than 1,000 holes in order to reduce its weight

Hand-punched dots like these (to impart spin to the ball) help to date a club—most later examples were punched mechanically

A Spalding, Gold Medal No. 4 jigger, with a hammer stamp and patent marks. *c. 1918, 39½ in (100 cm) long.*

$2,000–2,800

Three Dutch Delft tiles showing gentlemen golfers. *1880s, 5 in (12.5 cm) wide.*

$280–320

261

Golf

Top Tips

- Keep an eye out for large sales, which are often scheduled for the week leading up to the US Open Championship in June.
- Inspect golf clubs with wooden heads and shafts for undue wear and tear, as well as woodworm; irons should be checked for extensive rusting.
- Never clean antique golf clubs yourself; collectors value the soiling and patina accumulated over a lifetime of use. Ask a specialist to do the job for you instead.
- Look for golfing publications that are in excellent condition—with a strong binding, a clean, unmarked cover, and all the pages present and intact.

KEEP

Although now frowned upon, gathering stray balls from the edges of golf courses was a lucrative pursuit at one time and elderly relatives or friends might have indulged in this activity. If these balls are still around, hold on to those in good condition as prices should rise.

A North Berwick, square-mesh rubber-core ball. Although produced after the scarcer featheries and gutties, values for early 20th-century balls in good condition such as this one can still be relatively high. *1900–20, 1¾ in (4.5 cm) diam.*

$100–150

KEEP

Golfing memorabilia depicting women is at a premium. Modern young women took up the game in the 1920s. A golfing theme may add further period interest to an already attractive Art Deco figure.

A zinc, Art Deco lady golfer on a plinth base. The action has been captured at the end of the swing, which imparts a wonderful sense of movement to the piece. *1920s, 8 in (20.5 cm) high.*

$150–200

of gutta-percha (a whitish, rubbery substance). A genuine "gutty" can fetch more than $1,500, especially if it carries the stamp of a notable maker, such as Archie Simpson or Allan Robertson. Unbranded examples can be found for around $500–800.

At the end of the 19th century, rubber-core balls made by Haskell arrived on the scene and these were used until the more controllable dimple-patterned balls came into play some years later. Haskell balls are scarce: a standard example in good condition may fetch more than $120–180.

Celebrity links

Golf has been a favorite celebrity pastime since the mid-20th century, when Hollywood stars such as Bing Crosby and Bob Hope helped to popularize the sport. Any golfing items with a celebrity pedigree are attractive both to fans of the star and the sport. Equipment associated with professionals does have some worth, but unless it's linked to a truly international name, such as Jack Nicklaus or Tiger Woods, the effect on value will be minimal.

There is a strong market for golfing publications, particularly classic instruction manuals and books by renowned course architects and famous players, such as Ben Hogan and Bobby Jones. Books written by or about modern greats such as Seve Ballesteros or Nick Faldo can be picked up for $8–20 or less. But they could be worth around $30–100 if endorsed with a celebrity signature.

Other sporting memorabilia

is often kept by sports fans for purely nostalgic reasons, but clothing, equipment, photos, programs, and sporting souvenirs can be valuable too, if rare or associated with an important game or player. It is never too late to start collecting tomorrow's treasures.

From tickets for a world championship boxing match, which can be worth $15–100, to cycling medals of the 1890s that can fetch $100–500, there is a wealth of collectible ephemera for those of every sporting persuasion.

Slam-dunk junk

Basketball memorabilia has a big following. Basketball guides, programs, and record books from the 1950s to the 1970s generally sell for $20–60, while a Harlem Globetrotters yearbook from 1963 can be worth $90 or more. Signed photos of past players and teams can fetch anything up to $500. A rare basketball goal frame with its net from around 1910 can sell for up to $600. As with

baseball, basketball cards are also sought after, and can fetch anything from under $10 to hundreds or thousands of dollars for rare and early examples.

Hockey gear

A 1890s pair of hockey skates by Peck & Snyder, the premier sporting goods manufacturer during the second half of the 19th century, can fetch up to $120 or more. Other clothing, such as shin guards from the 1950s–60s, can be found for under $50. Game-worn hockey jerseys can be found for less than $50, but those worn for prestigious games or by big names can fetch $200 or more. Programs and tickets for teams such as The New York Rangers, the Buffalo Sabres, or the Chicago Black Hawks generally fetch $20–30. A 1920s puck with its original box can command $100–150, while more recent autographed hockey pucks fetch $10–30 or more.

A sealed can of three Wilson tennis balls. *c. 1950, 8 in (20.5 cm) high.*

$60–90

Tennis, anyone?

Tennis rackets from the 1870s can fetch up to $1,500 or more. Early aluminum rackets from the 1920s and 30s can be worth $100–300. These are rare since most pre-1980 rackets were wooden. Fiberglass rackets were introduced in the 1970s: early Wilson examples can cost around $50–100.

Unopened cans of tennis balls from the 1930s can cost about $80, and a 1960s can of Dunlop balls can sell for about $50. Programs from major tournaments usually cost only a few dollars, but a signature adds value.

Some sporting memorabilia to look for:
■ Programs ■ Equipment ■ Ceramics ■

OFFICIAL PROGRAM 50c

6th ANNUAL WORLD SERIES *of* **BASKETBALL**

HARLEM GLOBE TROTTERS vs **COLLEGE ALL★AMERICANS**

1955 NATIONAL TOUR

A Harlem Globetrotters 6th Annual Basketball National Tour Program, 1955 for Globetrotters vs. All-Stars. Items with impactive artwork or that are related to key games are generally more valuable. *1955, 10 in (25.5 cm) high.*

$50–80

A Wilding open-throat tennis racket, by Rawlins of St. Louis, Missouri. Tennis rackets can be dated by their shape and material, and often by their names. This example is named after the New Zealander Anthony Wilding, who won eight Wimbledon titles. *1910–14, 27¼ in (69 cm) high.*

$100–150

CLIPPERS

A Baltimore Clippers ice hockey nodder. Ceramic pieces add variety to a collection. Nodders are also a popular item among collectors, but only if in undamaged condition. Inspect the head carefully, and consider form and color since certain variations are rare.

$250–350

A Draper & Maynard basketball advertising paper blotter, with a color lithographed scene of children playing a game. c. 1920s, 9 in (15 cm) high.

$180–220

Formula One

A Grand Prix program from the last 30 years or so often fetches $30–80, but the one for the 1994 Imola race at which Ayrton Senna was killed can be worth $300. Press kits from the 1980s can fetch about $30; helmets worn by star drivers may cost $3,000 or more.

In the ring

Collectors look for signed boxing gloves, robes, and shorts, especially if fight-worn. A framed set of boxing shorts, signed by Mohammed Ali with a photo and certificate can cost $250–400, while items worn by Ali in significant fights can fetch thousands of dollars. Signed photographs of world champions from the 1950s to the present day can cost $80–300 or more.

Olympic gold

Memorabilia from the Olympic Games is varied and frequently sought after. A competitor's medal from 1932 with colored ribbon and Olympic bar can sell for $100–200. Olympics-related paper ephemera is often desirable: a program for the 1920 games can fetch $300 or more, early magazine advertisements featuring Olympic champions can fetch $30–80, and rare postcards can be worth $100.

Consider items for future high-profile, regular sporting occasions, such as the Olympic Games, the soccer World Cup, and world championships, as values could shoot up.

■ Replicas ■

A full-size replica Grand Prix racing helmet, the vizor signed by World Champion driver Michael Schumacher. This helmet, complete with Ferrari, Marlboro, and Asprey logos is identifiable as a replica, as it has a lipped base. Genuine race-used helmets are extremely scare. c. 2000, 17 in (43.5 cm) high.

$2,500–3,500

Top Tips

- Mohammed Ali's signature is often faked. Ali changed his name from Cassius Clay on March 6, 1964, and the majority of his signatures until the late 1960s include the word "from." Ali's handwriting has deteriorated due to Parkinson's, and from around 1982 onward his signatures are smaller.

- Establish the authenticity of equipment used by players—buy from reputable dealers and ask look for cast-iron provenance.

- Bear in mind that just because a sportsperson signed an item, he or she didn't necessarily own or use it.

KEEP

Look for photographs signed by sports heroes, especially those capturing a great sporting moment. A signature adds authenticity and value.

A Muhammad Ali signed press photograph. This photo shows a triumphant Muhammad Ali, standing over the prone Sonny Liston during their World Championship bout in May 1965. It is a terrific keepsake of one of the great nights in boxing history. 1965, 21½ in (55 cm) high.

$250–300

BUY

Pins are one of the most affordable and hot Olympic-related collecting areas. Desirability and prices should remain constant and may even rise for scarce examples.

A US Postal Service Olympic Games commemorative pin. The USPS is a regular sponsor of the Olympics. The good quality enamel design and presence of the Olympic logo also make this desirable. 1980s–90s, ¾ in (3 cm) high.

$4–6

The Written Word and Ephemera

From precious first edition books to holiday memorabilia, both the written word and ephemera are rich and diverse fields for collectors. Ephemera is an umbrella term for printed or handwritten objects, usually on paper or cardboard, made for a specific, often short-term, purpose before being discarded.

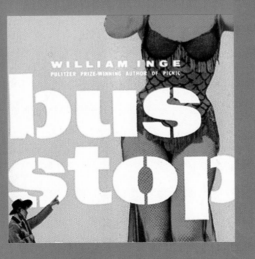

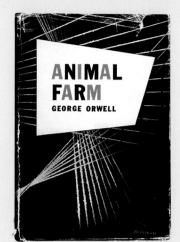

① Animal Farm by George Orwell, p. 268

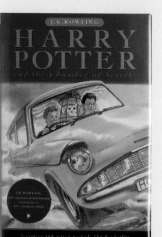

② J.K. Rowling Harry Potter book, p. 271

③ Dr. Seuss children's book, p. 271

Words and pictures......

From first editions of much loved books or favorite childhood comics to fashion magazines and old Valentine's cards, there are publications both vintage and modern to suit all tastes. Charming to read and look at, they bring back fond memories of leisure time in the past.

A first edition—the very first printing of a book—is the most valuable version. Search your bookcases for books that you may have bought new, or even secondhand, and stored away after reading —there may be a hidden gem. Titles by authors such as George Orwell **①** and Ian Fleming are highly sought after. Even more modern authors such as Brett Easton Ellis fire today's collectors' passions.

Children's writers like J. K. Rowling **②** and Dr. Seuss **③** are also collected and often fetch high prices, partly due to

nostalgia and the fact that children are hardly the most careful readers!

Childhood memories

Old comics such as *Spiderman* **④** and *Batman* are much appreciated by nostalgic adults eager to revisit the characters and stories they enjoyed as children. Like comics, old magazines **⑤** have their fans and because they are usually thrown away once read makes some surviving copies valuable.

Similarly, many of the growing army of Pez **⑥** collectors first came across the

⑥

⑦

Advertising trade card, p. 279

Batman PEZ dispenser, p. 289

⑧

Laurel and Hardy autograph, p. 284

Children's annuals have become valuable because they are only available for a limited period of time each year.

Marvel comic book, p. 275

1963 Life magazine, p. 277

.to treasure

distinctive candy dispensers as children and have carried their enthusiasm into their adult lives.

Don't throw it away!

Vintage advertising is an area full of surprises, from early 20th century whistles and clickers to tin signs, figurines and trade cards (7). Autographs of celebrities (8) can be lucrative, particularly when combined with photographs. Make sure yours are signed by the stars themselves and not by assistants or secretaries.

Joyful holiday occasions, especially Christmas and Halloween (9), are a time of year when decorations, cards, and costumes are often bought and then discarded. It can pay to hold on to these

items as they often have some value on the secondary market.

Some brands, such as Coca-Cola (10), are recognized worldwide. Promotional posters, glasses, badges, and trays are all worth keeping. Posters (11), particularly those for railroad lines, airlines, and steam cruisers offer a nostalgic trip back in time. Look for those by well-known artists or that are redolent of a particular era.

The condition for all books, cards, magazines, and ephemera is very important to collectors, as items made of paper and card can be easily damaged.

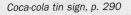

(9)

Halloween candy container, p. 280

(10)

Coca-cola tin sign, p. 290

(11)

French railroad poster, p. 294

Modern first editions offer

the newcomer one of the most accessible areas of book collecting. English-language books published since the 1890s are particularly sought after if they are in good condition and by notable authors.

When collecting new first editions, the trick is to spot up-and-coming writers who are likely to capture the public's imagination. Buying a first edition on publication and keeping it pristine may prove to be a good investment. For collectors of older books, there are many bookshops and websites that specialize in first editions.

Dust proof

Collectors generally define a first edition as the very first print run, or impression, of a book. Condition is vital, and the book must retain its original dust jacket. In the 19th century these were plain, but later they became more colorful and eye-catching to increase sales. The jacket on a second, or later, impression may differ from the first edition, perhaps with quotes added from book reviews. Print runs for many books published after World War II were larger than for prewar runs, so there is

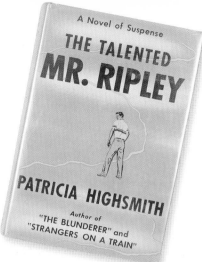

The Talented Mr. Ripley
by Patricia Highsmith (Coward-McCann, Inc., New York). *1955, 8 in (20.5 cm) high.*
$1,500–2,500

generally less of the scarcity factor that leads to high prices. Look also for "extras" such as the author's signature.

Talkin' about my generation

The work of the finest postwar writers, including the Americans William Burroughs, Jack Kerouac, Allen Ginsberg, and J. D. Salinger, and the Britons Lawrence Durrell, Anthony Burgess, and Kingsley Amis, is sought after. A first edition of J. P. Donleavy's

Some authors to look for:
- George Orwell ■ Tom Wolfe

Animal Farm, by George Orwell
(Harcourt Brace & Company, New York), with the dust jacket in poor condition. This political allegory continues to fascinate, so it is sought after. *1946, 8 in (20.5 cm) high.*
$120–180

A Moveable Feast, by Ernest Hemingway (Charles Scribner's Sons, New York). Hemingway's first editions are collectible and valuable, some fetching up to $1,000 or more. *1964, 8 in (20.5 cm) high.*
$300–400

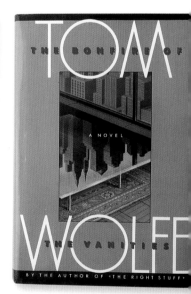

The Bonfire of the Vanities by Tom Wolfe (Farrar, Strauss, Giroux, New York). Wolfe typically engages closely with his subject in a highly journalistic manner. *1987, 8 in (20.5 cm) high.*
$350–450

Did You Know?

Collectors are as fascinated by the personality of Ian Fleming as by his books. His gold-plated typewriter sold at Christie's in London for over $84,000 in 1995. The buyer was the James Bond actor Pierce Brosnan.

1963 novel *A Singular Man* can cost around $30–50. On the other end of the scale, a J. D. Salinger first edition can fetch anywhere from $800 to $1,800, but a first edition of his first and best-known novel, *The Catcher in the Rye*, can command much higher prices of $10,000–15,000. A first edition of Anthony Burgess's *A Clockwork Orange* (1962) can be worth $1,500–2,000.

The here and now

Look for early works by today's popular writers such as John Grisham, Tom Wolfe, Dan Brown, Salman Rushdie, Sebastian Faulks, and Philip Roth. First editions by contemporary female authors, such as Margaret Atwood, Anne Rice, Alice Sebold, and Amy Tan, are in demand. Books often rise in value when made into films.

A first edition of Patricia Highsmith's *The Talented Mr. Ripley* (1955) can now reach up to $2,500 following the 1999 film adaptation.

Shock, horror

Science fiction, horror, spy stories, and detective fiction are popular themes. Ray Bradbury, Terry Pratchett, Brian Aldiss, Stephen King, and Thomas Harris are top names in the science fiction and horror genres. Most of Stephen King's titles are easy to find, and can be worth up to $2,000, with the better-known novels commanding the highest prices.

Spy novels by John Le Carré and Charles McCarry are favorites, and Ian Fleming remains popular. A pristine copy of *Casino Royale* (1953), the first James Bond novel, can fetch over $10,000.

Famous crime novels are also desirable. A first edition of Raymond Chandler's *The Big Sleep* (1939) can reach $10,000, with *Farewell My Lovely* fetching up to $4,000. More recent first editions such as the Dave Robicheaux books by James Lee Burke, may also be worth investing in.

BUY

Cult books by seminal authors that summed up a recent era are likely to be popular in the future as younger readers grow up and begin collecting books of their youth. If the author remains popular, his or her early works may also become sought after.

Less Than Zero, by Brett Easton Ellis (Simon and Schuster, New York). This first novel is deemed "the first MTV novel" and epitomized the 1980s. *1985, 8 in (20.5 cm) high.*

$200–300

KEEP

Memoirs are an increasingly popular genre. Books that describe successful attempts to overcome real-life setbacks appeal to a wide range of readers and are good investments.

Angela's Ashes by Frank McCourt (Scribner, New York). The story recalls the author's impoverished childhood in Ireland. The UK first edition, published by HarperCollins, fetching around $50–80, is currently less valuable than this US edition. *1996, 8¾ in (22.5 cm) high.*

$400–600

■ Tennessee Williams ■ Stephen King ■

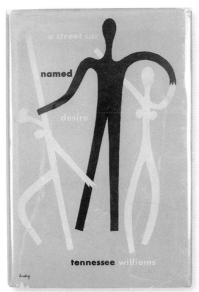

A Streetcar Named Desire, by Tennessee Williams (New Directions, New York). Considered a notable and prolific playwright, Williams drew upon his family and troubled life for inspiration. *1947, 8 in (20.5 cm) high.*

$1,800–2,800

The Shining by Stephen King (Doubleday & Company, Garden City, New York). This American author has written a wide variety of horror stories, many of them adapted for film. *1977, 7½ in (19 cm) high.*

$500–800

Children's books, treasured

for generations, are now highly sought after, both by collectors of first editions and by those for whom the rich heritage of children's literature is filled with nostalgia.

From beloved classics to tales of adventure and fantasy, there's plenty of scope for collecting children's books. Some, both traditional and modern, can reach high prices, but there are books to suit all budgets.

Enduring classics

First editions of well-known classics of children's literature are desirable, and tend to fetch high prices. A rare 1885 blue cloth-cover edition of Mark Twain's *Adventures of Huckleberry Finn*, published by Charles L. Webster & Company, is valued at around

$5,000–7,000. Frances Hodgson Burnett's *The Secret Garden* (1911) can be worth $500–800, while a Scribners first edition of Burnett's earlier *Little Lord Fauntleroy* (1886) can command up to $1,200. Works by E. B. White are sought after, and well-loved titles by this author can fetch high prices. *Stuart Little* (1945) is valued at up to $1,200, with 1952's *Charlotte's Web* fetching $2,000 or more, depending on condition. Other

Pippi Longstocking, by Astrid Lindgren (The Viking Press, New York), first edition. *1950, 8 in (20.5 cm) high.*
$580–680

The Hobbit by J. R. R. Tolkien, (Allen & Unwin, London). Partly due to the recent movies, first editions can fetch up to $30,000. This is the 7th impression of the 3rd edition, but retains its familiar dust jacket. *1972, 8 in (20.5 cm) high.*
$280–320

children's classics, especially rare or early books by Lucy Maud Montgomery, Washington Irving, Lewis Carroll, A. A. Milne, Laura Ingalls Wilder, and J. R. R. Tolkien, are also sought after. A first edition of Tolkien's *Lord of the Rings* can cost $15,000 or more.

Tales of adventure

L. Frank Baum created one of the best-loved fantasy adventures of all time, set in the land of Oz. The first

---

A closer look at... Roald Dahl's *The Gremlins*

Roald Dahl created such memorable characters as Willy Wonka and the BFG, thrilling generations of children. Many experts consider him to be one the few modern children's authors who will stand the test of time, making his books worth collecting. Consider examples carefully, as some are more desirable, or rarer, than others.

Gremlins were personifications of inexplicable problems experienced with World War II planes. Dahl was an ex-Royal Air Force pilot

The Gremlins, by Roald Dahl (Random House, New York). Since this book is also a rare first edition, it will appeal to collectors of first editions, such is Dahl's literary importance. *1943, 7½ in (19 cm) high.*
$3,000–4,000

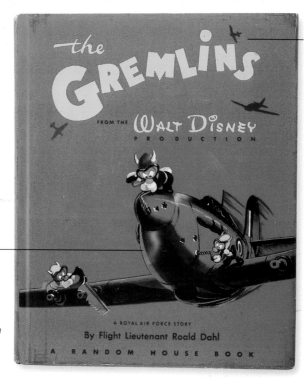

This was Dahl's first children's book—it was never reprinted and is very rare. A movie to be made by Disney was planned, but it was canceled

It was produced for Disney, and contains illustrations by Walt Disney Productions, making it desirable across another collecting market

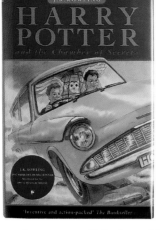

edition of the first book in the series, *The Wonderful Wizard of Oz*, published by Hill in 1900, can be worth up to $18,000, while prices for later and lesser-known Oz books range from around $700 to $3,000.

The British author Enid Blyton is best known for her *Famous Five* adventure stories (1942 onward), and her *Noddy* series (1949 onward). Prices for *Famous Five* titles range from around $50 to $800.

Modern originals

It may be worth investing in first editions of later classics by authors such as Walter Dean Myers, Mildred Taylor, or Ann Petry, whose *Tituba of Salem* (Cromwell first edition, 1964) can fetch up to $200. Books by Roald Dahl are sought after, particularly *James and the Giant Peach* (1961), worth over $1,000, and *Charlie and the Chocolate Factory* (1964), which can cost over $3,000, with many later books selling for $50–80 or less.

Picture books arouse interest—they can exert a powerful influence as collectors of such books were probably very young when they first

Harry Potter and the Chamber of Secrets by J. K. Rowling, first edition of the second book in the series (Bloomsbury, London); slightly damaged. *1998, 9½ in (24 cm) high.*

$2,500–3,000

read them. Look out for first editions by popular authors such as Dr. Seuss (creator of unforgettable characters such as The Grinch and The Cat in the Hat), Eric Carle, and Maurice Sendak.

World of wizards

First editions of J. K. Rowling's early Harry Potter books, particularly the first two volumes, can command high prices. In the UK, Bloomsbury issued an initial print run of only 500 copies of the first book, known there as *Harry Potter and the Philosopher's Stone* (1997). Many of these were sent to libraries, and were therefore stamped or worn through use. In 2003 a copy in mint, unread condition was sold for $29,250. The US Levine/Scholastic first edition of the same book, entitled *Harry Potter and the Sorcerer's Stone* (1998), is less rare, numbering 50,000, although examples in mint condition can still fetch a few thousand dollars.

In some cases, prices have not increased dramatically since 2000, because collectors may be waiting to see if Harry has staying power. Prices for a 1999 special limited edition of 4,000 copies of *Harry Potter and the Chamber of Secrets* range from around $120 to $170.

SELL

When books are turned into movies, prices of early editions of the original books usually rise, peak just after a movie has been released, and fall slowly from there.

Jumanji, by Chris van Allsburg (Houghton Mifflin Company, New York). It is best to sell this first edition to an avid collector, since prices are unlikely to rise again after the release of the moderately successful movie in 1995, starring Robin Williams as Alan Parrish. *1981, 10 in (25.5 cm) high.*

$500–700

KEEP

Certain characters are loved by adults as much as they are by children. If the author's work was enjoyed by many over the decades in different forms of media, it is likely that the demand for it will continue to grow.

It's a Mystery, Charlie Brown by Charles M. Schulz (Random House, New York), from the eighth printing of the first edition, signed. Schultz's death in 2000 and his lasting appeal mean prices may rise. *1975, 11 in (28 cm) high.*

$500–800

How The Grinch Stole Christmas! by Dr. Seuss (Random House, New York). This first edition is scarce and desirable, hence its high value. *1957, 11½ in (29 cm) high.*

$2,000–3,000

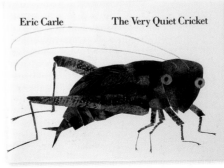

The Very Quiet Cricket, by Eric Carle, (Philomel Books, New York), first edition signed by the author. Carle's most famous book is *The Very Hungry Caterpillar*. *1990, 11¾ in (29 cm) long.*

$200–300

Paperbacks

are cult collectibles for many reasons. Although printed on the cheapest of paper—known as pulp—some have become important as social documents notwithstanding their cult appeal. While many can be had for under $50, a rarity can fetch up to $500.

The Written Word and Ephemera

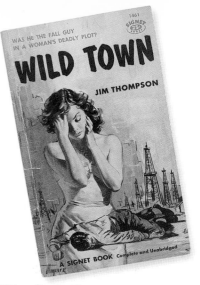

Wild Town, by Jim Thompson, (Signet Books, New York), first printing from The New American Library. *1957, 7 ¼ in (18 cm) high*

$80–120

Hardback books have traditionally attracted more attention than paperbacks (or "wraps"), although there is a growing market for these cheaply made books that appealed to a different type of reader. For the unitiated, it can seem crazy to pay so much for items that will probably deteriorate, but those in the know appreciate their uniqueness.

The Beat goes on

The earliest examples were made in the 1920s and 30s. First mass-produced by Avon from 1939, they are small and favored over the larger "trade" paperbacks. Other collectible publishers are Bantam, Pocket Books, Dell, Pyramid, Ace, and Anchor, although underground presses such as Grove also existed. Grove was associated with the Beat writers Jack Kerouac, Allen Ginsberg, and William Burroughs, thus attracting a young audience, many of whom have grown into avid collectors. As well as the often unwholesome content of pulp fiction, the unofficial status of some publishers made them cool.

Rare runs

Rarity seriously affects value, so hunt for small runs or books that didn't survive in quantity; a surprising number only came out in fragile paperback. Jack Kerouac's *Tristessa,* published by Avon, but not in hardback, can be worth $70–$100. Also rare is J. R. R. Tolkien's *Lord Of The Rings* trilogy by Ace, published illegally in the US in paperback and later withdrawn, but not before a few sets were scooped up; these can now fetch up to $400. Stephen King privately published *Six Stories* in 1997 and a copy can fetch $100–200, although a rare signed personal copy recently made $1,500.

Cover appeal

Books signed by the author and first editions command a premium, although some lesser editions are still collectible. For example, if a cover was created by a famous illustrator, it doesn't matter whether it's the 2nd or 10th edition, as long as it is in pristine condition. As paperbacks were designed to be sold on front-facing racks, they often had illustrative covers, particularly from the 1930s to the 60s, and relied on cover appeal to sell. If a book has artwork by Edward Gorey—a major illustrator for Anchor—it could cost $5–15, even for a later edition. Gorey illustrated Henry James's *What Maisie Knew,* Virgil's *The Aeneid,* and

Bus Stop, by William Inge, (Bantam Books, New York) first paperback edition, with Marilyn Monroe on the cover. *1956, 7¼ in (18 cm) high.*

$20–30

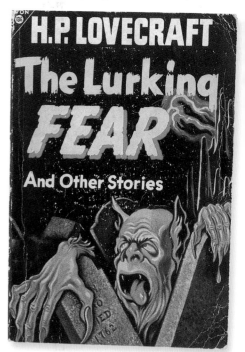

Lurking Fear, by H. P. Lovecraft, (Avon Book Company, New York). *1947, 6⅓ in (16 cm) high.*

$30–50

A closer look at... A paperback

Most paperbacks are collected for their rarity or the quality of their cover artwork alone. This is particularly true for the sex and crime genre, where the quality of the contents is usually poor, and many authors used one pseudonym. To make the right decisions, consider all features of the cover carefully.

Vice Rackets of Soho, by **Roland Vane** (Archer Press Ltd., London). The dual-currency pricing shows this was printed for both the US and the UK markets. The cover is crisp and in unmarked condition, with no fading. *1951, 6¼ in (16 cm) high.*

$80–120

The pseudonym Roland Vane was reused on postwar books to cash in on the name's excellent prewar reputation for similar novels—the author's real name was Ernest McKeag

The cover is typical of the genre, with a lewd lady exposing herself as she drapes provocatively across the cover

The subject would have been shocking at the time, as the title involves vice and the lady is being injected, perhaps with drugs, by a man

The cover was designed by Reginald Heade, whose cover designs are now highly collectible

BUY

Look for books that hold as many desirable features as possible, including genre, cover, artwork, and artist, as well as author and content. These make great buys while they are still inexpensive— prices are likely to rise.

Land of Terror by **Edgar Rice Burroughs**, (Ace Books, New York). This is from the popular fantasy genre and by a very well-known author. The cover is by the desirable artist Frank Franzetta and is typical of his work—all making this a superb buy. *1944, 6¼ in (16 cm) high.*

$10–15

The American Puritans. Particularly striking is the first edition of J. D. Salinger's *The Catcher in The Rye*, which shows a young man wearing a baseball cap backward and a sultry woman in the background; it often sells for $100, and even later editions can fetch $15–$25. Editions without this artwork are not as valuable, except to a collector who wants every publication.

Crime does pay

Enthusiasts collect by genre, too, and, as so much lewd material was published in paperback, high prices are paid for works with adult content. Sex, gangster, and crime stories are popular and often have salacious cover artwork. Popular artists include Reginald Heade and F. W. Perl; Hank Janson and Ben Sarto are known authors. Prices range from $30–80. Mysteries are also liked— look for "map backs" showing a map of a murder scene—and run $5–30. Science fiction was a national obsession in the 1950s and 60s, and paperbacks with great artwork can fetch $10–60.

Operation Outer Space, by Murray Leinster (Signet Books, New York) *1957, 7¼ in (18 cm) high.*

$10–15

Look too for horror stories, particularly by H. P. Lovecraft, children's books, travel, and romance. While high-end collectors prefer hardbacks, they too appreciate paperbacks as a record of the author's changes after an original printing. Country variations are of interest, as are original editions connected to a TV series, film, or a major character.

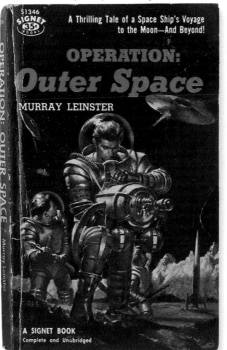

BUY

Many niche themes are becoming collecting categories of their own. Often produced in reaction to social feelings of their time, they are either as relevant today, or are valuable pieces of social history. Values are currently still low.

The Alcoholics, by **Jim Thompson** (Lion Books, New York). Substance abuse and delinquency are increasingly popular themes. The cover artwork is excellent and this is also a desirable first-edition paperback. *1953, 6½ in (16 cm) high.*

$80–120

Comics have long since ceased to be "just for kids." Many are now collectors' items and, with a vast range of titles stretching back nearly 70 years to choose from, there are comics for all tastes and budgets.

Generations of children grew up with comic books, and they are now a part of our consciousness. Superheroes have been battling the forces of evil—whether it be supervillains, gangsters, Nazis, aliens, or corrupt regimes—for so long that they reflect the shifting preoccupations of the nation and are important pieces of social history.

The gold standard
A comic book's value is determined by age, scarcity, condition, featured characters, and creative contributors. Some comics are valuable simply because of their topicality (Atoman No. 1, Feb.

1946, the first atomic explosion on a comic cover), others for their notoriety (the infamous severed head on Crime Suspenstories No. 22, May 1954). Some collectors concentrate on early comics, or on comics of the 1970s, while others aim for a complete run of a title from No. 1 to the present. How valuable a comic is depends on who is buying it. Condition is vital, and drastically affects price, although most serious enthusiasts would rather own a poor condition Action Comics No. 1 than a mint condition Action Comics No. 700.

The most prized period, known as the Golden Age (1938–c. 1955), began with the publication of Action Comics No. 1,

The Lone Ranger, No. 128, July 1959, published by Dell. *1959, 11¾ in (29 cm) high.*

$6–9

featuring the debut of a startling new hero—Superman. The success of Superman quickly gave rise to a host of rivals and imitators (Batman, Wonder Woman, Captain America) and led to an explosion in comic-book publishing. The leading lights of the Silver Age (c. 1956–69) were a new breed of psychologically complex heroes (Spider-Man, X-Men, The Fantastic

Fantastic Four, No. 29, Aug. 1965, published by Marvel Comics. *1965, 11¾ in (29 cm) high.*

$30–50

X-Men, No. 109, Feb. 1978, published by Marvel Comics. *1978, 11¾ in (29 cm) high.*

$20–30

Tom and Jerry, No. 136, Nov. 1955, published by D C Comics. *1955, 11¾ in (29 cm) high.*

$3–5

A closer look at... an Action Comic

Action Comics launched the very first true superhero character, Superman, in its first issue in June 1938. Considered the first comic of the Golden Age, a copy of this first issue in near mint condition could fetch up to $400,000 today! Superman gained his own comic in 1939, and Action Comics has become the second-longest running comic book in the US.

This 1946 copy is from the very desirable and early Golden Age, which covers comics from 1938–c. 1955

This issue deals with a core Superman theme—his secret identity as newspaper reporter Clark Kent

Superman is the most popular comic-book character of all time and one of the two most desirable and valuable characters from the Golden Age

Action Comics, No. 100, September 1946, in fine condition. Superman was an established character, so the comics had a large print run. Always look for comic books in as fine a condition as possible, as these have the best chance of appreciating further. *1946, 11¾ in (29 cm) high.*

$220–280

Four). The leaner years of the 1970s have been christened the Bronze Age (1970–79).

Faster than a speeding bullet...

The first issue of any comic is likely to be the most valuable; prices drop considerably for later issues. The superheroes command bigger prices than other characters, with Superman the most popular. A Superman No. 8 (c. 1941) can realize $6,000, but many later issues can be found for $5–10, depending on condition and age. A Batman No. 1, with a split spine, could fetch $4,500, and later, good condition examples $5–20. Wonder Woman is also desirable; she commands anything from $10 to $5,000. An affordable area to collect is Archie's line of children's comics, which have a wide fan base and are less expensive than the action heroes.

With established titles a particular run of issues can also attract a premium. Connoisseurs are eager to own anything that introduces a character or originates a storyline. Certain artists such as Jack Kirby, co-creator of Captain America, The Fantastic Four, The Hulk, and the X-Men, and Neal Adams, pioneer of a dynamic new style of comic-strip art in the 1960s, are also more collected than others. Some collectors look for popular writers such as Stan Lee, co-creator of The Fantastic Four and Spider-Man, and artist/writer Frank Miller, who came up with the dark, contemporary reimagining of Batman in the 1980s.

Most mainstream comic books have substantial print runs; in the Golden Age, over a million copies of Captain Marvel were printed monthly. However, there are scarcities and if a comic existed in small numbers its titles may be highly sought after, particularly if the characters or creators went on to bigger things. The first issues of Teenage Mutant Ninja Turtles (1984) were self-published by the creators and only 500 copies were printed. Despite being a relatively recent comic, it now fetches hundreds of dollars.

Captain America, No. 135, Mar. 1971, published by Marvel Comics. *1971, 11¾ in (29 cm) high.*

$8–12

BUY

DC Silver Age comics are underappreciated in comparison to Marvel and still affordable. Collectors like storylines that feature the introduction, death, or origins of popular characters. Buy now before the tide turns, which may happen as more characters make it to the silver screen.

Batman, No. 156, June 1963, by DC Comics. The death of Robin makes for an interesting story and the cover artwork is dramatic, representative, and eye-catching. *1963, 11¾ in (29 cm) high.*

$15–25

SELL

Films revitalize people's interests in or nostalgic affection for comic-book characters. As such, the value rises for a short time. Sell and catch the market at its peak, when more buyers will be prepared to pay a higher price for high-profile characters.

The Amazing Spider-Man, No. 29, Oct. 1965, published by Marvel Comics. Although Spider-Man is ever-popular, the two recent movies directed by Sam Raimi have encouraged many fans to collect afresh. *1965, 11¾ in (29 cm) high.*

$150–200

Vintage magazines can transport

the reader into an almost forgotten world. Their individual styles and contents provide a fascinating glimpse of the outstanding events, celebrities, fashions, and endlessly changing lifestyles of past decades.

I Love Lucy, issue No. 18 from 1958, published by Dell. *1958, 12¾ in (32 cm) high.*
$20–30

Dedicated collectors save magazines because an issue has an intriguing article or photograph, or because it covers an area of special interest such as fashion or movie stars.

In vogue

Fashion magazines offer a unique record of period styles and are filled with excellent photography showing the designs of the day. *Vogue*, launched in 1916, has documented decades of evolving fashions. The vintage of the edition is important, as is the style and subject of the cover, as striking covers are often associated with *Vogue*. Values vary from about $3–20 for a copy from the 1980s or 90s, to around $20–50 for a copy from the 1960s. Famous models such as Twiggy, or designers, such as Emilio Pucci or Giorgio Armani, can raise prices to $70–100 or more. An issue from the 1920s or 30s featuring the designs of a leading couturier like Elsa Schiaparelli can be worth $50–150, and some examples of early editions have changed hands for $250 or more.

Star attraction

Magazines featuring well-known personalities can attract anyone who collects subjects such as rock music or

Some magazines to look fo
- Vogue ■ House Beautiful ■

House Beautiful **from July 1949.** Founded in 1896, *House Beautiful* is the oldest continuously published interiors magazine in the US and has a reputation for covering the best in period styling. *1949, 12¾ in (32 cm) high*
$15–25

PRINT MANIA NINE WAYS TO A BEAUTIFUL BODY

APRIL 15 1964 THREE SHILLINGS

Vogue **from April 1964.** The fashionista's bible, *Vogue* is renowned for its coverage of the changing world of fashion. An eye-catching, well-photographed cover—as many were—makes an issue more collectible. *1964, 11½ in (29 cm) high.*
$20–50

movie stars. The face on the cover is a good indicator of value. The first issue of *Playboy* (December 1953), featuring a nude centerfold of Marilyn Monroe and a cover image of her waving, sold more than 54,000 copies, ensuring a second issue. As the centerfold was often removed, complete *Playboy* first issues in good condition are rare today and can command $800–2,500; some have been sold for $5,000 or more. Magazines featuring other enduring icons such as Grace Kelly or Audrey Hepburn are always desirable. Another sought-after example is the October 1961 issue of *Life* with a cover shot of Elizabeth Taylor as Cleopatra, which can be found for up to $40. The value of music magazines such as *Rolling Stone* is also often determined by the cover story.

Landmarks in history

Magazines vividly capture moments in history, and certain subjects are popular with collectors. Titles such as *Life*, *Time*, *Newsweek*, *Collier's*, and the *Saturday Evening Post* are collectible. Magazines featuring events of lasting importance, such as the assassination of President Kennedy, the death of Elvis Presley, or the 1969 Moon landing, are very common, as people tended to save these issues and throw others away. Yet there is a continuing demand for such mementos. *Life* magazines generally fetch $5–20, but, though it is not particularly scarce, a JFK memorial edition of *Life* can sell for up to $30.

Magazines from the 1940s showing events from World War II also have crossover appeal for collectors of war paraphernalia, and therefore tend to fetch higher prices.

Inner beauty

Lifestyle and interiors magazines are generally not as valued as other niche publications, but *House Beautiful* and *Better Homes and Gardens* have a small following. The value of 1950s, 60s, and 70s issues may rise, as there is a growing market in retro styles.

Many people collect by cover image or inside illustrations. Values vary depending on the artwork, but range from about $8–20 for a lesser-known publication with simple artwork up to $150 or more for classic examples of Art Nouveau or Art Deco.

Some people buy magazines for their advertisements, focusing on a brand name or a particular product. Values can vary from less than $1 to around $30–50. Wear and tear is to be expected and will affect value.

Top Tips

- Choose early issues: the first 10 issues—before a publication's sales became established—are rare and can be more desirable.
- Keep issues that feature modern celebrities with enduring popularity, such as Madonna or George Clooney, on the cover—you could realize a profit in a few years.

BUY

Key titles featuring outstanding photography of well-known personalities are sought after. Examples that were not marketed as specials or souvenir issues are the most likely to appreciate.

Vogue from December 1991, featuring the Princess of Wales. The continuing interest in Diana and the iconic photography by Patrick Demarchelier make this issue likely to rise in value. *1991, 11¾ in (30 cm) high.*

$15–25

SELL

Issues of magazines covering unpopular people or distasteful events often sold poorly. This makes them rare today. Specialized collectors may be prepared to pay a premium for them.

Life from December 1969, with a Charles Manson cover and story. This is a rare issue: few copies were sold or kept. *1969, 14 in (35.5 cm) high.*

$20–40

■ Life ■ Playboy ■

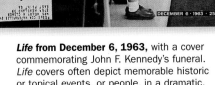

Life from **December 6, 1963,** with a cover commemorating John F. Kennedy's funeral. *Life* covers often depict memorable historic or topical events, or people, in a dramatic, hard-hitting way. *1963, 14 in (35.5 cm) high.*

$10–30

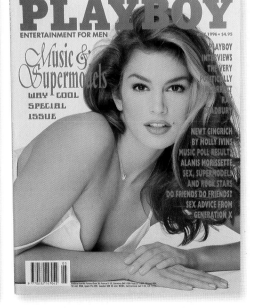

Playboy from **May 1996,** with Cindy Crawford cover. Hugh Hefner's *Playboy*, with its kitsch elements and series of clubs, has grown into a global brand hotly collected and sought after. *1996, 32 cm (12.75 in) high*

$10–15

Printed ephemera allows a

glimpse into past events, interests, styles, and trends. Small, easy to store and display, and often rare, these items appeal, through their fleeting nature, to design historians and enthusiasts alike.

Ephemera, such as cards, menus, and invitations, has been produced in large quantities for about the last 200 years. Values vary from less than $10 to upward of $2,000–3,000. Most examples date from the late 19th and early 20th centuries, with some items fetching $500–800 or more.

Stock-in-trade

Originating in London, England, during the early 17th century, trade cards, advertising products and services, were among the first forms of publicity. Eighteenth and early 19th-century woodcut or letterhead cards are rare and fetch $300–800 or more. Trade cards became popular in the US in the 1870s and 80s, helped by developments in chromolithography. Many stock cards had a generic picture with a blank space for the trader's details. Trade cards that were custom designed and those with colorful artwork are more sought after. By the 1900s, other forms of publicity, such as magazine advertisements and postcards,

A color lithographed advertising trade card for Columbus Buggy Co. of Columbus, Ohio. *c. 1900, 5 in (12.5 cm) high.*

$80–120

took over and the pictorial trade card declined. Examples with finely printed, complex designs, embossing, or gilt details, can cost $10–150 or more.

From the 1880s, cigarette packs carried advertisement cards and, later, collectible picture cards, to encourage brand loyalty. Collectors look for condition and complete sets of cards.

Sentimental scraps

Scraps, also known as swaps or die cuts, are brightly colored, shaped

Some Victorian scraps to look for:
▪ Ladies ▪ Animals ▪ Flowers ▪ Exoticism ▪

A large scrap of an elegant lady. Ladies featured on scraps often conform to ideas of Victorian beauty, with tiny noses and rosebud mouths. *c. 1880s, 4 in (10 cm) high.*

$8–12

Four die-cut, joined roosters. Complete pages of scraps are desirable and generally fetch more than the equivalent sum of individual pieces. *c. 1880s, 4¾ in (12 cm) wide.*

$30–40

cards printed with designs such as flowers, animals, and people. Their popularity peaked from the 1870s to the early 1910s. They were either cut from cards or torn from precut strips, and were placed into albums, made into bookmarks, or used to decorate screens and small pieces of furniture or boxes—a decorative process known as découpage. Prices start at less than $15 and rarely exceed $30–60. Look for large, well-printed, intact examples. Scraps can be found at flea markets, junk stores, or specialized dealers.

A color lithographed advertising trade card for Thurber's No. 41 coffee. *c. 1900, 4½ in (11 cm) wide.*
$10–20

Broad horizons

Broadsides are advertisements printed on one side, and were used in the 19th and early 20th centuries for publicizing merchandise or events. They proved to be an inexpensive way to reach a large audience, and were pasted onto surfaces in prominent locations. They usually favor text over imagery and were truly ephemeral in nature, being intended for short-term immediate use and then discarded.

Broadsides tend to be sought after by a small but dedicated group of collectors. Prices vary, and a broadside can sell for $50 or $3,000, with the higher prices reserved for rare pieces, items with intricate and colorful artwork, and those from unusual events.

BUY ▶

Inexpensive Victorian ephemera can be found. Choose good-quality printing and design, and items in still-vibrant colors and unusual shapes. 19th-century sentimentalism is still popular, and pieces with all these qualities should rise in value.

A die-cut card in the form of a tambourine. This card is unusual in shape; and the well-printed image makes it a good example of Victorian sentimentalism. *c. 1895, 6 in (15 cm) wide.*
$15–25

An Asian lady with fan. The Victorians loved exotic places and customs, and scraps featuring people in traditional dress or objects from a foreign country are common. *c. 1880s, 2¼ in (6 cm) high.*
$3–5

KEEP ▶

Items that were printed in large numbers for every-day purposes, but that were usually destroyed or discarded in the course of daily life, can be rare and desirable.

A printed label for a ream of paper made by I. Anderson of Milton, Massachusetts. The early date and the complex and patriotic artwork with flags and an eagle makes this example desirable, even though it is a little worn with age. *1810, 9 in (23 cm) high.*
$150–200

A large scrap of a man's hand bearing a lily-of-the-valley bouquet. Flowers are a common subject for scraps; the largest examples and those with finer detailing and intricately cut shapes are the most valuable. *c. 1890s, 4¾ in (12 cm) high.*
$5–8

Halloween collectibles,

from postcards to costumes, masks, and candy containers, are fun, varied, and evoke precious nostalgic memories. The delights of collecting are perhaps not yet fully appreciated.

Halloween is a custom that has been with us since the 1880s and originates from the Celtic harvest celebrations brought over by Scottish immigrants. Many items reflect the rural roots of the holiday, with candy containers, figurines, table centerpieces, and lanterns made in the shapes of vegetable characters. Yet it is the dark side of October 31, and its ghoulish objects, that collectors particularly appreciate, and the demand for scary stuff could mean an upturn in values.

Night frights

Some early Halloween memorabilia relates to courting parties held for young people at harvesttime, and includes costumes, invitations, and crepe-paper decorations. As trick-or-treating took off in the northeastern states from the 1920s, a whole array of merchandise appeared, from mass-produced ratchets, squeakers, tambourines, and horns in lithographed tin and paper to bright orange candy bags. Vintage paper bags can cost as little as $1–20, while a tin horn can sell for $15–70 and wooden ratchet noisemakers $70–350—depending on artwork, quality, and condition. Collectibles from this time are some of the most desirable, and often pricey, items on the market and were primarily imported from Germany. Typical materials are screen-printed tinplate and painted ceramic, papier-mâché, and composition.

An articulated, printed-and-die-cut cardboard skeleton, by H. E. Lehr. *1930s–40s, 22¾ in (58 cm) tall.*
$30–40

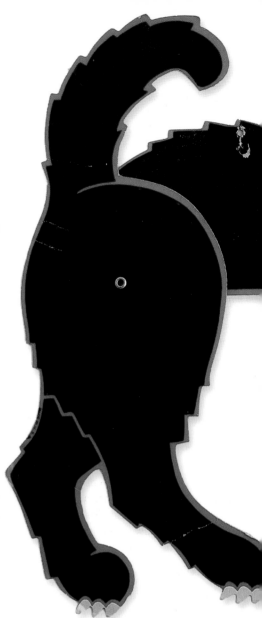

An articulated, printed-and-die-cut cardboard creeping cat hanging display piece. *1930s, 13¼ in (34 cm) long.*
$25–35

Essential Halloween collectibles

CARDS Examples in mint condition with evocative artwork are valuable, especially if rare, like this US card by Dennison. c. 1930s, 20¾ in (52 cm) high.
$30–40

CARDBOARD LATERNS German examples are prized, and 1950s US items are growing in popularity. 1920s, 4⅞ in (12cm) high.
$100–150

FIGURINES Bisque figurines in particular are scarce. Look for well-modeled figures, bright colors, and typical forms. 1920s–30s, 5½ in (14 cm) high.
$150–250

NOISEMAKERS These come in various forms such as this horn. German and Czech pieces from the 1920s–30s are scarce and valuable. 1950s, 4⅛ in (10.5 cm) diam.
$20–30

CONTAINERS German containers for trick-or-treating often look like ornaments, like this rare 1920s pumpkin lady. 8 in (20 cm) high.
$200–300

CANDY CONTAINERS Those made in plastic are affordable. Look for fun, colorful, intact pieces in complex shapes. 1950s–60s, 3 in (7.5 cm) high.
$30–50

Boo!

Postcards with Halloween themes appeared in the late 1880s and millions were produced by the early 20th century, with those from around 1910 being the most collectible. Styles range from simple greetings and graphics to ornate embossed examples with poems, which are the most valuable. Cards in mint condition by known artists such as Brundage, Clapsaddle, and Schmucker can reach $100–200, but an impressive display can be built with unnamed, yet attractive, cards costing $5–15 each.

Candy is dandy

Early printed party invitations in styles such as Art Nouveau and Art Deco fetch from $15–50, while crepe-paper decoration rolls run from $20 to $80. Made by manufacturers such as Dennison, Bainbridge, and American Tissue Mills, the evocative imagery was silk-screened in three or more colors on 10-feet (3-m) rolls and included witches, pumpkins, bats, and other motifs—the more the better. A set of Halloween napkins from the 1940s–50s can cost $8–12, whereas those from 1920–30 can be up to $50 each. Other paper ephemera include embossed wall decorations, party plates, place cards, doilies, fans, and stickers. Party plates are inexpensive now, but this area could be on the upswing, since so many were discarded. Condition is important, with an unopened set of 6–8 paper plates worth up to $50. Highly decorative magazine covers such as the *New Yorker* are prized and can cost $10–40.

Other Halloween treasures include pipecleaner party favors, felt dolls, wax candles, and Bakelite stickpins, but it is the composition candy containers, figurines, and jack o' lanterns that have the broadest appeal. Early examples (1910s–30s) are in papier-mâché or ceramic and marked "Japan"; those marked "Made in Japan" date from c. 1930–60s. From the Fifties, plastic was increasingly used. Plastic candy containers are found in great variety and make an excellent and affordable collection full of youthful nostalgia. Prices are $15–300 for rare shapes or colors, large sizes, or pieces with complete, but easily damaged, protruding parts. Early cardboard or ceramic items are valuable, the best fetching $1,000. Containers with removeable heads and good modeling are favored over simple ones with slots. As always, price depends on date, condition, rarity, and visual appeal.

A painted, pressed-cardboard German candy container in the form of a vegetable man, on a base. *1920s–30s, 3 in (7.5 cm) high.*

$220–280

Top Tips

- Look for postcards from Germany; they are more collectible than homegrown items. These predate World War I, when German imports were halted and production centered in Portland, Maine.

- Candy containers with an extra detail or mechanical aspect are favored. German makes are expensive; Japanese works and plastic pieces by the Rosen Company of Rhode Island are cheaper.

- Buy the best you can afford. Damage and missing parts reduce value by up to 30 percent.

- A piece with a slightly worn patina is preferred to one that has been refinished. Repairs almost certainly decrease value.

BUY

Noisemakers come in many materials and shapes, forming a good collection. Many are still affordable, but less common examples are likely to rise in value as demand for a finite supply grows. Examine the motifs as well as the condition to make sure you have an example that will rise in value.

A printed tinplate noisemaker. The combined devil and witch motif make this a rarity, as does the mark showing it was made in Japan. *1930s, 6½ in (16.5 cm) high.*

$40–50

KEEP

Variations in color and form are scarce and hotly sought after, particularly on more common plastic memorabilia. Prices rise consistently, since these pieces depart from standard production, are rarely found, and add variety to a collection.

A Halloween plastic snowman candy holder, with removeable pipe. Halloween colors for a Christmas shape are very rare. Here, orange plastic remained in the mold as the maker changed the shape, making accidental Halloween snowmen. *1950s–60s, 5¼ in (13 cm) high.*

$70–100

Christmas memorabilia—

glistening glass baubles, Victorian Christmas cards, and Santa Claus figurines—is much sought after for its charm and nostalgia. Mementos of a bygone age, these often fragile pieces conjure up visions of snowy Christmases past.

Sir Henry Cole, founder of the Victoria and Albert Museum in London, is credited with sending the first illustrated Christmas card in 1843. About a thousand were printed, a dozen of which survive. In 2001, one of these cards fetched $37,000 at auction.

Charles Goodall & Son was an early manufacturer of Christmas cards, as were Marcus Ward and Raphael Tuck & Sons. Louis Prang cards are also highly collectible. Late 19th-century cards are fairly easy to find and range from $8 to $80. Look for intact cards that fold in a complex way, are intricately decorated, or have moving parts.

From the early 20th century onward, other Christmas items were produced on a large scale. Santa figurines from before the 1940s are particularly desirable. Look for German Belsnickles made from papier-mâché: these large figures are valuable and can fetch from around $500 to $2,000 or more. Santas with clockwork parts and celluloid Santas from the late 1940s are also sought after. "Made in Japan" items are generally popular with collectors.

Early German Christmas trees made from colored goose feathers are prized. Other memorabilia, usually priced from $5–15 upward, includes early glass baubles, cake decorations, tree lights, and tins. By the 1960s, cheaper glass and plastic ornaments were being mass-produced and the Golden Age of the Christmas decoration was over. Beware of reproduction ornaments, which are shinier and brighter in color than the originals.

▲ **A German Christmas snowman candy container** made from pressed cardboard coated with plaster. Novelty-shaped containers that used to contain treats are a relatively common and very collectible form of memorabilia for both Christmas and Halloween. *1940s, 5½ in (14 cm) high.*
$120–180

▶ **An American papier-mâché Santa roly-poly,** by notable toymaker Alfred Schoenhut. Santa figurines produced before 1930 are particularly collectible. *1920s–30s, 5 in (12.5 cm) high.*
$150–250

▶ **An early English moveable Christmas card,** by Goodall, with four vignettes of little girls. Charles Goodall first made Christmas cards in 1859 and its cards are marked "CG & S." *c. 1870, 4¾ in (12 cm) high.*
$60–80

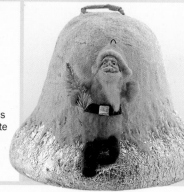

◀ **A Japanese Suzuki windup cycling Santa,** made from celluloid and tinplate, with a ringing bell. Many festive toys were produced in the late 1940s and 50s. Moving toys with tinplate parts like this are sought after. *c. 1946, 4¼ in (10.5 cm) high.*
$180–250

◀ **A "Made In Japan" foil, plaster, and cardboard bell,** with a papier-mâché Santa on the front and a candle and holly cardboard decal on the reverse side. *1950s, 4 in (10 cm) high.*
$30–50

◀ **A Hi-Ho Santa plastic pull-along toy.** Unusual color variations can add value, especially if they don't match the season's colors. The red, green, and tan color combination shown here is hard to find. *1960s, 10 in (25 cm) high.*

$100–150

▶ **A ceramic snowbaby.** Snowbabies were first made in Germany in the early 20th century, possibly based on cake decorations. Their condition and size affect their value, and larger sizes fetch higher prices than the standard 1½ in (3.5 cm) sizes. *1930s, 1½ in (3.5 cm) high.*

$40–50

▲ **A plastic Santa Claus candy container.** Plastic figures were produced in great variety from the 1950s onward, and make a fun, affordable collection. Complex shapes are usually more valuable. *1960s, 5 in (13 cm) high.*

$15–20

Collectors' Tips

- Look for incomplete sets of Christmas tree decorations, since full sets are rarely found
- Seek out fine-quality printed cards, preferably with complex cutout details
- Take care when storing Christmas cards: those that have been stuck in albums lose value

▶ **A Christmas tree,** in goose-feather style. Larger versions of such trees are more valuable, as are those in unusual colors such as blue or burgundy. *1920s, 8½ in (21.5 cm) high.*

$80–100

◀ ▲ **Two Victorian chromolithographed paper scraps.** Scraps were popular "cut out and collect" objects stuck in albums or used as bookmarks. Santa in a different colored suit is unusual and desirable. *1880s, largest 2¾ in (7 cm) high.*

$8–10 each

◀ **A small plastic nativity scene.** Given away by religious organizations from the 1950s on, these have recently become collectible. This example is undamaged and includes palm trees, which makes it desirable. Original boxes add value. *1950s, 18 cm (7 in) wide.*

$15–25

Autographs are the trophies

of today's celebrity-obsessed culture—whether scribbled on a napkin or sold as part of the luminary's public relations. A star's signature in a rare medium can fetch an aptly astronomical price.

A pair of Stan Laurel and Oliver Hardy autographs, mounted together with a publicity photograph. *13½ in (39.5 cm) high.*

$800–1,200

Famous personalities sign their names on a wide variety of collectible artifacts, including handwritten or typed letters, official documents such as contracts, driver's licenses, photographs, manuscripts, books, and programs, as well as items such as guitars and menus—and, of course, autograph albums.

Focus group

Many new collectors concentrate on one subject, such as movie stars, or sports heroes. Enthusiasts often take into account the accessibility of the personalities involved if they are still alive—for many, the thrill of the chase is as important as the satisfaction of ownership. Anyone considering collecting should look into prices before choosing their special interest; it can cost as little as $15–25

to buy a page from an autograph album signed by a minor star, but thousands of dollars for a rare document or object with biographical interest—such as a letter or a contract.

Reach for the stars

Before the 20th century, it was fashionable to collect the letters and autographs of writers and political figures. The advent of modern media shifted the focus to entertainers. By the 1930s and 40s many movie stars and, later, TV personalities, pop stars, sports heroes, and models, became so besieged

Main image: Brigitte Bardot signs her autograph for admiring fans. **Inset: A postcard-sized color photograph of Brigitte Bardot,** signed by her across the lower portion of the image in bold black ink. *1960s, 15 cm (5¾ in) high.*

$200–250

by autograph hunters that a minion often signed their photos for them.

In the past, movie stars working with the major studios were often contractually obliged to sign autographs and be friendly to fans, but today's entertainers are freer to opt out of what many regard as the irksome business of signing their names. A handful of stars, among them Britney

A closer look at... two Marilyn Monroe signatures

The kind of item, wording, presentation, and display appeal are important to a signature's value. Monroe's enduring fame and the rarity of her autograph influence value, but other characteristics cause price differences too. Checks, for example, make excellent display pieces, as they are larger and visually more interesting than autograph album pages.

A check signed by Marilyn Monroe, drawn on her company's account at the Bankers Trust Company in New York City, dated August 11, 1961. It is made payable for the sum of $127.90 to May Reis, who is known to have been a close friend of Monroe. *1961, 9¾ in (25 cm) long.*

$6,000–9,000

The date of the check helps attest to its period authenticity

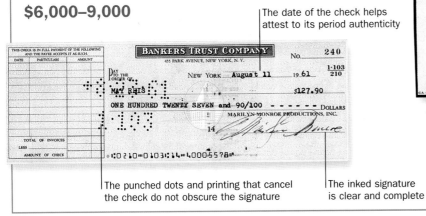

The punched dots and printing that cancel the check do not obscure the signature

The inked signature is clear and complete

The personal dedication to someone whose relationship to the star is unknown reduces the appeal to buyers

The signature, which is cramped to one side and on the diagonal, is less well placed here

The back of a picture postcard is less attractive to display

A Marilyn Monroe signature on a United Airlines DC-7 postcard. The card is signed and dedicated in blue ballpoint pen on the reverse (shown here) "To Judy Love & Kisses Marilyn Monroe." *1960s, 5¾ in (15 cm) wide.*

$3,000–5,000

Spears and Tobey Maguire, generally refuse to sign autographs. Others, such as George Clooney and Angelina Jolie, give them as "payback" to their loyal fans.

The value of an autograph often depends more on rarity than historical status. Trends also play a part: prices rise as people become more popular or are "rediscovered." An autograph including all the members of the band Abba can fetch up to $300 today, more than it would have done during the late 1980s. Signatures on artifacts with added visual appeal such as photographs are also desirable.

Professional autograph collectors can make six-figure salaries simply by selling signed photographs to fans. Be warned, autograph collecting provides easy pickings for forgers and swindlers too, especially through internet sites devoted to sales.

The genuine article

It can be difficult to distinguish between fakes and the real thing—few signatures are consistent—so seek the advice of a reputable dealer first. Experts will spot clues such as styles of lettering or, in the case of historical documents, old inks and papers.

Top Tips

- Examine the signature to ensure it was written and not printed.
- Look for a complete, clear signature.
- Consider whether the signature's position on the object allows for easy display.
- Handwritten letters tend to be more valuable than typed, hand-signed ones.
- For maximum investment value, pick signatures that are not dedicated to an individual.
- Only choose a dedicated signature if there is a relationship between the signer and recipient, or if the recipient is also famous.

KEEP

Autographs enhanced with personal drawings are highly sought after, particularly if the image is a hallmark of the artist. Values should rise if the artist does not sign any more.

A card signed by the late Charles M. Schulz. The addition of Schultz's drawing of Snoopy makes this well worth keeping.

1980s, 5¼ in (13 cm) wide.

$1,200–1,800

SELL

Beatles material is consistently collectible, but signatures by other people on their behalf reduce the appeal.

An autograph album page signed by Paul McCartney and George Harrison. Harrison also signed "Ringo Starr" (who signed "John Lennon" is unknown). Damage from tape reduces appeal. *1967, 4¼ in (11 cm) wide.*

$1,500–2,000

SELL

Leonardo DiCaprio is a major movie star, with roles in such movies as Titanic and The Aviator. He will almost certainly produce many more autographs to add to the large number already in circulation, so a plain DiCaprio signature is unlikely to appreciate much in the long term.

A Leonardo DiCaprio autograph on a plain white card. *1990s, 5¼ in (15 cm) wide.*

$100–150

Vintage advertising has

spawned a wealth of objects that speak volumes about our changing values, desires, and needs. And with its vibrant artwork, quirky slogans, and nostalgic qualities, there's something for everyone.

A diverse range of vintage promotional items has been created over the years, all with the express purpose of imprinting a brand on to our consciousness to encourage repeat purchases. Collectors may focus on a type of promotional item, such as point-of-sale displays, posters, tin signs, toys, or on all kinds of giveaway objects, from mirrors and money banks to figurines and novelties. Certain industries, such as beer brewing or tobacco production, are also popular, as are major brands, like Coca Cola and Planter's Peanuts. The brand can also have a bearing on value, with the best known brands having large followings and, as such, higher prices.

It pays to look good

The artwork is a vital factor to consider when collecting. Usually bold and colorful, it reflects the style of the period in its imagery and lettering. An interesting collection might, for instance, show how designs developed through the decades. Many collectors seek out artwork characteristic of a particular brand. The style can also be used to date a piece. A sign from 1900 may have traditional motifs, while 1930s artwork may be simpler and more modern, in keeping with the Art Deco taste of the period. The artwork also gives an insight into life in the past, showing what people wore and used in their homes. Such nostalgia is important to collectors.

Sign language

Some of the most collectible and often valuable pieces are the lithographed and enameled metal signs that were popular from the late

A Picobac tobacco-store advertising sign, with tinplate frame and blank area for writing prices. *c. 1920s, 10 in (25.5 cm) high.*

$30–50

A color, printed-cardboard shop standee for Orange Crush soft drink. *1940s, 11⅛ in (29 cm) high.*

$120–180

19th century to the 1950s, when radio and TV began to take over. These could run from $100 to $2,000 or more, depending on the popularity of the product and how distinctive and appealing the artwork appears. A 30-inch wide 1960s Sunbeam bread sign could cost around $400, while a rare, patriotic-themed Yankee Girl cigar sign from the late 19th century could make as much as $20,000. Variations abound, and include glass and neon examples, flange signs (viewable from both sides), festoons (hanging signs), as well as grocery-cart cards and menu boards. Countertop cardboard signs, known as standees, are also popular, as are dispensers for small items such as candy or chocolate. These point-of-

Essential advertising collectibles

TRADE CARDS The came in novelty shapes and eccentric artwork. This is for Thurber's coffee. c. 1900, 4½ in (11 cm) wide.
$12–18

FIGURINES These are popular. A Japanese Colonel Sanders plastic bank; eyes indicate country of origin. 1970s, 7⅞ in (20.5 cm) high.
$180–220

POCKET MIRRORS Made in the early 20th century, this Campbell's Soup pocket mirror advertises a popular brand. 1930s, 1¾ in (4.5 cm) wide.
$120–180

TAPE MEASURES This is a Goodyear Tires tape measure. Look for unusual materials, known brands, and iconic designs. c. 1920s, 1¾ in (4 cm) diam.
$50–80

TRAYS Look for tip trays with drinks or tobacco ads and fun artwork like this Brewing & Malting Co. tin tray. c. 1909, 4¼ in (11 cm) diam.
$100–150

TIN SIGNS Advertising signs like this Mayo's Plug example fetch high prices, but ensure they are authentic. Tobacco advertising is popular. c. 1910, 30 in (76 cm) high.
$300–500

sale display items were often adorned with the same artwork as signs and posters, but are usually less expensive, selling for $20–300. However, as always, value depends on condition, so make sure items are not faded by light or otherwise damaged.

A good tip

Metal trays, made as giveaways by beverage companies, can fetch high prices and have colorful printed artwork, particularly those designed by respected artists such as Norman Rockwell for Coca Cola. Trays are either oval or round and usually came in two sizes—large, round drink trays and small tip trays. It's the brand, style, rarity of the artwork, and condition that count for both types. Many smaller trays are still affordable, usually priced from $30–500, although attractive, vintage serving trays in great condition can command $200 to $1,500, since they usually saw plenty of use in their day

and those in pristine condition are hard to come by. An appealing 20th Century Ale tip tray with a rising sun design may fetch $500, although other examples can be picked up for $60–120; a Fairy Soap tip tray showing a girl seated on a bar of soap could be $70–100.

Prize inside

Giveaways and prizes have been used for almost every product on the market, and those with strong, characteristic branding or high nostalgia value can be of huge interest to advertising enthusiasts. Don't ignore mass-produced lighters, pens, key rings, or novelties; although these are still affordable—usually under $5–15— they often represent a brand well and may become tomorrow's sought-after collectibles as examples are thrown away or become damaged through use. One of the canniest prize incentives ever conceived was the prize that appeared inside every Cracker Jack popcorn box from 1912. Gifts included plaster charms, tinplate whistles, flip booklets, and baseball cards. Items from the last 25 years usually cost $3–10, with values rising to around $100 for rare or early prizes. Keep an eye out for associations with celebrities, such as the football player "Broadway Joe" Namath, who advertised Arrow shirts and Dingo boots, and characters such as Mickey Mouse or Little Orphan Annie. They usually add value to advertising memorabilia, and many comic-book heroes, cartoon favorites, and characters from books and TV were appropriated to sell goods. Also sought after are the characters created specifically for a product such as Kellogg's Frosted Flakes' Tony the Tiger, Alka-Seltzer's Speedy, and Planters' Peanuts' Mr. Peanut. The latter originated in 1916, and was soon depicted in coloring books, made into dolls, and adorned items from spoons to serving dishes. A 1920s papier-mâché Mr. Peanut container can sell for $100–150.

A color lithographed-tin advertising clicker for Peter's Weatherbird Shoes. c. 1930s, 1¾ in (4.5 cm) long.
$20–30

Top Tips

- Fakes are widespread. Genuine articles feature period artwork and are not as bright or clean as reproductions.
- Tin trays can be dated by the lithographer's name—printed on the edge—as company dates are recorded.
- Items with famous slogans, characters, or brands are particularly prized.
- The appeal of vintage advertising is the strength of images and colors; avoid anything that's worn or faded.
- Look for artwork with crossover appeal; higher demand means higher prices.

BUY ▷

Nostalgia is a key driver for the collectibles market. Favorite breakfast cereals are often remembered fondly. Look for memorabilia from popular brands that also have longevity, as this will increase the number of fans, and possibly the values of vintage pieces.

A Captain Crunch vinyl advertising money bank, back stamped "Captain Crunch." Created in 1963 for Quaker Oats, Captain Crunch is still used today. c. 1975, 7 in (17.5 cm) high.
$30–40

KEEP ▷

Certain brands have a cult status all their own and are a separate collecting area altogether. If the character has become iconic, a large variety of objects are currently available, and he is still in the public eye, vintage pieces are likely to increase in value as desirability grows.

An American Mr. Peanut black-and-tan painted plastic advertising bank. This appealing vintage piece shows Mr. Peanut in typical form, with his cane, top hat, and monocle. 1960s, 8 in (21 cm) high.
$50–80

PEZ dispensers were

launched in the US in the Fifties. With an infinite variety of character heads, PEZ have become hot to collect and, since they're still for sale today, collections can grow for less than $2 at a time.

Collecting clubs, newsletters, websites, and even conventions are devoted to the hobby of collecting PEZ candy holders. The earliest PEZ date to 1952, when the product was imported from Europe for American children. Originally conceived as adult breath mints in 1927 by Austrian Edward Haas, the PEZ brand name was created from the first, middle, and last letters of the German word for peppermint (pfefferminz). Early on, the mints were packaged in tins, but by 1948 they were given an "easy, hygienic dispenser." The owners later decided to aim their product at children by adding character heads to the dispensers and filling them with fruit-flavored candy. About 300 different heads have been made over the years, not including variations in color and (from 1987) dispensers with feet bases.

Head shots

Generally, new dispensers don't appeal to serious enthusiasts, although at just $2 they make a great starting point for a novice, and, if the current passion for PEZ continues, may one day be valuable. Items from the Nineties are already changing hands for about $20: a Bugs Bunny from 1993 with removable clothing can be $15–20, while a Daffy Duck of the same year with fixed parts can be $5–10. Looney Tunes characters Speedy Gonzales, Yosemite Sam, Tweety, and Sylvester (all mid-1990s) can be $5–10 each, as can Flintstones characters from around 1992.

Early birds

It is, however, the early dispensers and the rarities that are most prized; extremely rare PEZ have sold for

A Maharajah PEZ dispenser, made in Hong Kong. *c. 1973, 4¼ in (11 cm) high.*
$60–90

over $6,000. A rare bride or groom, which were discontinued in the Seventies, can fetch $1,000 each. These were never sold as a pair, but are often rented out together to be placed on wedding cakes—so intense is the nostalgia for these whimsical plastic figures. Early "regular" PEZ dispensers have a squared shape and notched plain block in place of the character head, and are valued for their age. Older, collectible PEZ run from $30–60 up to $100. Only real rarities command prices of $100–150 or more, even up to $1,000. Two of the most valuable non-characters are the baseball-themed PEZ with a bat, ball, and glove, and the Calculator PEZ with a slide rule. Other early favorites are the One-Eyed Monster and Disney examples (made under license from 1962) such as Captain Hook and Bambi.

Numbers game

Patent numbers on the sides of dispensers help to date a piece to a period, and indicate the earliest

A 1970s Walt Disney Mickey Mouse PEZ dispenser. *c. 1973, 4 in (10 cm) high.*
$8–12

A 1970s Cockatoo PEZ dispenser. *c. 1975, 4 in (10 cm) high.*
$60–80

A Warner Bros. Daffy Duck PEZ dispenser, with separate eye pieces. *c. 1978, 4¼ in (11 cm) high.*
$20–25

date a PEZ could have been made. For instance, a 2.620.061 patent idicates the item was made between 1952–68, when the next patent, 3.410.455, was introduced (1968–69). This was followed by patent 3.432.074. Some models were made for only part of these periods, so patents provide a starting point for dating PEZ.

It is important to be able to date pieces since some designs were made at different times: the 1920s black Batman has a 3.9 patent number, while the less valuable 1990s black Batman carries a 4.9 patent number. The number in the corner (IMC number) corresponds to the country: 6 is Hong Kong/China and 9 refers to the US factory.

The mouse that roared

PEZ is marketed in over 60 countries, and enthusiasts want characters known in one country but not another. Some collectors also aim to own every design of a character. Mickey Mouse, a top seller, has been issued in the US in about 56 versions (counting stem colors), although collectors usually count a variation only if it differs "from the neck up." Values range from $300–400 for a 1960s painted Mickey with a die-cut stem to $2–3 for a 1990s example.

The PEZ company often reissues popular characters. These are not as valuable as originals but are a way to obtain otherwise unavailable characters. Some enthusiasts even create "fantasy" PEZ—for example, sets resembling Elvis Presley or the rock band KISS—and although not authentic, some are desirable among avid collectors.

A **dark green Incredible Hulk PEZ dispenser**, made in Hong Kong. *c. 1978, 4 in (10 cm) high.*

$50–70

Top Tips

- Post-1987 PEZ have feet, although this is an unreliable indication of age, since recent reissues of "regulars"—early designs—have no feet.

- Beware of fakes; because it is relatively easy to swap parts, they are common.

- To be of interest, a dispenser should be in complete and original condition. Moving or removable parts are often lost, so check carefully.

- Incomplete dispensers can have value as collectors sometimes buy for parts.

BUY ▶

PEZ dispensers in the form of well-known characters, or related to popular films or TV series, will have cross-market appeal. This translates into increased demand from collectors that may cause values to rise.

A *Star Wars* **Darth Vader and Stormtrooper PEZ dispensers**. As they are modern and in unopened packaging, these items are likely to appreciate. *c. 1997, 8½ in (21.25 cm) high.*

$2–4 each

KEEP ▶

Dispensers in an unusual color or with additional parts or accessories that were easily lost are often more valuable. Often also denoting an earlier date, they can be rarer and prices should increase as demand begins to outstrip limited supplies.

A **Batman PEZ dispenser, with moving cape**. This is the earliest version of Batman, but beware of reproduction capes that are not as thick as originals. *c. 1967, 4¼ in (10.5 cm) high.*

$120–180

A closer look at... a PEZ dispenser

Often ignored by flea-market hunters, dispensers that are not of the standard form with molded character heads can fetch high values. As with other examples, consider the form and color to ensure you buy the best.

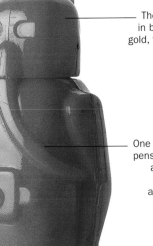

These were made in blue, yellow and gold, the latter being the rarest

One of the first dispensers made, it is also among the most visually appealing of the early examples

This is one of the very few "full body" figured dispensers, and, as such, is highly desirable to collectors

The robot form is typical of the 1950s, when science fiction and outer-space themes and movies were popular

A **red-plastic, robot-shaped Spacetrooper PEZ dispenser**. The backpack is molded "PEZ," helping to identify it. *c. 1955, 3¾ in (9.5 cm) high.*

$350–450

Coca-Cola is one of the world's most recognized brands. Ranging from Hamilton King's advertising calendars in the early 20th century to the Coca-Cola millennium bottle, this collecting area continues to grow.

Originally developed as a pick-me-up drink in 1886 by Dr. John Pemberton of Atlanta, Georgia, Coca-Cola's popularity grew swiftly from the 1900s onward, partly due to its long-standing rivalry with competing brands, such as Pepsi. Coca-Cola is now found in more than 200 different countries, with advertising, promotional material, and packaging designed specifically to reflect the culture of each market.

Coke memorabilia can be separated into either promotional advertising or packaging but, due to the vast amount available, collectors often focus on an object type or area, such as trays or a specific country. Pieces from the 1890s and early 20th century are rare; most objects date from the 1950s onward. Items displaying Coke's varying slogans are popular, and can also help to date the pieces. Since the 1970s, Coca-Cola has produced reproductions of vintage designs. It has also produced designs specifically to look old, so check for signs of wear to identify truly vintage pieces. Cans and promotional material produced for special occasions are particularly collectible: 200 cans were made to mark the presence of Coca-Cola on the ill-fated space shuttle *Challenger* in 1985, and the empty cans can sell for more than $200.

▲ **A lithographed tin sign.** This incorporates a thermometer and its imagery and relatively early date make it sought after. *1930s, 16½ in (42 cm) high.*
$300–400

▶ **A Coca-Cola "push plate,"** which would have been placed on the doors of shops that sold Coca-Cola, to advertise the product as the customer entered. This example is made of enameled metal. *1950s, 12 in (30 cm) high.*
$300–400

PUSH
Refresh Yourself
DRINK
Coca-Cola
REG. U.S. PAT. OFF.

▶ **A Matchbox No. 37 Coca-Cola Karrier Bantam truck.** Like other advertising toys, this crosses collecting fields, appealing to both collectors of the toy manufacturer and the product it advertises. *c. 1960s, 5 in (12 cm) long.*
$80–120

◀ **A color lithographed tin sign.** Cardboard six packs for Coca-Cola bottles, as shown on this sign, were introduced in 1929. Condition is important; if this example had not been faded, the value would have been higher. *1930s, 13 in (33 cm) wide.*
$50–80

◀ **A free sample cup.** An enormous number were made so they remain more common than other pieces. Although this example is more than 50 years old, it is still affordable. *1950s, 2¾ in (7 cm) high.*
$7–10

◄ **A tray** made for the Mexican market. Although trays showing smiling ladies are relatively common, this example features rare artwork. *1950s, 13¼ in (33.5 cm) high.*

$300–400

◄ **A card advertising Coca-Cola.** These command a premium when found in good condition, due to their fragile nature. If Santa had been cut out and assembled, this piece would have been worth a fraction of its value. *1950s, 7¼ in (18.5 cm) high.*

$80–120

▶ **A laminated cardboard sign** made for the German market. This sign's artwork is indicative of the varying styles produced for different countries. *1950s, 13 in (33 cm) high.*

$400–600

..das erfrischt

Collectors' Tips

- Beware of fakes: tin trays, novelties, and mirrors are the most commonly faked items
- Handle as many different objects as you can to learn the feel and appearance of authentic pieces

Drink **Coca-Cola** Delicious and Refreshing

To YOU!

Lupe Velez

▲ **A boxed bottle opener** of the kind that would have been attached to dispensing machines or to a bar. The box is rare, and without it the value would be lower. *1950s–60s, 8 in (20 cm) wide.*

$20–30

▶ **A rare, restored, cardboard advertising standee.** The model is Lupe Velez, a popular film star from the 1920s–40s, who starred in *The Mexican Spitfire* in 1939. Unrestored and mint-condition examples are rarer and worth more. *1930s, 20½ in (52 cm) high.*

$1,000–1,500

Vintage posters capture the

aspirations of past consumers. Their popularity is fueled by nostalgia and, judging by the way their appeal is growing, collectors will soon be pining for the era when they were less expensive.

Notices advertising products, sales, and events have existed for centuries, but they were largely unillustrated. The modern advertising poster was born in the 1860s when the French artist Jules Chéret exploited developments in color lithographic printing, which made the mass-production of attractive designs and eye-catching images possible for the first time. Chéret's fame grew, and his Art Nouveau designs advertising the Moulin Rouge and Folies-Bergère music halls in Paris in the 1890s are now legendary.

All in a brand

Progressive firms soon recognized the power of this new promotional tool to fix a brand image in the minds of consumers. Pioneering designers such as Chéret and Leonetto Cappiello were skilled in using striking artwork to convey a sales message. Cappiello's "L'Apéritif" for Campari (1921) captures the product's appeal—a bittersweet slice of sophistication—by using the image of a clown inside a twist of lemon.

An American store display poster for Konjola ("A Splendid Medicine of Proven Merit"), color lithographed. *1920, 27¾ in (70.5 cm) wide.*
$250–300

Such posters are beyond most people's budget, but there are plenty of others that can be found for $80–300.

Although France led the way, other countries followed. Posters for Coca-Cola first appeared in the 1920s. Early posters for this and other enduring brands are desirable and fetch high prices. A Hires Root Beer advertising poster can be worth as much as $1,600. Wrigley's Gum posters from the 1940s can fetch anything from $400 to $10,000, depending on size, design, and condition. Although posters for many well-known brand names may be expensive since they have a strong following, a great many inexpensive examples of beautifully styled posters from all periods can still be found.

Patriotic pieces

Governments were quick to spot the potential of the poster. During World Wars I and II, posters were used extensively: for example, to recruit soldiers and to encourage women to contribute to the war effort. An Air Service poster from c. 1918 by the artist Louis Fancher can fetch around $1,200, while a YWCA recruitment poster from World War II can sell for $500–600.

Give Us The Faith And Courage Of Our Forefathers, designed by Howard Chandler Christy in 1942 for World War II and reused for the Korean War. *1950, 35¼ in (90 cm) high.*
$1,200–$1,800

The prices of posters featuring patriotic images, such as Uncle Sam or President Kennedy, reflect their iconic status. A "Kennedy For President" election campaign poster from 1960 can fetch up to $12,000–18,000 if in mint condition.

Period details

Vintage advertising posters have both an aesthetic and a nostalgic value. Those with strong, colorful artwork tend to be the most desirable, particularly if they evoke the styles or trends of their period. A 1950s Du Maurier cigarettes poster showing an elegant woman in a foreign seaside location reflects the glamour and sophistication attached to overseas travel at a time when it was just beginning to become popular.

The typography of the poster is important too. It should complement the artwork and reflect the style of the time, such as the swirling lines of Art Nouveau or the angular, linear lettering used during the Art Deco period.

Sizing it up

Posters can vary greatly in size. Some were made for large billboards, but smaller ones were made for retail outlets. Larger posters are generally

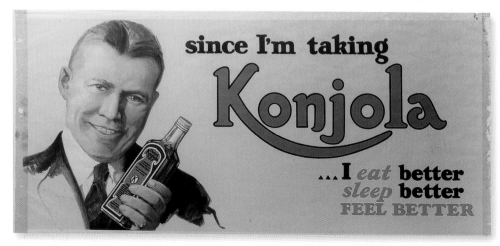

A closer look at... two Art Nouveau posters

The Art Nouveau period was the first Golden Age of poster design. Examples from this era usually fetch high prices, although the overall appearance and style of a poster can be important in determining value, as this comparison shows.

The inconsistent levels of detail (for example, between the intricate statues and the simple figure of the woman) give an uneven effect

The layout is comparatively "flat," with large expanses of plain, muted color and a lack of typically stylish Art Nouveau elements

The design is intricate and well composed, with strong Art Nouveau elements such as the flowing hair and clouds

The name of the brand of ink is boldly displayed in Art Nouveau-style lettering, which fits onto the table— a seamless component of the design

The Girl & the Gods, [a novel] **by Charlotte Mansfield,** designed by John Hassall, printed by David Allen. *c. 1910s, 30 in (76 cm) high.*

$300–500

Encre L. Marquet, designed by Eugène Grasset, published by Galérie de Malherbe, Paris. *1892, 47½ in (120.5 cm) high.*

$1,000–1,500

more valuable, often fetching $1,200–1,500 or more. They usually come in two or more parts. Smaller examples—30 inches (75 cm) or less in height or width—can be found for $80–800. They provide an ideal opportunity to own fine pieces of period artwork that are easy to display.

Lucky finds

The best places to look for vintage posters are estate sales and auction houses. Richer, but usually more expensive, sources include collectors' shows and specialized advertising memorabilia and poster dealers. Prices at general auctions tend to start at $100. A good way to start a collection is to buy group lots of posters, rather than individual items. Those found will probably be rolled up or more often folded. Open them with care to check for damage.

Pick a theme

Collectors often focus on one theme, such as automobile advertising—a potentially expensive niche. One of

the most sought after posters in this genre is "A Votre Santé Le Pneu Michelin Boit L'Obstacle" ("Michelin Tires Wish You Good Health by Swallowing Obstacles"), designed by Marius Rossillon in 1898. It can fetch $15,000–25,000, mainly because it marks the debut of the Michelin Man.

Posters featuring entertainments from years gone by are also sought after. Vintage theater posters can be worth up to $1,000–5,000 or more, such as one from 1930 advertising *The Wolf* at the New York Lyric Theater. Circus and fair posters are also desirable. A 1940s poster publicizing the Barnum and Bailey circus can sell for $500–1,000.

Posters that have local interest are also worth looking out for, as are those with ephemeral appeal—such as posters advertising a product with a limited run, or those publicizing key one-time events. A poster advertising the Greater Texas Pan Am Expo of 1950 can be worth $100–500, while a 1933 Chicago World's Fair poster is valued at around $400–600.

Du Maurier cigarette advertising poster. *1950s, 30 in (76 cm) high.*

$150–250

While some enthusiasts look for brand-name posters, others choose named artists, such as those known for Art Nouveau or Art Deco styles, including Chéret or Alphonse Mucha. These command top prices, often fetching thousands of dollars.

All aboard

Rail posters are a popular collecting area. Chicago Transit is one name highly sought after today. Its posters were designed to promote travel within Chicago and the surrounding areas using the electric rail systems of the Chicago Rapid Transit and the Chicago North Shore and Milwaukee lines. These posters presented beautiful views of the Windy City, showing cultural institutions, landmarks, parks, and monuments. Posters from the mid-1920s showing views such as "Golf By The North Shore," or "Evanston Lighthouse" can fetch $8,000–20,000 or more.

From the 1880s to the 1970s, the Canadian Pacific Railway Company produced more than 2,500 different lithographic and silk-screen poster designs, a thousand of which were created in its own graphic studio.

TRAVEL Canadian Pacific ACROSS CANADA!

A closer look at... a Cassandre travel poster

When collecting posters, always consider the artist. The work of the most renowned can fetch high prices. Most artists worked in a particular style and those that are highly representative of a period will always be popular. Using the pseudonym "Cassandre," Adolphe Mouron is one of the most respected poster artists of the 20th century, with much of his work in the Art Deco style.

The image of the train steaming across Europe is immensely powerful, and strongly suggests speed

The clear shapes, exaggerated perspective, and restrained use of color are typical of Cassandre's work

Nord Express, designed by Cassandre, printed by Hachard & Cie, Paris. It is mounted on Japanese paper; there is a repaired tear at the top margin and slight fading. *1927, 41¼ in (105 cm) high.*
$6,000–9,000

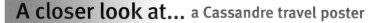

CHEMIN DE FER DU NORD
A.M.CASSANDRE

NORD EXPRESS

SOUTHERN RAILWAY — CHEMINS DE FER BELGES

LONDRES BRUXELLES RIGA
PARIS LIEGE BERLIN VARSOVIE
COMPAGNIE DES WAGONS-LITS

The posters promoted travel on its transcontinental railroad, and were designed to attract settlers to Canada. Posters can typically fetch $1,000–3,000, with Art Deco designs fetching the highest prices. The company also operated luxury hotels, ocean liners, and an airline, and posters advertising these services are also desirable.

The Chief attraction

In the first half of the 20th century, railroad companies made use of the fascination with Native American culture in their posters in order to encourage tourism and consequently the use of the railroads. The Santa Fe Railroad Company was one such business that used a series of posters attractively depicting the places and peoples encountered on the Santa Fe route. The most famous of these was "The

Travel Canadian Pacific Across Canada, designed by Peter Ewart for Canadian Pacific. *c. 1950, 35¾ in (89 cm) high.*
$2,000–3,000

Chief," painted by Hernando Villa, who worked as an illustrator for the Santa Fe Railroad Company for many years. "The Chief" became an emblem for the company, and gave its name to the fast train that ran between Chicago and Los Angeles. Original Santa Fe Railroad posters fetch around $400, with rarer ones fetching more. Vintage posters of Villa's "The Chief," have sold at auction for over $2,000. Look also for work by Louis Treviso, who was instrumental in creating the Santa Fe Railroad poster style.

Iconic images

Transportation companies often employed the talents of high-profile avant-garde artists to design their posters. In the UK, London Transport often commissioned posters by artists such as Edward McKnight Kauffer, Horace Taylor, and Man Ray. Prices for McKnight Kauffer's posters start at about $1,000, although some experts consider them undervalued.

Art Deco images are sought after, and rail posters in this style are no exception. Sascha Maurer created

America Welcomes You: United States Lines

designed by Genders, showing passengers relaxing or playing tennis or shuffleboard on the deck. *1930s, 38½ in (96 cm) high.*

$1,000–1,500

posters for the Pennsylvania Railroad. A 1930s poster of a train designed by Maurer for the New Haven Railroad can fetch up to $6,000–7,000. The work of Leslie Ragan (1897–1972) is particularly desirable. Creating artwork for the New York Central Line Railroad, his posters include landscapes, such as "Moonlight In Duneland," and trains, such as the "Empire State Express" and "Night Train." An original poster of his most famous train design, "The 20th Century Limited," can be worth up to $20,000.

Although many of the works by the leading artists are already in collections or change hands for thousands of dollars, there are plenty of other striking posters to choose from for between $100 and $800. Invest in those that show styles of the period, and those that you find appealing: if you like them, other collectors probably will too. Look for bright, fresh colors and evocative depictions of popular resorts.

Cruising in luxury

The romance associated with foreign travel began in the early 20th century with luxury cruise liners such as the *Mauretania*, the *Olympic*, the ill-fated *Titanic*, and the *Normandie*. Posters that show the ships themselves are popular, especially if they feature

Did You Know?

The most expensive travel poster ever sold at auction in the United States is a British poster depicting the sleeper train from Edinburgh to London known as "The Night Scotsman." Published by the London and North Eastern Railway in 1931, the poster sold for around $50,000. Its stunning, finely colored image of a train steaming through a dreamscape of Moon, stars, and clouds, was designed by the avant-garde designer, animator, and filmmaker Alexander Alexeieff.

period design—again most notably the Art Deco style. Perhaps the most famous example is the 1935 poster for the *Normandie* by Adolphe Mouron (Cassandre). Using his typical bold colors, simple lines, and clean design with large, flat forms, he depicts the mighty ship powering through the sea. Although this poster can fetch $8,000–15,000, its design and stylistic hallmarks are worth bearing in mind when looking at other examples. Less

expensive liner and ship posters can be found by lesser-known artists. For example, a Nelson Steam Navigation Company stylized poster from the 1930s depicting a line-up of ships, in a similar style to Cassandre, can fetch around $900.

Brand names also count. Partly owing to the immense public interest in the *Titanic*, owned by the White Star Line, prices for their posters will generally be high, as will those for

295

Vintage posters

other giants such as United States Lines and Cunard, particularly if the artwork is noteworthy. But such was the popularity of travel by liner that many other companies operated overseas. These smaller lines offer a more accessible option, with prices often ranging between $250 and $800.

Journey's end

Part of the attraction of ocean travel was the exotic destinations. Look for alluring images of foreign climes, with bright and saturated colors. These posters can be found from around $250—for example, a Blue Star Line poster for Mediterranean cruises showing a North African view with a man riding a camel amid Moorish buildings can fetch about $300. Canadian Pacific ocean liner posters feature the liners in exotic locations such as the West Indies, Rio de Janeiro, Hawaii, and China.

Later posters for liners in the 1950s and 60s, when sea travel began to fall out of fashion, are often less valuable than those from the 1920s and 30s

and can fetch $80–400 or more for known brand names, those by notable designers, or those with superb designs in period styles. As the best posters become too expensive for most collectors, these later posters may make a good investment.

Come fly with me

Air travel offered a swifter alternative to journeys by sea. The slogan, "Africa in days instead of weeks," on an Imperial Airways poster of 1937 neatly makes this point. Many of these 1930s posters can fetch $250–900 or more. Until Pan American (Pan Am) and Imperial Airways had airplanes with the range to make the trip across the Atlantic, flying boats provided the glamorous competition for liners.

After World War II, passengers grew to expect the convenience

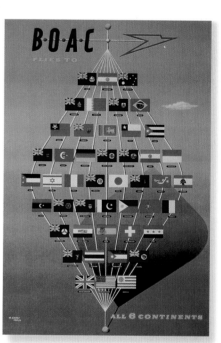

Blue Star Line: Mediterranean Cruises, designed by Maurice Randall and printed by Philip Reid, London; there are small areas missing and folds. *c. 1920s, 40¼ in (102 cm) wide.*

$250–350

Some airline posters to look for:
■ American Airlines ■ Pan American World Airways ■ BOAC ■

American Airlines to New York, in a very modern design typical of the era. It is designed by Weimer Pursell, who is known for his 1933 Chicago World's Fair poster, among others. *c. 1950, 40 in (101.5 cm) high.*

$1,800–2,200

Flying Down To Rio: Pan American, designed by Paul George Lawler. The now-defunct Pan Am is a very recognizable and collectible brand. The Rio theme is also desirable. *c. 1938, 41 in (104 cm) high.*

$1,200–1,800

BOAC Flies to all 6 Continents. BOAC was a popular airline of the 1950s, when airlines expanded their reach. The poster's designer, Abram Games, is rapidly becoming a sought-after name. *1953, 39¾ in (101 cm) high.*

$300–400

of a plane flying from a nearby airport. In the 1950s, foreign vacations by air became cheaper and services expanded. Planes became less luxurious and emphasis was placed on speed. Posters with images of speeding planes are desirable, and many have their stylistic origins in the 1930s, with clean lines, flat areas of bold color, and angular shapes. Those showing a multitude of foreign destinations, all conveniently served by the featured airline, are popular.

Posters for well-known airlines such as Pan Am and Air France have loyal followings and can be worth $800–1,500 or more, with some Pan Am posters fetching up to $7,000–10,000.

Less expensive posters in the style of the period can also be found.

Going supersonic

The Concorde represented the ultimate in luxury travel, and poster prices are probably yet to reach their peak. The withdrawal of the Concorde from service in 2003 may cause values to rise. A Concorde poster from 1977 (the year in which the plane first took paying passengers) can fetch under $100. Since the Concorde was operated by only two airlines, Air France and British Airways, examples are rare compared to posters for the more widespread Boeing 747, for example, and could prove to be a wise investment.

Top Tips

- Store posters flat between sheets of acid-free tissue paper. Never roll them, as this can crease the poster.
- Make sure your hands are clean before touching a poster; keep handling to a minimum.
- Avoid posters that are extensively faded or damaged, especially if a tear extends into the image.
- Frame posters using acid-free museum mounts and hang them away from direct light and heat to protect colors from fading.
- Do not undertake conservation work yourself—this is a job for an expert.
- Learn to spot a reproduction: the image will be made up of pixels (dots) and the paper will often be glossier and thicker than on an original.

297

BUY

Posters with striking graphics and that adhere to period style and design are likely to have lasting appeal and should rise in value.

International Industries Fair Brussels 1939, by an anonymous designer, printed by Créations Brussels. The strong colors, clean lines, and integration of lettering into the artwork are typical of the late 1930s and make this poster collectible; there are a few tears and folds. *1939, 40¼ in (101 cm) wide.*

$120–180

KEEP

Skiing posters are becoming increasingly sought after, combining travel, sports, and fashion. Look for vibrant colors, striking designs, and famous resorts. As skiing becomes a more accessible sport, prices are likely to increase.

Ski New York designed by H. W. The colors and angular design are strong and dynamic. If the destination were more globally famous for skiing, the value could be higher. *c. 1950s, 26 in (56 cm) high.*

$1,000–1,500

BUY

Look for posters that cross collecting areas as the increased number of potential buyers can cause values to rise. Desirability, and as such values, is likely to increase further if the design is modern or is representative of its era.

New York World's Fair: American Airlines" designed by Henry K. Bencathy. This poster will continue to appeal to both airline and World's Fair collectors. *1964, 40 in (101.5 cm) high.*

$500–700

KEEP

Look for recent posters advertising objects by brands that are known for their great design and that have become ubiquitous in everyday life.

"Yum: Think Different," by Apple Computers. The iMac is now a design classic, and Apple's fashionable advertisements are likely to increase in value. *c. 1999, 36 in (91 cm) high.*

$80–120

SELL

Smoking memorabilia is likely to appeal only to a comparatively small group due to its unhealthy, antisocial connotations. Sell to avid collectors when prices peak, since they may not appreciate in the long term.

A Marlboro advertising poster. The Marlboro Man is an icon, but the late date and unappealing design mean this is likely to appeal to hardcore collectors only. *1980s, 81 in (205 cm) high.*

$200–300

SELL

Most posters were stored folded, leaving fold marks and creases. Tears that affect the image are more serious and lower value. Unless extremely rare, these posters are unlikely to rise in price.

Messageries Maritimes, by an anonymous designer. This poster is by an unknown artist and is missing a substantial area at the bottom of the poster, which is irreparable. *c. 1920s, 40¼ in (102 cm) high.*

$40–60

Technology
and Travel

From the first radios to TVs, early calculators
to sophisticated personal organizers, the
romance of luxury cruise liners to the fascinating
possibilities of space travel, no century has
seen so much technological change. Objects
representing each of these advances are
available to own.

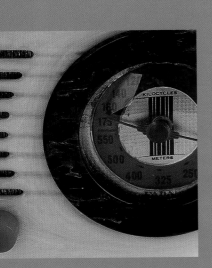

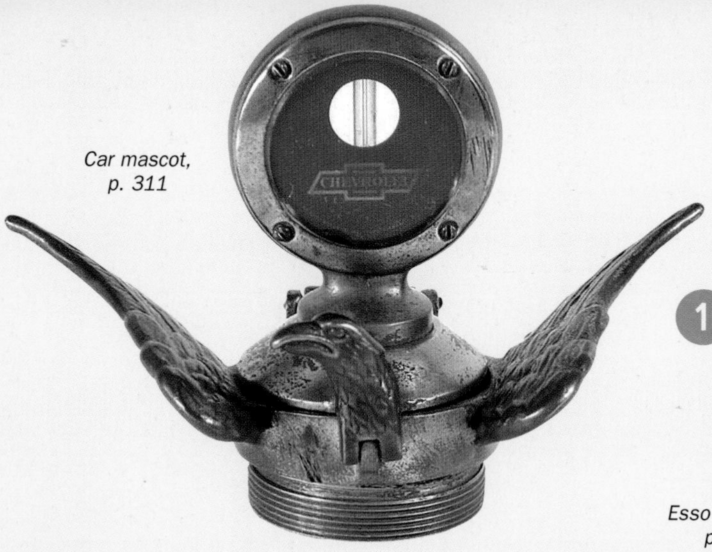

Car mascot,
p. 311

①

Esso Gas sign,
p. 311

The changing face.........

No one would have thought in 1900 that cars would come to dominate our roads, that leisure time would be centered around the TV, or that it would be possible to travel faster than the speed of sound. Objects that reflect technological change can be surprisingly valuable.

One of the most world-changing developments of the 20th century was surely the motor car, although pimping your ride in the 1920s and 30s usually meant nothing more than adding a mascot ① to the bonnet. These attractive adornments are often beautifully modeled and will be eagerly snapped up by today's vintage car enthusiasts. Marketing paraphernalia for gas companies and garages is also very desirable, particularly if it features good graphic design and big brand names.

Home entertainment

The first televisions appeared in the late 1920s. Sets from the 1930s and 40s are rare, so many enthusiasts prefer to look out for sets from the 1960s and 70s. Examples such as the JVC Videosphere TV ② are truly Space Age in design—a far cry from the first wireless sets. Radios from the 1920s to the 1950s are very popular, especially those with colorful Bakelite or shaped cases. Some more modern transistor radios such as those by Sony and Panasonic are also collectible.

Travelers moved on from the glorious steam cruise liners of the past to embrace the supersonic flights of Concorde and beyond.

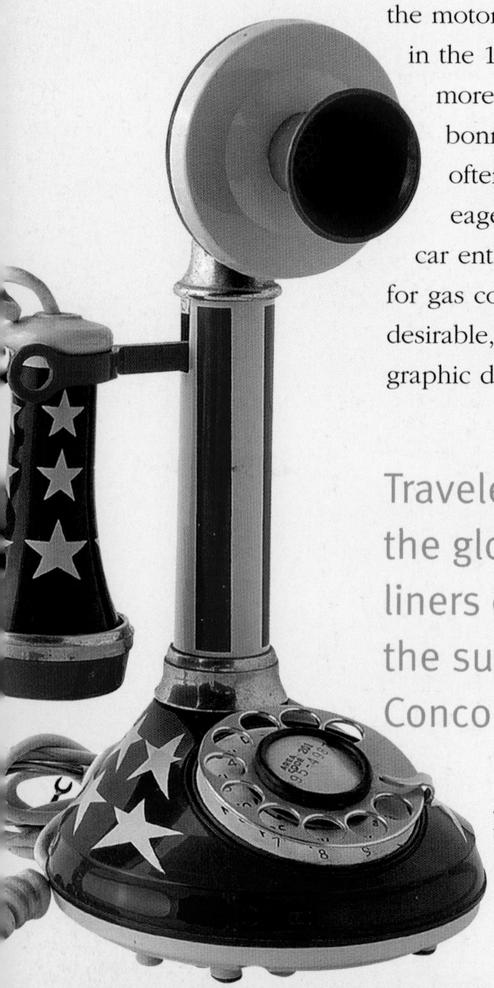

Stars-and-Stripes
telephone, p. 308

④

Commemorative
shuttle patch, p. 314

⑤

JVC Videosphere TV, p. 303

②

③

19th-century camera, p. 305

.of technology

Snap shot

From early plate cameras ③, with their brass-bound wood cases and bellows, to the first Leicas and the Kodak Box Brownie, there are plenty of cameras to look for. High-quality Leicas are especially popular as so many different types were made. The opposite is the case with the Box Brownie—mass production has meant that values are low for vintage examples.

On call

Another area where technology has leaped ahead is communications. Early and novelty telephones ④ are becoming sought after, as are some of the first cellular phones.

Now we are firmly in the Space Age ⑤ it is hard to imagine a time when the most extreme voyages undertaken by man took place on the ocean. Travelers moved on from the glorious steam cruise liners of the past to embrace the supersonic flights of Concorde and, possibly, beyond. Souvenirs from any of these modes of transport are highly desirable today, including *Titanic* memorabilia such as photographs and commemorative toys ⑥.

Titanic teddy bear, p. 313

Titanic picture, p. 312

⑥

Radios and TVs are reminders

of an era when families sat together to enjoy their favorite programs. Their attractive cases and the immense variety available make them highly collectible today—even if not in working order.

The phenomenon of radio began to take hold after 1910. Valve radio receivers were expensive, so many enthusiasts built their own more affordable "crystal sets" to pick up radio waves. A 1923 Marconiphone V2A valve radio receiver can fetch around $800–1,200 or more, but a more common, homemade crystal set often sells for under $70. Finer-made crystal sets, by noted makers such as Ericsson, can cost about $400–600.

Fine tuning

During the 1920s and 30s, radios became simpler to use and more affordable. The "superhet" (Supersonic Heterodyne) was introduced in the mid-1920s, enabling the user to tune the radio by turning a knob.

In the 1930s, Bakelite and Catalin, plastics that were simple to produce and less costly than other materials, were used to make radios. Popular examples include the FADA Bullet or Emerson Tombstone, which can fetch $800–1,200 or more. Some, like the FADA Bullet, had a tendency to overheat, causing scorch marks to the case. Brown and black Bakelite radios, made in large numbers, can be inexpensive—many models cost around $30–150 and often no more than $300–600 for more desirable ones. Brightly colored Catalin radios tend to attract higher prices, especially two-color examples, but check that their cases are not cracked. White Catalin radios often became discolored with age and can look similar in color to butterscotch examples. The case can usually be restored through intensive cleaning, but this should be done by a professional.

Look for radios with the clean lines associated with the Art Deco period, from the 1930s and late 40s. Radios produced in the 1950s in a modern or Art Deco style are popular, and stylish

A Fada Bullet All American model 189 radio in Catalin, with smooth knobs. This color was produced just before the US entered World War II. *1941, 10¼ in (26 cm) wide.*

$3,000–5,000

wooden radios of the period are also desirable. Value is primarily affected by the design of the radio, so look for striking examples.

Exceptional finds

Available in a variety of colors, the 1930s geometrical Air King Skyscraper is particularly sought after and examples can be worth $2,000–4,000 or more, depending on condition. The Sparton Bluebird is also a favorite with collectors. The large floor-standing version with a mirrored finish can be worth over $10,000. Other important makers include Addison, Motorola, Bendix, and General Electric. Radios by these makers can often be found for up to $2,000–4,000 or more.

Some radios to look for:
- Emerson ▪ Crosley ▪ Panasonic ▪ Tomy ▪

An Emerson Tombstone model BT245 butterscotch radio. This famous shape was introduced in 1935 and changed in style over the years, gaining a louvered grille. Earlier, more rounded models and red, blue, and brown colors are rarer and usually more valuable. *1937, 9¾ in (25 cm) high.*

$1,500–2,500

A Crosley model 11-103 U radio, known as "the Bullseye." This radio is much sought after, due to its typical 1950s styling that almost resembles a car's dashboard. It can be found in many different colors, with the color often being sprayed on. *c. 1951, 10½ in (26.5 cm) wide.*

$250–350

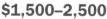

Smart sets

The first domestic, wooden-cased TV sets appeared in 1936. These pre-1940s sets are rare and can command high prices (as much as $7,500 or more). By 1949, about three million sets were in use, both floor-standing and tabletop models. Ten years later, this figure had rocketed to nearly 60 million. RCA, Philco, and Motorola are names to look for—1950s sets by these makers can cost $50–800.

TV sets from the 1960s and 70s can cost from $80–300 for portable models, to $500–1,200 or more for larger, floor-standing types. Look for sets that represent technological advances, such as the first portable TV, or those with strong design elements.

Shape of the future

The JVC Videosphere or "Sputnik" set from the late 1960s, was shaped like a space helmet and could be suspended from the ceiling. Some sets had a radio and alarm clock in the base, too, although these models

are less common. Values range from about $300 to $800.

The floor-standing Keracolor TV from around 1970, shaped like a globe on a tapered circular plinth, is desirable. The starkly modern black, white, or orange versions can sell for around $800–1,000, with the rarer teaklike finish being even more costly.

An orange JVC Videosphere TV. *1970s, 13 in (33 cm) high.*
$400–600

Top Tips

- Consult a specialist before you decide to restore a valve radio.
- Ask an electrician to inspect vintage radios or TVs before plugging them in.
- Look for a radio with its original speaker cloth; make sure that it isn't torn—replacements can be too bright.
- Chips and cracks on Bakelite radios lower value, so run your finger over the surface to feel for imperfections.
- Consider collecting transistor radios— they are inexpensive and compact.

BUY

Sinclair's electrical products were often groundbreaking. Many pieces can still be found for less than $150, but they may appreciate as interest grows and recognition of their importance increases.

A Sinclair TV80 Flat Screen pocket TV. This was an iconic development during the 1980s, but was not successful— today they are sought after in good condition. *c. 1981, 5½ in (14 cm) wide.*
$70–90

KEEP

Transistor radios, introduced in the late 1950s, are growing in popularity. Early Japanese models can be rare. Good condition is vital, especially for later models. The more innovative designs should hold their value or appreciate.

A National Panasonic PanaPet R-70 radio. The Panapet was one of the most popular transistor radios of the 1970s. Without its original box the value would be at least halved. *1970s, box 5½ in (14 cm) wide.*
$70–90

A Panasonic Tootaloop R-72 bangle radio. When closed, this radio could be worn around the wrist. Design classics like this are always popular. *1970s, closed 6 in (15 cm) diam.*
$80–100

A Japanese Tomy Mr. DJ Robot radio. The trend for robot toys in the 1980s was dominated by Tomy. These radios are now highly sought after. *1980s, 7 in (18 cm) high.*
$80–120

Cameras have come a long way since the first unwieldy wet-plate models of the 19th century. From Brownies to SLRs, and from Instamatics to spy cameras, the changing technology can make for a fascinating collection.

The first photograph was taken in 1826 by a Frenchman, Joseph Niépce, and the photographic plate was invented 12 years later by Louis Daguerre. In 1880 George Eastman set up the Eastman Dry Plate Company, later renamed Kodak, and its full developing and printing service first brought photography to a wide market. Kodak produced the Brownie camera between 1900 and 1930, but so many were made that they are not worth much today.

That's not the case with the Leica camera. Produced in Germany since 1925, it was one of the first really practical, compact 35 mm film cameras. Some Leicas are now worth $5,000 or more, so inspect any engraving—it may indicate a rare version. The serial number on the top can be used to date the camera.

Generally, though, many vintage cameras are affordable. A 1930s folding camera can be bought for just $20–30, and late 19th-century mahogany and brass cameras can fetch from $150 to $550, so check out specialty camera shows as well as all the usual places, such as flea markets, auctions, and junk shops.

At present, the market for modern cameras such as digital and disposable models is small, but they may prove to be a worthwhile investment in time.

▲ **A Franke & Heidecke Rolleiflex 2.8f,** in working order. Twin reflex cameras such as this example allowed the photographer to look at the image through one lens, while the second lens took the picture. Classic Rolleiflexes are highly collectible. *1950s, 7 in (17.5 cm) high.*
$200–250

▶ **A brown Bakelite Coronet Midget subminiature camera,** with case. This camera came in five colors including brown, mottled green, and blue. Bright colors fetch higher prices than the black or brown versions. *c. 1936, 3 in (7.5 cm) high.*
$150–200

▶ **A silver Corfield Periflex I SLR camera,** with a case. This camera has a moveable periscope, which allows the user to examine a shot for fine focus before pressing the shutter. *1955, 6½ in (16.5 cm) long.*
$200–250

◀ **An early Zeiss Ikon Contax III camera,** with a Sonnar f2 25mm lens. The Contax was a sophisticated camera and used fine quality Zeiss lenses and optical equipment. *c. 1936, 6¾ in (17.5 cm) long.*
$200–300

◀ **A Leica IIIa, with a Summar f2.50 mm lens and case.** Although one of the more common Leicas, it is in excellent condition—a real plus to collectors. *1939, 6½ in (16.5 cm) long.*
$300–500

◀ **A Bakelite Kodak Baby Box Brownie camera,** with box. A huge number of Brownies were produced for the young and those who wanted to take inexpensive photos. This one is worth more because it has its original box. *c. 1935, 4½ in (11.5 cm) high.*

$15–25

◀ **A Kodak Disc 4000** in near mint condition and boxed. Disc-format cameras came to the fore in the mid-1980s, spurred on by this, Kodak's first model. It was not successful and the format did not last, making it scarce and desirable today. Potentially, a good investment. *c. 1985, 4 in (10 cm) wide.*

$20–30

Collectors' Tips

- Look for accessories, such as extra lenses, carrying cases and light meters, as they add value to a camera
- Examine a Leica for military markings for the British or German armies or air forces, as these are desirable
- Seek out cameras with their original packaging and instruction booklets

▶ **A brown No. 1A Pocket Kodak.** Many of these "pocket folding" cameras were made by Kodak so their value is generally low. The brown version is less common than the black, which is worth about $15–30. *c. 1930, 8½ in (21.5 cm) long.*

$80–120

▼ **A Russian spy camera,** disguised as a pack of John Player cigarettes. It has a metal body with a box and a Russian-language information sheet. Hidden or disguised cameras—called detective cameras—can command high prices. *1970s, 4¾ in (12 cm) high.*

$200–250

▶ **A 19th-century, mahogany, Lancaster International, quarter-plate camera,** with rare blue bellows and a rotary shutter. Folding dry-plate cameras often come in leather cases and with many different accessories. *c. 1880.*

$500–700

Fountain pens

and other writing instruments from the 20th century are always stylish and can be an expression of their owner's personality. Leading makers include Parker, Waterman, and Montblanc.

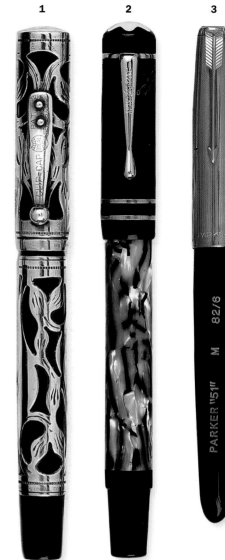

The mass-market fountain pen is a late 19th-century invention, introduced when two Americans, Lewis Edson Waterman and George S. Parker, separately patented reliable ink-feed systems. Within a few years the industry was booming and many different ink-filling mechanisms were introduced, as well as a variety of barrel designs, colors, and sizes.

A splash of color

Although early pens do attract interest, most had barrels made from hard black rubber, so later, more attractive, colored pens are often preferred. In the 1920s, Waterman released a range of "ripple" pens in bold colors. Today, they may fetch $50–500, depending on size, color, and condition.

Parker's Duofold, introduced in the early 1920s, was a landmark design, initially offered in a red-orange color, earning it the nickname "Big Red."

From the mid-1920s, the Duofold was sold in Senior and Junior sizes in blue, jade green, and the prized Mandarin yellow. While a standard Big Red may be worth around $200–300 today, a Duofold Senior in yellow may cost as much as $1,500–2,000.

Produced between 1941 and 1972, the Parker 51, with its futuristic rocket shape and hooded nib, was snapped up by the public—total sales ran to more than 20 million units over 30 years. It came in various colors and cap finishes. Used 51s, with a standard cap, can be bought for around $20–50, while an early American 51, or one in a rare color or with an unusual cap, can sell for up to $1,200. Prices rise for pens in mint condition and those with a precious metal overlay.

Jotting down the names

Makers to look out for include Conklin, Conway Stewart, De la Rue

---

A closer look at... a Dunhill Namiki maki-e Balance

During the 1930s, the British company Alfred Dunhill and Japan's Namiki Mfg. Co. Ltd. collaborated on a series of pens, employing various artists to decorate them. The designs, painted in lacquer, are works of art. Those by Kohkyo are highly sought after and valuable.

A Dunhill Namiki maki-e Balance by Kohkyo, decorated with an exotic bird on a black *roiro-nuri* lacquer background, with a Pilot 14K nib. The pen is signed with a red-lacquered signature on the reverse side (below the lever) in Japanese by the artist, using his art name, Kohkyo. *1930s, 5 in (13 cm) long.*
$3,000–5,000

The lacquerwork is unworn and the pen is in mint condition

The whole composition is skillfully contrived to draw the eye to the flying bird

The maki-e lacquerwork decoration is painstakingly applied by hand over many weeks, using different colored lacquers, shell fragments, and gold dust

---

1 **A Waterman Filigree,** hard, black-rubber eyedropper filler, overlaid with sterling-silver three leaf decorated filigree with a fine Waterman No. 4 nib; in good condition with some wear. *1915–20, 5½ in (14 cm) long.*
$180–220

2 **A limited-edition Montblanc Oscar Wilde 13300/20000,** with a pearl and black-resin barrel, a vermeil clip, and a medium 18K (18 karat gold) Montblanc nib, complete with box and papers; in mint condition. *1994, 5½ in (14 cm) long.*
$600–800

3 **A Parker 51 Custom,** black plastic aerometric filler, with a medium nib; in mint condition with original shop chalk rubbing over the name stamp on the barrel. *1950s, 5¼ in (13.5 cm) long.*
$120–180

4   5   6

(Onoto), Esterbrook, Mabie Todd/Swan, Moore, Sheaffer, and Wahl-Eversharp. Look for bright or unusual colors, such as Parker's Vacumatic (produced 1930s–40s). This was made from laminated celluloids in different colors, such as silver, green, and burgundy striped, with blue being the rarest. Examples in good condition fetch around $250–350 or more.

Size matters

Size is a key factor in the value of a pen. Small "lady" pens slipped easily into a handbag and often had rings on their caps to take a ribbon, but larger pens, with their impressive size and showy nibs, are more sought after. The name of a former owner engraved on the pen can lower its value, unless the owner was famous, but a presentation box usually makes a piece more desirable. A pen with its original nib is worth more than one with a replacement. The nib's value alone is not high, unless it is large or rare.

Writing in style

Dip pens, pencil holders, and propelling pencils from the 19th century and earlier are all desirable. Usually found in solid or plated gold or silver, propelling pencils may also have inlaid or enameled decoration.

Look for makers such as W. S. Hicks or Sampson Mordan, who produced a range of novelty-shaped pencils in the late 19th century. Values vary, but expect to pay from $30 and up. Good examples of Mordan's novelty pencils can fetch around $500 or more.

Good penmanship

Collecting modern limited editions by major makers is a new phenomenon. Many are high-priced luxury goods and collectors keep them unopened in the hope of increasing their value. The German-made Montblanc Lorenzo de Medici retailed at about $1,200 in 1992; now rare and desirable, it can fetch up to $3,000. But later editions, such as the Oscar Wilde, still sell for less than their original price.

The size of the edition, the maker, and the look of the pen are important. Small editions of elegant pens by the best makers are likely to appreciate.

4 A Conway Stewart Dinkie 540, gray jazz, multicolored, celluloid, ring-top lever filler, with a broad Conway Stewart nib; boxed, in fine condition. *1920s, 3¼ in (8 cm) long.*
$120–180

5 A Mabie Todd & Co. 44 ETN, jade green celluloid lever filler, with a No. 4 Eternal nib; in very good condition with a little discoloration. *c. 1928, 5½ in (14 cm) long.*
$120–180

6 A Montblanc 144 Meisterstück, black celluloid piston filler with a two-color 4810 nib; in good condition. *1949–60, 5½ in (14 cm) long.*
$100–150

Top Tips

- Do not dismiss pens with perished ink sacs, as these can easily be restored to working order by a professional.
- Avoid plastic pens with cracks, burn marks, or scratches, and metal-overlaid pens with dents or splits—all will devalue a pen.
- Make sure that a pen and pencil sold as a set really do match.

BUY

High-quality rolled-gold pens were luxury items during the 1920s. Any mint-condition, plated, or precious-metal pen with fine details such as engravings will make an excellent investment, as it should at least hold its value and is likely to appreciate.

A Waterman 0552 Pansy Panel, black, hard-rubber lever filler, with a yellow rolled-gold overlay, decorated with panels of pansy flowers, with a fine Waterman Ideal No.2 nib, in near-mint condition. *1924–27, 5½ in (14 cm) long.*
$200–300

BUY

Examples of Conway Stewart pens from the 1930s–50s are of good quality, are easy to repair, and are still usable. Decoration includes gold veining, herringbone, and the popular Cracked Ice pattern. They are beginning to be appreciated by collectors internationally, so prices should rise.

A Conway Stewart 58 green and black, line-marbled celluloid lever filler, with a fine Conway Stewart Duro nib, in very good condition. *c. 1949, 5½ in (14 cm) long.*
$60–90

SELL

The Big Red Parker Duofold from the 1920s and 30s is a classic vintage pen, but prices have remained static for years. Sell now and speculate elsewhere, as values are unlikely to rise substantially in the near future.

A Parker Lucky Curve Duofold Senior in red Permanite with a button filler, with a Parker Duofold nib, box, and leaflet; in excellent condition. *c. 1927, 5½ in (14 cm) long.*
$200–400

Telephones have undergone numerous design changes in the past 120 years, from wall-mounted to touch-tone versions. Not only are they fascinating, but most period models can be updated for use today.

The evolution of the telephone has been so rapid that we look back at models we used just a decade or so ago with nostalgia. Telephone technology was developed in the US in the late 19th century, and the American Bell Company began producing wall-mounted phones in the 1880s. These early models are rare, which is reflected in their prices. A complete wooden phone with brass fixtures from around 1900 can be worth up to $400–800 or more, while scarcer wall phones can command $3,000 or more if the cases are decoratively carved and in good condition.

Off the wall

Smaller, tabletop telephones were introduced toward the end of the 19th century. Designed by the Swedish Ericsson company, the skeleton phone had exposed workings and was made from 1895 to 1931. It also featured gilt transfers and a black base. Early examples in excellent condition can command from $800 to $1,200 or more. The first enclosed table phone was made in the early 1900s. Prices range from $75–150 for an Ericsson model from 1910, to $500 or more for rarer, decorative continental examples. Another design, the candlestick phone, was popular from about 1900 to the 1920s. Expect to pay about $150–250

A reproduction candlestick telephone, with Stars-and-Stripes decoration, produced in advance of the Bicentenial. *c. 1974, 11¼ in (28.5 cm) high.*
$150–200

A Northern Telecom plastic Graham Bell Plane telephone, in two-tone orange, also available in white and camouflage. *Late 1970s, 9 in (23 cm) wide.*
$80–120

for a phone in good condition, but if it has Bakelite fittings, or is made in mahogany and brass, it can be worth $200–400 or more.

Modern Bakelite

By the early 1930s, telephones with bells in the base rather than in a separate unit were available. Coupled with the use of Bakelite in their construction, they introduced a style of "modern" phone that remained in production for more than 50 years.

Seminal models include the Western Electric Model 302 telephone, in service from 1939 until 1954, and now worth between $150–450. Earlier versions had Bakelite receivers and a brown cloth cord, while thermoplastic was used in later examples. The company's earlier 202 model can be worth $300–500. Bakelite phones from

A closer look at... a 1970s telephone

The range of telephones available expanded greatly after World War II, but some were more innovative—and are therefore more collectible—than others. When building a collection or investing in a single piece for use, consider features such as the form, color, and positioning of the elements.

Orange is a rare color—gray, green, and blue are more common

A 1970s orange plastic Trimphone. This is now considered by many to be a design classic. *1970s, 8 in (20 cm) long.*
$120–150

This was the first telephone with a handset cradled over the keypad or dial, rather than at right-angles to it

This phone has buttons—earlier models had a dial

The design is modern and minimal, with simple, clean lines and forms, and no surface decoration

A red plastic Hot Lips telephone.
1980s, 8½ in (21.5 cm) wide.
$50–80

the 1930s generally sell for $150–250, but classic models can often fetch more. Other notable Bakelite phones from the decade include the Kellogg 925 Ashtray phone, usually worth $200–300, and the Stromberg Carlson 1234, often worth over $150.

Pushing the right buttons

Western Electric replaced the 302 with the 500, which was made in a wide variety of appealing colors. Versions of this phone were produced by a number of companies in large quantities; these can now be picked up for $30 upward. The Princess telephone, with a light-up dial, was introduced in 1962, and was followed by a push-button version. These can cost $50–100, while pink and rare black examples may cost $75–150.

Design classics

Based on a 1940s design, Ericsson's Ericofon (also known as "the Cobra") was one of the first successful single-piece phones. Launched for domestic use in 1956, the phone's dial was housed in the base of the unit. Prices range from about $75–150 for a standard phone to around $150–250 for a special reprise edition to mark the company's centenary in 1976. Slim rectangular phones, such as the Automatic Electric Slimline and

the Western Electric Trimline, became popular in the 1970s and early 80s, and can now be worth $15–60. An original box will increase the value. Other designer phones of note include the Grillo, a 1960s Italian model with a body that flips open, that can be worth around $200–300; Dawn, a pancake-shaped late rotary-dial phone, worth about $30–60; and the 1970s Genie, worth about the same.

Engaging novelties

Many novelty phones were made in the US. Examples include the R2-D2 *Star Wars* phone, valued at about $50–80; a teddy bear phone worth about $60–90; and phones from the 1970s and 80s featuring Snoopy, Mickey Mouse, and Kermit the Frog, which can fetch $75–300. Specialized phones, including models for cruise liners or hotels, and early speaker-phones, are also popular.

Top Tips

- Be wary of fake Bakelite phones. Look for uneven moldings and models painted over in rarer colors.
- Feel the numbers on the handset of a Bakelite phone: those on a copy are not as raised as ones on an original.
- Be careful of the many reproduction phones currently on the market, particularly copies of early telephones.

BUY

Recent telephones by important and influential designers are likely to have lasting appeal and interest and should at least hold their current values.

A blue plastic Ola T1000GD telephone by Thomson. This telephone was designed by the noted French designer Philippe Starck. Starck is also famous for his interiors, furniture, and bath and kitchenwares. *c. 1996, 11 in (28 cm) long.*
$70–100

KEEP

Key designs from the second half of the 20th century are most likely to hold their value, since they represent period design trends and can usually be converted for modern use. Visit design museums so you can identify those that are considered important, as these are more likely to hold, or even increase, their value.

A cream plastic Ericsson Ericofon telephone, with dialing buttons on the underside of the base. The New York Museum of Modern Art described this telephone—nicknamed "the Cobra"—as one of the best industrial designs of the 20th century. *1970s, 8¼ in (21 cm) high.*
$100–150

Automobilia is an exciting collecting field that offers a range of objects in striking designs and colors. From sleek Deco-style car mascots to old-time road signs, these records of the excitement and glamour of early motoring drive collectors wild.

A Ferrari large enamel commemorative key ring.
c. 1985, 1¾ in (4.5 cm) high.
$60–90

The Golden Age of driving conjures up a time when the American landscape was very different, and collectors hoard anything and everything that evokes the romanticism of the road. The earliest memorabilia from pre-1900 to 1910 (Duryea was the first licensed manufacturer of gas vehicles, c. 1893) is very rare and expensive. Items predating 1970 are considered collectible, while

anything pre-World War II (when driving was a joy, not a stress) has extra cachet. Automobilia from the Fifties and Sixties has become valuable to a whole new generation of nostalgic collectors.

Crossover collectibles

Sought-after objects vary from roadmaps and advertising signs to accessories and spare parts. Motometers—engine temperature gauges mounted on radiator caps—were made in the 1920s and are particularly desirable if by the US firm Boyce. For those with less cash, there are more affordable trinkets such as key rings ($10–100), lithographed oil cans ($25–150), and even car brochures ($15–20, although early examples can fetch up to $150). As automobilia is a diverse collecting area that crosses other fields, objects frequently hold their value. Many gas companies lent their logos to toy tankers and these can be valuable as vintage toys as well.

Giveaway goodies

As driving became popular, gas stations sprang up all over the country, and

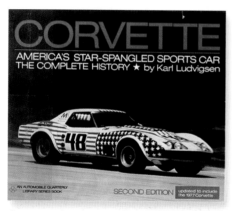

Corvette: America's Star-Spangled Sports Car, by Karl Ludvigsen, (*Automobile Quarterly*), second-edition hardback with transparent dust jacket. *1977, 12 in (30.5 cm) wide.*
$100–150

maps showing happy explorers were given out from the 1930s to 50s. If early, in great condition, and with bold graphics they can reach $300–400, although most are $30–100. Gas stations also gave away ashtrays, toys, calendars, matchbooks, or lemonade sets either emblazoned with logos or promoting products. A Mobil Oil cast-bronze ashtray (c. 1930) in Art Deco style with the distinctive Pegasus can fetch $350–400. Early gas pumps can be $1,000–4,000 or more, depending on condition.

Signs of the times

Automotive sign collecting is very popular, with the best examples costing hundreds of dollars. Signs come in many metals as well as glass, porcelain-enamel, wood, paper, and plastic. Other metal advertising objects include door push-plates, trays, and restroom signs. Collectors may specialize in a particular make—Oldsmobile, Buick, or Chevrolet—and many favor anything depicting cars

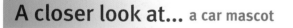

A closer look at... a car mascot

Car mascots are a very popular collecting area within automobilia, with high prices paid for those by renowned names. Character mascots are among the most varied and sought after. Although many visually represent speed and are often fine examples of Art Deco style, some also have hidden meanings and appeal, and interesting makers, making them very desirable.

A Billiken character car mascot, probably designed by L. V. Aronson who in 1910 patented the first cigarette lighter; the company later became Ronson Corp. *1909–10, 5 in (12.5 cm) high.*
$250–350

The Billiken is a good-luck symbol popularized by illustrator Florence Pretz of Kansas City, Missouri, from around 1908

This was made by Aronson Art Metal Works of Newark, New Jersey. It retains its original nickel-plated finish and is display-mounted on a radiator cap

The Billiken reached the peak of popularity in 1910–11 and is now closely connected to Saint Louis University sports teams

that are no longer made, such as Studebaker, Franklin, and Desoto. Items may be emblazoned with an oil company name or that of a tire supplier such as Goodyear or Michelin. Anything featuring the latter's Bibendum tire man is prized. A Bakelite ashtray can fetch $80–120 and a poster $3,000–5,000, or $12,000 for a rare, early image. Before the Highway Beautification Act of 1965 banned them, colorful signs brightened journeys, with the series of rhyming ones for Burma Shave being one of the most famous, long-lasting ad campaigns. Such signs are valuable since they were made of wood, which degrades easily when outside. Poster collectors snap up examples that illustrate the glamour of speed, and countless of these were made for ordinary domestic cars, although they rarely fetch the prices of, say, the Paris to Monaco race posters.

Stylish mascots

The crème de la crème of automobilia, however, is the elegant car mascot hood ornaments that ooze Art Deco style. The most coveted were conceived by the French maker René Lalique, who created 29 models from 1925 to 1932. Sought-after designs in top condition go for $35,000 or more, and most are over $5,000. Similar, more affordable, glass mascots were made by Red-Ashay in Britain, Sabino in Paris, and the Corning Glass Co. of New York. Other mascots were made in zinc, pewter, or aluminum. Most were British- or French-made; American producers include Doehler, Avard Fairbanks, and L. V. Aronson. Metal mascots cost $250–2,000, with the best ones fetching thousands.

An Esso Gas enameled-metal, two-sided advertising sign, with various chips to the edges. *c. 1920s, 30 in (76 cm) wide.*

$700–800

A Ford Motor Company Ford Mustang printed-tin advertising tray. *c. 1979, 13¼ in (33.5 cm) wide.*

$20–30

Top Tips

- Choose images of speed, classic cars, or the romance or nostalgia of driving.
- Look for radiator caps with mascots.
- Fake Lalique mascots are badly molded and finished and made of frosted glass.
- Go for undented gas cans and tin signs.

BUY

Motometers can be found in great variety, both in terms of shape and manufacturer. Boyce is one of the largest and most prolific makers. Produced during the Golden Age of motoring, at the same time as car mascots, motometers currently offer great value for money, although that may be set to change for the best examples.

A Boyce motometer temperature gauge, for Chevrolet. The wings add appeal, as does the Chevrolet branding and intact glass measuring tube. *c. 1920s, 6 in (15 cm) wide.*

$200–300

KEEP

Look for advertising materials such company brochures, particularly vintage examples from before the Seventies. These show how the car was marketed at the time and give details of specifications, which are of interest to collectors. Publicity materials for big names in excellent condition and with stylish period graphics are likely to rise in value in the future.

A "Cadillac for 1960" brochure. Showing the interior of a period Cadillac, the cover is stylish. The inside gives details about cars available at this time. *1960, 10 in (25.5 cm) wide.*

$15–20

Ocean liner memorabilia

reminds us of a more glamorous era when the only way to travel the world was by ship, usually in some style. Nostalgia and the chance to own a tiny slice of liner luxury spurs on the modern collector.

At the beginning of the 20th century, the giant luxury liners of shipping companies such as Cunard and White Star plied the transatlantic passenger trade. Notable ships included the *Olympic*, the *Britannic*, and the *Mauretania*, but the market for ocean- and cruise-liner collectibles is dominated by the ill-fated *Titanic*.

The tip of the iceberg

Titanic artifacts and memorabilia have increased in price since the 1997 movie. Items produced after the sinking of the *Titanic* in 1912 are generally of less value. Top prices of $5,000–15,000 or more are paid for rare memorabilia owned or used by survivors or rescuers, such as watches, spoons, menus, and plates.

Postcards and photographs are more reasonably priced, as so many were made. They can fetch around $40–150 each, often less. Handwritten postcards that mention the *Titanic* are valuable, depending on the message, date, and sender. Cards sent from the ship when it docked at Cherbourg, France, or Queenstown, Ireland, attract premium prices. A small framed photograph of the liner can fetch around $100–250.

Art Deco opulence

In the 1920s and 30s, ships such as the French *Normandie*, launched in 1932, set new standards of luxury, speed, and safety. Her first-class dining room was an extraordinarily lavish Art Deco creation of bronze, hammered glass, and Lalique fixtures. She was in New York when World War II broke out in Europe and was commandeered. Unfortunately, an accidental fire caused her to capsize, and she was scrapped in 1942.

Sister ships

Memorabilia from the *Queen Mary* is commonly found, and usually fetches less than $150. Launched in 1934, she is now a tourist attraction in California. Commemorative ceramics, which were often sold in the onboard souvenir shop, can cost $80–120, while a souvenir tin can fetch around $70–100.

A *Titanic* in memoriam picture, in a shell frame. *1912, 6 in (15 cm) diam.*

$180–220

Did You Know?

Memorabilia from passengers who were rescued from the Titanic are in the top league and have shot up in value. In 1999 an original painted cast-iron plaque from one of the lifeboats fetched more than $30,000 at auction, and in 2002 a rare first-class dinner menu dated April 10, 1912 (the day she sailed), made a world record price of $40,500.

A *Queen Mary* souvenir cup and saucer, made by Aynsley to commemorate her maiden voyage, May 1936. *1936, saucer 5½ in (14 cm) diam.*

$150–250

Cunard's *Queen Elizabeth* entered passenger service in 1946. Like her sister ship, she had luxurious Art Deco-inspired interiors. Memorabilia related to her tends to be less expensive than *Queen Mary* souvenirs. A menu from her last voyage can cost less than $30 and a 1964 course book, enabling passengers to follow her route, can fetch around $50–80.

The growth in air travel brought to an end the era of the great liners. The *Queen Mary* was withdrawn from service in 1967 and the *Queen Elizabeth* the following year.

Ship stock and souvenirs

In general, collectors focus on the best-known liners and shipping companies—Cunard, the White Star Line, Union Castle, P&O, Canadian Pacific, and Compagnie Générale Transatlantique. Memorabilia associated with lesser-known foreign lines, and those not operating the transatlantic route, are usually less costly. Objects showing the ship or boldly displaying the company logo are the most prized.

Items taken from the liners themselves can fetch high prices, depending on the type of object, with pieces related to first-class travel being the most desirable. Official souvenirs are popular too, but are often confused with ship stock—the former usually show an image of the ship while the latter have a more discreet logo or wording. Many official souvenirs (as opposed to items that were taken from the ship and kept

Essential ocean liner memorabilia

PLAYING CARDS
Card games were a favorite pastime on cruises. Cards showing the liner or the company's logo, such as these, are popular. 1930s, 3½ in (9 cm) high.
$30–40

TIMETABLES Sailing schedules give details of different cruises and often display attractive period artwork—as on this example. 1938, 10 in (25 cm) high.
$20–30

FIXTURES AND FITTINGS Original fixtures and fittings, such as this *Queen Mary* brass oil lamp, are rare and often valuable. 1936, 25¼ in (64 cm) high.
$600–700

BROCHURES Earlier brochures from 1910–1940, like this Hamburg-Amerika Line souvenir, are usually more valuable than later examples. c. 1937, 11¾ in (32 cm) high.
$50–80

SOUVENIRS Giftware from onboard shops is sought after, especially if well made or from a famous ship, like the *Normandie*, as with this ashtray. c. 1935, 5 in (13 cm) diam.
$80–120

MENUS Standard menus are easy to find, but first-class or special-occasion examples, such as this *QEII* Coronation gala dinner menu, are more desirable. 1953, 11 in (28 cm) high.
$20–30

as mementos) were bought and saved, so prices are usually lower than for pieces from the ship itself. Items from the ocean liners' Golden Ages (1900–10 and the 1930s) usually fetch the highest prices, while a brochure for the P&O *Canberra* from 1965 may fetch less than $15. Brochures often feature period artwork and show how companies attempted to draw passengers in an age when faster modes of travel were preferred.

In addition to the more obvious mementos—menus, deck plans, and brochures—often kept by passengers as keepsakes, look for items such as packaging, luggage tags, and magazines or newspapers. Prices remain low (usually under $15–50), but these items exist in finite numbers and form the backbone of many collections. They may yet rise in value.

A P&O Orient Line paper bag, with an image of the *Chusan* on one side and the *Arcadia* on the other. c. 1960s, 16 in (40 cm) high.
$10–15

Top Tips

- Hunt for postcards, particularly in Art Deco style, and sepia photographs from original negatives.
- Favor items from before World War II—prewar travel had the glamour factor.
- Look for objects in good condition, since these are more likely to rise in value.

BUY

Items from notable ships from the Golden Age have huge appeal. Paper items are often damaged, so any in good condition are a worthwhile investment.

A *Normandie* deck plan. The stunning artwork makes this deck plan both attractive and useful as a historical record. c. 1936, 13 in (33 cm) high.
$120–180

KEEP

The centenary of the Titanic tragedy is in 2012, and renewed interest may cause prices to rise. Keep more recent collectibles from small limited editions, by good quality makers, in mint condition.

A Merrythought limited-edition reproduction of a teddy bear saved from the *Titanic*, from an edition of 5,000. 1992, 6 in (15 cm) high.
$180–220

Space memorabilia is one

of the most exciting collecting fields—and surprisingly accessible. There's everything from mission patches and space toys for a few dollars to rare spacecraft components costing thousands.

A NASA Apollo program animation cel, created by NASA artists during the Apollo era for use by the networks during televised coverage of the Apollo space flights. *1960s, 8 in (20 cm).*
$180–220

The sheer scale, historical importance, and inherent danger of space exploration is awe-inspiring, which is why space artifacts so fascinate collectors. A premium is placed on items flown in missions and on anything that has been to the lunar surface, with a toothbrush taken to the Moon by Buzz Aldrin fetching over $16,000 at auction! Spacesuit components like an upper gas connector ($500–750) or the life-support system straps clipped to the backpacks of each spacesuit are also popular, although perhaps not as visually recognizable or quirky.

Along for the ride

Heat-resistant tiles that were made for a craft, but never used, can fetch $150–250. A tiny piece of *Columbia's* shuttle door removed for maintenance before disaster struck, or a flag patch carried aboard *Apollo 11* can be as much as $15,000–20,000. These are, of course, rare, as are flown objects carried by astronauts in their PPKs (personal preference kits) or in the mission's OFK (official flight kit). Sought-after items include flags, mission patches, maps, small cue cards, or excess hardware—all small, compact, light-weight items. Big ticket items include a backup Moon glove (worth over $5,000) and a US flag flown on *Apollo 11* (over $25,000).

Space race

Mass-produced commemoratives such as toys or money banks are an inexpensive way to start a collection. Space collecting also crosses many collecting fields. For example, cookie jars were made to celebrate major space events—a 1970 McCoy jar of *Apollo 13* with the American flag can be worth $800–900, while a 1968 Apollo 8 cast-iron bank shaped as the Moon with a rocket flying around it costs about $150.

A very popular space collectible is mission patches, available for as little as $5–10. Designed by the crews they celebrate, the patches made for flying astronauts contain silver and gold threads and are worth the most, up to $1,000–4,000, primarily because of their rarity. Postage stamps commemorating Moon landings and missions are also sought after. A good starting point is "first day" or "event" covers: these are envelopes bearing canceled stamps, mailed on the day the stamp was issued or from the location of a space exploration event the day it occurred. Covers can can be bought for $1–10.

Look for:

■ Flags ■ Autographs ■ Photographs ■ Patches ■

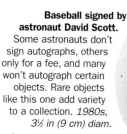

Baseball signed by astronaut David Scott.
Some astronauts don't sign autographs, others only for a fee, and many won't autograph certain objects. Rare objects like this one add variety to a collection. *1980s, 3½ in (9 cm) diam.*
$1,000–1,500

Flag from the International Space Station, August 2001; stamped on board. Type and size of flag affect value, as does the mission. Flown flags are preferred, especially with signatures or stamps. *2001, 6 in (15 cm) wide.*
$500–700

STS 51L commemorative shuttle patch.
Patches were made for everyone from security agents to astronauts and are a great way to start a collection. Some patches, like this one, are rare. *1986, 4 in (10 cm) wide.*
$150–250

Signed portrait of Sally Ride, the first American woman in space. Look for notable personalities—they are likely to have a long-term following. Informal scenes of astronauts are rarer than official portraits. *1983. 10 in (25.5cm) high.*
$50–90

We come in peace

The crème de la crème of commemoratives, however, is the gold and silver medallions made for astronauts by The Robbins Company. This practice began with Apollo 7 and continues today. Very rarely do the gold ones—made for the crew—come on the market, whereas the silver ones—purchased by any astronaut irrespective of whether he flies—are more likely to be sold. A gold Robbins medallion is $800–1,000 or more, while a silver one can be $200–300.

Signed autographs, most often on crew photographs, since many astronauts are reluctant to sign other objects, are sought after. Signatures of the pioneers of space exploration (e.g., the early American astronauts of Apollo, Mercury, and Gemini) attract top prices, as do autographs from those who died in accidents, such as the Russian cosmonauts Patsayev and Dobrovolsky, or are reluctant to sign anything at all, as with Toyohiro Akiyama. Since there are have been almost 400 space travelers, affordable autographs can be found, although as demand rises and the obvious names become increasingly unavailable prices will go up. An Apollo 11 moonwalk photo showing Buzz Aldrin by a US flag, signed "We come in peace for all mankind" can fetch around $400. The broad appeal of the famous name and iconic image is obvious, compared to a signed Jim McDivitt press portrait at $60–80. Neil Armstrong's autograph is not rare, but as he was the first man on the Moon, it will always be sought after and valuable.

A NASA publicity photograph signed by Buzz Aldrin and Neil Armstrong, with trimmed edges. *c. 1969, 3½ in (9 cm) high.*

$500–700

315 | Space memorabilia

KEEP

Those in the know say that supplies of space memorabilia are beginning to dry up, while interest continues to grow. The advice is buy now, before items related directly to astronauts or important missions or programs become unavailable. Look for unique pieces or those produced in small quantities.

An Apollo 1 gold-plated Robbins medallion. Gold medallions were only available to astronauts. The Apollo program would not have been as successful as it was had it not been for the lessons learned in the tragedy of Apollo 1. *c. 1967, 1½ in (3 cm) long.*

$1,000–1,500

■ Parts ■ Memorabilia ■

Apollo 11 gold foil from the first landing. Flown items are very rare and desirable. Parts of life-support systems are sought after, heat-resistant tiles less so. Mission is also crucial. *1969, ¾ in (1.5 cm) wide.*

$250–350

Cast iron bank from Apollo 8. Commemorative items are often affordable. Mission, design, and period affect value, with 1960s items, like this one, regular favorites. *c. 1968, 7 in (18 cm) high.*

$100–150

SELL

Items made in quantity are unlikely to rise in value, especially if they commemorated a landmark event, as many people will have kept them. Sell to a collector building a comprehensive collection and invest in rarer and more desirable pieces.

Life **magazine from July 16, 1966.** This issue contains six pages of images of the first color pictures taken of the lunar surface. Since it is not in mint condition, its value is reduced slightly. *1966, 14 in (35.5 cm) high.*

$30–40

Modern Design

Our homes often accumulate an eclectic mix of the styles from the past 70 years. From the sleekness of Art Deco to the flamboyant optimism of 1950s kitsch, and the vibrant looks of the 1960s to the clean lines of Scandinavian design, we all remember something from every era of our lives.

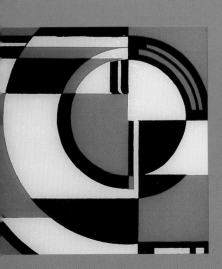

1930s teapot, p. 321

1

The 1930s were the years when plastic came into its own, whether Bakelite, celluloid, or Catalin.

Stylish designs in a......

Modern design, which took off in the 1930s, is increasing in desirability as people look to the past for inspiration. While some are content with modern copies of old favorites, others demand the real thing. And, thanks to mass production, they are still able to buy it.

The stylized lines of Art Deco can be found on household items as simple as a 1930s teapot ① or a clock. The style's bright colors are also in evidence in contemporary posters for trains and cruise liners. The 1930s were the years when plastic came into its own, whether Bakelite ②, celluloid, or Catalin. Clocks, radios, napkin rings, and picnic sets made from any form of early plastic are an inexpensive way to achieve the Art Deco look, but prices are rising.

Brave new world

After the austerity of World War II, the public embraced the colorful, New Look pieces of the late 1940s and 50s. As new types of materials were developed, the rationing of other materials ended and a new optimism took hold. Fifties designs to look for include glass by Blenko, furniture by Charles and Ray Eames, and Fiesta's colorful

5

1950s chair, p. 324

6

Plaster TV lamp, p. 327

Bakelite mantel clock, p. 322

2

3

*1950s pin-up girl
glass, p. 325*

4

*1950s side
table, p. 325*

.modern world

tablewares, which retained their pre-war popularity. These featured bold monochrome or brightly colored designs and innovative stylized motifs. Calendars, drinking glasses, and ashtrays featured pin-up girls ③ and furniture ④ was often rounded ⑤, with tubular-metal legs.

Pop is everything

From the kitsch of the 1950s ⑥, the 1960s took the Modern look even further with flower power and psychedelia. UFO-shaped heaters, lava lamps, and swirling patterns all show the 1960s look at its most extreme. Pop artists such as Peter Max ⑦ took their cue from Andy Warhol and incorporated popular culture into art and design, with colorful results. During the 1970s some designers continued to develop the funky look of the previous 20 years, while others went back to basics. The former attitude is encapsulated by the Smiley design ⑧ that appeared everywhere at the time. Pin-up girls continued to decorate men's accessories —thanks in part to the runaway success of *Playboy* magazine. The order of the day was love, and this word was emblazoned on everything from drinking glasses ⑨ to rugs.

7

Peter Max tin tray, p. 330

8

Smiley sneakers, p. 331

9

Love drinking glass, p. 331

The 1930s are epitomized by Art Deco, a distinctive style based on clean lines, geometric shapes, and architectural influences. As many objects in this style suit a modern home and are often inexpensive, they remain popular today.

A ceramic pitcher, with the handle modeled as a stylized saxophone player. *1930s, 9½ in (24 cm) high.*
$250–300

Art Deco, also referred to as Moderne, takes its name from the 1925 Paris exhibition of modern decorative arts—the *Exposition Internationale des Arts Décoratifs et Industriels Modernes*—where this distinctive style first gained widespread exposure. The flowing lines of Art Nouveau and the sober tones of a wartime world gave way to the strikingly modern objects exhibited by American, French, and Swiss designers.

An instant success

The exhibition featured items in many new materials, such as plastics and laminates, made with new industrial processes. Objects were brightly colored and decorated with geometric lines and angular shapes. The look was hugely popular and mass-production techniques enabled many people to buy these glamorous and fashionable objects at affordable prices for their own homes.

The shape of things

Early Art Deco items are often rounded, and feature Art Nouveau-inspired decoration, such as flowers, deer, and pearls. Later Deco objects frequently favor modern rectilinear or geometric forms with stylized motifs, including sunbursts, spirals, and chevrons. Popular objects decorated with this look include vases, lamps, and clocks. Items can be found from around $50–80 or more, depending on the style and maker, with items by leading names, such as Clarice Cliff or Roseville Futura, or that exhibit key designs, often fetching upward of $200–1,200.

Worldly wise

Designs of the period were influenced by changes in the world at large. Jazz, athletics, and travel were in vogue and had an impact on many 1930s objects. Bronze and spelter (a zinc-based metal) figures were made in large numbers. Unmarked painted plaster or spelter pieces can be found for up to $150–500, while signed ivory or bronze figures will cost around $600–15,000 or more.

Decorative objects of the period sometimes reflected the bold, abstract patterns of African art, Egyptian and Oriental styles, and Cubism.

▼ **The interior of a house** used as a movie set for MGM in the Jazz Age comedy *Our Modern Maidens*. Typical of the look of the period are the sweeping curves of the armchair and the clean lines of the stylish fireplace with its elegant marble slip, hearth, and firedogs. *c. 1929.*

▶ **A walnut-veneered display cabinet,** in a circular shape, raised on a paneled base, with twin glazed doors enclosing two glass shelves. *1930s, 73½ in (187 cm) high.*
$600–800

A closer look at... an Art Deco tray

Geometric patterns are typical of the Art Deco style. Look at the form, design, and materials to identify the best examples. Objects that are quintessentially 1930s should maintain their price and are likely to rise in value.

An Art Deco glass tray. Trays such as this would have been used to serve cocktails in fashionable bars or homes of the 1930s. Barware from this period is eminently collectible—and useable. *1930s, 18 in (45.5 cm) wide.*

$350–450

The typical geometric fragments cleverly map out part of a speeding car—a typical 1930s theme

Strong, vibrant colors, especially black, white, and red, are typically Art Deco

The pattern also alludes to early 20th-century Cubist paintings, such as those by Picasso, that influenced the Art Deco style

---

The glamour of early Hollywood led to a rise in luxury materials such as shagreen (a mottled, often green, shark skin), mirrored objects, and cocktail and smoking accessories. American designers began to streamline objects, with lines becoming cleaner and more curved. Chrome and Bakelite were used to mass-produce items of style, such as radios and lamps.

The best—and the rest, for less

Ceramics by Russel Wright and Paul Schreckengost, opalescent glass by René Lalique, and furniture by Donald Deskey and Paul Frankl are all collectible. Prices can be high (often $3,000–15,000 or more) but smaller items, or less popular designs, tend to be more affordable. The best designs were often copied—a 1930s Lalique bowl with a geometric design may cost $900–1,500 or more, but a similar bowl by Etling may fetch $400–500.

Items do not need to be by major names to be valuable, but they should be representative of the style of the period and in excellent condition. Bronze figures are expensive, so look for attractive spelter figures, such as elegant ladies with outstretched arms—but beware of fakes or poor quality.

Stylish living

Art Deco furniture from lesser-known designers can be bought for similar prices to new furniture. A dressing table with a column-shaped chest of drawers, large mirror, and curving top can be found for around $400–600. Look for circular display cabinets on rectangular bases, since these are typical of the period—they can cost upward of $500–900. Deco-styled leather armchairs may command around $2,000 or more for a pair, but many wood-framed examples can usually be found for about $500–800 or less.

Top Tips

- Visit architectural salvage merchants if you are looking for Art Deco fixtures.

- Beware of fake or reproduction spelter and bronze Art Deco figures—if pieces have resin or plastic parts, or the metal detailing is poor, they are unlikely to be original.

- Look for chrome items, such as picture frames, that have no pitting. If you really like a piece, though, you may have to accept a *little* pitting.

BUY

Many utilitarian but comparatively inexpensive pieces displaying key features of Art Deco style can be found. Those that can still be used and that are in excellent condition should at least retain their values, if not rise.

A copper teapot, with Bakelite handle and knob. The undecorated surface and the angular form of the body, spout, and knob make this typically Art Deco. *1930s, 6 in (15 cm) high.*

$60–90

KEEP

Art Deco furniture is popular, especially small, practical pieces that fit into the increasingly compact homes of today. Those that display or incorporate typical 1930s traits, such as light-colored wood, clean lines and designs, chrome, and mirrors, are more likely to rise in value.

A walnut occasional table, with mirrored top. The excellent condition of this table makes it desirable and likely to increase in value. *c. 1930s, 23 in (58.5 cm) diam.*

$400–600

Plastics and Bakelite

epitomize the energy of modern design of the
1920s and 30s. Their bright colors, exciting styling, and
new, affordable materials caught people's imaginations.
Now their appeal has been discovered anew.

Bakelite, the first synthetic plastic, was
developed in 1907 by a Belgian, Dr. Leo
Baekeland. In its heyday in the 1920s and
30s, it was known as the "material of 1,000
uses." Bakelite and its imitations ushered
in a new age of colorful and stylish, yet
inexpensive, household goods.

Bakelite can be identified by the strong
carbolic smell it gives off when it is rubbed.
It was made in mottled and plain browns,
black, green, red, and blue. Other early
plastics that are also avidly collected
include Lucite, which is usually either
clear or translucent, and cast phenolic
resins such as Catalin, which are often
brightly colored.

Colors other than browns and
black make any plastic object more
desirable. Styling is equally important.
Pieces that reflect the Art Deco style
of the 1930s—typified by stepped
forms, streamlining, and clean lines—
are especially collectible.

Plastics from the 1950s onward tend
to be less desirable and valuable, as
styling is not as strong and quality
generally poorer than plastics from
around 1910 to the 30s. Later plastics
are also usually lighter and less robust.

Classic radios can sell for many hundreds
of dollars or more, so most collectors
concentrate on other themes.

▲ **Two polythene duck-shaped
clothes brushes in their
holders.** These quirky animal
brushes with their holders are
easily found and still usable.
1950s, 11¼ in (28.5 cm) high.

**gray duck $15–25
blue duck $20–30**

▶ **Three novelty,
animal-shaped, cast-
phenolic napkin rings**
in different colors.
Napkin rings mounted on
tiny wheels are more
valuable than these
plain ones.
*1930s, squirrel
2¾ in (7 cm) high.*

**$15–40
each**

▲ **A French Bakelite mantel
clock by Blangy.** The distinctive
Art Deco styling of this clock,
with its stepped form and
clean lines, makes the piece
desirable. *1930s, 5¼ in
(13 cm) high.*

$150–250

◀ **A blue, urea-formaldehyde
lemon squeezer.** Plastics were
used for a huge array of kitchen
items in the 1930s, and many
are still inexpensive today. Look
for bright colors (especially the
comparatively rare blue) and
good condition. *1930s,
5¼ in (13.5 cm) diam.*

$30–50

◄ A pair of Lucite pineapple buttons. Lucite was particularly popular in the 1950s, and it was made in a variety of colors. *1950s 1½ in, (4 cm) diam.*

$6–9 each

◄ A Carvacraft double pen holder by Dickinson Products. In a move away from the typical dark colors of early Bakelite, these streamlined items were made in three bright colors—amber, yellow, and green. The green is rare and more valuable. *c. 1948, 6½ in (16.5 cm) wide.*

$100–150

► A Bakelite toast rack. The design incorporates the strong, angular lines of Art Deco. The brown and red mottling is typical of Bakelite. *1930s, 5½ in (14 cm) wide.*

$20–30

► A Catalin magnifying glass with a folding handle. As well as being brightly colored, this piece is also molded and carved, which makes it more desirable. *1930s, 4¼ in (11 cm) long.*

$40–60

▼ A Bandalasta ware plate, cup, and saucer. Bandalasta ware was a urea-formaldehyde, often marked with the name "Beatl" or "Beetleware." It was used extensively for 1930s picnic sets. *1930s, saucer 5 in (13 cm) diam.*

$30–50

Collectors' Tips

- Avoid chipped or cracked objects, unless rare—damage devalues a piece
- For cohesion, focus your collection on items from a specific room or area such as the kitchen or a dressing table
- Look in particular for large objects made of Bakelite, as these are rare and therefore valuable

◄ A Bakelite ashtray with folding cigarette rests (shown closed and open). This design was made in several color combinations for Dunlop. *c. 1930, 4¾ in (12 cm) diam.*

$150–250

◄ A urea-formaldehyde egg cup. Egg cups were produced in many styles and colors and can form a varied collection. The most desirable examples are those with good period styling and attractive colors, such as this mottled red and yellow. *1940s, 1¾ in (4.5 cm) diam.*

$5–8

The 1950s was a time for people to make a fresh start. Postwar optimism and hope were reflected by an enthusiasm for new products, materials, and designs—from sofa beds to kidney-shaped tables and tulip chairs.

At the start of the 1950s, manufacturing resources were channeled away from the war effort, and austerity gave way to affluence. More technological innovations appeared in the home, along with materials such as plastic, fiberglass, and nylon. Objects were designed in abstract shapes and patterns, breaking away from the utilitarian ideals of wartime. Today, there is a renewed interest in objects from this era.

Practical living

Modern houses called for more compact furniture, and the decade saw the popularization of carts, ironing boards, and sofa beds. Practical stacking furniture made its first appearance, as did flat-packed furniture. Tiered stands for plants were popular and can fetch around $80–150.

Kitchen tables were made from easy-to-clean Formica. Look out for dinette sets—a matching kitchen table and four chairs. Plain versions, or those with flecked designs in the laminated surfaces, cost about $100–250. Those with abstract patterns can fetch about $200–300 or more.

Rectangular coffee tables printed with plain designs can sell for $30–50, but those with abstract patterns or stars can fetch around $150–200. Kidney-shaped tables are usually worth less than $100, but the more popular artist's palette-shaped and three-tiered tables may cost

A cream Bakelite Goblin Teasmade, combining an alarm clock and tea maker. *1950s, 10½ in (26.5 cm) wide.*

$120–180

from around $80 up to $250–300. In 1945, there were around 7,000 TV sets in the US; by 1953, two-thirds of American homes had at least one TV. Manufacturers spotted a market and created TV lamps and chairs. Ceramics makers, such as Midwinter, Beswick, and Gladding McBean, launched compartmentalized TV-dinner plates.

Designer furniture

Many designers used materials such as bent plywood and molded plastic or fiberglass combined with metal tubular frames to create strong, simple designs.

Some 1950s chairs to look for:
- RAR - Cone - Tulip - Ant -

An RAR rocking chair, designed by Charles and Ray Eames and produced by The Herman Miller Furniture Company. The RAR chair—Rocking Armchair Rod—was designed in 1950 with a fiberglass shell on a wire and wood frame. This chair was produced around 1980—original 1950s examples can fetch twice this price. *c. 1980, 35½ in (90 cm) high.*

$600–900

A swiveling Cone chair, designed by Verner Panton. Panton moved away from preconceived ideas of how a chair should be shaped in developing the Cone. The frame was made from wire with an upholstered seat and back pad. *1950s–70s, 23¼ in (59 cm) wide.*

$400–500

Two ceramic cat vases made in West Germany. *1950s, 4 in (10 cm) high.*

$30–50 each

Look for pieces by Charles and Ray Eames, Arne Jacobsen, and Eero Saarinen. Values can range from less than $150 for a stacking chair, up to $2,500–3,000 or more for one of their larger or more classic designs.

From atoms to abstraction

Atoms, molecules, and boomerangs dominated surface design, and abstract patterns appeared on everything from drapes to plates. Parisian-style street scenes, palettes, poodles, and Siamese cat designs were also fashionable. Patterns on textiles became brighter, bolder, and more abstract. Designs by Lucienne Day and Alexander Girard are popular.

The homemaker's terrain

Electrical gadgets aimed at helping with domestic chores, such as the Goblin Teasmade, can cost around $150–500. Collectors value them for their period styling rather than as functional pieces.

◀ **A family clusters around a TV** in the 1950s.

Top Tips

- Look for the key motifs of the period—playing cards, glamour girls, and atomic abstract designs—in bright colors or strong pastels.

- Choose eccentric shapes—kidney, palette, and asymmetrical, curving forms—and materials such as bent plywood, fiberglass, and plastics.

- Angled spindle legs, ball feet, and finials are typical of the period.

- Check for wear in any drinking glasses bearing painted transfers. Do not scrub a transfer—it may wear off.

- Look for original upholstery fabric, as this adds value to a chair.

BUY

When buying furniture look for pieces that exhibit the typical themes, materials, and shapes of the period, as these are more likely to at least hold their value in the long term. Space-saving objects were popular in the 1950s.

An artist's palette-shaped side table by Dennis & Robin Portslade. The legs can be clipped flat to the top to resemble a palette with brushes, then the table can be hung on a wall. *1950s, 19¾ in (50 cm) high.*

$100–150

BUY

Typical 1950s motifs include gambling and glamorous girls. Even small objects from the period are desirable, as values have risen, but only choose pieces in excellent condition.

One of a pair of Tulip chairs, designed by Eero Saarinen, comprising one armchair and one side chair (not shown). By attaching the molded white fiberglass chair to an enameled metal base, Saarinen removed "troublesome" legs in this iconic design. The red woven slip seats are original. *c. 1956, 32 in (81 cm) high.*

$250–300 each

An Ant chair, designed by Arne Jacobsen and manufactured by Fritz Hansen; this is design 3105, comprising a one-piece plywood back and seat on tubular supports. Released in a series from 1951, each with slightly different back shapes, these successful stacking chairs are still in production today. *1950s, 32 in (81 cm) high.*

$100–150

A pin-up girl glass, with a double-sided transfer of a dancing girl. Unusually for a utilitarian piece, this is in top condition—the transfer is an attractive and desirable feature. *1950s, 4¼ in (11 cm) high.*

$60–90

Lamps from the 1930s to the 60s, often idiosyncratic, were beacons of contemporary style. As they fell out of favor, they were consigned to garages and attics. Now they are being hunted out again, since they are in great demand once more.

The styles that enthralled a public eager for the latest fashions in past decades are casting a bright light in today's homes, where retro fashions are back in vogue.

Lamps of the 1930s often have the sharp angular lines, architectural styling, and chrome features typical of the Art Deco period. In the 1940s, lamp designs emulated the streamlining of speeding cars and trains.

After wartime austerity, designs became stunningly innovative in the 1950s and 60s. Brass and painted plaster were used a great deal, often in exotic or kitsch forms. Look for typical 1950s examples featuring glamour girls, playing-card motifs, and polka dots. The Italian Castiglioni brothers dominated the designer end of the market.

Psychedelic colors—orange, purple, and lime green—were the hallmarks of the 1960s. Lamps of the period still look fresh today and are rising in value. Those by admired designers such as Verner Panton can fetch up to $300–1,200 or more, but less expensive look-alikes often fetch under $150. Look for shapes inspired by outer space, such as rocket-shaped lava lamps, and disk-shaped UFOs.

▲ **A dancer lamp.** The body is of plaster and the fabric skirt forms the shade. Such fine condition is rare in figural lamps, as painted plaster is fragile. *1950s, 37 in (94 cm) high.*
$1,000–1,500

▶ **A cast-bronze and pot-metal lamp,** with two Scottie dogs and a frog. This lamp would interest Scottie-dog enthusiasts. The value would be greater if the lamp had its original shade. *1930s, 14½ in (37 cm) high.*
$200–300

▶ **A floor lamp.** The ledge doubles as a table. The ball feet, angled legs, and plastic rocket-shaped shade are pure 1950s. *1950s, 39 in (99 cm) high.*
$80–120

◀ **A pair of chrome face Art Deco table lamps,** by the Revere Company, possibly designed by Doris Marks Dreyfuss. An unmistakably Art Deco design. *1930s, 10 in (25.5 cm) high.*
$400–600

◀ **A brown Bakelite French Jumo table lamp.** The streamlined form of this folding table lamp makes it a design classic. Look for the rarer versions in white Bakelite. *c. 1945, 19½ in (50 cm) high.*
$1,200–1,800

◀ **A pair of speckled, black-and-gold plaster table lamps,** typical of Modernist design. The original shades add to the value. *1950s, 24 in (61 cm) high.*

$300–400

◀ **A Bakelite-and-chrome airplane lamp,** with clock; by Sessions. The propellers on this example are Lucite replacements; they were originally chrome. *c. 1948, 20½ in (52 cm) wide.*

$500–600

▶ **A Flower Pot table lamp,** designed by Verner Panton. The bright orange color and mushroom shape of the shade show the vigor and playfulness of 1960s design. *c. 1968, 13½ in (34 cm) high.*

$400–600

Collectors' Tips

- Look for lamps with the original shade
- Before using a lamp, have it checked by an electrician to ensure that the wiring is safe
- Buy pairs of lamps when you can—they are worth more than two single items

▶ **A pair of Art Deco table lamps,** with chromed gazelles and black vitriolite glass bases. The stepped bases, figures, and frosted glass shades mimicking the work of René Lalique are quintessential Art Deco. *1930s, 8¾ in, (22 cm) high.*

$400–600

▶ **A Cosmo Designs chrome table lamp,** with a four-piece revolving shade. The shape and color of the shade embody 1960s psychedelia. *1960s, 13 in (33 cm) high.*

$40–60

◀ **A painted-plaster backlit TV lamp.** In the 1950s, these lamps were set on the TV to even the contrast between screen and room. *1950s, 17¾ in (45 cm) wide.*

$120–180

◀ **A pair of plaster fairy lamps** with their original shades. The complex shapes and kitsch figures make these lamps sought after. *1950s, 33¾ in (86 cm) high.*

$700–1,000

The 1960s brought a mix of colorful, modern, space-age, and anti-traditional styles with a dash of nostalgia. The current trend for retro styles has renewed interest in the fun and optimism of 60s design.

Modern Design |

The 1960s was the decade that brought psychedelia, free love, and flower power. Objects with the distinctive look of the period—from designer chairs to everyday homeware such as teakettles and pen holders—are eagerly sought after. The current interest in revisiting styles from past decades and the popularity of an eclectic look in interior design have led many people to choose 1960s-style pieces for their homes.

Colorful collage

In the Sixties, homes of the fashion-conscious became brighter and more open-plan. Plastic, upholstered foam, loud—even clashing—colors, and the exoticism of foreign lands such as

India and Morocco typified the 1960s look. Ovenware that stylishly matched the tableware in form and decoration was extremely popular, and stainless-steel items also found their way onto fashionable dining tables.

The 1950s had moved away from traditional tastes and historical influences, but the Sixties promiscuously ransacked the past, adopting styles from the late 19th and early 20th centuries, and updating them with a splash of vibrant color. An excellent example is the revival of Art Nouveau's sinuous, whiplash lines and stylized flower motifs—transformed by bold, bright psychedelic colors such as purple, orange, acid green, and yellow.

A *Pussycats* vinyl lunch box and thermos, by Aladdin Incorporated, the thermos with a paper label. *c. 1966, 12 in (30.5 cm) wide.*
$100–150

Look to the stars

Not all 1960s design looked backward—much looked forward too. The mysteries of outer space fascinated the public, from the UFO and sci-fi films of the 1950s up to 1969 when Neil Armstrong set foot on the Moon. Androgynous clothes designed in futuristic materials such as plastic by cutting-edge designers such as André Courrèges, or miniskirts and high boots were the look to acquire. In the home, furniture designed to resemble space pods, such as the Garden Egg

A Paul Cadovius 291–00 chair, made by Cado. The fabric seat can be detached from the white fiberglass shell. *c. 1969, 30 in (76 cm) high.*
$60–90

▼ **The Futuro House** was a portable home made entirely of glass-filled polyester resin by Oy Polykem AB, Helsinki, Finland. Shaped like a UFO and featuring futuristic furnishings, it reflected the general interest in outer space in the 1960s. Only 20 were made before the early 1970s oil crisis rendered the design uneconomical. *c. 1969.*

chair, typifies this style and can be found from around $500 upward.

Top tables

Tables also followed the decade's general trends, with many smaller examples being produced in brightly colored plastic and larger items made in a combination of wood and metal tubing. The smaller pieces are often desirable, as they fit in modern homes. Depending on the designer, size, and condition, values range from about $150 to more than $1,500–3,000.

Sitting pretty

Geometric shapes, including spheres, circles, and symmetrical curves, were popular. Plastic and upholstered foam overtook the use of laminated woods and could be easily formed into futuristic shapes. Foam furniture by the Danish designer Verner Panton or the Frenchmen Olivier Mourgue and Pierre Paulin can command about $900–2,000 or more, although plastic examples can be less expensive.

A closer look at... a Reuter Produkts Garden Egg chair

Consider the material, shape, and color, as well as the design, of 1960s chairs. Ideally all these factors should be in keeping with the trends and styles of the decade.

A Reuter Produkts Garden Egg chair, with a hinged lid enclosing a blue upholstered seat. It was designed by the German Peter Ghyczy in 1968 and has been in production ever since. *c. 1968, 32¼ in (82 cm) long.*

$700–1,000

The hinged cover has a seal to prevent water from damaging the fabric seat

The clean-lined Space-Age pod shape reflects interest in outer space in the Sixties

The casing is made from fiberglass, allowing it to be used both indoors and out, and its molded-plastic look is typical of the 1960s

Molded plastic stacking chairs by Joe Columbo and Panton's curving one-piece stacking chair, first mass-produced in 1967, can cost up to $150–1,000 or more.

Other Space-Age forms include Eero Aarnio's Ball chair, introduced in 1966 and featured in the cult 1960s TV show *The Prisoner* and the movie *The Italian Job* (1969). The chair was shaped like a giant sphere with a cutout section that allowed access to the upholstered interior, and stood on a swiveling base. Its film and TV links make this chair desirable and valuable, fetching around $3,000 or more.

Inflatable chairs were also popular in the 1960s—they were part of the Pop Art movement championed by Andy Warhol, which highlighted the growing trend toward ephemeral objects that were thrown away once they went out of fashion. New materials such as plastic made the disposable society possible, and much was produced in bright, primary colors.

A metal UFO-shaped floor heater by ITHO. *1960s, 13¾ in (35 cm) diam.*

$80–100

A Flower Power printed tin document storage box. *1960s, 10¼ in (26 cm) high.*

$30–50

Did You Know?

The most notable name in lava lamps still producing today is Mathmos. The company took its current name from the gloopy substance that sucked away the life force and lived under the inhabitants of the futuristic city of Sogo, in the cult 1960s sci-fi movie Barbarella.

Lighting the way

One of the most innovative objects of the 1960s was the lava lamp, designed by Edward Craven Walker and launched in 1963. It was shaped like a clear plastic rocket, and filled with a brilliantly colored, illuminated "lava" of oil and wax that rose and fell in liquid. The lamp came in different sizes and was widely imitated. New lamps cost around $80, but vintage pieces from the 1960s and 70s may sell for $100–250 or more, depending on shape, size, and condition.

Lighting also became more exciting. The variety was enormous, from plastic chandeliers to table lamps, floor lamps, up-lighters, and spotlights. Many were made in plastic or metal and had a Space-Age look. The

A closer look at... a pair of Piero Fornasetti pen holders

The Italian designer Piero Fornasetti was largely ignored by the Modern design movement in the 1950s and 60s, although he was popular with the public. His ceramics and furniture with opulent and intricate surface decoration are uncharacteristic of the period. His more individual pieces have the most appeal, and show consistent or rising values.

A pair of ceramic pen holders, designed by Piero Fornasetti. Fornasetti's unique designs have undergone a revival in popularity since the 1980s, and continue to be sought after today. *c. 1960s, each 2¾ in (7 cm) high.*

$60–90 each

Black and white are key colors

A bold, "flat" gold background is characteristic of his designs

Typical motifs include medallions, buildings, and architectural features

The Sun is another typical motif

spherical Moon lamp shade by Verner Panton is an excellent example. Made up of layers of curving strips of colored aluminum, it can be moved to reveal more or less of the bulb and so adjust the brightness. Examples can be found for about $150–500. Other

shades that copied this idea, which were made of cut plastic strips that were assembled at home, can fetch about $30–100.

Follow the pattern

Fabrics followed either the flowing lines of Art Nouveau or the startling optical illusions of Op Art, best seen in the work of British artist Bridget Riley. As a result, many fabrics had bold, geometrical, or abstract patterns in a palette that included oranges, browns, and creams, as well as the brighter colors associated with the decade. Value is determined by the size of the piece of fabric as well as by the designer and pattern. Pieces large enough to make a standard-sized pair of drapes usually cost around $150–300. Smaller pieces—suitable mainly for cushion covers—will generally cost less than $30–50.

The distinctive and influential designs of one of the best-known pop culture artists of the 1960s, Peter Max, are also very desirable. His vibrant psychedelic art, which drew inspiration

A Peter Max Happy tin tray. *1960s–70s, 13 in (32.5 cm) diam.*

$40–60

from comic books, can be found on an array of objects from book covers to dishes. Posters and original artworks can fetch sums of over $1,000, but even mass-produced items, such as tin trays, can be worth $40–60. Everyday objects from the 1960s were also brightly colored, with clean Space-Age lines. Small ceramic items such as creamers, plates, and jam jars, decorated with bold multicolored flowers can be found for $30 or less.

Play power

Objects that capture the era are desirable, especially items that evoke a sense of nostalgia, such as children's toys. Slinky, the toy spring that "walked" down stairs, was immensely popular, and boxed examples from the 1950s and early 60s can be worth $20 or more depending on condition. Vinyl trolls are also desirable and can be worth $40–60 or more, particularly examples by Thomas Dam.

Geometric glass

Scandinavian design continued to have a major impact on ceramics, and also on glassware. Geometric forms and textured surfaces became the most notable styles: brightly colored vases can be found for around $40–150 or less. The Blenko company helped popularize modern glass in the US—bold and vibrant pieces from the 1960s can be worth $30–150. Also look for glass by Viking or Pilgrim, which looks like, but can cost less than, Blenko glass.

A Slinky, by James Industries Inc., with original box and instructions. *1960s, box 3¼ in (8 cm) wide.*

$20–30

A screenprinted LOVE drinking glass, in excellent condition. *1960s, 5¾ in (14.5 cm) high.*

$15–20

BUY

The 1960s saw many innovations in design and use of materials. These often became icons of the decade—and of modern design—and their popularity is likely to last.

An inflatable PVC Blow chair, made by Zanotta. PVC can discolor, so this still-clear example is desirable. *c. 1967, 33½ in (85 cm) wide.*

$80–100

KEEP

Bright colors, simple lines, and use of materials such as laminate and plastic are typical of the 1960s. Pieces that reflect the character of the decade are worth keeping.

A Pop Art style desk, with laminate frame and plastic drawers. Elements such as the futuristic handles are typical of the period. *1960s, 47¼ in (120 cm) wide.*

$300–400

Top Tips

- Choose original pieces where possible. Many 1960s furniture designs are still produced today, but originals or limited editions are more desirable.

- To learn about 1960s themes and designers, study magazines and catalogs of the period. They are often inexpensive, at less than $5–25.

- If you want an item by a top designer, look for smaller or more common pieces, as they can be found more easily and are usually less expensive than bigger pieces.

- To date a Verner Panton chair, look for marks, including the name of the maker, on the underside of the piece.

- Marks on the base of the Ball chair identify the date it was made; those marked "Adelta" date from after 1992.

BUY

Lighting can be a relatively inexpensive way to add a 1960s touch to your home. The best investments will both sum up the style of the era and display the materials used.

A pair of Italian Artemide Dalu plastic table lamps, designed by Vico Magistretti. The curving design and bright plastic are typical. *c. 1969, 10½ in (26.5 cm) high.*

$200–300

KEEP

Iconic characters or images that summed up the 1960s prove constantly popular. Many have been used later, but original memorabilia featuring them is generally worth keeping, as demand may soon outweigh supply—leading to rising prices.

A pair of yellow Smiley sneakers, by the Newport Rubber Co. Largely unworn pairs such as this are scarce. The Smiley is an iconic symbol of the late 1960s and early 1970s that is still seen today. *Late 1960s–70s, 10¼ in (26 cm) long.*

$120–180

Glossary

Art Deco A style known for its geometric shapes, bright, bold colors, and architectural inspirations that was popular from c. 1918 to 1940.

Art Nouveau Popular from the 1890s to c. 1910, a style based on sinuous curves, flowing lines, asymmetry, and organic forms.

Arts and Crafts Movement A late 19th-century movement, led by the British designer William Morris, advocating a return to simple design and quality craftsmanship.

aventurine A type of translucent glass with metallic specks; the term also applies to other finishes with a similarly shiny appearance such as lacquer and glaze.

backstamp The mark printed on the base of a ceramic object that identifies the manufacturer, the model name and/or number, and sometimes the designer.

Bakelite A type of plastic made of phenolic resin and formaldehyde, patented by Dr. Leo Baekeland in 1907. When rubbed, it gives off a benzenelike smell. Brown and black are the most common colors.

baluster A double-curved form with a slender neck and bulbous body.

base metal Any nonprecious metal such as brass, iron, and steel or an alloy. It may be coated with a precious metal such as gold or silver. Often known as pot metal.

bisque A type of unglazed porcelain used for making dolls from c. 1860 to c. 1925.

bone china A durable porcelain made of kaolin (china clay), petuntse (china stone), and dried, powdered bone. It was developed as a way to compete with Chinese imports made of hard-paste porcelain. The Spode factory began producing it in England in 1794, and it is still made today.

cabochon A large, domed stone with a polished, unfaceted surface.

cameo A hardstone, gem, glass object, or shell with a carved design in relief, usually contrasting with the background. Commonly depicted subjects include portraits, classical groups, and landscapes.

cane A stick of glass that is made by fusing together a bundle of glass rods, or lengths. The rods may be colored to form a multicolored cane.

carded A term used when referring to merchandise still in its original packaging, comprising a cardboard backing with a plastic cover that allows the enclosed objects to be seen. "Loose" refers to an object no longer in its packaging.

cartouche A framed area, often in the shape of a paper scroll or shield, which can be inscribed.

cased glass Glassware consisting of two or more layers of glass in different colors. The thick outer layer is the first to be blown; subsequent layers are blown into the first layer.

Catalin A type of cast phenolic plastic made in bright colors. It was used from c. 1938 to c. 1946 to produce radio cabinets, costume jewelry, and other small items.

celadon Used in China for more than 2,000 years, this distinct grayish-green or bluish-green glaze serves to imitate jade. It can also be found on wares from Japan and South Korea.

chinoiserie A style popular in Europe during the late 17th and 18th centuries, in which oriental-style figures and motifs—including pagodas, birds, dragons, and lotus flowers—were used to decorate Western-style wares.

chronograph Any precision watch that can measure time accurately to the nearest second or fraction of a second, often to determine elapsed time in sporting events or to record speed.

composition A plasterlike substance consisting of whiting (chalk), resin, and size (glue) or other substances. It is used for producing dolls and other toys.

cranberry glass Also known as ruby glass, a type of 19th-century glass with copper oxide or gold chloride added to create a pink hue.

crazing A network of fine cracks in a ceramic glaze caused by uneven shrinking when the object was fired in the kiln. The term can also apply to cracks on a painted surface.

creamware A type of durable earthenware with a cream-colored body and lead glaze, first produced c. 1720. Wedgwood referred to it as Queen's ware.

cut glass Glass that has been decorated by cutting patterns—such as blazes, combs, diamonds, flutes, stars, steps, and swags—into the surface of the glass.

die cast Metal items, such as toy cars or figures, made inexpensively from metal alloys cast in a reusable mold.

earthenware Pottery that is fired in a kiln at a low temperature to a porous state. It then requires a glaze and a second firing to make it waterproof.

Elastolin A generic term for early 20th-century toy soldiers made from a mixture of sawdust, casein, kaolin, and glue around a wire figure.

embossed A large-scale relief design on metal (or leather) created by hammering or pressing on the reverse side of the material.

ephemera A term for all printed matter originally intended for immediate use and disposal, including packaging and wrappers, tickets, cards, and postage stamps.

escapement The part of a watch that governs the delivery of power to its movement, determining the speed at which the hands turn.

filigree An open ornamental work of fine gold or silver wire or plate that has been twisted or formed into a decorative shape.

finial A decorative knob on a lid or as the terminal of a piece, such as the decorative form at the end of a the handle on a spoon.

flambé A type of glaze produced to mimic the ancient *sang de boeuf* glaze. Introduced by Royal Doulton in 1902, the copper oxide formula creates a lustrous, crimson-red glaze.

flange The projecting disklike rim of a glass object, such as a vase.

frieze Originally an architectural term, it refers to the horizontal band found below the cornice on a piece of case furniture such as a cabinet or bookcase; a frieze rail is the wooden support below the top of a table.

gilt The gold finish applied to a silver or electroplated object or to a ceramic, wood, or glass item by one of several techniques.

glaze A glassy material applied to ceramics that forms a smooth, shiny, decorative, and protective surface when fired in a kiln. Tin and celadon glazes are opaque, while a lead glaze is transparent.

gold filled Jewelry made with a thin outer surface of solid gold bonded to another less expensive metal. It has many of the same physical characteristics as solid gold, such as strength and durability.

good condition A term used to refer to an item that is complete but shows some sign of age or use, perhaps with slight wear and tear, but nothing that dramatically affects its overall appearance.

guilloche A continuous pattern consisting of a pair of bands that twist to form interlacing plaits; these are sometimes filled with rosettes or other floral motifs and are often covered with colored enamel.

impressed marks Marks that have been made in the surface of a ceramic, glass, or metal body, usually on the base of the piece. They may provide information such as the manufacturer, designer, or pattern.

intaglio An Italian term for incised decoration, where the design is cut into the surface of a glass, ceramic, metalwork, or hardstone object. Unlike a cameo, where the design protrudes, the design in intaglio is recessed.

jet A type of black fossilized wood, or coal. In the 19th century it was carved and polished to create mourning jewelry. It was usually sourced from Whitby, in Yorkshire, England.

Kakiemon Used to decorate Japanese porcelain from c. 1660, a distinctive palette of colors, including dark blue, turquoise, iron red, yellow, black, and sometimes brown. The term is taken from the name of a Japanese potter. European factories copied the style in the early 18th century.

kapok A fiber similar to cottonballs used as a stuffing for teddy bears and other soft toys.

knop A rounded, bulbous part on the stem of a drinking glass, or a rounded, bulbous handle on a lid.

lithography The technique for making a print by taking an absorbent stone block and drawing on it with a special greasy crayon. When ink is applied to the block, it sticks to the greasy areas; by pressing paper on top of the block, the ink is transferred to the paper. It was developed in Germany by Aloys Senefelder c. 1798.

lithophane A panel or plaque made of thin, translucent, unglazed porcelain with a three-dimensional picture or design pressed into it.

loose *See carded.*

Lucite Also known as Plexiglass and later, Perspex, a transparent plastic first produced commercially in the 1930s. It sometimes yellows or cracks with age.

maki-e A Japanese decorative technique for lacquerwork, in which gold or colored dust is sprinkled onto wet lacquer to form a design.

millefiori The Italian term for "a thousand flowers," a glassmaking technique in which different-colored glass canes are cut into sections and embedded into a glass body so that their cross-section forms a pattern. The technique is often associated with glass paperweights made since the 19th century.

mint condition A term used to describe an item that is pristine, as if brand new, unused, and complete, showing no signs of age or any other damage. This is the most desirable condition for an object and can enhance value considerably.

mon The badge of a Japanese family, most commonly circular and in the form of a 16-petaled chrysanthemum, but also seen depicting other natural motifs.

mold-blown Molten glass that is blown into a mold to form a shape. The mold may be full size, or it may be a smaller dip mold, which forms a shape that is then reblown to a larger size.

murrine A type of Murano glassware in which short lengths or slices of colored glass canes (*murrine*) are used to form a mosaic pattern on the surface of an object.

Op Art The popular abbreviation for Optical Art, a 1960s art movement that created an illusion of space, movement, and volume by using abstract compositions of spirals, grids, undulating lines, and spots.

overglaze decoration Enamel colors that are applied by hand, or by a transfer print, onto a glazed ceramic object, which is then fired a second time at a low temperature.

paste A hard, versatile glass compound, which can have many of the properties of gemstones when certain minerals and oxides are added to it. Pastes have been used in a wide range of colors to make jewelry since the 18th century.

pastille burner A ceramic object used to hold a pastille—a small perfumed tablet—which was lit to scent a room. They were popular during the 18th and 19th centuries.

plate A term referring to items made of gold, silver, or another metal, often for domestic purposes, but also for ceremonial use, especially in churches. It is sometimes used as an abbreviation for Sheffield plate.

pontil mark Found on the base of a blown-glass object, a disk or irregular-shaped mark created where the object was held by a pontil rod while it was being blown.

poor condition A term used to refer to an item that shows considerable signs of wear and damage, possibly with missing parts.

Pop Art A style where everyday and mass-produced items—such as advertisements, packaging, and comic strips—were seen as possible forms of art. The style emerged in Britain in the mid-1950s and peaked in New York City in the 1960s.

porcelain A hard, white, translucent ceramic made from kaolin (china clay) and petuntse (china stone). It should ring when tapped.

porringer A silver, pewter, or ceramic cup with two handles and a cover.

pot metal *See base metal.*

Potteries, the An area in Staffordshire, England, known for its ceramics factories.

provenance Documentation or a verifiable account that is supplied with an object to identify its origins or history, or both. The provenance of an object can increase its value, especially if it is interesting, or links the object to a renowned maker, owner, event, or location.

reeding A type of decorative relief molding formed of thin, parallel, convex rods, or reeds; it is most commonly found on furniture and silver. The effect is similar to fluting.

reign mark Used on ceramics and works of art in China from the beginning of the Ming dynasty (1368–1644), an Imperial Chinese mark written as either four or six characters in script or seal form to provide the name of the emperor and usually the dynasty.

relief decoration Ornamentation that is made by a mold, stamped, or carved so that it is raised above the background surface; the depth of the decoration is referred to as high, medium, or bas (low) relief.

repeating mechanism Also known as a repeater, a mechanism found in clocks and watches that repeats the strike of the previous hour, quarter hour or last five minutes when a cord or button is touched.

resist In ceramic decoration, an area or sections on the body covered with wax or paper to block a luster solution applied to the rest of the piece. Once the solution has been applied, the resist is removed.

rhinestone This term originally referred to a type of clear quartz used in costume jewelry, but it now includes any colorless paste or rock crystal used in costume jewelry to imitate diamonds.

ruby glass *See cranberry glass*

salt glaze A type of glaze applied to stoneware, which is created by throwing salt into the kiln during firing. It vaporizes, leaving behind a thin, clear glaze.

Satsuma A general term for potteries on the island of Kyushu, Japan, which made simple wares for export to the West. These had a cream-colored body and a clear yellowish glaze that was often crackled. The wares were often decorated in colored enamel and with gilding.

scrap A small novelty piece of paper or thin cardboard color-printed and shaped in the form of an animal, flowers, people, or other popular motifs. Fashionable during the Victorian period, they were collected in albums or glued to small pieces of furniture, among other uses.

seconds Ceramic items in which the body or the glaze is damaged or becomes imperfect in some way during manufacture.

sgrafitto A decorative effect created by scratching or scoring through the surface of unfired slip applied to a ceramic object. *See slip.*

sleeping eyes A type of doll's eyes, weighted internally so that they remain open while the doll is upright but close when the doll is lying down.

slip A term meaning liquid clay; slip is often applied to a ceramic body as a finish, as decoration, or to bond two pieces together.

SLR The abbreviation for a single lens reflex camera. When the button is pressed, light enters through the lens and continues to the film as the viewfinder mirror is retracted.

sommerso From the Italian for "submerged," a glassmaking technique where one or more layers of differently colored glass are encased in a thick layer of clear glass. Up to around four different layers of colored glass may be used.

stoneware A hard, dense nonporous type of ceramic that is often decorated with a salt or lead glaze. It was first produced in China during the Shang dynasty (c. 1500–1028 BC) and rediscovered during the Middle Ages in Germany. It eventually spread to Britain in the late 17th century.

tessuto An Italian glassmaking technique in which finely striped canes decorate the body in a crisscrossing pattern.

tin plate A coating of tin or a tin alloy applied to steel, then decorated with hand painting or a transfer. Tinplate was used for toys between the mid-19th and mid-20th centuries.

transfer print A ceramic decorating technique which involves printing paper with a copper-plate engraving and then transferring the design to the object by pressing the paper on to it while the ink is still wet. The design is made permanent when the object is glazed and fired.

tube lining Decoration formed by piping or trailing thick slip clay onto the surface of a ceramic piece.

underglaze Decoration applied to a ceramic object before it is glazed and fired in the kiln.

vermeil Derived from the French word for "rosy," meaning silver that has been plated, or covered, with a thin layer, or wash, of gold.

Victorian era The period in Britain during the reign of Queen Victoria, from 1837 until 1901. This era was dominated by the Industrial Revolution, which led to the growth of mass-produced objects for the increasingly prosperous middle classes. A general fascination for a range of historical and exotic styles meant that there was no one definable style that characterized the period. Revival styles were also popular.

vignette Derived from the French word for vine, a carved ornament with a continuous design of grapevine leaves and tendrils. The word is also used when referring to a photograph or a drawing in which the edges fade away, or to a small room setting.

Find out more

CERAMICS

20–21 Clarice Cliff
- *Clarice Cliff and Her Contemporaries: Susie Cooper, Keith Murray, Charlotte Rhead, and the Carlton Ware Designers,* Helen Cunningham. Schiffer, 1999
- *Clarice Cliff: The Art of Bizarre,* Leonard Griffin. Pavilion, 2001
- *Taking Tea with Clarice Cliff: A Celebration of Her Art Deco Teaware,* Leonard Griffin. Pavilion, 1998

22–23 Fiestaware
- *Collecting Fiesta, Lu-Ray, and Other Colorware,* Mark Gonzalez. L-W Book Sales, 2000
- *Collectors Encyclopedia of Fiesta: Plus Harlequin, Riviera, and Kitchen Kraft,* Bob Huxford, Sharon Huxford. Collector Books, 2000
- *Modern Fiesta, 1986-Present,* by Terri Polick. Schiffer, 2003
- *Fiesta: The Homer Laughlin China Company's Colourful Dinnerware,* Jeffrey B Snyder. Schiffer Books, 2002

24–25 1930s ceramics
- *Carlton Ware,* Julie McKeown. Francis Joseph, 1994
- *Collecting Art Deco Ceramics: Shapes and Patterns from the 1920s and 1930s,* Pat Watson, Howard Watson. Francis Joseph, 1998
- *Cowan Pottery and the Cleveland School,* Mark T. Bassett, Victoria Naumann. Schiffer, 1997
- *McCoy Pottery Collectors Reference and Value Guide,* Bob Hanson. Collector Books, 2001

28–29 Rookwood
- *Rookwood Pottery: Identification & Value Guide: Bookends, Paperweights, and Animal Figurals,* Nick Nicholson, Marilyn Nicholson, Jim Thomas. Collector Books, 2002

30–31 Roseville
- *Collector's Encyclopedia of Roseville Pottery,* Sharon Huxford. Collector Books 2001
- *Introducing Roseville Pottery,* Mark T. Bassett. Schiffer, 2001
- *Warman's Roseville Pottery: Identification & Price Guide,* Mark F. Moran. Krause, 2004

32–33 American Arts and Crafts
- *DK Collector's Guides: Arts & Crafts,* Judith Miller. Dorling Kindersley, 2005
- *American Art Pottery,* David Rago. Knickerbocker Press, 1997
- *American Art Pottery: A Collection of Pottery, Tiles, and Memorabilia, 1880–1950: Identification & Values.*

Collector Books, 1997
- *The Collector's Encyclopedia of Van Briggle Art Pottery: Indentification & Value Guide,* Richard Sasicki, Josie Fania. Collector Books, 1992

34 Stoneware and redware
- *Blue and White Stoneware,* K. McNerney. Collector Books, 1981
- *Collector's Guide to Country Stoneware and Pottery,* Don Raycroft, Carol Raycroft. Collector Books, 1990
- *Redware: America's Folk Art Pottery,* Kevin McConnell. Schiffer Publishing, 1999

36–37 Lusterware
- *19th-Century Lustreware,* Michael Gibson. Antique Collectors' Club, 1999
- Royal Ontario Museum, 100 Queen's Park, Toronto, Ontario M5S 2C6 Canada. Tel: 416 586 5549, www.rom.on.ca

38–41 Floral ceramics
- *Chintz Ceramics,* Jo Anne P. Welsh. Schiffer, 1999
- *The Chintz Collectors Handbook.* Francis Joseph, 1999
- *Moorcroft: A Guide to Moorcroft Pottery 1897–1993,* Paul Atterbury and Beatrice Moorcroft. Richard Dennis, 1993

42–43 Oriental ceramics
- *Guide to Oriental Ceramics,* Elizabeth Wilson. Tuttle, 1995
- *Imari, Satsuma and Other Japanese Export Ceramics,* Nancy N. Schiffer. Schiffer, 1977
- *Marks and Monograms on European and Oriental Pottery and Porcelain,* William Chaffers. Reeves, 1965

44–45 Traditional ceramic ware
- *American Pottery & Porcelain,* William C. Ketchum. Black Dog & Leventhal, 2000
- *The Doulton Burslem Wares,* Desmond Eyles. Barrie and Jenkins, 1987
- *An Illustrated Encyclopaedia of British Pottery and Porcelain,* Geoffrey Godden. Herbert Jenkins, 1966
- *Sotheby's Concise Encyclopedia of Porcelain,* David Battie, Sotheby's, 1995

46–47 Cups and saucers
- *Collector's Encyclopedia of English China: Identification and Values,* Mary Frank Gaston. Collector Books, 2002
- *British Tea and Coffee Cups,* Steven Goss. Shire, 2000

- *Collectible Cups and Saucers,* Jim and Susan Harran. Collector Books, 2000

48–49 Cottage ware
- *Cottage Ware: Ceramic Tableware Shaped as Buildings 1920s–1990s,* Eileen Rose Busby. Schiffer, 1997
- *The Royal Winton Collector's Handbook: From 1925,* Muriel M. Miller. Krause Publications, 1999
- *Lilliput Lane Cottages,* Annette and Tom Power. Charlton Press, 2000

50–51 Nursery ware
- *Gifts for Good Children: The History of Children's China 1890–1990,* Maureen Batkin. Richard Dennis, 1996

52–53 Royal Doulton figurines
- *Royal Doulton Figurines (7th Edition),* Jean Dale. Charlton Press, 2000
- *Royal Doulton Figures: Produced at Burslem Staffordshire 1892–1994,* Desmond Eyles and Louise Irvine. Richard Dennis, 1994

54–55 Hummel figurines
- *Luckey's Hummel Figurines and Plates,* Carl F Luckey. Krause Publications, 2003
- *No. 1 Price Guide to M.I. Hummel Figurines,* Robert L. Miller. Portfolio Press, 2003.

56–57 Lady head vases
- *Collecting Head Vases: Identification and Value Guide,* David Barron. Collector Books, 2003
- *Head Vases, Identification and Values,* Kathleen Cole, Collector
- *Lady Head Vases,* Mary Zavada. Schiffer Publishing, 2003
- *Headhunters Newsletter,* c/o/ Maddy Gordon, P.O. Box 83H, Scarsdale, New York, NY 10583

HISTORICAL MEMORABILIA
62–63 Elizabeth II
- *British Royalty Commemoratives,* Douglas H. Flynn and Alan H. Bolton. Schiffer, 1999

64–65 Later royal memorabilia
- *Diana – an Illustrated Collection and Price Guide: Porcelain Plates,* Mary McMaster and Jose P. Torres. First Books Library, 2003
- *Diana: Collecting on a Princess,* Charles Nobles. Hobby House Press, 1999

66–67 Political memorabilia
- *200 Years of Political Campaign Collectibles,* Mark Warda. Galt, 2004

68–69 Stanhopes
- *Stanhopes – A Closer View,* Jean Scott. Greenlight, 2002

70–71 Philately
- *Stamp Collecting for Dummies,* Richard Sine. Hungry Minds, 2001

72–73 Coins and paper money
- *Standard Catalogue of World Paper Money volume 1 – General Issues,* Colin Bruce II and Neil Shafer. Krause Publications
- *Standard Catalogue of World Coins vols 1–4,* Chester L. Krause and Clifford Mishler. Krause Publications

74–75 New York World's Fairs
- *World's Fair Collectibles: Chicago, 1933 and New York, 1939,* Howard M. Rossen. Schiffer, 1998
- *NY World's Fair Collectibles, 1964–1965,* Joyce Grant. Schiffer, 1999

76–77 Native American art
- *North American Indian Artifacts: A Collector's Identification & Value Guide,* Lar Hothe. Krause, 1998
- *Warman's Native American Collectibles: A Price Guide & Historical Reference,* John A. Schuman, John A. III Schuman. Wallace-Homestead, 1998

HOUSEHOLD & KITCHENALIA
82–83 Old brass and copper and 84–85 Vintage wooden objects
- *300 Years of Kitchen Collectibles,* Linda Campbell Franklin. Krause Publications, 2003
- *Antique Brass and Copper – An Identification and Value Guide,* Mary Frank Gaston. Collector Books, 1992
- *Kitchen Antiques,* Mary Norwak. Ward Lock, 1975

86–87 Jelly molds
- *Jelly Moulds,* Sally Kevill-Davies. Lutterworth Press, 1999

88–89 Blue-and-white ware
- *Transfer Printed Pottery,* Robert Copeland. Shire, 1999
- *The Dictionary of Blue and White Printed Pottery: Vols I & II,* A.W. Coysh and R.K. Henrywood. Antique Collectors Club, 2001
- *Blue and White Pottery: A Collector's Guide,* Gillian Neale. Miller's, 2000
- *Fascinating Flow Blue,* Jeffrey B. Snyder, Schiffer, 1997

90–91 Quilts
- *The American Quilt : A History of Cloth and Comfort 1750–1950*, Roderick Kiracofe, Mary Elizabeth Johnson. Clarkson Potter, 2004
- *Antique Quilts & Textiles: A Price Guide to Functional and Fashionable Cloth Comforts*, Bobby Aug, Gerald Roy. Collector, 2004
- *Clues in the Calico: A Guide to Identifying and Dating Antique Quilts*, Barbara Brackman. Howell Press Inc., 1989
- *America's Glorious Quilts*, Dennis Duke and Deborah Harding. Value Publishing, 1989

92–93 Vintage packaging
- *Shelf Space: Modern Package Design, 1945–1965*, Jerry Jankowski. Chronicle Books, 1998

94–95 Scottie dogs
- *Scottie Showcase: A Pictorial Introduction to Scottie Dog Collectibles*, Donna Newton. Country Scottie, 1988

96–97 Cookie jars
- *An Illustrated Value Guide to Cookie Jars*, Ermagene Westfall. Collector, 1983
- *The Wonderful World of Cookie Jars: A Pictorial Reference and Price Guide*, Mark Supnick, Ellen Supnick. L-W, 1996

98–101 Tins
- *Antique Tins: Identification & Values*, Fred Dodge. Collector Books, 1999
- *Encyclopedia of Advertising Tins (Vol. 2)*, David Zimmerman. Collector Books, 1998
- *Decorative Printed Tins: The Golden Age of Printed Tin Packaging*, David Griffith. Studio Vista, 1979

102–103 Vintage kitchen equipment
- *Collecting Kitchenware*, Christina Bishop. Octopus, 2000
- *300 years of Kitchen Collectibles (3rd Edition)*, Linda Campbell Franklin. Books Americana, 1991
- *Price Guide to Collectible Kitchen Appliances – from Aerators to Waffle Irons 1900–1950*, Gary Miller and K.M. Scotty Mitchell. Wallace-Homestead, 1991
- *Kitchen Antiques*, Mary Norwak. Ward Lock, 1975
- *Kitchen Collectibles – The Essential Buyer's Guide*, Diane Stoneback. Wallace-Homestead, 1994

104–105 Jadeite
- *Jadeite: An Identification and Price Guide*, Joe Keller, David Ross. Schiffer Publishing, 2000

106–107 Vintage sewing tools
- *Antique Needlework Tools*, Nerylla Taunton. Antique Collectors' Club, 1997
- *The Encyclopedia of Early American Sewing Machines: Identification & Values*, Carter Bays. Collector Books, 2005

- *Sewing Tools & Trinkets: Collector's Identification & Value Guide*, Helen Lester Thompson. Collector, 1996

108–109 Salt and pepper shakers
- *The Complete Salt and Pepper Shaker Book*, Mike Schneider. Schiffer, 1997
- *Collecting Salt & Pepper Shaker Series*, Irene Thornburg. Schiffer, 1995
- *The Big Book of Salt and Pepper Shakers*, Irene Thornburg. Schiffer, 1999

110–111 Corkscrews
- *The Ultimate Corkscrew Book*, Donald Bull. Schiffer, 1999
- *A Guide to Corkscrew Collecting*, Peter Coldicott. BAS Printers, 1993
- *Corkscrews and Bottle Openers*, Evan Perry. Shire, 1999

112–113 Decanters and cocktail shakers
- *The Cocktail Shaker*, Simon Khachadourian. Philip Wilson, 2000
- *The Decanter*, Andy McConnell. Antique Collectors' Club, 2004

GLASS
118–119 Carnival glass
- *A Century of Carnival Glass*, Glen Thistlewood. Schiffer, 2001
- *Collector's Companion to Carnival Glass: Identification and Values*, Bill Edwards and Mike Carwile. Collector Books, 2003

120–121 Perfume bottles
- *The Art of Perfume: Discovering and Collecting Perfume Bottles*, Christie Mayer Lefkowith. Thames & Hudson, 1998
- *Perfume, Cologne and Scent Bottle*, Jacqualyne North, Duane A. Young. Schiffer, 1999

122–125 Scandinavian glass
- *DK Collector's Guides: 20th-Century Glass*, Judith Miller. Dorling Kindersley, 2004
- *Scandinavia: Ceramics and Glass in the 20th Century*, Jennifer Opie. V&A Publications, 1989
- *Nineteenth-Century British Glass*, Hugh Wakefield. Faber and Faber, 1982

128–129 Depression Glass
- *Collector's Encyclopedia of Depression Glass*, Gene Florence, Cathy Florence. Collector, 2003
- *Warman's Depression Glass: A Value & Identification Guide*, Ellen T. Schroy. Krause, 2003

130–131 Paperweights
- *The Encyclopaedia of Glass Paperweights*, Paul Hollister. Paperweight Press, 1986
- *All About Paperweights*, Lawrence H. Selman. Paperweight Press, 1992

132–133 Steuben
- *Steuben Glass: An American Tradition in Crystal*, Mary Jean Madigan, E. Mari McKee. Harry N Abrams, 2003

134–135 Fenton
- *The Big Book of Fenton Glass*, John Walk, Bibliotechnology, 2004
- *Fenton Art Glass Patterns 1939-1980: Identification & Value Guide*, Margaret Whitmyer, Kenn Whitmayer. Collector, 2004
- *The Big Book of Fenton Glass: 1940–1970*, John Walk. Schiffer Publishing, 1998

136–137 Blenko
- *Blenko: Cool '50s & '60s Glass*, Leslie Pina, Ramon Pina. Schiffer, 2000

138–139 Other glassware
- *DK Collector's Guide: 20th-Century Glass*, Judith Miller. Dorling Kindersley, 2004

140–143 Murano glass
- *Murano Glass (1910–1970): Theme and Variations*, Marc Heiremans. Arnoldsche Art Publishers, 2003
- *Venetian Glass 1890–1990*, Rosa Barovier Mentasti. Arsenale Editrice, 1997
- *Murano Glass: A History of Glass*, Gianfranco Toso. Arsenale Editrice, 2001

BEAUTY AND FASHION
148–149 Vintage fashions
- *Art Deco Fashion*, Suzanne Lussier. V&A Publications, 2003
- *Twentieth-Century Development in Fashion and Costume: Performing Arts*, Alycen Mitchell. Mason Crest, 2002
- *Chanel: Her Style and Her Life*, Janet Wallach. Bantam Doubleday Dell, 1998

150–151 1940s and 50s fashions
- *Christian Dior*, Richard Martin and Harold Koday. Metropolitan Museum of Art, 2000
- *Forties Fashion and the New Look*, Colin McDowell. Bloomsbury, 1997
- *Reconstructing Italian Fashion*, Nicola White. Berg, 2000

152–153 Hats
- *The Century of Hats*, Susie Hopkins. Aurum, 1999
- *Hats: Status, Style and Glamour*, Colin McDowell. Thames & Hudson, 1997
- *Women's Hats of the 20th Century: For Designers and Collectors*, Maureen Reilly and Mary Beth Detrich. Schiffer, 1997

154–155 1960s fashions
- *Biba: The Biba Experience*, Alwyn W. Turner. Antique Collectors' Club, 2004
- *Emilio Pucci*, Katel Le Bourhis, Stefania Ricci and Luigi Settembrini (eds). Skira Editore, 1997
- *Ossie Clark: 1965–74*, Judith Watt. V&A Publications, 2003
- *Pierre Cardin: Past, Present, Future*, Valerie Mendes. Dirk Nishen, 1990

- *Psychedelic Chic: Artistic Fashions of the Late 1960s & Early 1970s*, Roseann Ettinger. Schiffer, 1999

156–157 Post-1960s fashions
- *Dressing Up Vintage*, Tracey Tolkien. Rizzoli, 2000

158–159 Sunglasses
- *Spectacles: Utility Article and Cult Object*, B. Michael Andressen. Arnoldsche Art Publishers, 1998
- *Spectacles, Lorgnettes and Monocles*, D.C. Davidson and R.J.S. MacGregor. Shire, 2002
- *Specs Appeal: Extravagant 1950s and 1960s Eyewear*, Leslie Pina and Donald-Brian Johnson. Schiffer, 2001

160–161 Purses
- *Vintage Purses at Their Best*, Lynell K. Schwatz. Schiffer, 2004
- *Whiting & Davis Purses: The Perfect Mesh*, Leslie Pina. Schiffer, 2002

162–163 Vintage shoes
- *Salvatore Ferragamo: The Art of the Shoe, 1898–1960*, Salvatore Ferragamo, Stefania Ricci and Edward Maeder. Rizzoli International, 1993
- *Shoes: Fashion and Fantasy*, Colin McDowell. Thames & Hudson, 1994
- *Shoes: A Celebration of Footwear*, Linda O'Keeffe. Workman, 1997

164–165 Fans
- *Fans*, Hélène Alexander. Shire, 1994
- *Fans*, Avril Hart and Emma Taylor. V&A Publications, 1998
- *Fans: Ornaments of Language and Fashion*, James Mackay. Parkgate Books, 2000
- The Fan Museum, 12 Crooms Hill, Greenwich, London SE10 8ER, UK Tel: +44 (0)20 8305 1441

166–167 Gentlemen's accessories
- *Fit to be Tied: Vintage Ties of the Forties and Early Fifties*, Rod Dyer and Ron Spark. Abbeville Press, 1991
- *Fashion Accessory Series: Ties*, Avril Hart. V&A Publications, 1998
- *Cufflinks*, Bertrand Pizzin and Jean-Noel Liaut. Editions Assouline, 2002

168–169 Smoking accessories
- *Collector's Guide to Cigarette Lighters*, James Flanagan. Collector Books, 1997
- *Collectible Lighters*, Juan Manuel Clark. Flammarion, 2003
- *Matchsafes*, Deborah Sampson Shinn. Scala, 2001

170–171 Powder compacts
- *Vintage and Vogue Ladies' Compacts*, Roselyn Gerson. Collectors Books, 2001
- *Collector's Encyclopedia of Compacts, Carryalls and Face Powder Boxes (Volumes 1 & 2)*, Laura M. Mueller. Collectors Books, 1994 & 1997

■ *Vintage Compacts and Beauty Accessories*, Lynell Schwartz. Schiffer, 1997

172–175 Costume jewelry
■ *DK Collector's Guide: Costume Jewelry*, Judith Miller. Dorling Kindersley, 2003
■ *Hollywood Jewels: Movies, Jewelry, Stars*, Penny Proddow, Debra Healy, and Marion Fasel. Harry N. Abrams Inc., 1996
■ *The Jewels of Miriam Haskell*. Antique Collectors Club, 1997
■ *Jewelry by Chanel*, Patrick Mauries. Thames & Hudson, 2000
■ *Kenneth Jay Lane: Faking It*, Kenneth Jay Lane and Harrice Simons Miller. Harry N. Abrams Inc., 1996

176–177 Jewelry
■ *Art Deco Jewelry*, Sylvie Raulet. Thames & Hudson, 2002
■ *An Illustrated Dictionary of Antique Jewelry*, Harold Newman. Thames & Hudson, 1987
■ *Illustrated Guide to Jewelry Appraising, 3rd Edition: Antique, Period, and Modern*, Anna M. Miller. Gemstone Press, 2004
■ *How to Be a Jewelry Detective: Antiques Detectives How to Series*, C. Jeanenne Bell, Krause, 2001

178–179 Watches and 180–181 Digital watches
■ *The Wristwatch Almanac*, Michael Balfour. Eric Dobby, 1994
■ *The New Collector's Guide to Pocket Watches*. Barry S. Goldberg
■ *Collectible Wristwatches*, René Pannier. Flammarion, 2001
■ *History of the Modern Wrist Watch*, Pieter Doensen. Snoeck-Ducaju & Zoon, 1994

TOYS, DOLLS, AND TEDDY BEARS
186–187 Tinplate toys
■ *The Book of Penny Toys*. New Cavendish Books, 1999
■ *Tinplate Toys: From Schuco, Bing & Other Companies*, Jurgen Franzke. Schiffer, 1997
■ *Tin Toys 'The Collector's Corner'*, R. Kingsley. Grange Books, 1999
■ *The Art of the Tin Toy*, David Pressland. New Cavendish Books, 1990

188–189 Dinky toys
■ *Dinky Toys*, Edward Force. Schiffer, 1996
■ *Ramsay's British Die-Cast Model Toys Catalogue (9th Edition)*, John Ramsay. Swapmeet Publications, 2001
■ *The Great Book of Dinky Toys*, Mike and Sue Richardson. New Cavendish Books, 2000

190–191 Corgi toys
■ *The Great Book of Corgi 1956–1983*, Marcel Van Cleemput. New Cavendish Books, 1989
■ *Corgi Toys*, Edward Force. Schiffer, 1996

■ *Ramsay's British Die-Cast Model Toys Catalogue (9th Edition)*, John Ramsay. Swapmeet Publications, 2001

192–193 Hot Wheels
■ *Tomart's Price Guide to Hot Wheels Collectibles*, Micheal Thomas Strauss. Tomart, 2002
■ *Hot Wheels: 35 Years of Speed, Power Performance and Attitude*, Randy Leffingwell. Motorbooks International, 2003

194–195 Metal automobile toys
■ *Toy Car Collectors Guide: Identification and Values for Diecast, White Metal Other Automotive Toys & Models*, Dana Johnson. Collector Books, 2002

196–197 Model trains
■ *The American Toy Train*, Gerry Souter, Janet Souter. Motorbooks International, 1999
■ *Ramsay's British Model Trains Catalogue*, Pat Hammond (ed). Swapmeet Publications, 2002
■ *Christie's Toy Trains*, Hugo Marsh and Pierce Carlson. Watson-Guptill Publications, 2002

198–199 Marbles
■ *Marbles – Identification & Price Guide*, Robert Block. Schiffer, 1999

200–203 Teddy bears
■ *125 Years of Steiff*, Gunther Pfeiffer. Heel Verlag Gmbh, 2005
■ *The Teddy Bear Encyclopaedia*, Pauline Cockrill. Dorling Kindersley, 2001
■ *Bears*, Sue Pearson. De Agostini Editions, 1995

204–205 Soft toys
■ *Schroeder's Collectible Toys Antique to Modern Price Guide*, Sharon Huxford. Collector, 2003
■ *Steiff Identification and Price Guide*, Linda Mullins. Hobby House Press, 2001

206–207 Snow globes
■ *Collectible Snowdomes*, Lélie Carnot. Flammarion, 2002
■ *Snow Globes: The Collector's Guide to Selecting, Displaying, and Restoring Snow Globes*, Connie A. Moore and Harry L. Rinker. Courage Books, 1993

208–209 Bisque dolls, 212–213 Fabric dolls, and 214–215 Plastic dolls
■ *The Collector's Encyclopaedia of Dolls: Volumes 1 & 2*, Elizabeth A. Coleman, Dorothy S. Coleman, and Evelyn J. Coleman. Crown, 1976
■ *The 14th Blue Book: Dolls & Values*, Jan Foulke. Hobby House Press, 1999
■ *Doll Registry: A Guide to the Description and Value of Antique and Collectible Dolls*, Florence Thériault. Doll Masters, 1988

210–211 Half dolls
■ *Half-Dolls Price Guide*, Sally Van Luven and Susan Graham. Hobby House Press, 2004
■ *The Collector's Encyclopedia of Half-Dolls*, Frieda Marion and Norman Werner. Crown, 1979

216–217 Barbie
■ *Identifying Barbie Dolls: The New Compact Study Guide and Identifier*, Janine Fennick. Chartwell, 1999
■ *Barbie Doll Collector's Handbook*, A. Glenn Mandeville. Hobby House Press, 1997
■ *Collectibly Yours Barbie Doll 1980–1990: Identification & Price Guide*, Margo Rana. Hobby House Press, 1998

218–219 Dollhouses
■ *Collecting Dolls' Houses and Miniatures*, Nora Earnshaw. New Cavendish Books, 1999
■ *Collector's History of Dolls' Houses: Doll House Dolls and Miniatures*, Constance Eileen King. Smithmark Publishing, 1987

220–221 Nursery playthings
■ *Rocking Horses: The Collector's Guide to Selecting, Restoring, and Enjoying New and Vintage Rocking Horses*, Tony Stevenson and Eva Marsden. Courage Books, 1993
■ *Jigsaw Puzzles: An Illustrated History and Price Guide*, Anne D. Williams. Chilton Books, 1990

222–223 Games
■ *American Games: Comprehensive Collector's Guide*, Alex G. Malloy. Antique Trader Books, 2000
■ *Board Games*, Desi Scarpone. Schiffer, 1995
■ *Victorian Board Games*, Olivia Bristol. St Martins Press, 1995

ENTERTAINMENT AND SPORTS
228–229 Star Wars
■ *Tomart's Price Guide to Worldwide Star Wars Collectibles*, Stephen Sansweet. Tomart Publications, 1997
■ *A Universe of Star Wars Collectibles: Identification and Price Guide (2nd Edition)*, Stuart W. Wells III. Krause Publications, 2002

230–231 Cult TV
■ *Collector's Guide to TV Memorabilia 1960s & 1970s: Identification and Values*, Greg Davis, Bill Morgan. Collector, 1996
■ *A Collector's Guide to TV Toys and Memorabilia: 60 & 70s (22nd Edition)*, Bill Morgan. Collector Books, 1998

232–233 Character collectibles
■ *Cartoon Toys & Collectibles Identification and Value Guide*, David Longest. Collector Books, 1998

234–235 Sci-Fi TV memorabilia
■ *Star Trek Collectibles*, Sue Cornwell and Mike Kott. House of

Collectibles, 1997
■ *Trekkies' Guide to Collectibles*, Jeffrey B. Snyder. Schiffer, 1999

236–237 James Bond and 238–239 Movie memorabilia
■ *Official Price Guide to Star Wars Memorabilia*, Jeremy Beckett. House of Collectibles, 2005

240–243 Animation
■ *Animation Art at Auction: Since 1994*, Jeff Lotman. Schiffer, 1998
■ *Animation Art: The Later Years 1954–1993*, Jeff Lotman. Schiffer, 1996
■ *Animation Art: The Early Years 1911–1953*, Jeff Lotman and Jonathan Smith. Schiffer, 1995
■ *Stern's Guide to Disney Collectibles*, Michael Stern. Collector Books, 1995

244–245 Computer games
■ *Electronic Plastic*, Jaro Gielens (ed). Die Gestalte Verlag, 2001
■ *The Ultimate History of Video Games: From Pong to Pokemon – The Story Behind the Craze that Touched Our Lives*, Steve L. Kent. Prima Publishing, 2001

246–247 Elvis Presley
■ *Elvis Presley Memorabilia: An Unauthorized Collector's Guide*, Sean O'Neal. Schiffer, 2001
■ *The Official Price Guide to Elvis Presley Records & Memorabilia*, Jerry Osborne. House of Collectibles, 1994

248–249 The Beatles
■ *The Official Price Guide to The Beatles' Records and Memorabilia*, Perry Cox. Random House, 1999
■ The Beatles Story, Britannia Pavilion, Albert Dock, Liverpool L3 4AA, UK Tel: + 44 (0)151 709 1963

250–253 Rock and pop music
■ *A Music Lover's Guide to Record Collecting*, Dave Thompson. Backbeat UK, 2002
■ *Rare Record Price Guide: 2004*. Omnibus Press, 2004

254–257 Baseball
■ *Collecting Baseball Memorabilia: A Handbook*, Duke Snider, Dan Zachofsky. McFarland & Company, 2000
■ *Complete Guide to Baseball Memorabilia*, Mark K. Larson. Krause, 1996
■ *Tuff Stuff's Baseball Memorabilia Price Guide*, Larry Canale. Krause, 2001

258–259 Football
■ *The Official Beckett Price Guide to Football Cards 2005, Edition #24*, James Beckett. House of Collectibles, 2004

260–261 Golf
■ *Beyond the Links: Golfing Stories, Collectibles and Ephemera*, Sarah Fabian. Studio Editions, 1992
■ *Vintage Golf Club Collectibles:*

Find out more

Clubs and societies

ADVERTISING
Antique Advertising Association of America
PO Box 1121, Morton Grove, IL 60053
Tel: 708 446 0904
www.pastimes.org

Coca-Cola Collectors' Club International
PO Box 49166, Atlanta, GA 30359-1166

AERONAUTICA
The Aviation Postcard Club (International)
Phil Muson, 25 Kerill Avenue, Old Coulsdon, Surrey CR5 1QB, UK
Tel: +44 (0) 1737 551 817

AUTOGRAPHS
International Autograph Collectors' Club and Dealers' Alliance
4575 Sheridan St. Ste.111, Hollywood, FL 33021-3515
Tel: 561 736 8409
www.iacc-da.com

Universal Autograph Collectors' Club
PO Box 6181, Washington, DC 20044
Tel: 202 332 7388
www.uacc.com

AUTOMOBILIA
Automobile Objets d'Art Club
252 N. 7th St., Allentown, PA 18102-4204
Tel: 610 432 3355

BOOKS
Antiquarian Bookseller's Association of America
20 W. 44th St., 4th Floor, New York, NY 10036
Tel: 212 944 8291

CAMERAS
Daguerreian Society
3045 W, Liberty Ave. Ste. 7, Pittsburgh, PA 15216-2460
Tel: 412 343 5525

Photographic Historical Society of Canada
P.O. Box 54620, Toronto, Ontario M5M 4N5, Canada
Tel: 416 736 2100

Vintage Camera Club
2562 Victoria St., Wichita, KS 67216
Tel: 316 265 0393

CERAMICS
American Art Pottery Association
PO Box 834, Westport, MA 02790-0697
www.amartpot.org

American Ceramic Circle
520 16th St., Brooklyn, NY 11215
www.amercercir.org

American Stoneware Collectors' Society
PO Box 281, Point Pleasant Beach, NJ 08742-0281
Tel: 732 899 8707
libertyforever@home.com

The Belleek Collectors' International Society
9893 Georgetown Pike, Ste. 525, Great Falls, VA 22066
Tel: 800 235 5335
or 703 847 6207
Fax: 703 847 6201

Blue and White Pottery Club
224 12th St. NW, Cedar Rapids, IA 52405-3913
Tel: 319 362 8116

Enesco Lilliput Lane Collector's Club
225 Windsor Drive, Itasca, IL 60143
Tel: 630 875 5300
or 800 436 3726
caffairs@enesco.com
www.enesco.com

The Homer Laughlin China Collectors Association (including Fiestaware)
PO Box 26021, Crystal City, VA 22215-6021
www.hlcca.org

Hummel Collectors Club
1261 University Dr., Yardley, PA 19067-2857
Tel: 888 548 6635
Fax: 215 321 7367
www.hummels.com

Minnesota Art Pottery Association
10120 32nd Ave., Minneapolis, MN 55441
Tel: 612 724 1734

Noritake Collectors' Society
145 Andover Place, West Hempstead, NY 11552-1603
Tel: 516 292 8355
or 718 464 9009
Fax: 718 464 8448
ttrapani@aol.com

Northern California Doulton Collectors' Club
PO Box 214, Moraga, CA 94556
Tel: 925 376 2221
royaldoultonwest@yahoo.com
www.royaldoultonwest.com

Pottery Lovers Reunion
4969 Hudson Drive, Stow, OH 44224
potlvrs@neo.lrun.com

Royal Doulton International Collectors' Club
700 Cottontail Lane, Somerset, NJ 08873
Tel: 800 682 4462
Fax: 732 764 4974

Valley of the Sun Roseville Collectors Club
4681 N. 84th Way, Scottsdale, AZ 85251-1864
Tel: 888 255 0664
or 480 947 5693
Fax: 480 994 4382

Van Briggle Collectors Society
600 S. 21st St., Colorado Springs, CO 80901
Tel: 719 633 7729
Fax: 719 633 7720
vanpottery@aol.com
www.vanbriggle.com

Wisconsin Pottery Association
PO Box 46, Madison, WI 53701-0046
Tel: 608 301 0185
Fax: 608 241 8770
webmaster@wisconsinpottery.org
www.wisconsinpottery.org

CHARACTER COLLECTIBLES
Howdy Doody Memorabilia Collectors' Club
8 Hunt Court, Flemington, NJ 08822-3349
Tel: 908 782 1159
Fax: 908 782 0188
jjudson@ptd.net

Official Popeye Fan Club
1001 State St, Chester, IL 62233
Tel: 618 826 4567
Fax: 618 826 2809
spinach@midwest.net
www.popeyethesailor.com

CHRISTMAS
Golden Glow of Christmas Past
6401 Winsdale St., Minneapolis, MN 55427-4250
Tel: 612 544 8933
Morrison@aracnet.com

CLOTHING & ACCESSORIES
The Costume Society of America
55 Edgewater Dr., PO Box 73, Earleville, MD 21909-0073
Tel: 410 275 1619
www.costumesocietyamerica.com

American Fan Collectors' Association
PO Box 5473, Sarasota, FL 34277-5473
Tel: 817 267 9851

California Purse Collector's Club
PO Box 572, Campbell, CA 95009

COINS
American Numismatic Association
818 N. Cascade Avenue, Colorado Springs, CO 80903-3279
Tel: 719 632 2646
Fax: 719 634 4085
rochette@money.org
www.money.org

COMIC BOOKS
The Comic Book Club of Ithaca
PO Box 701, Ithaca, NY 14851

COMPUTERS
Historical Computer Society
1 Oakleigh Court, Richmond, VA 23233-3125
Tel: 804 754 1951
david@classiccomputing.com
www.classiccomputing.com

COSTUME JEWELRY
Leaping Frog Antique Jewelry & Collectible Club
4841 Martin Luther King Blvd, Sacramento, CA 95820-4932
Tel: 916 452 6728

Vintage Fashion & Costume Jewelry Club
PO Box 265, Glen Oaks, NY 11004-0265
Tel: 718 939 3095
www.lizjewel.com

DISNEYANA
National Fantasy Club For Disneyana Collectors & Enthusiasts
PO Box 106, Irvine, CA 92713-9212
Tel: 714 731 4705
info@nffc.org
www.nffc.org

Walt Disney Collectors' Society
500 South Buena Vista St, Burbank, CA 91521-8028
Tel: 800 932 5749

EPHEMERA
The Ephemera Society of America, Inc.
PO Box 95, Cazenovia, NY 13035-0095
Tel: 315 655 9139
Fax: 315 655 9139
info@ephemerasociety.org
www.ephemerasociety.org

The Ephemera Society of Canada
36 Macauley Drive, Thornhill, Ontario L3T 5S5, Canada
Tel: 416 492 5958
ephemera@tht.net

GLASS
The National American Glass Club
Po Box 8489, Silver Spring, MD 20907-8489
nagc@att.net
www.glassclub.org

Fenton Art Glass Collectors of America
P.O. Box 384, Williamstown, WV 26187
Tel: 304 375 6196
fagcainc.wirefire.com

International Carnival Glass Association
P.O. Box 306, Mentone, IN 46539-0306
Tel: 219 353 7678

Lalique Collectors' Society
400 Veterans Boulevard, Carlstadt, NJ 07072-2704
Tel: 800 274 7825

The National Depression Glass Association
5871 Vista Drive, Apt. 725,
West Des Moines, IA 50266
Tel: 515 223 9364

National Fenton Glass Society
PO Box 4008, Marietta,
OH 45750-7008
Tel: 614 374 3345

Murano Glass Society
32040 Mount Hermon Road,
Salisbury, MD 21804
Tel: 410 546 5881
Fax: 410 546 5881

KITCHENALIA
American Cookie Jar Association
1600 Navajo Rd, Norman,
OK 73026
davismj@ionet.net

International Correspondence of Corkscrew Addicts
670 Meadow Wood Road,
Mississauga Ontario, L5J 2S6,
Canada
dugohuzo@aol.com
www.corkscrewnet.com

Jelly Jammers (Jelly molds)
6086 W. Boggstown Rd.,
Boggstown, IN 46110
Tel: 317 835 7121

Kitchen Antiques & Collectibles News
4645 Laurel Ridge Dr.,
Harrisburg, PA 17119

Kollectors of Old Kitchen Stuff
354 Route 206 North,
Chester 07930
Tel: 908 879 0976

Novelty Salt & Pepper Shakers Club
P.O. Box 67738, Orlando,
FL 32867-7388
Tel: 407 678 1219

MARBLES
Marble Collectors Unlimited
PO Box 206, Northborough,
MA 01532-0206
marblesbev@aol.com

MOVIES, TV, AND ENTERTAINMENT
The Animation Art Guild
330 W. 45th St, Ste 9D
New York, NY 10036-3864
Tel: 212 765 3030
theaagltd@aol.com

The James Bond International Fan Club
PO Box 1570, Christchurch,
Dorset BH23 4XS, UK
www.bondbooks.biz

Starfleet - The International Star Trek Fan Association
www.sfi.org

Star Wars Collectors Archives
lopez@halcyon.com
www.toysrgus.com

NATIVE AMERICAN ART
Indian Arts & Crafts Association
PO Box 29780, Albuquerque,
NM 87592-9780
Tel: 505 265 9149
Fax: 505 474 8924
iaca@ix.netcom.com
www.iaca.com

NEW YORK WORLD'S FAIRS
World's Fair Collectors' Society,
c/o Mike Pender, P.O. Box 20806,
Sarasota, FL 34276-3806
wfcs@aol.com

OCEAN LINER MEMORABILIA
Oceanic Navigation Research Society
P.O. Box 8005, Universal City,
CA 91618-8005
Tel: 818 985 1345

Steamship Historical Society of America
300 Ray Drive, Ste. #4,
Providence, RI 02906
Tel: 401 274 0805
www.sshsa.net

Titanic International Society
P.O. Box 7007, Freehold,
NJ 07728-7007
Tel: 732 462 1413
or 973 742 8747

PAPERWEIGHTS
Paperweight Collectors' Association, Inc.
PO Box 40, Barker, TX 77413-0040
Tel: 281 579 7413
Fax: 281 579 7413
albates@worldnet.att.net
www.paperweight.org

PENS
Pen Collectors of America
PO Box 80, Redding Ridge,
CT 06876
www.pencollectors.com

PEZ
Pez Collectors' News
PO Box 14956, Surfside Beach,
SC 29587
info@pezcollectorsnews.com
www.pezcollectorsnews.com

PHILATELY
American Philatelic Society
PO Box 8000, State College,
PA 16803-8000
Tel: 814 237 3803
Fax: 814 237 6128
relamb@stamps.org
www.stamps.org

American Stamp Dealers Association
3 School Street, Ste. 205,
Glen Cove, NY 11542-2548
Tel: 516 759 7000
www.asdaonline.com

POLITICAL MEMORABILIA
American Political Items Collectors
PO Box 340339, San Antonio,
TX 8234-0339
www.collectors.org/apic

Kennedy Political Items Collectors
P.O. Box 922, Clark,
NJ 07066-0922
Tel: 732 382 1325

POWDER COMPACTS
Compact Collectors Club
PO Box 40, Lynbrook,
NY 11563-0040
Tel: 516 593 8746
compactldy@aol.com

QUILTS
American Quilter's Society
P.O. Box 3290
Paducah, KY 42002-3290
Tel: 800 626 5420
or 270 898 7903
www.aqsquilt.com

The National Quilting Association, Inc.
PO Box 393, Ellicott City,
MD 21043-0393
Tel: 410 461 5733
Fax: 410 461 3693

RADIOS
Antique Wireless Association, Inc.
Box E, Breesport, NY 14816
Tel: 607 739 5443
Fax: 607 796 6230
www.antiquewireless.org

International Antique Radio Club, div. of RGB Enterprises
P.O. Box 5367, Old Bridge,
NJ 08857
Tel: 732 607 0299

ROCK N ROLL
Elvis Forever TCB Fan Club
PO Box 1066, Miami,
FL 33780-1066

The Official Elvis Collectors Club
www.elvisinsiders.com

Working Class Hero Beatles Club
3311 Niagara St., Pitsburgh,
PA 1213-4223

SCENT BOTTLES
International Perfume Bottle Association
396 Croton Rd, Wayne, PA 19087
Tel: 610 995 9051
www.perfumebottles.org

Miniature Perfume Bottle Collectors
28227 Paseo El Siena,
Laguna Niguel,
CA 92677-4500
Tel: 949 364 9510

SCOTTIE DOGS
Wee Scots
David Bohnlein, P.O. Box 450,
Danielson, CT 06239-0450
Tel: 860 564 6660
www.campbellscotties.com

SMOKING
Cigarette Lighter Collectors' Club
SPARK International
http://members.aol.com/intspark

Pocket Lighter Preservation Guild & Historical Society, Inc.
PO Box 1054, Addison,
IL 60101-8054
Tel: 708 543 9120

SNOW GLOBES
Snowdome Collectors' Club
PO Box 53262, Washington,
DC 20009-9262

SPORTING MEMORABILIA
Boxing & Pugilistica Collectors International
PO Box 83135, Portland,
OR 97283-0135
Tel: 502 286 3597

Golf Collectors' Society
PO Box 24102, Cleveland, OH 44124
Tel: 216 861 1615
www.golfcollectors.com

Society for American Baseball Research
812 Huron Road, E. 719, Cleveland,
OH 441155
www.sabr.org

TELEPHONES
Antique Telephone Collectors' Association
P.O. Box 94, Abilene,
KS 67410-0094
Tel: 785 263 1757
www.atcaonline.com

Telephone Collectors International, Inc.
3207 Bend Drive, Algonquin,
IL 60102-9664
Tel: 847 658 7855
info@singingwires.org
www.singingwires.org

TINS
Tin Container Collectors' Association
PO Box 440101, Aurora,
CO 80044

TOYS AND GAMES
American Game Collectors Association
P.O. Box 44, Dresher, PA 19025
www.agca.com

The Antique Toy Collectors of America, Inc
c/o Carter, Ledyard & Milburn,
Two Wall St (13th Floor), New York,
NY 10005

Barbie Doll Collectors Club International
PO Box 245, Garnerville, NY 10923
Tel: 914 362 4657
info.bdcci@juno.com

National Model Railroad Association
4121 Cromwell Rd, Chattanooga,
TN 37421
Tel: 423 892 2846
nmra@tttrains.com

United Federation of Doll Clubs
10920 N. Ambassador Dr., Kansas
City, MO 64153
Tel: 816 891 7040
ufdc@aol.com

WATCHES
Early American Watch Club
PO Box 81555, Wellesley Hills,
MA 02481-1333

National Association of Watch and Clock Collectors
514 Poplar St, Columbia,
PA 17512-2130
Tel: 717 684 8261
www.nawacc.org

WORLD'S FAIRS
World's Fair Collectors Society, Inc.
PO Box 20806, Sarasta,
FL 34276-3806
Tel: 941 923 2590
http://members.aol.com/bbqprod/
wfcs.html

Internet resources

Over the past decade or so, the internet has revolutionized the buying and selling of collectibles. Many millions of items are offered for sale and traded daily, with sites varying from global online marketplaces, such as eBay, to specialist dealers' websites. Most collectibles are easily defined, described, and photographed. Shipping is also comparatively easy, as most items are relatively small and light. Prices are generally more affordable and accessible than for many antiques and the internet can provide a cost-effective way of buying and selling, avoiding the overheads of shops and auction rooms—particularly for collectibles valued at less than $100. Nevertheless, if you are selling, you should be aware that all of the administration, including describing, photographing, packing, and shipping the item, as well as dealing with payment, is your responsibility.

When searching online, remember that some sellers may not know how to describe their item accurately—if in doubt, always ask questions politely. General category searches, even though more time-consuming, can yield otherwise hidden results, as can deliberately misspelling a name—this can reveal interesting items that have been incorrectly described. If something looks too good to be true, it probably is. On eBay, always look at a seller's feedback rating—this shows how many items they have sold and how happy buyers are with their service. If a seller has negative ratings, take the time to read about the reasons why—a third party problem (such as a postal strike) may be to blame.

As you will understand from using this book, color photography is vital—look for online listings that include as many images as possible and check them carefully. Be aware that colors may not be reproduced accurately, and can vary even from one computer screen to another.

It is crucial to ask the vendor questions about the object, particularly regarding condition. If there is no image, or you want to see another aspect of it—ask. Most sellers (private or trade) will want to realize the best price for their items so will be happy to help if approached sensibly.

On top of the "e-hammer" price, you will have to pay additional fees such as packing, shipping, and possibly regional or national import or sales taxes. It is best to ask for an estimate of these transactional costs before bidding. This will also help you to tailor your bid, as you will have an idea of the maximum price the item will cost if you are successful.

Beyond well-known names such as eBay, the internet has a host of useful online auction resources for buying and selling, including sites which publish date listings for fairs and auctions.

AuctionBytes
www.auctionbytes.com
Auction resource with community forum, news, events, tips, and a weekly newsletter.

Auctiontalk
www.auctiontalk.com
Auction news, online and offline auction search engines, and live chat forums.

Collectors Online
www.collectorsonline.com
An online global aggregator for art, antiques, and collectibles dealers who showcase their stock online, allowing users to browse and buy.

eBay
www.ebay.com
The largest and most diverse of the online auction sites, allowing users to buy and sell in an online marketplace with over 62 million registered users. Collectors should also view eBay Live Auctions (www.ebayliveauctions.com) where traditional auctions are combined with real-time online bidding, allowing users to place real-time bids over the internet as the auction takes place.

La Gazette Drouot
www.drouot.com
The online home of the magazine listing all auctions to be held in France at the Hotel de Drouot in Paris and beyond. An online subscription enables you to download the magazine online.

GoAntiques
www.goantiques.com
An online global aggregator for art, antiques, and collectibles dealers who showcase their stock online, allowing users to browse and buy.

Invaluable
www.invaluable.com
A subscription service that allows users to search selected auction house catalogs from the United Kingdom and Europe. Also offers an extensive archive for appraisal uses.

Live Auctioneers
www.liveauctioneers.com
A free service that allows users to search catalogs from selected auction houses in the USA, Europe, and the United Kingdom. Through its connection with eBay, users can bid live via the Internet into salerooms as auctions happen. Registered users can also search through an archive of past catalogs and receive a free newsletter by email.

Maine Antiques Digest
www.maineantiquesdigest.com
The online version of this trade newspaper, including news, articles, fair and auction listings, and more.

Tias
www.tias.com
Showcase for art, antiques, and collectibles. Users can browse and buy online.

Specialist dealers

ADVERTISING
Phil & Karol Atkinson
May–Oct: 713 Sarsi Tr, Mercer,
PA 16137
Tel: 724 475 2490
Nov–Apr: 7188 Drewry's Bluff
Road, Bradenton, FL 34203
Tel: 941 755 1733

Toy Road Antiques
Canal, Winchester,
OH 43110
Tel: 614 834 1786
toyroad@aol.com

AMERICANA
Richard Axtell Antiques
1 River St, Deposit, NY 13754
Tel: 607 467 2353
Fax: 607 467 4316
raxtell@msn.com
www.axtellantiques.com

Buck County Antique Center
Route 202, Lahaksa, PA 18931
Tel: 215 794 9180

Burlwood Antique Center
149 Daniel Webster Highway,
Route 3, Meredith, NH 03253
Tel: 603 279 6387
Fax: 603 253 3866
www.burlwood-antiques.com

Olde Hope Antiques
P.O. Box 718, New Hope, PA 18938
Tel: 215 297 0200
info@oldehope.com
www.oldehope.com

AERONAUTICA AND SPACE
Peter DeNevai
20th C. Aviation Collectibles
HC63 Box 5, Duchesne,
UT 84021-9701
Pinyon99@yahoo.com

The Space Source
PO Box 604, Glenn Dale,
MD 20769
Tel: 301 871 6367
space@thespacesource.com
www.thespacesource.com

ANIMATION AND DISNEYANA
MuseumWorks
525 East Cooper Avenue, Aspen,
CO 81611
www.mwhgalleries.com

Wonderful World of Animation Art
51 E. 74th Street, Ste. 1R,
New York, NY 10022
Tel: 212 472 1720
debbiew@animationartgallery.com
www.animationartgallery.com

ART DECO
Deco Etc
122 West 25th Street, between 6th
& 7th Aves, New York, NY 10001
Tel: 212 675 3326
deco_etc@msn.com,
www.decoetc.net

AUTOGRAPHS
Autographs of America
P.O. Box 461, Provo,
UT 84603-0461

tanders3@autographsofamerica.com
www.autographsofamerica.com

Platt Autographs
PO Box 135007, Clermont,
FL 34711
Tel: 352 241 9164
ctplatt@ctplatt.com
www.ctplatt.com

AUTOMOBILIA
Dunbar's Gallery
54 Haven St. Milford,
MA 01757
Tel: 508 634 8697
Fax: 508 634 8697
dunbarsgallery@comcast.net
dunbarsgallery.com

BOOKS
Abebooks
www.abebooks.com

Aleph-Bet Books
85 Old Mill River Rd.,
Pound Ridge, NY 10576
Tel: 914 764 7410
Fax: 914 764 1356
helen@alephbet.com
www.alephbet.com

Bauman Rare Books
535 Madison Ave, between
54th & 55th Streets, New York,
NY 10022
Tel: 212 751 0011
brb@baumanrarebooks.com
www.baumanrarebooks.com

CANADIANA
The Blue Pump
178 Davenport Road,
Toronto M5R 1J2, Canada
Tel: 416 944 1673

Toronto Antiques Centre
276 King Street West,
Toronto, Ontario M5V 1J2,
Canada
Tel: 416 260 5662
yank@yank.ca
www.antiquesformen.com

CERAMICS
Blue and White Dinnerware
4800 Crestview Dr, Carmichael,
CA 95609
Tel: 916 961 7406
thefourls@aol.com

Charles & Barbara Adams
By appointment only,
289 Old Main St, South
Yarmouth, MA 02664
Tel: 508 760 3290
adams_2430@msn.com

Fayne Landes Antiques
593 Hansell Road, Wynnewood,
PA 19096
Tel: 610 658 0566

Greg Walsh
P.O. Box 747, Potsdam,
NY 13676-0747
Tel: 315 265 9111
gwalsh@northnet.org
www.walshauction.com

The Perrault-Rago Gallery
333 North Main Street,
Lambertville, NJ 08530
Tel: 609 397 1802
www.ragoarts.com

Keller & Ross
47 Prospect Street, Melrose,
MA 02176
Tel: 781 662 7257
kellerross@aol.com
http://members.aol.com/kellerross

Ken Forster
5501 Seminary Road,
Ste 1311, South Falls Church,
VA 22041
Tel: 703 379 1142

Mellin's Antiques
P.O. Box 1115, Redding,
CT 06875
Tel: 203 938 9538
remellin@aol.com

Mark & Marjorie Allen
300 Bedford St. Suite 421,
Manchester, NH 03101
Tel: 1-603-644-8989
Fax: 1 603 627 1472
mandmallen@adelphia.net
www.antiquedelft.com

CHARACTER COLLECTIBLES
What A Character!
hugh@whatacharacter.com
www.whatacharacter.com

COINS
Brad Shiff
Cybercoins, net, Inc. 1000
Greentree Road, Pittsburgh,
PA 15220
Tel: 412 937 1999
cybercoins@aol.com
www.cybercoins.net

COMICS
Carl Bonasera
A1-American Comic Shops,
3514 W. 95th St,
Evergreen Park, IL 60642
Tel: 708 425 7555

Metropolis Collectibles Inc.
873 Broadway, Suite 201,
New York, NY 10003
Tel: 212 260 4147
Fax: 212 260 4304
orders@metropoliscomics.com
www.metropoliscomics.com

The Comic Gallery
4224 Balboa Ave,
San Diego,
CA 92117
Tel: 619 483 4853

COOKIE JARS
Krazy Cat Collectibles
PO Box 1192,
Emmitsburg,
MD 21727
Tel: 301 271 9851
KrazyCatCo@aol.com
www.krazycatcollectibles.com

COSTUME AND ACCESSORIES
Andrea Hall Levy
P.O. Box 1243, Riverdale,
NY 10471
Tel: 646 441 1726
barangrill@aol.com

Colette Donovan
98 River Road, Merrimacport,
MA 01860
Tel: 978 346 0614

Fayne Landes Antiques
593 Hansell Road,
Wynnewood, PA 19096
Tel: 610 658 0566
fayne@comcast.net

Lucy's Hats
1118 Pine Street,
Philadelphia, PA,
USA

Neet-O-Rama
93 West Main Street,
Somerville, NJ 08876
Tel: 908 722 4600
www.neetstuff.com

Vintage Clothing Company
PO Box 20504, Keizer,
OR 97307-0504
retrothreads@aol.com

Vintage Eyeware of New York
Tel: 646 319 9222

Yesterday's Threads
206 Meadow St, Branford,
CT 06405-3634
Tel: 203 481 6452

COSTUME JEWELRY
Aurora Bijoux
aurora@aurorabijoux.com
www.aurorabijoux.com

Barbara Blau
c/o South Street Antiques Market
615 South 6th Street, Philadelphia,
PA 19147-2128 USA
Tel: 215 739 4995 / 592 0256
bbjools@msn.com

Baubles
South Street Antiques Center,
615 South 6th Street,
Philadelphia, PA 19147-2128
Tel: 215 487 0207

The Junkyard Jeweler
www.junkyardjeweler.com

Mod-Girl
South Street Antiques Center,
615 South 6th Street,
Philadelphia, PA 19147
Tel: 215 592 0256

Roxanne Stuart
gemfairy@aol.com

Terry Rodgers & Melody LLC
30 & 31 Manhattan Art & Antique
Center, 1050 2nd Avenue,
New York, NY 10022
Tel: 212 758 3164
melodyjewelnyc@aol.com

Bonny Yankauer
bonnyy@aol.com

DISNEYANA
MuseumWorks
525 East Cooper Avenue,
Aspen, CO 81611
Tel: 970 544 6113
Fax: 970 544 6044
www.mwhgalleries.com

Sign of the Tymes
Mill Antiques Center, 12 Morris
Farm Road, Lafayette,
NJ 07848
Tel: 973 383 6028
www.millantiques.com

DOLLS
Memory Lane
45-40 Bell Blvd, Suite 109,
Bayside, NY 11361
Tel: 718 428 8181
memlnny@aol.com
www.tias.com/stores/memlnny

Treasure & Dolls
518 Indian Rocks Rd,
N. Belleair Bluffs, FL 33770
Tel: 727 584 7277
dolls@treasuresanddolls.com
www.treasuresanddolls.com

EPHEMERA
De Wolfe and Wood
P.O. Box 425, 2 Waterboro Rd.
(Rt. 202) Alfred, Maine 04002
dewolfeandwood@adelphia.net
www.dwbooks.com

The Nostalgia Factory
Original Movie Posters & Related
Ephemera, Charlestown Commerce
Center, 50 Terminal St., Bldg. 2,
Boston, MA 02129
Tel: 617 241 8300
Fax: 617 241 0710
posters@nostalgia.com
www.nostalgia.com

FIFTIES, SIXTIES, AND SEVENTIES DESIGN
Lois' Collectibles
Market III, 413 W Main St,
Saint Charles, IL 60174-1815
Tel: 630 377 5599

Neet-O-Rama
93 West Main Street, Somerville,
NJ 08876
Tel: 908 722 4600
www.neetstuff.com

Off The Deep End
712 East St, Frederick,
MD 21701-5239
contact@offthedeepend.com
www.offthedeepend.com

General
Anastacia's Antiques
617 Bainbridge Street, Philadelphia,
PA 19147

Black Horse Antique Showcases
2180 North Reading Road, Denver
PA, 17517
Tel: 717 335 3300

Bucks County Antique Center
Route 202, Lahaska,
PA 18931
Tel: 215 794 9180

Burlwood Antique Center
Route 3, Meredith, NH 03523

Tel: 603 279 6387
www.burlwood-antiques.com

Manhattan Art & Antiques Center
1050 Second Avenue, between 55th
& 56th Street, New York, NY, 10022
Tel: 212 355 4400
Fax: 212 355 4403
www.the-maac.com

South Street Antiques Market
615 South 6th Street, Philadelphia,
PA 19147
Tel: 215 592 0256.

The Lafayette Mill Antiques
12 Morris Farm Road, Just off Rte
15, Lafayette NJ 07848
Tel: 973 383 0065
millpartners@inpro.net
www.millantiques.com

Toronto Antiques Centre
276 King Street West, Toronto,
Ontario M5V 1J2 Canada
Tel: 416 345 9941

GLASS
Block Glass Ltd.
Tel: 203 556 0905
blockglass@aol.com
www.blockglass.com

Glassfinders
32040 Mount Hermon Road,
Salisbury, MD 21804
Tel: 410 546 5881

Jeff E. Purtell
PO Box 28, Amherst,
NH 03031-0028
Tel: 603 673 4331
Fax: 603 673 1525

Paul Reichwein
2321 Hershey Ave,
East Petersburg,
PA 17520
Tel: 717 569 7637
paulrdg@aol.com

Paul Stamati Gallery
1050 2nd Ave, New York,
NY 10022
Tel: 212 754 4533
Fax: 212 754 4552
www.stamati.com

Suzman's Antiques
P.O. Box 301, Rehoboth,
MA 02769
Tel: 508 252 5729

**Walk Memory Lane
(Fenton Glass)**
jwalk@swetland.net,
www.walkmemorylane.com

HISTORICAL MEMORABILIA
Rowan S. Baker, USA Stamps
28 Bedfordbury, London,
WC2N 4RB, UK
Tel: +44 (0) 207 379 1448
Fax: +44 (0) 207 836 3100
rowanbaker@btopenworld.com
www.usa-stamps.com

HOLIDAY MEMORABILIA
Sign of the Tymes
Mill Antiques Center,
12 Morris Farm Road, Lafayette,
NJ 07848
Tel: 973 383 6028
jhap@nac.net
www.millantiques.com

HOUSEHOLD & KITCHENALIA
Dynamite Antiques & Collectibles
eb625@verizon.net

Jazz'e Junque
1648 W.Belmont Ave,
Chicago,ILL60657
Tel 773 4726450
cookiejarlayde@aol.com
www.jazzjunqe.com1648

Village Green Antiques
Port Antiques Center, 289 Main
Street, Port Washington, NY 11050
Tel: 516 625 2946
amysdish@optonline.net

MAGAZINES
Million Magazines
221 E. Sixth Street, #125 (rear),
Tucson, AZ 85705
Tel: 800 877 9887
www.millionmagazines.com

MARBLES
Auction Blocks
P.O. Box 2321,
Huntington Station,
CT 06484
Tel: 203 924 2802
auctionblocks@aol.com
www.auctionblocks.com

NATIVE AMERICAN
David Summers
Native American Artifacts
45 W. Parkway
Victor, NY 14564-1243
Tel: 716 924 5167
naasummers@aol.com

OCEAN LINER MEMORABILIA
ShipShape
1041 Tuscany Place, Winter Park,
FL 32789-1017
Tel: 407 644 2892
shipshape@shipshape.com
www.shipshape.com

PAPERWEIGHTS
Betty and Larry Schwab
The Paperweight Shoppe, 2507
Newport Drive, Bloomington,
IL 61704-4525
Tel: 309 662 1956

PENS AND WRITING
Gary & Myrna Lehrer
16 Mulberry Rd, Woodbridge,
CT 06525-1717
Tel: 203 389 5295
Fax: 203 389 4515
www.gopens.com

David Nishimura
Vintage Pens, P.O. Box 41452
Providence, RI 02940-1452
Tel: 401 351 7607
www.vintagepens.com

PEZ
Gary Doss
Burlingame Museum of PEZ
Memorabilia
214 California Drive,
Burlingame, CA 94010
Tel: 650 347 2301
www.burlingamepezmuseum.com

PHILATELY
Henry Gitner Philatelists, Inc.
2–20 Low Ave., Ste. 311,
P.O. Box 3077, Middletown,

NY 10940
Tel: 800 947 8267
hgitner@hgitner.com
www.hgitner.com

Carlton King
L & C Stamps, PO Box 421,
Sedalia, MO 65302-0421
Tel: 660 826 0897
lncking@iland.net
www.landcstamps.com

PLASTICS
Dee Battle
9 Orange Blossom Trail,
Yalaha, FL 34797
Tel: 352 324 3023

Malabar Enterprises
172 Bush Lane, Ithaca,
NY 14850
Tel: 607 255 2905
Fax: 607 255 4179

POSTERS
Poster America
138 West 18th St,
New York,
NY 10011-5403
Tel: 212 206 0499
Fax: 212 727 2495
pfair@dti.net
www.posterfair.com

Vintage Poster Works
Debra Clifford-Angela Amato
P.O. Box 88, Pittsford,
NY 14534
Tel: 585 381 9355
www.vintageposterworks.com

QUILTS
**Marie Miller
Antique Quilts**
Route 30, PO Box 968,
Dorset, VT 05251
Tel: 802 867 5969
www.antiquequilts.com

**The Antique
Quilt Source**
385 Springview Road, Carlisle,
PA 17013-0372
Tel: 717 245 2054
www.antiquequiltsource.com

RADIOS
Catalin Radios
Tel: 419 824 2469
Mob: 419 283 8203
steve@catalinradio.com
www.catalinradio.com

ROCK & POP
Heinz's Rare Collectibles
P.O. Box 179, Little Silver,
NJ 07739-0179
Tel: 732 219 1988
Fax: 732 219 5940

Tod Hutchinson
P.O. Box 915, Griffith,
IN 46319-0915
Tel: 219 923 8334
toddtcb@aol.com

SCENT BOTTLES
Oldies But Goldies
860 NW Sorrento Ln.
Port St. Lucie,
FL 34986
Tel. 772 873 0968
email@oldgood.com
www.oldgood.com

Monsen & Baer Inc
P.O. Box 529, Vienna,
VA 22183-0529
Tel: 703 938 2129
monsenbaer@erols.com

SEWING
Can-Sew
3 Davick Drive, Toronto,
Ontario M8W 2C8, Canada
Tel: 416 253 5165
canseweadmin@sew2go.com
www.sew2go.com

**SCIENTIFIC AND
TECHNICAL**
George Glazer Gallery
28 East 2nd St, New York,
NY 10021
Tel: 212 535 5706
Fax 212 658 9512
worldglobe@georgeglazer.com
www.georgeglazer.com

The Olde Office
68-845 Perez Rd, Ste 30,
Cathedral City, CA 92234
Tel: 760 346 8653
Fax: 760 346 6479
info@thisoldeoffice.com
www.thisoldeoffice.com

Jane Hertz
Fax: 941 925-0487
auction@breker.com
www.breker.com

SMOKING
Richard Weinstein
International Vintage Lighter
Exchange, 30 W. 57th St,
New York, NY 10019
vinlighter@aol.com
www.vintagelighters.com

SPORTING MEMORABILIA
Classic Rods & Tackle
P.O. Box 288, Ashley Falls, MA 01222
Tel: 413 229 7988

Larry Fritsch Cards Inc
735 Old Wassau Rd, P.O. Box 863,
Stevens Point, WI 54481
Tel: 715 344 8687
Fax: 715 344 1778
larry@fritschcards.com
www.fritschcards.com

George Lewis
Golfiana, P.O. Box 291,
Mamaroneck, NY 10543
Tel: 914 698 4579
findit@golfiana.com
www.golfiana.com

Golf Collectibles
P.O. Box 165892, Irving, TX 75016
Tel: 800 882 4825
www.golfforallages.com

The Hager Group
P.O. Box 952974, Lake Mary, FL 32795
Tel: 407 788 3865

Tom & Jill Kaczor
1550 Franklin Rd, Langhorne,
PA 19047
Tel: 215 968 5776
Fax: 215 946 6056

Vintage Sports Collector
3920 Via Solano,
Palos Verdes Estates,
CA 90274
Tel: 310 375 1723

TEDDY BEARS & SOFT TOYS
Harper General Store
10482 Jonestown Rd, Annville,
PA 17003
Tel: 717 865 3456
Fax: 717 865 3813

lauver5@comcast.net
www.harpergeneralstore.com

Marion Weis
Division St Antiques,
P.O. Box 374,
Buffalo, MN 55313-0374
Tel: 612 682 6453

TELEPHONES
AndHow! Antique Telephones
www.andhowantiques.com

TOYS & GAMES
Atomic Age
318 East Virginia Road,
Fullerton, CA 92831
Tel: 714 446 0736
Fax: 714 446 0436

Litwin Antiques
PO Box 5865, Trenton,
NJ 08638-0865
Tel/Fax: 609 275 1427

Memory Lane
18 Rose Lane, Flourtown,
PA 19031-1910
Tel: 215 233 4094
toyspost@aol.com

Milezone's Toys
4025 South Franklin St,
Michigan City, IN 46360
Tel: 219 874 6629
sales@milezone.com,
www.milezone.com

Neet-O-Rama
93 West Main Street,
Somerville, NJ 08876
Tel: 908 722 4600
www.neetstuff.com

TV AND MOVIE
STARticles
58 Stewart St, Studio 301, Toronto,

Ontario, M5V 1H6 Canada
Tel/Fax: 416 504 8286
info@starticles.com

Norma's Jeans
3511 Turner Lane, Chevy Chase,
MD 20815-2313
Tel: 301 652 4644
Fax: 301 907 0216

George Baker
CollectorsMart, P.O. Box 580466,
Modesto, CA 95358
Tel; 290 537 5221
Fax: 209 531 0233
georgeb1@thevision.net
www.collectorsmart.com

WATCHES
Early American Watch Club
P.O. Box 81555, Wellesley Hills,
MA 02481-1333

**National Association of Watch &
Clock Collectors**
514 Poplar St, Columbia,
PA 17512-2130
Tel: 717 684 8261
www.nawcc.org

Mark Laino
c/o South Street Antiques Market,
615 South 6th Street,
Philadelphia, PA 19147-2128

WRITTEN WORD
Mori Books
141 Route 101A, Amherst,
NH 03031
Tel: 603 882 2665
richard@moribooks.com
www.moribooks.com

Specialist auction houses

ALABAMA
Flomaton Antique Auctions
P.O. Box 1017, 320 Palafox Street,
Flomaton, AL 36441
Tel: 251 296 3059, Fax: 251 296 1974
www.flomatonantiqueauction.com

ARIZONA
Dan May & Associates
4110 N. Scottsdale Road, Scottsdale,
AZ 85251
Tel: 602 941 4200

ARKANSAS
Ponders Auctions
1504 South Leslie, Stuttgart, AR 72160
Tel: 501 673 6551

CALIFORNIA
Aurora Galleries International
30 Hackamore Lane, Ste 2,
Bell Canyon, CA 91307
Tel: 818 884 6468, Fax: 818 227 2941
www.auroragalleriesonline.com

Butterfield & Butterfield
7601 Sunset Blvd, Los Angeles, CA 90046
Tel: 323 850 7500, Fax: 323 850 5843
info@butterfields.com
www.butterfields.com

Butterfield & Butterfield
220 San Bruno Ave, San Francisco,
CA 94103
Tel: 415 861 7500
Fax: 415 861 8951
info@butterfields.com
www.butterfields.com

L.H. Selman
123 Locust St, Santa Cruz,
CA 95060
Tel: 800 538 0766
Fax: 408 427 0111
leselman@got.net

Malter Galleries
17003 Ventura Blvd, Encino,
CA 91316
Tel: 818 784 7772
Fax: 818 784 4726
www.maltergalleries.com

Poster Connection Inc.
43 Regency Dr, Clayton,
CA 94517
Tel: 925 673 3343
Fax: 925 673 3355
sales@posterconnection.com
www.posterconnec tion.com

Profiles in History
110 North Doheny Dr, Beverly Hills,
CA 90211
Tel: 310 859 7701
Fax: 310 859 3842
www.profilesinhistory.com

San Rafael Auction Gallery
634 Fifth Avenue,
San Rafael, CA 9490
Tel: 415 457 4488
Fax: 415 457 4899
www.sanrafael-auction.com

Slawinski Auction Co.
The Scotts Valley Sports Center,
251 Kings Village Road,
Scotts Valley,
CA 95066
Tel: 831 335 9000
www.slawinski.com

CONNECTICUT
Alexander Autographs
100 Melrose Ave,
Greenwich, CT 06830
Tel: 203 622 8444
Fax: 203 622 8765
info@alexautographs.com
www.alexautographs.com

Norman C. Heckler & Co.
79 Bradford Corner Road,
Woodstock Valley, CT 0682
Tel: 860 974 1634
Fax: 860 974 2003
www.hecklerauction.com

Lloyd Ralston Gallery
350 Long Beach Blvd, Stratford,
CT 016615
Tel: 203 386 9399
Fax: 203 386 9519
lrgallery@sbcglobal.net
www.lloydralstontoys.com

DELAWARE
Remember When Auctions Inc.
Tel: 302 436 4979
Fax: 302 436 4626
sales@history-attic.com
www.history-attic.com

FLORIDA
Auctions Neapolitan
995 Central Avenue,
Naples,
FL 34102
Tel: 941 262 7333
www.auctionsneapolitan.com

Burchard Galleries
2528 30th Ave N, St Petersburg,
FL 33713
Tel: 727 821 1167
www.burchardgalleries.com

Dawson's
P.O. Box 646, Palm Beach, FL 33480
Tel: 561 835 6930
Fax: 561 835 8464
info@dawsons.org
www.dawsons.org

Kincaid Auction Company
3809 East CR 542, Lakeland, FL 33801
Tel: 800 970 1977
www.kincaid.com

Sloan's Auction Galleries
8861 NW 19th Terace, Ste 100,
Miami, FL 33172
Tel: 305 751 4770
sloans@sloansauction.com
www.sloansandkenyon.com

GEORGIA
Great Gatsby's
5070 Peachtree Industrial Blvd, Atlanta, GA
Tel: 770 457 1903
Fax: 770 457 7250
www.gatsbys.com

My Hart Auctions Inc
P.O. Box 2511, Cumming, GA 30028
Tel: 770 888 9006
www.myhart.net

IDAHO
**The Coeur D'Alene
Art Auction**
P.O. Box 310, Hayden, ID 83835
Tel: 208 772 9009
Fax: 208 772 8294
cdaartauction@cdaartauction.com
www.cdaartauction.com

ILLINOIS
Leslie Hindman Inc.
122 North Aberdeen Street,
Chicago, IL 60607
Tel: 312 280 1212,
Fax: 312 280 1211
www.lesliehindman.com

Joy Luke
300 East Grove Street, Bloomington,
IL 61701
Tel: 309 828 5533
Fax: 309 829 2266
www.joyluke.com

Mastronet Inc
10S 660 Kingery Highway, Willobrook,
IL 60527
Tel: 630 471 1200
info@mastronet.com
www.mastronet.com

INDIANA
**Curran Miller Auction &
Realty Inc.**
4424 Vogel Rd, Ste 400, Evansville,
IN 47715
Tel: 812 474 6100, Fax: 812 474 6110
www.curranmiller.com

Kruse International
5540 County Rd 11A, Auburn, IN 46706
Tel: 800 968 4444
info@kruseinternational.com
www.kruseinternational.com

Lawson Auction Service
P.O. Box 885, North Vernon, IN 47265
Tel: 812 372 2571
www.lawsonauction.com

Stout Auctions
529 State Road 28 East,
Willamsport, IN 47993
Tel: 765 764 6901
Fax: 765 764 1516
info@stoutauctions.com
www.stoutauctions.com

IOWA
Jackson's Auctioneers & Appraisers
2229 Lincoln St, Cedar Falls, IA 50613
Tel: 319 277 2256
Fax: 319 2771252
www.jacksonsauction.com

Tom Harris auctions
2035 18th Ave, Marshalltown, IA 50158
Tel: 641 754 4890
Fax: 641 753 0226
www.tomharrisauctions.com

Tubaugh Auctions
1702 8th Ave, Belle Plaine, IA 52208
Tel: 319 444 2413 / 319 444 0169
www.tubaughauctions.com

KANSAS
Manions International Auction House
P.O. Box 12214, Kansas City, KS, 66112
Tel: 913 299 6692
Fax: 913 299 6792
www.manions.com

CC Auctions
416 Court St, Clay Center, KS 67432
Tel: 785 632 6021
www.cc-auctions.com

Brian Spielman Auctions
PO Box 884, Emporia, KS 66801
Tel: 620 341 0637 or 620 437 2424
www.kansasauctions.net/spielman

KENTUCKY
Hays & Associates Inc
120 South Spring Street, Louisville,
KY 40206
Tel: 502 584 4297
www.haysauction.com

Steffens Historical Militaria
P.O. Box 280, Newport, KY 41072
Tel: 859 431 4499
Fax: 859 431 3113
www.steffensmilitaria.com

LOUSIANA
**Morton M. Goldberg Auction
Galleries**
547 Baronne Street
New Orleans, LA 70113
Tel: 504 592 2300
Fax: 504 592 2311

New Orleans Auction Galleries
801 Magazine Street, New Orleans,
LA 70130
Tel: 504 566 1849
Fax: 504 566 1851
info@neworleansauction.com
www.neworleansauction.com

MAINE
**James D. Julia
Auctioneers Inc.**
P.O. Box 830, Fairfield, Maine 04937
Tel: 207 453 7125
www.juliaauctions.com

**Thomaston Place
Auction Galleries**
P.O. Box 300, 51 Atlantic Highway,
US Rt 1 Thomaston ME 04861
Tel: 207 354 8141
Fax: 207 354 9523
www.thomastonauction.com

MARYLAND
Guyette & Schmidt
PO Box 1170, St. Michaels,
MD 21663
Tel: 410 745 0485
Fax: 410 745 0457
www.guyetteandschmidt.com

**Hantman's Auctioneers
& Appraisers**
P.O. Box 59366, Potomac,
MD 20859
Tel: 301 770 3720
Fax: 301 770 4135
hantman@hantmans.com
www.hantmans.com

**Isennock Auctions
& Appraisals**
4106B Norrisville Road,
White Hall, MD 21161
Tel: 410 557 8052
Fax 410 692 6449
isennock@isennockauction.com
www.isennockauction.com

MASSACHUSETTS
Eldred's
P.O. Box 796, 1483 Route 6A
East Dennis,
MA 02641
Tel: 508 385 3116
Fax: 508 385 7201
info@eldreds.com
www.eldreds.com

Groz gan & Company
22 Harris St, Dedham,
MA 02026
Tel: 800 823 1020
Fax: 781 461 9625
grogans@groganco.com
www.groganco.com

**Simon D. Hill &
Associates**
420 Boston Turnpike,
Shrewsbury, MA 01545
Tel: 508 845 2400
Fax: 978 928 4129
www.simondhillauctions.com

Skinner Inc
The Heritage on the Garden,
63 Park Plaza, Boston, MA 02116
Tel: 617 350 5400
Fax: 617 350 5429
and 357 Main Street, Bolton,
MA 01740
Tel: 978 779 6241
Fax: 978 779 5144
info@skinnerinc.com
www.skinnerinc.com

Willis Henry Auctions
22 Main St, Marshfield,
MA 02050
Tel: 781 834 7774
Fax: 781 826 3520
www.willishenry.com

MICHIGAN
DuMouchelles
409 East Jefferson Ave,
Detroit, MI 48226
Tel: 313 963 6255
Fax: 313 963 8199
info@dumouchelles.com
www.dumouchelles.com

MINNESOTA
Buffalo Bay Auction Co
825 Fox Run Trail, Edmond,
OK 73034

Tel: 405 285 8990
buffalobayauction@hotmail.com
www.buffalobayauction.com

Rose Auction Galleries
3180 Country Drive, Little Canada,
MN 55117
Tel: 651 484 1415 / 888-484-1415
Fax: 651 636 3431
auctions@rosegalleries.com
www.rosegalleries.com

MISSOURI
Ivey-Selkirk
7447 Forsyth Blvd, Saint Louis,
MO 63105
Tel: 314 726 5515,
Fax: 314 726 9908
www.iveyselkirk.com

MONTANA
Allard Auctions Inc
P.O. Box 1030 St Ignatius,
MT 59865
Tel: 406 745 0500
Fax: 406 745 0502
www.allardauctions.com

Cope Sports Collectibles
2504 Suite D, West Main,
Bozeman, MT 59718
Tel: 406 587 1793,
Fax: 406 586 3460
cope@copesportscollectibles.com
www.copesportscollectibles.com

NEW HAMPSHIRE
Northeast Auctions
93 Pleasant St, Portsmouth,
NH 03801-4504
Tel: 603 433 8400,
Fax: 603 433 0415
contact@northeastauctions.com
www.northeastauctions.com

NEW JERSEY
333 Auctions
333 North Main Street, Lambertville,
NJ 08530
Tel: 609 397 9374
Fax: 609 397 9377

Bertoia Auctions
2141 Demarco Dr, Vineland, NJ 08360
Tel: 856 692 1881
Fax: 856 692 8697
www.bertoiaauctions.com

Craftsman Auctions
333 North Main St, Lambertville, NJ 08530
Tel: 609 397 9374
Fax: 609 397 9377
info@ragoarts.com
www.ragoarts.com

Dawson & Nye
128 American Road, Morris Plains,
NJ 07950
Tel: 973 984 6900, Fax: 973 984 6956
info@dawsonandnye.com
www.dawsonandnye.com

Greg Manning Auctions Inc
775 Passaic Ave,
West Caldwell, NJ 07006
Tel: 973 883 0004
Fax: 973 882 3499
info@gregmanning.com
www.gregmanning.com

Rago Modern Auctions LLP
333 North Main St, Lambertville, NJ 08530
Tel: 609 397 9374, Fax: 609 397 9377
info@ragoarts.com
www.ragoarts.com

NEW MEXICO

Manitou Gallery
123 West Palace Ave., Santa Fe,
NM 87501
Tel: 800 986 0440
info@manitougalleries.com
www.manitougalleries.com

Parker-Braden Auctions
P.O. Box 1897, 4303 National Parks
Highway, Carlsbad, NM 88220
Tel: 505 885 4874
Fax: 505 885 4622
www.parkerbraden.com

NEW YORK

TW Conroy
36 Oswego St, Baldwinsville,
NY 13027
Tel: 315 638 6434
Fax: 315 638 7039
info@twconroy.com
www.twconroy.com

Samuel Cottone Auctions
15 Genesee St, Mount Morris,
NY 14510
Tel: 585 658 3119
Fax: 585 658 3152
www.cottoneauctions.com

William Doyle Galleries
175 E. 87th St, New York,
NY 10128
Tel: 212 427 2730
Fax: 212 369 0892
info@doylenewyork.com
www.doylenewyork.com

Guernsey's Auctions
108 East 73rd St, New York, NY 10021
Tel: 212 794 2280
Fax: 212 744 3638
auctions@guernseys.com
www.guernseys.com

Phillips, De Pury & Luxembourg
450 West 15 Street, New York NY 10011
Tel: 212 940 1200
Fax: 212 924 3306
info@phillipsdepury.com
www.phillips-dpl.com

Swann Galleries Inc
104 E. 25th St, New York, NY 10010
Tel: 212 254 4710
Fax: 212 979 1017
swann@swanngalleries.com
www.swanngalleries.com

NORTH CAROLINA

Robert S. Brunk
P.O. Box 2135, Asheville,
NC 28802
Tel: 828 254 6846
Fax: 828 254 6545
auction@brunkauctions.com
www.brunkauctions.com

Historical Collectible Auctions
24 NW Court, SquareSuite 201,
Graham, NC 27253
Tel: 336 570 2803
Fax: 336 570 2748
auctions@hcaauctions.com
www.hcaauctions.com

NORTH DAKOTA

Curt D Johnson Auction Company
4216 Gateway Dr., Grand Forks,
ND 58203
Tel: 701 746 1378
figleo@hotmail.com
www.curtdjohnson.com

OHIO

The Cincinnatti Art Galleries
225 East Sixth St, Cincinnati,
OH 45202
Tel: 513 381 2128,
Fax: 513 381 7527
info@cincinnatiartgalleries.com
www.cincinnatiartgalleries.com

Cowans Historic Americana
673 Wilmer Avenue, Cincinnati, OH 45226
Tel: 513 871 1670
Fax: 513 871 8670
www.historicamericana.com

DeFina Auctions
1591 State Route 45 Sth, Austinburg,
OH 44010
Tel: 440 275 6674
Fax: 440 275 2028
info@definaauctions.com
www.definaauctions.com

Garth's Auctions
2690 Stratford Rd, Box 369, Delaware,
OH 43015
Tel: 740 362 4771
Fax: 740 363 0164
info@garths.com
www.garths.com

PENNSYLVANIA

Alderfer Auction Gallery
501 Fairgrounds Rd, Hatfield, PA 19440
Tel: 215 393 3000
Fax: 215 368-9055
info@alderferauction.com
www.alderferauction.com

Noel Barrett
P.O. Box 300, Carversville, PA 18913
Tel: 215 297 5109
www.noelbarrett.com

Dargate Auction Galleries
214 North Lexington, Pittsburgh, PA 15208
Tel: 412 362 3558
info@dargate.com
www.dargate.com

Freeman's
1808 Chestnut Ave, Philadelphia, PA 19103
Tel: 610 563 9275
info@freemansauction.com
www.freemansauction.com

Hunt Auctions
75 E. Uwchlan Ave, Ste 1, 30 Exton,
PA 19341
Tel: 610 524 0822
Fax: 610 524 0826
info@huntauctions.com
www.huntauctions.com

Morphy Auctions
2000 North Reading St, Denver PA
Tel: 717 335 3435
Fax: 717 336 7115
morphy@morphyauctions.com
www.morphyauctions.com

Pook & Pook Inc
463 East Lancaster Ave, Downington,
PA 19335
Tel: 610 269 4040
Fax: 610 269 9274
info@pookandpook.com
www.pookandpook.com

Skinner's Auction Co.
170 Northampton St,
Easton, PA 18042
Tel: 610 330 6933
skinnauct@aol.com
www.skinnersauction.com

Stephenson's Auctions
1005 Industrial Blvd, Southampton,
PA 18966
Tel: 215 322 618
Fax: 215 364 0883
info@stephensonsauction.com
www.stephensonsauction.com

RHODE ISLAND

WebWilson
P.O. Box 506, Portsmouth,
RI 02871
Tel: 800 508 0022
www@webwilson.com
www.webwilson.com

SOUTH CAROLINA

Charlton Hall Galleries Inc.
912 Gervais St Columbia,
SC 29201
Tel: 803 799 5678
Fax: 803 733 1701
www.charltonhallauctions.com

TENNESSEE

**Berenice Denton Estate Sales
and Appraisals**
2209 Bandywood Drive, Suite C
Nashville, TN 37215
Tel: 615 292 5765
info@berenicedenton.com
www.berenicedenton.com

Kimball M. Sterling Inc
125 W. Market St, Johnson City,
TN 37604
Tel: 423 928 1471
www.sterlingsold.com

TEXAS

Austin Auctions
8414 Anderson Mill Rd,
Austin, TX 78729-4702
Tel: 512 258 5479
Fax: 512 219 7372
www.austinauction.com

Dallas Auction Gallery
1518 Socum St, Dallas,
TX 75207
Tel: 213 653 3900
Fax: 213 653 3912
info@dallasauctiongallery.com
www.dallasauctiongallery.com

Heritage Galleries
3500 Maple Avenue
Dallas, Texas 75219
Tel: 214 528 3500
www.heritagegalleries.com

UTAH

America West Archives
P.O. Box 100, Cedar City, UT 84721
Tel: 435 586 9497
Fax: 435 586 9497
info@americawestarchives.com
www.americawestarchives.com

VERMONT

Eaton Auction Service
Chuck Eaton, 3428 Middlebrook Road,
Fairlee, VT 05045
Tel: 802 333 9717
eas@sover.net
www.eatonauctionservice.com

VIRGINIA

Ken Farmer Auctions & Estates
105A Harrison St, Radford, VA 24141
Tel: 540 639 0939
Fax: 540 639 1759
info@kfauctions.com
www.kfauctions.com

Phoebus Auction Gallery
14-16 E. Mellen St, Hampton, VA 23663
Tel: 757 722 9210
Fax: 757 723 2280
www.phoebusauction.com

Signature House
407 Liberty Ave, Bridgeport, WV 25330
Tel: 304 842 3386
Fax: 304 842 3001
www.signaturehouse.net

WASHINGTON DC

Weschlers
909 E St, NW Washington, DC 20004
Tel: 202 628 1281
Fax: 202 628 2366
fineart@weschlers.com
www.weschlers.com

WISCONSIN

Krueger Auctions
P.O. Box 275, Iola, WI 54945-0275
Tel: 715 445 3845

Schrager Auction Galleries
2915 North Sherman Blvd,
P.O. Box 100043, Milwaukee, WI 53210
Tel: 414 873 3738
Fax: 414 873 5229
www.schragerauction.com

WYOMING

Cody Old West Show & Auction
P.O. Box 2038, 37555 Hum Rd, Ste 101,
Carefree, AZ 85377
Tel: 307 587 9014
www.codyoldwest.com

CANADA

**Maynards Fine Art & Antique
Auction House**
415 W 2nd Ave., Vacouver
V5Y 1E3, Canada
Tel: 604 876 6787
www.maynards.com

Pinneys Auctions Les Encans
2435 Duncan Road, Montreal
H4P 2A2, Canada
Tel: 514 345 0571
Fax: 514 731 4081
pinneys@ca.inter.net
www.pinneys.ca

Ritchies
288 King Street East, Toronto, Ontario
M5A 1K4, Canada
Tel: 416 364 1864
www.ritchies.com

**Waddington's
Auctioneers & Appraisers**
111 Bathurst St., Toronto, Ontario
M5V 2R1, Canada
Tel: 416 504 9100
www.waddingtons.ca

Specialist auction houses

Index

Acknowledgments

The following images, photographed with permission from the sources itemized below, are copyright © Judith Miller and Dorling Kindersley. Abbreviations: t=top, b=bottom, r=right, l=left, c=center, R=row (eg, R3r=third row right).

10th Planet Limited, Unit 36 Vicarage Field Shopping Centre, Ripple Road, Barking, IG11 8DQ, UK. Tel: +44 (0)20 8591 5357. www.10thplanet.co.uk. 234bl. **Beth Adams,** Unit G043/044, Alfies Antique Market, 13–25 Church Street, London NW8 8DT, UK. Tel: +44 (0)20 7723 5613. 46bl, 108bl, 109tr. **All Our Yesterdays,** 6 Park Road, Kelvinbridge, Glasgow G4 9JG, Scotland. Tel: +44 (0)141 3347788. antiques@allouryesterdays.fsnet.co.uk. 40bl, 46cl, 47R2r, 222br, 222bc, 278br, 278bl, 279bl, 279cl. **Allard Auctions,** P.O. Box 1030, 419 Flathead St. 4, St. Ignatius, MT 59865. Tel: 460 745 0500. Fax: 406 745 0502. – 76tr, 76br, 76bc, 76bl, 77c, 77bc, 77bl. **American Jazz,** Box 302, Ossining, NY 10562. Tel: 917 217 6349. amjazz@optonline.net. 197cr. **Andrew Lineham Fine Glass,** The Mall, Camden Passage, London N1 8ED, UK. Tel: +44 (0)20 7704 0195 or 07767 702 722. www.andrewlineham.co.uk. 46br. **Animation Art Gallery,** 13–14 Great Castle Street, London W1W 8LS, UK. Tel: –Tel: +44 (0)20 7255 1456. www.animaart.com. 242tl, 243tr, 243cr, 243br, 243bl. **Anona Gabriel,** 26–28 High Street, Otford, Sevenoaks, Kent TN14 5PQ, UK. Tel: +44 (0)1959 522 025. Fax: +44 (0)1959 525 858. info@otfordantiques.co.uk. 55br. **Antique Textiles and Lighting,** 34 Belvedere, Lansdowne Road, Bath, Avon BA1 5HR, UK. Tel: +44 (0)1225 310 795. joannaproops@aol.co.uk. 165tl. **Bill & Myrtle Aquilino,** P.O. Box 9, Chalfont, PA 18914. Tel: 215 822 6867. 75bc, 75t 'Souvenir Pins.' **Art Deco Etc,** 73 Upper Gloucester Road, Brighton, East Sussex BN1 3NQ, UK. Tel: +44 (0)1273 329 268. johnclarke@artdecoetc.co.uk. 39tc. **Arthur Ivan Spike,** c/o South Street Antiques Center, 615 South 6th Street, Philadelphia, PA 19147–2128. Tel: 215 592 0256. 75t 'Maps.' **At the Movies,** 17 Fouberts Place, Carnaby Street, London W1F 7QD, UK. Tel: +44 (0)20 7439 6336. www.atthemovies.co.uk. 236tr, 236br, 236bl, 237bl. **Phil & Karol Atkinson,** May–Oct: 713 Sarsi Tr, Mercer, PA 16137; Nov–Apr: 7188 Drewry's Bluff Road, Bradenton, FL 34203. Tel: May–Oct: 724 475 2490; Nov–Apr: 941 755 1733. 92bl, 92br, 93bl. **Atomic Age,** 318 E. Virginia Road, Fullerton, CA 92831. Tel: 714 446 0736. atomage100@aol.com. 216cr, 217tc, 288tr, 288br, 288bc, 289br, 289bl, 290bl, 290tr, 291tl, 291R2l, 291br. **Auction Blocks,** P.O. Box 2321, Huntington Station, CT 06484. Tel: 203 924 2802. www.auctionblocks.com. 198tr, 198cr, 198br, 198bl, 198cl, 199tr, 199R2r, 199br, 199bl, 199cl, 199tl. **Auction Team Köln,** Postfach 50 1119, Bonner Str. 528–530, D–50971 Köln, Germany. Tel: +49 (0)221 38 70 49. www.breker.com. 103cr, 107br, 241tc 'Money Banks,' 253bl, 283bl(&bc), 304tr, 304cr, 304br, 304bl, 304cl, 305bl. **333 Auctions LLC,** 333 North Main Street, Lambertville, NJ 08530. Tel: 609 397 9374. Fax: 609 397 9377. www.333auctions.com. 31br. **Auktionshaus W.G. Herr,** Friesenwall 35, D–50672, Köln, Germany. Tel: +49 (0)221 25 45 48. www.herr-auktionen.de. 140bl, 140bc, 140br, 141bc, 141br, 143tl. **Aurora Galleries International,** 30 Hackamore Lane, Suite 2, Bell Canyon, CA 91307. Tel: 818 884 6468. www.auroragalleriesonline.com. 310cl, 314tr, 314bl, 314bcl, 314bcr, 314br, 315cr, 315br, 315bc, 315bl, 315cl. **Axtell Antiques,** 1 River Street, Deposit, NY 13754. Tel: 607 467 2353. Fax: 607 467 4316. www.axtellantiques.com. 102tr. **Colin Baddiel,** Stand B25, Stand 351–3, Grays Antique Market, South Molten Lane, London W1Y 2LP, UK. Tel: +44 (0)20 7408 1239. 190bl. **Baubles,** South Street Antiques Center, 615 South 6th Street, Philadelphia, PA 19147. Tel: 215 592 0256/215 487 0207. 170tr, 170cr. **Bauman Rare Books,** 4535 Madison Avenue, between 54th & 55th Streets, New York, NY 100022. Tel: 212 751 0011. www.baumanrarebooks.com. 268tr, 268br, 268bc, 269cr, 269br, 269bc, 269bl, 270cl, 270bc(&br), 271cr, 271br, 271bc, 271bl. **Bébés & Jouets,** c/o Post Office, 165 RestalrisRoad, Edinburgh EH7 6HW, Scotland. Tel: +44 (0)131 332 5650. bebesetjouets@u.genie.co.uk. 201br, 203tr, 204bcr, 209l. **Linda Bee,** Grays in The Mews, Antiques Market, 1–7 Davies Mews, London W1K 5AB, UK. Tel/Fax: +44 (0)20 7629 5921 or Tel: 07956 276 384. 120br, 121tr, 121R2r, 121br, 121bl, 121tl. **Belhorn Auction Services,** P.O. Box 20211, Columbus, OH 43220. Tel: 614 921 9441. Fax: 614 921 9447. www.belhorn.com. 24br, 30tr, 30br, 30bl, 31bl, 31tl, 31cr, 258c. **Below Stairs of Hungerford,** 103 High Street, Hungerford, Berkshire RG17 0NB, UK. Tel: +44 (0)1488 682 317. www.belowstairs.co.uk. 82bl, 83bl, 102br, 103bl. **Bertoia Auctions,** 2141 Demarco Drive, Vineland NJ 08360. Tel: 856 692 1881. Fax: 856 692 8697. www.bertoiaauctions.com. 194bc, 194bl, 195br. **Beverley,** 30 Church Street, London NW8 8EP, UK. Tel: +44 (0)20 7262 1576. 24bl, 25bl, 26cr, 26bcl, 27R3l, 27tl, 27bl, 27R2r, 39tl, 40tc, 41br, 41bl, 109R3r. **Beyond Retro,** 110–112 Cheshire Street, London E2 6EJ, UK. Tel: +44 (0)20 7613 3636. www.beyondretro.com. 154cl. **Biblion,** 1–7 Davies Mews, London W1K 5AB, UK. Tel: +44 (0)20 7629 1374. www.biblion.com. 270tr. **Black Horse Antique Showcases,** 2222 North Reading Road, Denver, PA 17517. Tel: 717 335 3300. Fax: 717 336 1110. info@antiques-showcase.com. 100br, 263br, 311tc, 311br. **Block Glass Ltd.** www.blockglass.com. 130tr, 130bl, 131tl, 131R2r, 131bl, 139cr. **Bloomsbury Auctions,** Bloomsbury House, 24 Maddox Street, London W1 S1PP, UK. Tel: +44 (0)20 7495 9494. Fax: +44 (0)20 7495 9499. www.bloomsburyauctions.com. 72tr, 73cr, 268bl. **The Blue Pump,** 178 Davenport Road, Toronto, Canada, M5R 1J2. Tel: 001 416 944 1673. 83br, 85tr, 85cr. **Bonhams,** 101 New Bond Street, London W1S 1SR, UK. Tel: +44 (0)20 7629 6602. www.bonhams.com. 20tr, 43cr, 44br, 50tr, 125tr, 125bc, 324bl. **Bonhams Edinburgh,** 65 George Street, Edinburgh EH2 2JL, Scotland. Tel: +44 (0)131 225 2266. www.bonhams.com. 131R3r, 328bl, 325bc. **Bonhams Knightsbridge,** Montpelier Street, London SW7 1HH, UK.www.bonhams.com. 200bl, 200br, 201tr, 2021bl, 202t 'Colored Bears,' 202t 'Gadget Bears,' 204bl, 204bcl, 212bl, 220br, 221tl, 331c. **Bonhams Knowle,** The Old House, Station Road, Solihull, West Midlands B93 0HT, UK. Tel: +44 (0)1564 776 151. www.bonhams.com. 164bl, 165br. **Joseph Bonnar,** 72 Thistle Street, Edinburgh EH2 1EN, Scotland. Tel: +44 (0)131 226 2811. 177cr, 177br. **Roger Bradbury,** Church Street, Coltishall, Norfolk NR12 7DJ, UK. Tel: +44 (0)1603 737 444. 43tl 'Nanking,' 43tc 'Diana,' 43tr 'Tek Sing.' **Branksome Antiques,** 370 Poole Road, Branksome, Poole, Dorset BH12 1AW, UK. Tel: +44 (0)1202 763 324. 118tr, 118br, 118bc, 118bl, 119t, 119cr, 119br, 119bc. **Bristol Auction Rooms,** (Collectors' Saleroom), Baynton Road, Ashton, Bristol BS3 2EB, UK. (Main Saleroom), St John's Place, Apsley Road, Clifton, Bristol BS8 2ST, UK. Tel: +44 (0)117 973 7201. www.bristolauctionrooms.co.uk. 21br, 37tc, 37bl, 169bc. **Brunk Auctions,** P.O. Box 2135, Ashville, NC 28802. Tel: 828 254 6846. Fax: 828 254 6545. www.brunkauctions.com. 90tr, 90br, 91tr, 91bc. **Bucks County Antique Center,** Route 202, Lahaska PA 18931. Tel: 215 794 9180. 34cr, 35tr, 35cr, 35br, 35bl, 85bl, 89br, 240tr, 241bl. **Cad van Swankster at The Girl Can't Help It,** Alfies Antique Market, Shop G115, Ground Floor, 13–25 Church Street, London NW8 8DT, UK. Tel: +44 (0)20 7723 0564. 159tr, 167l, 167cr, 230tr, 325br. **C.A.R.S. of Brighton,** 4–4a Chapel Terrace Mews, Kemptown, Brighton, East Sussex BN2 1HU, UK. Tel: +44 (0)1273 601 960. 310tr. **Catalin Radios,** 5443 Schultz Drive, Sylvania, OH 43560. Tel: 419 824 2469. www.catalinradio.com. 302tr, 302br, 302bl. **Cheffins,** The Cambridge Saleroom, 2 Clifton Road, Cambridge CB1 4BW, UK. Tel: +44 (0)1223 213 343. www.cheffins.co.uk. 37cr, 188b, 191bl, 231tl, 231bc, 235bl, 248b. **Chisholm Larsson,** 145 8th Avenue, New York, NY 10011. Tel: 212 741 1703. www.chisholm-poster.com. 297bc, 297bl. **Chiswick Auctions,** 1–5 Colville Road, London W3 8BL, UK. Tel: +44 (0)20 8992 4442. 119bl, 128tr, 128br, 129c, 129cr, 129br, 129bc. **Chris & Eddie's Collectibles,** c/o South Street Antiques Center, 615 South 6th Street, Philadelphia, PA 19147–2128. Tel: 215 592 0256. 75t 'Memorabilia.' **Christine Bertrand Collection.** 106b 'Bros,' 106b 'Dorcas,' 106b 'Horner,' 106b 'Fenton,' 106b 'Iles,' 107bl. **Christopher Sykes Antiques,** The Old Parsonage, Woburn, Milton Keynes MK17 9QL, UK. Tel: +44 (0)1525 290 259/467. www.sykes corkscrews.co.uk. 110tr, 110b, 110c, 111tc, 111cr, 111br, 111bc, 111bl, 112tr, 167tr. **Clevedon Salerooms,** The Auction Centre, Kenn Road, Clevedon, Bristol BS21 6TT, UK. Tel: +44 (0)1934 830 111. www.clevedon-salerooms.com. 47bl, 53bl, 53cr. **Cloud Cuckoo Land,** 6 Charlton Place, Camden Passage, London N1, UK. Tel: +44 (0)20 7354 3141. 151br, 155cr,158cr, 162tr. **Cobwebs,** 78 Old Northam Road, Southampton SO14 0PB, UK. Tel: +44 (0)2380 227 458. www.cobwebs.uk.com. 312tr, 312c, 313t 'Playing Cards,' 313t 'Timetables,' 313t 'Fixtures & Fittings,' 313t 'Menus,' 313t 'Souvenirs,' 313t 'Brochures,' 313cr, 313br, 313bl. **Collectors Cameras,** P.O. Box 16, Pinner, Middlesex HA5 4HN, UK. Tel: +44 (0)20 8421 3537. 305tr, 305cr, 305br. **Sheila Cook,** 283 Westbourne Grove, London W11 2QA, UK. Tel: +44 (0)20 7792 8001. www.sheilacook.co.uk. 149cr, 149tl, 162b '1900s,' 162b '1920s.' **Cowan's Historic Americana Auctions,** 673 Wilmer Avenue, Cincinnati, OH 45226. Tel: 513 871 1670. www.historicamericana.com. 166br, 166bl. **Cristobal,** 26 Church Street, London NW8 8EP, UK. Tel/Fax: +44 (0)20 7724 7230. www.cristobal.co.uk. 160b, 172bl(&bc), 173br, 173bc, 173bl, 174tr, 175c. **David Rago Auctions,** 333 North Main Street, Lambertville, NJ 08530. Tel: 609 397 9374. www.ragoarts.com. 24bc, 28tr, 28cl, 29cl, 29cr, 31bc, 32tr, 32br, 32bc, 32bl, 33bc, 33cr, 33bl, 33br, 83tl, 132br, 249bc 'Records,' 308tr. **Dawson & Nye Auctioneers & Appraisers,** 128 American Road, Morris Plains, NJ 07950. Tel: 973 984 6900. Fax: 973 984 6956. www.dawsons.org. 29br, 50b, 66tr. **Deco Etc,** 122 West 25thStreet, (between 6th & 7th Avenues), New York, NY 10010. Tel: 212 675 3327. deco_etc@msn.com. 113cr, 321t, 326tr, 326bl, 327tr, 327br, 327bl, 327R4l, 327tl. **Dee Carlton Collection.** qnoscots@aol.com. 94tr, 94cr, 94bl, 94cl, 95cr, 95cl, 95tl, 170bl. **Delage–Creuzet,** La Cité des Antiquaires, 117, Boulevard de Stalingrad, 69100 Lyon–Villeurbanne, France. Tel: +33 (0)4 78 89 70 21. depotventegdlyon@aol.com. 275cr. **Design Twentieth Century.** www.design20c.com. 303tc, 303bl, 303br, 331cr. **Dickins Auctioneers,** The Claydon Saleroom, Calvert Road, Middle Claydon, Buckinghamshire MK18 2EZ, UK. Tel: +44 (0)1296 714 434. www.dickins–auctioneers.com. 52bc, 85br. **DODO, Alfies Antique Market,** 1st floor (F073, 83 & 84), 13–25 Church Street, London NW8 8DT, UK. Tel: +44 (0)20 7706 1545. dodoposters@yahoo.com. 293br. **Doll Express,** 2222 N. Reading Road, Denver, PA 17517. Tel: 717 335 3300. www.thedollexpress.com. 205cr, 205l, 208br, 213bl, 213cr, 214r, 215tl(&tc), 215cr, 215br, 216tr, 216br, 216bl, 216cl, 217tl, 217bc, 217bl, 217r. **Donay Games & Pastimes,** 3 Pierrepont Row, Camden Passage, London N1 8EF, UK. Tel: 01444 416 412.donaygames@btconnect.com. 221cr, 222tr, 222bl, 223br, 223bc. **Dorotheum,** Dorotheergasse 17, A–1010 Vienna, Austria. Tel: +43 1 515 60 0. www.dorotheum.com. 326br, 327R2l. **Dreweatt Neate,** Donnington Priory Salerooms, Donnington, Newbury, Berkshire RG14 2JE, UK. Tel: +44 (0)1635 553 553. www.auctions.dreweattneate.co.uk. 39cr, 41tc 'Recent Pieces,' 42b, 42tr, 42br, 44tr, 45cr, 48bl, 51br, 52tr, 109tl, 113br, 124tr, 142bl, 143bc, 201bc, 201tl, 203tc, 204br, 220tr, 241cr. **Simon Dunlavey.** pennyblack@despammed.com. 71c. **Dynamite Antiques & Collectibles.** Tel: 301 652 1140. eb625@verizon.net. 103br, 56tr, 67bl. **Early Technology,** Monkton House, Old Craighall, Edinburgh, Scotland. Tel: +44 (0)131 665 5753. www.earlytech.com. 103tc, 203br. **Larry & Dianna Elman,** P.O. Box 415 Woodland Hills, CA 91365. 66b, 67tc, 212tc. **The End of History,** 548 1/2 Hudson Street, New York, NY 10014. Tel: 212 647 7598. Fax: 212 647 7634. 136tr, 136br, 136bl, 137tc, 137br, 137cl, 138tr, 138br, 138bl, 138cl, 139tl, 139br, 139bl. **Feljoy Antiques,** Shop 3, Angel Arcade, Camden Passage, London N1 8EA, UK. Tel: +44 (0)20 7354 5336. www.chintznet.com/feljoy. 38tr, 38cl, 38b, 41br. **Sandra Fellner,** Stand 125/B14, Grays Mews Antiques Market, Davies Mews, South Molton Lane, London W1Y 5AB, UK. Tel: +44 (0)20 8946 5613. fellner-sellers@grays. clara.net. 218tr, 219bc, 219br. **Fellow's & Sons,** Augusta House, 19 Augusta Street, Hockley, Birmingham B18 6JA, UK. Tel: +44 (0)121 212 2131. www.fellows.co.uk. 108cl, 116cl, 176br, 179cr, 179tc, 210tr, 210br, 210bl, 210cl, 210cr, 211tr, 211R3r, 211br, 211bl, 211R, 2l, 211tl, 221bl, 240c, 241tl 'Die-cast.' **Jill Fenichell,** 305 East 61st Street, New York, NY. Tel: 212 980 9346. jfenichell@yahoo.com. 48tr 'Coffee pots,' 48tr 'Jugs,' 48tr 'Cheese Dishes,' 48tr 'Jam Pots,' 49br. **Flo Blue Shoppe,** 22860 W.Thirteen Mile Road, Beverly Hills, MI 48025. Tel: 248 433 1933. 89cr. **France Antique Toys.** Tel: 631 754 1399. 248tr. **Fraser's Autographs,** 399 The Strand, London WC2 R0LX, UK. Tel: +44 (0)20 7836 9325. www.frasersautographs.com. 284br, 285tl, 285br, 285bl. **Freeman's,** 1808 Chestnut Street, Philadelphia, PA 19103. Tel: 215 563 9275. www.freemansauction.com. 20b, 24tr, 36br, 121R2l, 325bl, 331bc. **Gallery 1930 Susie Cooper Ceramics Art Deco,** 18 Church Street, London NW8 8EP, UK. Tel: +44 (0)20 7723 1555. www.susiecooperceramics.com. 25tc, 25br, 26br, 26bl, 27tr, 27br, 51tc, 51cr, 51bl. **Richard Gibbon,** 34/34a Islington Green, London N1 8DU, UK. Tel: +44 (0)20 7354 2852. neljeweluk@aol.com. 172tr, 175tl. **Gillian Neale Antiques,** P.O. Box 247, Aylesbury, Buckinghamshire HP20 1JZ, UK. Tel +44 (0)1296 423754 or 07860 638700. www.gilliannealeantiques.co.uk. 88br. **The Glass Merchant.** Tel: 07775 683 961. as@titan98.freeserve.co.uk. 122t, 123bc, 125br, 142r, 143tr, 143bl. **Goodwins Antiques Ltd,** 15 & 16 Queensferry Street, Edinburgh EH2 4QW, Scotland. Tel: +44 (0)131 225 4717. 168tr. **Gorringes,** 15 North Street, Lewes, East Sussex BN7 2PD, UK. Tel: +44 (0)1273 472 503. www.gorringes.co.uk. 21tc, 21bl, 21cr, 36bl(&cl), 37bc, 41tr 'Florian Ware,' 45br, 130cl, 131R3l, 306bl. **Graham Cooley Collection.** Tel: 07968 722269. grahamcooley_ffc@hotmail.com. 124bl, 125bl. **Ken Grant,** F109–111, Alfies Antique Market, 13 Church Street, London NW8 8DT, UK. 82tr, 83cr. **Griffin & Cooper Antiques,** South Street Antiques Center, 615 South 6th Street, Philadelphia, PA 19147. Tel: 215 582 0418/3594. 54tr, 55bl. **Guernsey's Auctions,** 108 East 73rd Street, New York, NY 10021. Tel: 212 794 2280. www.guernseys.com. 246cr, 247tl. **Halcyon Days,** 14 Brook Street, London W1S 1BD, UK. Tel: +44 (0)20 7629 8811. www.halcyondays.co.uk. 247cr. **Harper General Store,** 10482 Jonestown Road, Annville, PA, 17003. Tel: 717 865 3456. www.harpergeneralstore.com. 67bc, 200bc, 200tr, 202t 'Berlin Bears,' 202t 'Novelty Bears,' 202t 'Pandas,' 203cr, 205br, 241tr 'Badges.' **Heritage Comics,** Heritage Plaza, 100 Highland Park Village, 2nd Floor, Dallas, Texas 75205–2788. Tel: 800 872 6467/214 528 3500. Fax: 214 520 6968. www.heritagecomics.com. 275tr, 276tr. **Holiday Happening.** 280–281c, 280cl, 280b 'Cards,' 280b 'Figurines,' 280b 'Plastic,' 280b 'Containers,' 280b 'Noisemakers,' 281cr, 282br, 283br, 283tl. **Hope and Glory,** 131A Kensington Church Street, London W8 7LP, UK.

Tel: +44 (0)20 7727 8424. 62bl, 62br, 62tr, 63t, 63cr, 63bl, 64tr, 64br, 64bc, 65tl, 65tr, 65br, 65bc, 65bl, 67br. **Hunt Auctions,** 75 E. Uwchlan Avenue, Suite 130, Exton, PA 19341. Tel: 610 524 0822. www.huntsauctions.com. 163cr, 254tr, 254c, 254b, 256tl, 256b 'Cards,' 256b 'Advertising,' 256b 'Pins,' 256b 'Photos,' 257bc, 258tr, 258b 'Vintage Cleats,' 258b 'Programs,' 259br, 262br. **Huxtins,** 11 & 12 The Lipka Arcade, 288 Westbourne Grove, London W11, UK. Tel: 07710 132 200. www.huxtins.com. 98bl, 100l, 100tr, 101tc, 213br, 241tr 'Tins,' 260tr. **InterCol,** 114 Islington High Street, London W1X 3HB, UK. Tel: +44 (0)20 7354 2599. www.intercol.co.uk. 72bl, 73t, 73br, 73bc, 236bl. **Jacobs & Hunt Fine Art Auctioneers,** 26 Lavant Street, Petersfield, Hampshire GU32 3EF, UK. Tel: +44 (0)1730 233 933. www.jacobsandhunt.com. 109R2r. **James Bridges Collection.** james@jdbridges.fsnet.co.uk. 321bc, 322tr, 322br, 322cr, 323tl, 323br. **James D. Julia Inc.,** P.O. Box 830, Fairfield, Maine 04937. Tel: 207 453 7125. Fax: 207 453 2502. www.juliaauctions.com. 126tr, 126br, 126bc, 126bl, 127t,127cr, 127br, 127bc, 127bl, 132tr, 132bl, 133br, 133c, 134tr, 196t, 197br, 219t, 286b 'Tintray,' 311bl. **Jean Scott Collection,** Stanhope **Collectors' Club,** 42 Frankland Crescent, Parkstone, Poole, Dorset BH14 9PX, UK. www.stanhopes.info. 68tr, 68br 68cl, 69tc, 69tr, 69br, 69bc, 69cl, 106tr, 107tl, 107cr. **Jeanette Hayhurst Fine Glass,** 32A Kensington Church Street, London W8 4HA, UK. Tel: +44 (0)20 7938 1539. 112br, 112bc. **Karl Flaherty Collectables.** Tel: +44 (0)2476 445 627. kfckarl@aol.com. 228tr, 228b, 229bc, 229bcl, 229bcr. **Kathy's Korner.** Tel: 516 624 9494. 56cl, 56b 'Praying Girl,' 56b 'Jackie Kennedy,' 56b 'Engagement Girl,' 56b 'Headache Lady,' 56b 'Betty Lou Nichols,' 56b 'Little Sister,' 57cr, 57br, 57bl., 74b, 75br, 75t 'Money.' **Keller & Ross,** P.O. Box 783, Melrose, MA 02716. Tel: 978 988 2070. http://members.aol.com/kellerross. 22tr, 22bc, 22bl, 23cl, 23cr, 23bc. **Kitsch-N-Kaboodle,** South Street Antiques Center, 615 South 6th Street, Philadelphia, PA 19147-2128. Tel: 215 382 1354. 229tl. **Bill and Rick Kozlowski.** Tel: 215 997 2486. 166tr. **Lankes,** Triftfeldstrasse 1, 95182 Döhlau, Germany. Fax: +49 (0)92 8695 05 40. www.lankes-auktionen.de. 196-197b. **Law Fine Art Ltd,** Firs Cottage, Church Lane, Brimpton, Berkshire RG7 4TJ, UK. Tel: +44 (0)118 971 0353. www.lawfineart.co.uk. 45tc. **Lawrence's Fine Art Auctioneers,** South Street, Crewkerne, Somerset TA18 8AB, UK. Tel: +44 (0)1460 73041. www.lawrences.co.uk. 120R2l, 169br, 202t 'Unknown Bears.' **Hugo Lee-Jones.** Tel: +44 (0)1227 375 375 or 07941 1872027. electroniccollectables@hotmail.com. 229br, 244tr, 244cr, 244br, 244bl, 244cl, 245tr, 245R3r, 245br, 245bl, 245R3l, 245R2l, 245tl **L.H. Selman Ltd,** 123 Locust Street, Santa Cruz, CA 95060. Tel: 800 538 0766. www.selman.com/pwauction. 130cr, 130br, 131tr. **Lights, Camera, Action,** 6 Western Gardens, Western Boulevard, Aspley, Nottingham NG8 5GP, UK. Tel: +44 (0)115 913 1116 or 07970 342 363. www.lca-autographs.co.uk. 237tc, 284tr. **Lilliput Lane, Enesco Ltd.** www.lilliputlane.co.uk. 49tl, 49cr. **Lucy's Hats,** South Street Antiques Center, 615 South 6th Street, Philadelphia, PA 19147. Tel: 215 592 0256. shak06@aol.com. 152cl, 152bl, 152br, 152cr, 153tl. **Luna,** 323 George Street, Nottingham NG1 3BH, UK. Tel: +44 (0)115 924 3267. www.luna-online.co.uk. 108cr, 108tr, 303cr, 303bc, 308b, 309t, 309cr, 309br, 320br, 324tr, 329tr, 329bl. **Lyon and Turnbull Ltd,** 33 Broughton Place, Edinburgh EH1 3RR, Scotland. Tel: +44 (0)131 557 8844. www.lyonandturnbull.com. 37br, 41tc 'Native Flowers,' 41tl 'Art Nouveau,' 44bl, 44bc, 53tc, 62cl, 261t, 321br, 324br. **Mad Hatter Antiques,** Unit 82, Admiral Vernon Antique Market, 141-149 Portobello Road, London W11, UK. Tel: +44 (0)20 7262 0487 or 07931 956 705. madhatter.portobello@virgin.net. 46tr, 46cr, 46bl, 47tl, 47R3l, 47R3r, 47br, 47tr. **Manfred Schotten Antiques,** 109 Burford High Street, Burford, Oxfordshire OX18 4RH, UK. Tel: +44 (0)1993 822 302. Fax: +44 (0)1993 822 055. www.schotten.com. 262bc. **Manic Attic, Stand S011,** Alfies Antique Market, 13 Church Street, London NW8 8DT, UK. Tel: +44 (0)20 7723 6105. manicattic@alfies.clara.net. 26tr, 27R2l, 325tl, 325cr, 326cr. **Mark Hill Collection.** Tel: 07798 915 474. stylophile@btopenworld.com. 143br, 322bl, 323tr, 323R2r, 323R4r, 323bl, 323R2l. **Mark Slavinsky Collection.** 204tr, 213tl, 242b. **Francesca Martire,** Stand F. 131-137, First Floor, Alfies Antique Market, 13-25 Church Street, London NW8 0RH, UK. Tel: +44 (0)20 7724 4802. martire@alfies.clara.net. 141tl, 330tr(&tc). **Mary Ann's Collectibles,** South Street Antiques Center, 615 South 6th Street, Philadelphia, PA 19147. Tel: 215 592 0256/923 3247. 54bl, 153cr, 159R3r, 171R2r, 282bl. **Bob Mauriello.** Tel: 856 1312. Toystrains@comcast.net. 197t. **Memory Lane,** 45-40 Bell Blvd, Suite 109, Bayside, NY 11361. Tel: 718 428 8181. www.tias.com/store/memlnny. 74tr, 74c, 74b, 75br, 75t 'Money.' **Mendes Antique Lace and Textiles,** Flat 2, Wilbury Lawn, +44 Wilbury Road, Hove, East Sussex BN3 3PA, UK. Tel: +44 (0)1273 203 317. www.mendes.co.uk. 164tr, 164cr, 164br, 164cl, 165tr, 165c, 165bl. **Metropolis Collectibles, Inc.,** 873 Broadway, Suite 201, New York, NY 10003. Tel: 212 260 4147. Fax: 212 260 4304. www.metropoliscomics.com. 274tr, 274br, 274cr, 274bl, 275br, 275bc. **Mod-Girl,** South Street Antiques Center, 615 South 6th Street, Philadelphia, PA 19147.Tel: 215 592 0256/413 0434. 152tr. **Mood Indigo,** 181 Prince Street, New York, NY 10012. Tel: 212 254 1176. www.moodindigonewyork.com. 25bc. **Mori Books,** Amherst Book Center, 141 Route 101A, Amherst, NH 03031. Tel: 603 882 2665. www.moribooks.com. 272tr, 272br, 272bl, 273cr, 273cr, 273br, 273bl. **Mullock Madeley,** The Old Shippon, Wall-under-Heywood, Church Stretton, Shropshire SY6 7DS, UK. Tel: +44 (0)1694 771 771. www.mullock-madeley.co.uk. 261cr, 263cr, 263bl. **Mum Had That.** www.mumhadthat.com. 122bl, 122br, 123br, 123bl, 123tr, 137cr. **Neet-O-Rama,** 93 W. Main Street, Somerville, NJ 08876. Tel: 908 722 4600. www.neetstuff.com. 154r, 155tr, 156bc, 157bl, 157br, 192c, 193br, 234tr, 235tl, 235tc, 250b, 252br, 252cl, 253cr, 308cl, 328tr, 329br, 330bl, 331br, 331bl. **Nifty Fifties,** 20065 Inkster Road, Romulus, MI 48174. Tel: 734 782 3974. 96br, 97br, 97tc. **Nigel Wright Collection.** xab@dircon.co.uk. 109R3l, 206tr, 206cr, 206br, 206bl, 206cl, 207tr, 207R2r, 207br, 207bl, 207cl, 207tl. **Noel Barrett Antiques & Auctions Ltd,** P.O. Box 300, Carversville, Pennsylvania, 18913. Tel: 215 297 5109. www.noelbarrett.com. 186bl, 187cr, 187bl(&bc), 195cr, 195bl, 241tl 'Early Designs,' 241bl, 242tr. **Northeast Auctions,** 93 Pleasant Street, Portsmouth, NH 03801. Tel: 603 433 8400. Fax: 603 433 0415. www.northeastauctions.com. 89bl, 89tc. **Onslows,** The Coach House, Manor Road, Stourpaine, Dorset DT11 8TQ, UK. Tel/Fax: +44 (0)1258 488 838. www.onslows.co.uk. 293tr, 293tl, 294tr, 296tr, 296br, 297br, 297cl. **Otford Antiques and Collectors Centre,** 26-28 High Street, Otford, Kent TN15 9DF, UK. Tel: +44 (0)1959 522 025. www.otfordantiques.co.uk. 43br, 54bcl, 54bcr, 54br, 64bl, 214bc, 305tl. **Cooper Owen,** 10 Denmark Street, London WC2H 8LS, UK. Tel: +44 (0)20 7240 4132. www.cooperowen.com. 223t, 236bc, 238tr, 238br, 239c, 239cr, 239br, 246bl, 247br, 249tl, 249cr, 249bl 'Personal Items,' 249bl 'Merchandise,' 249bl 'Signatures,' 285bc, 285tr, 306tr 'Filigree,' 306tr 'Oscar Wilde,' 306tr 'Custom,' 307tr, 307cr, 307br, 307tl 'Dinkie,' 307tl 'Etn,' 307tl 'Meisterstück.' **Pantry & Hearth,** 994 Main Street South, Woodbury, CT 06798. Tel: 212 532 0535. http://www.nhada.org/pantryhearth.htm. 84tr. **Patricia Stauble Antiques,** 180 Main Street, P.O. Box 265, Wiscasset, ME 04578. Tel: 207 882 6341. 34tr, 218bl. **Paul Reichwein,** 2321 Hershey Avenue, East Petersburg, PA 17520. Tel: 717 569 7637. paulrdg@aol.com. 129bl. **Peter Chapman Collection.** pgcbal1@supanet.com. 273tc. **Petersham Books,** Unit 67, 56 Gloucester Road, Kensington, London SW7 4UB, UK. Tel/Fax: +44 (0)20 7581 9147. www.modernfirsts.co.uk. 271tl. **Phil Arthurhultz,** P.O. Box 12336, Lansing, MI 48901. Tel: 517 334 5000. 93cr, 286b 'Colonel Sanders,' 287br, 287cr. **Philip Weiss Auction Galleries,** 1 Neil Court, Oceanside, NY 11572. Tel: 516 594 0731. Fax: 516 594 9414. www.philipweissauctions.com. 194-195t, 194br, 257br. **Pook and Pook,** 463 East Lancaster Avenue, Downingtown, PA 19335. Tel: 610 269 4040/610 269 0695. Fax: 610 269 9274. www.pookandpook.com. 84br, 35bc, 90bl. **Port Antiques Center,** 289 Main Street, Port Washington, NY 11050. Tel: 516 767 3313. visualedge2@aol.com. 23br, 23bl, 30bc, 75t 'Set of Cards,' 75t 'Ceramic,' 134br, 134bc, 134bl, 135cl, 135cr, 135br, 135bl, 135bc. **Posteritati,** 239 Center Street, New York, NY 10013. Tel: 212 226 2207. www.posteritati.com. 238bc, 238bl, 239bc, 239bl. **Potteries Specialist Auctions,** 271 Waterloo Road, Cobridge, Stoke-on-Trent, Staffordshire ST6 3HR, UK. Tel: +44 (0)1782 286 622. www.potteriesauctions.com. 49bl, 49bc, 52bl, 52br, 53bc, 53br, 65cr. **Private Collection.** 36tr, 43tc 'Hatcher,' 63br, 143tc, 148tr, 171tl, 175br, 177bc, 221br, 251tr, 279cr, 282cr. **Quittenbaum Kunstauktionen München,** Hohenstaufenstraße 1, D-80801, München, Germany. Tel: +49 (0)89 33 00 756. 140tr, 141bl. **R. & G. McPherson Antiques,** 40 Kensington Church Street, London W8 4BX, UK. Tel: +44 (0)20 7937 0812 or 07768 432 630. www.orientalceramics.com. 43tl 'Hoi an Hoard,' 43tr 'Vung Tao.' **Rennies, 13 Rugby Street,** London WC1 3QT, UK. Tel: +44 (0)20 7405 0220. info@rennart.co.uk. 151cr, 153bl. **Richard Ball Lighters.** richard@lighter.co.uk. 169tr. **Rick Hubbard Art Deco,** 3 Tee Court, Bell Street, Romsey, Hampshire S051 8GY, UK. Tel/Fax: +44 (0)1794 513 133. www.rickhubbard-artdeco.co.uk. 25cr, 39bl. **Ritchie's Auctioneers & Appraisers,** 288 King Street East, Toronto, Ontario, Canada M5A 1KA. Tel: 001 416 364 1864. www.ritchies.com. 155bc. **Rogers de Rin,** 76 Royal Hospital Road, Paradise Walk, Chelsea, London SW3 4HN, UK. Tel: +44 (0)20 7352 9007. www.rogersderin.co.uk. 41cr. **Rosie Palmer,** 26-28 High Street, Otford, Kent TN15 9DF, UK. Tel: +44 (0)1959 522 025. Fax: +44 (0)1959 525 858. www.otfordantiques.co.uk. 29bc, 33c, 77br, 77cr, 256b 'Pennants.' **Rowan S. Baker,** The Covent Garden Stamp Shop, 28 Bedfordbury, London, WC2N 4RB, UK. Tel: +44 (0)20 7379 1448. Fax: +44 (0)20 7836 3100. www.usa-stamps.com. 70br, 70tr, 71tr, 71cr, 71br, 71bc, 71bl. **Sanford Alderfer Auction Company,** 501 Fairgrounds Road, Hatfield, PA 19440. Tel: 215 393 3000. www.alderferauction.com. 34br, 34bc, 34bl, 55cr, 148l, 150bl, 279br.**Sara Covelli Collection.** 148br, 161cr. **Seaside Toy Center,** 179 Main Street, Westerly, Rhode Island 02891. Tel: 401 596 0962. 229cr. **Seventies Watches.** Tel: +44 (0)20 7274 4342. www.70s-watches.com. 178br, 178bc, 178bl, 179bcr, 179bcl, 179bl, 180tr, 180br, 180bc, 180bl, 181tr, 181br, 181bl, 181R2l, 181tl, 181R3l. **Sign of the Tymes,** 2 Morris Farm Road, Lafayette, NJ 07848. Tel: 973 383 6028. www.millantiques.com. 93bl, 192tr, 192b, 193t, 193cr, 193bl, 202br, 232br, 232bc, 232bl, 233br, 233bc, 233bl, 256-257c, 257cr, 280b 'Cardboard Lanterns,' 281br, 281bl, 282tr, 282cl, 283tr, 283r, 288bl, 289tc, 290br, 290cr, 290cl, 291tr, 291bl, 331tc. **Skinner,** 63 Park Plaza, Boston, MA 02116, & 357 Main Street, Bolton, MA 01740. Tel: 617 350 5400/978 779 6241. Fax: 617 350 5429/978 779 5144. www.skinnerinc.com. 91br, 218br. **Sloans.** No longer trading. 91cr. **Sparkle Moore at The Girl Can't Help It,** Alfies Antique Market, Shop G100 & G116, Ground Floor, 13-25 Church Street, London NW8 8DT, UK. Tel: +44 (0)20 7724 8984 or 07958 515 614. www.sparklemoore.com. 109R4r, 150tr, 158br, 162bc '1950s,' 163br, 163bl, 170br, 170cl, 171tr, 171R3l, 171br, 171bl. **Sylvie Spectrum,** Grays Antique Market, Stand 372, 58 Davies Street, London W1Y 2LB, UK. Tel: +44 (0)20 7629 3501. 167br, 176tr. **Steinberg and Tolkien,** 193 King's Road, Chelsea, London SW3 5ED, UK. Tel: +44 (0)20 7376 3660.149br, 153br, 154bl, 155br, 156tr, 156br, 156bl, 157tl, 157cr, 160tr, 161tl, 161br, 162bc '1940s,' 162br '1960s,' 162br '1970s,' 163tc. **Strand Stamp Centre,** The Stamp Centre, 79 Strand, London, WC2R 0DE, UK. Tel: +44 (0)20 7240 3778. Fax: +44 (0)20 7240 5419. www.spamp-centre.co.uk. 70bl. **Roxanne Stuart.** Tel: 888 750 8869/215 750 8868. 94br, 95tr, 95bl, 96tr, 96bl, 97cr, 97bc, 97bl, 109b, 172br, 174br(&bc), 175bc, 326cl. **Sue Norman at Antiquarius,** Stand L4, Antiquarius, 135 King's Road, Chelsea, London SW3 4PW, UK. Tel: +44 (0)20 7352 7217. www.sue-norman.demon.co.uk. 88tr, 88c, 88bl, 89bc 'Ponte Rotto,' 89bc 'Willow Pattern.' **Sue Scrivens Collection.** 84bl, 85bc, 86tr, 86cr, 86br, 86bl, 86cl, 87tr, 87R2r, 87R3r, 87br, 87bl, 87tl. **Swann Galleries,** 104 East 25th Street, New York, New York 10010. Tel: 212 254 4710. Fax: 212 979 1017. www.swanngalleries.com. 292tr, 294bl, 295r, 296bc, 296bl, 297c, 297cr. **T.W. Conroy,** 36 Oswego Street, Baldwinsville, NY 13027. Tel: 315 638 6434. www.twconroy.com. 35cr, 102bl. **T.W. Gaze & Sons,** Diss Auction Rooms, Roydon Road, Diss, Norfolk IP22 4LN, UK. Tel: +44 (0)1379 650 306. www.twgaze.co.uk. 249br, 250tr, 251bc, 252tr, 253tr, 253br, 327cr. **Tagore Ltd,** Stand 302, Grays Antique Market, 58 Davies Street, London W1Y 2LP,UK. Tel: +44 (0)20 7499 0158. tagore@grays.clara.net. 113bl. **Take-A-Boo Emporium,** 1927 Avenue Road, Toronto, Ontario M5M 4A2, Canada. Tel/Fax: 001 416 785 4555. www.takeaboo.com. 128bc, 176bl, 177tc, 178tr, 179br. **Tennants Auctioneers,** The Auction Centre, Leyburn, North Yorkshire DL8 5SG, UK. Tel: +44 (0)1969 623780. www.tennants.co.uk. 260bl, 261br, 261cl, 262tr. **Terry Rodgers & Melody,** 30 & 31 Manhattan Art and Antique Center, 1050 2nd Avenue, New York, NY 10022. Tel: 212 758 3164. melodyjewelnyc@aol.com. 175cr. **Thomas Drelling Collection.** 133tr. **Toy Heroes,** 42 Westway, Caterham-on-the-Hill, Surrey CR3 5TP, UK. Tel: +44 (0)1883 348 001. www.toyheroes.co.uk. 230bl, 231cr, 231br, 231bl, 235cr, 235br. **Toy Road Antiques,** 2200 Highland Street, Canal Winchester, OH 43110. Tel: 614 834 1786. toyroad@aol.com. 92tr, 93tc, 98tr, 99b, 99tl, 99tc, 100bc, 101cr, 101br, 278tr, 279tc, 286tr, 286cl, 286b 'Trade Cards,' 286b 'Campbell's,' 286b 'Mayo's Plug,' 286b 'Goodyear,' 287bl, 292bl. **Transport Car Auctions,** 14 The Green, Richmond, Surrey TW9 1PX, UK. Tel: +44 (0)20 8940 2022. www.tc-auctions.com. 310bc, 311cr. **Trio,** Stand L24, Grays Antique Market, 1-7 Davies Mews, London W1Y 2LP, UK. Tel: +44 (0)20 7493 2736. www.trio-london.fsnet.co.uk. 120bl, 120bc, 120tr. **Vectis Auctions Limited,** Fleck Way, Thornaby, Stockton-on-Tees, Cleveland TS17 9JZ, UK. Tel: +44 (0)1642 750 616. www.vectis.co.uk. 190bl, 191br, 191cr, 230br. **Ventisemo,** 4 Unit S001, Alfies Antique Market, 13-25 Church Street, London NW8 8DT, UK. Tel: 07767 498 766. 168l, 189bl. **Victoriana Dolls,** 101 Portobello Rd, London W11 2BQ, UK. Tel: +44 (0)1737 249 525. heather.bond@total-serve.co.uk. 208bcl, 208bcr, 209cr. **Village Green Antiques,** Port Antiques Center, 289 Main Street, Port Washington, NY 11050. Tel: 516 625 2946. amysdish@optonline.net. 104tr, 104br, 104bl, 105tl, 105cr, 105br, 105bc(&br), 128bl, 130bl. **VinMag,** 39/43 Brewer Street, London W1R 9UD, UK. Tel: +44 (0)20 7439 8525. www.vinmag.com. 237cr, 276br, 276bl, 277cr, 277br, 277bc, 277bl. **Vintage Eyeware.** Tel: 917 721 6546. www.vintage-eyeware.com. 158tr, 158bl, 158cl, 159tl, 159R2r, 159b, 159R3l. **Vintage Sports Collector,** 3920 Via Solano, Palos Verdes Estates, CA 90274. Tel: 310 375 1723. 255cr, 255br, 255bl, 255b 'Yearbooks,' 258b 'Cover,' 258b 'Vintage,' 258b 'Balls,' 259cr, 259bl, 262bl, 262tl. **Vintage to Vogue,** 28 Milsom Street, Bath, Avon BA1 1DG, UK. Tel: +44 (0)1225 337 323. www.vintagetovoguebath.com. 151bl.**W. & H. Peacock,** 26 Newnham Street, Bedford MK40 3JR UK. Tel: +44 (0)1234 266 366. www.peacockauction.co.uk. 189br, 208tr, 209br, 212tr, 240b, 241tc 'Pottery Figures.' **Wallis and Wallis West Street Auction Galleries,** Lewes, East Sussex BN7 2NJ, UK. Tel: +44 (0)1273 480 208. www.wallisandwallis.co.uk. 131br, 187tl, 187br, 188tr, 189tc, 189cr, 190tr, 190bc, 191t, 237br, 289cr. **What A Character!** www.whatacharacter.com. 232tr, 233t, 233cr. **Woolley and Wallis,** 51-61 Castle Street, Salisbury, Wiltshire SP1 3SU, UK. Tel: +44 (0)1722 424 500.www.woolleyandwallis.co.uk. 45bl, 89tl, 112bl, 320tr. **Bonny Yankauer.** bonnyy@aol.com. 173tr.

ARCHIVE PICTURE ACKNOWLEDGEMENTS

The publisher would like to thank the following people, museums, and photographic libraries for permission to reproduce their material. Every care has been taken to trace copyright holders. However, if we have omitted anyone we apologise and will, if informed, make corrections to any future edition.

Alamy Images/Janine Wiedel Photolibrary, 12bl. **Camera Press,** London/Heilemann. 280b. **Elizabeth Whiting Associates,** London. 375tl. **Hulton Archive/Getty Images,** London. 34br, 92br, 129bc, 316bl, 360bl, 365tc, 368br. **Mary Evans Picture Library,** London. 230bl. **The Museum of London.** 156bl. **Rex Features/Nils Jorgensen.** 10bc. **Stoke-on-Trent City Archives.** 22bl.

PUBLISHER'S ACKNOWLEDGEMENTS

Dorling Kindersley would like to thank Caroline Hunt for editorial assistance, and Claire Bowers and Lucy Claxton for digital image co-ordination.